# SAP S/4 HANA FINANCE & TRANSITION FROM ECC

## CONFIGURATIONS & TRANSACTIONS

YOGI KALRA

# ACKNOWLEDGMENTS

I am very thankful foremost to my clients and their employees who have given me the opportunity to work on their SAP systems, always learning from them and their Businesses. Without their support and my learning their Business Processes, this manual would not have been possible.

I am grateful to my family for tolerating my absence while I composed this manual ignoring them most of the time. I will have to make up to them one day! I am thankful to my wife Michelle for helping me edit the proof of this manual and finding it's numerous errors.

Finally, and not the least, I am grateful to you, the reader for selecting this book among the thousands available, never an easy choice and I hope it met or exceeded your expectations. I am happy to answer any questions you may have on the topic - info@shefaria.com The author will be grateful for your review and feedback on the public fora if the book helped you increase your understanding of the subject.

# CONTENTS

# FOREWORD

This manual, written with the objective of providing detailed training to both, consultants and users goes deep into the subject from initial configurations to setting up the Income Statement and Balance Sheet of the company. The book was originally written on ECC 6.0 a few years ago and recently completely re-written on HANA 1809, the latest HANA version at the time of writing. During the re-writing of the book, various changes and differences were observed between ECC and HANA which have been documented all along in the book. Thus, apart from being a first book for users in HANA, it is also a transitionary book for consultants and users who have worked on ECC and need to understand what has changed to prepare them for the HANA world. These differences have been recorded wherever they are applicable and they exist in many sections of the book. They have been explicitly shown as **HANA CHANGE** in both, configurations and transactions.

The integration points of Finance with Purchasing/Inventory and Shipping/Billing are explained in detail and the chapters marked clearly if it is a Configuration (C) or Transaction (U) or both. Since most of the book has been written in standard SAP, once a company code is set up along with some other basic configurations defined in the first few pages, a SAP user, if so desires, can stay only with the areas marked 'U', by passing the 'C' since not everything in standard SAP depends on specific company code configurations. Consultants or to-be consultants, of course, need to understand both sides of SAP. The effects of changes done in configuration are immediately followed by their effect on the transactions, thereby making the learning relational in real time for better understanding. From the user's perspective, not much from the subject has been left out in writing this manual and every effort has been taken to keep it relevant to the Corporate Finance functions of day-to-day working on SAP in an orderly flow.

This manual has been written keeping standard Business processes proposed by SAP. In writing this book, I have stayed away from all frills and concentrated on providing only useful subject matter with tips and tricks based on over my many years of experience in SAP implementations and consulting. This book is not a result of overnight arrangement but a composition of several years of training and understanding of Business processes across multiple industries in various disciplines. I believe it is as comprehensive as any book can be for users and consultants, new and old, to conducting any Corporate Finance and Banking functions in SAP.

For New users: One of the primary learning curves in SAP is navigation. The data in SAP is so well organized that first time users are often astonished to see the integrative nature of this ERP system. It is no exaggeration to say that everything you need to know in SAP is at one, two or maximum three clicks away. Mastering navigation in SAP is half the battle won. This becomes even more vital in Finance, being at the tail end of all the processes. Good navigation skills will guide you in finding sources of the data in the documents. It would be very worth the while to spend time on navigation on the different screens and get familiar with them as for the most part, there is a commonality in the way SAP is structured across different areas in terms of screen layouts. To get a better understanding of Navigation in a structured form, read the author's book *SAP Navigation & General Components*. Use the F1 key for help liberally – it will help you wade through the screens understanding everything thoroughly. As is the case with all seemingly multifaceted structures, the base is very simple. In spite of SAP's complexity as an ERP system, it's edifice is built on very elementary processes as you will notice while going through this book. Processes that are uniform, scalable and easily comprehensible. One of SAP's masterstrokes is the Transaction code and the philosophy that drives it. Usually a 4 alpha-numeric or alpha code (but can be often longer, especially in Finance reporting), it is used to invoke a program which will guide you through the entire process. Thus, a user need only to remember this transaction code for the function to be performed and entering it in the transaction window to begin your activity. This manual endeavors to cover over 400 such transactions; bear in mind, each of them will perform a related and unique business function. Further, to simplify learning, a transaction code is usually ended as 01, 02 or 03 signifying create, change or display respectively. Thus, FB01, FB02 and FB03 become Post (Create) Accounting document, Change Accounting document and Display Accounting document, respectively. Also, for the most part, transaction codes and configurable objects are case insensitive i.e. FB01 is same as fb01.

For SAP Users and Process Owners: This book covers over 110 standard processes and transactions in Corporate Finance and daily banking in depth in easily understandable language and with only relevant screen shots. It is unlikely that any organization will be required to call upon any other substantial transactions other than these in its normal functioning. Towards the end, the book also touches on some cross application components, which if you have access to, will simplify your work in SAP tremendously. Anyone new to the SAP world is advised to read the chapter on 'Variants' after getting a good feel of the first couple of transactions while leaving the rest to the end. Again, for users new to SAP, the best and perhaps fastest way to learn from this book is to think of what you do or did in your legacy system and look up this manual on how to perform the same process in SAP. The transaction code to perform that function is provided right in the beginning of the chapter.

For Consultants: This book covers most configurations relating to Finance and some Controlling in depth. The effect of the changes in configurations in real time is explained as you go along, making your learning easier. The entire book has been developed on S/4 HANA 1809 and since it was originally done on ECC 6.0 EHP 7, all changes from ECC to HANA have been recorded where ever they occur. This will help you transition to HANA if you are familiar with ECC. If you have never worked on ECC before, this is your stepping stone into HANA as a new consultant. If you prefer to learn on ECC only you may want to get the author's earlier version of this book which is available from the same store you bought this from. Also detailed are the relationship between Finance and MM/SD wherever applicable to enable you to become more robust consultants. The ability to understand how FI gets it's data from Sales & Distribution and Purchasing/Inventory is critical to setting up the FI module. Most importantly, you will learn a lot by diving into the details of the transactions also as explained in this book and that will help you face the users more confidently. I can't recount the number of times I was embarrassed in my early days at client's sites when the experienced users explained to me navigation on the screens I did not know myself!

Your inputs and criticism are very welcome. If there is anything the author can do to help you understand the subject better or guide you in any way, please feel free to drop an email to info@shefaria.com noting the name of the book and topic in the subject of the email. Since nothing is perfect, there may be some errors and omissions in the book. I will be very grateful for your comments and responses if you find them or even otherwise give your suggestions since they will work to make the next edition better.

# FINANCIAL ACCOUNTING MENU (C)

T Code SPRO

SAP Implementation begins from the IMG (Implementation Guide) screen.

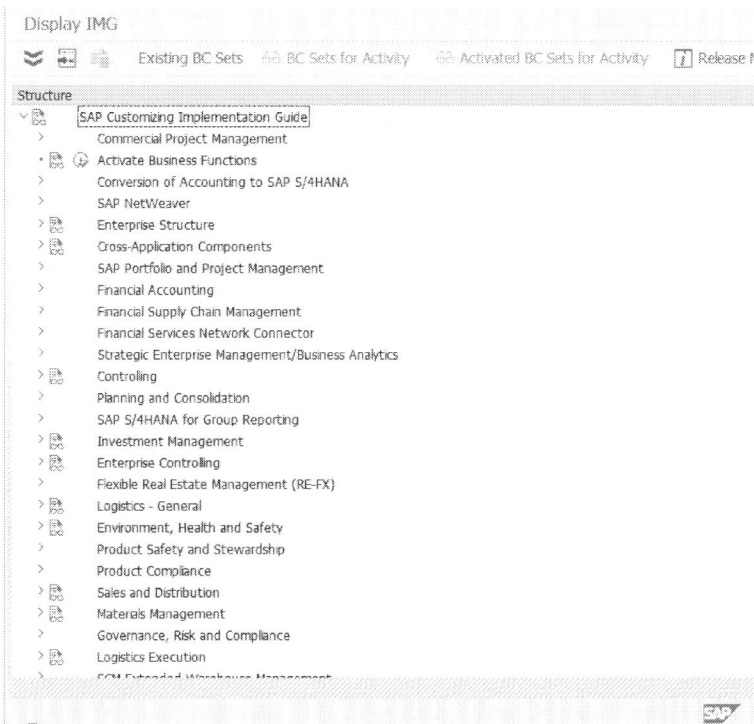

Fig 1

To go to the above screen, log in to SAP and in the transaction window, type SPRO and Hit Enter:

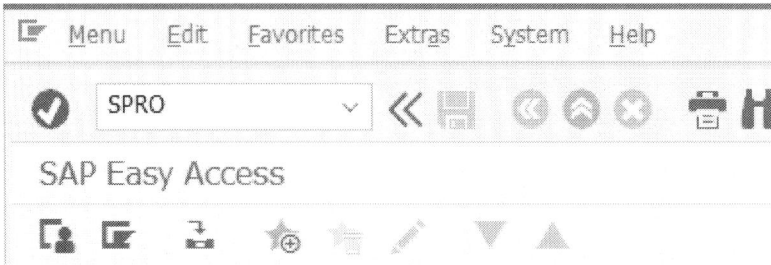

Fig 2

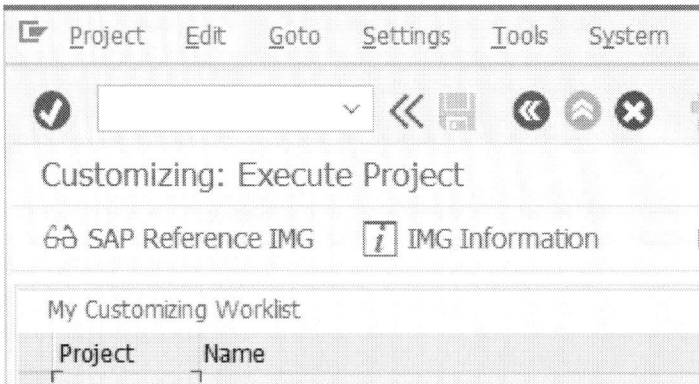

Fig 3

Click on the above button – SAP Reference IMG:

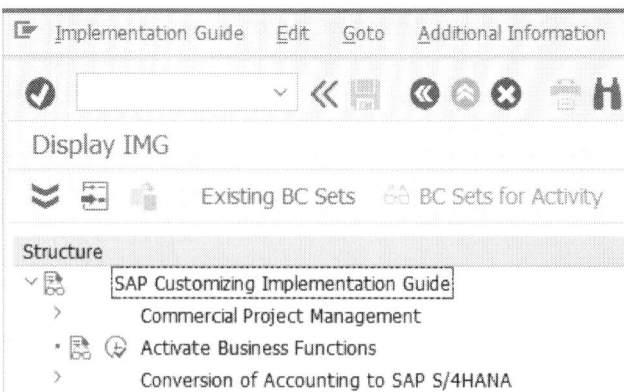

Fig 4

The IMG is divided into different modules arranged in no particular order. Within each module there are more sub-modules relating to specific areas. Within each sub-module one can find configuration areas at each node for each particular activity, some of which we will explore in this course.

# SETTING UP A COMPANY (C)

T Code SPRO

The first step in SAP is to set up a company, much in the same way as we would in the real world. The path to set up a company is:

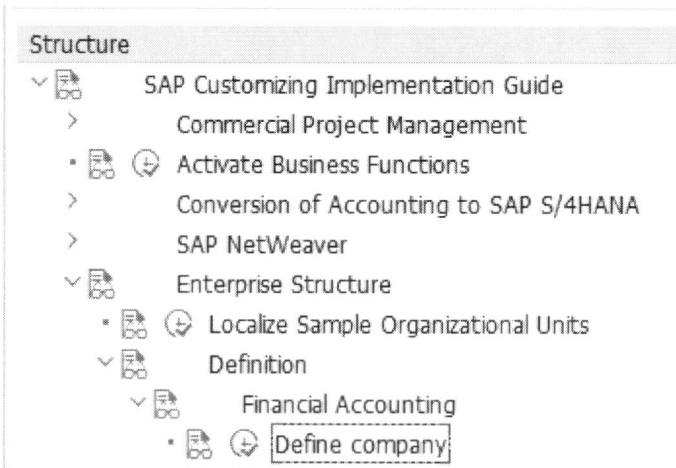

Fig 1

The company is the highest level of organizational structure that is created in SAP in FI. A company is used to consolidate the financial statements of the legal entities of any Business group. Usually a company will comprise of many CCs (discussed next). On the FI side, the use of a company is to consolidate this data and pass it on to the Controlling module, which is set up separately based on how the group company needs to do their filings or otherwise use this data.

Clicking on the Execute - 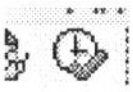 button will lead us into a table in which the company will be set up:

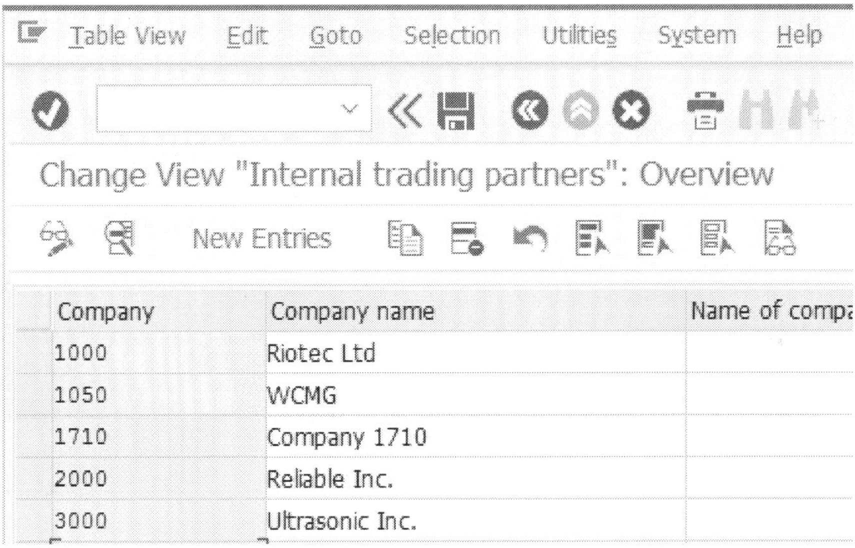

Fig 1

Click on New Entries to define your own company (up to 6 alphanumeric code) and its address.

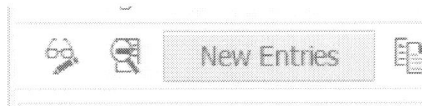

Fig 2

At many places in SAP, based on countries and their formats, there are inbuilt error checks like the Postal Code check for country Canada as below:

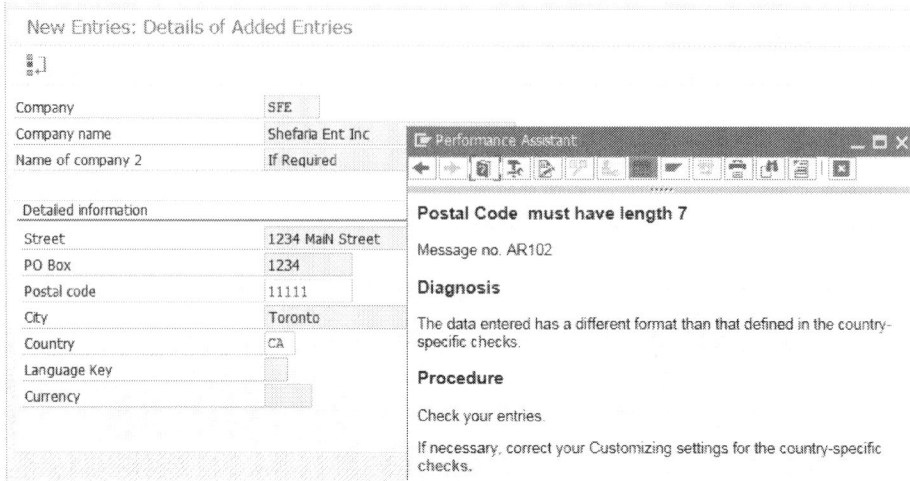

Fig 3

Thereby forcing the user to enter the correct data:

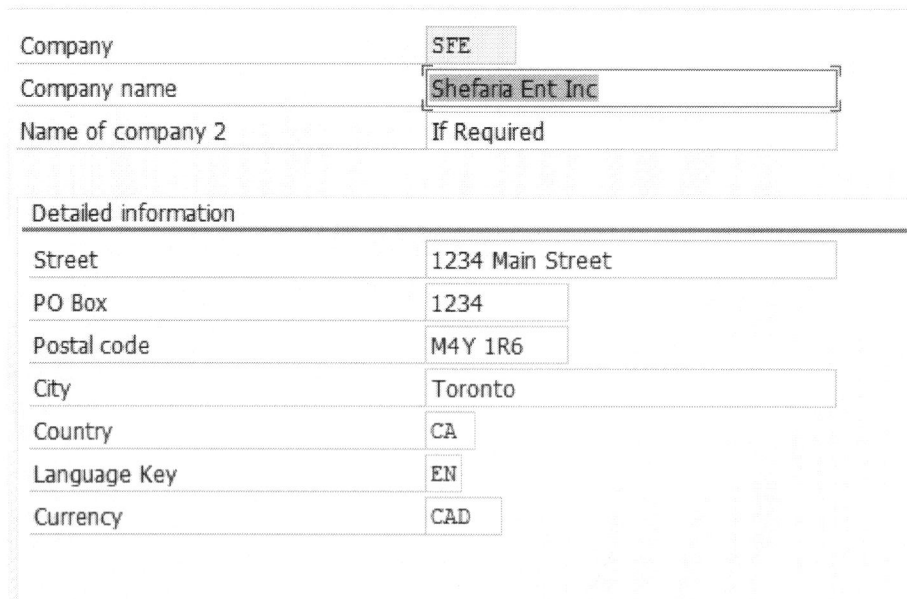

Fig 4

Save the data. A window pops up asking the user to create a transport:

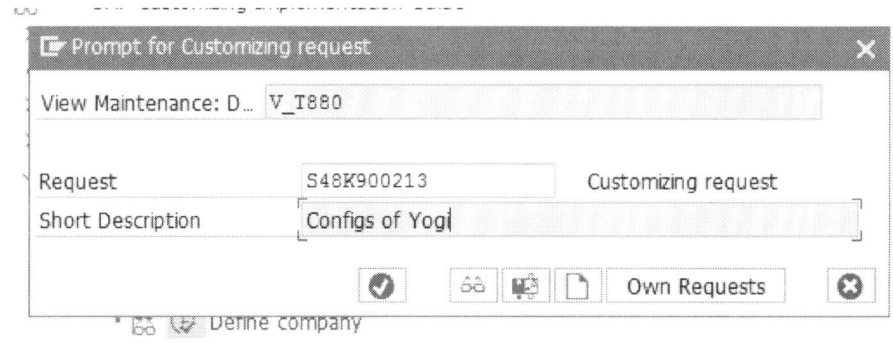

Fig 5

You should create a new transport if it proposes any transport number which is not your own. This transport number will be moved from one system to another carrying with it all the changes done. To create a new transport, click on [image]. If you want to add this change to your own pre-existing transport, you have the ability to choose that from Own Requests also.

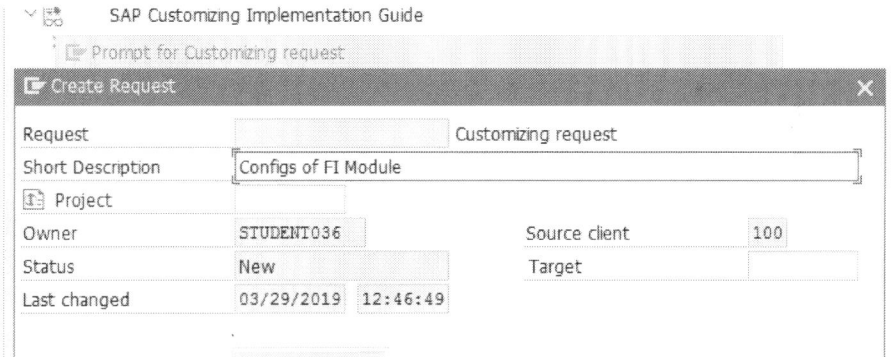

Fig 6

Give a description that will make sense to you or is specific to the change being done e.g. we will collect all the configurations relating to FI in this one transport.

Clicking on Save will give you a different (new) number as below:

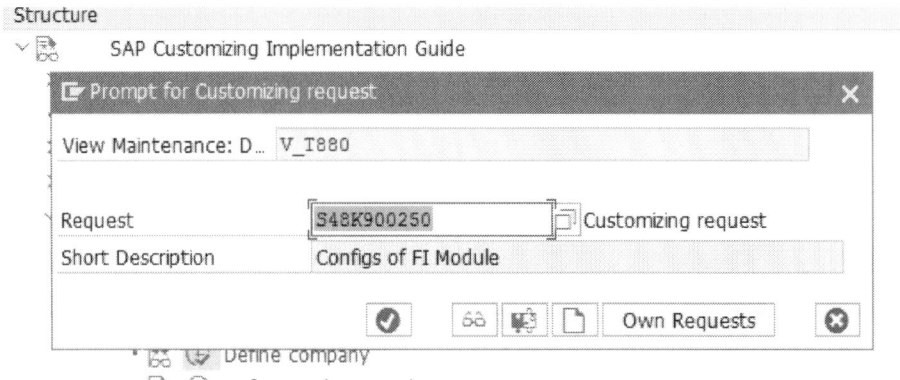

Fig 7

Hit Enter and the system will have saved your changes under the transport Number as above. As we go along, we will add more changes onto this same number so that we do not have to have multiple unnecessary numbers to remember and look for.

# SETTING UP THE COMPANY CODE (C)

T Code SPRO

A Company Code (CC) is a legal entity in whose name the Income statements and Balance Sheet will be filed. It is different from the Company. One company may have multiple CCs, which may require to be set up depending on the prevailing legal requirements. The path to it is after the option to set up the CC in the same tree.

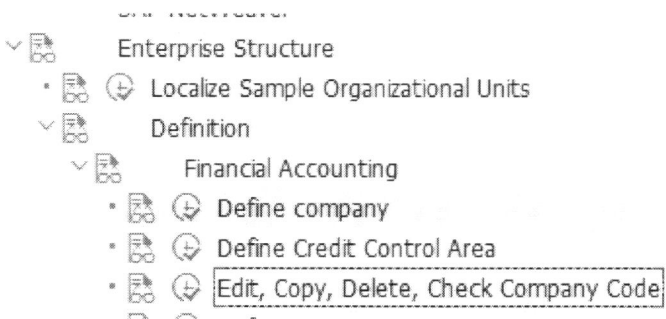

Fig 1

The company code we will set up is SFE1 on which this entire manual is based.

Double click the second option (Edit CC Data) in the below window:

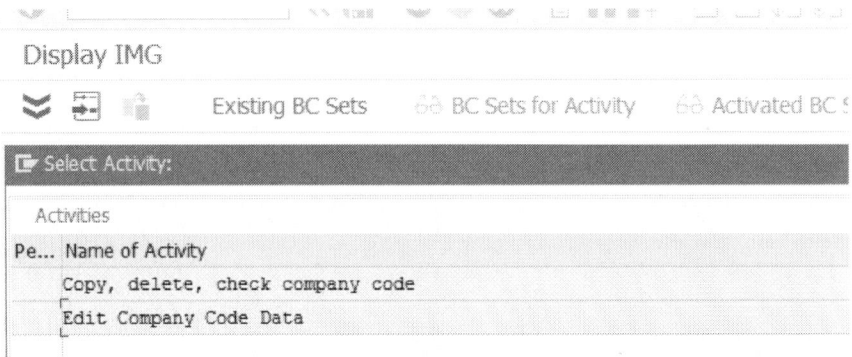

Fig 2

Alternatively, simply place the cursor in the 2nd line and Hit Enter.

Click on New Entries as previously and add your CC (4 characters maximum):

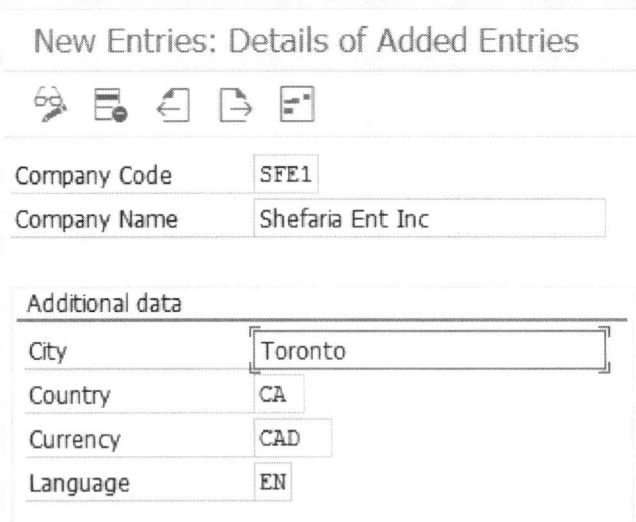

Fig 3

On Hitting Save, a window comes up asking for the address:

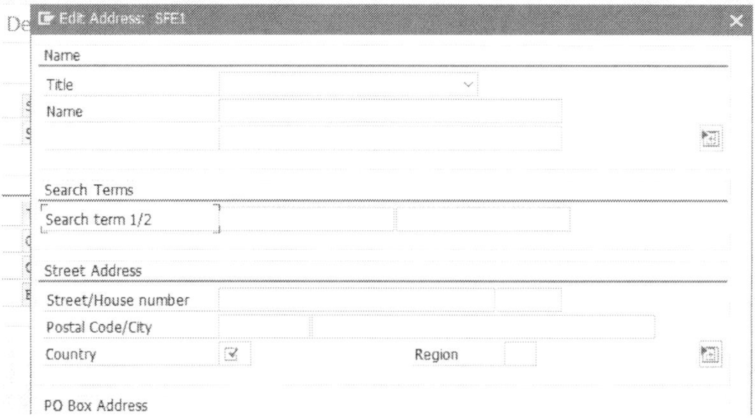

Fig 4

While only the country is mandatory (shown by the Check Mark inside the field), it is advisable to enter the complete address as it may be used for printing on documents later.

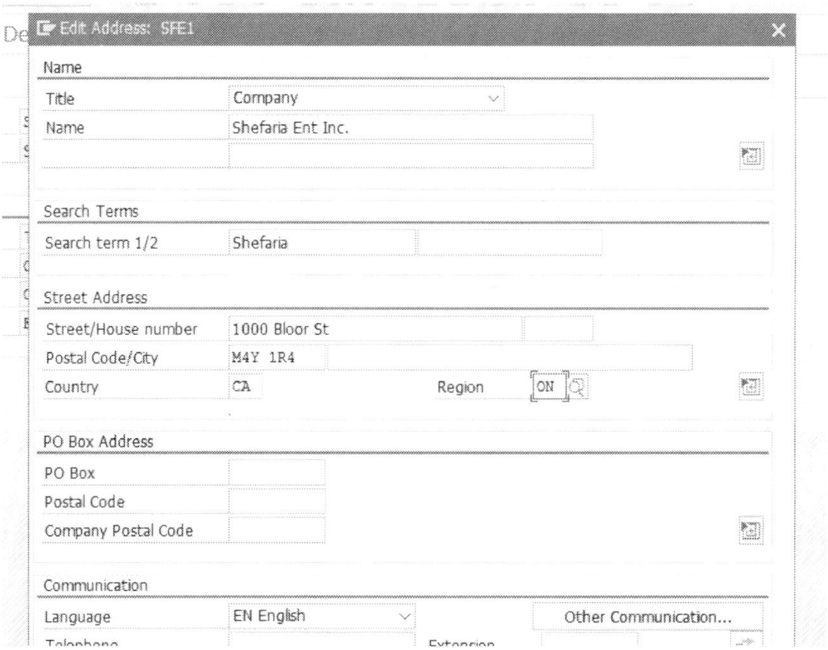

Fig 5

Hit Enter and Save. If a window asking for a transport comes up, use the same number as above. At the bottom, a message will come up saying your data was saved:

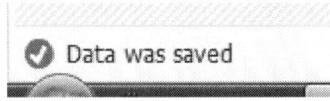

Fig 6

# ASSIGNMENTS (C)

T Code SPRO

All objects in SAP are mere placeholders and have no real use unless they are connected with each other in a meaningful way. In our case, since a company is representing multiple CCs, which are legal entities on their own, it is necessary to form a link between them. This link is called 'assignment' and these assignments are done across all modules for their respective organizational objects. This assignment is done in the Menu tree right after Definition in the respective module:

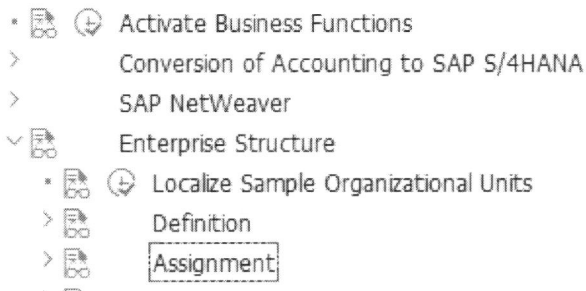

Fig 1

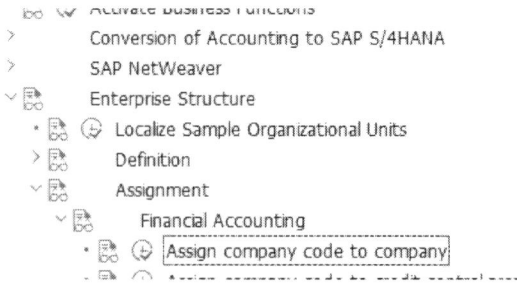

> Activate Business Functions
> Conversion of Accounting to SAP S/4HANA
> SAP NetWeaver
∨ Enterprise Structure
• Localize Sample Organizational Units
> Definition
∨ Assignment
∨ Financial Accounting
• Assign company code to company

Fig 2

Click on the Position window at the bottom and search for the CC
SFE1 by typing it in and hitting Enter:

Position...

Fig 3

Change View "Assign Company Code -> Company": Overview

| CoCd | City | Company | |
|------|------|---------|---|
| SFE1 | Toronto | | |
| STUD | SANTO ANDRE | | |
| TEAM | | | |

Fig 4

Add the company SFE in the field on the right most column and
save:

Change View "Assign Company Code -> Company": Overvie

| CoCd | City | Company |
|------|------|---------|
| SFE1 | Toronto | SFE |
| STUD | SANTO ANDRE | |
| TEAM | | |
| US01 | Flint, MI | |
| USFM | San Diego | USFM |

Fig 5

Add it to the same transport #.

# CHART OF ACCOUNTS (C)

T Code SPRO

A Chart of Accounts (CoA) is a list of the General ledger accounts that will be used to enter or post the balances originating out of the transactions in SAP. These accounts can be of many kinds- the 2 primary categories being – *Income statement accounts* that record the Profit and loss numbers and the other that record balances i.e. *balance sheet accounts*. Often, large corporations retain the same CoA across all CCs for ease of reporting, however that is not mandatory and each CC can have its own CoA. In SAP, the same CC can have, depending on requirements, up to 3 CoAs:

1 **Operational CoA** – in which it does its own postings

2 **Country CoA** – set up to meet the legal requirements of specific countries

3 **Group CoA** – for multi-national corporations, this is used to amalgamate the postings from different CoAs of different CCs in multiple countries to report 'as a group'

For our purpose here, we will set up only the Operational CoA. It is set up in transaction OB13 or by following the path in IMG as below:

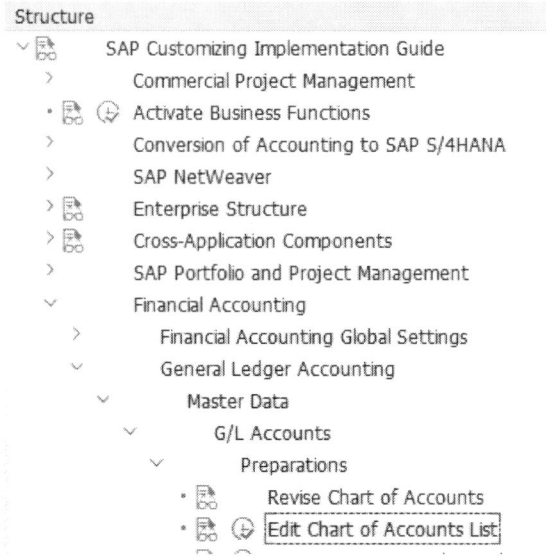

Fig 1

Click on New Entries and define the CoA as below. Since a COA can be used by many CCs concurrently for ease of operations and accounting, it is best to give them a generic or group name instead of one based on the CC:

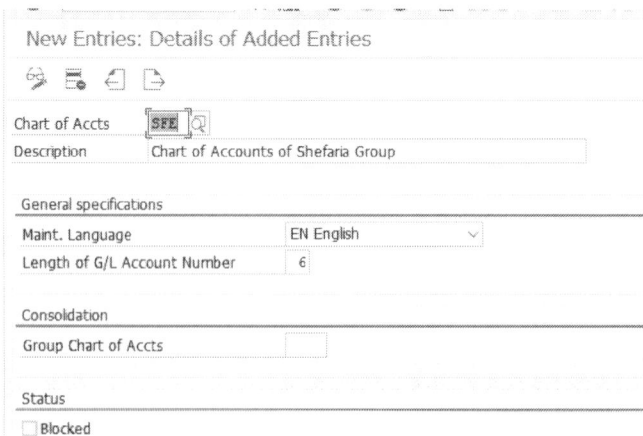

Fig 2

16

The G/L accounts can range from 4 to 10 digits and depending on a nomenclature that a company may choose, they can be defined as such. Normally, 6 digit good enough for the # of G/L accounts a CoA will have so we will choose 6 too. For the moment, since we are not doing consolidation, we will not define the Group CoA.

Save and the familiar window comes up to save the changes, which can be done in the same transport:

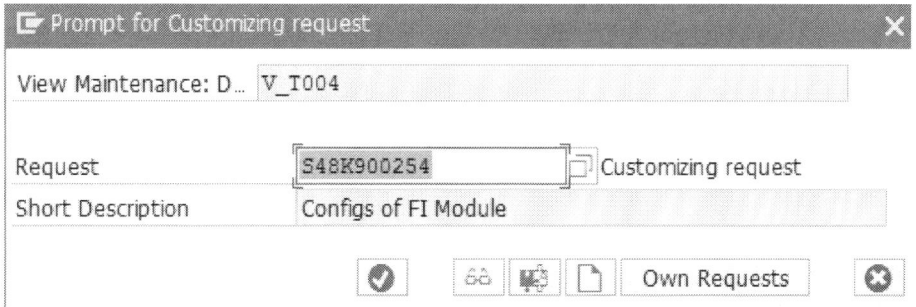

Fig 3

# ASSIGNING CO CODE TO COA (C)

T Code SPRO

Now we need to make our CC recognize the CoA to enable postings from its transactions into this CoA. To do that, we assign the CoA to the CC in the path:

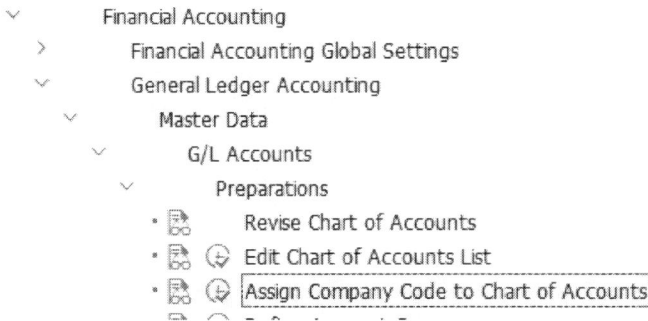

```
∨    Financial Accounting
  >       Financial Accounting Global Settings
  ∨       General Ledger Accounting
    ∨         Master Data
      ∨           G/L Accounts
        ∨             Preparations
          ·  ⧉          Revise Chart of Accounts
          ·  ⧉  ⊕       Edit Chart of Accounts List
          ·  ⧉  ⊕      Assign Company Code to Chart of Accounts
```

Fig 1

Alternatively, simply use transaction code OB62:

Search for the CC as previously, assign the CoA to it, and save:

Change View "Assign Company Code -> Chart Of Accounts": Overview

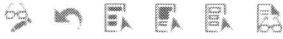

| CoCd | Company Name | City | Chrt/Accts | Cty ch/act |
|---|---|---|---|---|
| F120 | F100 NW | Seattle | | |
| FAZ1 | SAPFAZ CONSULTING 1 | LAUSANNE | FAZ1 | |
| NG01 | NG Company Code NG01 | Mumbai | | |
| NG02 | NG Company Code NG02 | Basel | | |
| PHNX | Phoenix Consulting | Stuttgart | YCOA | |
| SFE1 | Shefaria Ent Inc | Toronto | SFE | |

Fig 2

This now makes the CC hold its numbers in the G/L accounts of the CoA of the group. Later, we will set up some G/L accounts and see how all this aligns together.

# CREATING G/L ACCOUNT GROUPS (C)

T Code SPRO

To meet the statutory requirements of most countries, 2 account groups are mandatory – the Income statement group and the Balance sheet group. Some others could be like Fixed assets accounts, Data Conversion Acts (to hold temporary balances esp. at times of mergers/acquisitions) etc. The different account groups will drive how postings will be done, and what fields will be mandatory to fill in while setting up different G/L accounts. This configuration will also define the number ranges we give to the different account groups, which will also differentiate them from each other.

## Menu path:

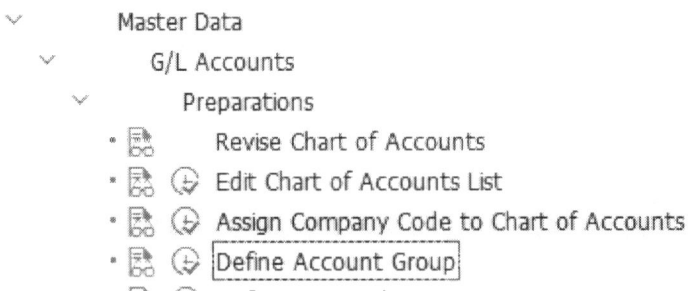

Fig 1

Alternatively, use transaction OBD4.

For our purpose we will set up 2 account groups for PL and BS and give them appropriate number ranges:

New Entries: Overview of Added Entries

Field status

| Chrt/Accts | Acct Group | Name | From Acct | To Account |
|------------|-----------|------|-----------|------------|
| SFE | BS | Balance Sheet Accounts | 100000 | 399999 |
| SFE | PL | L & L Accounts | 400000 | 999999 |

Fig 2

These ranges mean that when we set up a Balance sheet G/L Account, SAP will require us to give a number between 100000 and 399999 and for an Income statement account, between 400000 and 999999. The numbers cannot overlap between the 2 groups thus keeping them independent of each other.

This is also a good time to set up the Retained Earnings account. Without a RE account, the other P&L accounts can't be set up. This account is a configuration also unlike others, which are master data only and can be set up directly in all systems.

The RE account is set up in transaction OB53 or in the path:

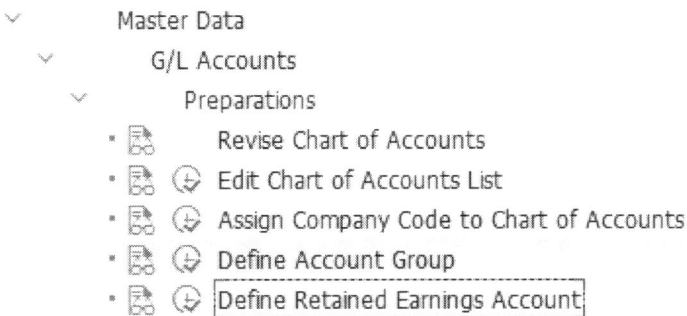

- Master Data
  - G/L Accounts
    - Preparations
      - Revise Chart of Accounts
      - Edit Chart of Accounts List
      - Assign Company Code to Chart of Accounts
      - Define Account Group
      - Define Retained Earnings Account

Fig 3

Enter the CoA when the window prompts you to and Set the account you wish the retained earnings to be posted to, keeping in mind it is a BS account:

21

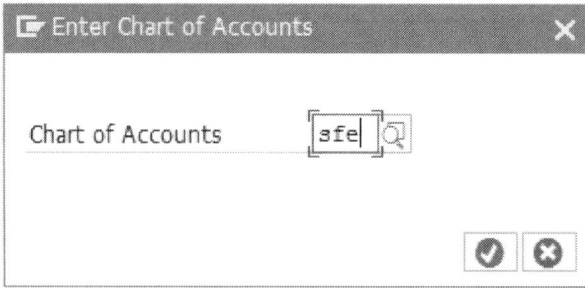

Fig 4

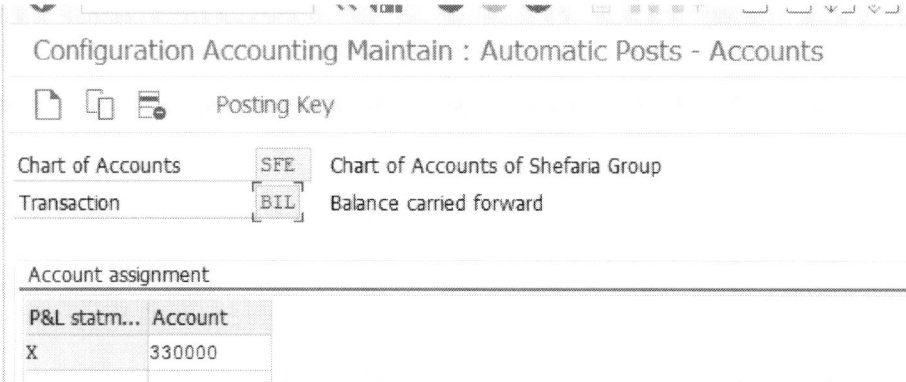

Fig 5

You may get a message at the bottom:

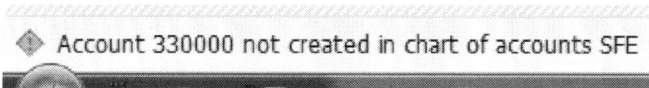

Account 330000 not created in chart of accounts SFE

Fig 6

This message is because we have not actually set up any GL account with this number, for the moment, Hit Enter and ignore the message. Save as usual.

# FISCAL YEAR VARIANT AND POSTING PERIODS (C)

## I.    FISCAL YEAR VARIANT

T Code SPRO

A fiscal period variant determines the period a company will adopt to keep its accounts. It may be the calendar year or one in which a company can make it's own periods – e.g. begin the year in July with period 1, August period 2 etc. or follow a different methodology which could even include half periods. Most companies prefer to set up 16 periods - 12 of them could be used as normal posting periods and the rest 4 for special postings. Normally, it is helpful to keep one such 'extra' period per quarter for tax adjustments and companies often do that. To mirror the actual posting periods in the real world to open and close the books, SAP provides the ability to set up fiscal year variants, which can be replicated to multiple CCs thereby making the process of setting up fiscal year variants, a lot simpler.  The path to assigning a fiscal year variant is in Fig 1.

Financial Accounting
    Financial Accounting Global Settings
       Regenerate CDS Views and Field Mapping
         Ledgers
           Fields
           Ledger
           Fiscal Year and Posting Periods
             Maintain Fiscal Year Variant
             Edit Fiscal Year Calendar
             Assign Company Code to a Fiscal Year Variant

Fig 1

Choose your company using the Position Key if it is not visible on the screen:

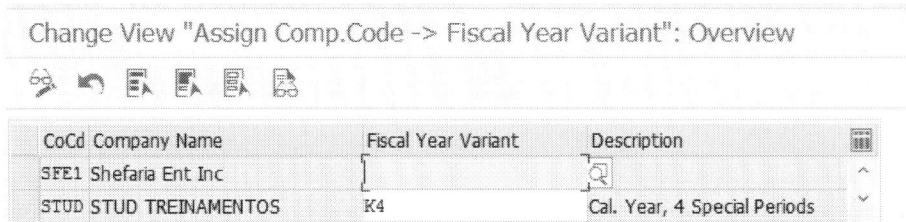

Change View "Assign Comp.Code -> Fiscal Year Variant": Overview

| CoCd | Company Name | Fiscal Year Variant | Description |
|------|--------------|---------------------|-------------|
| SFE1 | Shefaria Ent Inc | | |
| STUD | STUD TREINAMENTOS | K4 | Cal. Year, 4 Special Periods |

Fig 2

Press F4 in the field Fiscal Year Variant or click on the Desc icon to bring up the possible entries:

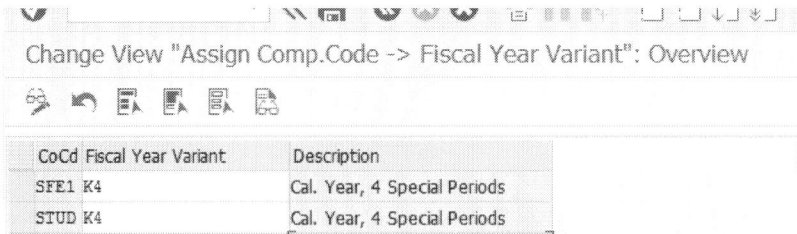

Change View "Assign Comp.Code -> Fiscal Year Variant": Overview

| CoCd | Fiscal Year Variant | Description |
|------|---------------------|-------------|
| SFE1 | K4 | Cal. Year, 4 Special Periods |
| STUD | K4 | Cal. Year, 4 Special Periods |

Fig 3

Normally the K4 period which divides an year into 4 quarters is most commonly used and there should be no need to set up any new ones as an available one will suffice.

We choose K4 and Save.

If a new one is required for any reason, it can be set up in the previous step:

Fig 4

## II.        POSTING PERIOD

T Code SPRO

Posting Period is the actual time during which documents can be posted to the accounting database. They usually mirror the actual dates for which the fiscal year variants are valid e.g. if we have a variant that is set up to divide the entire year into 12 calendar months, then the Finance dept. will maintain the posting period from the 1st to the end of the month. Thus, on July 18th the period open will be July, on August 1, the period open August and so on. Documents have to be necessarily posted in the open periods only. If, for any reason, documents are created later, then, quite likely, they will have to be posted in a later period as one normally does not go back and open closed periods.

Posting periods are also set up as posting period variants to reduce redundancy of set up.

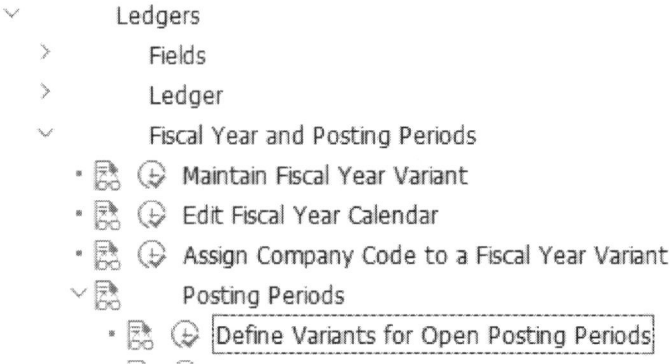

Fig 5

Again, make your entry as earlier:

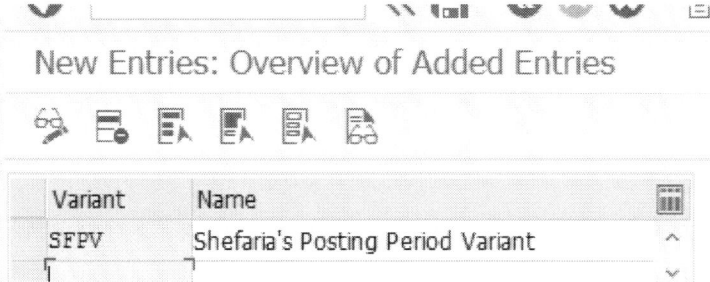

Fig 6

Normally, different CCs under the same company can share the same posting period variant unless dictated differently for legal reasons. It is not necessary though it helps in keeping the books in sync with each other and the business users then have to open/close only the variant and automatically it affects all the CCs that are using that variant.

In the next step, we will assign this variant to the CCs, in our case, just one for the moment

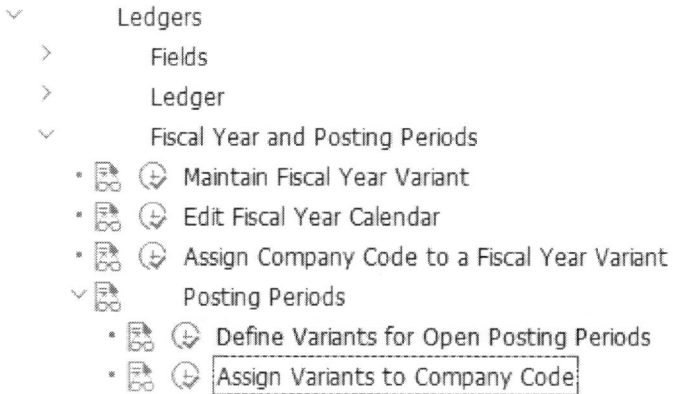

```
  ∨        Ledgers
     >        Fields
     >        Ledger
  ∨        Fiscal Year and Posting Periods
      · ▨ ⊕  Maintain Fiscal Year Variant
      · ▨ ⊕  Edit Fiscal Year Calendar
      · ▨ ⊕  Assign Company Code to a Fiscal Year Variant
      ∨ ▨     Posting Periods
          · ▨ ⊕  Define Variants for Open Posting Periods
          · ▨ ⊕  Assign Variants to Company Code
```

Fig 7

Search for your CC using the Position tab or otherwise by scrolling and assign the posting period variant to it:

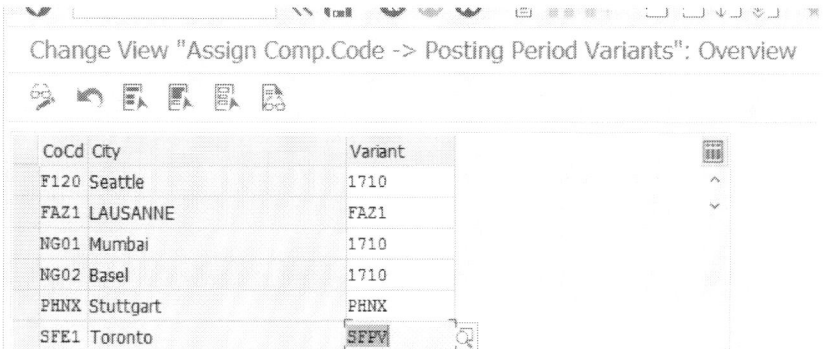

Change View "Assign Comp.Code -> Posting Period Variants": Overview

| CoCd | City | Variant | |
|------|------|---------|---|
| F120 | Seattle | 1710 | |
| FAZ1 | LAUSANNE | FAZ1 | |
| NG01 | Mumbai | 1710 | |
| NG02 | Basel | 1710 | |
| PHNX | Stuttgart | PHNX | |
| SFE1 | Toronto | SFPV | |

Fig 8

Save.

Now we look at how posting periods are opened and closed. T Code to Open and close posting periods is OB52 or S_ALR_87003642.

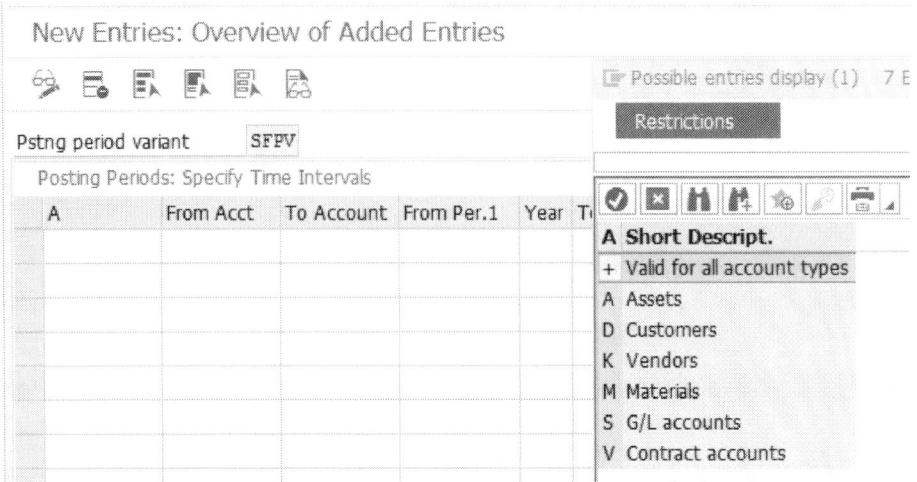

Fig 9

There are different kinds of accounts in SAP represented in the 2nd column:

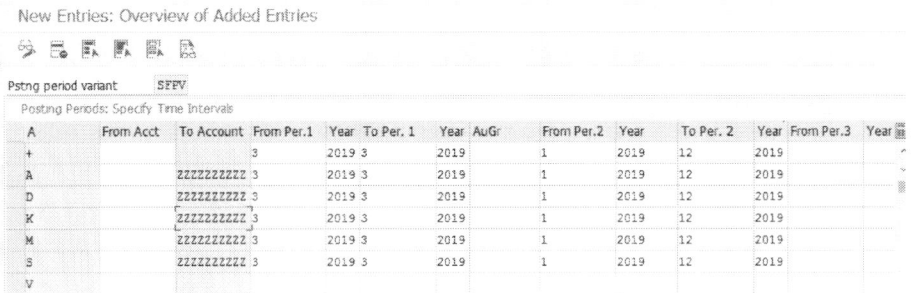

Fig 10

The entry in Fig 10 simply tells us that for SFE1 only 03/2019 i.e. Mar 2019 is open. Everything else, before and after this month, is closed. So based on this, on this day, we can post documents in the co code SFE1 only with a posting date of Mar, 2019 because it's posting period variant SFPV has only this one month as open.

We would normally define the posting periods for all kinds of accounts separately but not differently from each other though it is technically possible to close vendors, keep customers open etc. This overview simply states that only Mar 2019 is open to post accounting documents to, no other. Therefore, we can't pre-date or post-date documents other than of 03/2019 and post them. We can, in reality allow only vendor postings to be posted while preventing the AR (customers) or vice versa etc., though most companies would follow the right business practice of closing all of them as the period ends.

The field AuGr is a feature that validates the user who is changing the posting periods with their ability i.e. authorization to do so. A posting period can be made available to only a limited set of users using the authorization group.

Now, all the CCs that get the posting period variant SFPV attached to them will have their posting periods open and close together based on SFPV. Create these entries for all these kinds of G/L accounts for your posting period variant in the above table.

# FIELD STATUS GROUPS & VARIANTS (C)

T Code SPRO or OBC4

Every document has bits of data, which is necessary for some functional area of the organization to understand its impact on their particular domain. That data is often carried from the beginning to the end of the transaction's life cycle. It would be very cumbersome as well as prone to errors if that data were to be entered manually at every stage. Field status groups are one of the many such objects in SAP that enable us to keep fields as necessary – as mandatory, optional, suppressed or only to display (i.e. no change possible). Thus, configuration is done to mark them as such so that this data like plant, profit centers, cost centers, once determined, are allowed to flow from one preceding document to the next, with some of it unchangeable.

The transaction code is OBC4 or the path to set these field statuses and field status variants is:

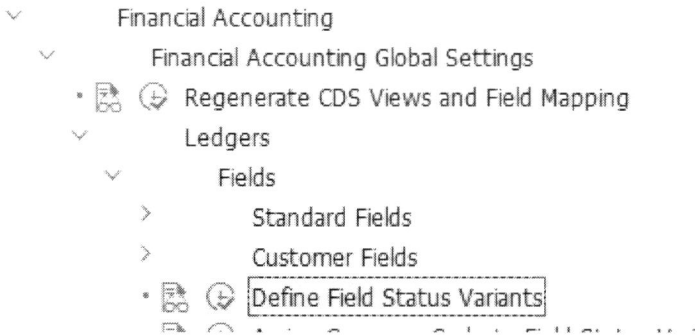

Fig 1

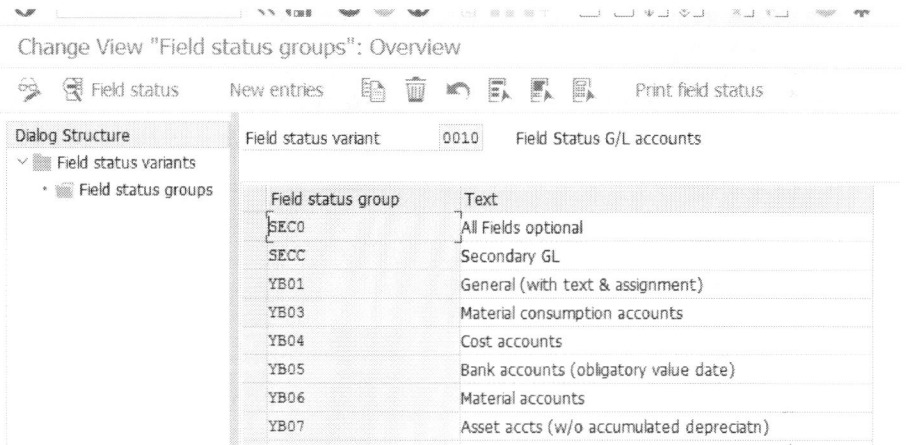

Fig 2

We will use 0010 for our purpose. As their names suggest, SAP has created them with the view of utilizing them for specific kinds of G/L accounts, e.g. YB04 for Cost accounts, YB07 for Asset accts (w/o accumulated depreciation). (see Fig 7).

Then, we have the ability to modify it as needed without disturbing the existing one. Select 0010 as above and click on the Copy button:

Fig 3

In the window that comes, replace 0010 with SFE1.

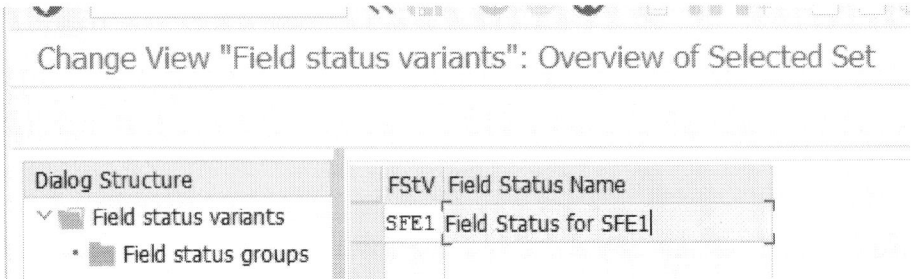

Change View "Field status variants": Overview of Selected Set

| Dialog Structure | | FStV | Field Status Name |
|---|---|---|---|
| ∨ ▦ Field status variants | | SFE1 | Field Status for SFE1 |
| • ▦ Field status groups | | | |

Fig 4

Hit Enter

In the window, say Copy All:

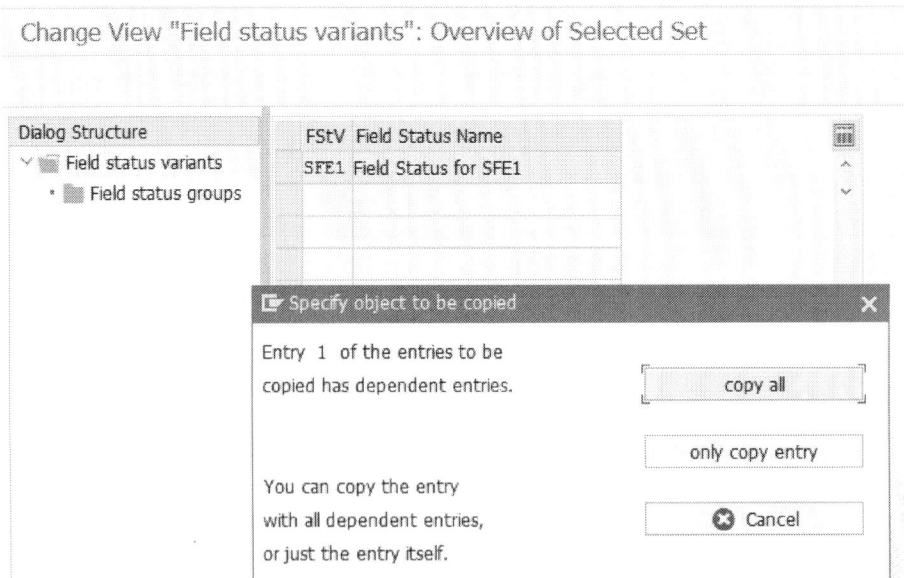

Change View "Field status variants": Overview of Selected Set

| Dialog Structure | | FStV | Field Status Name |
|---|---|---|---|
| ∨ ▦ Field status variants | | SFE1 | Field Status for SFE1 |
| • ▦ Field status groups | | | |

**Specify object to be copied**

Entry 1 of the entries to be copied has dependent entries.

| copy all |
|---|
| only copy entry |
| ⊗ Cancel |

You can copy the entry with all dependent entries, or just the entry itself.

Fig 5

A window informs you the copying was done.

Hit Enter again and we can see our field status variant:

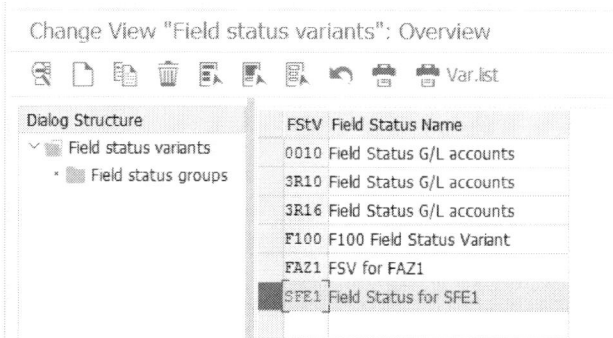

Change View "Field status variants": Overview

| FStV | Field Status Name |
|------|-------------------|
| 0010 | Field Status G/L accounts |
| 3R10 | Field Status G/L accounts |
| 3R16 | Field Status G/L accounts |
| F100 | F100 Field Status Variant |
| FAZ1 | FSV for FAZ1 |
| SFE1 | Field Status for SFE1 |

Fig 6

The 46 entries it had in 0010 are the underlying field status groups. These can be seen by checking the line SFE1 and double clicking on the line Field Status groups:

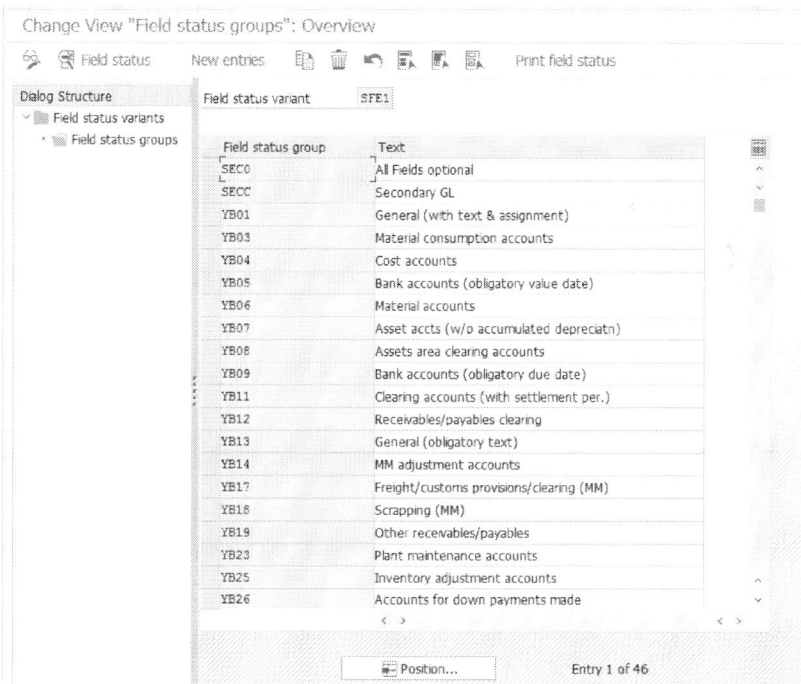

Change View "Field status groups": Overview

Field status variant    SFE1

| Field status group | Text |
|--------------------|------|
| SEC0 | All Fields optional |
| SECC | Secondary GL |
| YB01 | General (with text & assignment) |
| YB03 | Material consumption accounts |
| YB04 | Cost accounts |
| YB05 | Bank accounts (obligatory value date) |
| YB06 | Material accounts |
| YB07 | Asset accts (w/o accumulated depreciatn) |
| YB08 | Assets area clearing accounts |
| YB09 | Bank accounts (obligatory due date) |
| YB11 | Clearing accounts (with settlement per.) |
| YB12 | Receivables/payables clearing |
| YB13 | General (obligatory text) |
| YB14 | MM adjustment accounts |
| YB17 | Freight/customs provisions/clearing (MM) |
| YB18 | Scrapping (MM) |
| YB19 | Other receivables/payables |
| YB23 | Plant maintenance accounts |
| YB25 | Inventory adjustment accounts |
| YB26 | Accounts for down payments made |

Position...    Entry 1 of 46

Fig 7

Note the same number 46 at the bottom. This is what was copied.

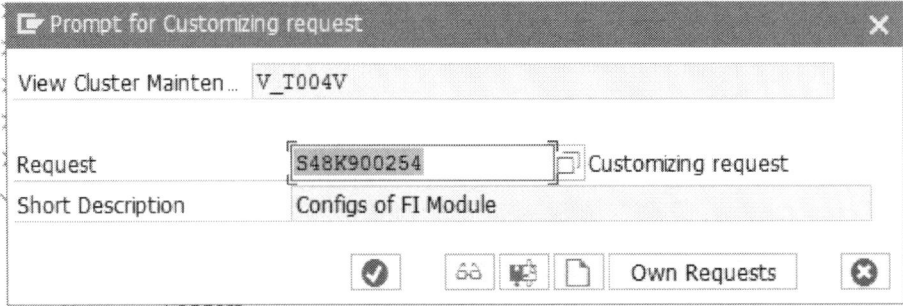

**Prompt for Customizing request** ✕

| | |
|---|---|
| View Cluster Mainten... | V_T004V |
| Request | S48K900254 ⬜ Customizing request |
| Short Description | Configs of FI Module |

✓    👓   🗐   🗋   Own Requests   ✕

Fig 8

To see more detail about them, let's look at an example like YB03 relating to Material consumption accounts:

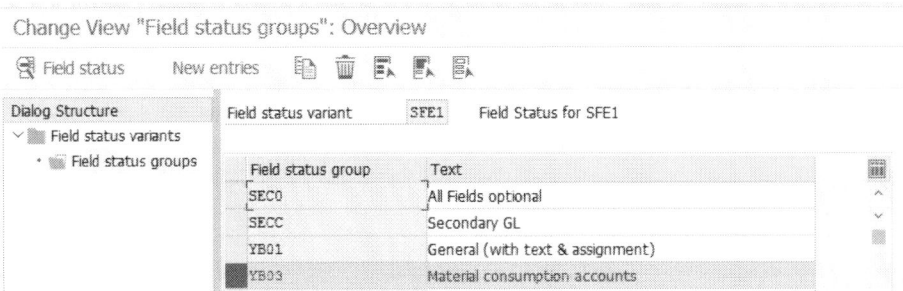

Change View "Field status groups": Overview

🗐 Field status    New entries   🗐 🗑 🗐 🗐 🗐

Dialog Structure
∨ 🖿 Field status variants
  • 🖿 Field status groups

Field status variant   SFE1   Field Status for SFE1

| Field status group | Text |
|---|---|
| SEC0 | All Fields optional |
| SECC | Secondary GL |
| YB01 | General (with text & assignment) |
| YB03 | Material consumption accounts |

Fig 9

Check the first one and click on the field 'Field Status'

🗐 Field status    |

Fig 10

Underlying each variant (here YB03) is a list of the field group:

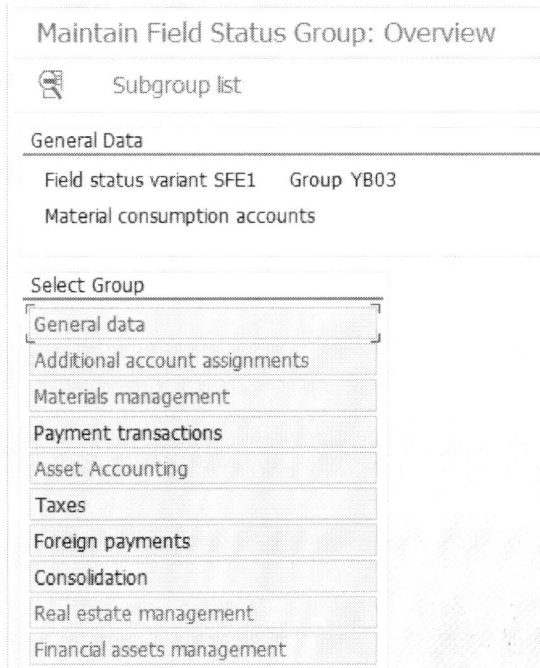

**Fig 11**

These field status groups relate to different data on the document and each signifies a kind of data. Double clicking each one of them gives more details about the fields and how they have been set up (ROS – Required/Optional/Suppress):

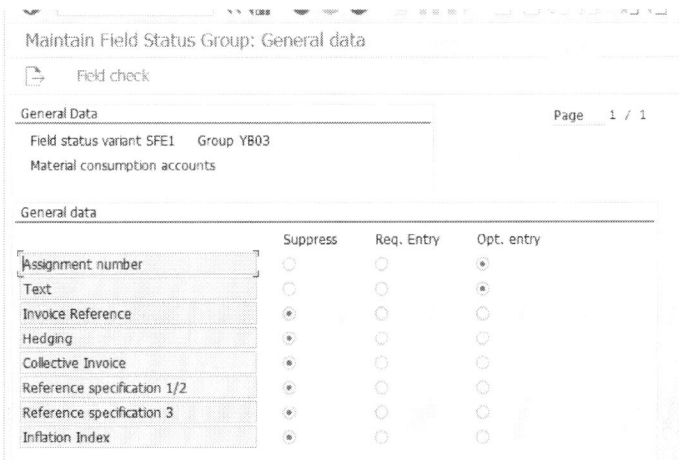

**Fig 12**

The next step is to assign our field status variant to the CC so it can be used. The T code for that is OBC5 or we can follow the path:

```
v        Financial Accounting
   v        Financial Accounting Global Settings
      · 🗟 🕒 Regenerate CDS Views and Field Mapping
         v        Ledgers
            v        Fields
               >        Standard Fields
               >        Customer Fields
            · 🗟 🕒 Define Field Status Variants
            · 🗟 🕒 Assign Company Code to Field Status Variants
```

Fig 13

Find your CC using the Position key or by scrolling and then add the FSV SFE1 to it:

Change View "Assign Company Code -> Field Status Variant": Overview

🔧 ↩ 🗟 🗟 🗟 🗟

| CoCd | Company Name | City | Fld stat.var. | 🔢 |
|------|-------------|------|---------------|---|
| SFE1 | Shefaria Ent Inc | Toronto | SFE1 | ^ |
| STUD | STUD TREINAMENTOS | SANTO ANDRE | 0010 | v |

Fig 14

Hint: If there will be multiple CCs i.e. more to be set up down the road and normally, since in larger organizations, the CoA is common to all the CCs, it may be advisable to give a more 'generic' FSV code name like 1000 or SFV etc.

# NUMBER RANGES (C)

T Code SPRO or FBN1

The entire SAP is a litany of numbers and dates. With the combination of the two plus some other relevant data the entire data flow can be constructed. Every document that posts in FI must have some sort of a number, system either generated or external. The users have the ability to decide on any number range they wish. The number range can be repeated over different CCs though it is advisable that for clear accounting and audit trails, it is not done. It can also be repeated over different document types (we will discuss this later) i.e. different types of documents can share one number range. Number ranges are set up in different systems separately, a concept we will visit when we discuss testing of the system at the end of the course. The ranges on the FI side are set up in transaction FBN1. Alternatively, the path:

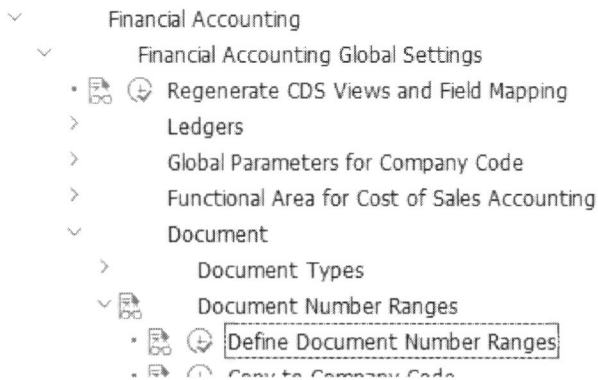

Fig 1

Since SAP has already pre-defined ranges for the template in this system, co code 0001, we will merely copy it, later, if we need to re-visit it, we can.

Enter 0001 as below and then click on the Copy button -

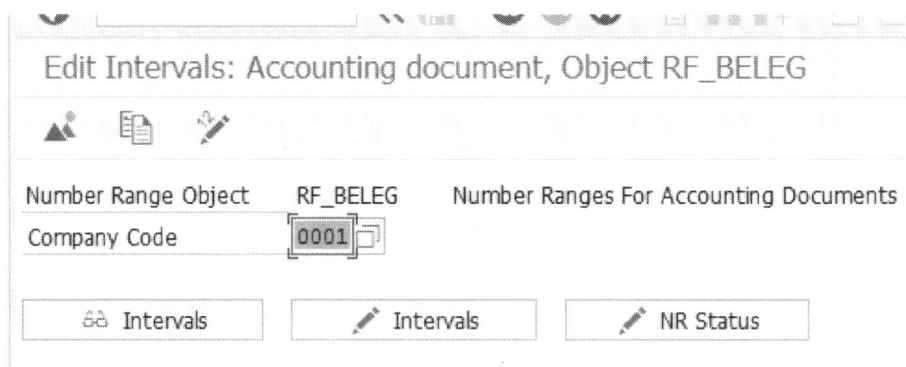

Fig 2

In the window, enter your CC – copying from '0001' to 'your CC':

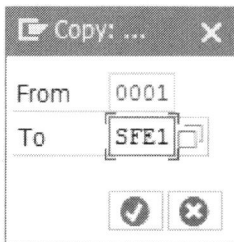

Fig 3

Click on the Copy button again and a window comes up advising you to transport them separately. Normally, they can also be set up separately in the systems as noted above.

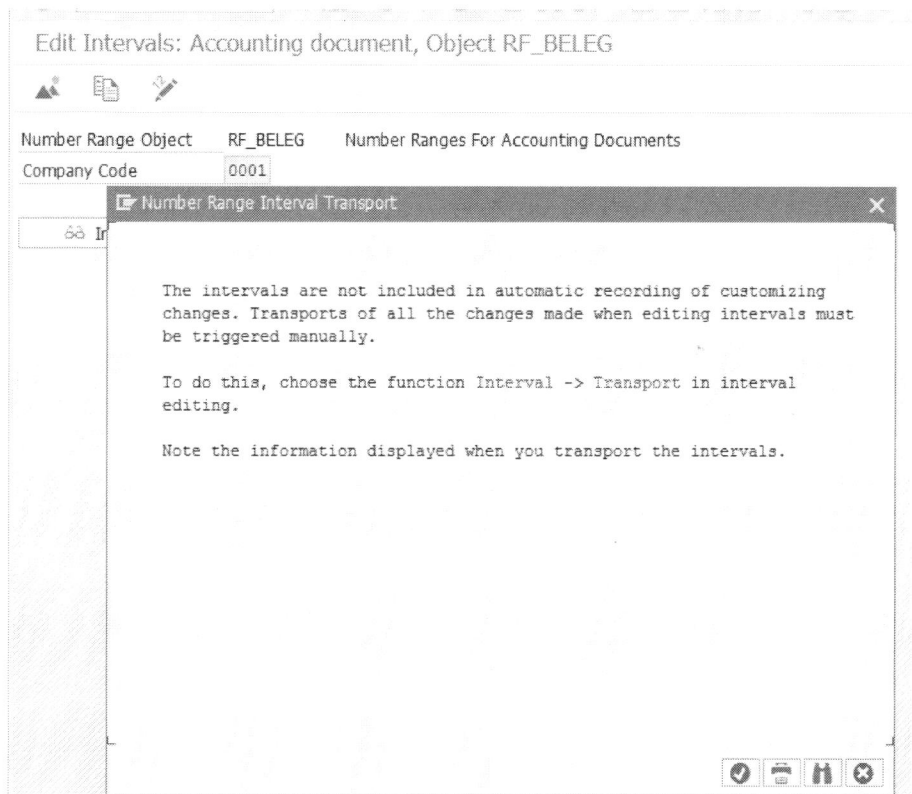

**Edit Intervals: Accounting document, Object RF_BELEG**

Number Range Object    RF_BELEG    Number Ranges For Accounting Documents
Company Code         0001

**Number Range Interval Transport**

The intervals are not included in automatic recording of customizing changes. Transports of all the changes made when editing intervals must be triggered manually.

To do this, choose the function Interval -> Transport in interval editing.

Note the information displayed when you transport the intervals.

Fig 4

Hit Enter and you get a message at the bottom:

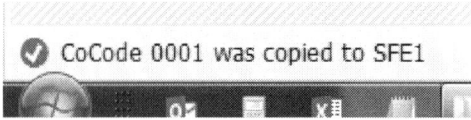

CoCode 0001 was copied to SFE1

Fig 5

To verify, enter your CC on the screen and click on Display or Change mode of the intervals:

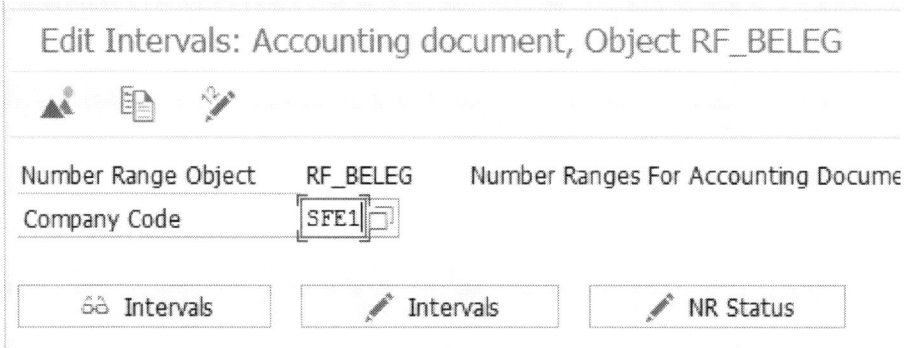

Edit Intervals: Accounting document, Object RF_BELEG

| Number Range Object | RF_BELEG | Number Ranges For Accounting Docume |
| Company Code | SFE1 | |

| 👓 Intervals | 🖉 Intervals | 🖉 NR Status |

Fig 6

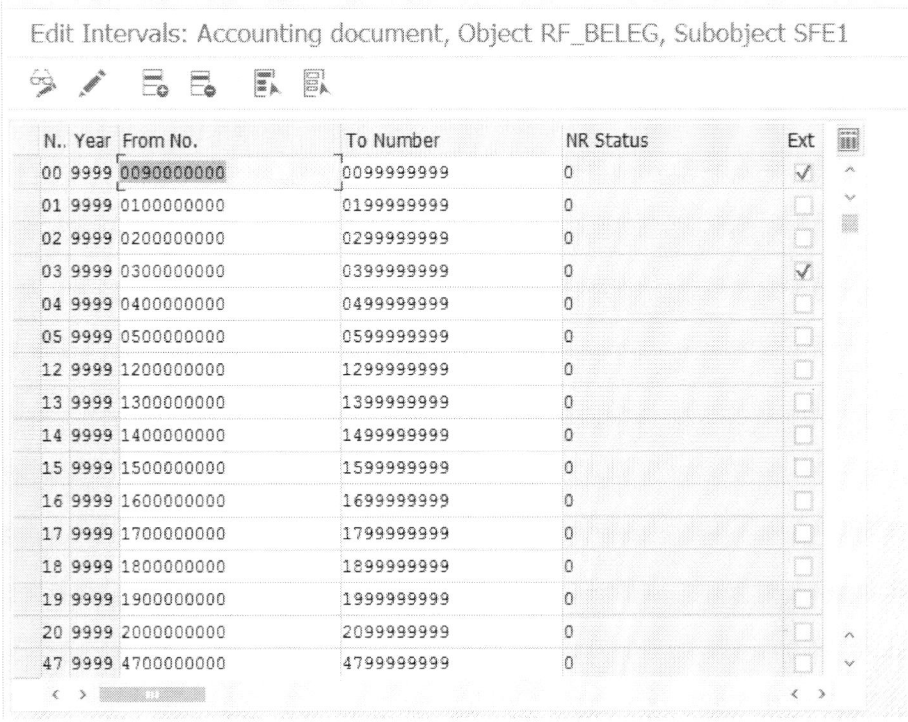

Edit Intervals: Accounting document, Object RF_BELEG, Subobject SFE1

| N.. | Year | From No. | To Number | NR Status | Ext | |
|-----|------|----------|-----------|-----------|-----|---|
| 00 | 9999 | 0090000000 | 0099999999 | 0 | ✓ | |
| 01 | 9999 | 0100000000 | 0199999999 | 0 | ☐ | |
| 02 | 9999 | 0200000000 | 0299999999 | 0 | ☐ | |
| 03 | 9999 | 0300000000 | 0399999999 | 0 | ✓ | |
| 04 | 9999 | 0400000000 | 0499999999 | 0 | ☐ | |
| 05 | 9999 | 0500000000 | 0599999999 | 0 | ☐ | |
| 12 | 9999 | 1200000000 | 1299999999 | 0 | ☐ | |
| 13 | 9999 | 1300000000 | 1399999999 | 0 | ☐ | |
| 14 | 9999 | 1400000000 | 1499999999 | 0 | ☐ | |
| 15 | 9999 | 1500000000 | 1599999999 | 0 | ☐ | |
| 16 | 9999 | 1600000000 | 1699999999 | 0 | ☐ | |
| 17 | 9999 | 1700000000 | 1799999999 | 0 | ☐ | |
| 18 | 9999 | 1800000000 | 1899999999 | 0 | ☐ | |
| 19 | 9999 | 1900000000 | 1999999999 | 0 | ☐ | |
| 20 | 9999 | 2000000000 | 2099999999 | 0 | ☐ | |
| 47 | 9999 | 4700000000 | 4799999999 | 0 | ☐ | |

Fig 7

# GENERAL LEDGER IN SAP (U)

T Code FS00 (Area Menu)

The General ledger, henceforth, G/L Accounts in SAP is simply 'buckets' in which amounts pertaining to different activities or balances are held. We saw previously there are different types of account groups under which G/L accounts are set up. Further, the G/L accounts usually belong to a Chart of Accounts and a CoA may be repeated over multiple CCs, thereby indirectly assigning the G/L account to a CC. However, the G/L accounts then need to be created/extended to the CC itself also.

## There are 3 different types of G/L accounts in SAP:

1. Accounts to which we must post via transactions i.e. no direct JEs are possible to these accounts. Typically, these entries are posted from a different module like SD posts revenues/receivables and MM posts purchases/payables. No direct entry to these accounts is possible. Instead, the entries emanate from a sub ledger – there are also reconciliation accounts, which fall in this definition.
2. Direct entry accounts like direct purchases e.g. consumption accounts, balance sheet accounts etc.
3. Indirect accounts where postings take place as a part of a different posting – typically a tax account will be like that where the taxes are a certain % of the revenue or expense and get posted accordingly

Alternatively, we can set up G/L accounts in a CoA and later extend them to the CCs we wish to. The G/L account must exist in the CC to enable postings to take place to the account.

G/L accounts are best explained by creating one to represent different business activities or balances. For the sake of brevity, we will set them up in 2 major groups that represent the P & L and a Balance sheet:

1. Balance Sheet
2. P & L

Re-visiting our numbering sequence will tell us what numbers we can give them:

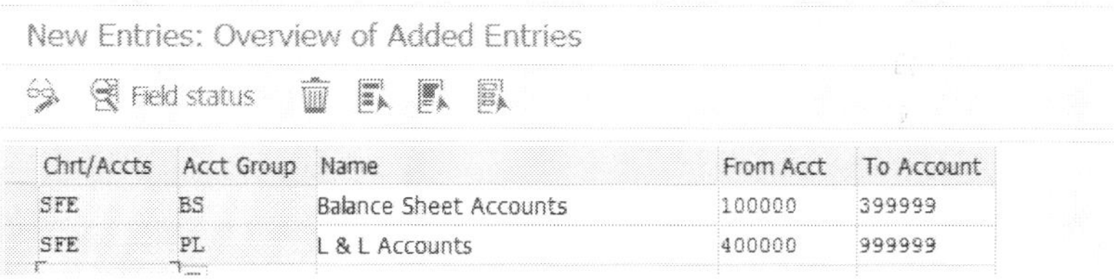

New Entries: Overview of Added Entries

🔗 🔍 Field status  🗑 📑 📑 📑

| Chrt/Accts | Acct Group | Name | From Acct | To Account |
|---|---|---|---|---|
| SFE | BS | Balance Sheet Accounts | 100000 | 399999 |
| SFE | PL | L & L Accounts | 400000 | 999999 |

Fig 1

The people running the accounting and finance areas in the organization generally set up G/L accounts. Let us set up a G/L account and understand the significance of each field in this set up. The transaction to set up a G/L account is in a menu called FS00 or we can follow the below path on the transactional SAP menu (not IMG/SPRO).

This is on the Menu at log in time:

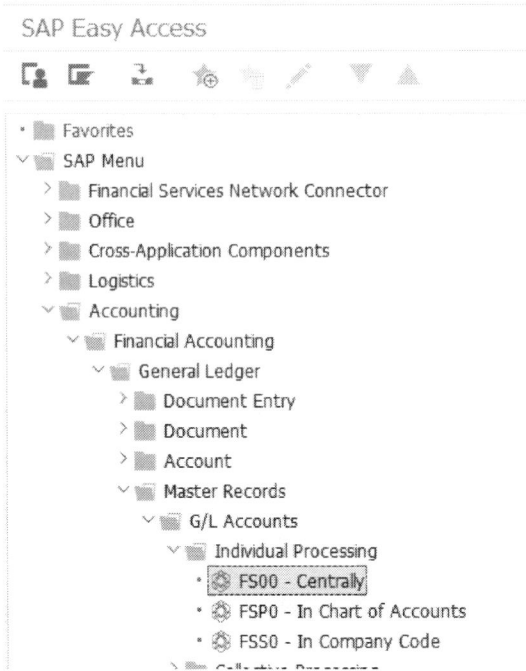

Fig 2

Enter the G/L account and company code in the window. Let us create a revenue account 451010:

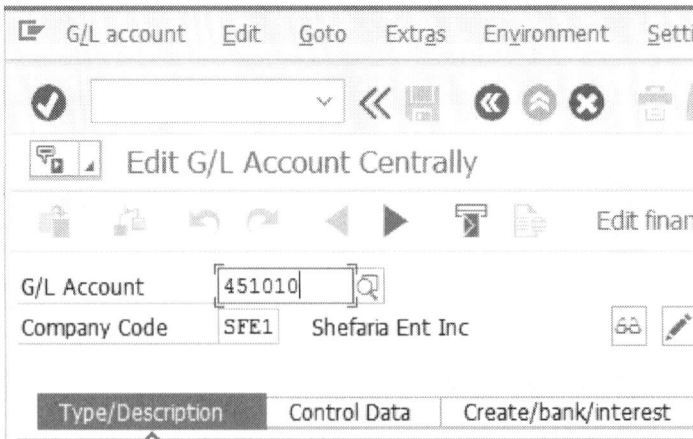

Fig 3

Enter the Account # and CC as in Fig 3, and Go to G/L Account> Create:

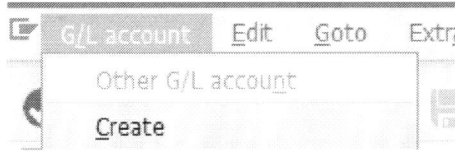

Fig 4

Select Primary Costs or Revenue if we will use it as for posting revenues or costs directly e.g. from Sales or Purchase:

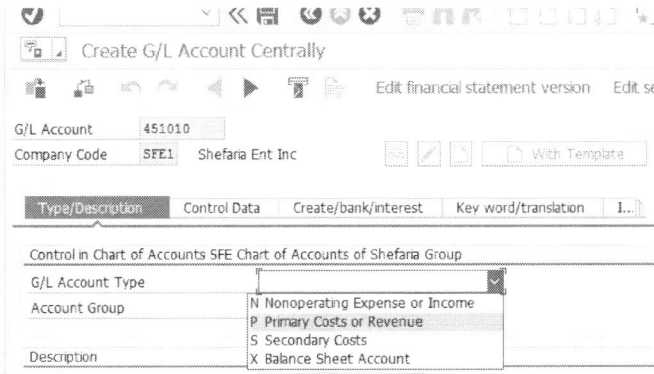

Fig 5

As for the Account group, we already know the numbering series is PL accounts and select that:

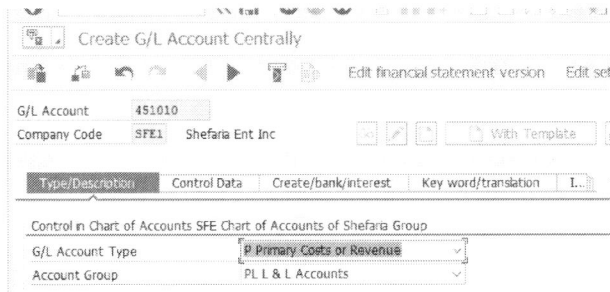

Fig 6

Give it the appropriate description i.e. it's purpose:

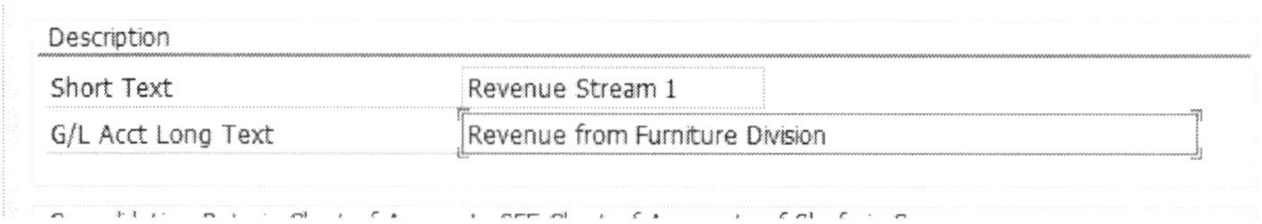

| Description | |
|---|---|
| Short Text | Revenue Stream 1 |
| G/L Acct Long Text | Revenue from Furniture Division |

Fig 7

On the next tab, the main field is currency, which should auto, populate from the CC currency e.g. CAD in our case:

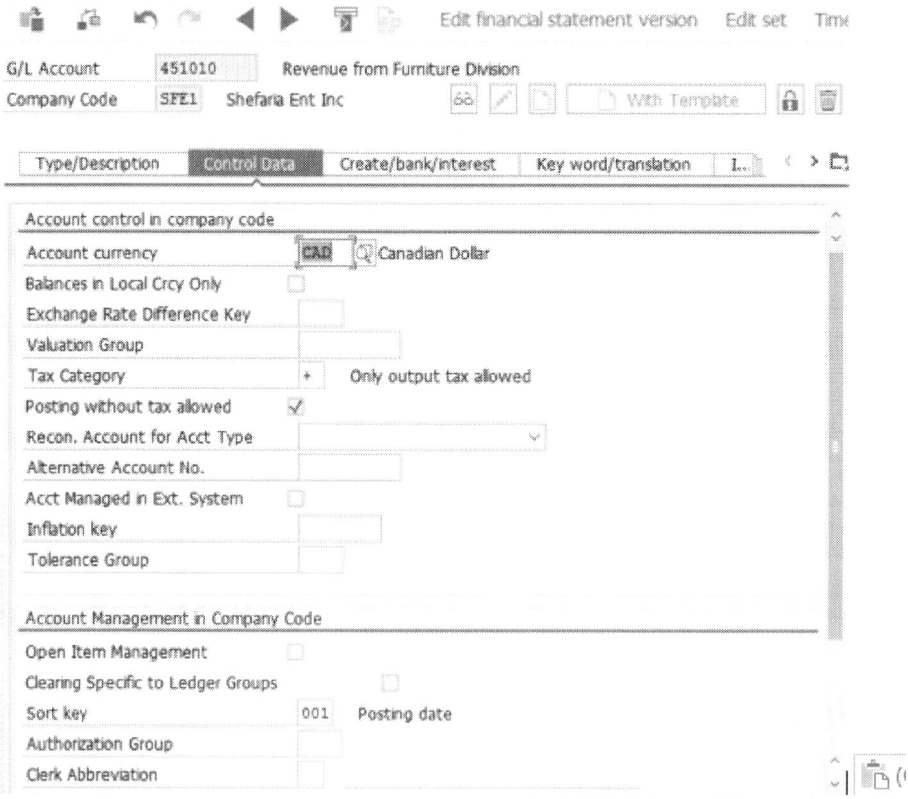

G/L Account 451010 Revenue from Furniture Division
Company Code SFE1 Shefaria Ent Inc

Type/Description | Control Data | Create/bank/interest | Key word/translation | 1..

Account control in company code

| Account currency | CAD | Canadian Dollar |
| Balances in Local Crcy Only | | |
| Exchange Rate Difference Key | | |
| Valuation Group | | |
| Tax Category | + | Only output tax allowed |
| Posting without tax allowed | ✓ | |
| Recon. Account for Acct Type | | |
| Alternative Account No. | | |
| Acct Managed in Ext. System | | |
| Inflation key | | |
| Tolerance Group | | |

Account Management in Company Code

| Open Item Management | |
| Clearing Specific to Ledger Groups | |
| Sort key | 001 Posting date |
| Authorization Group | |
| Clerk Abbreviation | |

Fig 8

- **Tax category** – in SAP the output taxes (on sales) and input taxes (on purchases) are different categories. Since this is a revenue account, it makes sense to mark it as such

- **Posting without tax allowed** – generally, keep this checked for nontaxable customers.
- **Sort Key** – this enables the reporting sequence. Usually 001 is the preferred one as it gives the listing in sequence of the Posting Date.

**Click on the Create/Bank/Interest tab:**

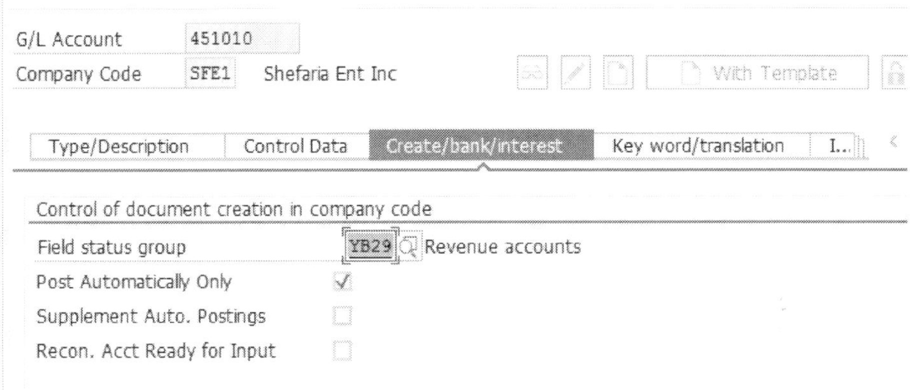

| G/L Account | 451010 | | | | |
| Company Code | SFE1 | Shefaria Ent Inc | | With Template | |

| Type/Description | Control Data | Create/bank/interest | Key word/translation | I... |

**Control of document creation in company code**

| Field status group | YB29 | Revenue accounts |
| Post Automatically Only | ✓ | |
| Supplement Auto. Postings | ☐ | |
| Recon. Acct Ready for Input | ☐ | |

Fig 9

- **Field Status group** – this is the same that we saw in the step of Field Status variants. Use the one that exists for revenue accounts – YB29
- **Post automatically** – this button ensures no manual postings can be done to this G/L account. Since it is an account that will collect the revenue and since revenue is a result of sales orders from customers, the postings into this account should originate from Sales side. Thus, we ensure nobody can post revenue directly in the system.
- **Supplemental Auto Postings** - Indicates that line items which are generated automatically by the system for this account can be supplemented manually.
- **Recon. Acct Ready for Input** - Indicator which determines that the reconciliation account is ready for input when posting a document. The indicator is used in Financial Assets Management.

The other tabs are not important for anything specific that can affect the postings.

**HANA CHANGE:** In HANA, SAP has taken away the choice to ask for line item display or not in the G/L account set up. All items by default are now open to line item display. This is likely due to a faster database as well as how the report is structured which we will see later.

Save the account and it is ready for use. Because it was created in the CC SFE1, it automatically is also in the CoA SFE.

# RECONCILIATION ACCOUNTS (C/U)

T Code SPRO, FS00

Reconciliation accounts are provided by SAP as secondary accounts into which the main accounts pour their numbers. These accounts merely act as a 'one point' storage to see amounts relating to total receivables, payables, assets etc and are very useful at the time of generating the P&L and Balance Sheet. When we set up customers and vendors, this account is a mandatory field that needs to be filled up so the system can recognize the account that needs to be updated with the sale or purchase transaction with that customer or vendor.

A typical transaction will occur like this:

A purchase of $1000 of a product has occurred and the vendor has submitted an invoice for it, which is posted to AP.

This transaction will perform the Vendor and expense direct entries:

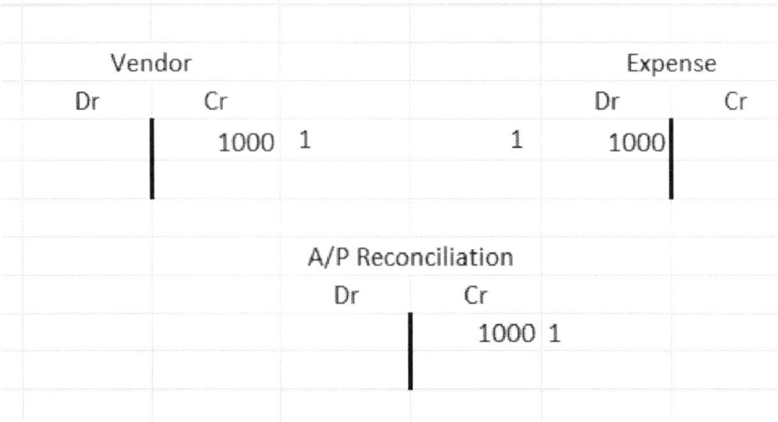

| Vendor | | | | | Expense | |
|---|---|---|---|---|---|---|
| Dr | Cr | | | Dr | | Cr |
| | 1000 1 | | 1 | 1000 | | |

| A/P Reconciliation | |
|---|---|
| Dr | Cr |
| | 1000 1 |

Fig 1

Based on the reconciliation account defined in the customer master, SAP will post another entry in the background to it to the A/P Reconciliation account. Thus, with hundreds of such vendor invoice receipts taking place, the A/P Reco account will hold all those balances and one can look up the payables amount at one spot. The Recon acct is the general ledger account, which is updated via the sub-ledger accounts.

Once the vendor is paid, the following will happen in the system:

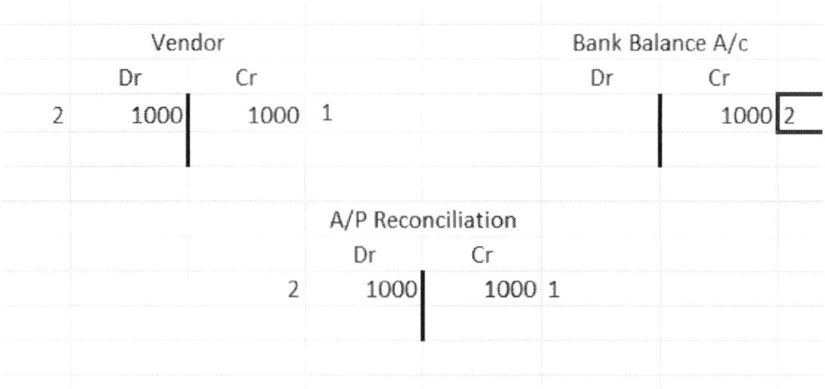

| | Vendor | | | | Bank Balance A/c | |
|---|---|---|---|---|---|---|
| | Dr | Cr | | | Dr | Cr |
| 2 | 1000 | 1000 1 | | | | 1000 2 |

| | A/P Reconciliation | |
|---|---|---|
| | Dr | Cr |
| 2 | 1000 | 1000 1 |

Fig 2

Let us create a reconciliation account 211000 for Trade Payables – Domestic for the vendors that will provide goods or services to the SFE1. Again, the T Code is the same, FS00:

Since, this account will hold the total amount of payables at any point of time; it must be a Balance sheet account:

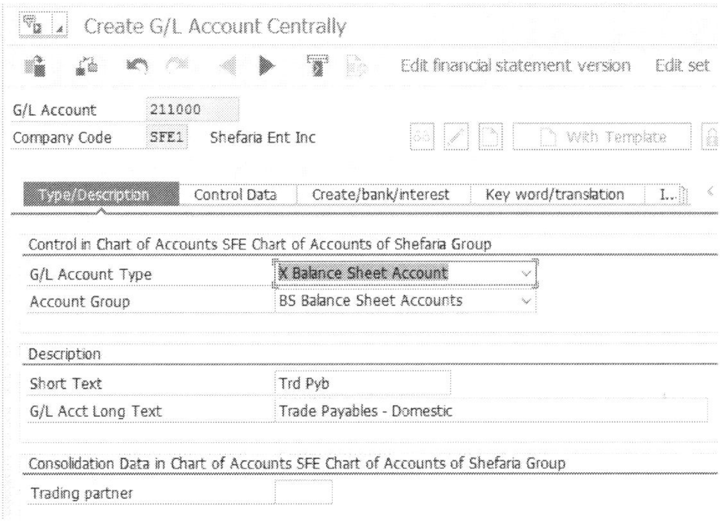

Fig 3

Control Data tab:

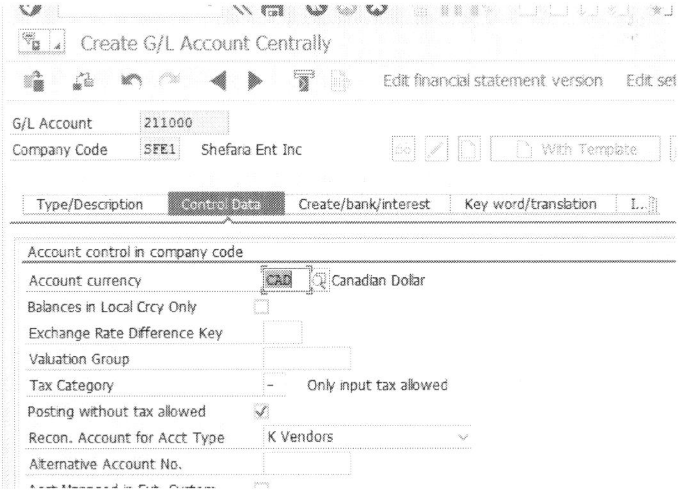

Fig 4

The notation 'K' is the same 'K' we saw in the posting period open/close screen. It is K here because this account 211000 (a part of the BS sheet series of accounts) is for trade payables (to vendors). Had it been for trade receivables, we would have used D (from customers). We have to open or close posting periods for the account type K to enable the postings to flow in the same way as they would for the normal revenue G/L accounts thus, to maintain balance between the two, it is generally recommended to open and close all kinds of accounts synchronously.

Again, the currency will pre-populate based on the CC of the CoA. It is recommended to allow all kinds of tax categories by using a '*'.

It is not recommended to check the boxes Open line item management or line item display as the former is unnecessary since postings take place only indirectly to the recon accounts and the latter will cause a lot of time to be taken to run the reports relating to the recon accounts due to the high volume of transactions with each transaction also posting to the recon account. However, it is possible to select line item display if one really feels the need to.

### Create/Bank/Interest Key tab:

Use YB67 for recon accounts:

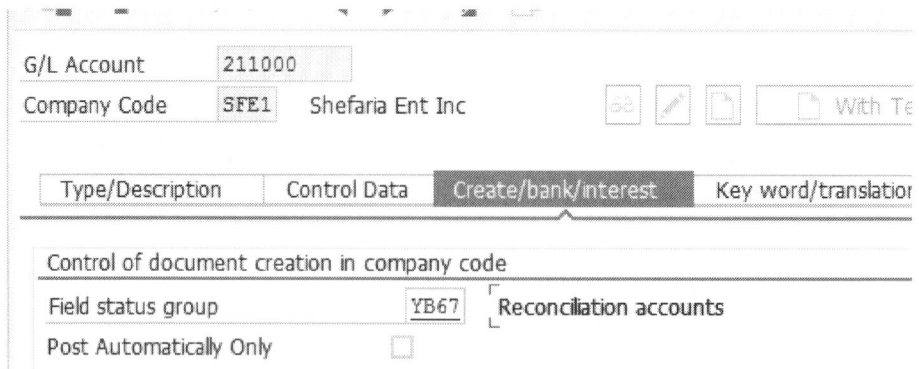

Fig 5

Do not check any other boxes are they are not relevant to a recon account. A recon account by default can only be posted to automatically via a transaction from the sales or purchasing side.

The other tabs are not significant and mainly relate to descriptions in different languages, relationships to cost elements etc.

Save the G/L account, the message should come at the bottom:

Fig 6

Along with the others, at this stage, also set up the retained Earnings G/L account we configured earlier – 330000. It is a BS sheet account.

### HANA CHANGE:

If you input a G/L that does not exist (and this is true across many other data across SAP HANA), the system displays a message stating 'no Results Found':

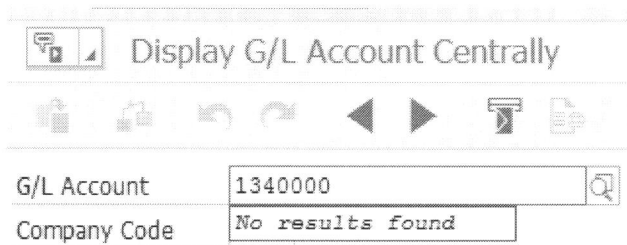

If it exists, it will find it for you:

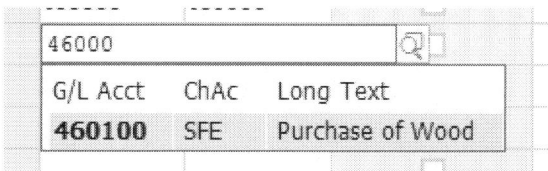

# DEFINING EMPLOYEE TOLERENCE (C)

T Code SPRO

Before we can make any real postings to a G/L account, we must define Employee tolerance limits. These limits set up the following information:

1. Maximum amount that can be posted in a single accounting document
2. Maximum amount that can be posted to a vendor or customer account. This field restricts the amount that can be paid to a vendor or cleared from receivables for a customer.
3. Maximum percentage for a cash discount that can be applied to a line item in this field.
4. Maximum acceptable tolerance for payment differences

These tolerance limits are defined in employee groups which in turn are attached to the user's profiles in the area of SAP roles/authorizations and security. The path to set this up is:

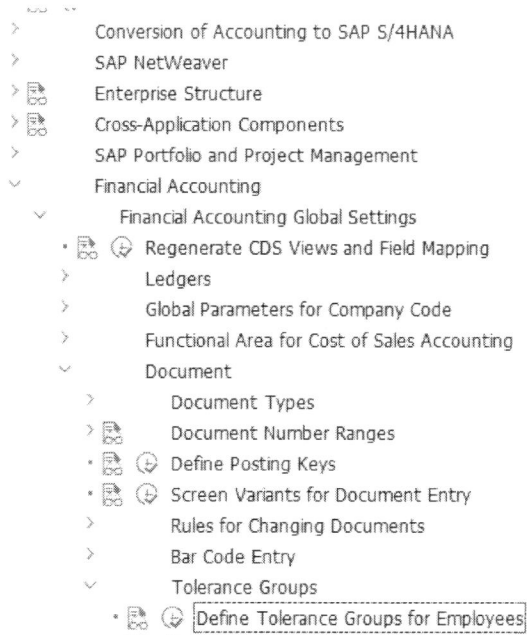

Fig 1

For the purpose of keeping this simple, we will define for only one employee, not as any group of employees. We make the entry for the CC in the table below by clicking on New Entries tab:

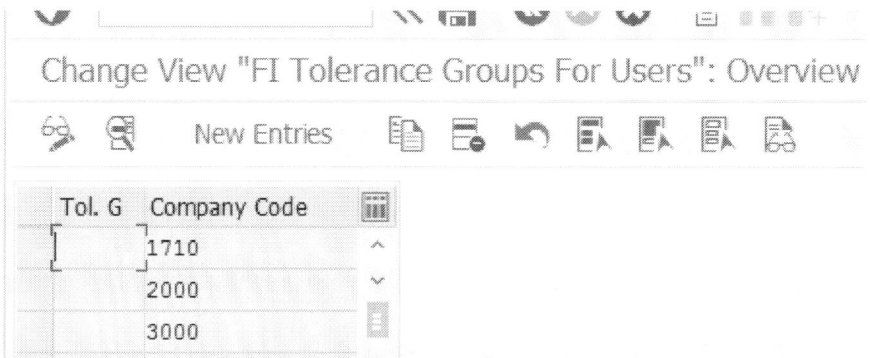

Fig 2

| Group | | | |
|---|---|---|---|
| Company code | SFE1 | Shefaria Ent Inc | Toronto |
| Currency | CAD | | |

**Upper limits for posting procedures**

| | |
|---|---|
| Amount per document | 100,000,000.00 |
| Amount per open item account item | 100,000,000.00 |
| Cash discount per line item | 10.000 % |

**Permitted payment differences**

| | Amount | Percent | Cash discnt adj.to |
|---|---|---|---|
| Revenue | 100.00 | 99.9 % | |
| Expense | 100.00 | 99.9 % | |

Fig 3

## This means:

- The employee can post a total document till 100 mn CAD and each line of a max 100 mn
- The differences the employee is allowed to apply against the receivable or payable compared to the actual transaction value is 100 dollars or up till 99.9%. The % is valid only for a gain, not loss. SAP chooses the lower of the two, hence if we want to define the limits in absolute terms, the percentage must always be kept to 99.9.

Save this configuration.

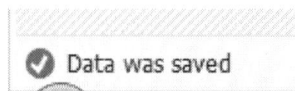

✓ Data was saved

Fig 4

# POSTING G/L ENTRIES (U)

T Code FB50 or FB50L

At this point, we have defined the following:

1. Our company code and it's CoA
2. A few G/L accounts, of type P&L, Balance sheet and reconciliation; some allow direct postings, some not
3. Employee tolerances which determine how much an employee can post, both in absolute terms of a manual JE and in relative terms as a % or $ difference from the actual transaction document.

While there are some more configurations like tax codes for accounts that mandatorily require taxes in the amounts to be posted, we will for the moment, proceed with minimal and simplest posting to see how it is done.

When G/L entries are done, every entry must have a debit and credit side to it and both must balance else SAP will not allow the posting to take place. Thus, 2 or more different accounts are needed to make one posting in the system. SAP allows until 999 line items for every document.

The books in SAP are posted to from the point of view of the corporation. The accounting rules that drive them are:

1. To increase the value of an expense or asset account, we post a debit entry to it
2. To decrease the value of the expense or asset account, we post a credit entry to it
3. To increase the value of a revenue or liability account, we post a credit entry to it
4. To decrease the value of a revenue or liability account, we post a debit entry to it

Before we actually create any recurring entries, we need to look at the concept of posting keys in SAP. Posting keys control the line item posting in a document screen. They also control the data underlying them:

> A/c Type (A-assets, D-customer, K-vendor and S-GL),
> Transaction Type and
> Nature of the Transaction (debit/credit)

A unique combination of these 3 elements is a different posting key. Just by knowing the # of the posting key, one can identify what kind of transaction it is. Though not a major utility, it facilitates daily work when posting manual JEs. There should not be any reason to set up any new ones, SAP provided standard ones will always suffice. The different posting keys can be seen in the configuration:

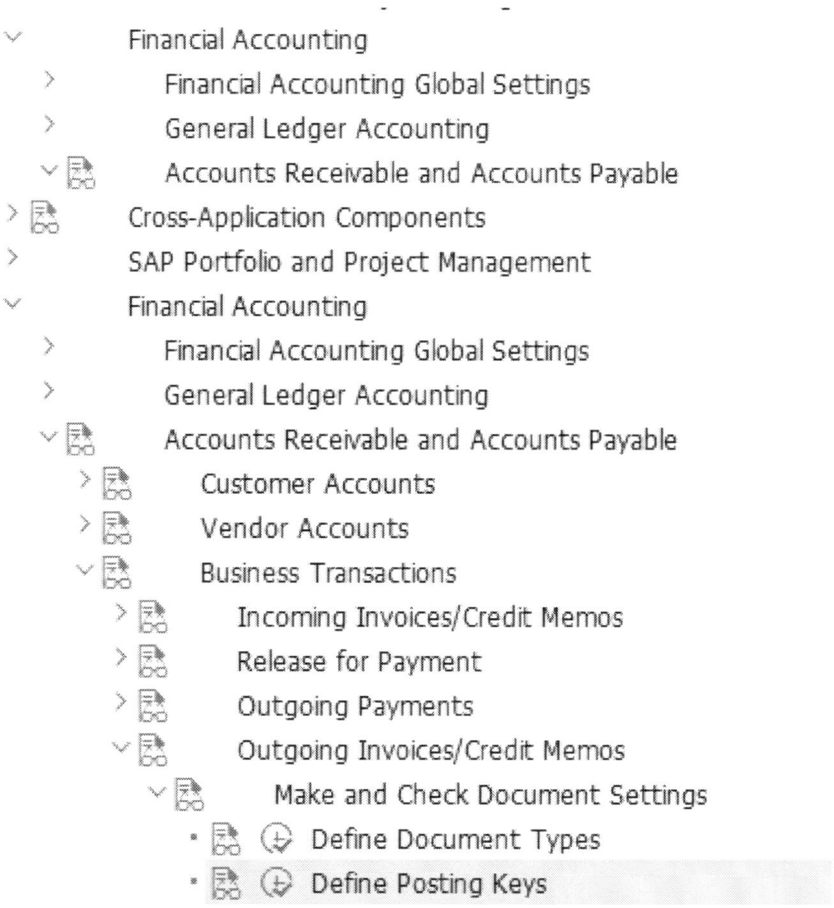

Financial Accounting
> Financial Accounting Global Settings
> General Ledger Accounting
˅ Accounts Receivable and Accounts Payable
> Cross-Application Components
> SAP Portfolio and Project Management
˅ Financial Accounting
> Financial Accounting Global Settings
> General Ledger Accounting
˅ Accounts Receivable and Accounts Payable
   > Customer Accounts
   > Vendor Accounts
   ˅ Business Transactions
     > Incoming Invoices/Credit Memos
     > Release for Payment
     > Outgoing Payments
     ˅ Outgoing Invoices/Credit Memos
       ˅ Make and Check Document Settings
         • Define Document Types
         • Define Posting Keys

Fig 1

Maintain Accounting Configuration : Posting Keys - List

| Posting Key | Name | Debit/Credit | Account Type |
|---|---|---|---|
| 01 | Invoice | Debit | Customer |
| 02 | Reverse credit memo | Debit | Customer |
| 03 | Expenses | Debit | Customer |
| 04 | Other receivables | Debit | Customer |
| 05 | Outgoing payment | Debit | Customer |
| 06 | Payment difference | Debit | Customer |
| 07 | Other clearing | Debit | Customer |
| 08 | Payment clearing | Debit | Customer |
| 09 | Special G/L debit | Debit | Customer |
| 0A | CH Bill.doc. Deb | Debit | Customer |
| 0B | CH Cancel.Cred.memoD | Debit | Customer |
| 0C | CH Clearing Deb | Debit | Customer |
| 0X | CH Clearing Cred | Debit | Customer |
| 0Y | CH Credit memo Cred | Debit | Customer |
| 0Z | CH Cancel.BillDocDeb | Debit | Customer |
| 11 | Credit memo | Credit | Customer |
| 12 | Reverse invoice | Credit | Customer |
| 13 | Reverse charges | Credit | Customer |
| 14 | Other payables | Credit | Customer |

Fig 2

**They are categorized into 4 groups:**

- Customer (01 to 20)
- Vendor (21-39)
- GL (40&50)
- Asset (70&75)

A detail screen of 01 reveals more:

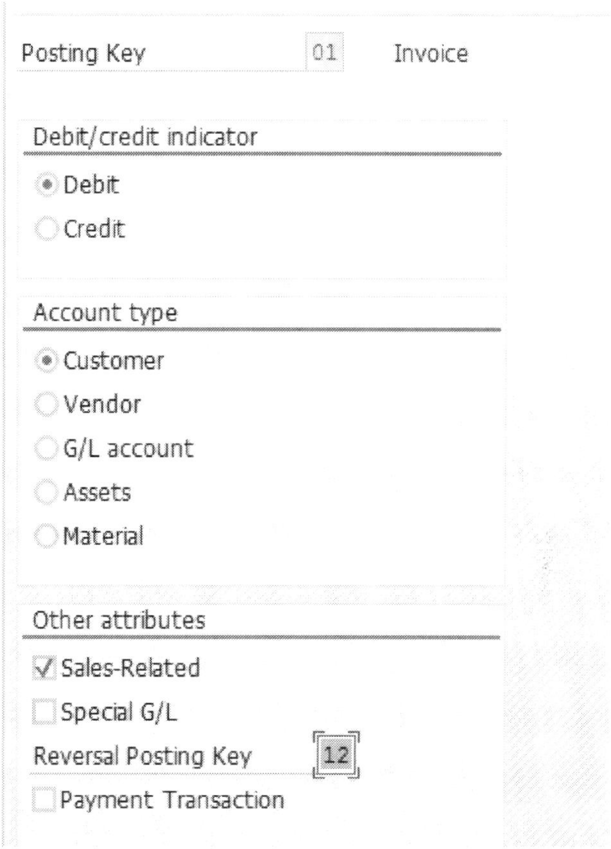

Posting Key                01    Invoice

Debit/credit indicator
⦿ Debit
○ Credit

Account type
⦿ Customer
○ Vendor
○ G/L account
○ Assets
○ Material

Other attributes
☑ Sales-Related
☐ Special G/L
Reversal Posting Key    12
☐ Payment Transaction

Fig 3

Therefore, now we know, when we have to post a sales related debit entry on a customer, we should use the key 01. One of the most commonly used ones are 40 and 50 (for G/L postings) with both of them also being each other's reversal posting keys.

| | Special G/L credit | Credit | Vendor |
|---|---|---|---|
| 40 | Debit entry | Debit | G/L account |
| 50 | Credit entry | Credit | G/L account |
| 70 | Debit asset | Debit | Asset |

Fig 4

As noted, there should not be any reason to create a new posting key, the configuration though lies in the below path to view the details of the keys:

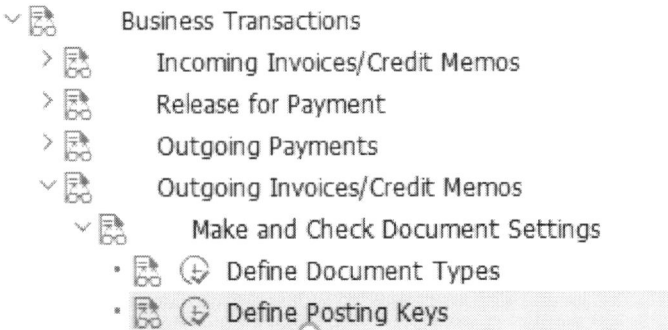

Fig 5

**HANA CHANGE:** In HANA SAP has introduced new concepts relating to connecting the FI side with the CO side in Finance.

1. In S4, it is mandatory to have document splitting so configurations need to be made accordingly. Create the controlling area in customizing:

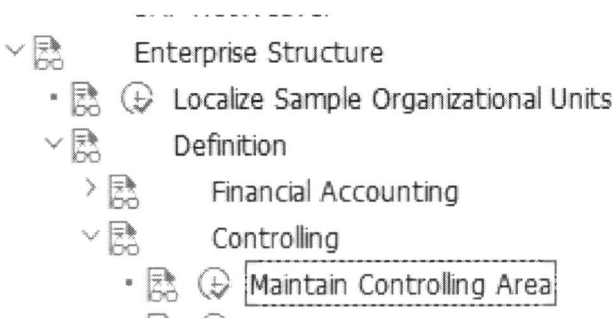

Fig 6

SAP will recognize the other elements from the company code as default – use this option only if you have 1 controlling area per company code (which will usually be the case). For multiple, you will need to assign the different ones to each other in the assignment configuration option as in fig 8.

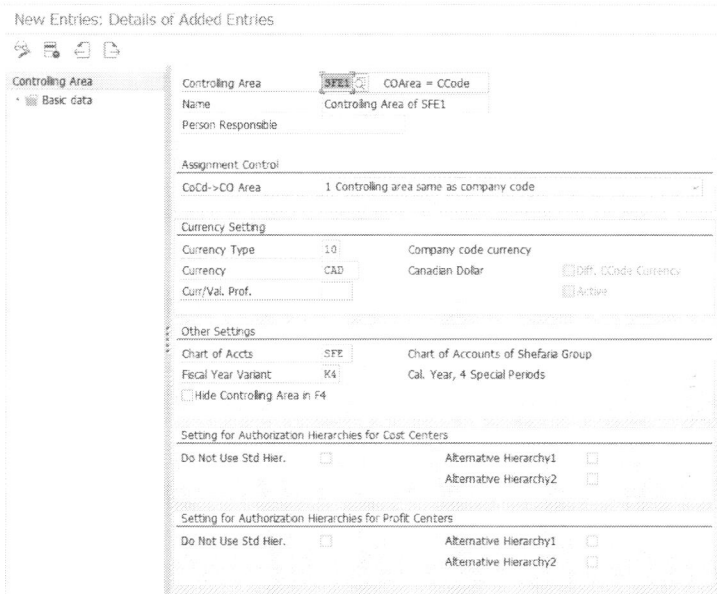

Fig 7

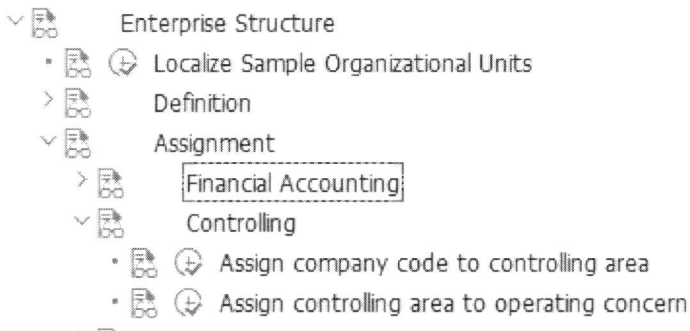

Fig 8

2. As a result of the above, you also need the CO module to recognize the GL your company code is using. In the step below, attach the GL

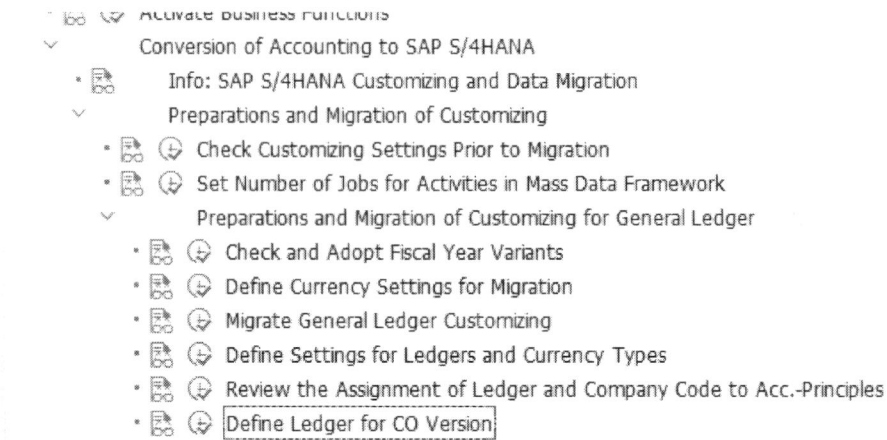

Fig 9

Fig 10

Making an entry via a transaction will make the usage of posting keys more clear. The T Code to make an entry directly is FB50 or follow the path:

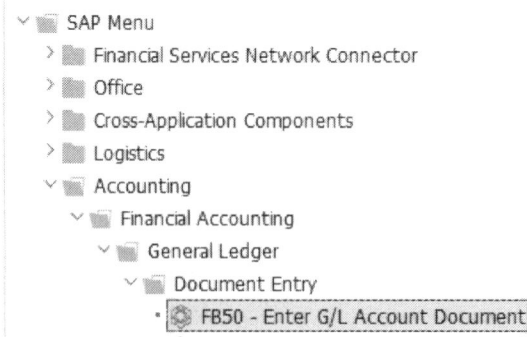

Fig 11

The transaction took us directly to post into SFE1 because we have been working in it, SAP holds that data in it's memory.

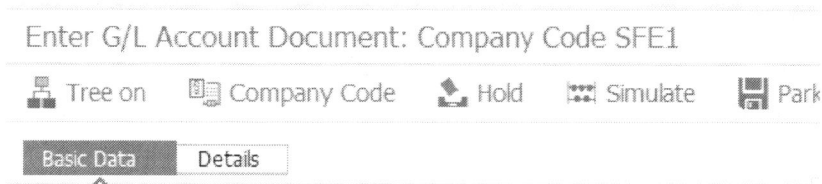

Fig 12

If, however, the correct CC does not show up as 'default', it must be made so by clicking on the option

Company Code

Fig 13

Then choose your co code from the drop down list or enter it directly:

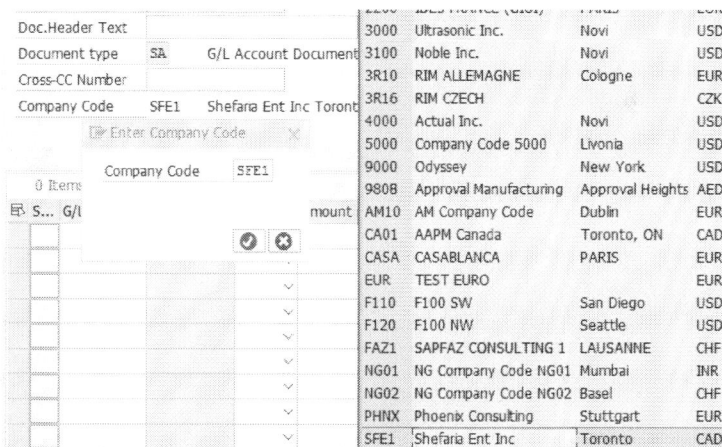

Fig 14

Let us try to purchase goods and increase the inventory. A typical JE will require this header (document level) information:

Enter G/L Account Document: Company Code SFE1

Tree on　Company Code　Hold　Simulate　Park　Editing options

**Basic Data**　Details

| Document Date | 04/02/2019 | Currency | CAD |
| Posting Date | 04/02/2019 |
| Reference | TEST INV |
| Doc.Header Text | HANA BOOK |
| Document type | SA | G/L Account Document |
| Cross-CC Number | |
| Company Code | SFE1 | Shefaria Ent Inc Toronto |

Amount Information

| Total Dr. | | 0.00 | CAD |
| Total Cr. | | 0.00 | CAD |

OO■

Fig 15

Enter the dates and texts to give the JE a meaning.

In the lower part of the screen, let us try the first line item, debiting the purchase account:

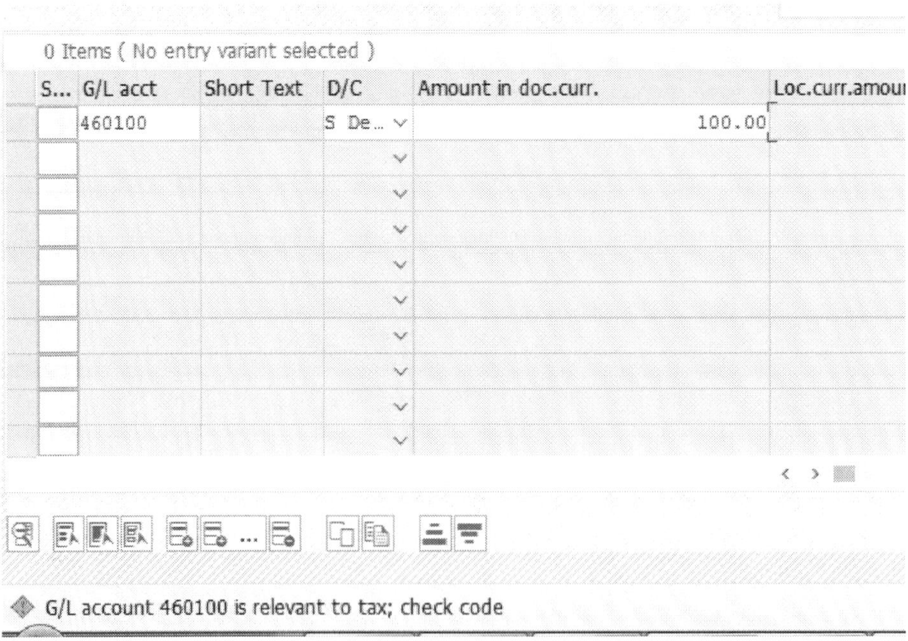

0 Items ( No entry variant selected )

| S... | G/L acct | Short Text | D/C | Amount in doc.curr. | Loc.curr.amoul |
|------|----------|------------|-----|---------------------|----------------|
| | 460100 | | S De... ∨ | 100.00 | |
| | | | ∨ | | |
| | | | ∨ | | |
| | | | ∨ | | |
| | | | ∨ | | |
| | | | ∨ | | |
| | | | ∨ | | |
| | | | ∨ | | |
| | | | ∨ | | |

< > ■

◆ G/L account 460100 is relevant to tax; check code

Fig 16

On the 2nd line, enter the corresponding inventory account to credit it – an asterisk in the amount column will 'copy' the amount from the 1st line, thereby preventing the need to manually enter and make any mistake:

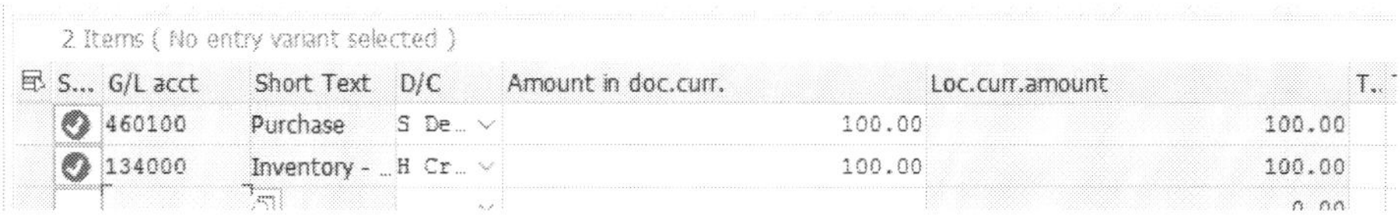

| S... | G/L acct | Short Text | D/C | | Amount in doc.curr. | Loc.curr.amount | T.. |
|------|----------|------------|-----|---|---------------------|------------------|-----|
| ✓ | 460100 | Purchase | S | De.. ∨ | 100.00 | 100.00 | |
| ✓ | 134000 | Inventory - ..H | Cr.. ∨ | | 100.00 | 100.00 | |
| | | | | ∨ | | 0.00 | |

2 Items ( No entry variant selected )

Fig 17

A message in yellow may appear if the G/L account is set up to reflect taxes in it. However entry of taxes is not mandatory as there may not be any taxes to pay/collect.

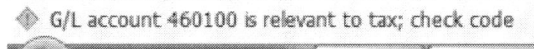

◈ G/L account 460100 is relevant to tax; check code

Fig 18

Hit Enter and the data screen changes to a balancing sign at the top right in Green (right most position on the 3 circles)

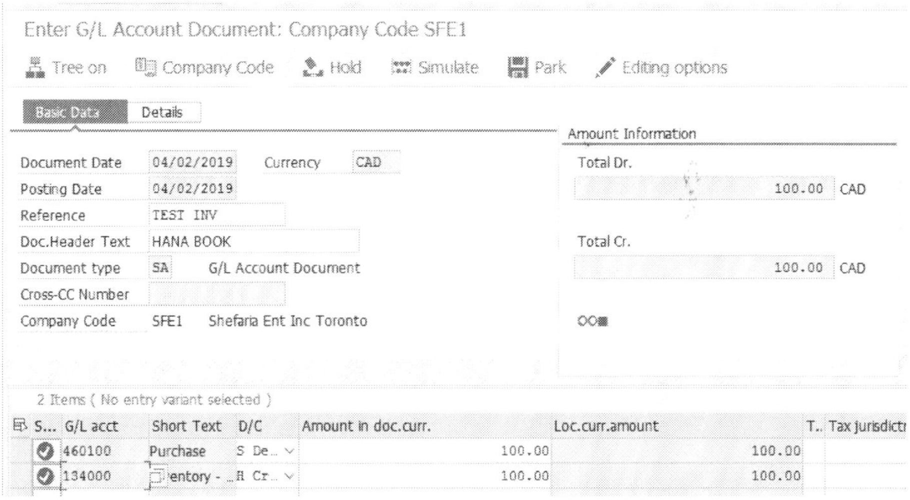

Enter G/L Account Document: Company Code SFE1

🔲 Tree on    📖 Company Code    🔼 Hold    ▦ Simulate    💾 Park    ✏ Editing options

**Basic Data**    Details

| | | | | | Amount Information | |
|--|--|--|--|--|--|--|
| Document Date | 04/02/2019 | Currency | CAD | | Total Dr. | |
| Posting Date | 04/02/2019 | | | | | 100.00 CAD |
| Reference | TEST INV | | | | | |
| Doc.Header Text | HANA BOOK | | | | Total Cr. | |
| Document type | SA | G/L Account Document | | | | 100.00 CAD |
| Cross-CC Number | | | | | | |
| Company Code | SFE1 | Shefaria Ent Inc Toronto | | | ○○▪ | |

2 Items ( No entry variant selected )

| S... | G/L acct | Short Text | D/C | | Amount in doc.curr. | Loc.curr.amount | T.. | Tax jurisdict |
|------|----------|------------|-----|---|---------------------|------------------|-----|---------------|
| ✓ | 460100 | Purchase | S | De.. ∨ | 100.00 | 100.00 | | |
| ✓ | 134000 | entory - ..H | Cr.. ∨ | | 100.00 | 100.00 | | |

Fig 19

As we know, SAP will allow to make an entry only if the credit and debit balance match as they do in this case. If the amounts do not match, the screen would display the red light (left most position on the 3 circles) as below:

**Fig 20**

It is also possible to 'simulate' to ensure everything is in sync and correct before posting. Click on the tab:

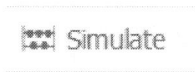

**Fig 21**

**Fig 22**

The above posting keys 40 and 50 were self-determined by SAP based on the G/L transaction that is being posted.

At this point, we have the option to Park or Post the document or to go back and make changes. Let us post this document by clicking on the Save button:

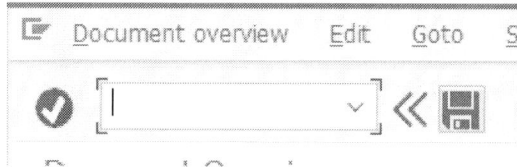

Fig 23

A message appears at the bottom informing the document was posted:

Document 100000000 was posted in company code SFE1

Fig 24

Note the numbering sequence, it posted this document and took the number from the sequence we set up earlier for the CC:

*Display Number Range Intervals*

| NR Object | Accounting document | | | | |
| Subobject | SFE1 | | | | |

Intervals

| No | Year | From number | To number | Current number | Ext |
|----|------|-------------|-----------|----------------|-----|
| 01 | 1992 | 0100000000 | 0199999999 | 0 | |
| 01 | 1993 | 0100000000 | 0199999999 | 0 | |
| 01 | 1999 | 0100000000 | 0199999999 | 0 | |
| 01 | 9999 | 0100000000 | 0199999999 | 100000000 | |

Fig 25

**HANA CHANGE:(U)** A new t code FB50L has been introduced to make postings based(U) on the Ledger group:

Enter G/L Acct Document for Ledger Group: Company Code SFE1

Tree on | Company Code | Hold | Simulate | Park | Editing options

Basic Data | Details

Amount Information

| | | | | |
|---|---|---|---|---|
| Document Date | | Currency | CAD | Total Dr |
| Posting Date | 04/17/2019 | | | |
| | | Ledger Grp | | |

Ledger Group (1) 16 Entries found

| Ledger Grp | Ledger Contained in Group | Text |
|---|---|---|
| 0C | 0C | Management Accounting |
| 0E | 0E | Commitment/Order Entry |
| 0L | 0L | Ledger 0L |
| 2L | 2L | Ledger 2L |
| B1 | B1 | |
| C1 | C1 | |

| | | | |
|---|---|---|---|
| Reference | | | |
| Doc.Header Text | | | |
| Document type | SA | G/L Account Document | |
| Cross-CC Number | | | |
| Company Code | SFE1 | Shefaria Ent Inc Toronto | |

Other than that, the process for posting remains the same as in FB50.

# RECLASSING ENTRIES (U)

T Code F-02

Occasionally mistakes occur in which a posting to be made manually or automatically in a certain G/L account is inadvertently made to another G/L. Balances can be moved around from one G/L to another using transaction F-02:

Enter the data as necessary relating to the G/L you made the incorrect entry to. E.g. we need to move some amount from G/L 460100 to 460300:

Enter data in F-02 crediting 460100 with the amount:

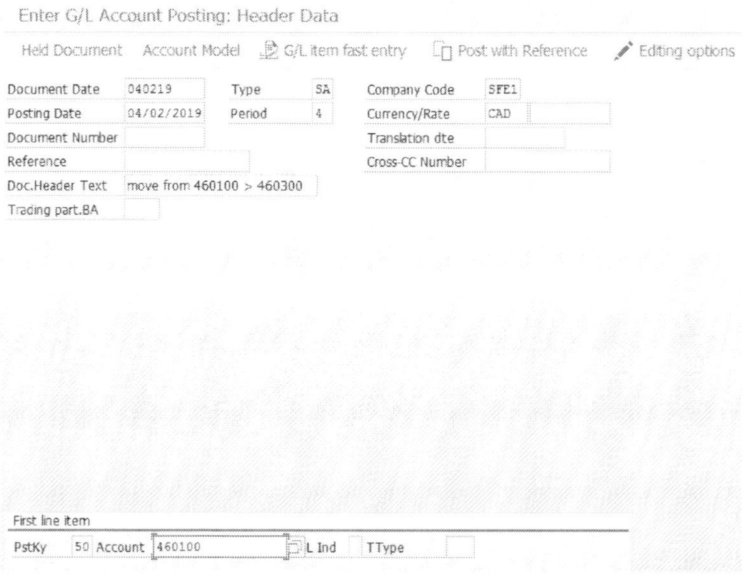

Fig 1

Hit Enter and on the next screen enter the amount and the account to be debited:

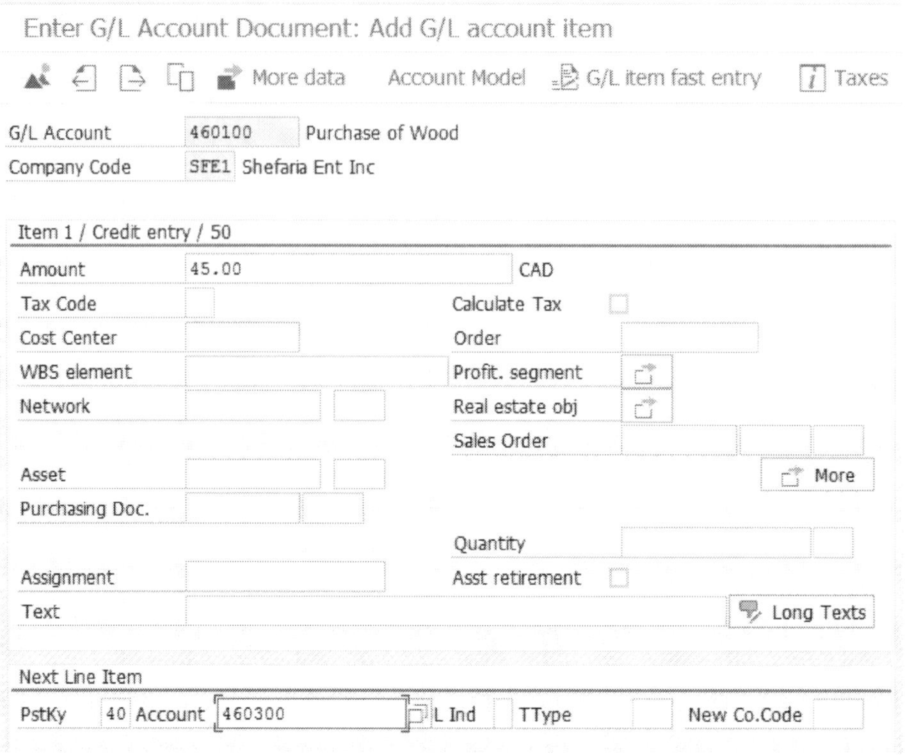

Enter G/L Account Document: Add G/L account item

More data    Account Model    G/L item fast entry    Taxes

G/L Account     460100    Purchase of Wood
Company Code    SFE1    Shefaria Ent Inc

Item 1 / Credit entry / 50

| Amount | 45.00 | | CAD |
| Tax Code | | Calculate Tax | |
| Cost Center | | Order | |
| WBS element | | Profit. segment | |
| Network | | Real estate obj | |
| | | Sales Order | |
| Asset | | | More |
| Purchasing Doc. | | | |
| | | Quantity | |
| Assignment | | Asst retirement | |
| Text | | | Long Texts |

Next Line Item

PstKy   40  Account  460300    L Ind    TType    New Co.Code

Fig 2

Hit Enter again and on the following screen copy the amount to be debited using * or entering it:

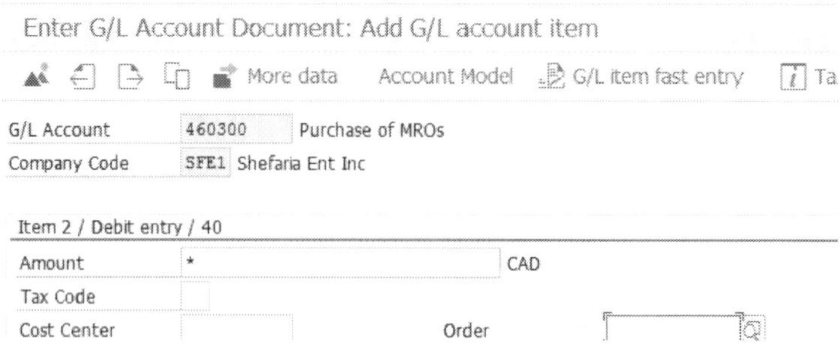

Enter G/L Account Document: Add G/L account item

More data    Account Model    G/L item fast entry    Ta

G/L Account     460300    Purchase of MROs
Company Code    SFE1    Shefaria Ent Inc

Item 2 / Debit entry / 40

| Amount | * | | CAD |
| Tax Code | | | |
| Cost Center | | Order | |

Fig 3

72

Now you can simulate the document to see the effects of your changes:

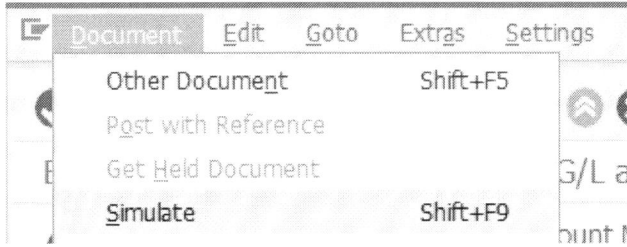

Fig 4

Fig 5

In addition, post:

Fig 6

Run FBL3N transaction for the date you did the postings and you will find the 2 corresponding entries:

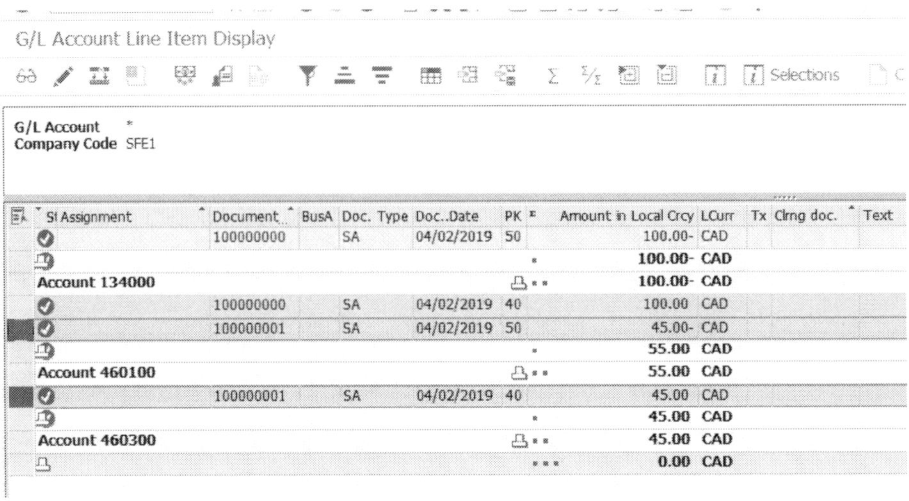
G/L Account Line Item Display

Selections

G/L Account *
Company Code SFE1

| St | Assignment | Document | BusA | Doc. Type | Doc..Date | PK | Σ | Amount in Local Crcy | LCurr | Tx | Clrng doc. | Text |
|---|---|---|---|---|---|---|---|---|---|---|---|---|
| | | 100000000 | | SA | 04/02/2019 | 50 | | 100.00- | CAD | | | |
| | | | | | | | • | **100.00-** | **CAD** | | | |
| **Account 134000** | | | | | | | •• | **100.00-** | **CAD** | | | |
| | | 100000000 | | SA | 04/02/2019 | 40 | | 100.00 | CAD | | | |
| | | 100000001 | | SA | 04/02/2019 | 50 | | 45.00- | CAD | | | |
| | | | | | | | • | **55.00** | **CAD** | | | |
| **Account 460100** | | | | | | | •• | **55.00** | **CAD** | | | |
| | | 100000001 | | SA | 04/02/2019 | 40 | | 45.00 | CAD | | | |
| | | | | | | | • | **45.00** | **CAD** | | | |
| **Account 460300** | | | | | | | •• | **45.00** | **CAD** | | | |
| | | | | | | | ••• | **0.00** | **CAD** | | | |

Fig 7

# DISPLAYING BALANCES IN G/L ACCOUNTS (U)

T Code FAGLB03

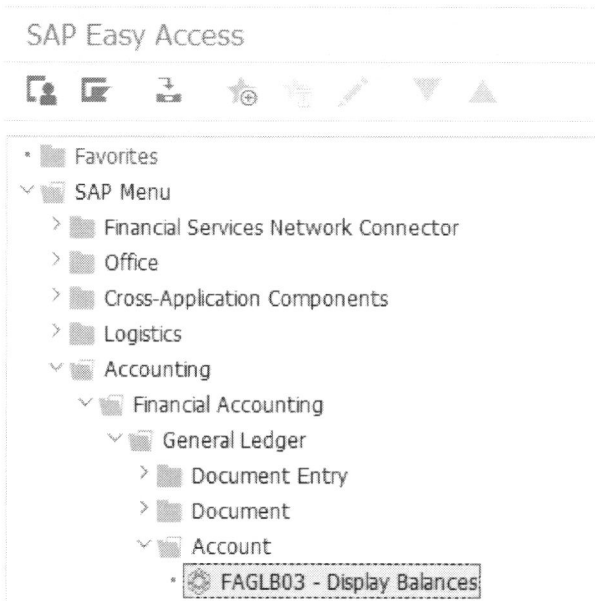

Fig 1

FAGLB03 will be a transaction every SAP FI user will use fairly often. On the main screen, enter the G/L account, CC (since in a common CoA, a G/L account can be across several CCs) and the year you wish to look up in:

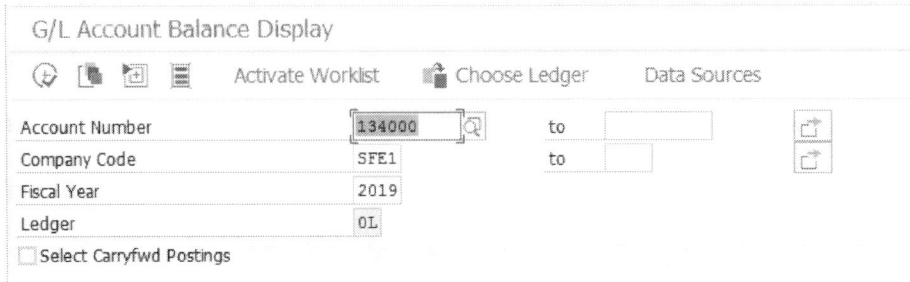

Fig 2

Multiple G/L accounts can be entered at the same time by clicking on the button  and in the screen that comes up:

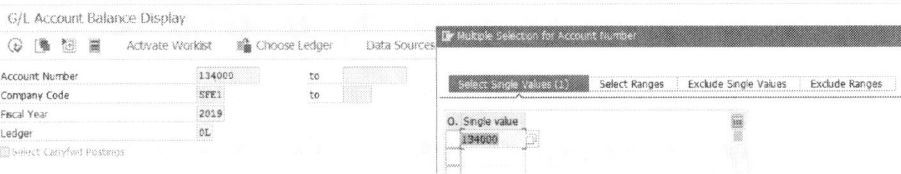

Fig 3

G/L accounts can also be included or excluded as needed in the above tabs. For the moment, we will run this transaction for the G/L 134000.

Fig 4

Click on the Execute button or hit F8. A new screen comes up giving the balances as in the different months:

Balance Display: G/L Accounts For the Ledger 0L

Document Currency    Document Currency    Document Currency

| Account Number | 134000 | Inventory - FG |
| Company Code | SFE1 | Shefaria Ent Inc |
| Fiscal Year | 2019 | |

Display More Chars

| All Documents in Currency | * | Display Currency | CAD | Company cod‹ |

| Period | Debit | Credit | Balance | Cumulative Balance |
|---|---|---|---|---|
| Bal.Carryfor... | | | | |
| 1 | | | | |
| 2 | | | | |
| 3 | | | | |
| 4 | | 100.00 | 100.00- | 100.00- |
| 5 | | | | 100.00- |
| 6 | | | | 100.00- |
| 7 | | | | 100.00- |
| 8 | | | | 100.00- |
| 9 | | | | 100.00- |
| 10 | | | | 100.00- |
| 11 | | | | 100.00- |
| 12 | | | | 100.00- |
| 13 | | | | 100.00- |
| 14 | | | | 100.00- |
| 15 | | | | 100.00- |
| 16 | | | | 100.00- |
| Total | | 100.00 | 100.00- | 100.00- |

Fig 5

As we notice above, the amount is the G/L entry we did in the section on Posting G/L entries in the account 134000 as a credit entry, which is reflected here. A debit entry would have reflected in the first column.

If we double click on the highlighted line below, we can find more details about the balances. Depending on which cell/column you click (Debit or credit or balance), you can see either only the debit, or only the credit or all the postings in that G/L.

Fig 6

A very neat way of looking at this table to sort the data is by switching the layout mode in Settings>Switch List:

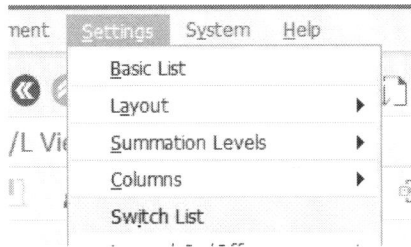

Fig 7

A more pleasing layout emerges:

Fig 8

# DISPLAYING LINE ITEMS (U)

**HANA CHANGE:** T Code FBL3N from ECC is now FBL3H with a lot more enhanced selection criteria. In fact, for Reporting, many transactions have got similar changes from N to H as the suffix while some have also got N as the new suffix.

Further, the old report FBL3N that was available from the Menu is no longer there with the activation of New G/L. To get it, one needs to find the transaction and put it on the Favorites manually.

However, in the HANA system we now have FAGLL03H and FAGLL03 as below in the menu:

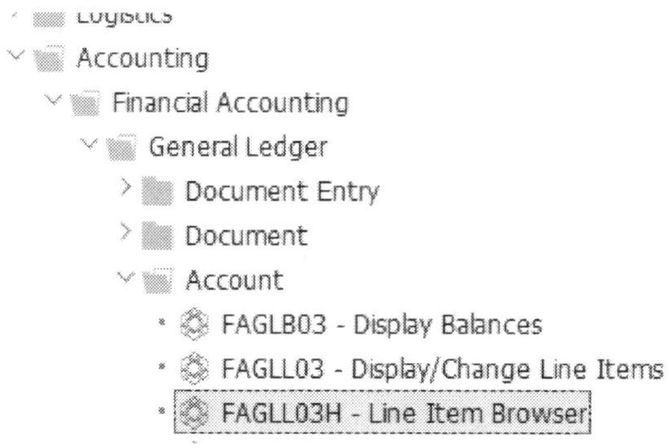

```
    Logistics
  Accounting
    Financial Accounting
      General Ledger
        Document Entry
        Document
        Account
          FAGLB03 - Display Balances
          FAGLL03 - Display/Change Line Items
          FAGLL03H - Line Item Browser
```

Fig 1

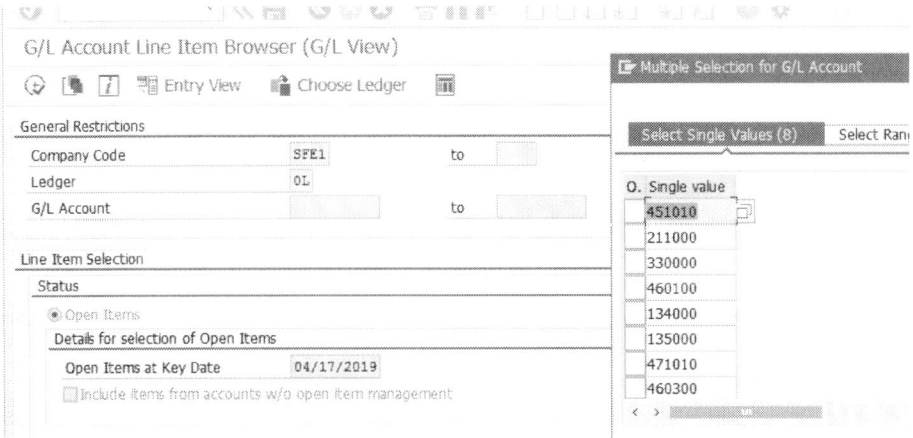

Fig 2

FAGLL03H is an improvement over FAGLL03 in a few ways:

1. It gives the ability to choose the ledger you want the display from by clicking on 'Choose Ledger':

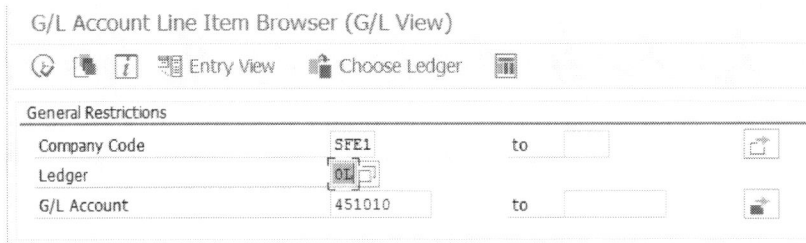

Fig 3

2. It can also fetch the balances for the G/L accounts that are *not* set up for line item display by clicking on the button:

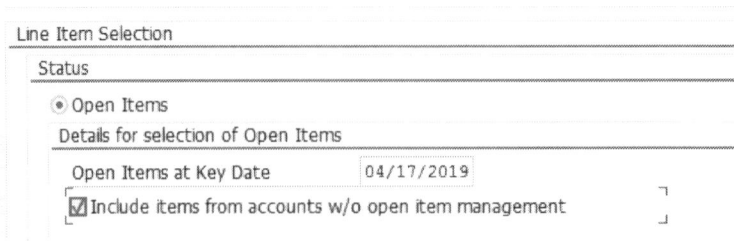

Fig 4

In the above case, none of the GLs are set to Open Line item management:

GL Account Details

| ChAc | G/L Acct | B/S acct | Short Text | OI Management | G |
|------|----------|----------|------------|---------------|---|
| SFE | 451010 | | Revenue Stream 1 | | 4 |
| SFE | 211000 | X | Trd Pyb | | 2 |
| SFE | 330000 | X | RE | | 3 |
| SFE | 460100 | | Purchase | | 4 |
| SFE | 134000 | X | Inventory - FG | | 1 |
| SFE | 135000 | X | Inventory - MRO | | 1 |
| SFE | 471010 | | Revenue Stream 2 | | 4 |
| SFE | 460300 | | Purchase MRO | | 4 |

Fig 5

However, by selecting the check box shown in Fig 4, the report does give the balances in all these G/Ls if they exist:

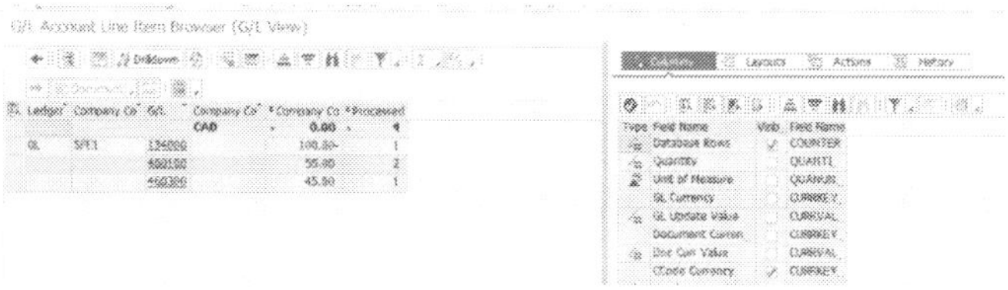

Fig 6

3. As shown in the screen shot above, we now have the ability to play around with the layout as well as to perform certain actions which were till now, either not available or had to be performed through the menu:

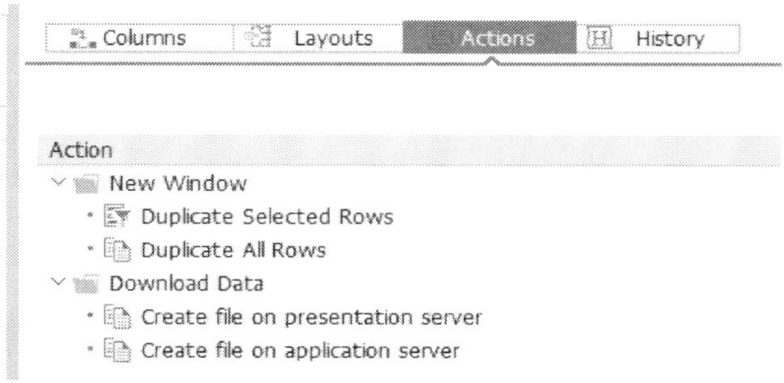

Fig 7

On execution, the report gives a condensed version of the balances per G/L account:

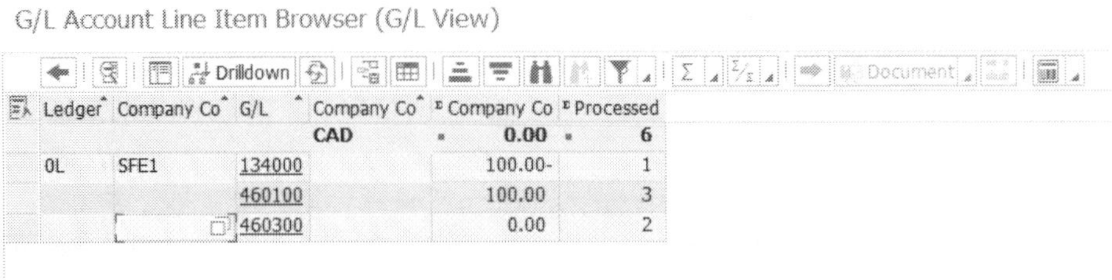

G/L Account Line Item Browser (G/L View)

| Ledger | Company Co | G/L | Company Co | Company Co | Processed |
|--------|-----------|-----|-----------|-----------|-----------|
| | | | CAD | 0.00 | 6 |
| 0L | SFE1 | 134000 | | 100.00- | 1 |
| | | 460100 | | 100.00 | 3 |
| | | 460300 | | 0.00 | 2 |

Fig 8

To view the details by line item for these G/Ls either select individually or select all of them by clicking on the top left corner till the required line/s are highlighted:

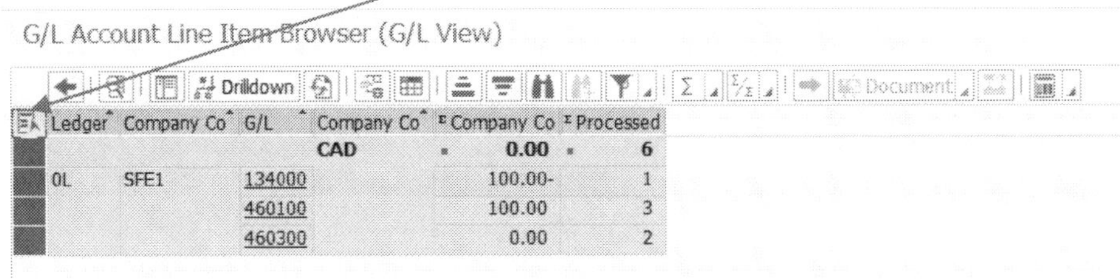

G/L Account Line Item Browser (G/L View)

| Ledger | Company Co | G/L | Company Co | Company Co | Processed |
|--------|-----------|-----|-----------|-----------|-----------|
| | | | CAD | 0.00 | 6 |
| 0L | SFE1 | 134000 | | 100.00- | 1 |
| | | 460100 | | 100.00 | 3 |
| | | 460300 | | 0.00 | 2 |

Fig 9

Next, choose Call Line item report from the far right icon:

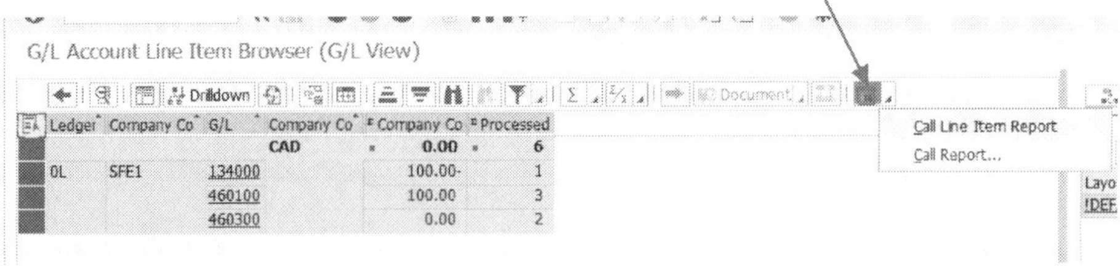

G/L Account Line Item Browser (G/L View)

| Ledger | Company Co | G/L | Company Co | Company Co | Processed | | |
|--------|-----------|-----|-----------|-----------|-----------|--|--|
| | | | CAD | 0.00 | 6 | Call Line Item Report | |
| 0L | SFE1 | 134000 | | 100.00- | 1 | Call Report... | |
| | | 460100 | | 100.00 | 3 | | Layo |
| | | 460300 | | 0.00 | 2 | | !DEF |

Fig 10

The old familiar layout will emerge:

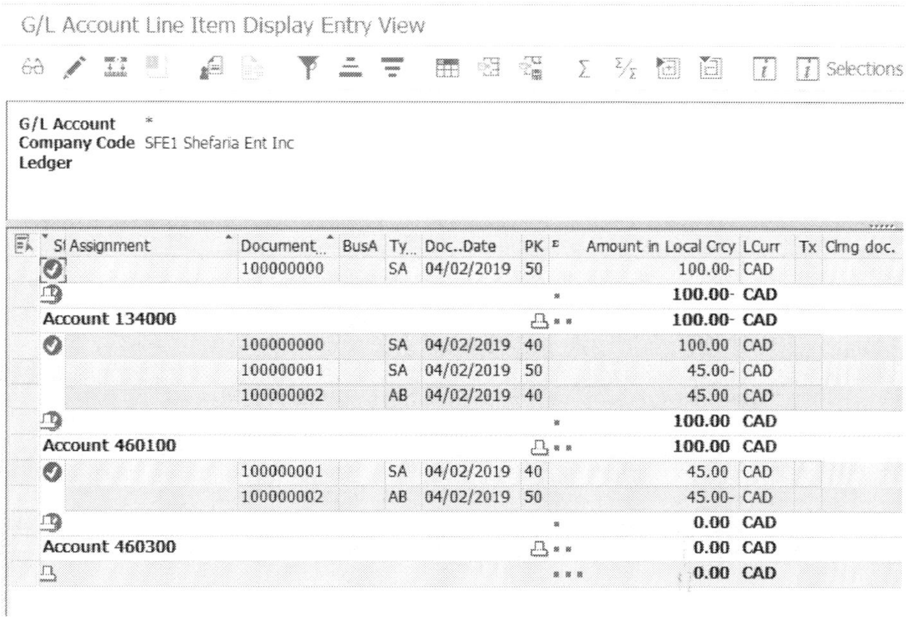

Fig 11

From here, you can select the other format also:

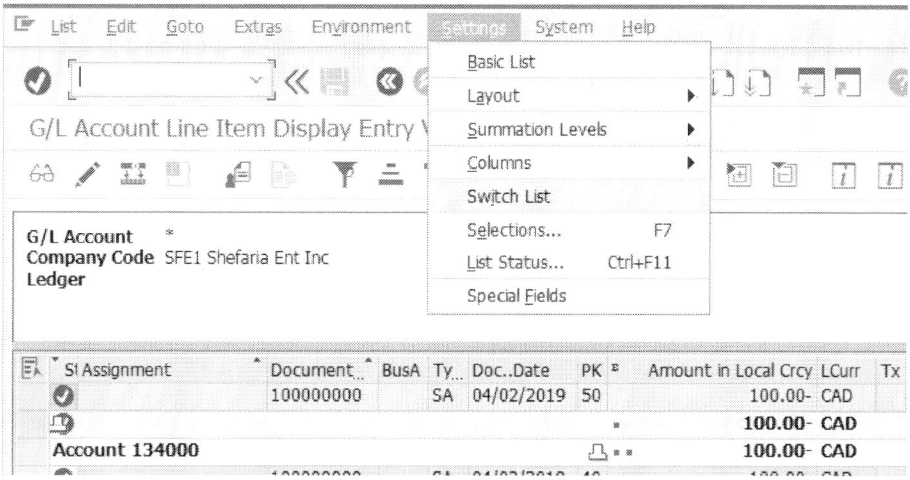

Fig 12

G/L Account         134000       Inventory - Finished Goods
Company Code      SFE1        Shefaria Ent Inc
Ledger

| | Stat | Assign. | DocumentNo | BusA | Type | Doc..Date | PK | LC Amount | LCurr | Tx | Clrng doc. | Profit Ctr | Segment | Text | OffsetAcc |
|---|---|---|---|---|---|---|---|---|---|---|---|---|---|---|---|
| ☐ | ⊘ | | 100000000 | | SA | 04/02/2019 | 50 | 100.00- | CAD | | | | | | |
| * | ⊘ | | | | | | | 100.00- | CAD | | | | | | |
| ** Account 134000 | | | | | | | | 100.00- | CAD | | | | | | |

G/L Account         460100       Purchase of Wood
Company Code      SFE1        Shefaria Ent Inc
Ledger

| | Stat | Assign. | DocumentNo | BusA | Type | Doc..Date | PK | LC Amount | LCurr | Tx | Clrng doc. | Profit Ctr | Segment | Text | OffsetAcc |
|---|---|---|---|---|---|---|---|---|---|---|---|---|---|---|---|
| ☐ | ⊘ | | 100000000 | | SA | 04/02/2019 | 40 | 100.00 | CAD | | | | | | |

## Fig 13

# REVERSING ACCOUNTING ENTRIES (U)

T Code FB08

A number once used up cannot be cancelled or deleted in accounting. This is to ensure a complete audit trail. However, it can be reversed. The path to do that is:

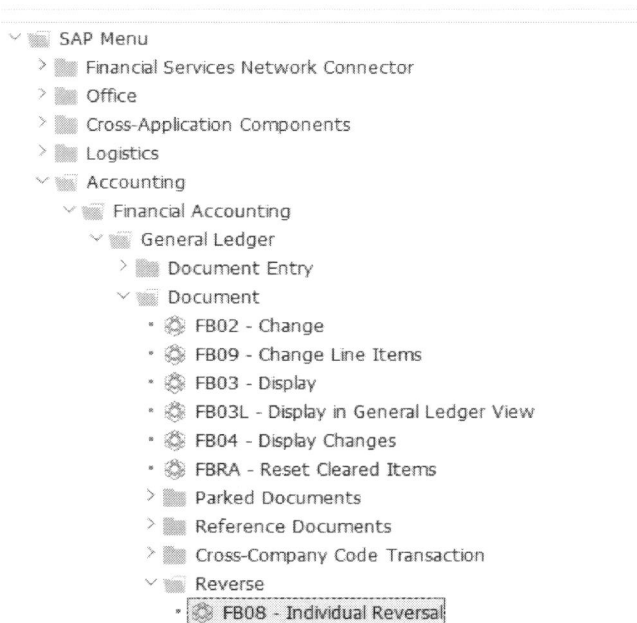

Fig 1

Enter the document # you need to reverse and give the reason thereof which is mandatory:

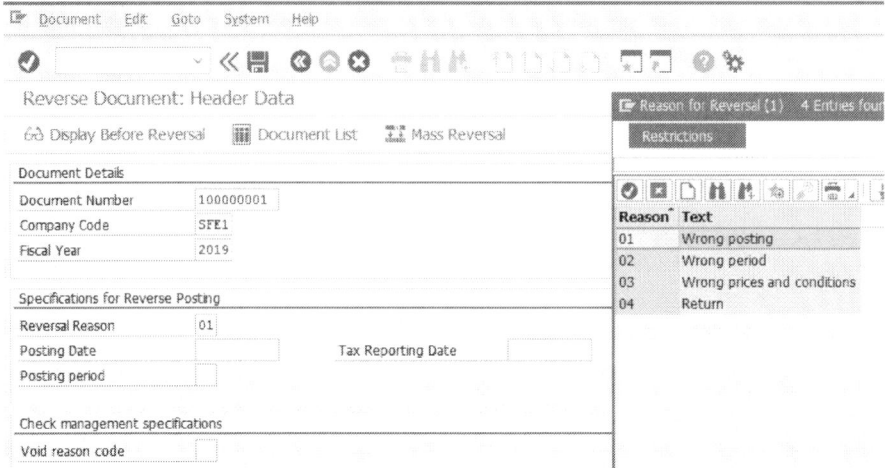

Fig 2

We can define our own reasons also via configuration though it is unnecessary and one of standard SAP ones will work fine, like 01 above.

You can also give a different date if the original posting date belonged to a period, which is now closed:

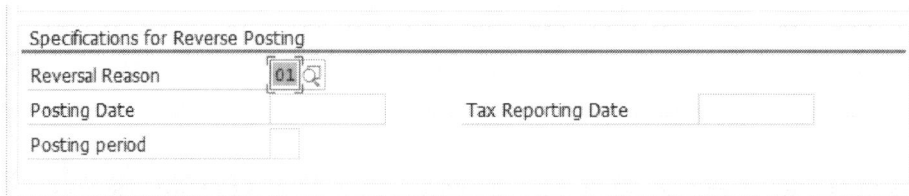

Fig 3

**HANA CHANGE:** SAP has introduced 2 changes here:

1. Your tax reporting date for the reversal document can be different and you can define your own rules in configuration to decide that

2. Previously there were many reason codes under which you could reverse a document – that is now limited to 4 standard codes only

Before reversing, you can also look at the original document if you need to for confirmation:

6ð Display Before Reversal

Fig 4

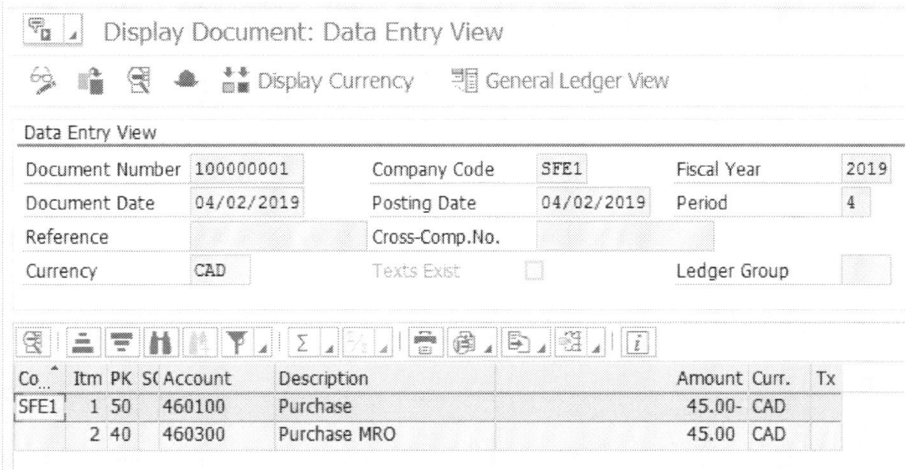

Display Document: Data Entry View

69 ♠ Display Currency   General Ledger View

Data Entry View

| Document Number | 100000001 | Company Code | SFE1 | Fiscal Year | 2019 |
| Document Date | 04/02/2019 | Posting Date | 04/02/2019 | Period | 4 |
| Reference | | Cross-Comp.No. | | | |
| Currency | CAD | Texts Exist | ☐ | Ledger Group | |

| Co | Itm | PK | SC | Account | Description | Amount | Curr. | Tx |
|-----|-----|-----|-----|---------|-------------|--------|-------|-----|
| SFE1 | 1 | 50 | | 460100 | Purchase | 45.00- | CAD | |
| | 2 | 40 | | 460300 | Purchase MRO | 45.00 | CAD | |

Fig 5

Save and a message is displayed at the bottom:

✔ Document 100000002 was posted in company code SFE1

Fig 6

Note that it took the next available number from the same series. It is possible to have different numbering for reversal documents and often companies do that to ensure better separation and visibility.

When we run the report again, we find the reversal entries have appeared together under the documents that posted them:

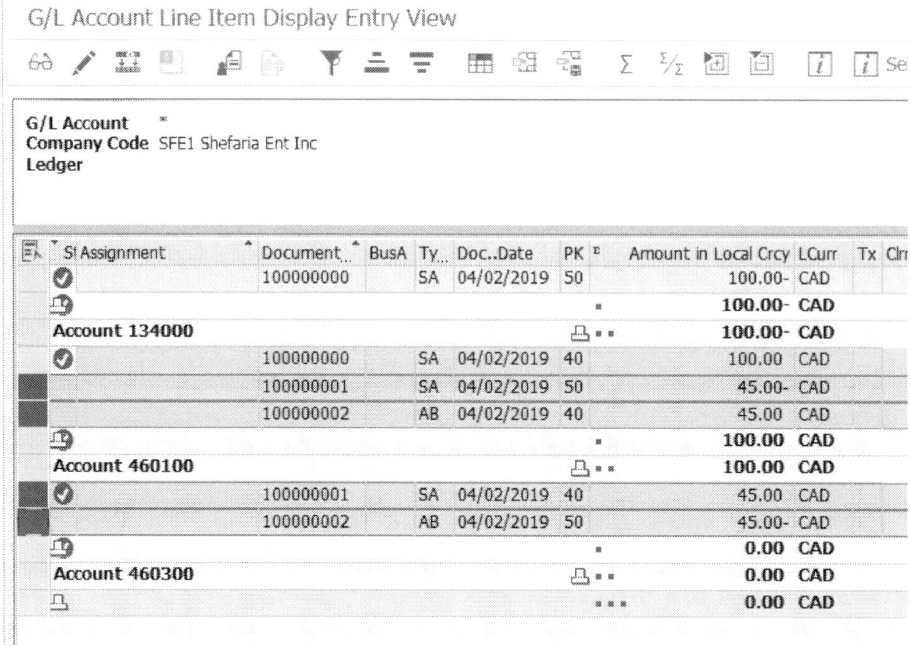

G/L Account Line Item Display Entry View

G/L Account       *
Company Code  SFE1 Shefaria Ent Inc
Ledger

| St | Assignment | Document | BusA | Ty | Doc..Date | PK | Amount in Local Crcy | LCurr | Tx | Clr |
|----|-----------|----------|------|-----|-----------|-----|---------------------|-------|-----|-----|
| ✓ | | 100000000 | | SA | 04/02/2019 | 50 | 100.00- | CAD | | |
| | | | | | | * | 100.00- | CAD | | |
| **Account 134000** | | | | | | | 100.00- | CAD | | |
| ✓ | | 100000000 | | SA | 04/02/2019 | 40 | 100.00 | CAD | | |
| | | 100000001 | | SA | 04/02/2019 | 50 | 45.00- | CAD | | |
| | | 100000002 | | AB | 04/02/2019 | 40 | 45.00 | CAD | | |
| | | | | | | * | 100.00 | CAD | | |
| **Account 460100** | | | | | | | 100.00 | CAD | | |
| ✓ | | 100000001 | | SA | 04/02/2019 | 40 | 45.00 | CAD | | |
| | | 100000002 | | AB | 04/02/2019 | 50 | 45.00- | CAD | | |
| | | | | | | * | 0.00 | CAD | | |
| **Account 460300** | | | | | | | 0.00 | CAD | | |
| | | | | | | *** | 0.00 | CAD | | |

Fig 7

# PARKING A DOCUMENT (U)

T Code FV50 or FV50L

Occasionally, we have situations where we may be expecting more information or changes to the postings in which case we can park the document until we are ready to post it. Documents may also be required to park if there is an informal or formal (like workflow) process of getting authorizations to make postings directly to the G/Ls or AP/AR. Parking the document has the same effect as posting in terms of obtaining a document number except that it does not update the posted balances. To park a document, we can go via the same route of FB50/FB50L:

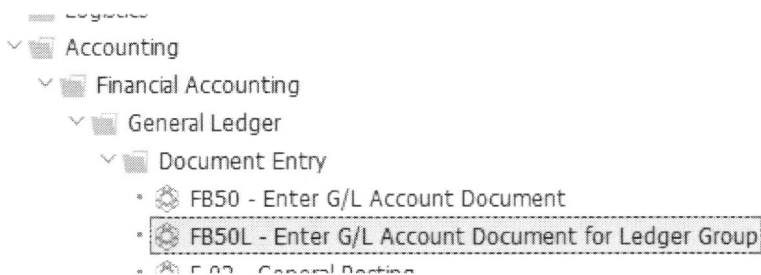

Fig 1

However, this time, choose the option to park instead of post (or save).

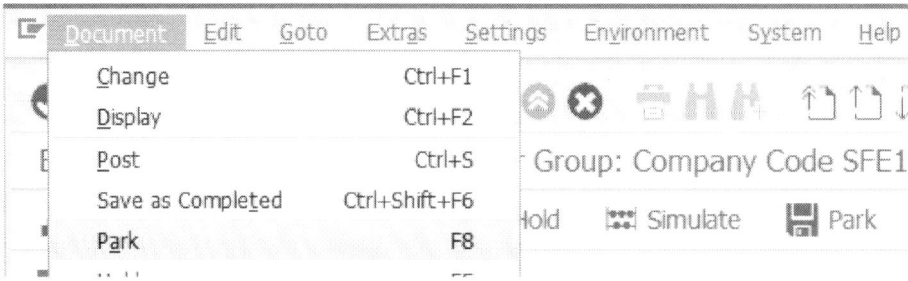

Fig 2

Alternatively, go directly to T Code FV50 or FV50L:

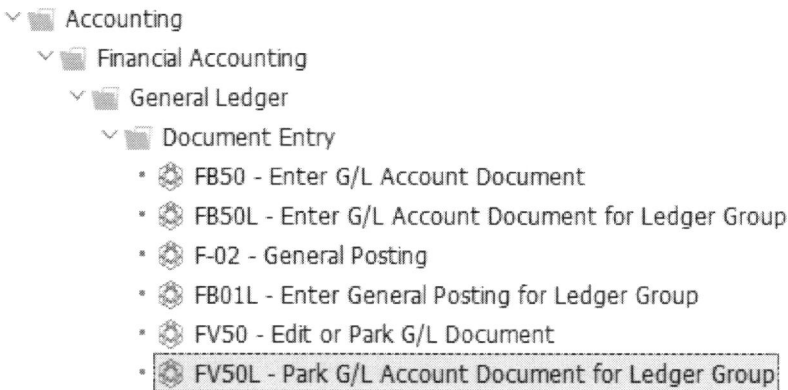

Fig 3

The screens look similar but are not same. FB50, because it is the transaction to post when saved, it will by default, post the document but gives the option to park also:

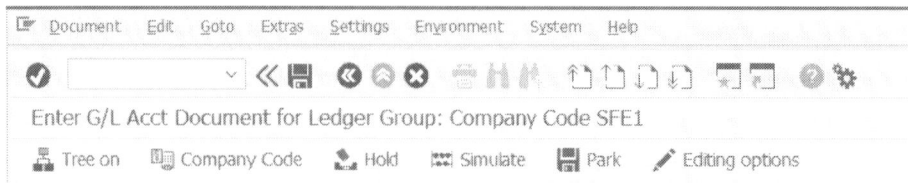

Fig 4

FV50, because it is the transaction to park, will by default, park the document when saved, but gives the option to post also:

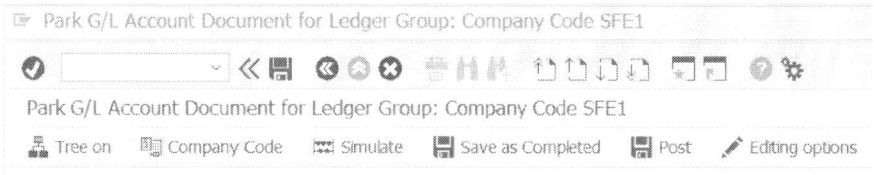

Fig 5

Saving as completed and parking are practically the same things. A list of parked documents for verification and action can be obtained through transaction FBV3.

Let us try to park a document using the same process as earlier.

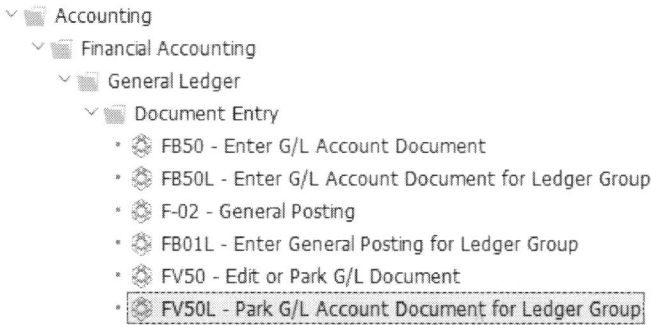

Fig 6

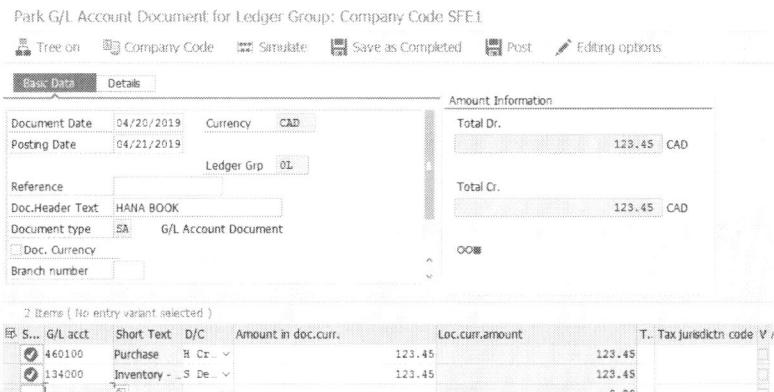

Fig 7

Save the document and SAP will give a number at the bottom:

✓ Document 100000003 SFE1 was parked

Fig 8

The difference between this and the posted document is that this number will not show up in G/L line balances when we run the report for these 2 G/L accounts in FBL3H/N or FAGLL03/FAGLL03H:

> ∨ 📁 Accounting
> > ∨ 📁 Financial Accounting
> > > ∨ 📁 General Ledger
> > > > 〉📁 Document Entry
> > > > 〉📁 Document
> > > > ∨ 📁 Account
> > > > > • ⚙ FAGLB03 - Display Balances
> > > > > • ⚙ FAGLL03 - Display/Change Line Items
> > > > > • ⚙ FAGLL03H - Line Item Browser
> > > > > • ⚙ F 02 Cl

Fig 9

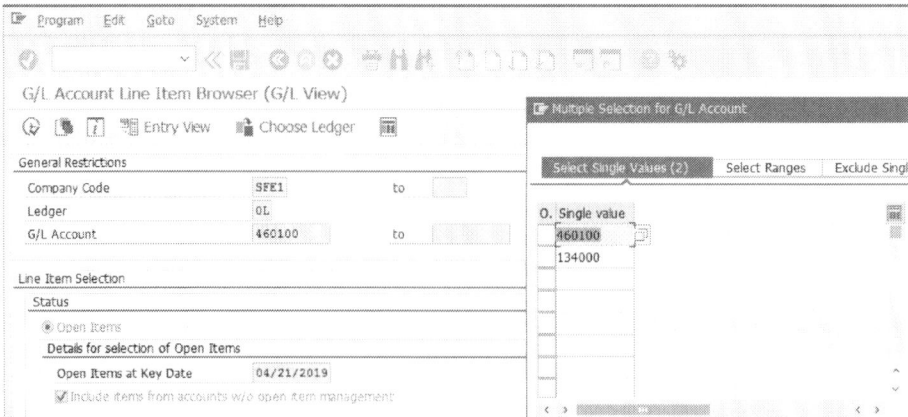

Fig 10

92

On executing the report for these 2 G/Ls, we see other numbers but not the parked one:

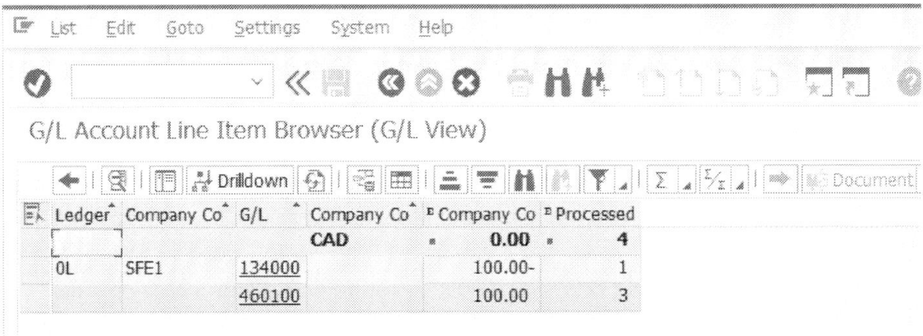
List Edit Goto Settings System Help
G/L Account Line Item Browser (G/L View)
Drilldown
Document
Ledger Company Co G/L Company Co Company Co Processed
CAD 0.00 4
0L SFE1 134000 100.00- 1
460100 100.00 3

Fig 11

However, if you do want to see them, check on the box in the previous selection screen:

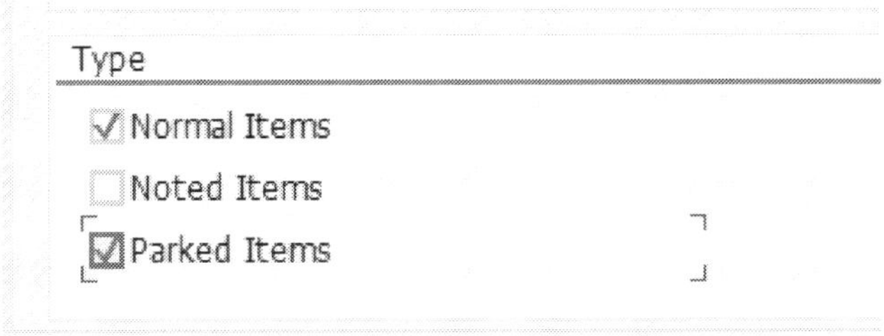
Type
Normal Items
Noted Items
Parked Items

Fig 12

The original report will show non line item managed G/L accounts like below:

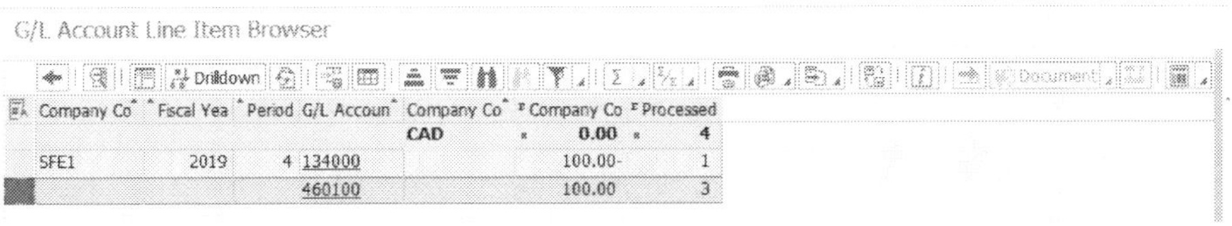
G/L Account Line Item Browser
Drilldown
Document
Company Co Fiscal Yea Period G/L Accoun Company Co Company Co Processed
CAD 0.00 4
SFE1 2019 4 134000 100.00- 1
460100 100.00 3

Fig 13

As earlier, to view the line items, we will have to ask for their display:

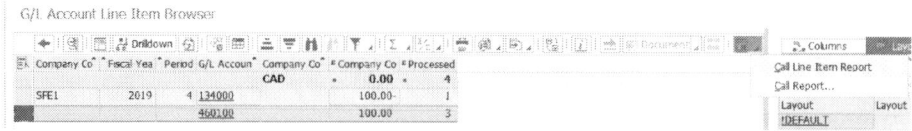

Fig 14

The Yellow upward triangle symbol in the first column tells you it is a parked document:

Fig 15

While Green check means it is posted:

Fig 16

To see just the list of parked postings by G/L for taking action on them, un-select the Posted button and re-run the report:

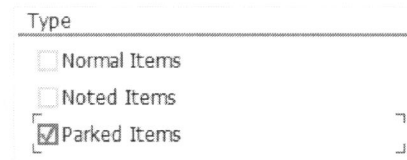

Type

☐ Normal Items

☐ Noted Items

☑ Parked Items

Fig 17

Alternatively, to just get a list of the parked documents, run the transaction FBV3:

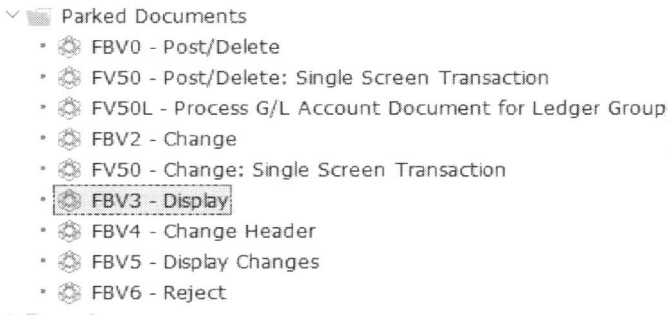

∨ 📁 Parked Documents
- ⚙ FBV0 - Post/Delete
- ⚙ FV50 - Post/Delete: Single Screen Transaction
- ⚙ FV50L - Process G/L Account Document for Ledger Group
- ⚙ FBV2 - Change
- ⚙ FV50 - Change: Single Screen Transaction
- ⚙ FBV3 - Display
- ⚙ FBV4 - Change Header
- ⚙ FBV5 - Display Changes
- ⚙ FBV6 - Reject

Fig 18

Various other options also exists to action the parked documents as seen above – change the header info, display the changes or reject the documents (useful in workflow)

Run FBV3 and enter the document # if you know and are specifically looking for it:

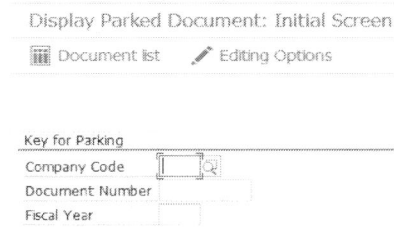

Display Parked Document: Initial Screen

🎞 Document list    ✏ Editing Options

Key for Parking

Company Code

Document Number

Fiscal Year

Fig 19

The fiscal year will also be needed to be entered in case the same document number exists in multiple fiscal years. In our case since it is only in current year, that is not necessary.

If you do not know the document # and just want a list to work on, click on:

Document list

Fig 20

Now you have many options – you can run it open i.e. for the report to display all the parked documents in any or all CC/s.

Alternatively, restrict the selection to specific times, people (Entered by), dates etc:

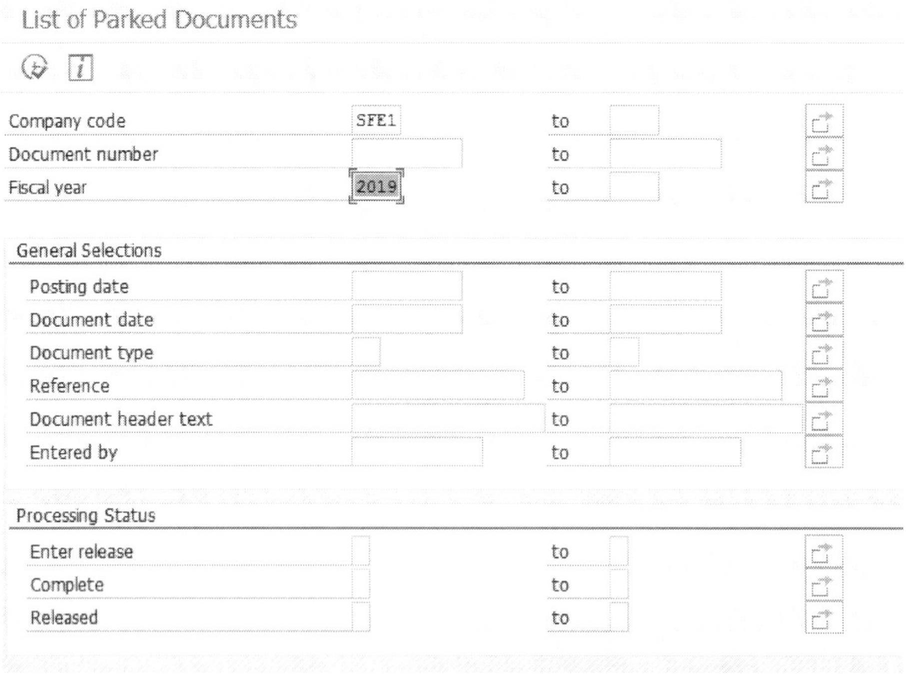

List of Parked Documents

| | | | |
|---|---|---|---|
| Company code | SFE1 | to | |
| Document number | | to | |
| Fiscal year | 2019 | to | |

General Selections

| | | | |
|---|---|---|---|
| Posting date | | to | |
| Document date | | to | |
| Document type | | to | |
| Reference | | to | |
| Document header text | | to | |
| Entered by | | to | |

Processing Status

| | | | |
|---|---|---|---|
| Enter release | | to | |
| Complete | | to | |
| Released | | to | |

Fig 21

Executing it will display the parked documents that were entered by IDES0164 in CC SFE1:

Fig 22

We saw this same document also appear in the G/L line item display earlier:

Fig 23

From the report in FBV3, we can also step into the document by choosing the line and clicking on Display:

Fig 24

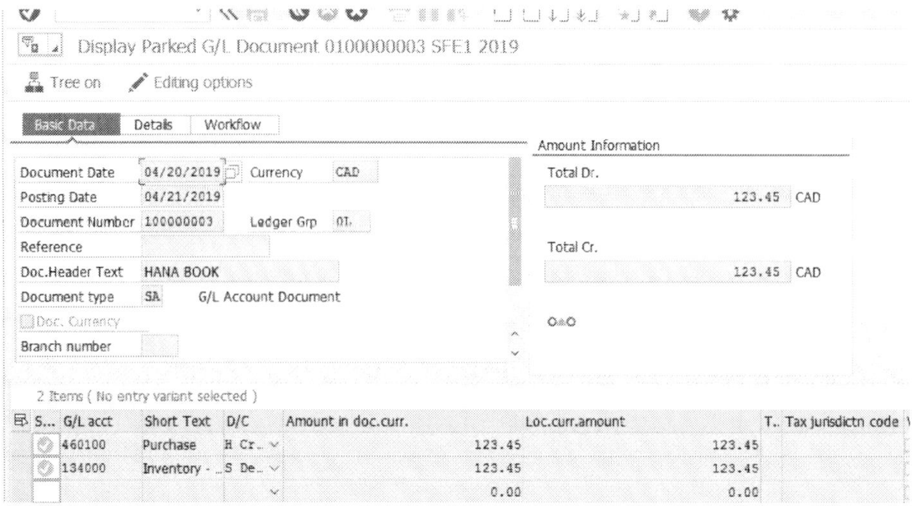

Display Parked G/L Document 0100000003 SFE1 2019

Tree on    Editing options

| Basic Data | Details | Workflow |

**Basic Data**

| | | | |
|---|---|---|---|
| Document Date | 04/20/2019 | Currency | CAD |
| Posting Date | 04/21/2019 | | |
| Document Number | 100000003 | Ledger Grp | 01 |
| Reference | | | |
| Doc.Header Text | HANA BOOK | | |
| Document type | SA | G/L Account Document | |
| ☐ Doc. Currency | | | |
| Branch number | | | |

**Amount Information**

| | | |
|---|---|---|
| Total Dr. | 123.45 | CAD |
| Total Cr. | 123.45 | CAD |
| O⊕O | | |

2 Items ( No entry variant selected )

| S... | G/L acct | Short Text | D/C | Amount in doc.curr. | Loc.curr.amount | T.. | Tax jurisdictn code |
|---|---|---|---|---|---|---|---|
| ⊘ | 460100 | Purchase | H Cr... ∨ | 123.45 | 123.45 | | |
| ⊘ | 134000 | Inventory - ... | S De... ∨ | 123.45 | 123.45 | | |
| | | | ∨ | 0.00 | 0.00 | | |

Fig 25

98

# POSTING PARKED DOCUMENTS (U)

T Code FBV0

Once you have obtained all the information and/or authorizations needed, the parked documents can be posted in the system. This will change their status from parked to posted and update the database accordingly. To post a parked document, go to the menu:

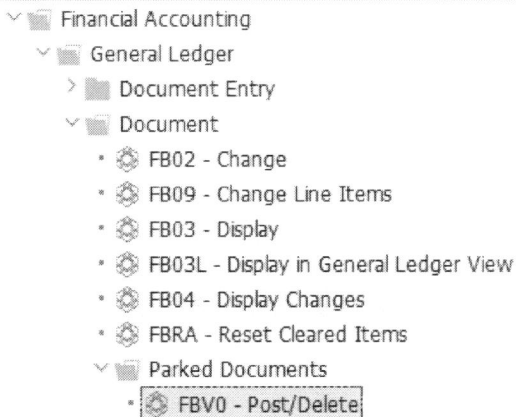

Fig 1

Enter the document #:

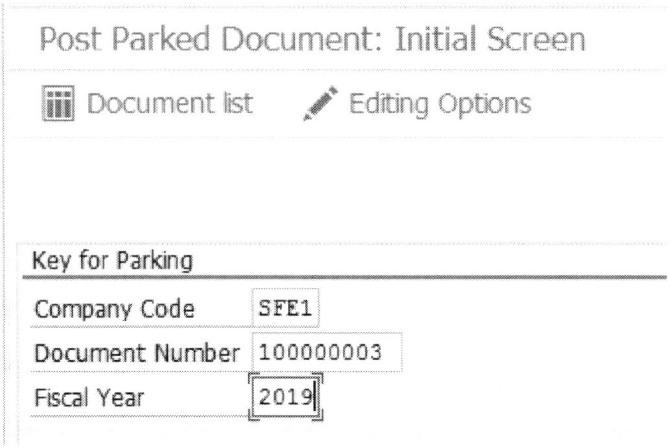

Post Parked Document: Initial Screen

📋 Document list      ✏️ Editing Options

**Key for Parking**

| | |
|---|---|
| Company Code | SFE1 |
| Document Number | 100000003 |
| Fiscal Year | 2019 |

Fig 2

Hit Enter:

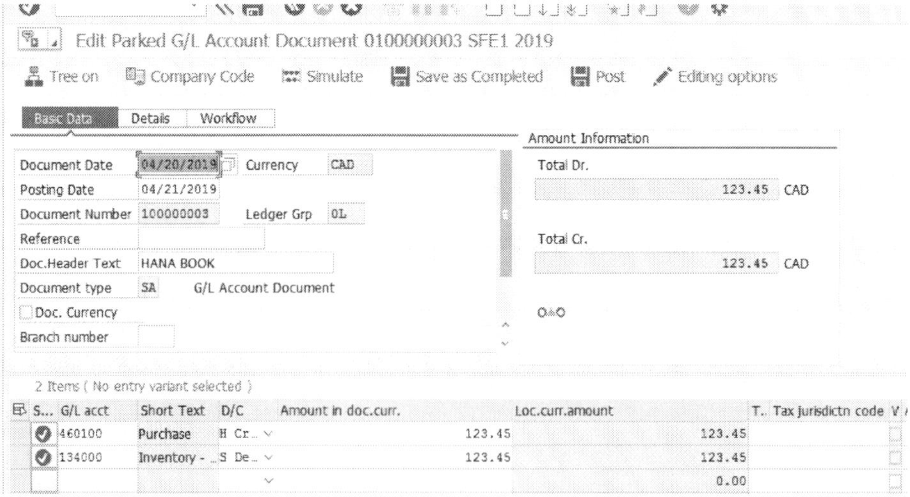

Edit Parked G/L Account Document 0100000003 SFE1 2019

🗂 Tree on    Company Code    Simulate    💾 Save as Completed    💾 Post    ✏️ Editing options

**Basic Data** | Details | Workflow

| | | | | | Amount Information | | |
|---|---|---|---|---|---|---|---|
| Document Date | 04/20/2019 | Currency | CAD | | Total Dr. | | |
| Posting Date | 04/21/2019 | | | | | 123.45 | CAD |
| Document Number | 100000003 | Ledger Grp | 0L | | | | |
| Reference | | | | | Total Cr. | | |
| Doc.Header Text | HANA BOOK | | | | | 123.45 | CAD |
| Document type | SA | G/L Account Document | | | | | |
| ☐ Doc. Currency | | | | | O▲O | | |
| Branch number | | | | | | | |

2 Items ( No entry variant selected )

| S... | G/L acct | Short Text | D/C | Amount in doc.curr. | Loc.curr.amount | T.. Tax jurisdictn code | V |
|---|---|---|---|---|---|---|---|
| ✔ | 460100 | Purchase | H Cr.. ∨ | 123.45 | 123.45 | | |
| ✔ | 134000 | Inventory - ..S De.. ∨ | | 123.45 | 123.45 | | |
| | | | ∨ | | 0.00 | | |

Fig 3

Note that in a parked document, we can practically change anything we need to, except the document # itself, as it has not yet his the database.

Post the document:

Fig 4

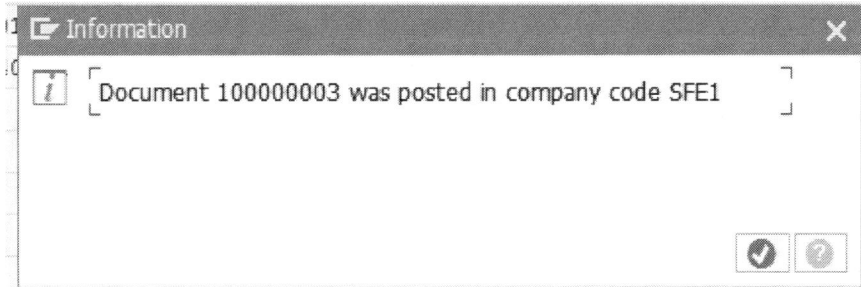

Fig 5

When we re-run the line items or G/L account balances reports, FBL3N/H, this document will change it's status from Yellow to Green:

G/L Account Line Item Display

G/L Account *
Company Code SFE1

| SI Assignment | Document | BusA | Doc. Type | Doc..Date | PK | Amount in Local Crcy | LCurr | Tx |
|---|---|---|---|---|---|---|---|---|
| | 100000000 | SA | | 04/02/2019 | 50 | 100.00- | CAD | |
| | 100000003 | SA | | 04/20/2019 | 40 | 123.45 | CAD | |
| | | | | | | 23.45 | CAD | |
| Account 134000 | | | | | | 23.45 | CAD | |
| | 100000000 | SA | | 04/02/2019 | 40 | 100.00 | CAD | |
| | 100000001 | SA | | 04/02/2019 | 50 | 45.00- | CAD | |
| | 100000002 | AB | | 04/02/2019 | 40 | 45.00 | CAD | |
| | 100000003 | SA | | 04/20/2019 | 50 | 123.45- | CAD | |
| | | | | | | 23.45- | CAD | |
| Account 460100 | | | | | | 23.45- | CAD | |
| | | | | | | 0.00 | CAD | |

Fig 6

Also, that document will no longer show up in the parked documents report FBV3:

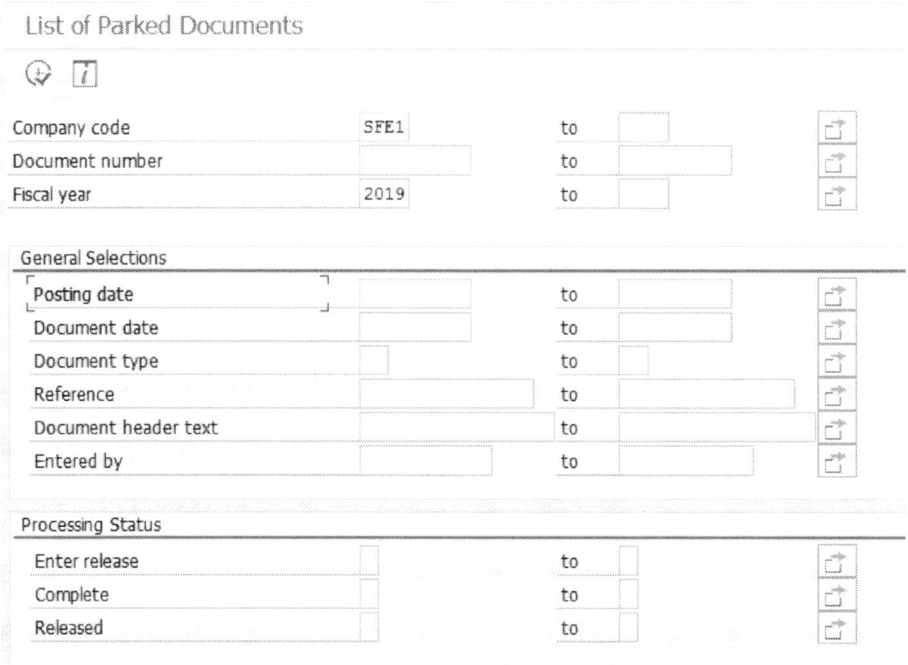

List of Parked Documents

| Company code | SFE1 | to | | |
|---|---|---|---|---|
| Document number | | to | | |
| Fiscal year | 2019 | to | | |

General Selections

| Posting date | | to | | |
|---|---|---|---|---|
| Document date | | to | | |
| Document type | | to | | |
| Reference | | to | | |
| Document header text | | to | | |
| Entered by | | to | | |

Processing Status

| Enter release | | to | | |
|---|---|---|---|---|
| Complete | | to | | |
| Released | | to | | |

Fig 7

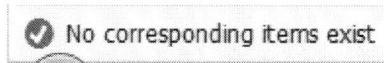 No corresponding items exist

Fig 8

# RECURRING OR REPEATED

# TRANSACTIONS (U)

## I.   SETTING UP FOR REPEATED TRANSACTIONS

T Code FBD1

We often have bills like of rents, telephone; insurance which are recurring amounts i.e. repeat themselves over at certain defined periods. SAP has provided the option of setting them up as recurring to avoid making repeated entries at every payment cycle. When the appropriate times come, the G/L entries are posted either automatically or by the user with the minimal intervention.

Let us now try posting a recurring entry in the system. The path is below or T Code FBD1:

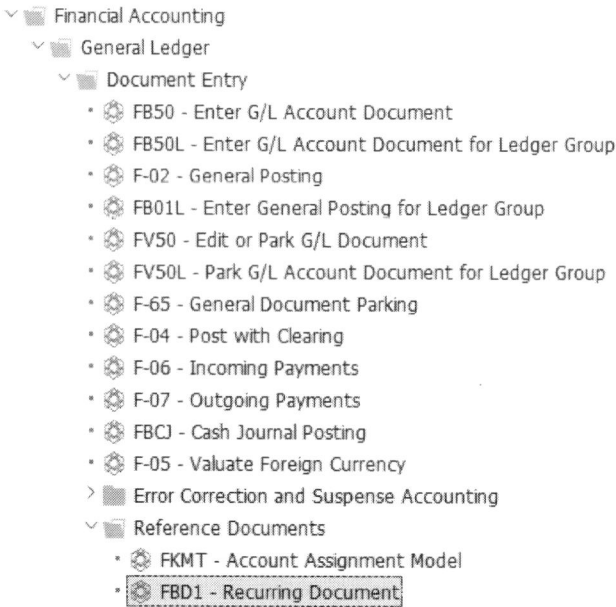

Fig 1

Enter the following information to enable the recurring entries to take place:

1. Company Code
2. When you want the first and the last runs of this fixed amount to occur
3. How often should they occur i.e. the time gap in months between each run
4. Run date – you can have this in lieu of the first run date
5. Reference – usually this would be provided by the vendor as it's invoice# on us
6. Document header text – to give some meaning to the entry
7. Document type – choose SA (G/L entry)

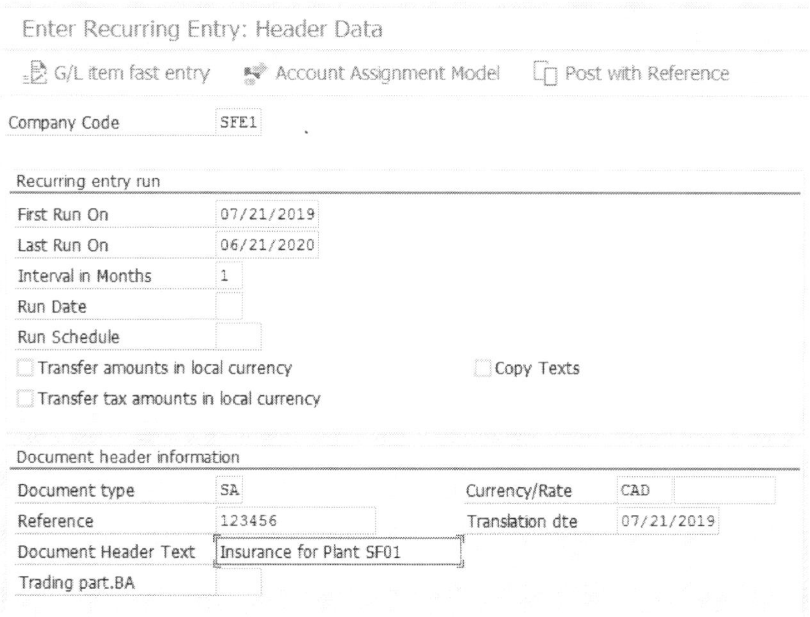

Fig 2

Hit Enter and the system takes you to the bottom of the screen to make the actual JEs:

Fig 3

Let us debit the Insurance account by the insurance amount:

Fig 4

Hitting Enter takes us to the next screen to make more entries. Enter the amount and tax code if applicable (more on tax codes later, for now leave it blank) and with posting key 50 (to offset

40), enter the bank account that will be credited for this transaction:

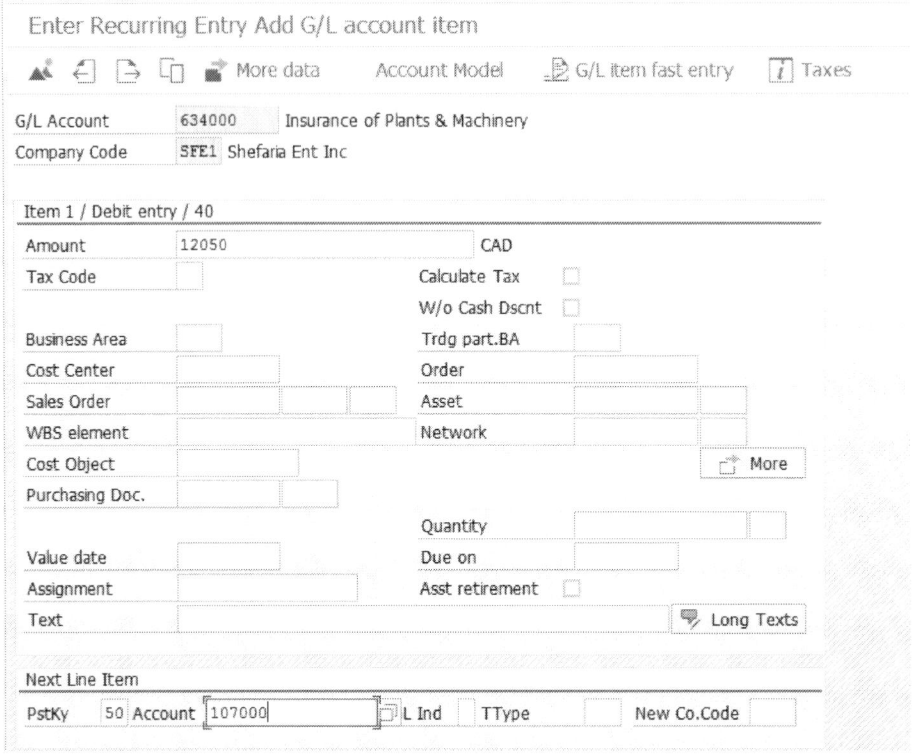

Enter Recurring Entry Add G/L account item

More data    Account Model    G/L item fast entry    Taxes

G/L Account        634000    Insurance of Plants & Machinery
Company Code       SFE1  Shefaria Ent Inc

Item 1 / Debit entry / 40

| Amount | 12050 | | CAD | |
|---|---|---|---|---|
| Tax Code | | | Calculate Tax | |
| | | | W/o Cash Dscnt | |
| Business Area | | | Trdg part.BA | |
| Cost Center | | | Order | |
| Sales Order | | | Asset | |
| WBS element | | | Network | |
| Cost Object | | | | More |
| Purchasing Doc. | | | | |
| | | | Quantity | |
| Value date | | | Due on | |
| Assignment | | | Asst retirement | |
| Text | | | | Long Texts |

Next Line Item

PstKy  50 Account 107000    L Ind    TType    New Co.Code

Fig 5

Hit Enter and a new screen will come up

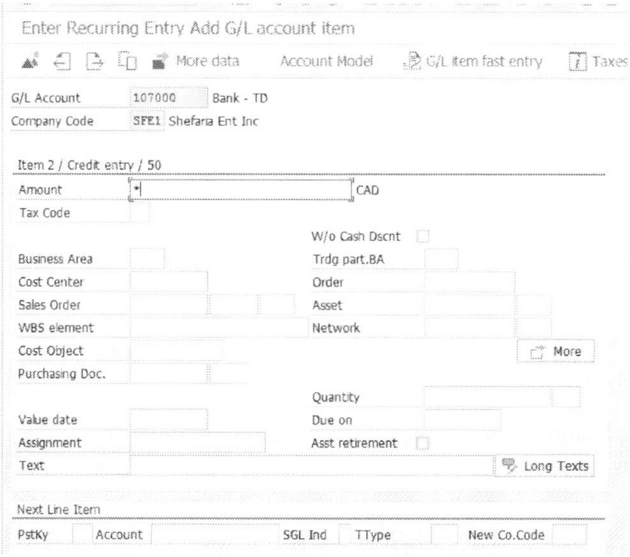

Fig 6

Amount: Enter the amount for your second line item. We can use '*' as before to copy this amount from the 1st line or if you want the amount to be taken from 2 or more bank accounts, the enter the amount you want taken from the G/L you entered on the previous screen in the field – Amount. Then, repeat the step for that G/L with the other G/L/s in the bottom of the screen. In our case, we are taking all this amount from one G/L only, hence the '*' in the line below:

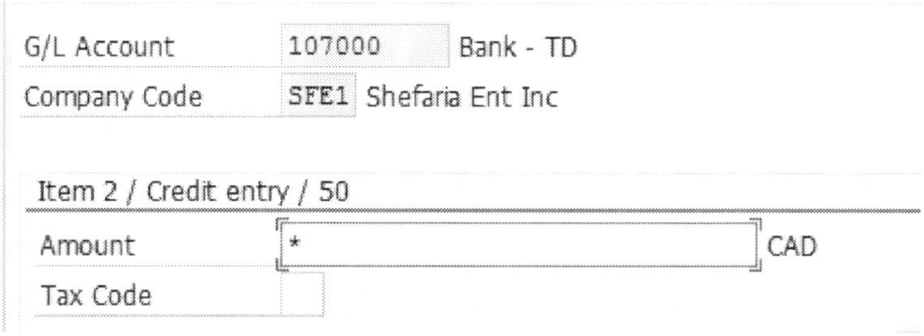

Fig 7

This is the complete data to be entered one time only for recurring transactions. We can use the icons to view an overview or scroll between the line items:

Fig 8

The overview screen shows the entries:

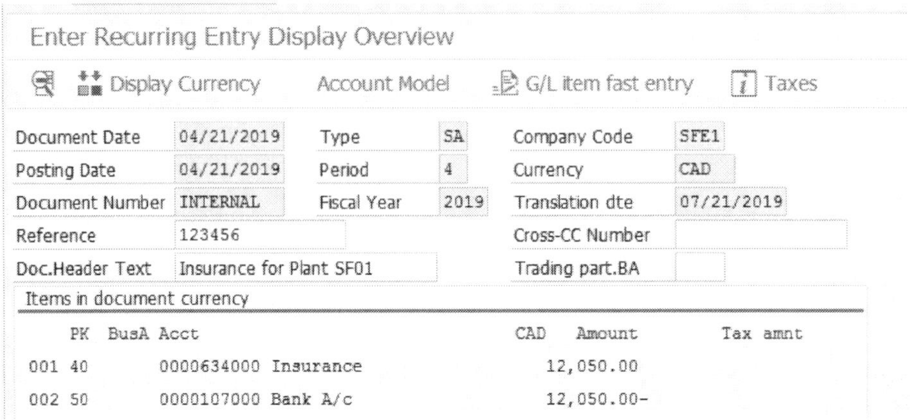

Fig 9

We can now save this entry using the save button and the system displays a message:

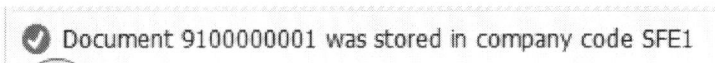

Fig 10

Note the different numbering sequence. Now SAP used the numbering sequence associated with the document type SA.

# II. PROCESSING RECURRING ENTRIES (U)

T Code F.14

Recurring entries can be processed manually or by sessions that can span across different periods. Use transaction code F.14 or follow the path:

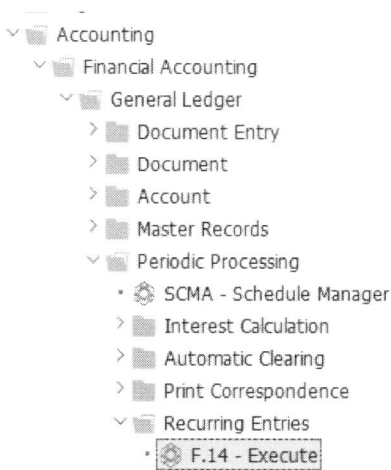

Fig 1

Enter as much data as you need for the runs – the more the restrictions, the lesser the runs will be created, as they will be restricted to only where the data matches up in the required transaction. The dates in the settlement period below will be set up in the variant dynamically and normally, the FI consultant or BASIS will set up a job to process this entry at the appropriate date based on the data entered in the FBD1 screen.

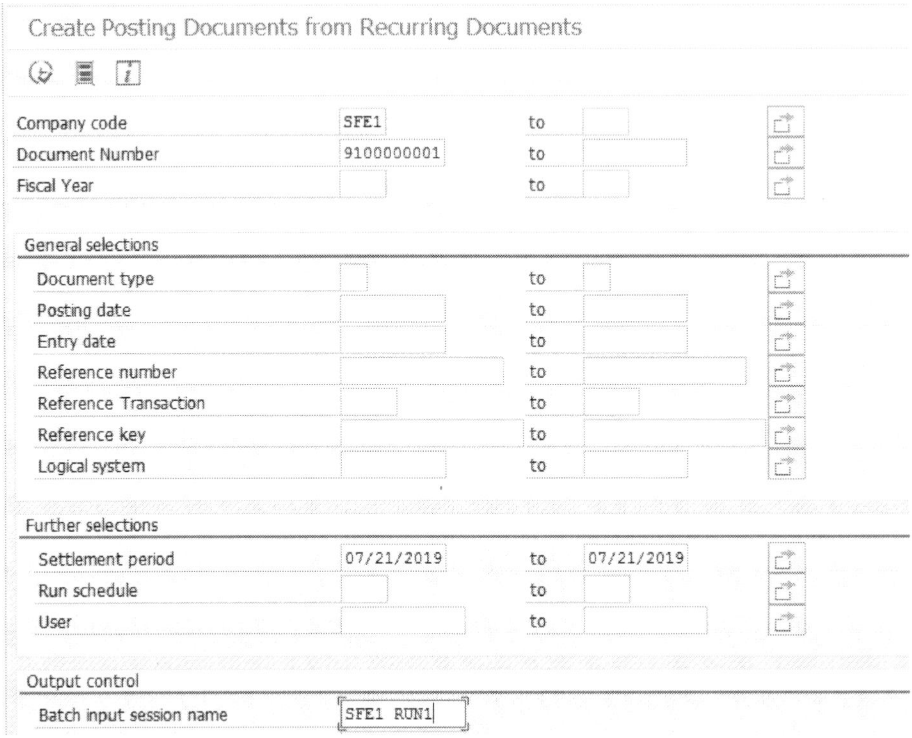

**Create Posting Documents from Recurring Documents**

| | | | | |
|---|---|---|---|---|
| Company code | SFE1 | to | | |
| Document Number | 9100000001 | to | | |
| Fiscal Year | | to | | |

General selections

| | | | | |
|---|---|---|---|---|
| Document type | | to | | |
| Posting date | | to | | |
| Entry date | | to | | |
| Reference number | | to | | |
| Reference Transaction | | to | | |
| Reference key | | to | | |
| Logical system | | to | | |

Further selections

| | | | | |
|---|---|---|---|---|
| Settlement period | 07/21/2019 | to | 07/21/2019 | |
| Run schedule | | to | | |
| User | | to | | |

Output control

| | |
|---|---|
| Batch input session name | SFE1 RUN1 |

Fig 2

Execute. At the bottom, it gives a message:

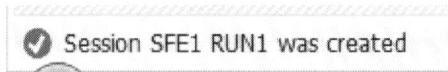

Session SFE1 RUN1 was created

Fig 3

# III.      RUNNING THE SESSION

T Code SM35

The creation of a run simply means that SAP has collected all the data it needs to post the actual JEs in the system. To actually post them, we have to run this session, which we do by following the path:

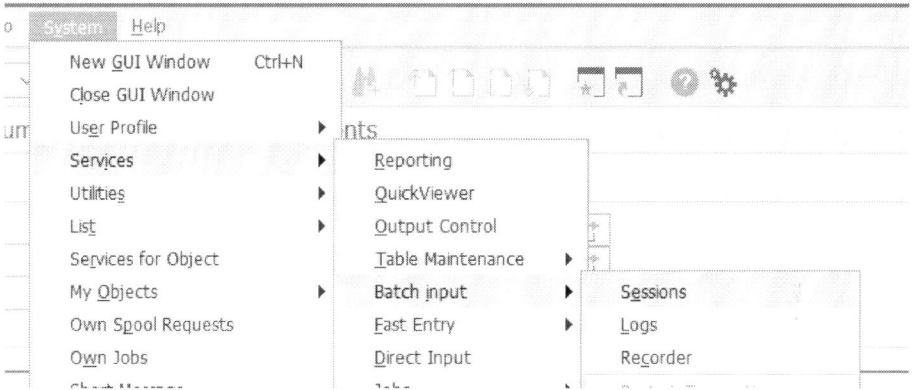

Fig 1

This brings us to a screen where we choose the run it shows under our respective IDs. Depending upon authorizations provided, we can run the sessions of other users also – again, this is something that the FI consultant or BASIS will set up in the background to run so the users' job really is to ensure that the entries in the original document created from FBD1 are correct as indeed, nobody other than the user themselves can know that data correctly.

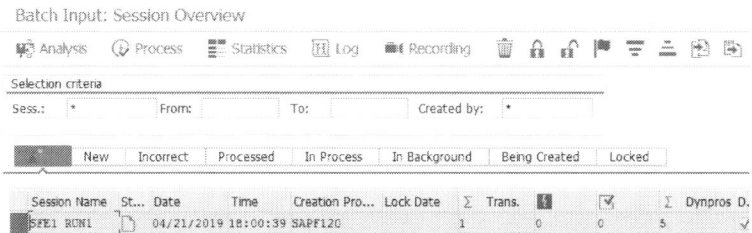

Fig 2

This screen can also be reached directly via transaction code SM35.

Check the line and click on the button to Process it:

⟳ Process

Fig 3

In the window, ask it to be processed in 'Display Errors only' mode:

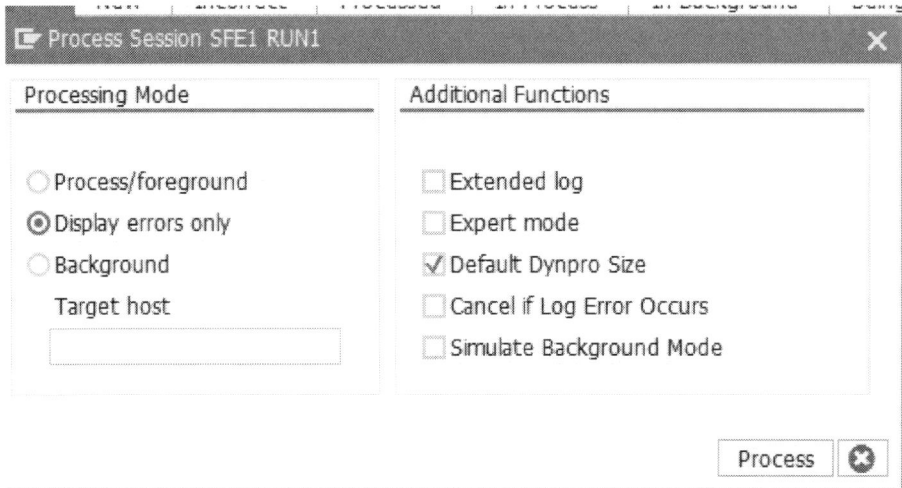

☞ Process Session SFE1 RUN1 ✕

**Processing Mode**

○ Process/foreground
◉ Display errors only
○ Background
  Target host
  [                    ]

**Additional Functions**

☐ Extended log
☐ Expert mode
☑ Default Dynpro Size
☐ Cancel if Log Error Occurs
☐ Simulate Background Mode

[ Process ] ✖

Fig 4

Click on Process and in the windows that appear as below, keep hitting Enter a few times till you see:

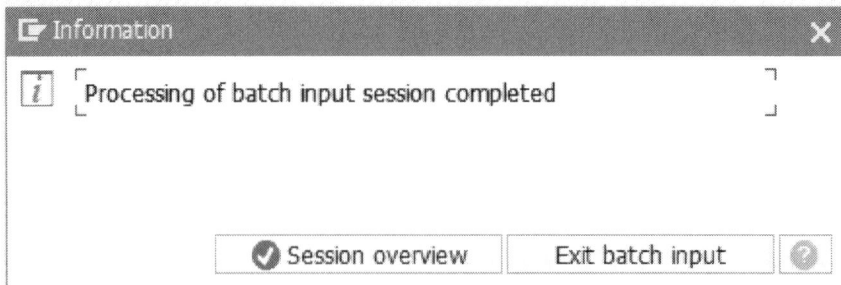

☞ Information ✕

ⓘ Processing of batch input session completed

[ ✔ Session overview ] [ Exit batch input ] [?]

Fig 5

Now if we go to run the G/L balance report FAGLB03H for these 2 accounts:

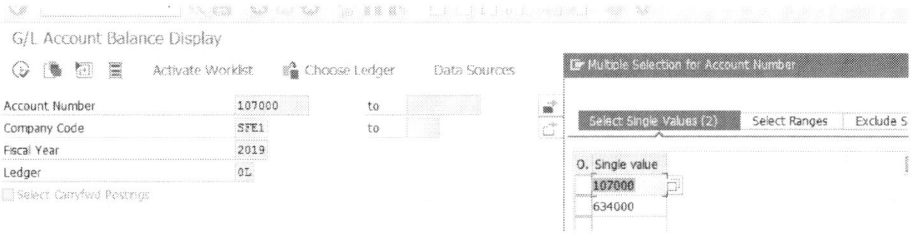

Fig 6

We find the amount appearing and double clicking it, it gives us the details or it's origin and the month as highlighted below:

Fig 7

Double clicking the cell under Cumulative Balance & the period of posting yields the 2 line items of this posting

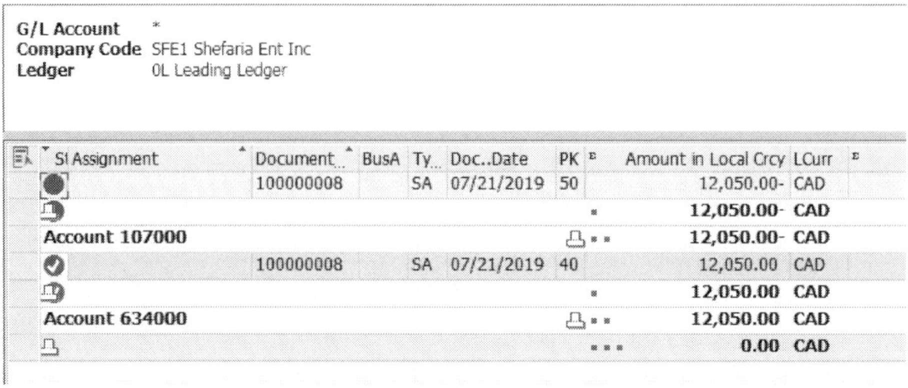

**G/L Account**    *
**Company Code**   SFE1 Shefaria Ent Inc
**Ledger**        0L Leading Ledger

| St Assignment | Document | BusA | Ty | Doc..Date | PK | Amount in Local Crcy | LCurr |
|---|---|---|---|---|---|---|---|
| ● | 100000008 | | SA | 07/21/2019 | 50 | 12,050.00- | CAD |
| | | | | | | 12,050.00- | CAD |
| Account 107000 | | | | | | 12,050.00- | CAD |
| ● | 100000008 | | SA | 07/21/2019 | 40 | 12,050.00 | CAD |
| | | | | | | 12,050.00 | CAD |
| Account 634000 | | | | | | 12,050.00 | CAD |
| | | | | | | 0.00 | CAD |

Fig 8

From here, you can also go directly into the document:

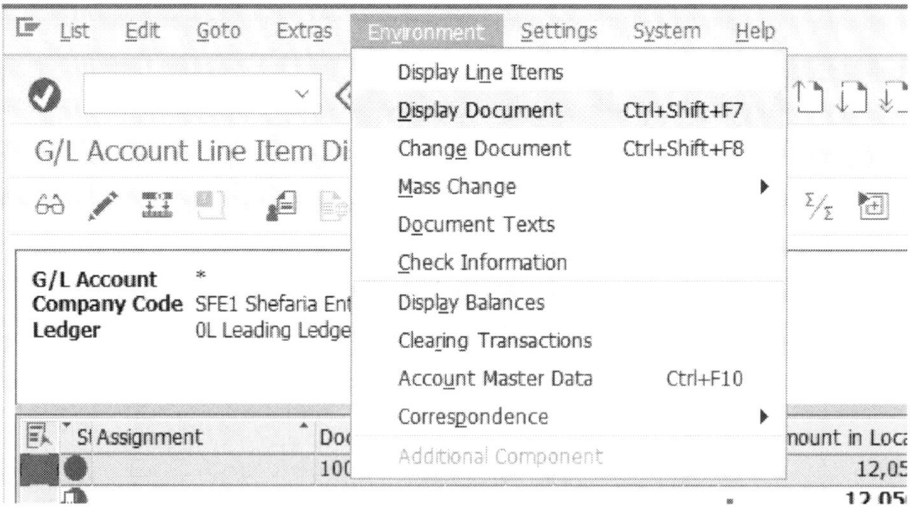

| List | Edit | Goto | Extras | Environment | Settings | System | Help |
|---|---|---|---|---|---|---|---|

G/L Account Line Item Di

- Display Line Items
- Display Document    Ctrl+Shift+F7
- Change Document    Ctrl+Shift+F8
- Mass Change ▶
- Document Texts
- Check Information
- Display Balances
- Clearing Transactions
- Account Master Data    Ctrl+F10
- Correspondence ▶
- Additional Component

**G/L Account**    *
**Company Code**   SFE1 Shefaria Ent
**Ledger**        0L Leading Ledge

| St Assignment | Doc | | nount in Loca |
|---|---|---|---|
| ● | 100 | | 12,05 |
| | | | 12.05 |

Fig 9

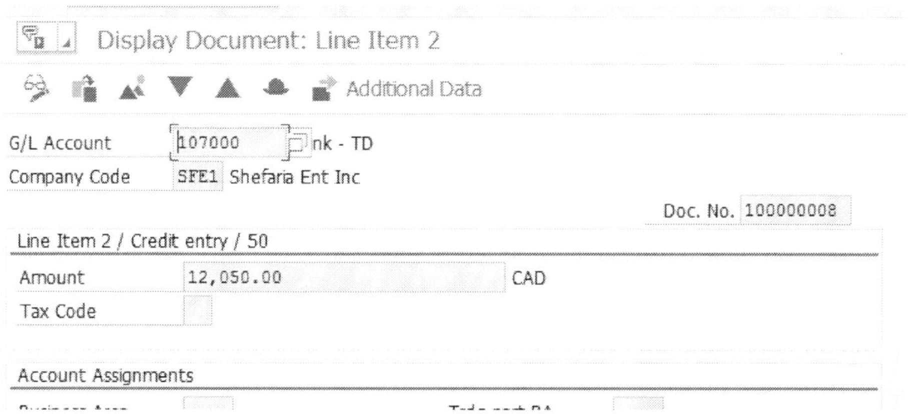

## Display Document: Line Item 2

⊕ 📋 ▲ ▼ ▲ ☁ 🗗 Additional Data

| G/L Account | 107000 | ⬚ nk - TD |
|---|---|---|
| Company Code | SFE1 Shefaria Ent Inc | |

Doc. No. 100000008

Line Item 2 / Credit entry / 50

| Amount | 12,050.00 | CAD |
|---|---|---|
| Tax Code | | |

Account Assignments

~~Business Area~~          ~~Trde cost BA~~

Fig 10

And then click on overview button 🏔

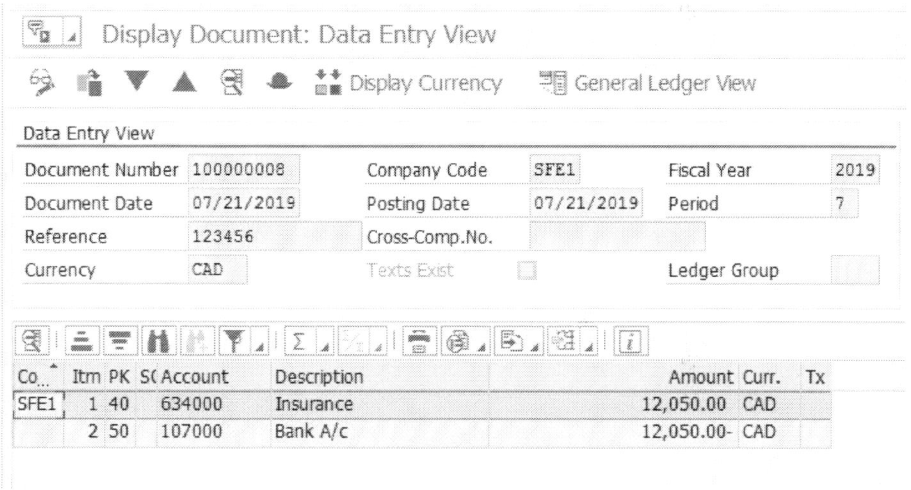

## Display Document: Data Entry View

⊕ 📋 ▼ ▲ 🗗 ☁ ⬆ Display Currency    ▤ General Ledger View

Data Entry View

| Document Number | 100000008 | Company Code | SFE1 | Fiscal Year | 2019 |
|---|---|---|---|---|---|
| Document Date | 07/21/2019 | Posting Date | 07/21/2019 | Period | 7 |
| Reference | 123456 | Cross-Comp.No. | | | |
| Currency | CAD | Texts Exist | ☐ | Ledger Group | |

| Co... | Itm | PK | SC | Account | Description | Amount | Curr. | Tx |
|---|---|---|---|---|---|---|---|---|
| SFE1 | 1 | 40 | | 634000 | Insurance | 12,050.00 | CAD | |
| | 2 | 50 | | 107000 | Bank A/c | 12,050.00- | CAD | |

Fig 11

115

The Header gives us more information about the origin of this document:

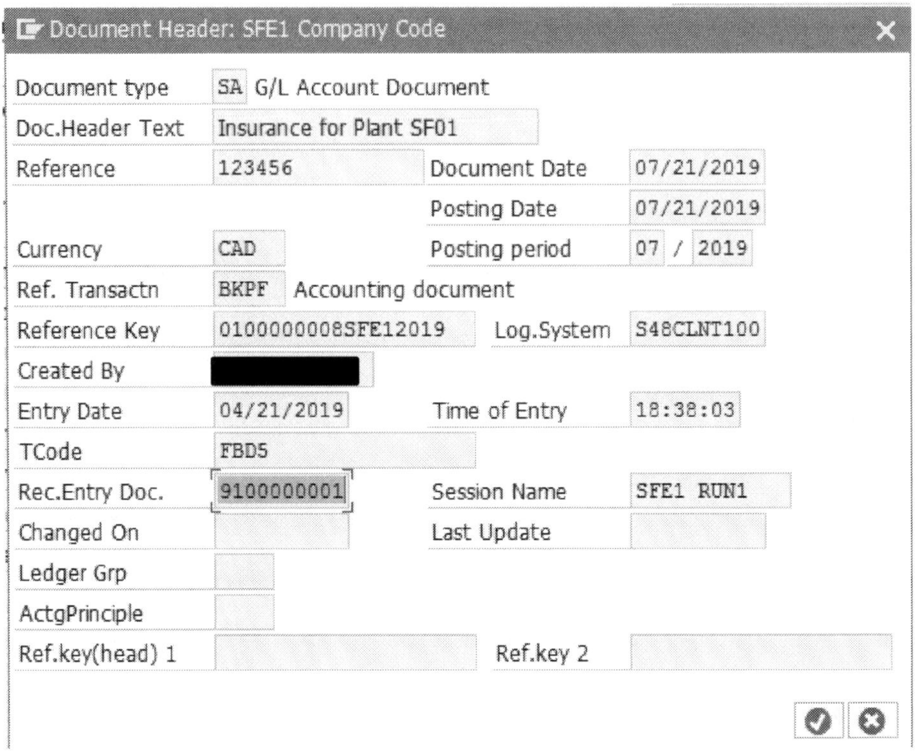

| Document Header: SFE1 Company Code | | |
|---|---|---|
| Document type | SA G/L Account Document | |
| Doc.Header Text | Insurance for Plant SF01 | |
| Reference | 123456 | Document Date | 07/21/2019 |
| | | Posting Date | 07/21/2019 |
| Currency | CAD | Posting period | 07 / 2019 |
| Ref. Transactn | BKPF Accounting document | |
| Reference Key | 0100000008SFE12019 | Log.System S48CLNT100 |
| Created By | ███████ | |
| Entry Date | 04/21/2019 | Time of Entry 18:38:03 |
| TCode | FBD5 | |
| Rec.Entry Doc. | 9100000001 | Session Name SFE1 RUN1 |
| Changed On | | Last Update |
| Ledger Grp | | |
| ActgPrinciple | | |
| Ref.key(head) 1 | | Ref.key 2 |

Fig 12

The Rec. Entry doc. in the above print was the # we got when we set this recurring entry up.

It converted that particular posting to an actual accounting entry, which is what we saw in the G/L report.

116

# CUSTOMER & VENDOR TOLERANCE (C)

T Code SPRO

Customer and vendor tolerances are required to be set up before we can make any posting of payment from or payment to them as the case may be. This is because it is not necessary that the amounts we post would be the same as the invoices we will raise or receive. SAP does not allow any postings to customer or vendor accounts if these limits are not defined in the configuration.

The path to do this configuration is:

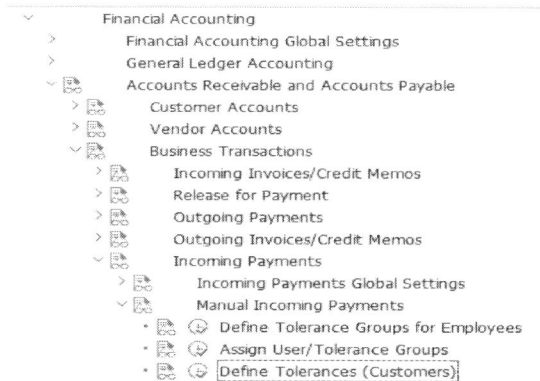

Fig 1

Click on **New Entries** to define one for your company, let us use the values below; the other fields are not important for this purpose:

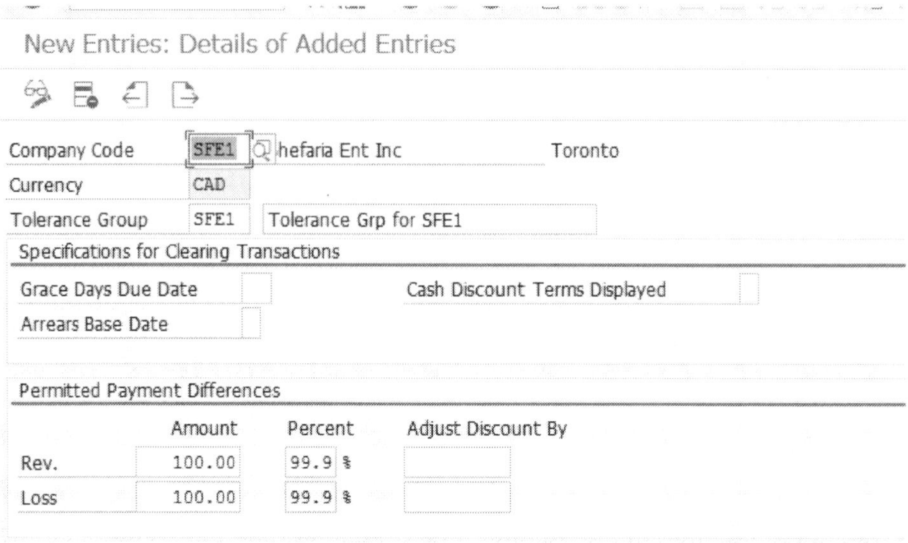

**New Entries: Details of Added Entries**

| | | |
|---|---|---|
| Company Code | SFE1 | hefaria Ent Inc          Toronto |
| Currency | CAD | |
| Tolerance Group | SFE1 | Tolerance Grp for SFE1 |

Specifications for Clearing Transactions

| | | |
|---|---|---|
| Grace Days Due Date | | Cash Discount Terms Displayed |
| Arrears Base Date | | |

Permitted Payment Differences

| | Amount | Percent | Adjust Discount By |
|---|---|---|---|
| Rev. | 100.00 | 99.9 % | |
| Loss | 100.00 | 99.9 % | |

Fig 2

Save the configuration. This configuration linking the CC with the tolerance group will work for both, customer and vendors. This configuration says that a deviation of $100 or .1% which ever is lower, from the amount of the document is allowed when posting payments.

# VENDOR GROUPS (C)

T Code SPRO

All master data in SAP is ordered by way of grouping them for specific purposes. These groups are fundamental to the way the master data will be required to be entered and be visible to the user. A master data record is for the most part, a 'proposal' of the most often repeated or expected scenario to be used in the transaction. Its primary purpose is to save time for the users from entering data repeatedly. Because SAP is such an integrated system, it requires a great amount of data to link different business process documents and modules with each other. It does that by making data relevant at different points in the business cycle of a document. For the most part, substantial elements of this data can be changed in the first document that is created from it.

Vendor group is the highest level of data organization of a vendor master. This is also the first step in setting up the vendor master in any SAP system. In most situations, standard vendor groups provided by SAP should suffice, though if custom ones need to be created, that is also an easy activity.

Vendor groups can be seen in the path:

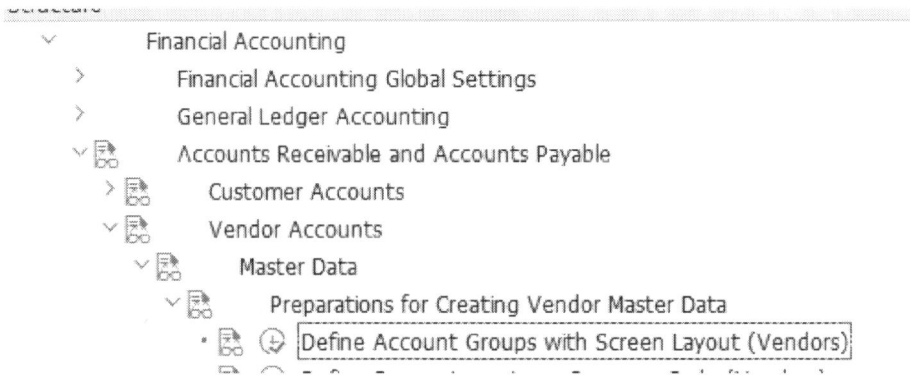

Fig 1

**HANA CHANGE:** For the customer and vendor side i.e. SD module and MM module respectively, one of the biggest changes in HANA are those related to the customer and vendor master. Both of them have been replaced by the term Business Partner. Business partner itself is not new to SAP – the CRM system has had them forever and now the concept has been lifted and shifted into the HANA system.

Instead of the old transactions to create vendors and customers via XK01/XD01, we now use BP. From the configuration angle as seen below, the groups Vendor, Payee, Goods supplier etc have been replaced with SUPL – Supplier. In the Business partner setup, the account groups are replaced by 'roles' i.e. the payee, instead of an account group is now a 'role' that the SUPL will/can play but is decided by the master data rather than by configuration as in ECC.

To change the existing vendors and customers, the t codes MK02, FK02, MK03, XD02 etc are still valid. Only new vendors or customers can't be created by the old codes, and we have to use BP for them. It can be expected that in the next versions of HANA, SAP may replace these also with BP.

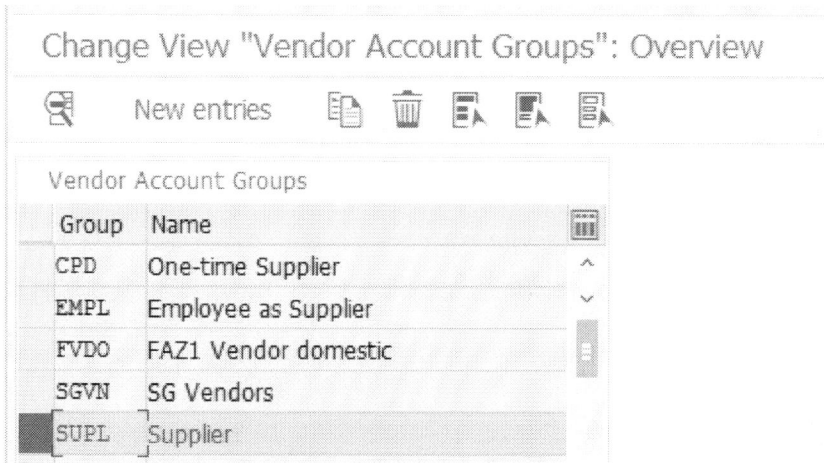

Fig 2

Double clicking on the above gives the detail of how the data will be organized, here, in account group 0001, it is split into 3 areas – General data, CC data and Purchasing data:

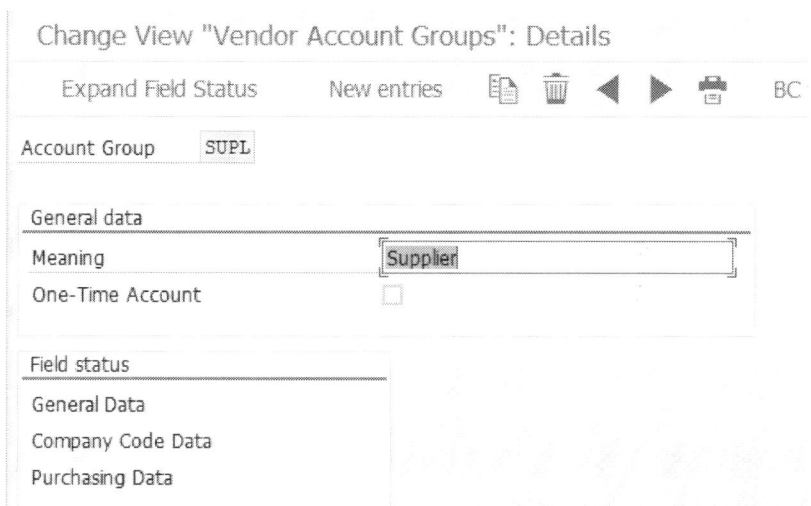

Fig 3

Double clicking on any one of them further reveals the sub-groupings/screens in that section:

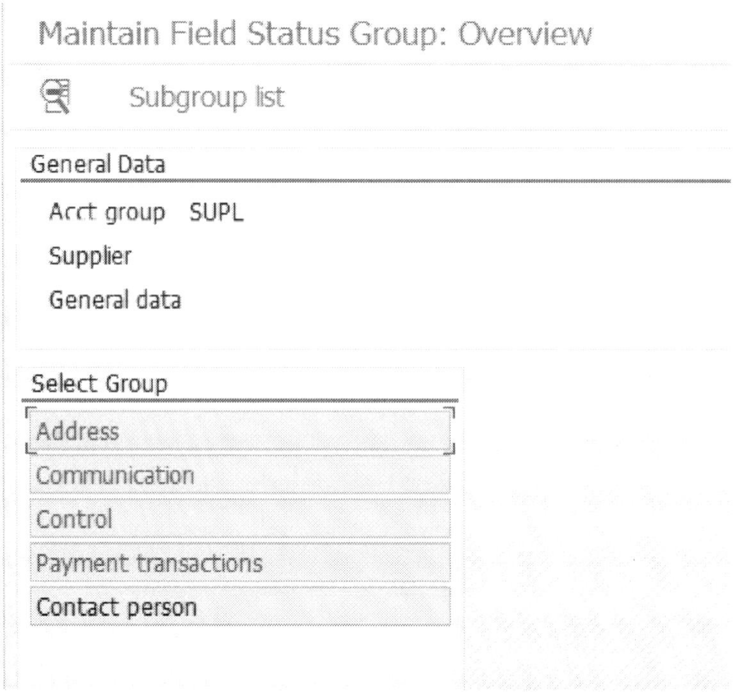

Maintain Field Status Group: Overview

⊟    Subgroup list

General Data

  Acct group   SUPL
  Supplier
  General data

Select Group

| Address |
| --- |
| Communication |
| Control |
| Payment transactions |
| Contact person |

Fig 4

For most business requirements, the existing vendor account groups will work though some companies may prefer to create their own. For our purpose, we will use the existing standard one – SUPL.

# VENDOR MASTER (U)

T Code FK01 or XK01 in ECC (Use account group 0001) OR in HANA, the T Code is BP. The below process is on HANA i.e. T code BP.

We are now ready to create our first vendor. The T Code to create a vendor is BP and then we decide what elements of the BP to create. To begin with we will create the Business partner's general data and then assign it the different roles required:

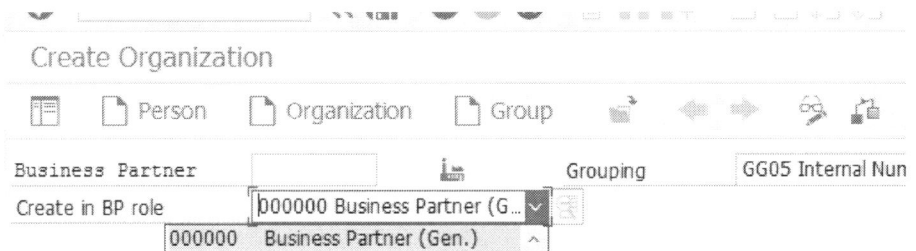

Fig 1

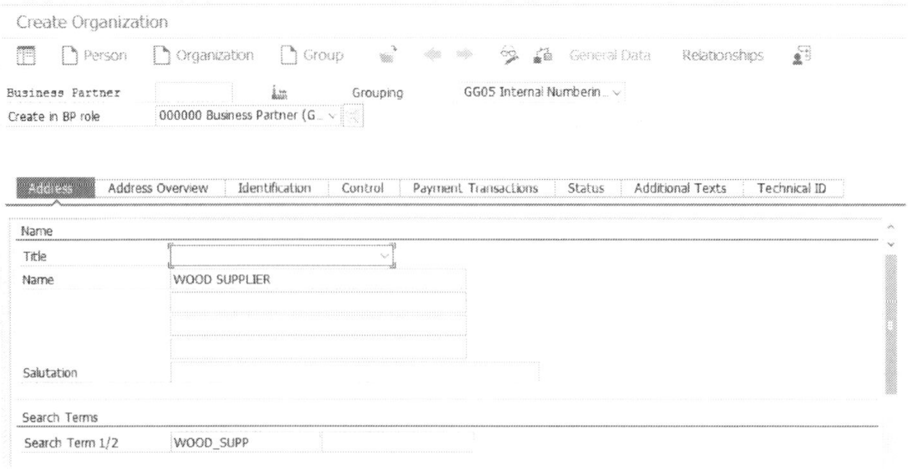

Fig 2

As seen above, there are different screens which require relevant data for the vendor to be entered. Since vendor master is essentially a part of Purchasing, we will not spend much time here and create the vendor with the minimum of data which, from the Finance perspective, really relates to payment terms, modes of payments, banking information if available, who will be responsible to make payments to, etc.

Saving the above data gave us our vendor number:

Fig 3

Next, we give our new vendor a role for Financial transactions and enter the appropriate data in the Company Code screen:

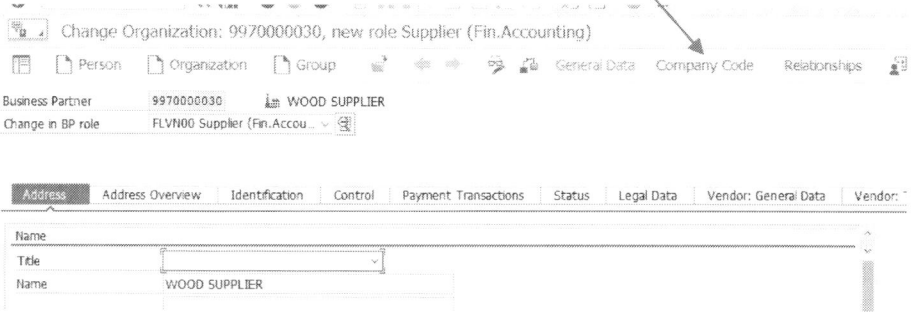

Fig 4

Company Code screens – Click on 'Company Code' and enter the company code and Adopt:

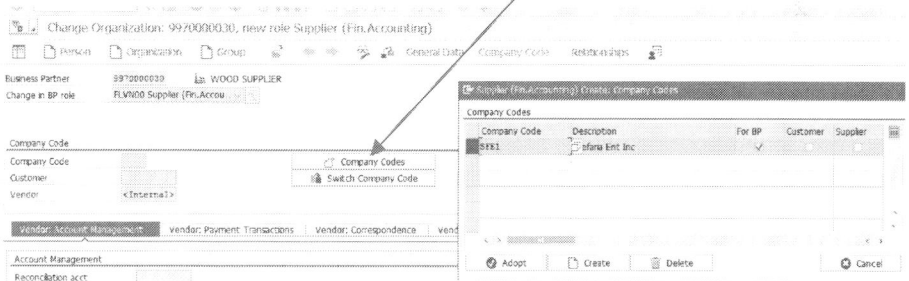

Fig 5

The fields open up to enter data as applicable for your company code. Insert the data as much as you know and save the BP:

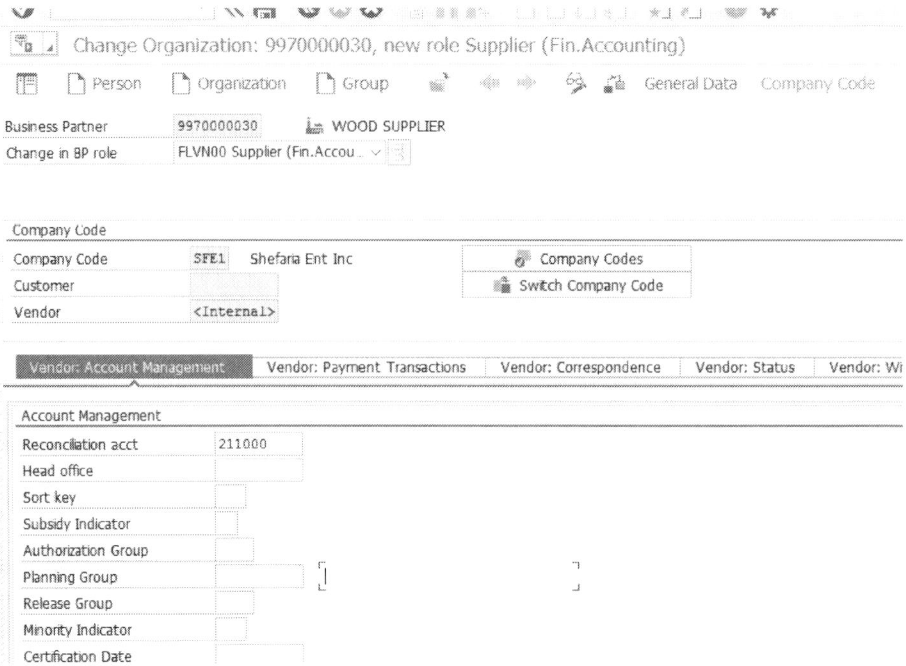

Fig 6

For all practical purposes the data required in the CC screens remains generally the same as in ECC, just the layouts are different and instead of reaching the screens through the menu, they are now laid out in plain view e.g. for blocking data we no longer have to go through Extras – there is a screen Vendor Status right there:

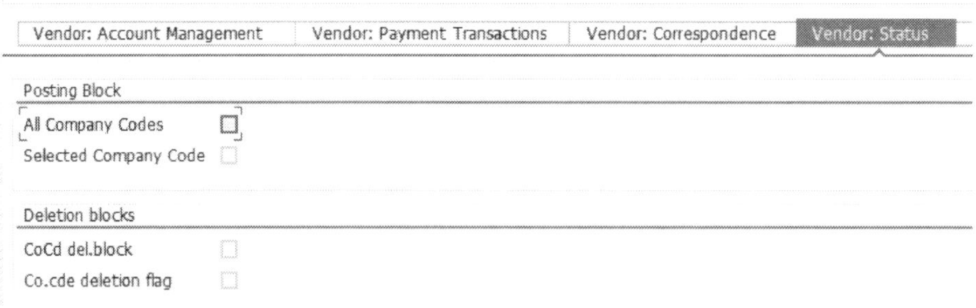

Fig 7

Customer in Vendor: General Data: If the vendor also happens to be a customer, enter its customer # here. This can also be used to adjust the payables against the receivables or vice versa once, some other data settings are done as we will see in transaction F.13 for auto clearing accounts. On this screen is also the field Alternative Payee which is used if this vendor is not the one to whom you will pay for it's goods and services supplied to you.

The field-trading partner under Control tab is used to denote if it is an inter-company vendor and then populated with it's Inter company customer number.

On the tab Payment Transactions, define the vendor's banking information where payments can be made:

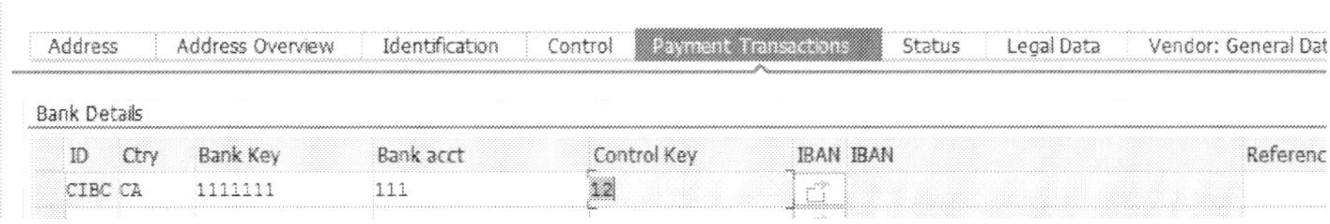

| Address | Address Overview | Identification | Control | Payment Transactions | Status | Legal Data | Vendor: General Dat |
|---------|------------------|----------------|---------|----------------------|--------|------------|---------------------|

Bank Details

| ID | Ctry | Bank Key | Bank acct | Control Key | IBAN IBAN | Referenc |
|----|------|----------|-----------|-------------|-----------|----------|
| CIBC | CA | 1111111 | 111 | 12 | | |

Fig 8

Alternative payee: If the vendor to be paid for the purchases is different from the current vendor #, enter that payee # here

On the Company code data the single most important field is the reconciliation account to which the sub ledger will post.

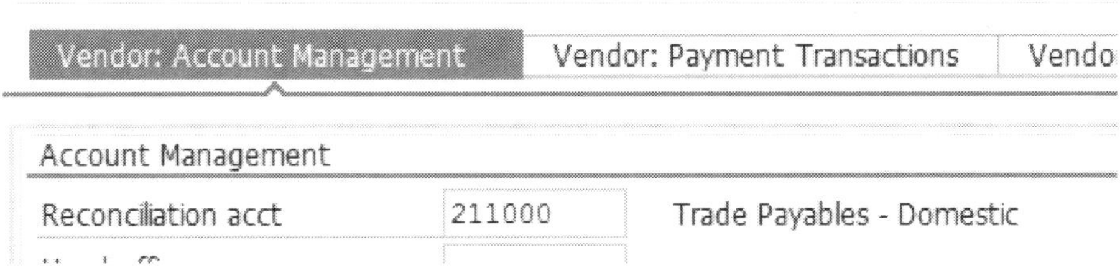

| Vendor: Account Management | Vendor: Payment Transactions | Vendo |
|---------------------------|------------------------------|-------|

Account Management

| Reconciliation acct | 211000 | Trade Payables - Domestic |
|---------------------|--------|---------------------------|

Fig 9

You will recall from the previous chapters that the reconciliation account is the account to which the account payables are posted via the sub-ledger. Enter the account we created or choose from the drop down or press F4 - the reconciliation account is a mandatory field as this is the account to which the account payables are posted via the sub-ledger. Enter the account we created or choose from the drop down or press F4 after positioning the cursor in this field:

Choose 211000 that is what is created for this purpose as it is a domestic vendor

On the screen Vendor: Payment Transactions we have the vendors' payment terms (from FI perspective, MM can/may have it's own payment terms but usually both are kept same). Mode of payment (check, transfer etc) can be entered in the Payment methods field and when doing the payment run, SAP will look at this field and pay the vendor in the manner specified.

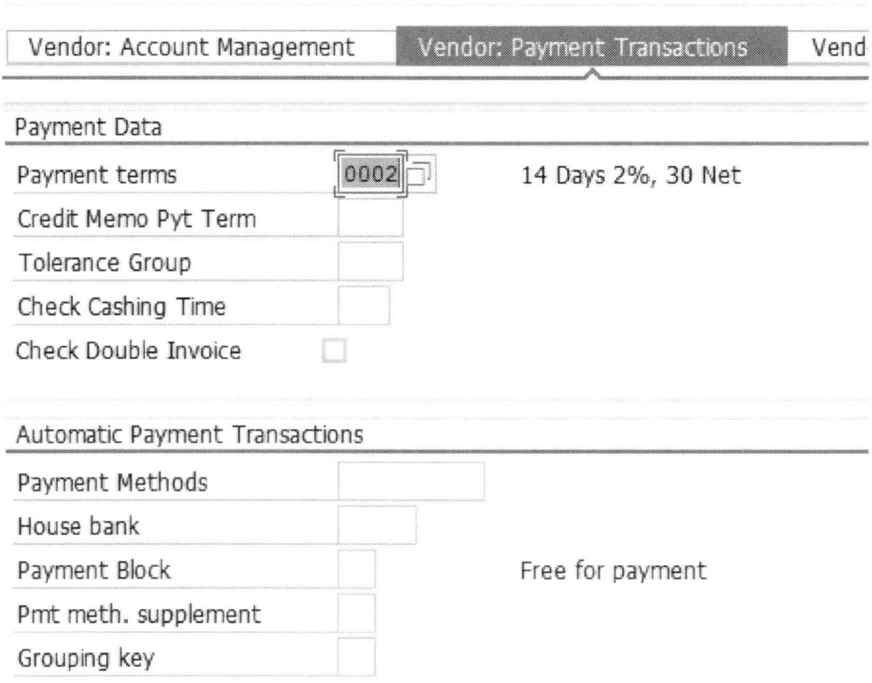

| Vendor: Account Management | Vendor: Payment Transactions | Vend |
|---|---|---|

**Payment Data**

| | | |
|---|---|---|
| Payment terms | 0002 | 14 Days 2%, 30 Net |
| Credit Memo Pyt Term | | |
| Tolerance Group | | |
| Check Cashing Time | | |
| Check Double Invoice | ☐ | |

**Automatic Payment Transactions**

| | | |
|---|---|---|
| Payment Methods | | |
| House bank | | |
| Payment Block | | Free for payment |
| Pmt meth. supplement | | |
| Grouping key | | |

Fig 10

The Check Double Invoice prevents the vendor from getting paid multiple times for the same invoice. Keep this indicator checked. The ramification of this is explained in a later chapter in this book.

In HANA SAP has introduced the concept of sending remittance invoices by XML to the vendor:

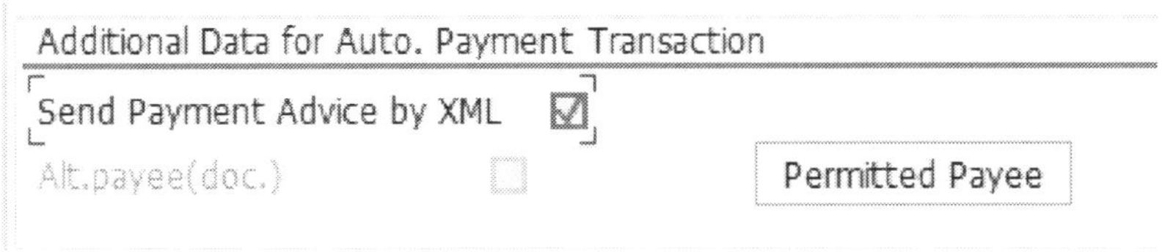

Additional Data for Auto. Payment Transaction

Send Payment Advice by XML ☑

Alt.payee(doc.) ☐          Permitted Payee

Fig 11

The next screen has data relating to how to correspond with this vendor:

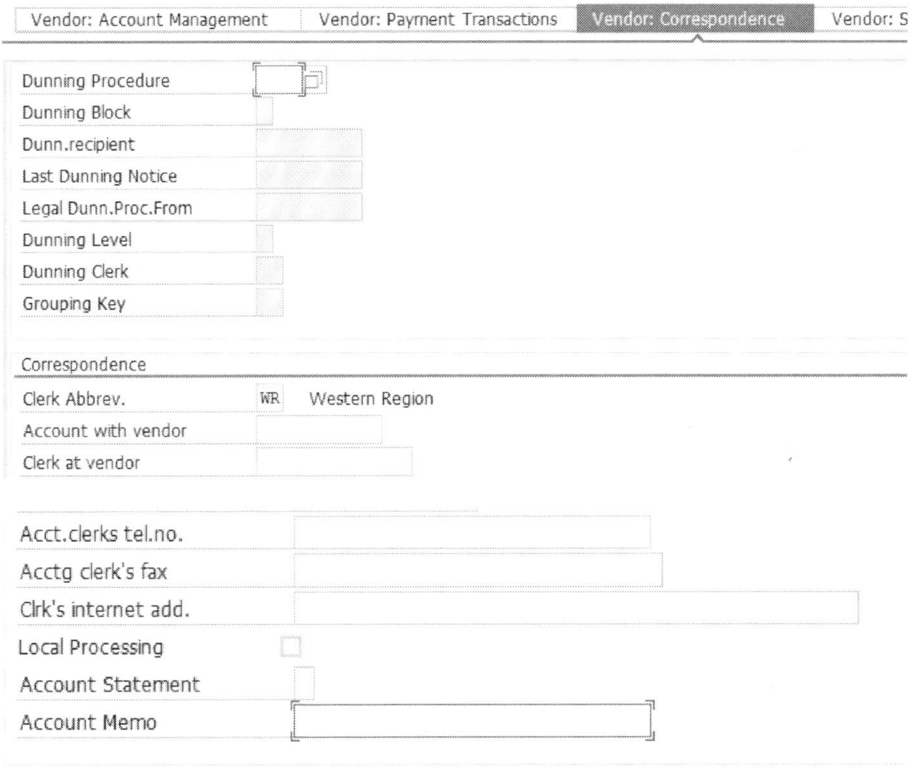

| Vendor: Account Management | Vendor: Payment Transactions | Vendor: Correspondence | Vendor: S |

Dunning Procedure

Dunning Block

Dunn.recipient

Last Dunning Notice

Legal Dunn.Proc.From

Dunning Level

Dunning Clerk

Grouping Key

Correspondence

Clerk Abbrev.          WR    Western Region

Account with vendor

Clerk at vendor

Acct.clerks tel.no.

Acctg clerk's fax

Clrk's internet add.

Local Processing

Account Statement

Account Memo

Fig 12

Data like Acct clerk is used to provide visibility to the vendor. The acct clerk is a person or group responsible to make payments to this vendor and if we run reports for accounting clerks, we get the

129

lists of vendors that clerk is responsible for and whose payments are due.

At this point, we have entered in all the data that the system needed on the screens we chose to set up. We now save this data for the vendor

When the data was saved, SAP gave it a vendor # which we will use in our transactions:

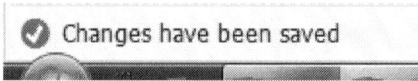

Fig 13

Fig 14

As we notice, the vendor # and the Business partner # are different. In the customer section later, we will learn how to keep both the numbers same via configuration.

At various times in this manual, we will come back to the vendor master to populate certain more data and see it's effect on our transactions.

# CUSTOMER GROUPS (C)

T Code SPRO

Conceptually, the customer master follows the same principles as the vendor master i.e. it proposes the customer related information in the transaction. Information such as which sales office of the company is responsible for the customer, who is responsible for the receivables from this customer, what is their credit terms, whom to contact, their banking information, method or preference of shipping and what locations they can be shipped to, and a lot more, can be made to 'default' from the customer master instead of entering into every transaction. This information though, is not cast in stone and is only a 'proposal' based on the most often repeated scenarios. The user can override most of this information in the transaction if it happens to be different for that particular situation.

Generally, the same rules apply in creation of customer account groups as they do for vendor account groups. SAP has provided some excellent customer account groups based on the way businesses are structured and it is always advisable to use the existing ones or create a custom one by copying and modifying an existing one as needed. As described in the earlier pages under the Vendor group section, in the HANA system, the same way as the Vendor groups, the old ECC customer groups have been replaced with one called CUST who assumes different roles in the customer master. The path to create or modify/view the customer groups is the same, under Financial Accounting in SPRO as below:

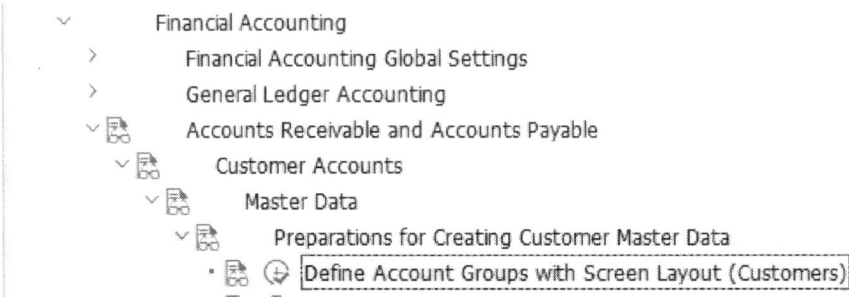

Fig 1

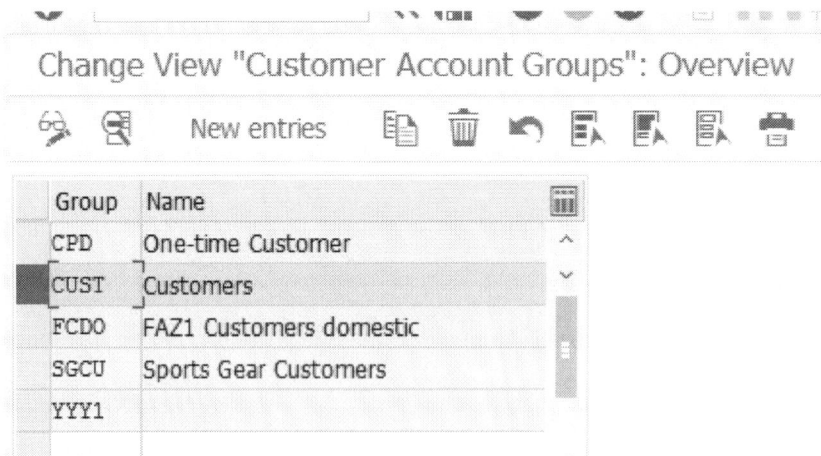

Fig 2

Again, we will use the standard account group CUST – Customers. The old CPD for one time customers as we had in ECC, is still available.

By default, all the fields on the various screens of the customer master are optional to fill in (Fig 5). However if we need to, we can make some mandatory e.g. if it is a company policy to always have an AR representative (called accounting clerk in SAP) assigned to every customer, then we can make this field mandatory in the CC data. This can be done by first going to the CC data under this account group by double clicking on it:

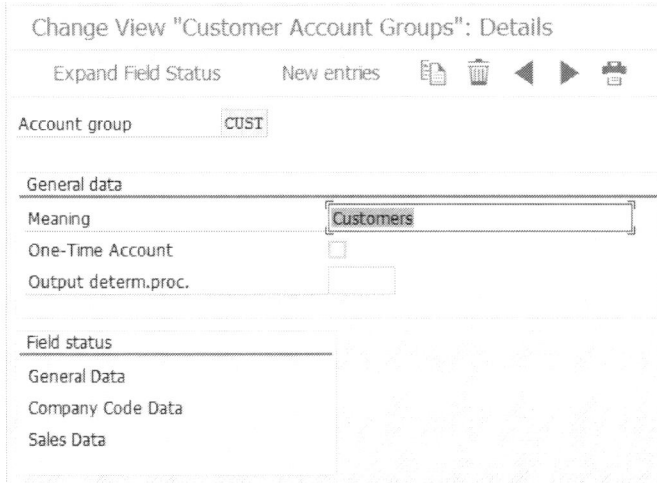

Fig 3

Next, double click on the Company Code data:

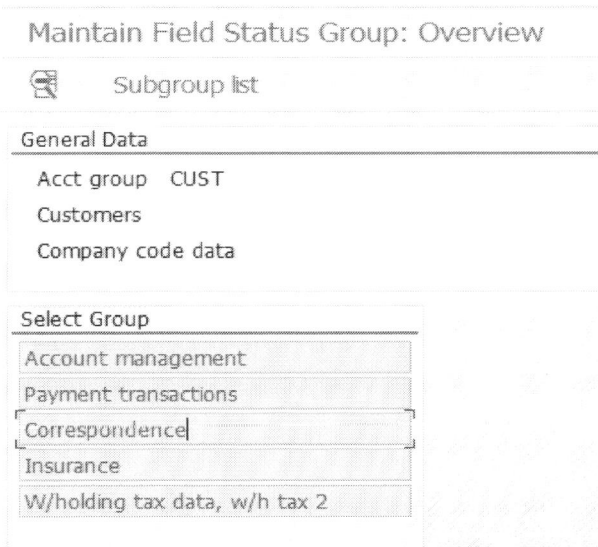

Fig 4

Finally, double click on the Correspondence tab and for the accounting clerk field, check on the radio button Req. Entry instead of Optional:

Maintain Field Status Group: Correspondence

⮐  🗋     Field check

| General Data | | | | Page   1 / 1 |
| --- | --- | --- | --- | --- |

Acct group   CUST
Customers
Company code data

Correspondence

| | Suppress | Req. Entry | Opt. entry | Display |
| --- | --- | --- | --- | --- |
| Payment notices | ○ | ○ | ⦿ | ○ |
| Acctng clerk's communication | ○ | ○ | ⦿ | ○ |
| Dunning data | ○ | ○ | ⦿ | ○ |
| Account statement | ○ | ○ | ⦿ | ○ |
| Local processing | ○ | ○ | ⦿ | ○ |
| Collective invoice variant | ○ | ○ | ⦿ | ○ |
| Account at customer | ○ | ○ | ⦿ | ○ |
| Accounting clerks | ○ | ⦿ | ○ | ○ |
| Users at customer | ○ | ○ | ⦿ | ○ |
| Account memo | ○ | ○ | ⦿ | ○ |

Fig 5

Save. Now, whenever we try to create a customer's financial accounting data, SAP will insist we fill in this field.

A caveat: One should not make changes to standard SAP configurations. This has been done only as a demo. If you need an accounting clerk to be mandatory, you should define a new group for yourself in which you can make it mandatory.

For this field to be filled, we must also have at least one accounting clerk set up in the particular CC. Account clerks are set up in the path below in the vendor tree or in a path under the customer node. Both lead to the same configuration and can be used interchangeably.

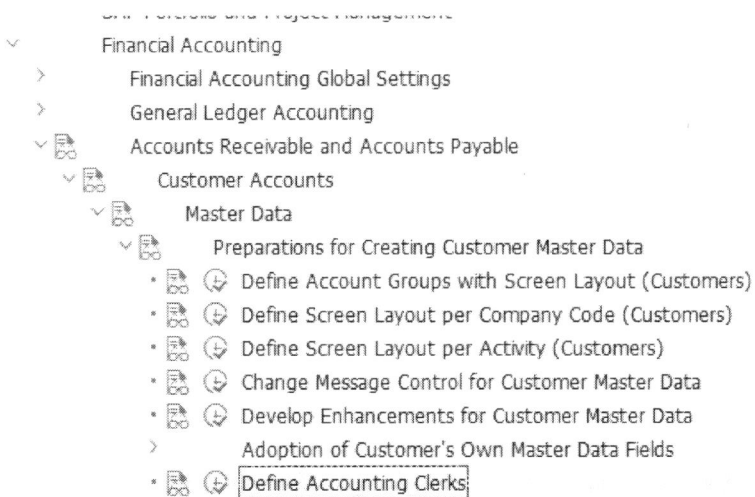

Financial Accounting
> Financial Accounting Global Settings
> General Ledger Accounting
∨ Accounts Receivable and Accounts Payable
  ∨ Customer Accounts
    ∨ Master Data
      ∨ Preparations for Creating Customer Master Data
        · Define Account Groups with Screen Layout (Customers)
        · Define Screen Layout per Company Code (Customers)
        · Define Screen Layout per Activity (Customers)
        · Change Message Control for Customer Master Data
        · Develop Enhancements for Customer Master Data
        > Adoption of Customer's Own Master Data Fields
        · Define Accounting Clerks

Fig 6

Click on New entries, define yours for your CC, and give it a description – a two-digit charter field:

New Entries

Fig 7

New Entries: Overview of Added Entries

| CoCd | Clerk | Name of Accounting Clerk | Office User |
|------|-------|--------------------------|-------------|
| SFE1 | WR | Western Region | |

Fig 8

Save the data in the transport.

# CUSTOMER MASTER (U)

T Code FD01 or XD01 in ECC (Use SAP standard account group 0001 for sold to party) OR in HANA, the T Code is BP. The below process is on HANA i.e. T code BP.

Choose the BP Role General for now to get the customer number.

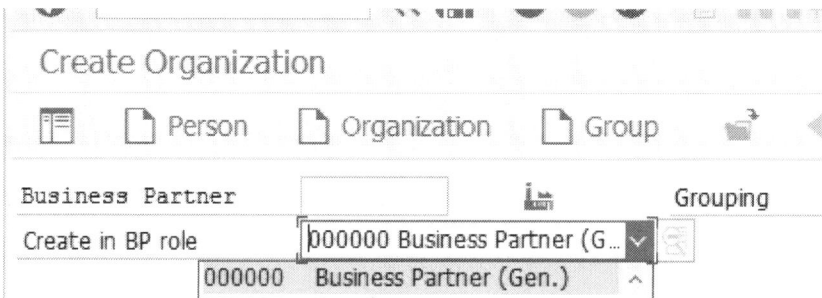

Fig 1

Leave the field Business partner blank, as SAP will auto generate the number. Enter as much data as you can in the various tabs – address etc, whatever is mandatory, SAP will ask for it and you can't save w/o it.

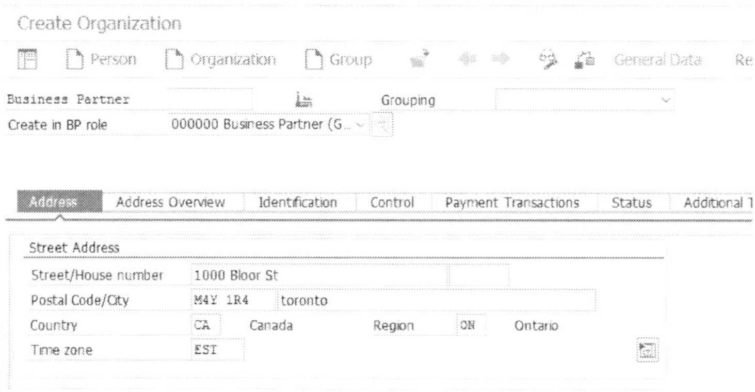

Fig 2

Save and recall it back in change mode to extend it to accounting:

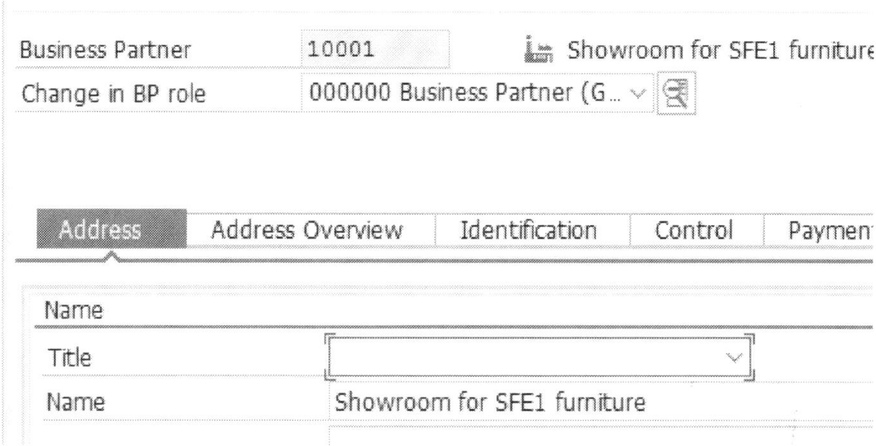

Fig 3

Having obtained the customer number, let us proceed to give this customer the 'roles' necessary for it to perform our functions. As discussed earlier these roles now replace the account groups in ECC.

Toggle to the Change mode using ✎ if you are in Display and/or enter the customer number to recall it's data you entered.

Choose the role Financial Accounting as below:

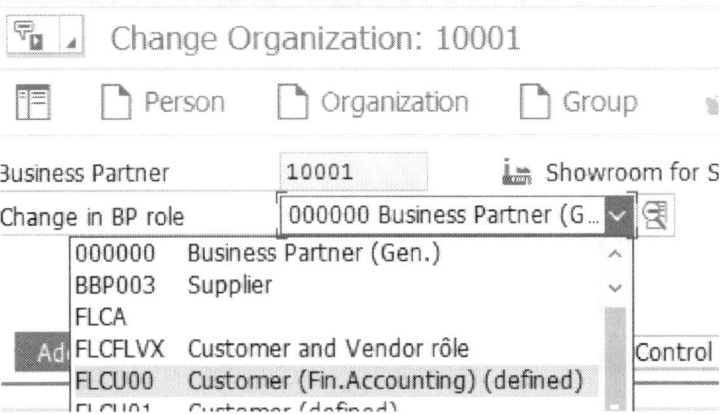

Fig 4

The tab Company Code should open up at top right. click on it to enter the company code and Hit Enter to open up the different tabs and fields for data entry:

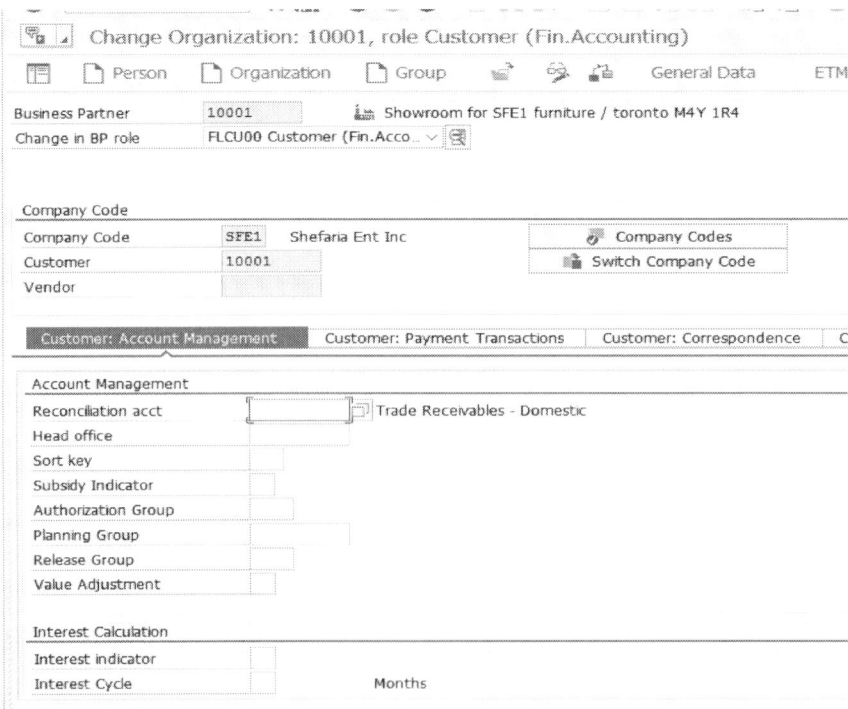

Fig 5

The reconciliation account must always be entered and for the most part this will always be mandatory – this enables SAP to keep track of the current assets i.e. receivables from the customers up to date for a quick view.

The accounting clerks are the same in the configuration and can also be entered if you have a policy of tracking customers in accounts based on job roles or regions.

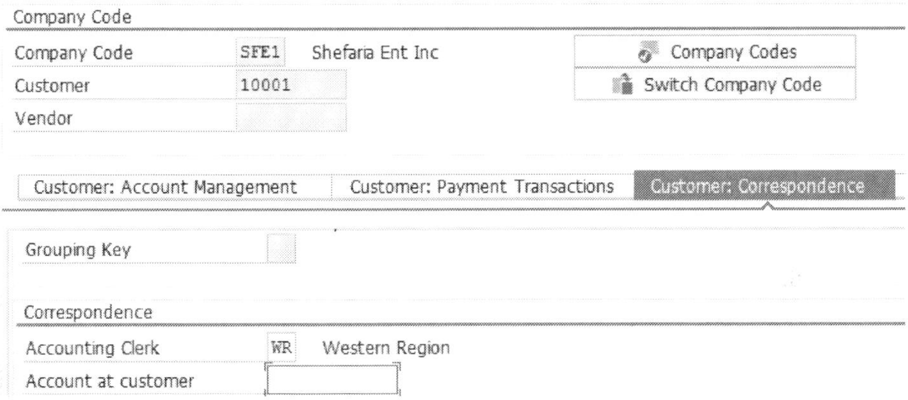

| Company Code | | | | |
|---|---|---|---|---|
| Company Code | SFE1 | Shefaria Ent Inc | | Company Codes |
| Customer | 10001 | | | Switch Company Code |
| Vendor | | | | |

| Customer: Account Management | Customer: Payment Transactions | Customer: Correspondence |
|---|---|---|

| Grouping Key | | |
|---|---|---|

Correspondence

| Accounting Clerk | WR | Western Region |
|---|---|---|
| Account at customer | | |

Fig 6

We see that the reconciliation account is mandatory, as was in the vendor master.

So let us enter the appropriate recon account as below:

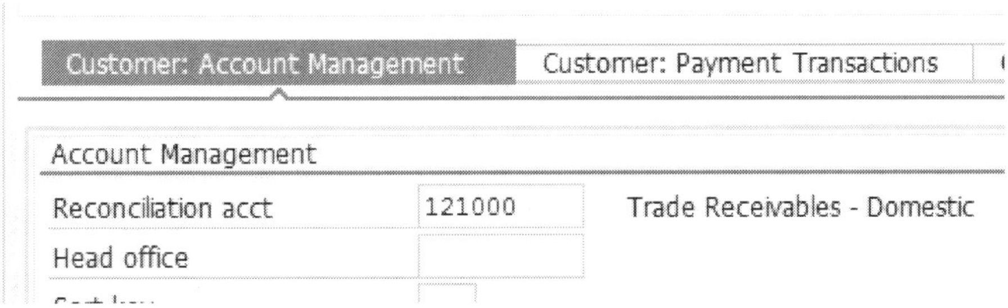

| Customer: Account Management | Customer: Payment Transactions |
|---|---|

Account Management

| Reconciliation acct | 121000 | Trade Receivables - Domestic |
|---|---|---|
| Head office | | |

Fig 7

139

On the next tab, payment Transactions we can enter the payment terms we have given the customer as well as the tolerance group we configured earlier in Customer and vendor tolerances.

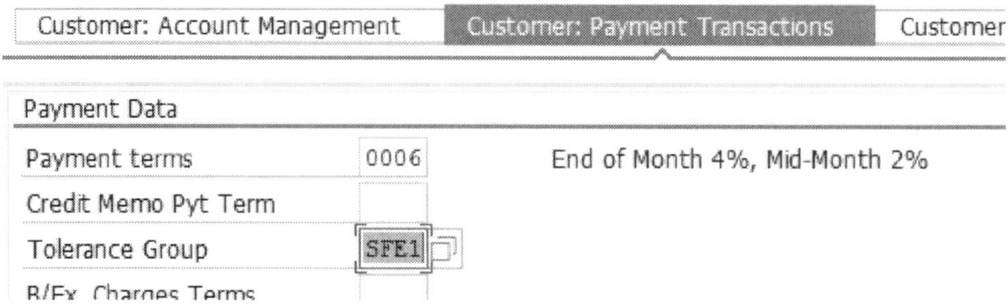

| Customer: Account Management | Customer: Payment Transactions | Customer |
| --- | --- | --- |

Payment Data

| Payment terms | 0006 | End of Month 4%, Mid-Month 2% |
| --- | --- | --- |
| Credit Memo Pyt Term | | |
| Tolerance Group | SFE1 | |
| B/Ex Charges Terms | | |

Fig 8

On the next tab, Correspondence, we find the field Accounting Clerk is mandatory:

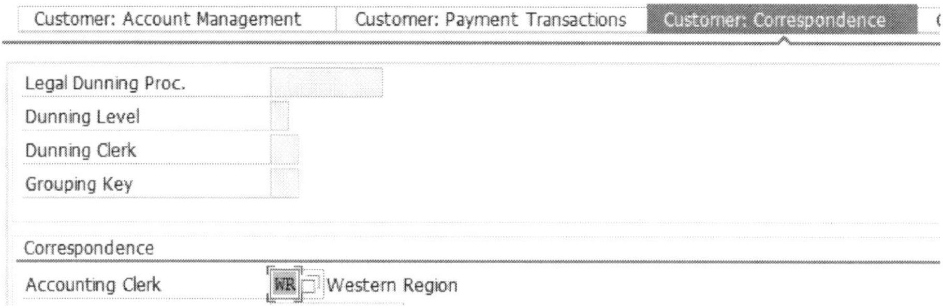

| Customer: Account Management | Customer: Payment Transactions | Customer: Correspondence | |
| --- | --- | --- | --- |

| Legal Dunning Proc. | |
| --- | --- |
| Dunning Level | |
| Dunning Clerk | |
| Grouping Key | |

Correspondence

| Accounting Clerk | WR | Western Region |
| --- | --- | --- |

Fig 9

This is because we made it so in the configuration. Populate it with the accounting clerk we had set up and save:

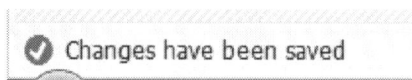

✅ Changes have been saved

Fig 10

At various times in this manual, we will come back to the customer master to populate certain data and see it's effect on our transactions.

# POSTING CUSTOMER INVOICES (U)

T Code FB70

Under normal times, customer invoices will be created as a part of a transaction in which services and/or goods were provided. In SAP, invoicing is a function performed under Sales & Distribution module, as they are a result of goods and/or services provided, however, in reality; the Finance department may do it as most non-SAP legacy systems have billing as a part of the accounting function. Billing in SAP is a very generic term and encompasses invoices, credit notes, cancellation documents, even pro-forma invoices. Every invoice in SAP except the pro-forma invoice, generally leads up to an accounting document.

There are rare times when customers are invoiced or credited directly in accounting and those transactions create accounting documents that show up in the AR reports of the customer. To create one such manual invoice, let us follow the path below:

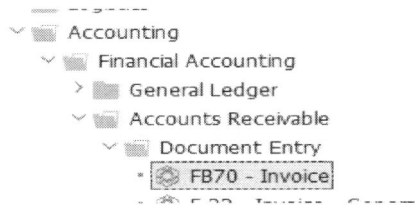

Fig 1

Enter your CC if/when prompted to do so:

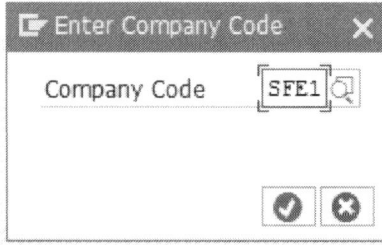

Fig 2

Enter your data, at the minimum, the customer #, date and amount and Hit Enter:

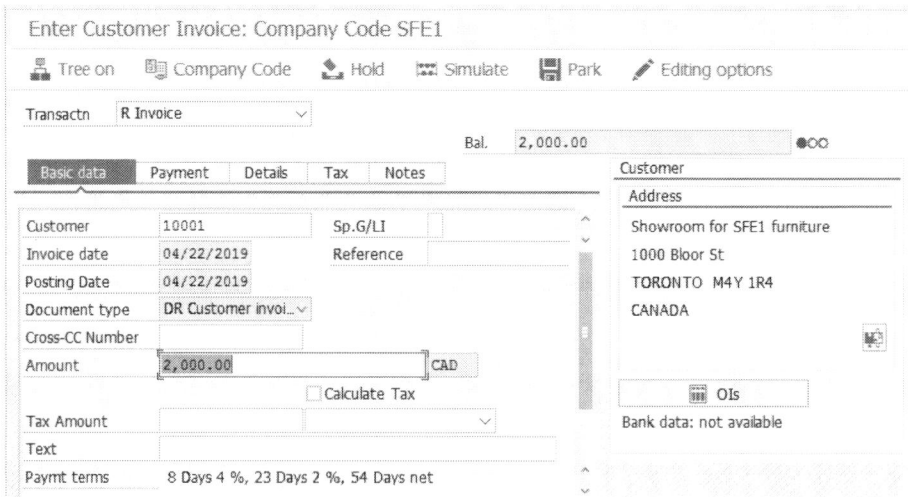

Fig 3

If tax is applicable, check *Calculate tax*, else leave it unchecked.

Enter the revenue account you want to post this amount against:

Fig 4

The * will copy the amount from the main line or, if multiple lines, will calculate the balance remaining to match debits with credits.

It is always a good idea, while one is learning, to simulate the entry

using the [☷ Simulate] button before posting it:

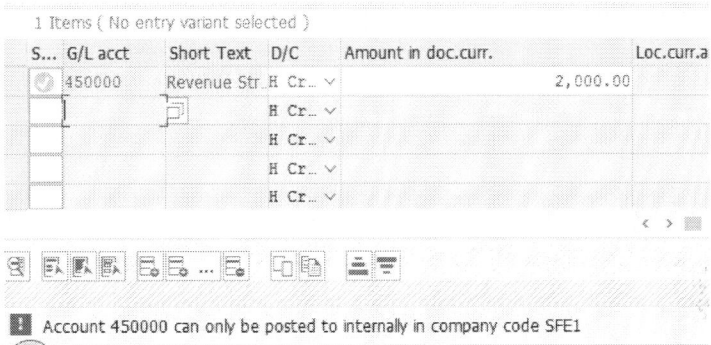

Fig 5

We get an error because the way the GL 450000 was defined prevents us from posting directly to it, only automatic postings (from Sales or Purchase) can be made:

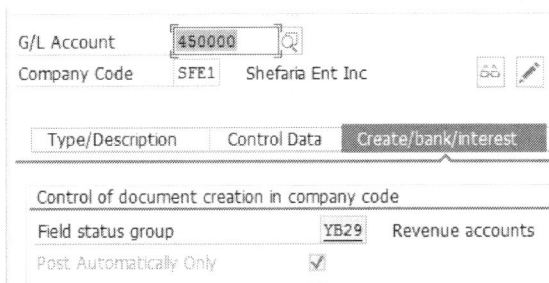

Fig 6

This setting determines that postings to this account can come only from the sales side. Therefore, this would not work obviously. We should change the account to a revenue account that allows direct postings. Normally, companies keep an account or two only for these purposes i.e. to make direct JEs.

We have account 450300 for this purpose. Let us substitute 450000 with 450300 and try the posting again and w/o any taxes to keep it simple:

| S... | G/L acct | Short Text | D/C | Amount in doc.curr. | Loc.cur |
|------|----------|------------|-----|---------------------|---------|
| ✓ | 450300 | Revenue Str.. | H Cr... ⌄ | 2,000.00 | |
| | | | H Cr... ⌄ | | |
| | | | H Cr... ⌄ | | |

*1 Items ( No entry variant selected )*

Fig 7

The simulation button gives no errors – only a message in yellow that can be by passed by hitting Enter:

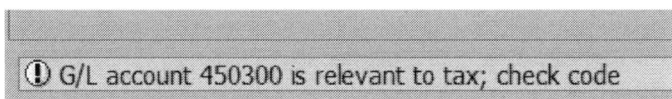

① G/L account 450300 is relevant to tax; check code

Fig 8

Simulation screen tells us the customer is being debited and G/L account is being credit for the same amount:

```
Doc.Type : DR ( Customer invoice ) Normal document
Doc. Number                Company Code    SFE1        Fiscal Year    2019
Doc. Date      04/22/2019   Posting Date   04/22/2019  Period         04
Calculate Tax  ☐
Doc. Currency  CAD
```

| Itm | PK | Account | Account Short Text | Assignment | Tx | Amount |
|-----|----|---------|--------------------|-----------|----|--------|
| 1 | 01 | 10001 | Showroom for SFE1 fu | | | 2,000.00 |
| 2 | 50 | 450300 | Revenue Stream 2 | | | 2,000.00- |

Fig 9

Since no errors were observed, we save this posting:

144

Fig 10

Note the numbering is yet another sequence. These numbers also tell us what kind of posting was made as they are linked to different document types.

# POSTING A VENDOR INVOICE (U)

T Code FB60

The process is the same as posting a customer's invoice except for the G/L accounts and the debit and credit side. FB60 can again be used to post this entry or the path:

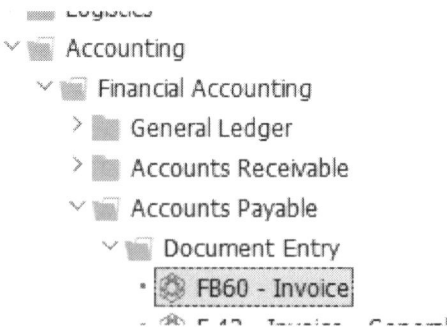

Fig 1

Enter appropriate data for vendor #, amount, G/L being debited and the dates and/or Reference # of the vendor:

Fig 2

The interesting thing to note is that SAP recognizes what we are doing and defaults the appropriate Dr or Cr indicator for the line item. In FB70, it was Cr and in FB60, it is Dr for the appropriate G/L line item.

Simulate:

Fig 3

Post and the system gives us yet another numbering sequence:

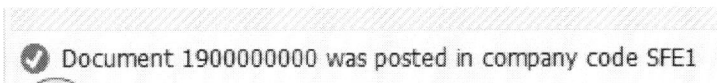

Fig 4

# DUPLICATE INVOICE CHECK (U)

T Code FB60

This functionality has been provided by SAP to ensure multiple bookings of the same vendor invoice do not take place. To activate this, some configurations have been done already; from the vendor master data point of view, the indicator *Chk double inv.* needs to be checked under the Payment Transaction tab in the vendor in FK01:

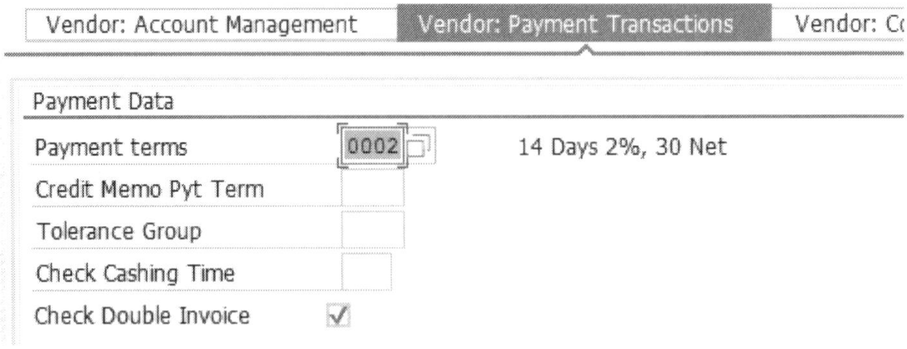

| Vendor: Account Management | Vendor: Payment Transactions | Vendor: C( |

**Payment Data**

| Payment terms | 0002 | 14 Days 2%, 30 Net |
| Credit Memo Pyt Term | | |
| Tolerance Group | | |
| Check Cashing Time | | |
| Check Double Invoice | ✓ | |

Fig 1

In the screen for posting a vendor invoice, there is a field called Reference:

Fig 2

Though a free field that can be used for anything, most companies prefer to insert the vendor's invoice # in this field. At the time of checking for duplicates, SAP looks at the following fields for complete match in data:

CC
Vendor
Currency
Invoice Date
Reference document number

If the reference field is not filled up, it looks for an exact match using these fields:

CC
Vendor
Currency
Invoice Date
Amount in document currency

i.e. replaces the Reference Number with the amount for validation.

Let us post a vendor invoice with the following data in FB60:

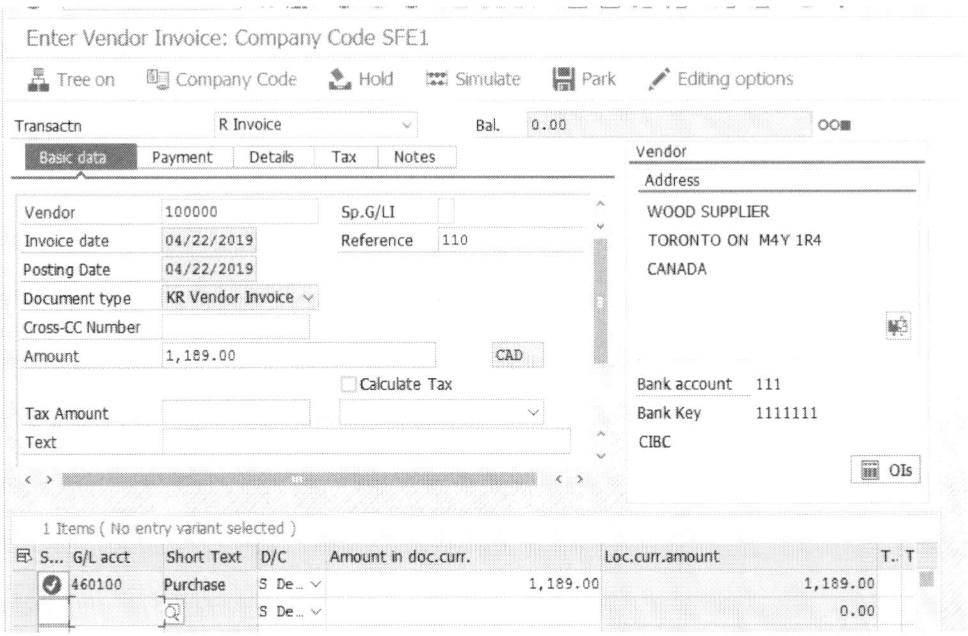

Fig 3

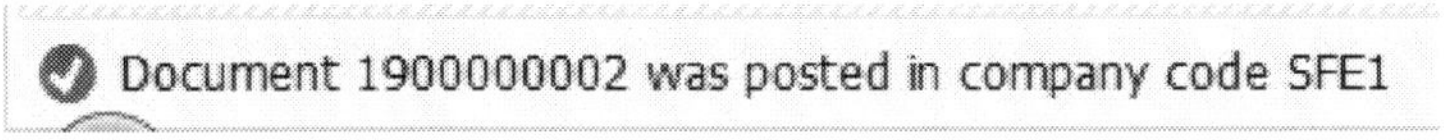

Fig 4

Now if we attempt another posting with the reference even if with a different amount we get the same message:

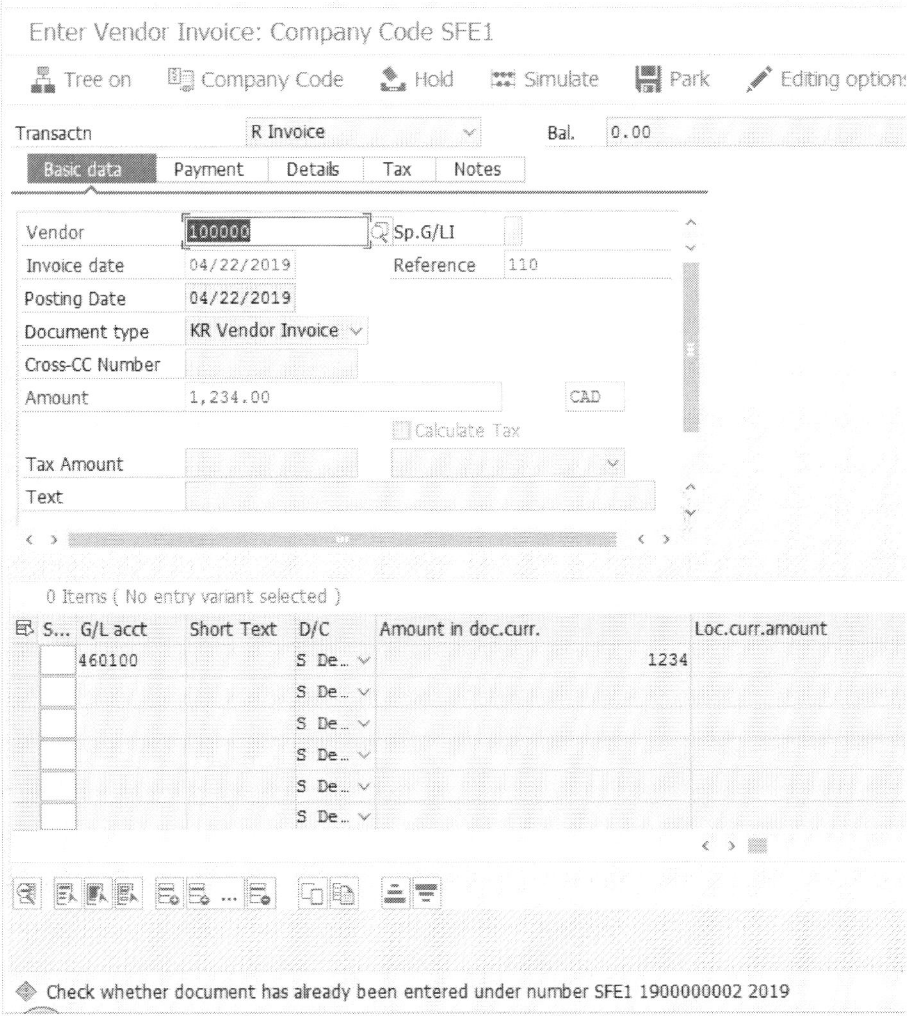

Fig 5

As noticed above, this is a warning message as it is in Yellow. Hitting Enter again will allow the user to post this one also. Normally, companies will go around this in 2 ways:

1. To prevent the posting itself i.e. make this into a hard error

2. Put a payment block on the document and then periodically run the report before paying the vendor.

The 2nd option will be through coding so not discussed here. the 1st option is through configuration via transaction OBA5 in which we insert this error (Area F5, error # 117) in the table:

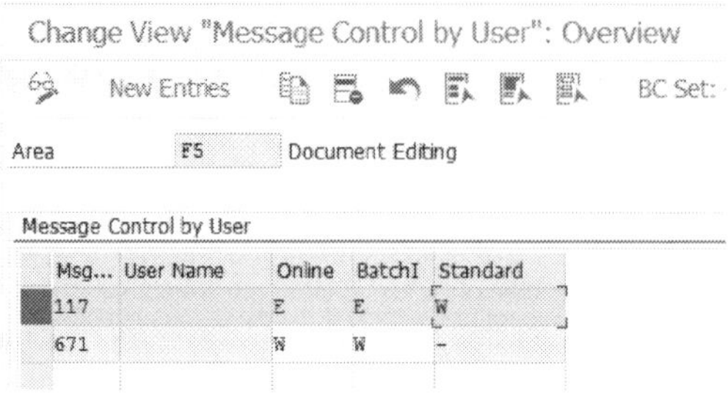

Change View "Message Control by User": Overview

New Entries    BC Set:

| Area | F5 | Document Editing |

Message Control by User

| Msg... User Name | Online | BatchI | Standard |
|---|---|---|---|
| 117 | E | E | W |
| 671 | W | W | - |

Now, when we attempt to post the same document with same data, it will prevent us from doing so:

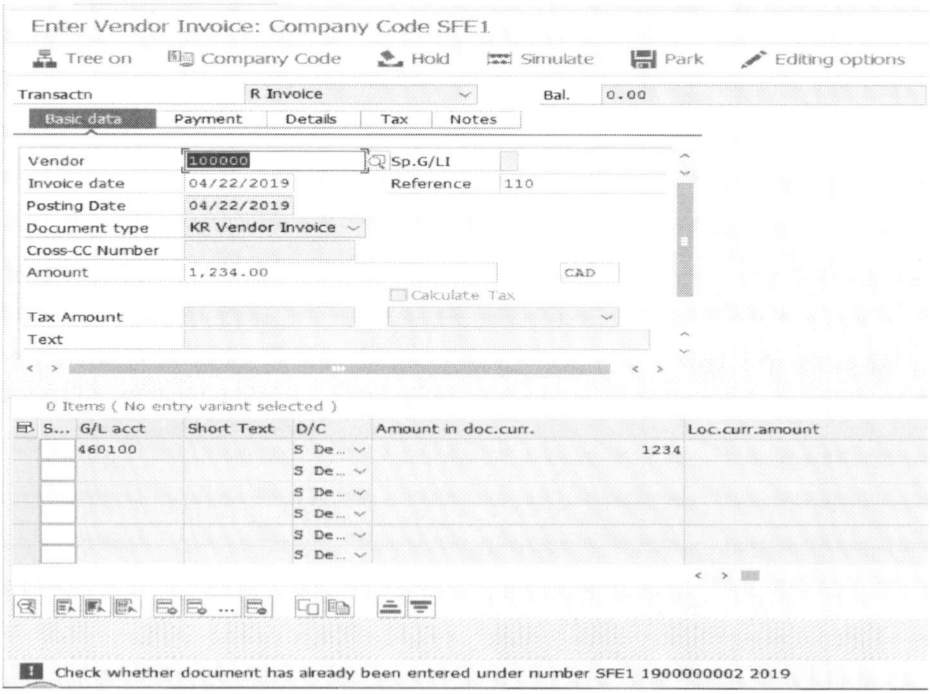

Enter Vendor Invoice: Company Code SFE1

Tree on    Company Code    Hold    Simulate    Park    Editing options

| Transactn | R Invoice | | Bal. | 0.00 |

Basic data | Payment | Details | Tax | Notes

| Vendor | 100000 | | Sp.G/LI | |
| Invoice date | 04/22/2019 | | Reference | 110 |
| Posting Date | 04/22/2019 | | | |
| Document type | KR Vendor Invoice | | | |
| Cross-CC Number | | | | |
| Amount | 1,234.00 | | | CAD |

Calculate Tax

| Tax Amount | | | |
| Text | | | |

0 Items ( No entry variant selected )

| S... G/L acct | Short Text | D/C | Amount in doc.curr. | Loc.curr.amount |
|---|---|---|---|---|
| 460100 | | S De... | | 1234 |
| | | S De... | | |
| | | S De... | | |
| | | S De... | | |
| | | S De... | | |
| | | S De... | | |

Check whether document has already been entered under number SFE1 1900000002 2019

Fig 7

Now we can post this 2nd invoice only if we remove the reference # from the field or change it to any other as below:

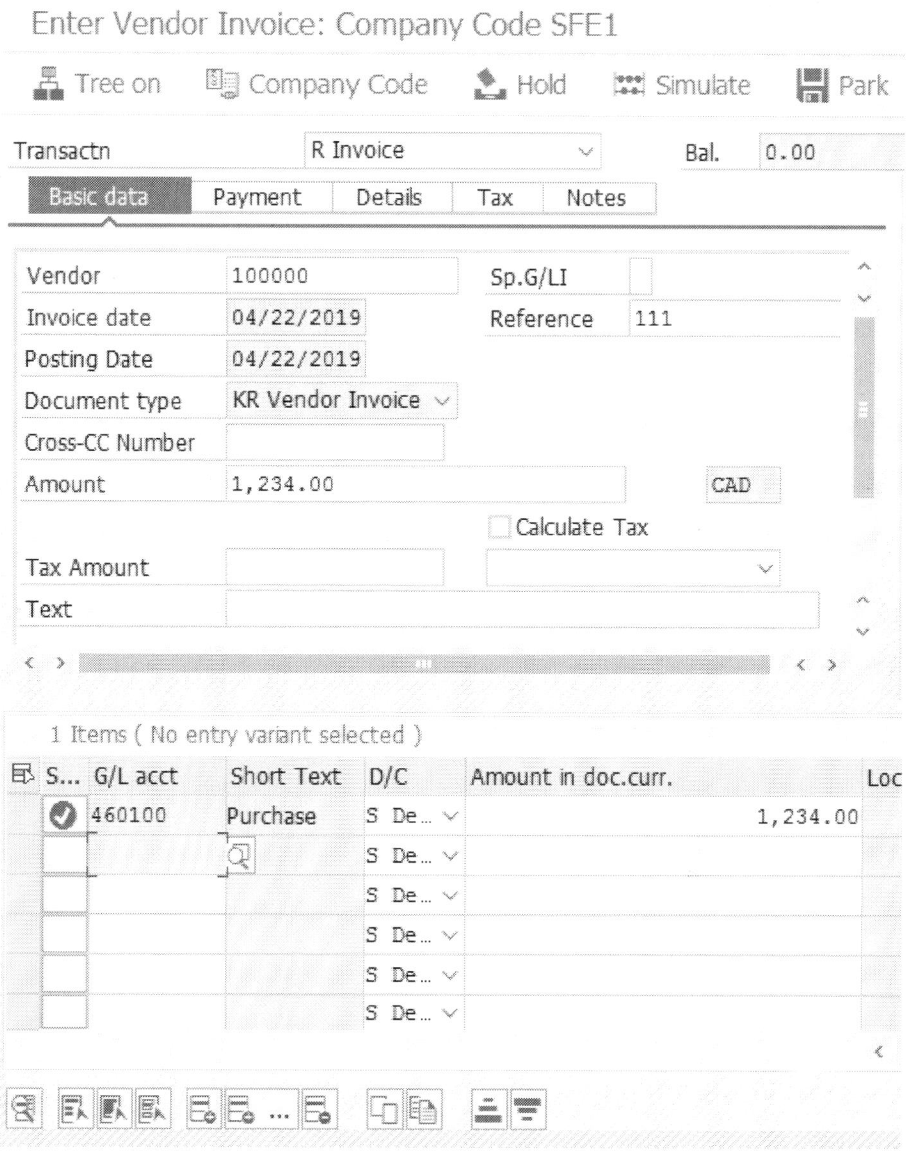

Enter Vendor Invoice: Company Code SFE1

🔲 Tree on    🗐 Company Code    ⬆ Hold    ⠿ Simulate    💾 Park

| Transactn | R Invoice | ∨ | Bal. | 0.00 |

**Basic data**    Payment    Details    Tax    Notes

| Vendor | 100000 | Sp.G/LI | |
| Invoice date | 04/22/2019 | Reference | 111 |
| Posting Date | 04/22/2019 | | |
| Document type | KR Vendor Invoice ∨ | | |
| Cross-CC Number | | | |
| Amount | 1,234.00 | | CAD |

☐ Calculate Tax

| Tax Amount | | ∨ |
| Text | | |

1 Items ( No entry variant selected )

| S... | G/L acct | Short Text | D/C | Amount in doc.curr. | Loc |
|------|----------|-----------|-----|---------------------|-----|
| ✅ | 460100 | Purchase | S De… ∨ | 1,234.00 | |
| | | 🔍 | S De… ∨ | | |
| | | | S De… ∨ | | |
| | | | S De… ∨ | | |
| | | | S De… ∨ | | |
| | | | S De… ∨ | | |

Fig 8

# LOOKING UP PAYABLES AND

# RECEIVABLES (U)

T Code FBL1N and FBL5N

## I. PAYABLES

T Code FBL1N in ECC and FBL1H in HANA

**HANA CHANGE**: FBL1H is a major improvement over ECC's FBL1N as is the customer line items FBL5H over FBL5N.

Now we can gie the command directly on the input screen to download the results instead of on the results page. It also has the ability to download in different format e.g. xlxs, xls, txt, csv etc. as demonstrated below.

The items not yet paid are called vendor open items or payables. These payables can be looked up with the transaction code FBL1H or follow the path below which has both the old and the new together:

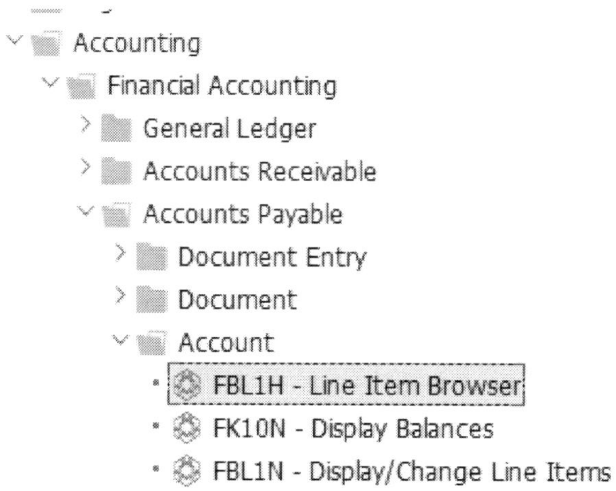

Accounting
  Financial Accounting
    > General Ledger
    > Accounts Receivable
    > Accounts Payable
      > Document Entry
      > Document
      > Account
        · FBL1H - Line Item Browser
        · FK10N - Display Balances
        · FBL1N - Display/Change Line Items

Fig 1

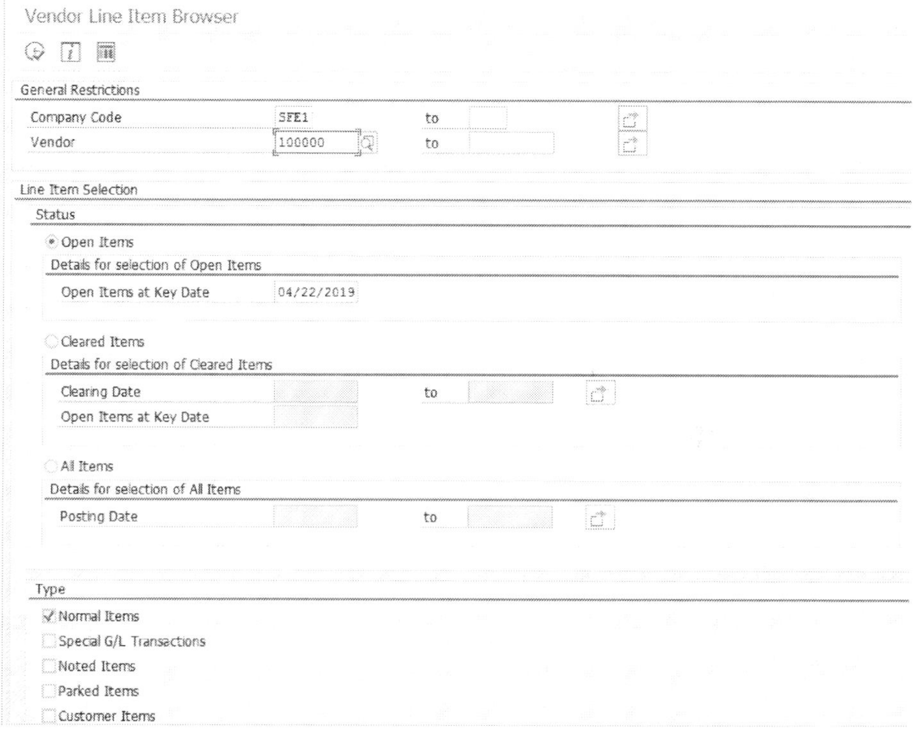

Vendor Line Item Browser

General Restrictions

| Company Code | SFE1 | to | |
| Vendor | 100000 | to | |

Line Item Selection

Status

● Open Items
Details for selection of Open Items

Open Items at Key Date     04/22/2019

○ Cleared Items
Details for selection of Cleared Items

| Clearing Date | | to | |
| Open Items at Key Date | | | |

○ All Items
Details for selection of All Items

Posting Date          to

Type

☑ Normal Items
☐ Special G/L Transactions
☐ Noted Items
☐ Parked Items
☐ Customer Items

Fig 2

This screen is almost identical to what you will see for receivables so let us understand the usage of some of the input fields here:

Vendor account:

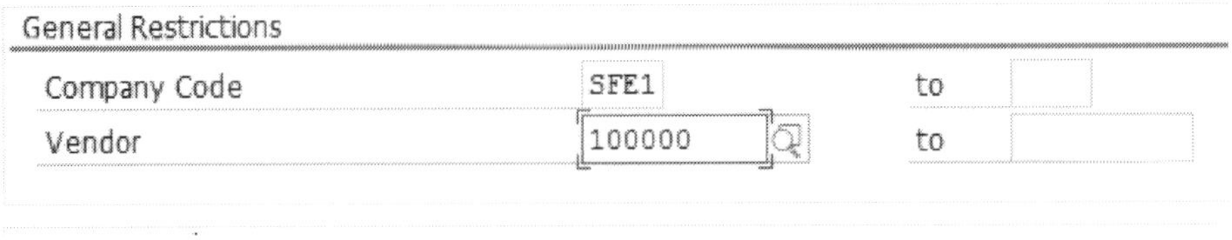

| General Restrictions | | | |
|---|---|---|---|
| Company Code | SFE1 | to | |
| Vendor | 100000 | to | |

Fig 3

This is the actual vendor #. We can look up the payables by including or excluding a range of vendors, or individual multiple vendors using the key

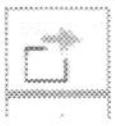

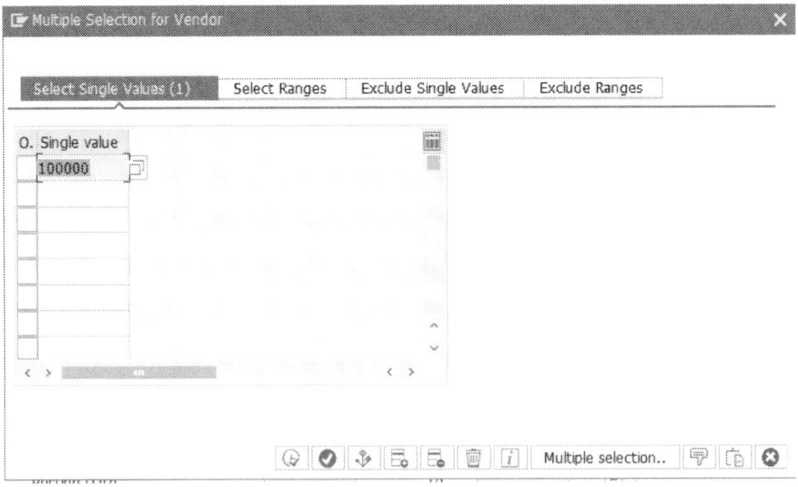

This screen is a multiple selection dialog titled "Multiple Selection for Vendor" with tabs: Select Single Values (1), Select Ranges, Exclude Single Values, Exclude Ranges. Under "O. Single value" the value 100000 is entered.

Fig 4

Using the same choices, the vendors' payables can be looked across multiple CCs at the same time:

| Company Code | SFE1 | to | |
|---|---|---|---|

Fig 5

The more data we give to restrict the inputs on this screen, the faster will be the results. For most people, when running day-to-day transactions, the selection key ⬚ in ECC will be very useful.

This option on the HANA instance has moved down on the main screen and is visible as:

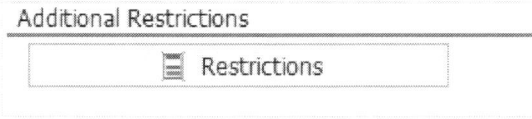

Additional Restrictions

▤ Restrictions

Fig 6

With a lot more selections possible in the screen that pops up:

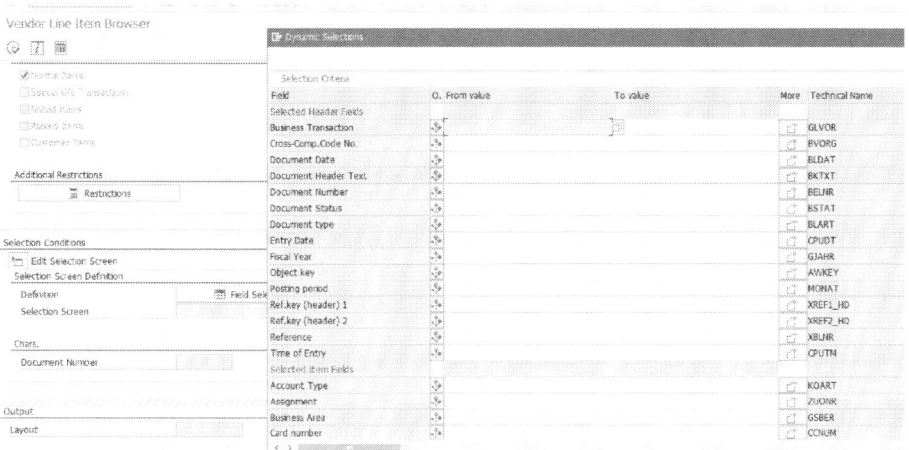

Fig 7

Normally, one will be responsible for certain groups of vendors or certain vendors. That person can be made the accounting clerk for those vendors in the vendor's master data and when the report is run for that accounting clerk selected in the above screen, then only the A/P for those vendors that have this accounting clerk in their master data will show up in the report. This input data can be saved as a 'variant' and whenever the user wants to run this report, he/she can call for that variant. Let us consider an example:

If we want to run this report for all vendors whose accounting clerk is as below we merely select the accounting clerk and leave the Vendor field blank; this way, it will pick up all the vendors for whom WR is responsible.

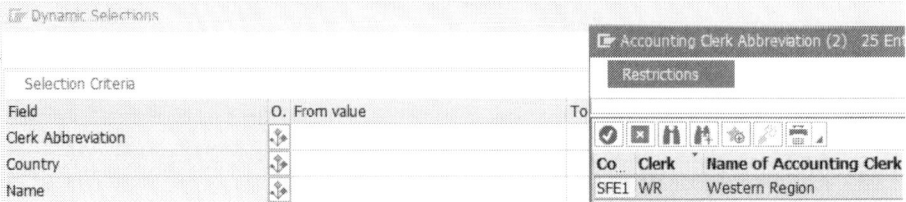

Fig 8

We select it and run the report.

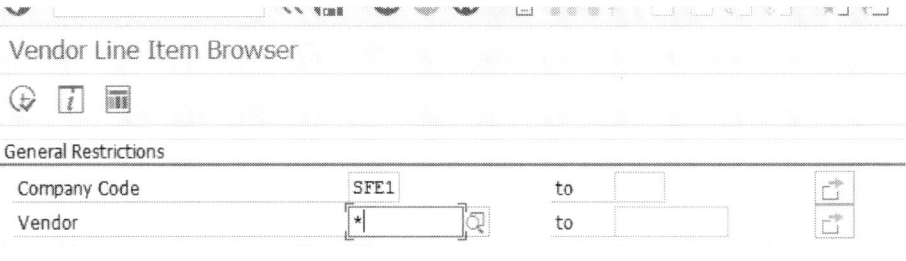

Fig 9

In FBL1H you can also restrict further by making more selections:

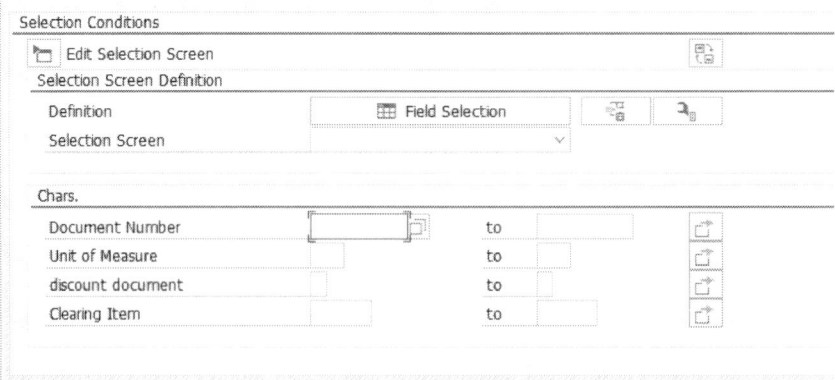

Fig 10

These selections are over and above the standard and this offers a lot more choices of selection by moving the required fields from left to right:

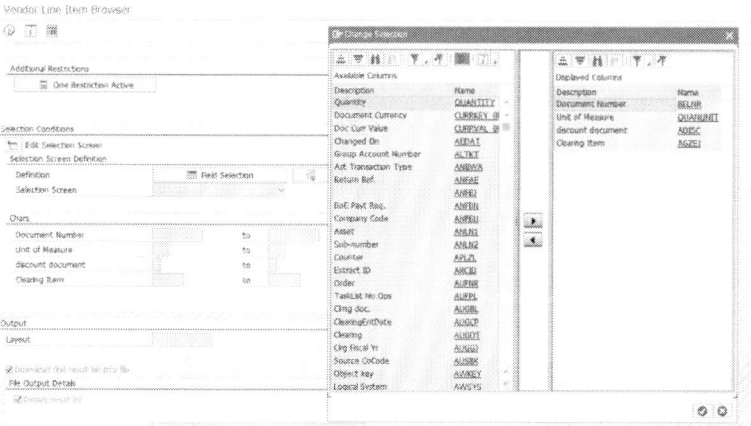

Fig 11

Downloading:

At the bottom of the screen you have various options of downloading the file. Since HANA is so data driven, various modes are possible like txt, csv which are 'lighter' files and can be downloaded faster. However you can download in Excel form also.

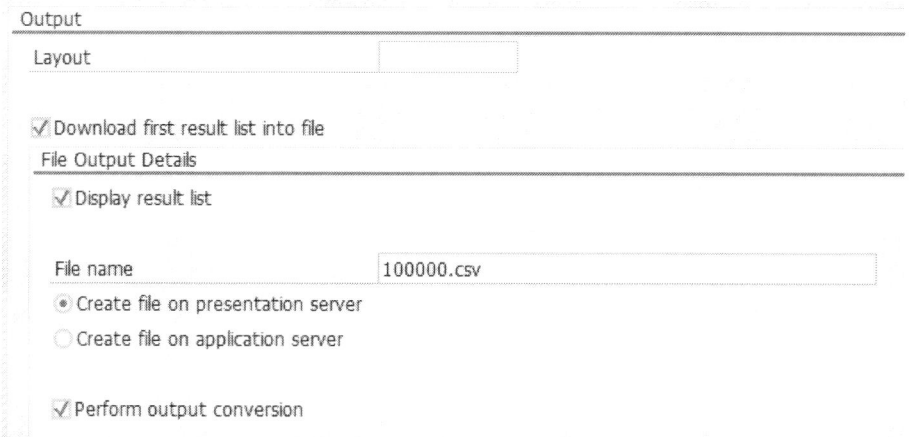

Fig 12

When you execute the transaction, the file (as in the above choice, a csv file) gets downloaded to your destination, in this case, the desktop:

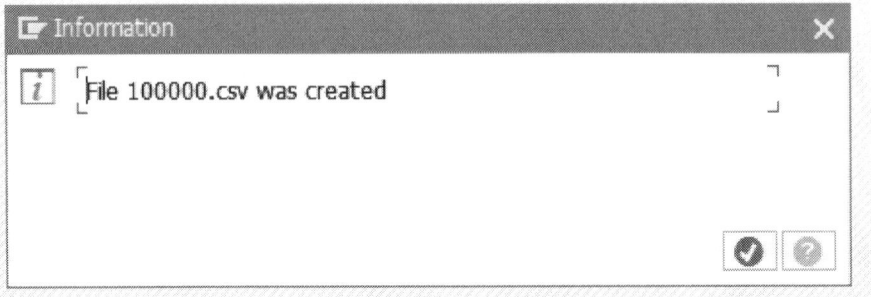

Fig 13

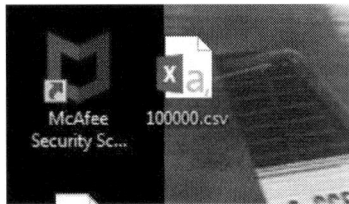

Fig 14

Report results:

It displays all balances payable to all vendors that have this as their accounting clerk – in our case only one vendor.

This link between the vendor and the accounting clerk is formed from the vendor master data.

To look at the detailed line items in the report, select the line and then click on 'Call line item report' as below:

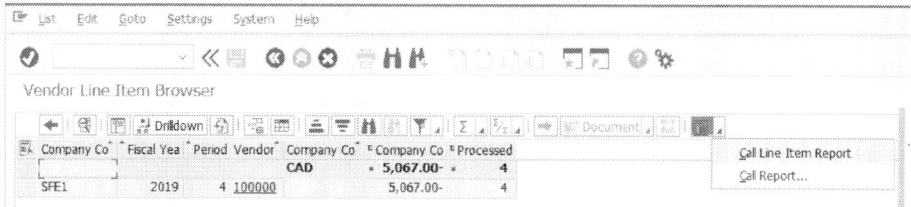

Fig 16

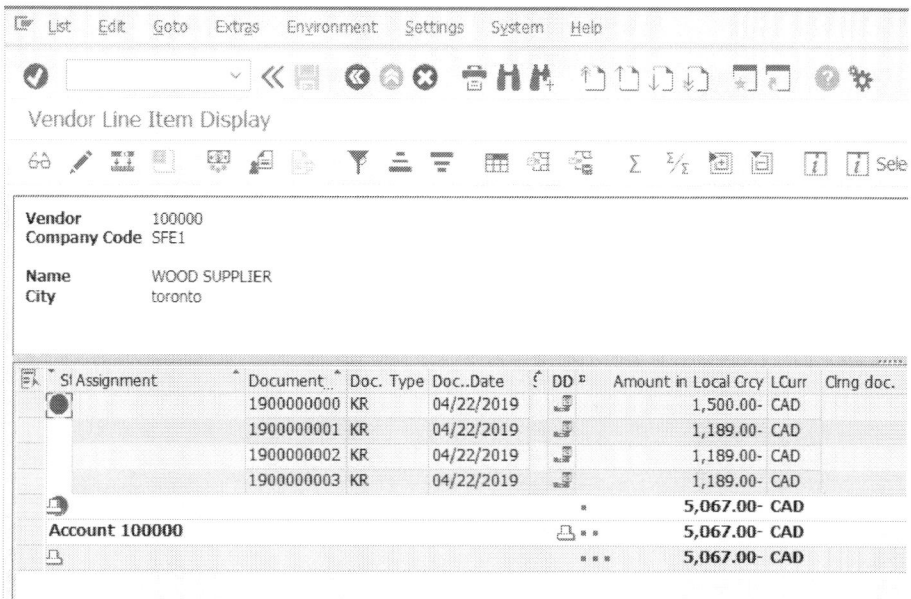

Fig 17

The new report will show all the line items open as of the date you put on the selection screen.

# II.    RECEIVABLES

T Code FBL5H for HANA and FBL5N for ECC

**HANA CHANGE:** The changes in HANA for customer receivables are exactly the same as for the vendor payables as described in the previous section so we won't repeat them in detail here:

1. More selection

2. Restrictions moved down on the screen

3. Report is downloadable from main screen

4. To view line items we have to call for them on the report screen

The items for which we have not been paid yet are called customer open items or receivables. These receivables can be looked up with the transaction code FBL5H or FBL5N or follow the path below:

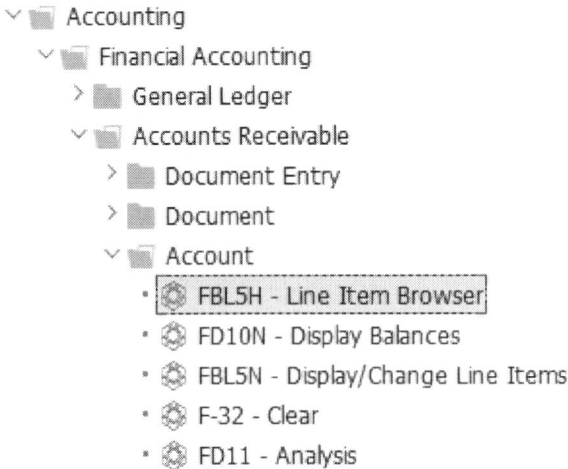

Fig 18

Conceptually, it is exactly the same as FBL1N/H so we will not go into details of the screen. The way we executed FBL1H, we can execute FBL5H to see the results of one, multiple or all customer open items in one or multiple company codes as on a date of our choosing. We can also look for all or only the cleared postings made during a date range:

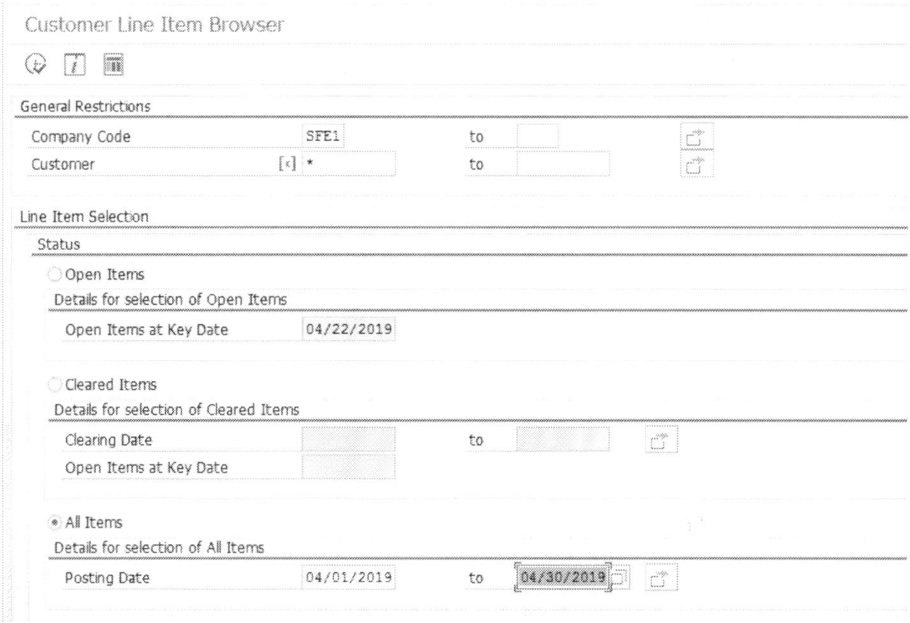

Fig 19

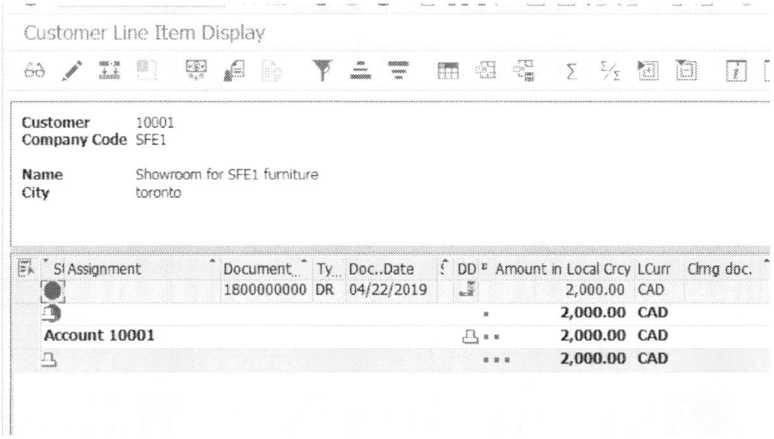

Fig 20

As we notice in the report above, it is similar to the vendor report and the layout can be customized to our choice to display whatever fields we desire.

# TRANSFER AR BETWEEN CUSTOMERS (U)

T Code F-30

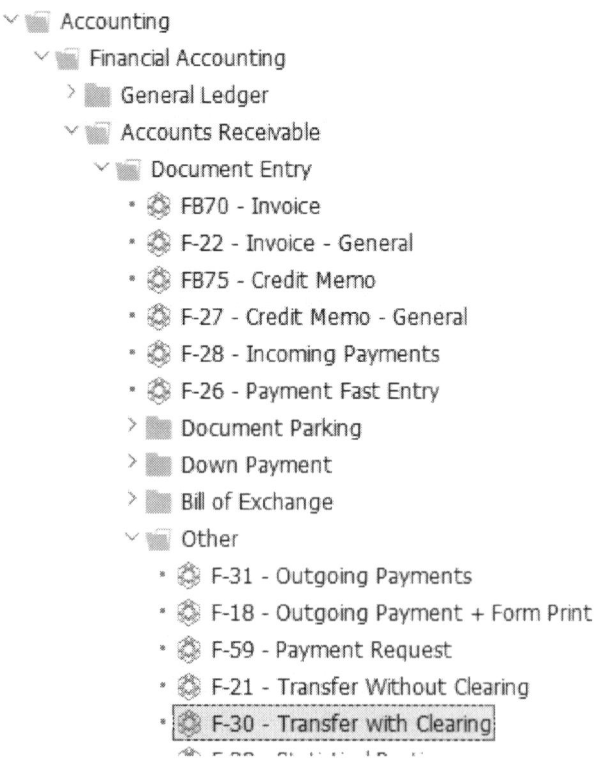

```
∨ 📁 Accounting
  ∨ 📁 Financial Accounting
    › 📁 General Ledger
    ∨ 📁 Accounts Receivable
      ∨ 📁 Document Entry
        • ⚙ FB70 - Invoice
        • ⚙ F-22 - Invoice - General
        • ⚙ FB75 - Credit Memo
        • ⚙ F-27 - Credit Memo - General
        • ⚙ F-28 - Incoming Payments
        • ⚙ F-26 - Payment Fast Entry
        › 📁 Document Parking
        › 📁 Down Payment
        › 📁 Bill of Exchange
        ∨ 📁 Other
          • ⚙ F-31 - Outgoing Payments
          • ⚙ F-18 - Outgoing Payment + Form Print
          • ⚙ F-59 - Payment Request
          • ⚙ F-21 - Transfer Without Clearing
          • ⚙ F-30 - Transfer with Clearing
```

Fig 1

AR can be transferred from one customer to another. Situations like these can arise at time of initial upload of data, re-alignment of customers, customer buyouts/takeover etc. The same can be achieved in the transaction code F-30. Choose the appropriate posting key for debiting/crediting the 2 customer numbers.

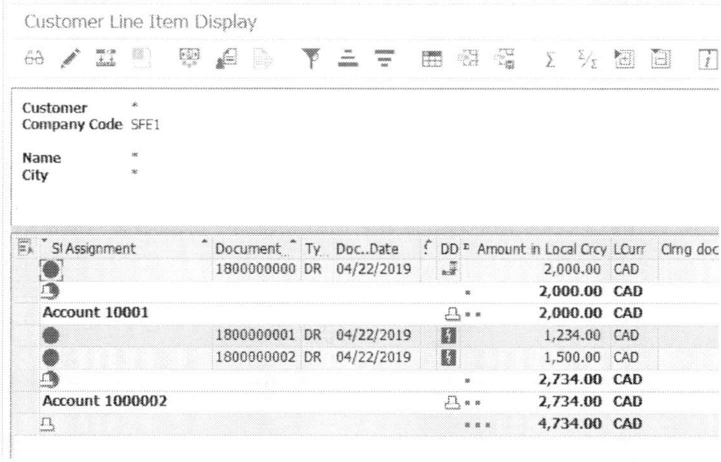

Fig 1

If we want any AR from one customer to move to the other for any reason, simply debit one and credit the other using the appropriate posting keys as shown next; the contra entries from the original entry remain intact.

In F-30:

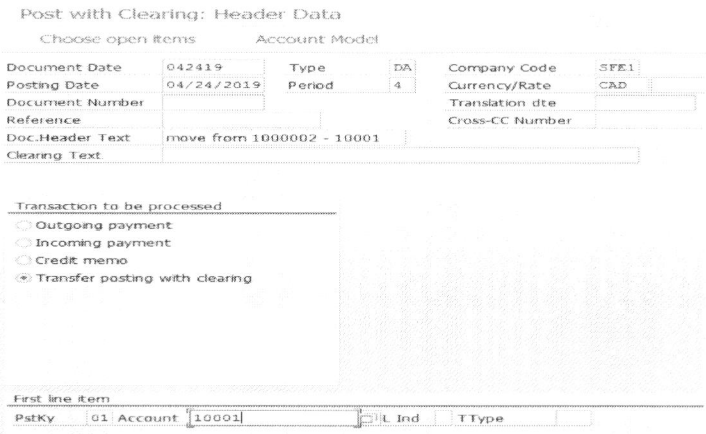

Fig 2

On the next screen, enter the amount and the offsetting data:

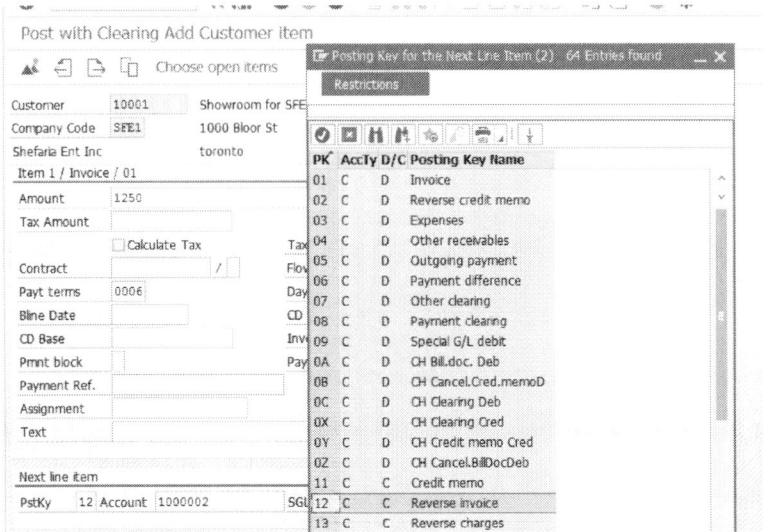

Fig 3

Hit Enter and on the next screen copy the amount using the '*' or if you want to transfer to multiple accounts, put the first amount on this screen along with the other customer # and repeat the process on the next screen:

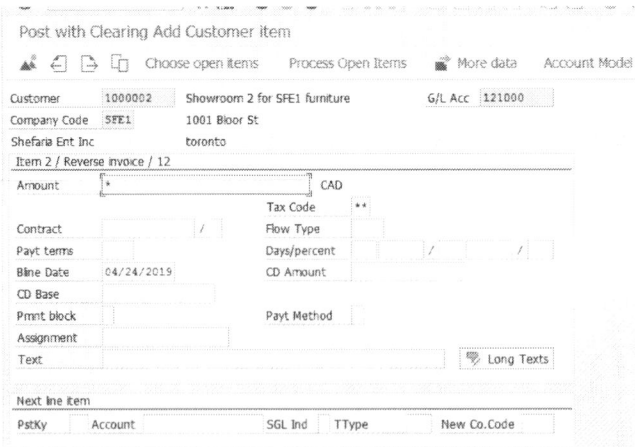

Fig 4

Simulate and/or save:

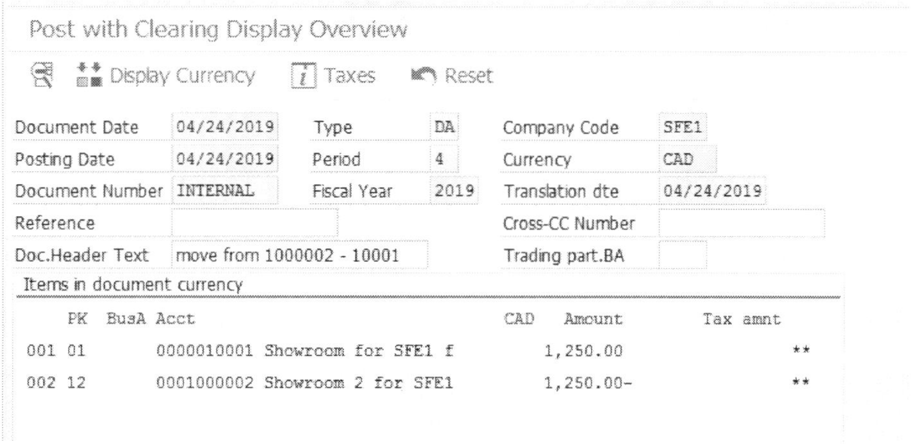
Post with Clearing Display Overview
Display Currency
Taxes
Reset
Document Date 04/24/2019
Type DA
Company Code SFE1
Posting Date 04/24/2019
Period 4
Currency CAD
Document Number INTERNAL
Fiscal Year 2019
Translation dte 04/24/2019
Reference
Cross-CC Number
Doc.Header Text move from 1000002 - 10001
Trading part.BA
Items in document currency
PK BusA Acct CAD Amount Tax amnt
001 01 0000010001 Showroom for SFE1 f 1,250.00 **
002 12 0001000002 Showroom 2 for SFE1 1,250.00- **

Fig 5

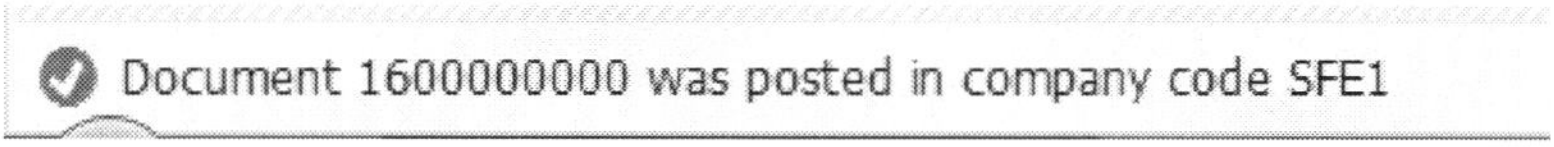
Document 1600000000 was posted in company code SFE1

Fig 6

When you run FBL5N for the customers, the 2 offsetting entries will be available in the line items of the 2 customers:

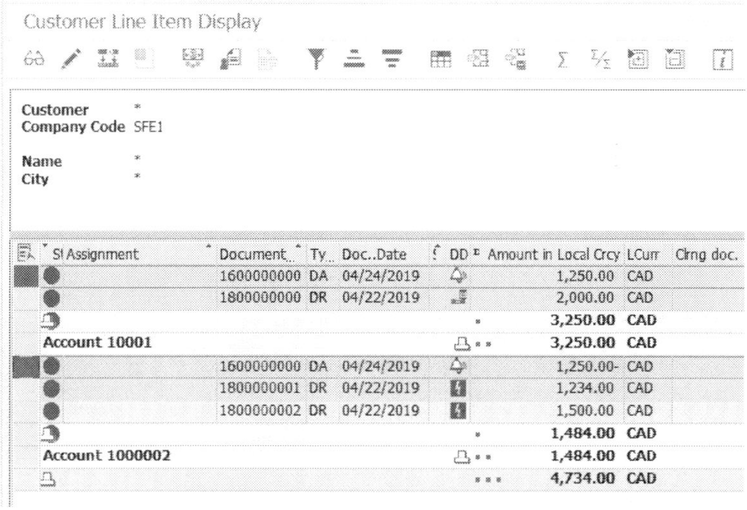
Customer Line Item Display
Customer *
Company Code SFE1
Name *
City *
St Assignment Document Ty Doc..Date DD Amount in Local Crcy LCurr Clrng doc.
1600000000 DA 04/24/2019 1,250.00 CAD
1800000000 DR 04/22/2019 2,000.00 CAD
3,250.00 CAD
Account 10001 3,250.00 CAD
1600000000 DA 04/24/2019 1,250.00- CAD
1800000001 DR 04/22/2019 1,234.00 CAD
1800000002 DR 04/22/2019 1,500.00 CAD
1,484.00 CAD
Account 1000002 1,484.00 CAD
4,734.00 CAD

Fig 7

# CLEARING RECEIVABLES & PARTIAL PAYMENTS (U)

T Code F-28

A customer invoice remains outstanding or open until it is paid or cancelled or adjusted in some other way. To clear a receivable we must first have an invoice. For this purpose, we will use one of the invoices we posted earlier.

| | | | | | | | | | | | |
|---|---|---|---|---|---|---|---|---|---|---|---|
| **Customer** | 10001 | | | | | | | | | | |
| **Company Code** | SFE1 | | | | | | | | | | |
| **Name** | Showroom for SFE1 furniture | | | | | | | | | | |
| **City** | toronto | | | | | | | | | | |

| SI Assignment | Document | Ty | DocDate | DD | Amount in Local Crcy | LCurr | Net Due Dt | DD | Discount Base Amount | Disc.1 | Curr. Cash Disc. Amt |
|---|---|---|---|---|---|---|---|---|---|---|---|
| ● | 1600000000 | DA | 04/24/2019 | | 1,250.00 | CAD | 04/24/2019 | | 1,250.00 | 0.000 | 0.00 |
| ● | 1800000000 | DR | 04/22/2019 | | 2,000.00 | CAD | 06/15/2019 | | 2,000.00 | 4.000 | 80.00 |
| ● | 1800000003 | DR | 04/22/2019 | | 2,341.00 | CAD | 06/15/2019 | | 2,341.00 | 4.000 | 93.64 |
| ● | 1800000004 | DR | 04/22/2019 | | 345.00 | CAD | 04/30/2019 | | 345.00 | 0.000 | 0.00 |
| ● | 1800000005 | DR | 02/22/2019 | | 10,000.00 | CAD | 05/22/2019 | | 10,000.00 | 0.000 | 0.00 |
| ● | 1800000006 | DR | 10/01/2019 | | 103.47 | CAD | 10/31/2019 | | 103.47 | 2.000 | 2.07 |
| ● | 1800000007 | DR | 01/12/2018 | | 200.00 | CAD | 01/15/2019 | | 200.00 | 4.000 | 0.00 |
| ● | 1800000008 | DR | 01/11/2018 | | 5,600.00 | CAD | 01/15/2019 | | 5,600.00 | 4.000 | 0.00 |
| ● | 1800000009 | DR | 05/11/2019 | | 237.00 | CAD | 09/15/2016 | | 237.00 | 4.000 | 0.00 |
| ● | 1800000010 | DR | 12/01/2019 | | 674.00 | CAD | 09/15/2016 | | 674.00 | 4.000 | 0.00 |
| | | | | | 22,750.47 | CAD | | | | | |
| Account 10001 | | | | | 22,750.47 | CAD | | | | | |
| | | | | | 22,750.47 | CAD | | | | | |

Fig 1

Let's assume the customer is making only a part payment against the invoice highlighted above. F-28 is the transaction code or the path to clear open items:

```
⌄ 🗃 Accounting
    ⌄ 🗃 Financial Accounting
        > 🗃 General Ledger
        ⌄ 🗃 Accounts Receivable
            ⌄ 🗃 Document Entry
                • ⚙ FB70 - Invoice
                • ⚙ F-22 - Invoice - General
                • ⚙ FB75 - Credit Memo
                • ⚙ F-27 - Credit Memo - General
                • ⚙ F-28 - Incoming Payments
                • ⚙ F-26 - Payment Fast Entry
```

Fig 2

A few fields are mandatory but one should try to fill in as much as known:

**Post Incoming Payments: Header Data**

Process Open Items

| | | | | | |
|---|---|---|---|---|---|
| Document Date | 042419 | Type | DZ | Company Code | SFE1 |
| Posting Date | 04/24/2019 | Period | 4 | Currency/Rate | CAD |
| Document Number | | | | Translation dte | |
| Reference | Payment | | | Cross-CC Number | |
| Doc.Header Text | CUST CHECK # 12345 | | | Trading part.BA | |
| Clearing Text | | | | | |

Bank data

| | | | | |
|---|---|---|---|---|
| Account | 107000 | | Business Area | |
| Amount | 1000.45 | | | |
| Amt.in loc.cur. | | | | |
| Bank Charges | | | LC Bank Charges | |
| Value date | | | Profit Center | |
| Text | | | Assignment | |

| Open item selection | | | Additional selections |
|---|---|---|---|
| Account | 10001 | | ◉ None |
| Account Type | D | ☐ Other Accounts | ○ Amount |
| Special G/L Ind | | ☑ Standard OIs | ○ Document Number |
| Payt Advice No. | | | ○ Posting Date |
| ☐ Distribute by Age | | | ○ Dunning Area |
| ☐ Automatic Search | | | ○ Others |

Fig 3

169

The document type DZ should be selected by default but if not, please enter DZ. The period should again be the current open posting period.

Document date is the date on which it is being entered, usually 'today'

Bank Data: Amount is the total amount on the check, Account is the Bank G/L account to which the posting will be made.

In the section Open Items selection, the Account is the customer #.

Enter data as above and click on

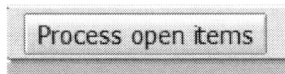

Process open items

Fig 4

or simply Press Enter.

These lines in Fig 5 are the same as what we saw in the customer receivable report in Fig 1. As we also notice in Fig 5, there are cash discounts against invoices if the customer is paying on/before the date when he receives this discount for early payment. We will discuss the applicability of discounts later; here we simply adjust the amount that is being paid against the invoice. Assume the customer has paid this amount against the 2nd invoice in the outstanding list and we have to adjust this amount against that invoice.

By default all lines get chosen and appear in Blue – the full amount getting assigned to the amount being paid as seen at the bottom right of the screen in Fig 5.

Post Incoming Payments Process open items

Distribute Difference    Charge Off Difference    Editing Options    Cash Disc. Due    Create Dispute Case

**Standard**   Partial Pmt   Res.Items   WH Tax

Account items 10001 Showroom for SFE1 furniture

| Document... | D. | Document... | P.. | Bu.. | Da... | CAD Gross | CashDiscount | | CDPer. |
|---|---|---|---|---|---|---|---|---|---|
| 1600000000 | DA | 04/24/2019 | 01 | | 0 | 1,250.00 | | | |
| 1800000000 | DR | 04/22/2019 | 01 | | 6- | 2,000.00 | | 80.00 | 4.000 |
| 1800000003 | DR | 04/22/2019 | 01 | | 6- | 2,341.00 | | 93.64 | 4.000 |
| 1800000004 | DR | 04/22/2019 | 01 | | 6- | 345.00 | | | |
| 1800000005 | DR | 02/22/2019 | 01 | | 28- | 10,000.00 | | | |
| 1800000006 | DR | 10/01/2019 | 01 | | 174- | 103.47 | | 2.07 | 2.000 |
| 1800000007 | DR | 01/12/2018 | 01 | | 99 | 200.00 | | | |
| 1800000008 | DR | 01/11/2018 | 01 | | 99 | 5,600.00 | | | |
| 1800000009 | DR | 05/11/2019 | 01 | | 951 | 237.00 | | | |

Am...   Gross<...   Currency   Items   Items   Disc.   Disc.

Processing Status

| | | | | |
|---|---|---|---|---|
| Number of Items | 10 | | Amount Entered | 1,000.45 |
| Display from Item | 1 | | Assigned | 22,574.76 |
| Reason Code | | | Difference Postings | |
| Display in clearing currency | | | Not Assigned | 21,574.31- |

Fig 5

To do that we need to be able to 'isolate' the 2nd line from the rest.

First, deactivate all the line items by

(i)     selecting Select All button:

All lines will turn Blue:

Account items 10001 Showroom for SFE1 furniture

| Document... | D.. | Document... | P.. | Bu... | Da... | CAD Gross | CashDiscount | | CDPer. |
|---|---|---|---|---|---|---|---|---|---|
| 1600000000 | DA | 04/24/2019 | 01 | | 0 | 1,250.00 | | | |
| 1800000000 | DR | 04/22/2019 | 01 | | 6- | 2,000.00 | | 80.00 | 4.000 |
| 1800000003 | DR | 04/22/2019 | 01 | | 6- | 2,341.00 | | 93.64 | 4.000 |
| 1800000004 | DR | 04/22/2019 | 01 | | 6- | 345.00 | | | |
| 1800000005 | DR | 02/22/2019 | 01 | | 28- | 10,000.00 | | | |
| 1800000006 | DR | 10/01/2019 | 01 | | 174- | 103.47 | | 2.07 | 2.000 |
| 1800000007 | DR | 01/12/2018 | 01 | | 99 | 200.00 | | | |
| 1800000008 | DR | 01/11/2018 | 01 | | 99 | 5,600.00 | | | |
| 1800000009 | DR | 05/11/2019 | 01 | | 951 | 237.00 | | | |

Fig 6

(ii)     Next, click on Deactivate all items:

Fig 7

All lines will now turn black making the assigned amount 0 thereby allowing us to assign to which ever line we want to.

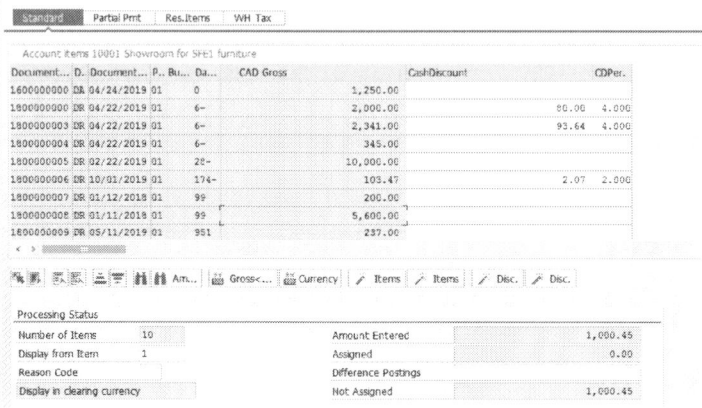

Fig 8

(iii)    Position the cursor in the line to be adjusted (here, the 2nd line):

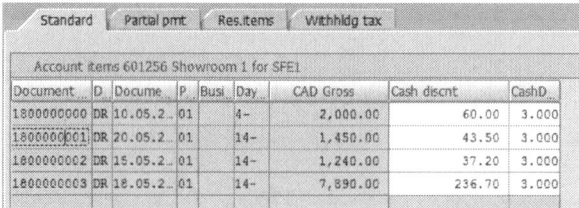

Fig 7

Then activate the line item with the activate item key:

Fig 8

Only that line (here, 2nd) will turn blue as below.

*Note: Alternatively, double clicking the actual amount also works the same way. Double clicking toggles between blue and black. It is not necessary to first make all of them inactive and then active...it merely depends on how many lines there are. E.g. if there are just 2 lines, double click on the one you want or don't want to select by toggling between Blue and Blank. As a general SAP process, Blue means active, Black means inactive. Practice this a few times to get a better understanding of it.*

Post Incoming Payments Process open items

Distribute Difference    Charge Off Difference    Editing Options    Cash Disc. Due    Create Dispute Case

Standard | Partial Pmt | Res.Items | WH Tax

Account items 10001 Showroom for SFE1 furniture

| Document... | D. | Document... | P.. | Bu... | Da... | CAD Gross | CashDiscount | CDPer. |
|---|---|---|---|---|---|---|---|---|
| 1600000000 | DA | 04/24/2019 | 01 | | 0 | 1,250.00 | | |
| 1800000000 | DR | 04/22/2019 | 01 | | 6- | 2,000.00 | 80.00 | 4.000 |
| 1800000003 | DR | 04/22/2019 | 01 | | 6- | 2,341.00 | 93.64 | 4.000 |
| 1800000004 | DR | 04/22/2019 | 01 | | 6- | 345.00 | | |
| 1800000005 | DR | 02/22/2019 | 01 | | 28- | 10,000.00 | | |
| 1800000006 | DR | 10/01/2019 | 01 | | 174- | 103.47 | 2.07 | 2.000 |
| 1800000007 | DR | 01/12/2018 | 01 | | 99 | 200.00 | | |
| 1800000008 | DR | 01/11/2018 | 01 | | 99 | 5,600.00 | | |
| 1800000009 | DR | 05/11/2019 | 01 | | 951 | 237.00 | | |

Am... | Gross<... | Currency | Items | Items | Disc. | Disc.

Processing Status

| Number of Items | 10 | | Amount Entered | 1,000.45 |
|---|---|---|---|---|
| Display from Item | 1 | | Assigned | 2,000.00 |
| Reason Code | | | Difference Postings | |
| Display in clearing currency | | | Not Assigned | 999.55- |

Fig 9

If we don't want to provide the customer discount due to any reason, we can simply clear it out and SAP will not post the discount i.e. not adjust the receivable accordingly.

Note the difference between the invoice value and the payment as the Not Assigned amount at the bottom right. To balance it, we need to move this amount to the difference postings cell by double clicking in it:

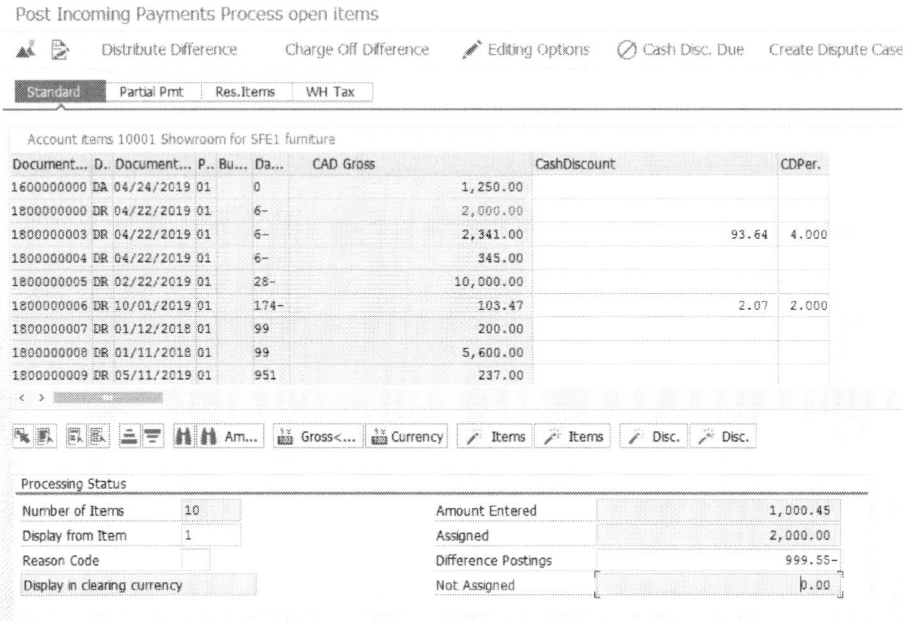

Post Incoming Payments Process open items

| | Distribute Difference | Charge Off Difference | Editing Options | Cash Disc. Due | Create Dispute Case |

| Standard | Partial Pmt | Res.Items | WH Tax |

Account items 10001 Showroom for SFE1 furniture

| Document... | D. | Document... | P.. | Bu... | Da... | CAD Gross | CashDiscount | CDPer. |
|---|---|---|---|---|---|---|---|---|
| 1600000000 | DA | 04/24/2019 | 01 | | 0 | 1,250.00 | | |
| 1800000000 | DR | 04/22/2019 | 01 | | 6- | 2,000.00 | | |
| 1800000003 | DR | 04/22/2019 | 01 | | 6- | 2,341.00 | 93.64 | 4.000 |
| 1800000004 | DR | 04/22/2019 | 01 | | 6- | 345.00 | | |
| 1800000005 | DR | 02/22/2019 | 01 | | 28- | 10,000.00 | | |
| 1800000006 | DR | 10/01/2019 | 01 | | 174- | 103.47 | 2.07 | 2.000 |
| 1800000007 | DR | 01/12/2018 | 01 | | 99 | 200.00 | | |
| 1800000008 | DR | 01/11/2018 | 01 | | 99 | 5,600.00 | | |
| 1800000009 | DR | 05/11/2019 | 01 | | 951 | 237.00 | | |

| | | | | | Am... | Gross<... | Currency | Items | Items | Disc. | Disc. |

Processing Status

| Number of Items | 10 | Amount Entered | 1,000.45 |
| Display from Item | 1 | Assigned | 2,000.00 |
| Reason Code | | Difference Postings | 999.55- |
| Display in clearing currency | | Not Assigned | 0.00 |

Fig 10

We can now either simulate this first or post directly. Simulation tells us:

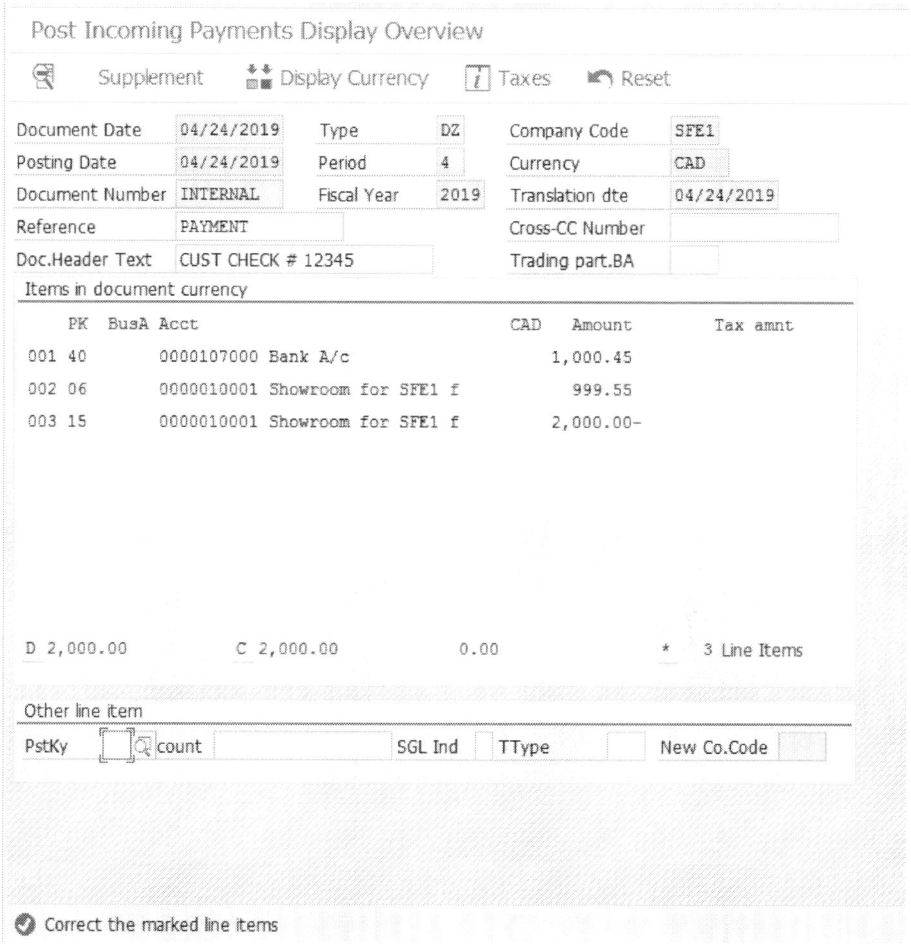
Post Incoming Payments Display Overview
Supplement
Display Currency
Taxes
Reset
Document Date 04/24/2019
Type DZ
Company Code SFE1
Posting Date 04/24/2019
Period 4
Currency CAD
Document Number INTERNAL
Fiscal Year 2019
Translation dte 04/24/2019
Reference PAYMENT
Cross-CC Number
Doc.Header Text CUST CHECK # 12345
Trading part.BA
Items in document currency
PK BusA Acct CAD Amount Tax amnt
001 40 0000107000 Bank A/c 1,000.45
002 06 0000010001 Showroom for SFE1 f 999.55
003 15 0000010001 Showroom for SFE1 f 2,000.00-
D 2,000.00 C 2,000.00 0.00 * 3 Line Items
Other line item
PstKy count SGL Ind TType New Co.Code
Correct the marked line items

Fig 11

The note – Correct the marked line items (not the 2nd line is in Blue) means SAP wants you to enter some note re the short payment. It can be done by double clicking the line and entering it in the Notes column:

**Post Incoming Payments Correct Customer item**

▲ ◁ ▷ ▯ 📑 More data  ↩ Reset

| Customer | 10001 | Showroom for SFE1 furniture | | G/L Acc | 121000 |
|---|---|---|---|---|---|
| Company Code | SFE1 | 1000 Bloor St | | | |
| Shefaria Ent Inc | | toronto | | | |

Item 2 / Payment difference / 06

| Amount | 999.55 | | CAD |
|---|---|---|---|
| Tax Amount | 0.00 | | |
| | ☐ Calculate Tax | Tax Code | |
| Contract | / | Flow Type | |
| Payt terms | | Days/percent | 0.000 / / |
| Bline Date | 04/24/2019 | CD Amount | 0.00 |
| CD Base | 999.55 | Invoice Ref. | / / 0 |
| Pmnt block | | Payt Method | |
| Assignment | | | |
| Text | Remainder from invoice | | |

Next line item

| PstKy | | Account | | SGL Ind | | New Co.Code | |
|---|---|---|---|---|---|---|---|

Fig 12

Step back and the message will gone with the line in Black:

**Post Incoming Payments Display Overview**

🔳 ⬆⬇ Display Currency  ⓘ Taxes  ↩ Reset

| Document Date | 04/24/2019 | Type | DZ | Company Code | SFE1 |
|---|---|---|---|---|---|
| Posting Date | 04/24/2019 | Period | 4 | Currency | CAD |
| Document Number | INTERNAL | Fiscal Year | 2019 | Translation dte | 04/24/2019 |
| Reference | PAYMENT | | | Cross-CC Number | |
| Doc.Header Text | CUST CHECK # 12345 | | | Trading part.BA | |

Items in document currency

| | PK | BusA | Acct | | CAD | Amount | Tax amnt |
|---|---|---|---|---|---|---|---|
| 001 | 40 | | 0000107000 Bank A/c | | | 1,000.45 | |
| 002 | 06 | | 0000010001 Showroom for SFE1 f | | | 999.55 | |
| 003 | 15 | | 0000010001 Showroom for SFE1 f | | | 2,000.00- | |

Fig 13

The balance of the receivable will be automatically put back in the AR of the customer.

Post the document and SAP gives us the posting #:

✓ Document 1400000000 was posted in company code SFE1

Fig 14

When we look up the customers' receivables in FBL5N/H again, we find this invoice now has only the remaining balance:

| Customer | 10001 | | | | | | | | | |
|---|---|---|---|---|---|---|---|---|---|---|
| Company Code | SFE1 | | | | | | | | | |

| Name | Showroom for SFE1 furniture | | | | | | | | | |
|---|---|---|---|---|---|---|---|---|---|---|
| City | toronto | | | | | | | | | |

| SI Assignment | Document | Ty | DocDate | DD | Amount in Local Crcy | LCurr | Net Due Dt | DD | Discount Base Amount | Disc.1 | Curr. Cash Disc. Amt |
|---|---|---|---|---|---|---|---|---|---|---|---|
| | 1400000000 | DZ | 04/24/2019 | | 999.55 | CAD | 04/24/2019 | | 999.55 | 0.000 | 0.00 |
| | 1600000000 | DA | 04/24/2019 | | 1,250.00 | CAD | 04/24/2019 | | 1,250.00 | 0.000 | 0.00 |
| | 1800000003 | DR | 04/22/2019 | | 2,341.00 | CAD | 06/15/2019 | | 2,341.00 | 4.000 | 93.64 |
| | 1800000004 | DR | 04/22/2019 | | 345.00 | CAD | 04/30/2019 | | 345.00 | 0.000 | 0.00 |
| | 1800000005 | DR | 02/22/2019 | | 10,000.00 | CAD | 05/22/2019 | | 10,000.00 | 0.000 | 0.00 |
| | 1800000006 | DR | 10/01/2019 | | 103.47 | CAD | 10/31/2019 | | 103.47 | 2.000 | 2.07 |
| | 1800000007 | DR | 01/12/2018 | | 200.00 | CAD | 01/15/2019 | | 200.00 | 4.000 | 0.00 |
| | 1800000008 | DR | 01/11/2018 | | 5,600.00 | CAD | 01/15/2019 | | 5,600.00 | 4.000 | 0.00 |
| | 1800000009 | DR | 05/11/2019 | | 237.00 | CAD | 09/15/2016 | | 237.00 | 4.000 | 0.00 |
| | 1800000010 | DR | 12/01/2019 | | 674.00 | CAD | 09/15/2016 | | 674.00 | 4.000 | 0.00 |
| | | | | | 21,750.02 | CAD | | | | | |
| Account 10001 | | | | | 21,750.02 | CAD | | | | | |
| | | | | | 21,750.02 | CAD | | | | | |

Fig 15

We can also look up this document in transaction FB03:

Display Document: Initial Screen

📊 Document List    ⟨ First Item    ✏ Editing Oj

Keys for Entry View

| Document Number | 1400000000 |
|---|---|
| Company Code | SFE1 |
| Fiscal Year | 2019 |

Fig 16

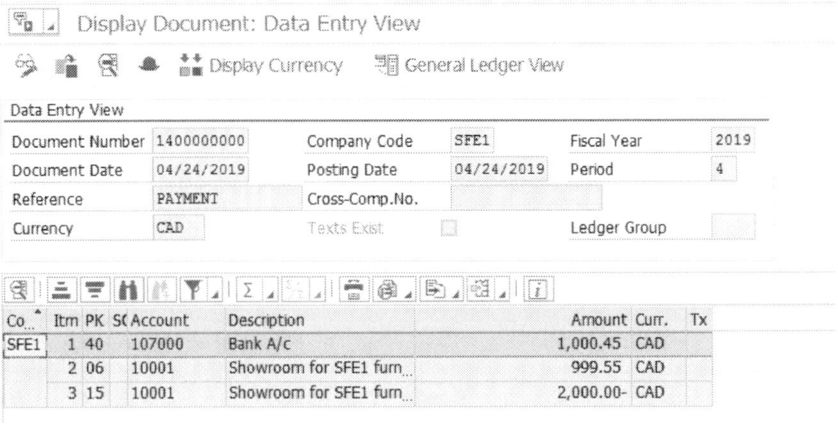

Fig 17

To see the notes, just double click the line that represents the full invoice:

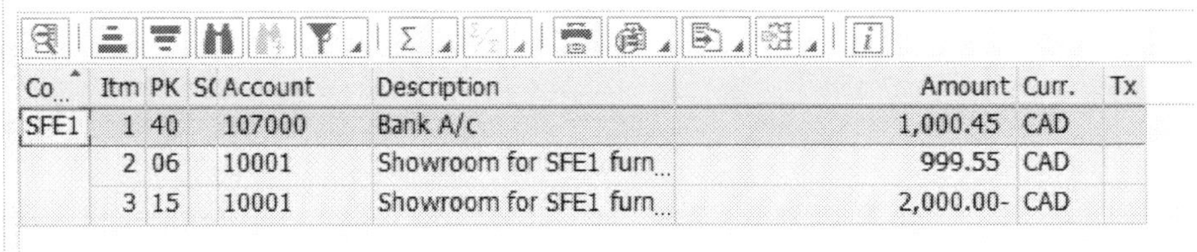

Fig 18

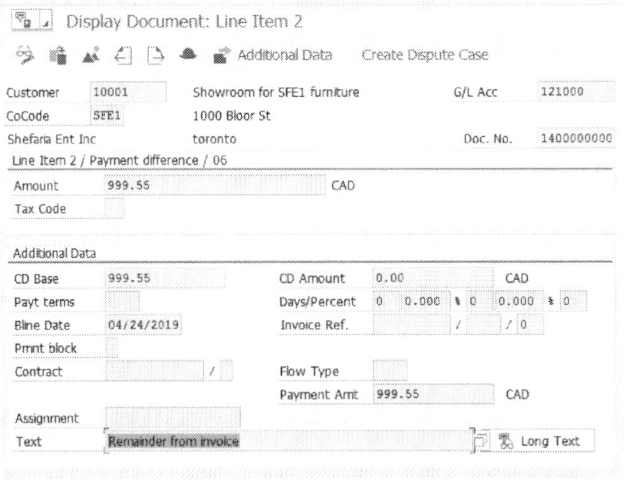

Fig 19

To look up documents in FB03: If we do not know the document #, then click on Document List,

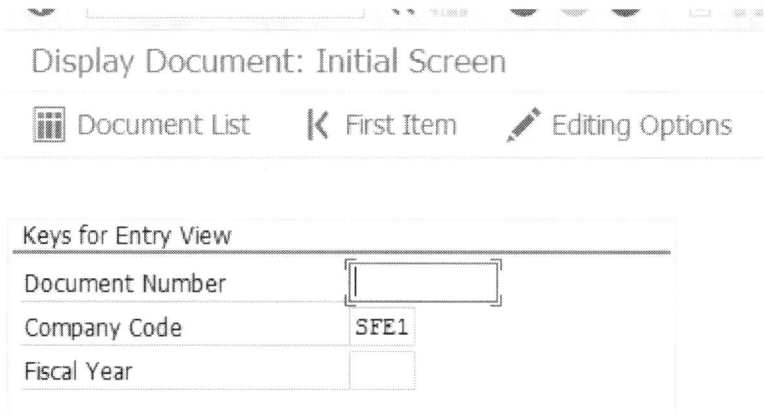

## Display Document: Initial Screen

📊 Document List    K First Item    ✏️ Editing Options

### Keys for Entry View

| | |
|---|---|
| Document Number | |
| Company Code | SFE1 |
| Fiscal Year | |

Fig 20

Enter as much data as you can on the screen and click Execute:

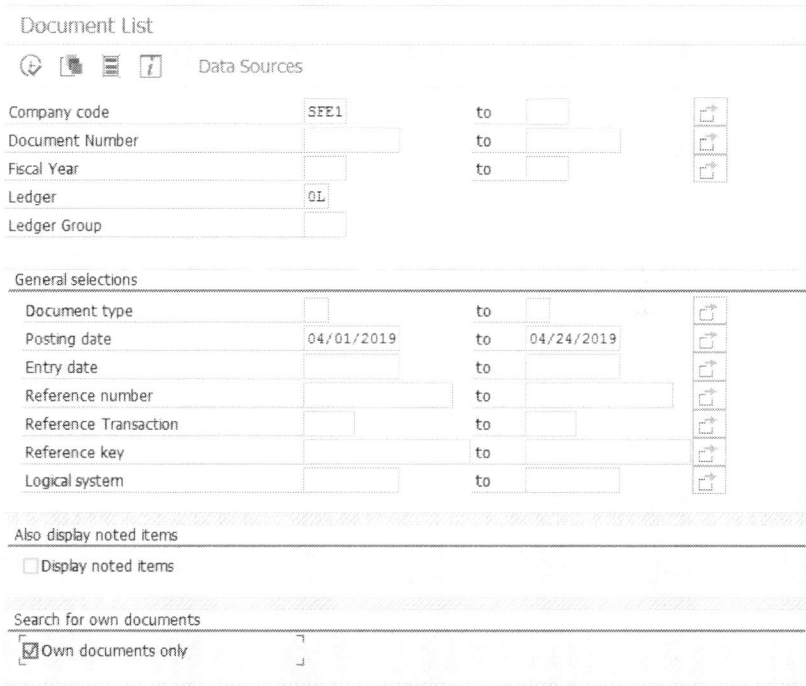

### Document List

⊕ 📋 ≡ ⓘ    Data Sources

| | | | |
|---|---|---|---|
| Company code | SFE1 | to | |
| Document Number | | to | |
| Fiscal Year | | to | |
| Ledger | 0L | | |
| Ledger Group | | | |

#### General selections

| | | | |
|---|---|---|---|
| Document type | | to | |
| Posting date | 04/01/2019 | to | 04/24/2019 |
| Entry date | | to | |
| Reference number | | to | |
| Reference Transaction | | to | |
| Reference key | | to | |
| Logical system | | to | |

#### Also display noted items

☐ Display noted items

#### Search for own documents

☑ Own documents only

Fig 21

You can also ask it to display only those documents that you may have posted by clicking on:

Search for own documents

☑ Own documents only

Fig 22

In the report that comes up, the document type DZ means a payment document:

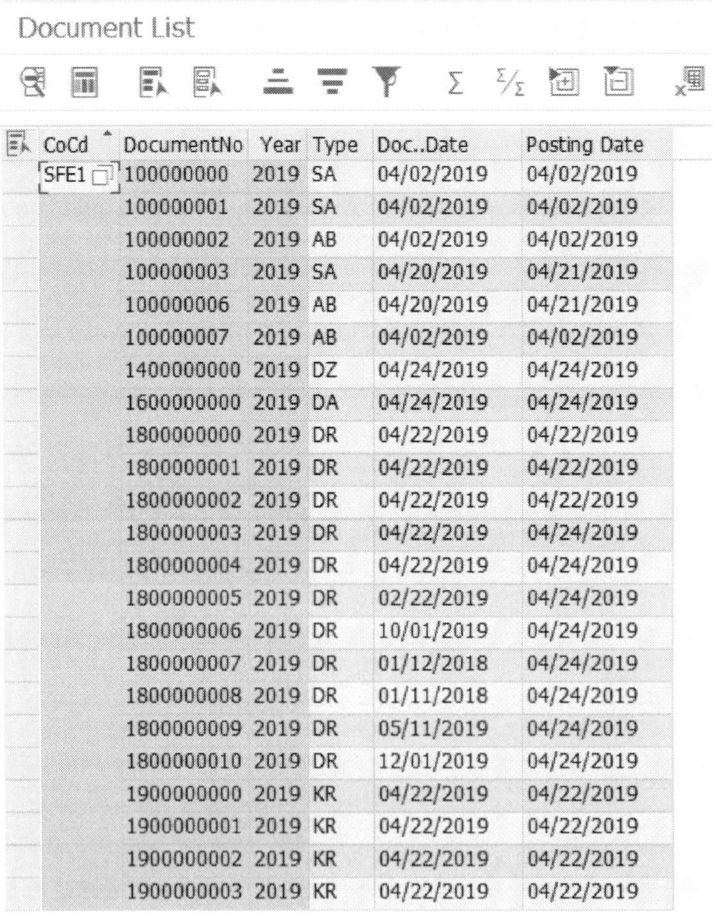

Document List

| CoCd | DocumentNo | Year | Type | Doc..Date | Posting Date |
|------|------------|------|------|-----------|--------------|
| SFE1 | 100000000 | 2019 | SA | 04/02/2019 | 04/02/2019 |
| | 100000001 | 2019 | SA | 04/02/2019 | 04/02/2019 |
| | 100000002 | 2019 | AB | 04/02/2019 | 04/02/2019 |
| | 100000003 | 2019 | SA | 04/20/2019 | 04/21/2019 |
| | 100000006 | 2019 | AB | 04/20/2019 | 04/21/2019 |
| | 100000007 | 2019 | AB | 04/02/2019 | 04/02/2019 |
| | 1400000000 | 2019 | DZ | 04/24/2019 | 04/24/2019 |
| | 1600000000 | 2019 | DA | 04/24/2019 | 04/24/2019 |
| | 1800000000 | 2019 | DR | 04/22/2019 | 04/22/2019 |
| | 1800000001 | 2019 | DR | 04/22/2019 | 04/22/2019 |
| | 1800000002 | 2019 | DR | 04/22/2019 | 04/22/2019 |
| | 1800000003 | 2019 | DR | 04/22/2019 | 04/24/2019 |
| | 1800000004 | 2019 | DR | 04/22/2019 | 04/24/2019 |
| | 1800000005 | 2019 | DR | 02/22/2019 | 04/24/2019 |
| | 1800000006 | 2019 | DR | 10/01/2019 | 04/24/2019 |
| | 1800000007 | 2019 | DR | 01/12/2018 | 04/24/2019 |
| | 1800000008 | 2019 | DR | 01/11/2018 | 04/24/2019 |
| | 1800000009 | 2019 | DR | 05/11/2019 | 04/24/2019 |
| | 1800000010 | 2019 | DR | 12/01/2019 | 04/24/2019 |
| | 1900000000 | 2019 | KR | 04/22/2019 | 04/22/2019 |
| | 1900000001 | 2019 | KR | 04/22/2019 | 04/22/2019 |
| | 1900000002 | 2019 | KR | 04/22/2019 | 04/22/2019 |
| | 1900000003 | 2019 | KR | 04/22/2019 | 04/22/2019 |

Fig 23

Double click on it to see more details:

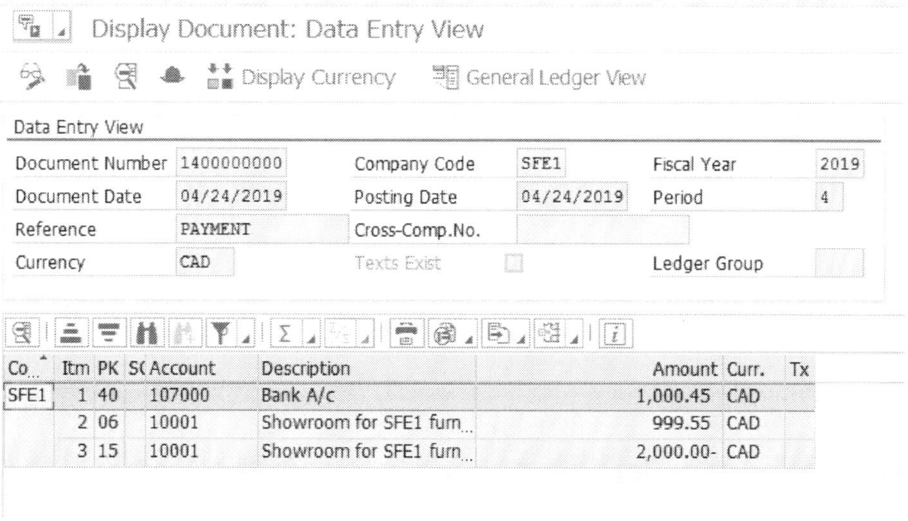

Display Document: Data Entry View

Display Currency    General Ledger View

Data Entry View

| | | | | | |
|---|---|---|---|---|---|
| Document Number | 1400000000 | Company Code | SFE1 | Fiscal Year | 2019 |
| Document Date | 04/24/2019 | Posting Date | 04/24/2019 | Period | 4 |
| Reference | PAYMENT | Cross-Comp.No. | | | |
| Currency | CAD | Texts Exist | | Ledger Group | |

| Co... | Itm | PK | S( | Account | Description | Amount | Curr. | Tx |
|---|---|---|---|---|---|---|---|---|
| SFE1 | 1 | 40 | | 107000 | Bank A/c | 1,000.45 | CAD | |
| | 2 | 06 | | 10001 | Showroom for SFE1 furn... | 999.55 | CAD | |
| | 3 | 15 | | 10001 | Showroom for SFE1 furn... | 2,000.00- | CAD | |

Fig 24

# POSTING RESIDUAL PAYMENTS (U)

T Code FB70

Residual payments in SAP are regarded as disputed amounts. The intent is to record those as such pending decisions. The effect they have is that the customer's credit balance/limits are not affected since they are disputed. If not paid, then at the end of the financial period they may find their way to bad debts depending on the company's policy.

We will post a new customer invoice using transaction FB70.

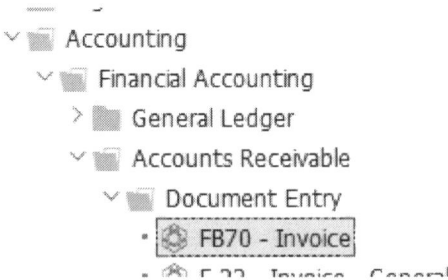

Fig 1

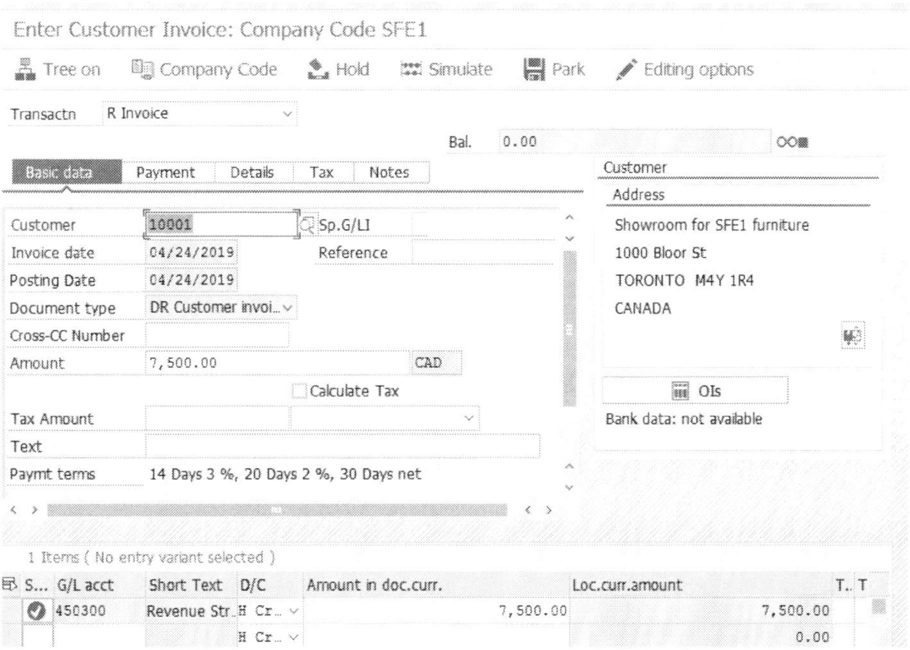

Fig 2

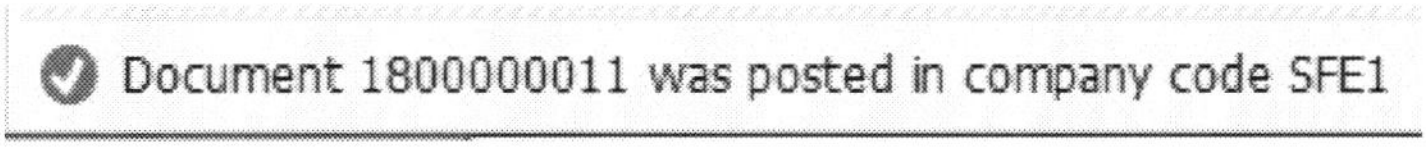

Document 1800000011 was posted in company code SFE1

Fig 3

This currently shows up in the customer's AR statements, FBL5N/H:

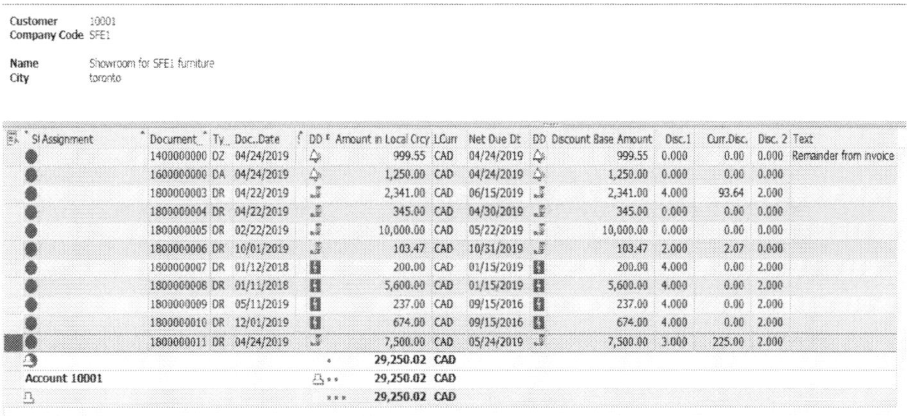

| Customer | 10001 | | | | | | | | | | |
| Company Code | SFE1 | | | | | | | | | | |
| | | | | | | | | | | | |
| Name | Showroom for SFE1 furniture | | | | | | | | | | |
| City | toronto | | | | | | | | | | |

| SI Assignment | Document | Ty | Doc..Date | DD E | Amount in Local Crcy | LCurr | Net Due Dt | DD | Discount Base Amount | Disc.1 | Curr.Disc. | Disc. 2 | Text |
|---|---|---|---|---|---|---|---|---|---|---|---|---|---|
| | 1400000000 | DZ | 04/24/2019 | | 999.55 | CAD | 04/24/2019 | | 999.55 | 0.000 | 0.00 | 0.000 | Remainder from invoice |
| | 1600000000 | DA | 04/24/2019 | | 1,250.00 | CAD | 04/24/2019 | | 1,250.00 | 0.000 | 0.00 | 0.000 | |
| | 1800000003 | DR | 04/22/2019 | | 2,341.00 | CAD | 06/15/2019 | | 2,341.00 | 4.000 | 93.64 | 2.000 | |
| | 1800000004 | DR | 04/22/2019 | | 345.00 | CAD | 04/30/2019 | | 345.00 | 0.000 | 0.00 | 0.000 | |
| | 1800000005 | DR | 02/22/2019 | | 10,000.00 | CAD | 05/22/2019 | | 10,000.00 | 0.000 | 0.00 | 0.000 | |
| | 1800000006 | DR | 10/01/2019 | | 103.47 | CAD | 10/31/2019 | | 103.47 | 2.000 | 2.07 | 0.000 | |
| | 1600000007 | DR | 01/12/2018 | | 200.00 | CAD | 01/15/2019 | | 200.00 | 4.000 | 0.00 | 2.000 | |
| | 1800000008 | DR | 01/11/2018 | | 5,600.00 | CAD | 01/15/2019 | | 5,600.00 | 4.000 | 0.00 | 2.000 | |
| | 1800000009 | DR | 05/11/2019 | | 237.00 | CAD | 09/15/2016 | | 237.00 | 4.000 | 0.00 | 2.000 | |
| | 1800000010 | DR | 12/01/2019 | | 674.00 | CAD | 09/15/2016 | | 674.00 | 4.000 | 0.00 | 2.000 | |
| | 1800000011 | DR | 04/24/2019 | | 7,500.00 | CAD | 05/24/2019 | | 7,500.00 | 3.000 | 225.00 | 2.000 | |
| | | | | | 29,250.02 | CAD | | | | | | | |
| Account 10001 | | | | | 29,250.02 | CAD | | | | | | | |
| | | | | | 29,250.02 | CAD | | | | | | | |

Fig 4
183

The net due date is being calculated based on posting date + days net due.

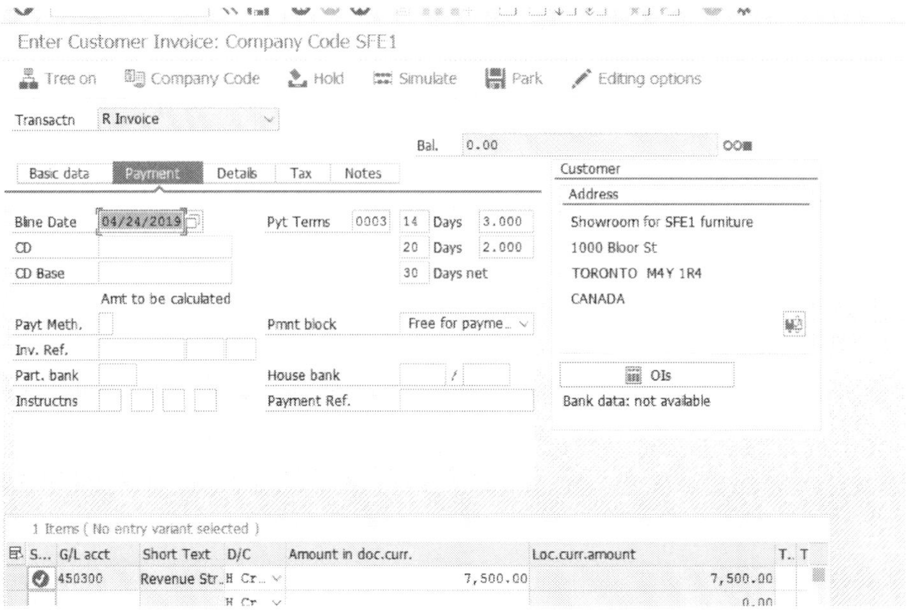

Fig 5

If the customer were to pay within 14 or 20 days, SAP would automatically apply 3% or 2% cash discounts respectively, which we will see later in this course.

Let's say the customer has paid only partial amount and the remaining needs to be cleared off via this process. The transaction to do this is previously used F-28 or, we can look at a new one here, F-26 which leads up to the same result as F-28. The only difference is, in F-28 if you already know the document you are posting against, it makes it simpler and we don't have to search, deactivate and re-activate the document we need.

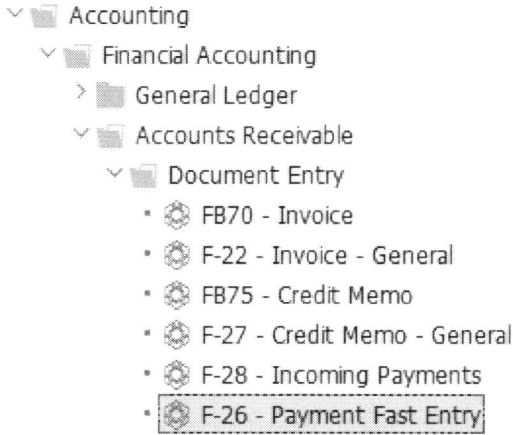

Fig 6

Enter the data as below for the bank account you will debit for this payment:

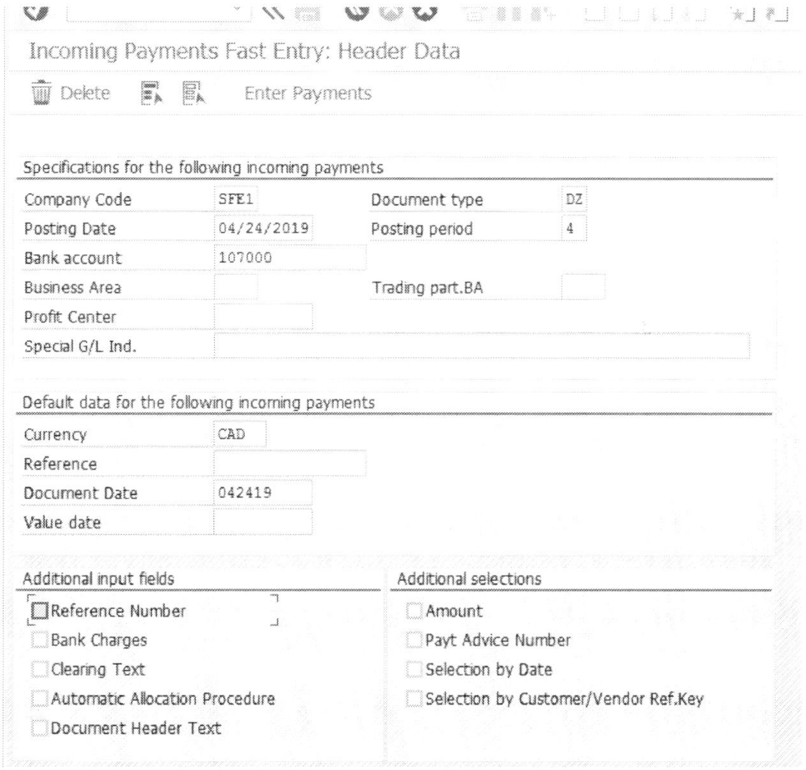

Fig 7

Now on  Enter Payments where you can enter the customer # and amount:

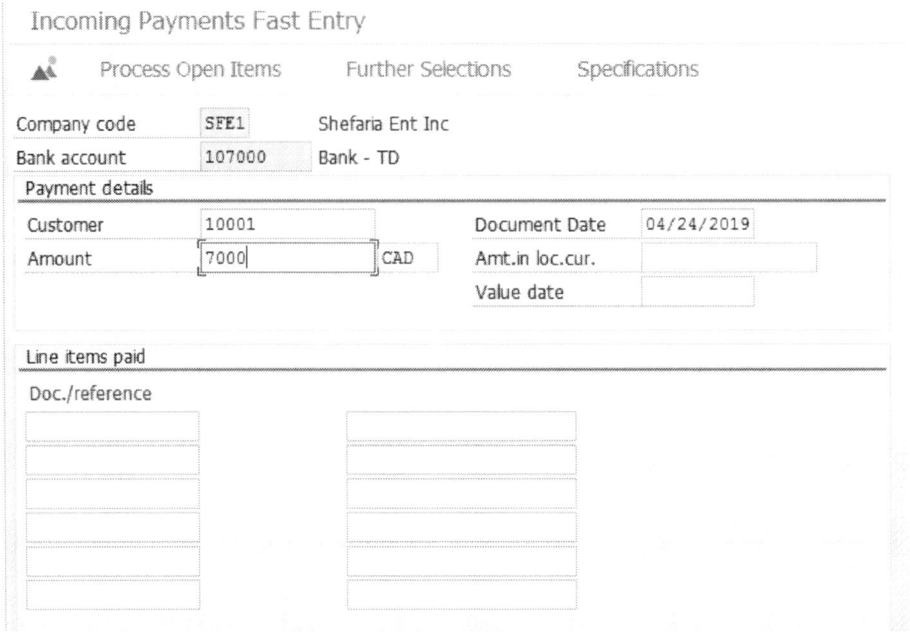

Incoming Payments Fast Entry

Process Open Items    Further Selections    Specifications

| Company code | SFE1 | Shefaria Ent Inc |
| Bank account | 107000 | Bank - TD |

**Payment details**

| Customer | 10001 | | Document Date | 04/24/2019 |
| Amount | 7000 | CAD | Amt.in loc.cur. | |
| | | | Value date | |

**Line items paid**

Doc./reference

Fig 8

Then on *Process Open Items* to bring up the invoices open for payment of this customer – our line is on the next screen so use the Windows bar on the right to scroll down:

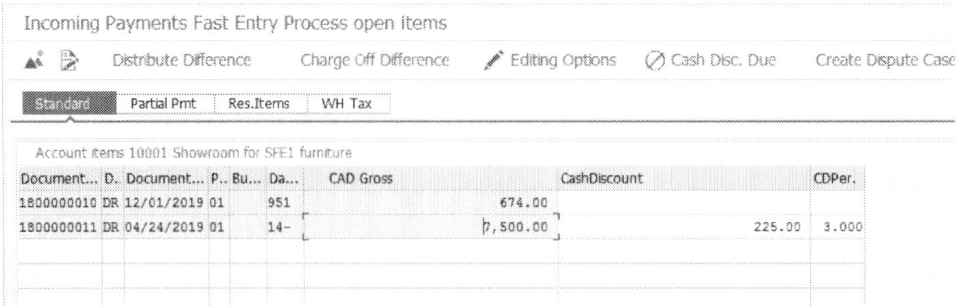

Incoming Payments Fast Entry Process open items

Distribute Difference    Charge Off Difference    Editing Options    Cash Disc. Due    Create Dispute Case

| Standard | Partial Pmt | Res.Items | WH Tax |

Account items 10001 Showroom for SFE1 furniture

| Document... | D.. | Document... | P.. | Bu... | Da... | CAD Gross | CashDiscount | CDPer. |
|---|---|---|---|---|---|---|---|---|
| 1800000010 | DR | 12/01/2019 | 01 | | 951 | 674.00 | | |
| 1800000011 | DR | 04/24/2019 | 01 | | 14- | 7,500.00 | 225.00 | 3.000 |

Fig 9

186

Double click on the line you need to apply this against to make it blue. Note that since the payment has come within 15 days, SAP has applied a cash discount automatically as done below in Fig 10 – note the amount at the bottom right – the residual is only 275 and not 500 in spite that the invoice was 7,500 and payment is 7,000.

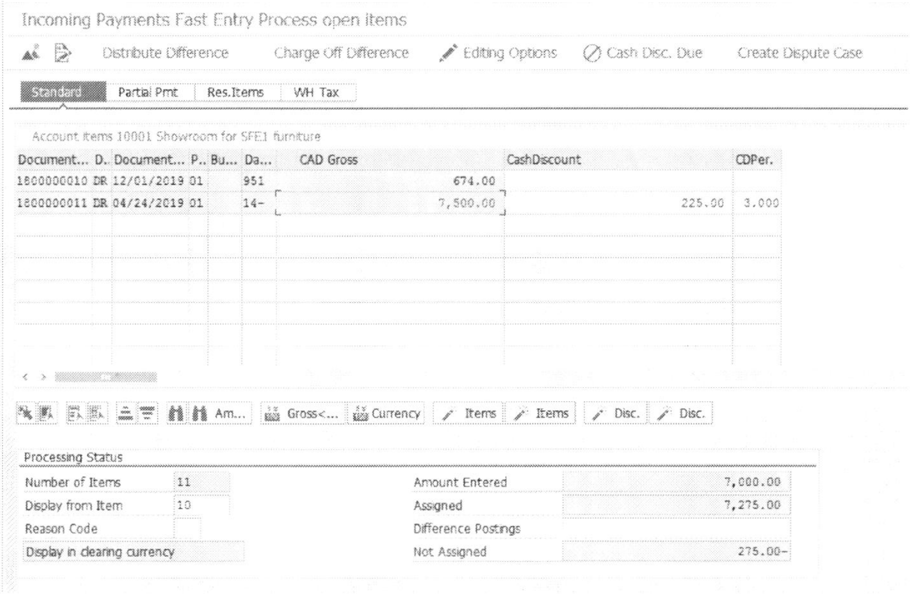

| Incoming Payments Fast Entry Process open items | | | | | | | | |
|---|---|---|---|---|---|---|---|---|
| ⚲ ➦ | Distribute Difference | | Charge Off Difference | ✎ Editing Options | ⊘ Cash Disc. Due | | Create Dispute Case | |
| Standard | Partial Pmt | Res.Items | WH Tax | | | | | |

Account items 10001 Showroom for SFE1 furniture

| Document... | D.. | Document... | P.. | Bu... | Da... | CAD Gross | CashDiscount | | CDPer. |
|---|---|---|---|---|---|---|---|---|---|
| 1800000010 | DR | 12/01/2019 | 01 | | 951 | 674.00 | | | |
| 1800000011 | DR | 04/24/2019 | 01 | | 14– | 7,500.00 | | 225.00 | 3.000 |

| Processing Status | | | | |
|---|---|---|---|---|
| Number of Items | 11 | Amount Entered | | 7,000.00 |
| Display from Item | 10 | Assigned | | 7,275.00 |
| Reason Code | | Difference Postings | | |
| Display in clearing currency | | Not Assigned | | 275.00– |

Fig 10

Since the customer has disputed the difference amount anyway, you have the choice of wiping out this discount by clearing out the line manually and then decide whether to give the discounts later once resolution for this difference happens. Therefore, we will clear the cash discounts (Fig 10) and apply the paid amount to the entire document.

We now need to account for this residual amount, we do this by going to the Residual items tab:

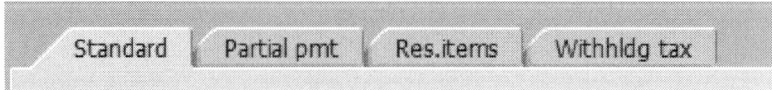

Standard | Partial pmt | Res.items | Withhldg tax

Fig 11

Fig 12

Either manually enter the amount in the cell Residual items next to the Net Amount or double click in it. and the Not Assigned amount at the bottom turns to 0 (Fig 13)

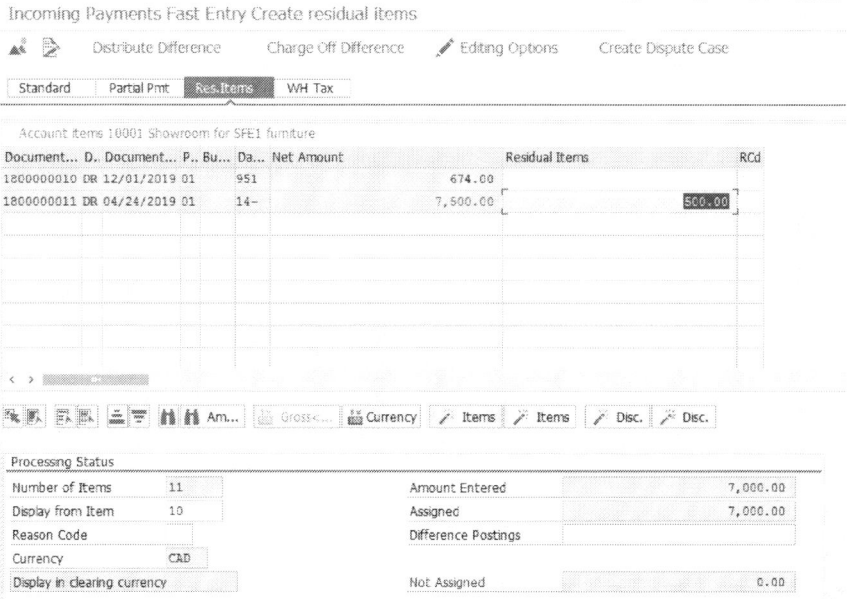

Distribute Difference    Charge Off Difference    Editing Options    Create Dispute Case

Standard    Partial Pmt    Res.Items    WH Tax

Account Items 10001 Showroom for SFE1 furniture

| Document... | D.. | Document... | P.. | Bu.. | Da... | Net Amount | Residual Items | RCd |
|---|---|---|---|---|---|---|---|---|
| 1800000010 | DR | 12/01/2019 | 01 | | 951 | 674.00 | | |
| 1800000011 | DR | 04/24/2019 | 01 | | 14- | 7,500.00 | 500.00 | |

‹ › 

Am...    Gross<...    Currency    Items    Items    Disc.    Disc.

Processing Status

| Number of Items | 11 | Amount Entered | 7,000.00 |
|---|---|---|---|
| Display from Item | 10 | Assigned | 7,000.00 |
| Reason Code | | Difference Postings | |
| Currency | CAD | | |
| Display in clearing currency | | Not Assigned | 0.00 |

Fig 13

Simulate if you would like to:

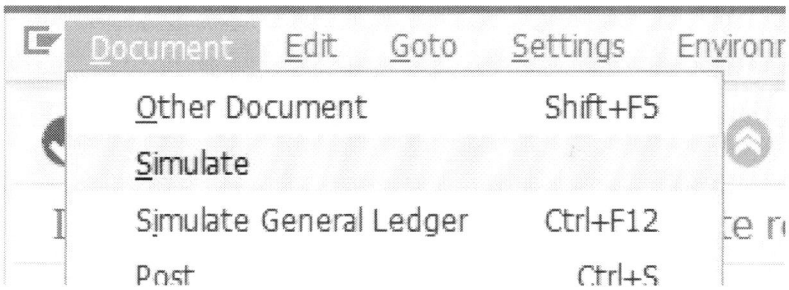

| Document | Edit | Goto | Settings | Environr |
|---|---|---|---|---|
| Other Document | | | Shift+F5 | |
| Simulate | | | | |
| Simulate General Ledger | | | Ctrl+F12 | |
| Post | | | Ctrl+S | |

Fig 14

To see 3 lines:

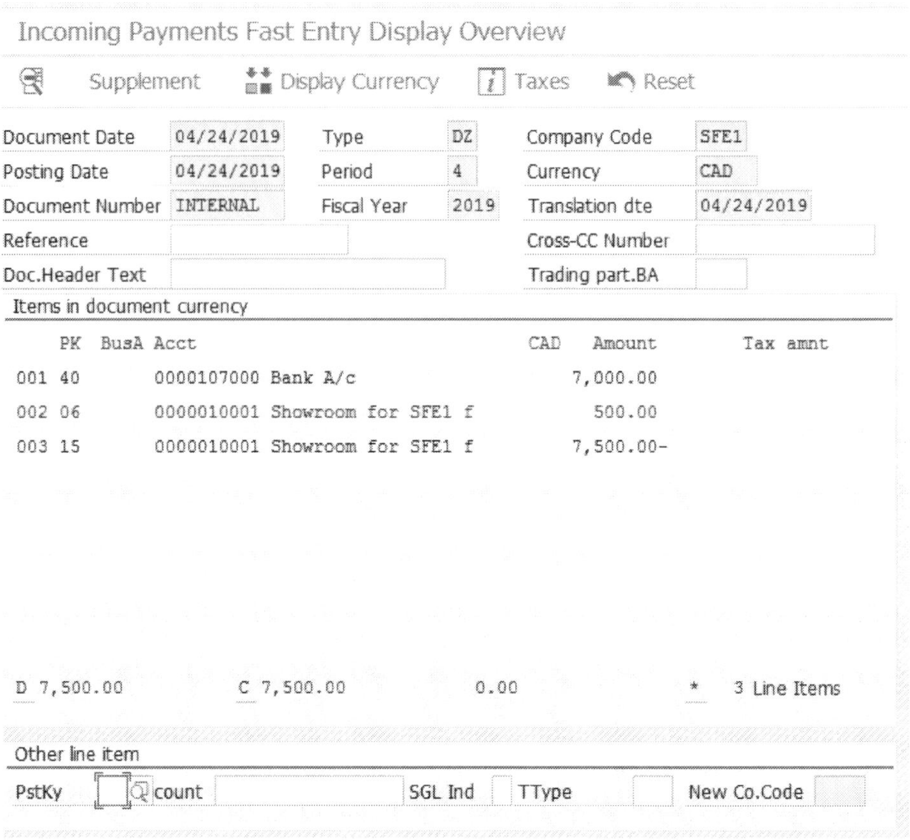

Incoming Payments Fast Entry Display Overview

| ⊞ | Supplement | Display Currency | ℹ Taxes | ↩ Reset |

| Document Date | 04/24/2019 | Type | DZ | Company Code | SFE1 |
|---|---|---|---|---|---|
| Posting Date | 04/24/2019 | Period | 4 | Currency | CAD |
| Document Number | INTERNAL | Fiscal Year | 2019 | Translation dte | 04/24/2019 |
| Reference | | | | Cross-CC Number | |
| Doc.Header Text | | | | Trading part.BA | |

Items in document currency

| PK | BusA | Acct | CAD | Amount | Tax amnt |
|---|---|---|---|---|---|
| 001 | 40 | 0000107000 Bank A/c | | 7,000.00 | |
| 002 | 06 | 0000010001 Showroom for SFE1 f | | 500.00 | |
| 003 | 15 | 0000010001 Showroom for SFE1 f | | 7,500.00- | |

D 7,500.00     C 7,500.00     0.00     *  3 Line Items

Other line item

| PstKy | ⊞ count | SGL Ind | TType | New Co.Code |

Fig 15

You may also want to make a note at this point to explain this remaining. To do that, double click on the difference line:

002 06        0000010001 Showroom for SFE1 f          500.00

Fig 16

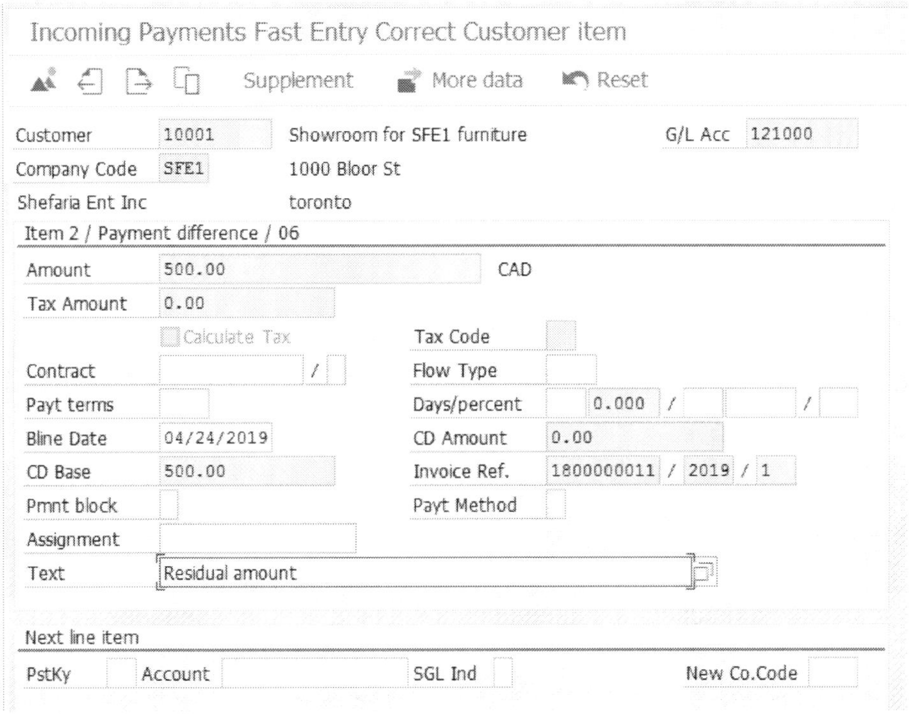

## Incoming Payments Fast Entry Correct Customer item

▲  ⬅  ➡  ⬛   Supplement   ➡ More data   ↩ Reset

| | | | | |
|---|---|---|---|---|
| Customer | 10001 | Showroom for SFE1 furniture | G/L Acc | 121000 |
| Company Code | SFE1 | 1000 Bloor St | | |
| Shefaria Ent Inc | | toronto | | |

Item 2 / Payment difference / 06

| | | | | | | |
|---|---|---|---|---|---|---|
| Amount | 500.00 | | CAD | | | |
| Tax Amount | 0.00 | | | | | |
| | ☐ Calculate Tax | | Tax Code | | | |
| Contract | | / | Flow Type | | | |
| Payt terms | | | Days/percent | 0.000 | / | / |
| Bline Date | 04/24/2019 | | CD Amount | 0.00 | | |
| CD Base | 500.00 | | Invoice Ref. | 1800000011 | / 2019 | / 1 |
| Pmnt block | | | Payt Method | | | |
| Assignment | | | | | | |
| Text | Residual amount | | | | | |

Next line item

| PstKy | | Account | | SGL Ind | | New Co.Code | |
|---|---|---|---|---|---|---|---|

Fig 17

Then save it:

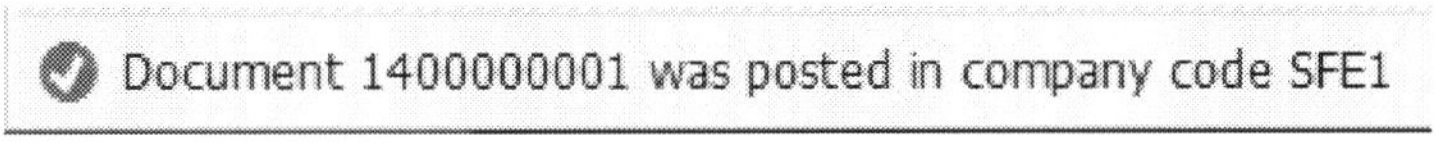

✔ Document 1400000001 was posted in company code SFE1

Fig 18

Let us now check the customer balance in FBL5N/H or FD10N:

Thus, this balance remains on the customer account as payable:

| SI | Assignment | Document | Ty | Doc..Date | DD | Amount in Local Crcy | LCurr | Net Due Dt | DD | Discount Base Amount | Disc.1 | Curr.Disc. | Disc. 2 | Text |
|----|-----------|----------|-----|-----------|-----|---------------------|-------|-----------|-----|---------------------|--------|-----------|---------|------|
| | | 1400000000 | DZ | 04/24/2019 | | 999.55 | CAD | 04/24/2019 | | 999.55 | 0.000 | 0.00 | 0.000 | Remainder from invoice |
| | | 1400000001 | DZ | 04/24/2019 | | 500.00 | CAD | 04/24/2019 | | 500.00 | 0.000 | 0.00 | 0.000 | Residual amount |
| | | 1600000000 | DA | 04/24/2019 | | 1,250.00 | CAD | 04/24/2019 | | 1,250.00 | 0.000 | 0.00 | 0.000 | |
| | | 1800000003 | DR | 04/22/2019 | | 2,341.00 | CAD | 06/15/2019 | | 2,341.00 | 4.000 | 93.64 | 2.000 | |
| | | 1800000004 | DR | 04/22/2019 | | 345.00 | CAD | 04/30/2019 | | 345.00 | 0.000 | 0.00 | 0.000 | |
| | | 1800000005 | DR | 02/22/2019 | | 10,000.00 | CAD | 05/22/2019 | | 10,000.00 | 0.000 | 0.00 | 0.000 | |
| | | 1800000006 | DR | 10/01/2019 | | 103.47 | CAD | 10/31/2019 | | 103.47 | 2.000 | 2.07 | 0.000 | |
| | | 1800000007 | DR | 01/12/2018 | | 200.00 | CAD | 01/15/2019 | | 200.00 | 4.000 | 0.00 | 2.000 | |
| | | 1800000008 | DR | 01/11/2018 | | 5,600.00 | CAD | 01/15/2019 | | 5,600.00 | 4.000 | 0.00 | 2.000 | |
| | | 1800000009 | DR | 05/11/2019 | | 237.00 | CAD | 09/15/2016 | | 237.00 | 4.000 | 0.00 | 2.000 | |
| | | 1800000010 | DR | 12/01/2019 | | 674.00 | CAD | 09/15/2016 | | 674.00 | 4.000 | 0.00 | 2.000 | |
| | | | | | * | 22,250.02 | CAD | | | | | | | |
| Account 10001 | | | | | ** | 22,250.02 | CAD | | | | | | | |
| | | | | | *** | 22,250.02 | CAD | | | | | | | |

Customer 10001
Company Code SFE1

Name Showroom for SFE1 furniture
City toronto

Fig 19

192

# CASH DISCOUNT ACCOUNTS (C/U)

We give cash discounts to customers and take them from vendors by receiving or making payments within certain agreed to specified days or for any other agreed reasons. These discounts require expense or income accounts as part of the P & L accounts to post these discounts. Part of this set up is data (setting up of the accounts themselves in the CoA) and part configuration (to make the cash discount process pick up these accounts at times of posting via the automatic account assignment process of SAP).

As the first step, we need to define 2 G/L accounts of the P & L type for cash discount given and taken.

Select your numbering (here, 450600 and 460600 for cash discount given and taken respectively) for the two types and enter data for both as in Figs 1 and 2.

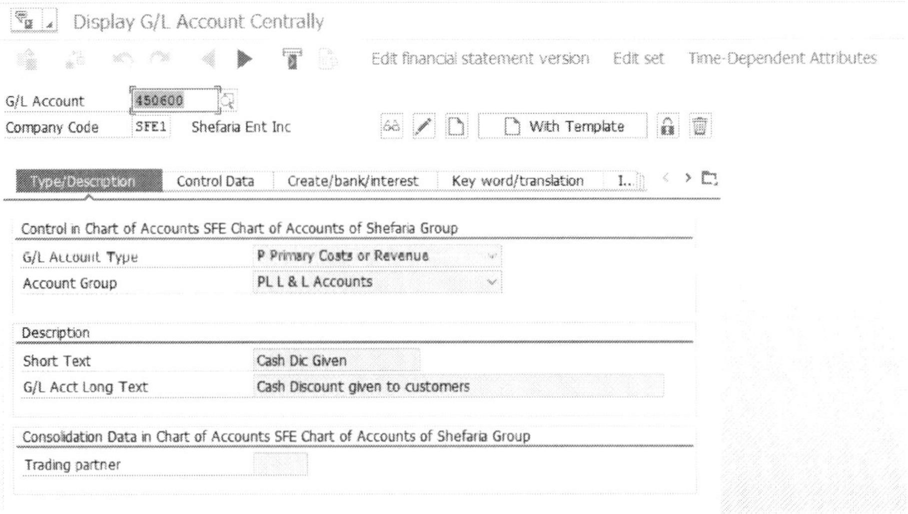

Fig 1

Fig 2

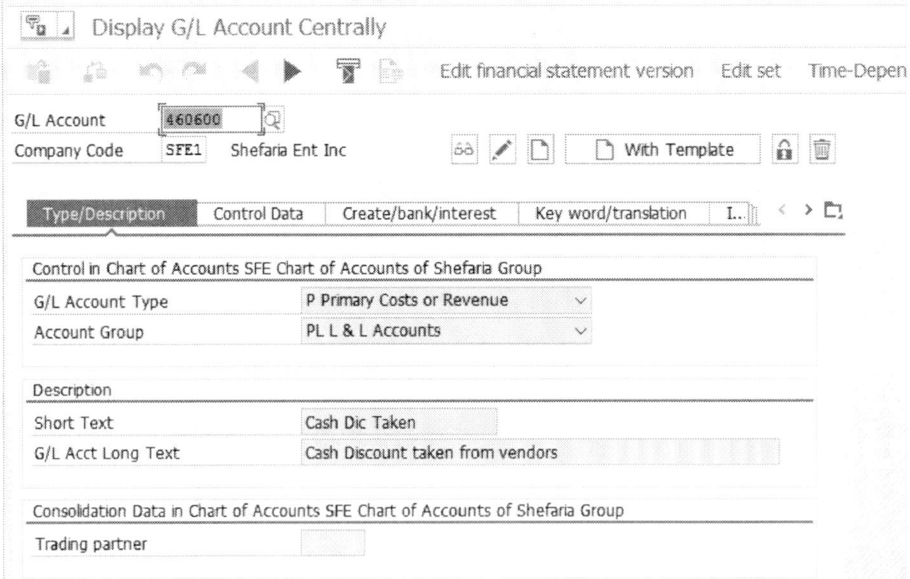

194

For both enter Control data and Create/Bank/Interest Data as:

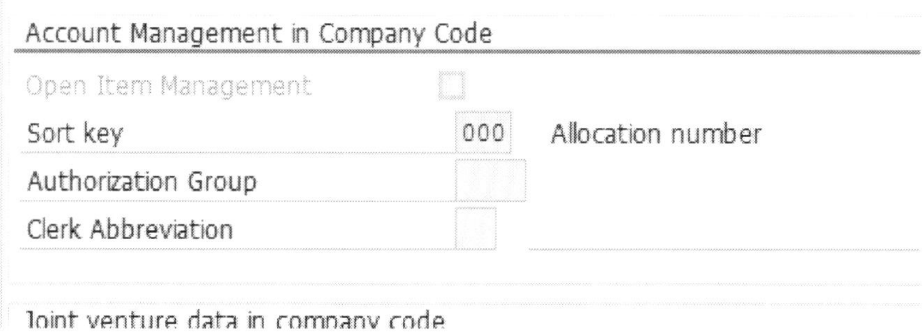

**Account Management in Company Code**

| | | |
|---|---|---|
| Open Item Management | ☐ | |
| Sort key | 000 | Allocation number |
| Authorization Group | | |
| Clerk Abbreviation | | |

Joint venture data in company code

Fig 3

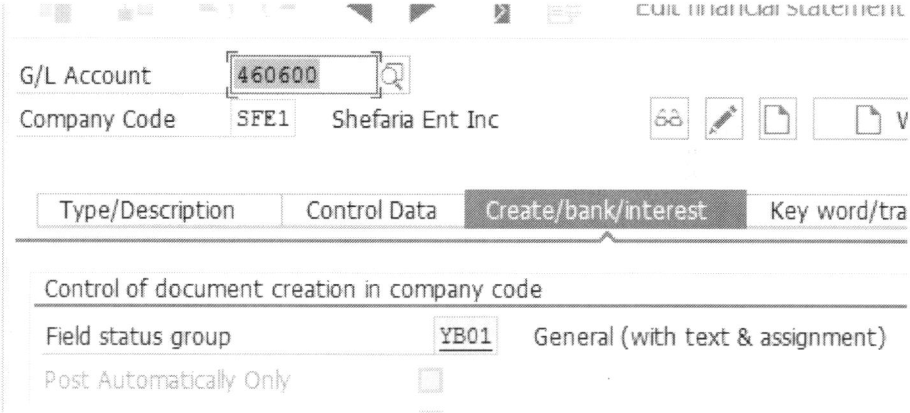

| | | | | | | | Edit financial statement |
|---|---|---|---|---|---|---|---|

| G/L Account | 460600 | 🔍 | | | | | | |
|---|---|---|---|---|---|---|---|---|
| Company Code | SFE1 | Shefaria Ent Inc | | | 👓 | ✏ | 🗋 | 🗋 V |

| Type/Description | Control Data | Create/bank/interest | Key word/tra |
|---|---|---|---|

**Control of document creation in company code**

| | | |
|---|---|---|
| Field status group | YB01 | General (with text & assignment) |
| Post Automatically Only | ☐ | |

Fig 4

Once we have 450600 and 460600 setup, we need to make the system recognize to make postings to these accounts, much in the same way as it recognizes the reconciliation accounts. This is done by assigning the process keys to these accounts in configurations. The process key for discounts given to customers is called SKT and this configuration is done in the following path in SPRO (Fig 5)

Fig 5

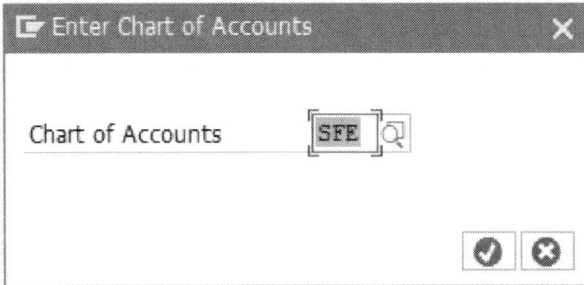

Fig 6

Ensure SKT exists on the screen:

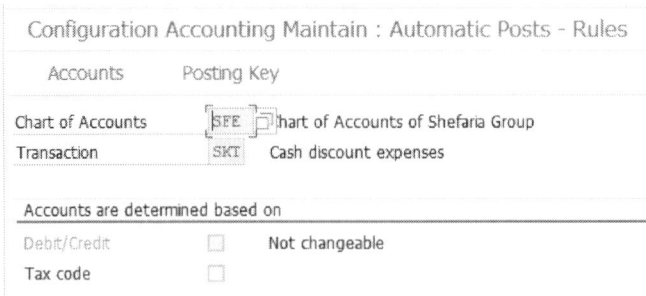

Fig 7

Click on Save to save this configuration linking the CoA SFE with SKT.

Next, click on 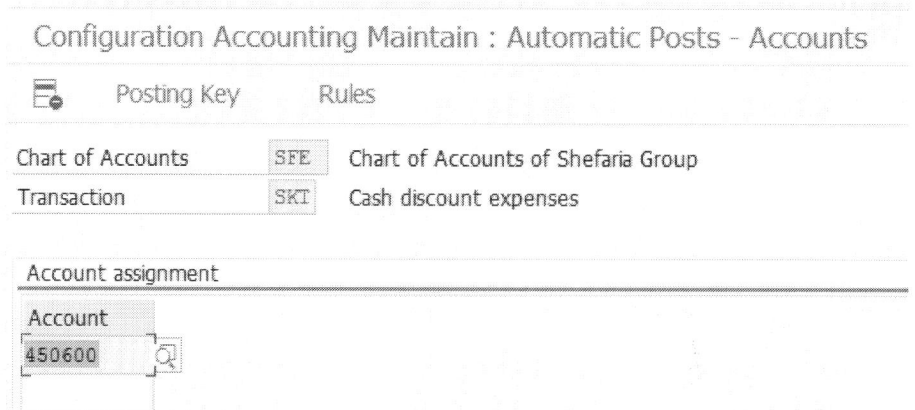 Accounts and enter the Cash discount given in the G/L account field:

Fig 8

Save:

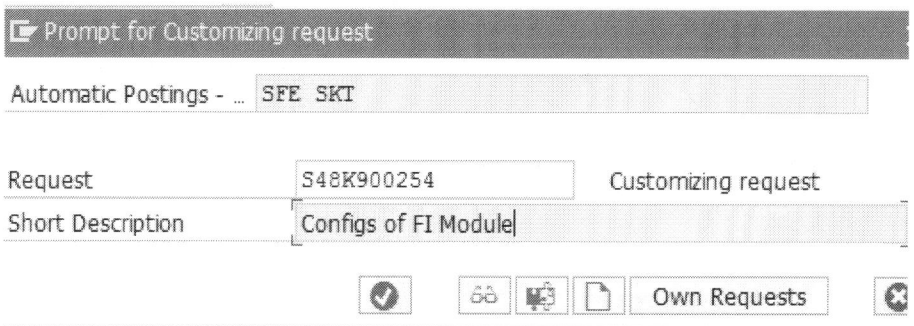

Fig 9

Repeat the same configuration for Cash Discount taken G/L account 460600 with process key SKE in the path

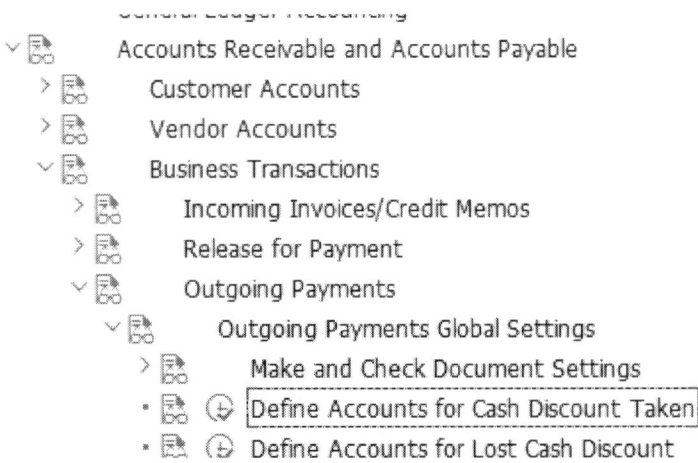

Fig 10

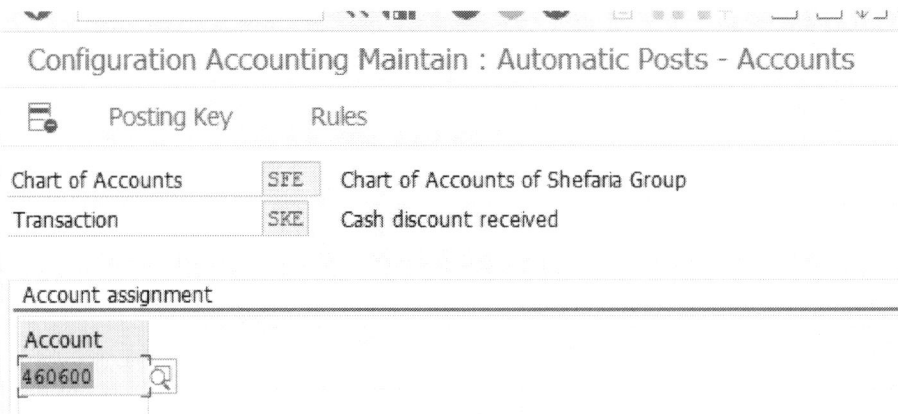

Fig 11

# UNDER AND OVER PAYMENTS (C/U)

T Code SPRO, FS00

These are also P & L (revenue & Expense) accounts in which SAP posts the differences when certain criteria are met:

1. There is a difference between the amount being posted vs the document value in this posting
2. This difference is within the tolerance limits for an automatically adjusted posting defined for that employee
3. Cash discount adjustments can't take care of this difference

Since these under and over payments can occur from customers and to vendors alike, often companies prefer to have a sub-group of "Other" accounts under P & L to set up such accounts in that group. In our case, we will keep it simple and like for cash discount accounts set up 2 G/L accounts 900100 and 900200 under P & L group for one Under Payment Account and the other Over Payment Account. Enter data as in Fig 1

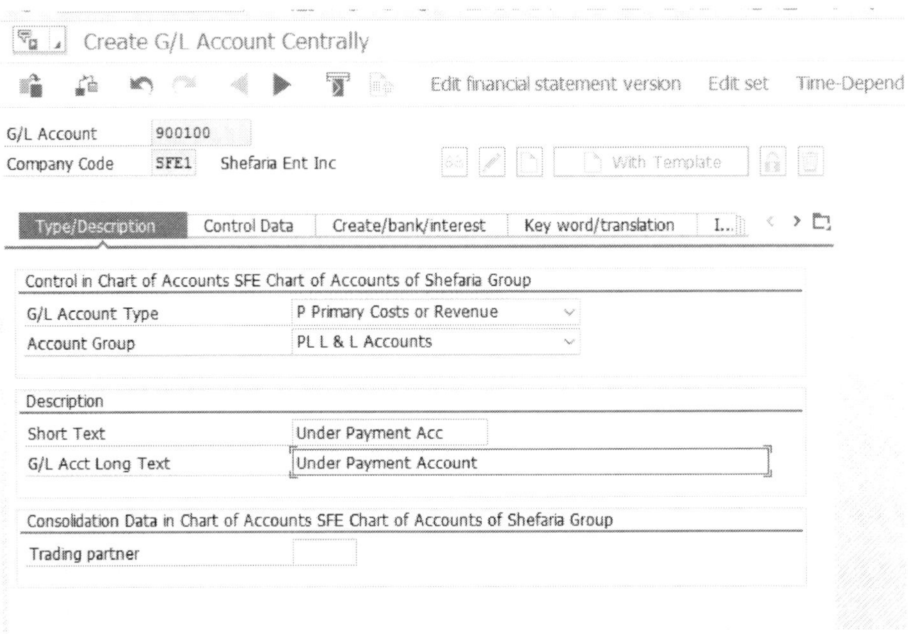

Fig 1

Fig 2

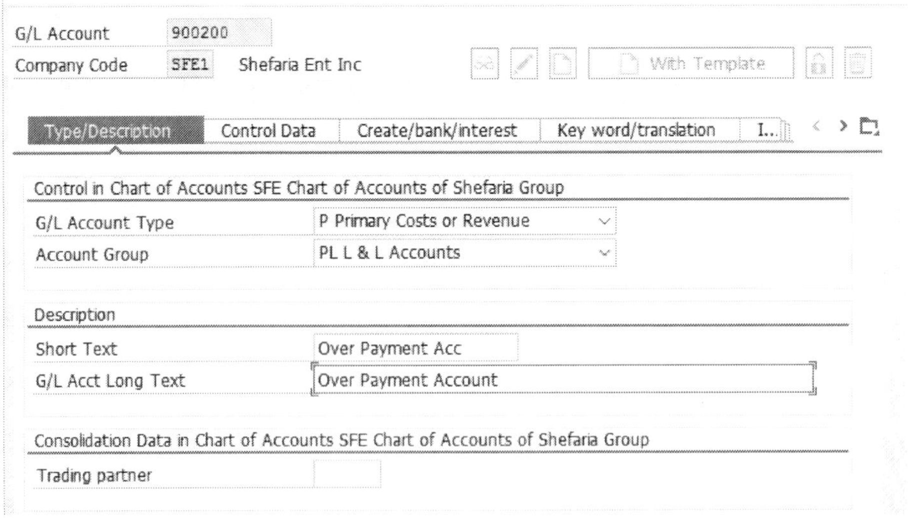

200

For both enter Control data and Create/Bank/Interest Data as:

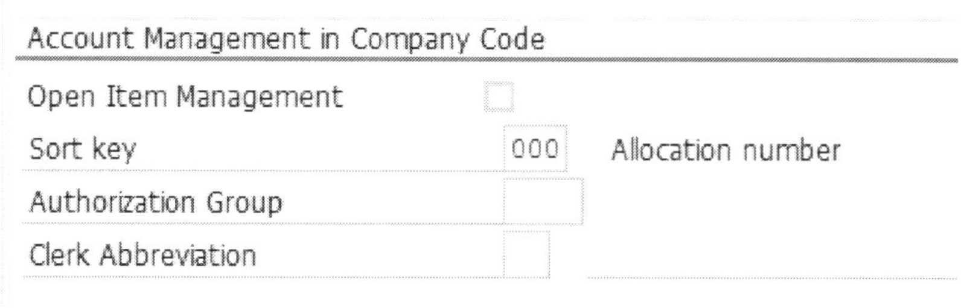

**Account Management in Company Code**

| | | |
|---|---|---|
| Open Item Management | ☐ | |
| Sort key | 000 | Allocation number |
| Authorization Group | | |
| Clerk Abbreviation | | |

Fig 3

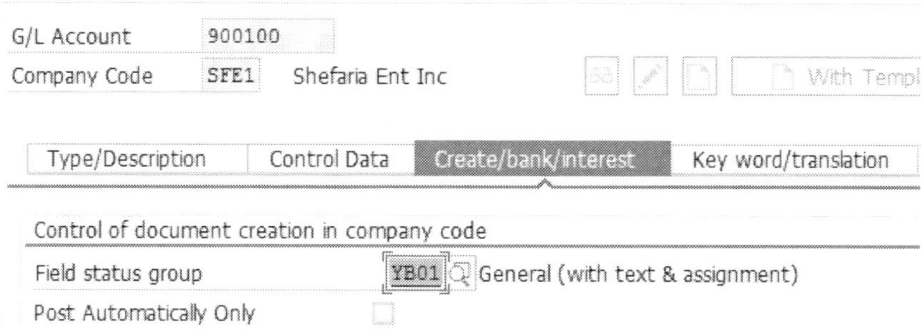

| G/L Account | 900100 | |
|---|---|---|
| Company Code | SFE1 | Shefaria Ent Inc |

| Type/Description | Control Data | Create/bank/interest | Key word/translation |

**Control of document creation in company code**

| | | |
|---|---|---|
| Field status group | YB01 🔍 | General (with text & assignment) |
| Post Automatically Only | ☐ | |

Fig 4

The next step is to make SAP recognize these 2 accounts 900100 and 900200 to post the Under and Over payments to via the process key ZDI:

The path to do that is:

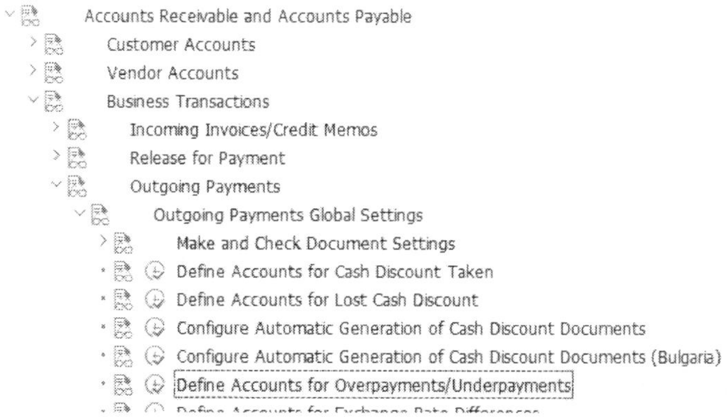

- Accounts Receivable and Accounts Payable
  - Customer Accounts
  - Vendor Accounts
  - Business Transactions
    - Incoming Invoices/Credit Memos
    - Release for Payment
    - Outgoing Payments
      - Outgoing Payments Global Settings
        - Make and Check Document Settings
        - Define Accounts for Cash Discount Taken
        - Define Accounts for Lost Cash Discount
        - Configure Automatic Generation of Cash Discount Documents
        - Configure Automatic Generation of Cash Discount Documents (Bulgaria)
        - Define Accounts for Overpayments/Underpayments
        - Define Accounts for Exchange Rate Differences

Fig 5

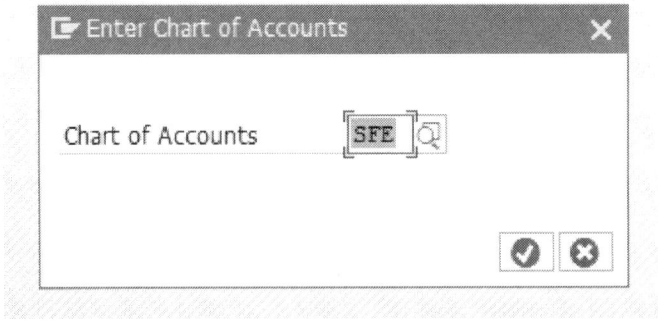

Fig 6

Ensure ZDI is present:

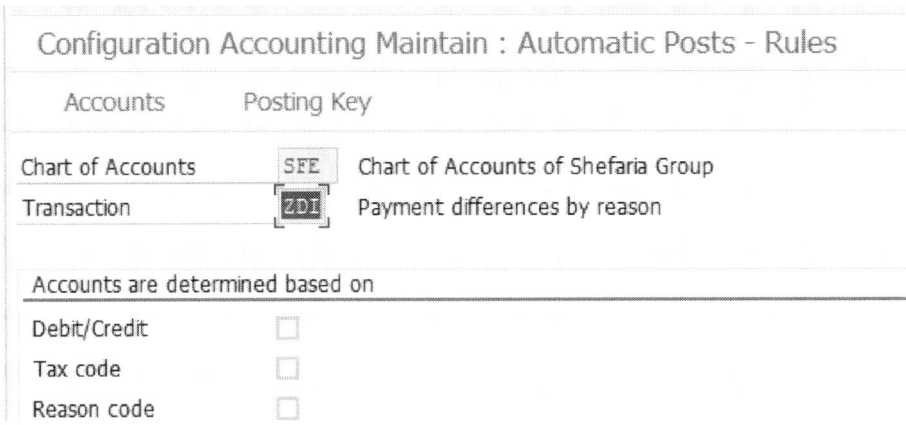

Fig 7

Click on the Debit/Credit Key and Save:

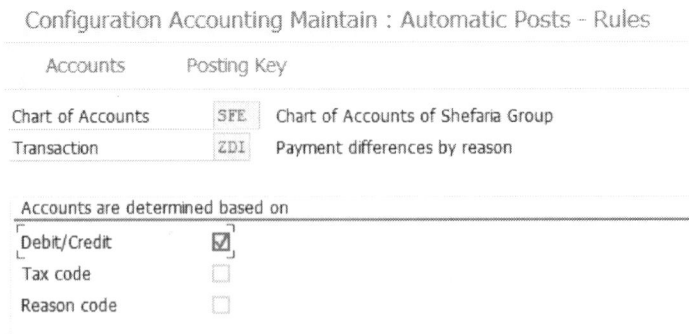

Fig 8

Along with the Save message at the bottom, a new window opens up to enter the 2 accounts:

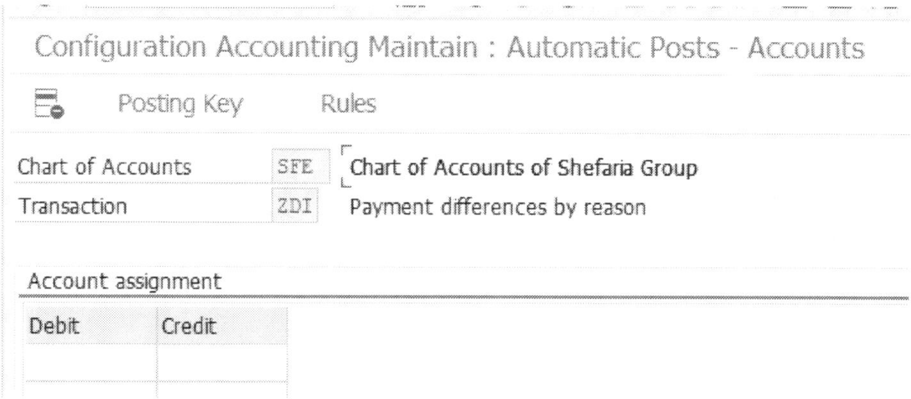

Configuration Accounting Maintain : Automatic Posts - Accounts

Posting Key          Rules

Chart of Accounts      SFE    Chart of Accounts of Shefaria Group
Transaction            ZDI    Payment differences by reason

Account assignment

| Debit | Credit |
|-------|--------|
|       |        |

Fig 9

The underpayment account in the Debit field and the over, payment account goes into Credit field:

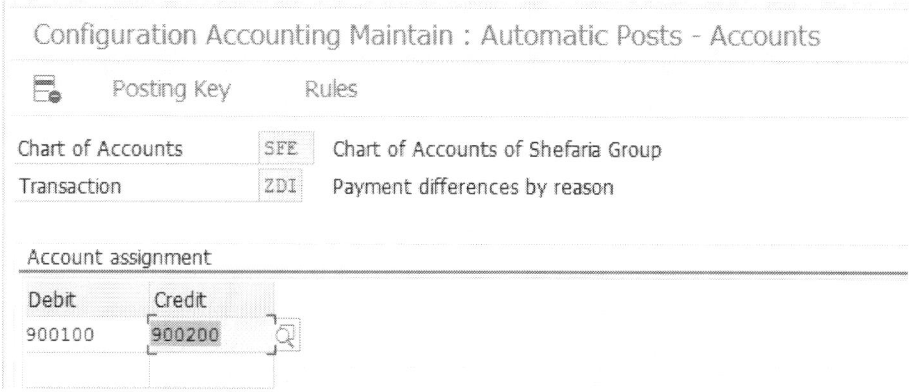

Configuration Accounting Maintain : Automatic Posts - Accounts

Posting Key          Rules

Chart of Accounts      SFE    Chart of Accounts of Shefaria Group
Transaction            ZDI    Payment differences by reason

Account assignment

| Debit  | Credit |
|--------|--------|
| 900100 | 900200 |
|        |        |

Fig 10

Save the configuration.

**HANA CHANGE:** Because document splitting is mandatory in HANA, SAP will require you to assign an item category since each document is assigned to a accounting transaction variant and each document row to an item category.

This is done in the following path in SPRO:

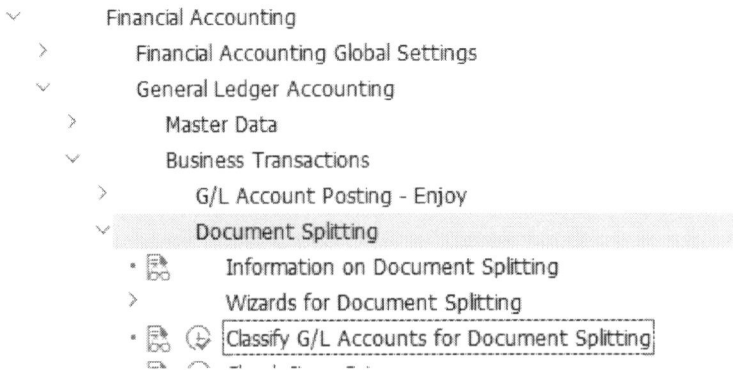

Fig 11

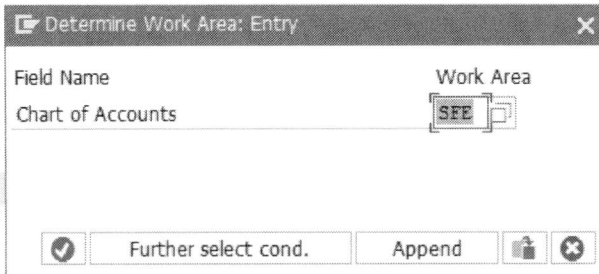

Fig 12

Add the new G/Ls to the list of those already there, if any by clicking on New Entries:

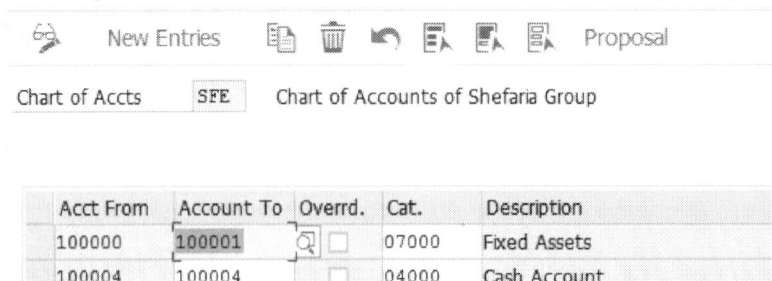

Fig 13

New Entries    Proposal

Chart of Accts    SFE    Chart of Accounts of Shefaria Group

| Acct From | Account To | Overrd. | Cat. | Description |
|---|---|---|---|---|
| 100000 | 100001 | ☐ | 07000 | Fixed Assets |
| 100004 | 100004 | ☐ | 04000 | Cash Account |
| 100005 | 100005 | ☐ | 03100 | Vendor: Special G/L Transaction |
| 100006 | 100006 | ☐ | 20000 | Expense |
| 100007 | 100007 | ☐ | 20000 | Expense |
| 100008 | 100008 | ☐ | 30000 | Revenue |
| 100009 | 100009 | ☐ | 04000 | Cash Account |
| 107000 | 107000 | ☐ | 20000 | Expense |
| 119000 | 119000 | ☐ | 20000 | Expense |
| 134000 | 134000 | ☑ | 20000 | Expense |
| 400015 | 400015 | ☐ | 20000 | Expense |
| 450000 | 459999 | ☑ | 30000 | Revenue |
| 460000 | 469999 | ☑ | 20000 | Expense |
| 634000 | 634000 | ☑ | 20000 | Expense |
| 900100 | 900100 | ☐ | 30000 | Revenue |
| 900200 | 900200 | ☐ | 20000 | Expense |

Fig 14

Say OK to the message if it comes:

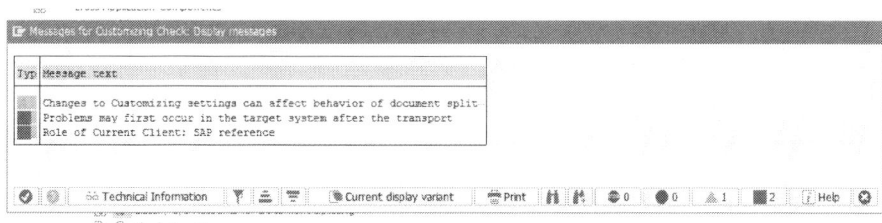

Messages for Customizing Check: Display messages

| Typ | Message text |
|---|---|
|  | Changes to Customizing settings can affect behavior of document split |
|  | Problems may first occur in the target system after the transport |
|  | Role of Current Client: SAP reference |

Technical Information    Current display variant    Print    0   0   1   2   Help

Fig 15

Save the configuration.

# POSTING INCOMING UNDER/OVER

# PAYMENTS WITH, W/O DISCOUNTS (U)

Now that we have our over/under and discount G/Ls in place along with employee tolerances, we can see the effects of the same via actual postings with various scenarios.

T Code F-28

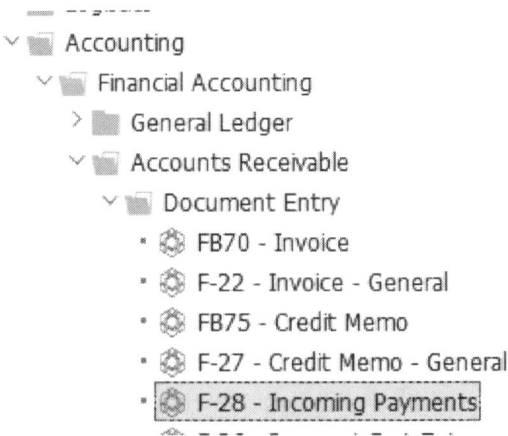

Fig 1

206

# I. POSTING AN AMOUNT WITHIN THE TOLERANCE LIMITS

## Post Incoming Payments: Header Data

### Process Open Items

| | | | | | | |
|---|---|---|---|---|---|---|
| Document Date | 042419 | Type | DZ | Company Code | SFE1 | |
| Posting Date | 04/25/2019 | Period | 4 | Currency/Rate | CAD | |
| Document Number | | | | Translation dte | | |
| Reference | | | | Cross-CC Number | | |
| Doc.Header Text | | | | Trading part.BA | | |
| Clearing Text | | | | | | |

**Bank data**

| | | | |
|---|---|---|---|
| Account | 107000 | Business Area | |
| Amount | 1200 | | |
| Amt.in loc.cur. | | | |
| Bank Charges | | LC Bank Charges | |
| Value date | | Profit Center | |
| Text | | Assignment | |

**Open item selection**

| | | | Additional selections |
|---|---|---|---|
| Account | 10001 | | ⦿ None |
| Account Type | D | ☐ Other Accounts | ○ Amount |
| Special G/L Ind | | ☑ Standard OIs | ○ Document Number |
| Payt Advice No. | | | ○ Posting Date |
| ☐ Distribute by Age | | | ○ Dunning Area |
| ☐ Automatic Search | | | ○ Others |

Fig 5

## Post Incoming Payments Process open items

Distribute Difference  Charge Off Difference  Editing Options  Cash Disc. Due  Create Dispute Case

**Standard** | Partial Pmt | Res.Items | WH Tax

Account items 10001 Showroom for SFE1 furniture

| Document... | D.. | Document... | P.. | Bu... | Da... | CAD Gross | | CashDiscount | CDPer. |
|---|---|---|---|---|---|---|---|---|---|
| 1400000000 | DZ | 04/24/2019 | 06 | 0 | | | 999.55 | | |
| 1400000001 | DZ | 04/24/2019 | 06 | 0 | | | 500.00 | | |
| 1600000000 | DA | 04/24/2019 | 01 | 0 | | | 1,250.00 | | |
| 1800000003 | DR | 04/22/2019 | 01 | 6- | | | 2,341.00 | 93.64 | 4.000 |
| 1800000004 | DR | 04/22/2019 | 01 | 6- | | | 345.00 | | |
| 1800000005 | DR | 02/22/2019 | 01 | 28- | | | 10,000.00 | | |
| 1800000006 | DR | 10/01/2019 | 01 | 174- | | | 103.47 | 2.07 | 2.000 |
| 1800000007 | DR | 01/12/2018 | 01 | 99 | | | 200.00 | | |
| 1800000008 | DR | 01/11/2018 | 01 | 99 | | | 5,600.00 | | |

‹ › 

Am...  Gross<...  Currency  Items  Items  Disc.  Disc.

**Processing Status**

| | | | |
|---|---|---|---|
| Number of Items | 11 | Amount Entered | 1,200.00 |
| Display from Item | 1 | Assigned | 1,250.00 |
| Reason Code | | Difference Postings | |
| Display in clearing currency | | Not Assigned | 50.00- |

Fig 6

When we try to simulate it this time, we find SAP determined the difference to post to the underpayment account from configuration as it is within $100:

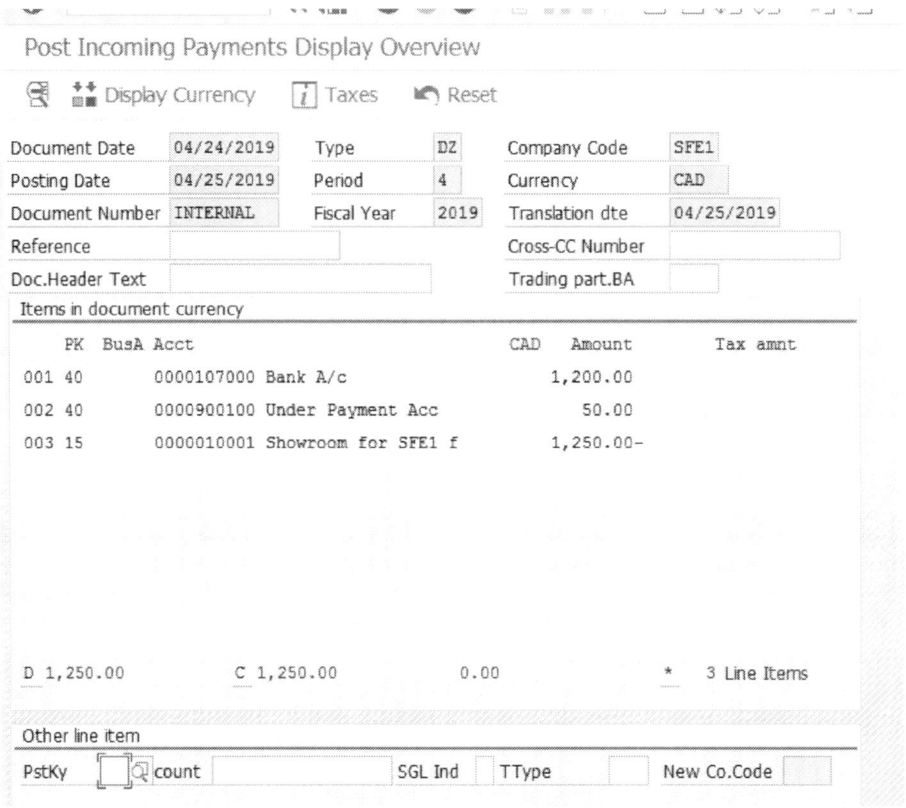

Post Incoming Payments Display Overview

⊟ ⠿ Display Currency  ⓘ Taxes  ↺ Reset

| Document Date | 04/24/2019 | Type | DZ | Company Code | SFE1 |
|---|---|---|---|---|---|
| Posting Date | 04/25/2019 | Period | 4 | Currency | CAD |
| Document Number | INTERNAL | Fiscal Year | 2019 | Translation dte | 04/25/2019 |
| Reference | | | | Cross-CC Number | |
| Doc.Header Text | | | | Trading part.BA | |

Items in document currency

| PK | BusA | Acct | | CAD | Amount | Tax amnt |
|---|---|---|---|---|---|---|
| 001 | 40 | 0000107000 | Bank A/c | | 1,200.00 | |
| 002 | 40 | 0000900100 | Under Payment Acc | | 50.00 | |
| 003 | 15 | 0000010001 | Showroom for SFE1 f | | 1,250.00- | |

D 1,250.00        C 1,250.00           0.00           *    3 Line Items

Other line item

| PstKy | | count | | SGL Ind | TType | | New Co.Code | |
|---|---|---|---|---|---|---|---|---|

Fig 7

Had there been any cash discounts associated with this, it would have first posted to that cash discount and then the remaining balance (subject to the balance being a max of $100, to this underpayment account) as in next section.

We can now post the document:

✓ Document 1400000002 was posted in company code SFE1

Fig 8

208

When we run the payables again, note there is no balance for this invoice, which we posted against earlier as it wrote off the amount since it was less than the tolerance limits we have defined.

Before:

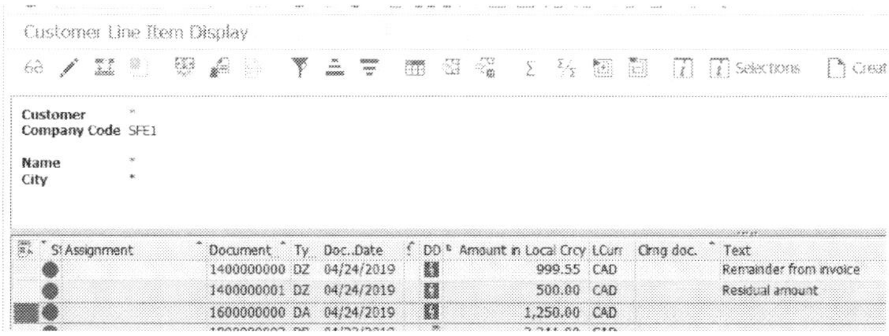

Fig 9

After – the document is missing:

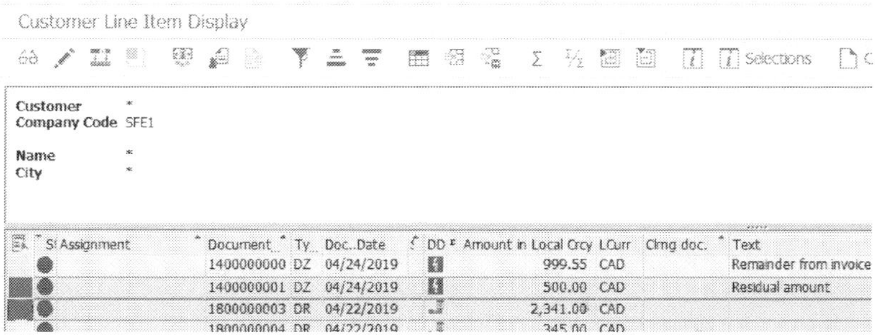

Fig 10

If we run FBL3N/H for the G/L 90100 we find this amount in the report:

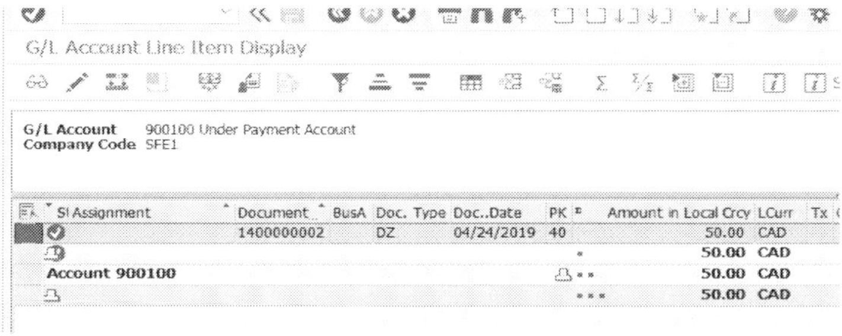

Fig 11

# I.    EFFECT OF TOLERANCE LIMITS

Let us try to first post an incoming payment *outside of tolerance limits* from a customer in F-28:

Ensure that account type D comes pre-entered. Enter the rest of the data in this by now familiar screen – Bank G/L account, amount, posting date, document date, value date, customer # etc:

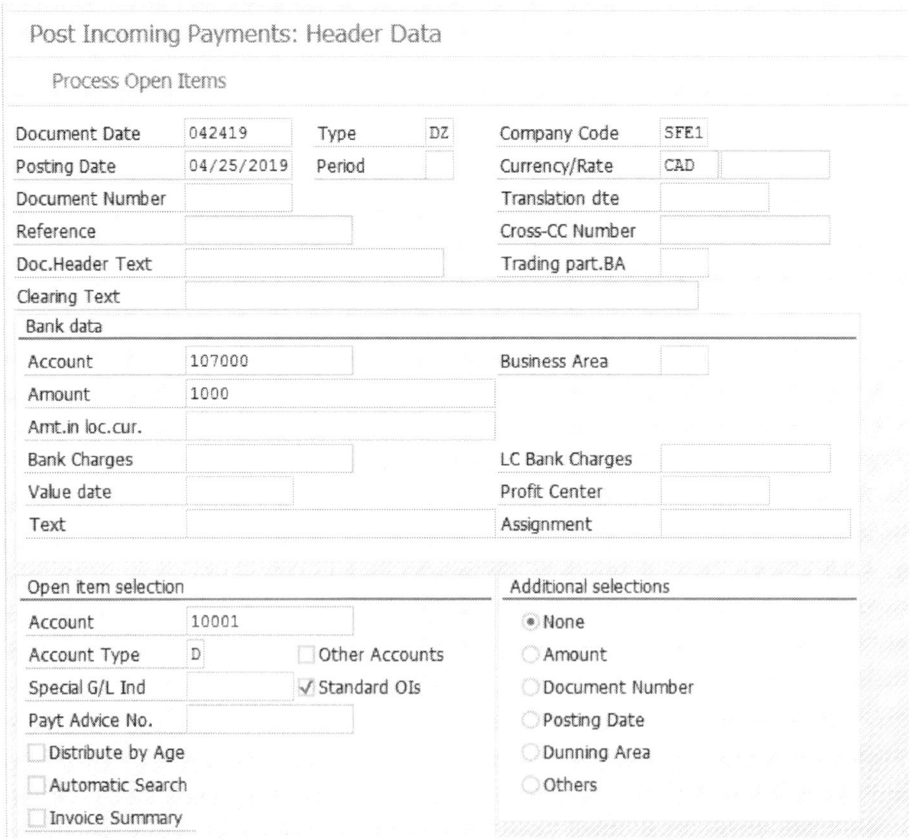

| Post Incoming Payments: Header Data | | | | | |
|---|---|---|---|---|---|
| Process Open Items | | | | | |
| Document Date | 042419 | Type | DZ | Company Code | SFE1 |
| Posting Date | 04/25/2019 | Period | | Currency/Rate | CAD |
| Document Number | | | | Translation dte | |
| Reference | | | | Cross-CC Number | |
| Doc.Header Text | | | | Trading part.BA | |
| Clearing Text | | | | | |

**Bank data**

| Account | 107000 | Business Area | |
|---|---|---|---|
| Amount | 1000 | | |
| Amt.in loc.cur. | | | |
| Bank Charges | | LC Bank Charges | |
| Value date | | Profit Center | |
| Text | | Assignment | |

**Open item selection**

| Account | 10001 | |
|---|---|---|
| Account Type | D | ☐ Other Accounts |
| Special G/L Ind | | ☑ Standard OIs |
| Payt Advice No. | | |
| ☐ Distribute by Age | | |
| ☐ Automatic Search | | |
| ☐ Invoice Summary | | |

**Additional selections**

- ● None
- ○ Amount
- ○ Document Number
- ○ Posting Date
- ○ Dunning Area
- ○ Others

Fig 2

Again, select the appropriate line against which this amount needs to be adjusted. In our example, we will adjust it against line 3:

| | Distribute Difference | Charge Off Difference | Editing Options | Cash Disc. Due | Create Dispute Case |
|---|---|---|---|---|---|

| Standard | Partial Pmt | Res.Items | WH Tax |
|---|---|---|---|

Account items 10001 Showroom for SFE1 furniture

| Document... | D.. | Document... | P.. | Bu... | Da... | CAD Gross | CashDiscount | CDPer. |
|---|---|---|---|---|---|---|---|---|
| 1400000000 | DZ | 04/24/2019 | 06 | | 0 | 999.55 | | |
| 1400000001 | DZ | 04/24/2019 | 06 | | 0 | 500.00 | | |
| 1600000000 | DA | 04/24/2019 | 01 | | 0 | 1,250.00 | | |
| 1800000003 | DR | 04/22/2019 | 01 | | 6- | 2,341.00 | 93.64 | 4.000 |
| 1800000004 | DR | 04/22/2019 | 01 | | 6- | 345.00 | | |
| 1800000005 | DR | 02/22/2019 | 01 | | 28- | 10,000.00 | | |
| 1800000006 | DR | 10/01/2019 | 01 | | 174- | 103.47 | 2.07 | 2.000 |
| 1800000007 | DR | 01/12/2018 | 01 | | 99 | 200.00 | | |
| 1800000008 | DR | 01/11/2018 | 01 | | 99 | 5,600.00 | | |

| | | | | | | Am... | Gross<... | Currency | Items | Items | Disc. | Disc. |
|---|---|---|---|---|---|---|---|---|---|---|---|---|

Processing Status

| Number of Items | 11 | Amount Entered | 1,000.00 |
|---|---|---|---|
| Display from Item | 1 | Assigned | 1,250.00 |
| Reason Code | | Difference Postings | |
| Display in clearing currency | | Not Assigned | 250.00- |

Fig 3

Note the Not assigned amount, the difference of the actual and the amount being posted. This amount needs to now be posted to the under payment account as the customer has underpaid us by this amount. To verify if it will work, simulate the document:

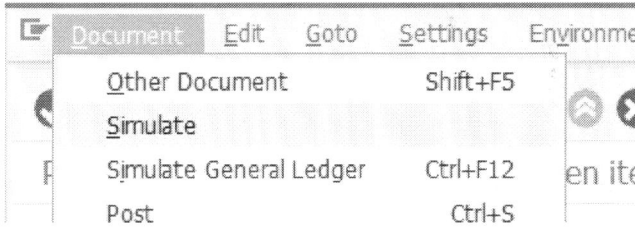

| | Document | Edit | Goto | Settings | Environme |
|---|---|---|---|---|---|
| | Other Document | | Shift+F5 | | |
| | Simulate | | | | |
| | Simulate General Ledger | | Ctrl+F12 | | en ite |
| | Post | | Ctrl+S | | |

And get the message at the bottom:

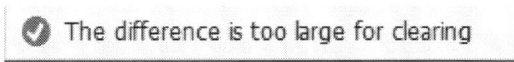

The difference is too large for clearing

Fig 4

This means we have not told SAP what to do with the difference of and the difference being outside of the employee's tolerance limits

211

that we defined earlier to be only $100, it will not post automatically. We do have the option to post it as partial payment and throwing this difference amount back into the customer's AR as we saw in the earlier chapter.

# II.   POSTING WITH A CASH DISCOUNT AND A DIFFERENCE WITHIN TOLERANCE LIMITS

Line 3 has applicable cash discounts and we can post an amount, which is within tolerance limits after the cash discount has been applied:

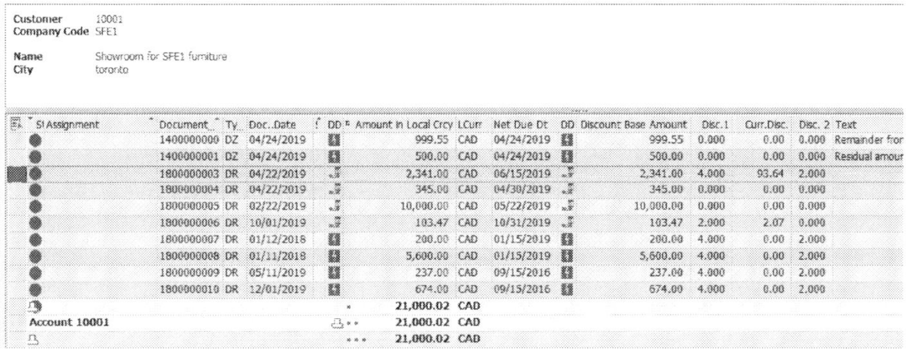

| SI Assignment | Document | Ty | Doc..Date | DD | Amount in Local Crcy | LCurr | Net Due Dt | DD | Discount Base Amount | Disc.1 | Curr.Disc. | Disc. 2 | Text |
|---|---|---|---|---|---|---|---|---|---|---|---|---|---|
| ● | 1400000000 | DZ | 04/24/2019 | | 999.55 | CAD | 04/24/2019 | | 999.55 | 0.000 | 0.00 | 0.000 | Remainder from |
| ● | 1400000001 | DZ | 04/24/2019 | | 500.00 | CAD | 04/24/2019 | | 500.00 | 0.000 | 0.00 | 0.000 | Residual amour |
| ● | 1800000003 | DR | 04/22/2019 | | 2,341.00 | CAD | 06/15/2019 | | 2,341.00 | 4.000 | 93.64 | 2.000 | |
| ● | 1800000004 | DR | 04/22/2019 | | 345.00 | CAD | 04/30/2019 | | 345.00 | 0.000 | 0.00 | 0.000 | |
| ● | 1800000005 | DR | 02/22/2019 | | 10,000.00 | CAD | 05/22/2019 | | 10,000.00 | 0.000 | 0.00 | 0.000 | |
| ● | 1800000006 | DR | 10/01/2018 | | 103.47 | CAD | 10/31/2019 | | 103.47 | 2.000 | 2.07 | 0.000 | |
| ● | 1800000007 | DR | 01/12/2018 | | 200.00 | CAD | 01/15/2019 | | 200.00 | 4.000 | 0.00 | 2.000 | |
| ● | 1800000008 | DR | 01/11/2018 | | 5,600.00 | CAD | 01/15/2019 | | 5,600.00 | 4.000 | 0.00 | 2.000 | |
| ● | 1800000009 | DR | 05/11/2019 | | 237.00 | CAD | 09/15/2016 | | 237.00 | 4.000 | 0.00 | 2.000 | |
| ● | 1800000010 | DR | 12/01/2019 | | 674.00 | CAD | 09/15/2016 | | 674.00 | 4.000 | 0.00 | 2.000 | |
| | | | | | 21,000.02 | CAD | | | | | | | |
| Account 10001 | | | | | 21,000.02 | CAD | | | | | | | |
| | | | | | 21,000.02 | CAD | | | | | | | |

Customer 10001
Company Code SFE1

Name Showroom for SFE1 furniture
City toronto

Fig 10

Post Incoming Payments: Header Data

Process Open Items

| Document Date | 042519 | Type | DZ | Company Code | SFE1 |
|---|---|---|---|---|---|
| Posting Date | 04/25/2019 | Period | 4 | Currency/Rate | CAD |
| Document Number | | | | Translation dte | |
| Reference | | | | Cross-CC Number | |
| Doc.Header Text | | | | Trading part.BA | |
| Clearing Text | | | | | |

Bank data

| Account | 107000 | | Business Area | |
|---|---|---|---|---|
| Amount | 2200 | | | |
| Amt.in loc.cur. | | | | |
| Bank Charges | | | LC Bank Charges | |
| Value date | | | Profit Center | |
| Text | | | Assignment | |

Open item selection

| Account | 10001 |
|---|---|
| Account Type | D | ☐ Other Accounts |
| Special G/L Ind | | ✓ Standard OIs |
| Payt Advice No. | |
| ☐ Distribute by Age | |
| ☐ Automatic Search | |

Additional selections

- ◉ None
- ○ Amount
- ○ Document Number
- ○ Posting Date
- ○ Dunning Area
- ○ Others

Fig 11

As before, we select the appropriate line:

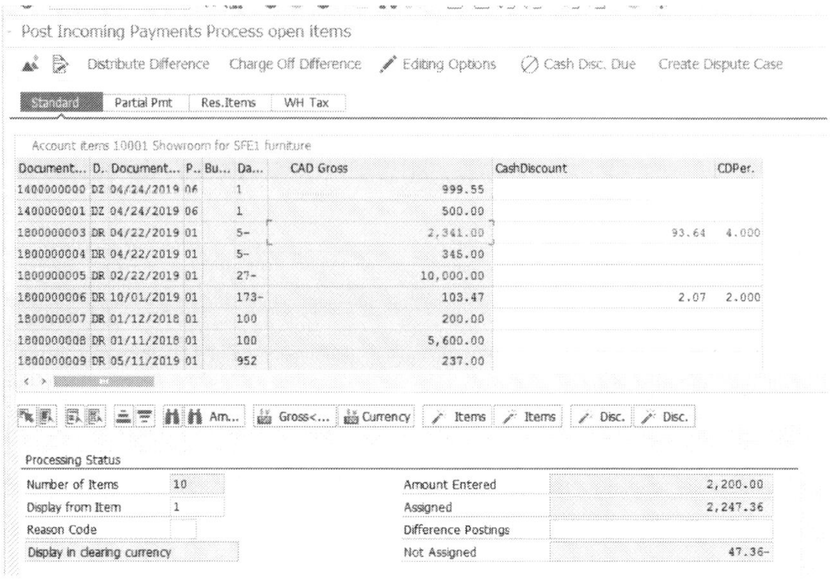

Fig 12

Note the difference, which is still unaccounted for after applying the cash discount. However, since this is within the tolerance limits, let us try to simulate this after allocating the difference:

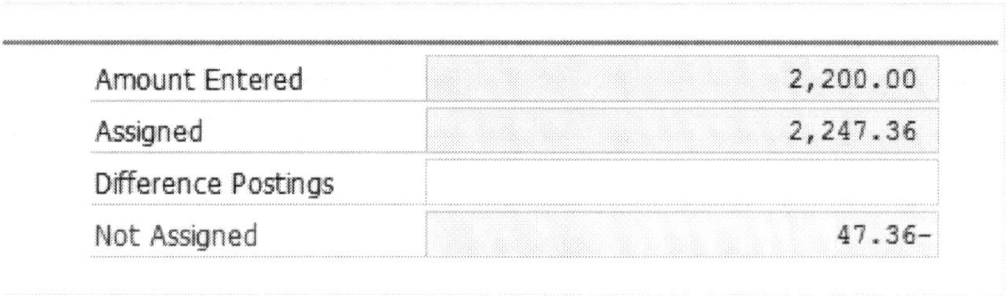

| Amount Entered | 2,200.00 |
|---|---|
| Assigned | 2,247.36 |
| Difference Postings | |
| Not Assigned | 47.36– |

Fig 13

## Post Incoming Payments Display Overview

🔲 ⁑ Display Currency  ℹ️ Taxes  🔙 Reset

| Document Date | 04/25/2019 | Type | DZ | Company Code | SFE1 |
|---|---|---|---|---|---|
| Posting Date | 04/25/2019 | Period | 4 | Currency | CAD |
| Document Number | INTERNAL | Fiscal Year | 2019 | Translation dte | 04/25/2019 |
| Reference | | | | Cross-CC Number | |
| Doc.Header Text | | | | Trading part.BA | |

Items in document currency

| | PK | BusA | Acct | | CAD | Amount | Tax amnt |
|---|---|---|---|---|---|---|---|
| 001 | 40 | | 0000107000 | Bank A/c | | 2,200.00 | |
| 002 | 40 | | 0000450600 | Cash Dic Given | | 93.64 | |
| 003 | 40 | | 0000900100 | Under Payment Acc | | 47.36 | |
| 004 | 15 | | 0000010001 | Showroom for SFE1 f | | 2,341.00- | |

Fig 14

We now find SAP returning with the G/L for cash discount given and posts the balance back into the customer A/R.

✅ Document 1400000004 was posted in company code SFE1

Fig 15

The entire document disappears from the AR, some for payment amount, some for the discount given and the rest written off:

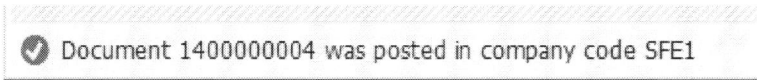

Fig 16

215

# III. OVERPAYMENT WITH CASH DISCOUNT

Let us attempt to post against an invoice an amount that will leave a difference more than the max permissible after the applicable cash discount is applied:

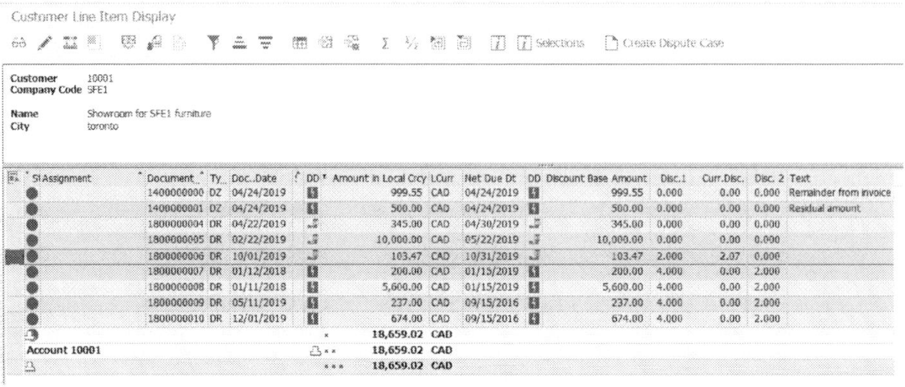

| St | Assignment | Document | Ty | Doc..Date | DD | Amount in Local Crcy | LCurr | Net Due Dt | DD | Discount Base Amount | Disc.1 | Curr.Disc. | Disc. 2 | Text |
|----|-----------|----------|-----|-----------|-----|--------------------|-------|-----------|-----|--------------------|--------|-----------|---------|------|
| | | 1400000000 | DZ | 04/24/2019 | | 999.55 | CAD | 04/24/2019 | | 999.55 | 0.000 | 0.00 | 0.000 | Remainder from invoice |
| | | 1400000001 | DZ | 04/24/2019 | | 500.00 | CAD | 04/24/2019 | | 500.00 | 0.000 | 0.00 | 0.000 | Residual amount |
| | | 1800000004 | DR | 04/22/2019 | | 345.00 | CAD | 04/30/2019 | | 345.00 | 0.000 | 0.00 | 0.000 | |
| | | 1800000005 | DR | 02/22/2019 | | 10,000.00 | CAD | 05/22/2019 | | 10,000.00 | 0.000 | 0.00 | 0.000 | |
| | | 1800000006 | DR | 10/01/2019 | | 103.47 | CAD | 10/31/2019 | | 103.47 | 2.000 | 2.07 | 0.000 | |
| | | 1800000007 | DR | 01/12/2018 | | 200.00 | CAD | 01/15/2019 | | 200.00 | 4.000 | 0.00 | 2.000 | |
| | | 1800000008 | DR | 01/11/2018 | | 5,600.00 | CAD | 01/15/2019 | | 5,600.00 | 4.000 | 0.00 | 2.000 | |
| | | 1800000009 | DR | 05/11/2019 | | 237.00 | CAD | 09/15/2016 | | 237.00 | 4.000 | 0.00 | 2.000 | |
| | | 1800000010 | DR | 12/01/2019 | | 674.00 | CAD | 09/15/2016 | | 674.00 | 4.000 | 0.00 | 2.000 | |
| | Account 10001 | | | | | 18,659.02 | CAD | | | | | | | |
| | | | | | | 18,659.02 | CAD | | | | | | | |
| | | | | | | 18,659.02 | CAD | | | | | | | |

**Customer Line Item Display**

Customer 10001
Company Code SFE1

Name Showroom for SFE1 furniture
City toronto

Fig 17

## Post Incoming Payments: Header Data

### Process Open Items

| | | | | | |
|---|---|---|---|---|---|
| Document Date | 042519 | Type | DZ | Company Code | SFE1 |
| Posting Date | 04/25/2019 | Period | | Currency/Rate | CAD |
| Document Number | | | | Translation dte | |
| Reference | | | | Cross-CC Number | |
| Doc.Header Text | | | | Trading part.BA | |
| Clearing Text | | | | | |

**Bank data**

| | | | |
|---|---|---|---|
| Account | 107000 | Business Area | |
| Amount | 120 | | |
| Amt.in loc.cur. | | | |
| Bank Charges | | LC Bank Charges | |
| Value date | | Profit Center | |
| Text | | Assignment | |

**Open item selection**

| | |
|---|---|
| Account | 10001 |
| Account Type | D |
| Special G/L Ind | ✓ Standard OIs |
| Payt Advice No. | |
| ☐ Distribute by Age | |
| ☐ Automatic Search | |
| ☐ Invoice Summary | |

☐ Other Accounts

**Additional selections**

- ⦿ None
- ○ Amount
- ○ Document Number
- ○ Posting Date
- ○ Dunning Area
- ○ Others

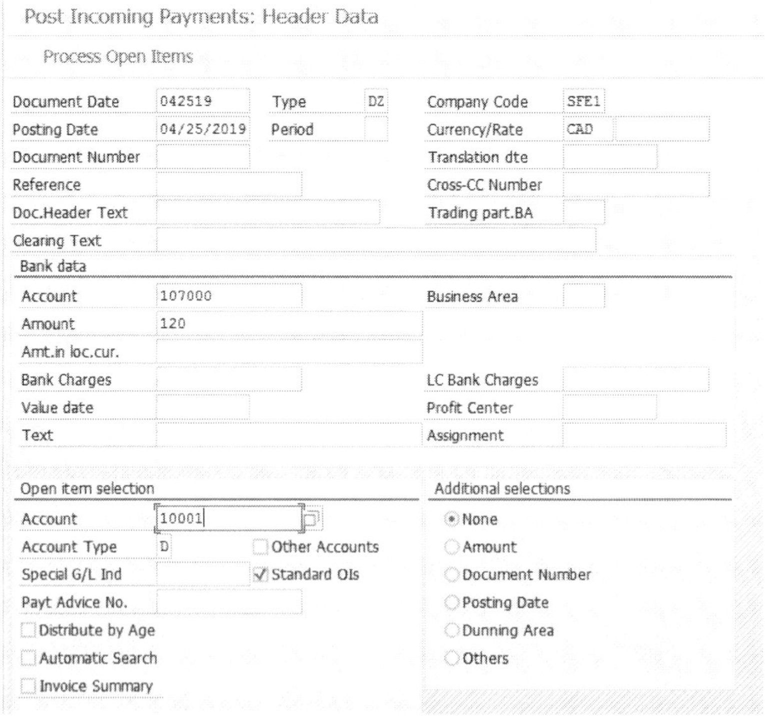

Fig 18

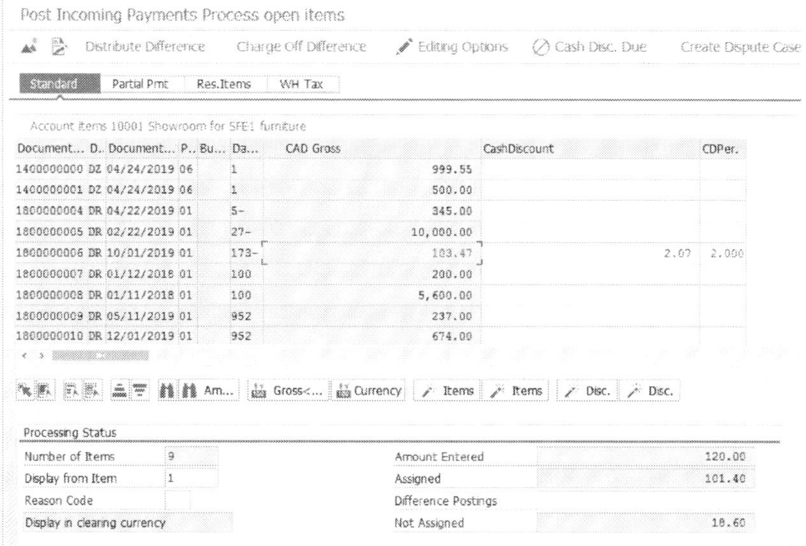

## Fig 19

When we try to simulate this, we notice the unassigned difference after adjusting the cash discount is being posted to the over payment account

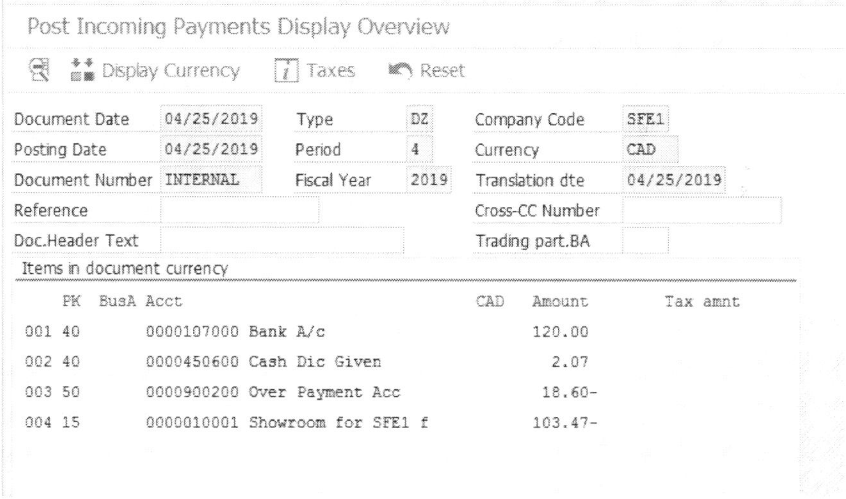

## Fig 20

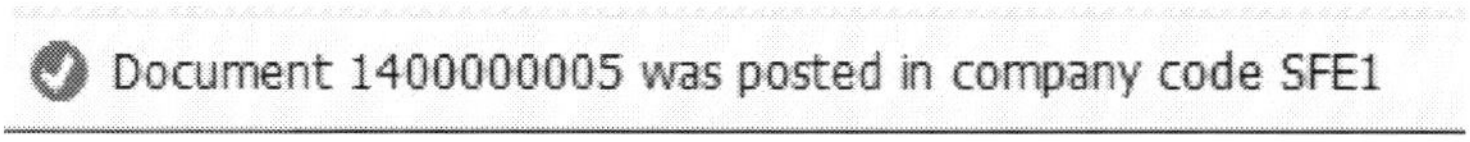

Document 1400000005 was posted in company code SFE1

# POSTING OUTGOING UNDER/OVER PAYMENTS WITH, W/O DISCOUNTS (U)

T Code F-53

Let us now post an outgoing payment to a vendor within tolerance limits using F-53:

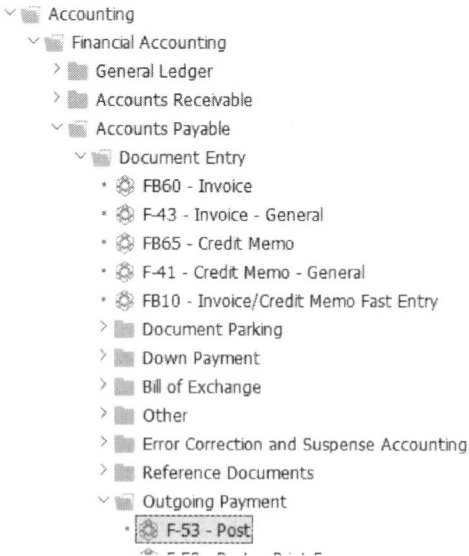

Fig 1

# I. EFFECT OF TOLERANCE LIMITS:

Let us look at and work off the AP of a vendor in FBL1N/H:

**Vendor** 100000
**Company Code** SFE1

**Name** WOOD SUPPLIER
**City** toronto

| | St | Assignment | Document | Doc. Type | DocDate | DD | Amount in Local Crcy | LCurr | Clrng doc |
|---|---|---|---|---|---|---|---|---|---|
| | ◉ | | 1900000000 | KR | 04/22/2019 | | 1,500.00- | CAD | |
| | | | 1900000001 | KR | 04/22/2019 | | 1,189.00- | CAD | |
| | | | 1900000002 | KR | 04/22/2019 | | 1,189.00- | CAD | |
| | | | 1900000003 | KR | 04/22/2019 | | 1,189.00- | CAD | |
| | | | 1900000004 | KR | 04/24/2019 | | 3,450.00- | CAD | |
| | | | | | | | 8,517.00- | CAD | |
| | Account 100000 | | | | | | 8,517.00- | CAD | |
| | | | | | | | 8,517.00- | CAD | |

Fig 1

F-53, enter details as you did for the customer AR:

**Post Outgoing Payments: Header Data**

Process Open Items

| | | | | |
|---|---|---|---|---|
| Document Date | 042519 | Type | KZ | Company Code | SFE1 |
| Posting Date | 04/25/2019 | Period | 4 | Currency/Rate | CAD |
| Document Number | | | | Translation dte | |
| Reference | | | | Cross-CC Number | |
| Doc.Header Text | | | | Trading part.BA | |
| Clearing Text | | | | | |

Bank data

| | | | |
|---|---|---|---|
| Account | 107000 | Business Area | |
| Amount | 1200 | | |
| Amt.in loc.cur. | | | |
| Bank Charges | | LC Bank Charges | |
| Value date | | Profit Center | |
| Text | | Assignment | |

| Open item selection | | | | Additional selections |
|---|---|---|---|---|
| Account | 100000 | | | ◉ None |
| Account Type | K | ☐ Other Accounts | | ○ Amount |
| Special G/L Ind | | ☑ Standard OIs | | ○ Document Number |
| Payt Advice No. | | | | ○ Posting Date |
| ☐ Distribute by Age | | | | ○ Dunning Area |
| ☐ Automatic Search | | | | ○ Others |

Fig 2

219

Hit Enter or click on                  and the vendor's open line items come up in the next screen:

Post Outgoing Payments Process open items

| | Distribute Difference | Charge Off Difference | Editing Options | Cash Disc. Due |
|---|---|---|---|---|

**Standard** | Partial Pmt | Res.Items | WH Tax

Account items 100000 WOOD SUPPLIER

| Document... | D.. | Document... | P.. | Bu... | Da... | CAD Gross | CashDiscount | CDPer. |
|---|---|---|---|---|---|---|---|---|
| 1900000000 | KR | 04/22/2019 | 31 | | 11- | 1,500.00- | 30.00- | 2.000 |
| 1900000001 | KR | 04/22/2019 | 31 | | 11- | 1,189.00- | 23.78- | 2.000 |
| 1900000002 | KR | 04/22/2019 | 31 | | 11- | 1,189.00- | 23.78- | 2.000 |
| 1900000003 | KR | 04/22/2019 | 31 | | 11- | 1,189.00- | 23.78- | 2.000 |
| 1900000004 | KR | 04/24/2019 | 31 | | 13- | 3,450.00- | 69.00- | 2.000 |

< >

| | | | | | Am... | Gross<... | Currency | Items | Items | Disc. | Disc. |
|---|---|---|---|---|---|---|---|---|---|---|---|

Processing Status

| Number of Items | 5 | | Amount Entered | 1,200.00- |
|---|---|---|---|---|
| Display from Item | 1 | | Assigned | 8,346.66- |
| Reason Code | | | Difference Postings | |
| Display in clearing currency | | | Not Assigned | 7,146.66 |

Fig 3

Once again, this is reflective of the vendor line item balance in FBL1N, except documents that may have already been selected in a payment run but have not yet processed. In that case, they still show up in FBL1N but not in F-53. Payment runs are discussed later in this manual.

**Vendor** 100000
**Company Code** SFE1

**Name** WOOD SUPPLIER
**City** toronto

| | St | Assignment | Document | Doc. Type | Doc..Date | DD | Amount in Local Crcy | LCurr | Clrng doc. |
|---|---|---|---|---|---|---|---|---|---|
| | | | 1900000000 | KR | 04/22/2019 | | 1,500.00- | CAD | |
| | | | 1900000001 | KR | 04/22/2019 | | 1,189.00- | CAD | |
| | | | 1900000002 | KR | 04/22/2019 | | 1,189.00- | CAD | |
| | | | 1900000003 | KR | 04/22/2019 | | 1,189.00- | CAD | |
| | | | 1900000004 | KR | 04/24/2019 | | 3,450.00- | CAD | |
| | | | | | | | 8,517.00- | CAD | |
| Account 100000 | | | | | | | 8,517.00- | CAD | |
| | | | | | | | 8,517.00- | CAD | |

Fig 4

As always, select, deactivate and activate the line we will post against, here the line of 1,500 and clear the cash discount amount, we will see that in the next section.

Fig 5

Since we are paying a lesser amount than the amount on the invoice, this must be an under payment to the vendor. Let us confirm by trying to simulate the document:

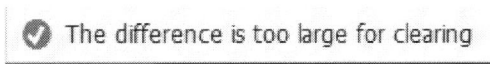

Fig 6

The above message tells us we do not have the authorization to post this document because the difference between the vendor's invoice and the payment we are making is more than what we are authorized for.

## II.    POSTING AN AMOUNT WITHIN TOLERANCE LIMITS:

Let us attempt the same posting with a bigger amount closer to the invoice amount:

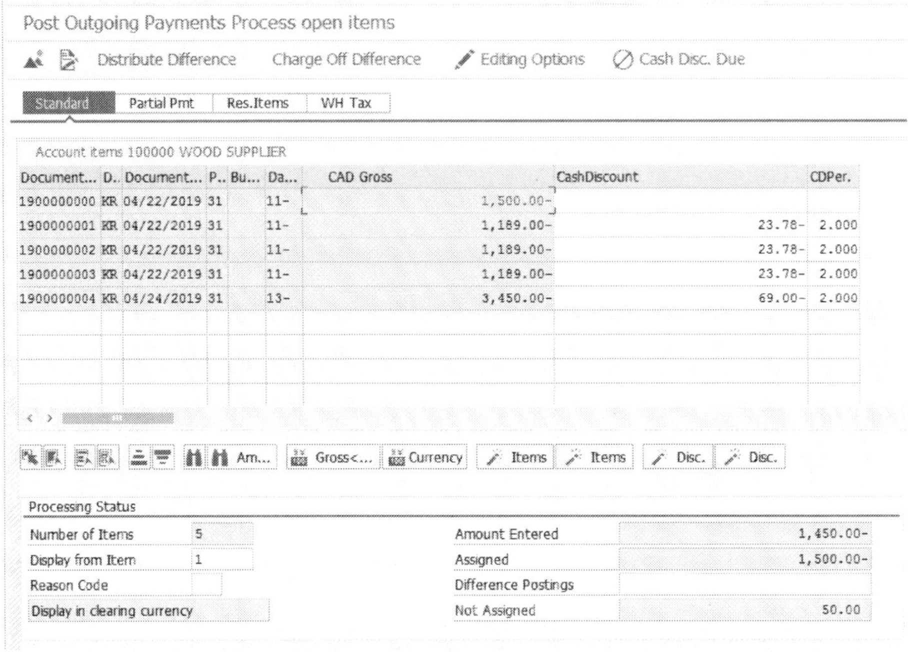

Post Outgoing Payments Process open items

▲ 📄  Distribute Difference    Charge Off Difference    ✎ Editing Options    ⊘ Cash Disc. Due

| Standard | Partial Pmt | Res.Items | WH Tax |

Account items 100000 WOOD SUPPLIER

| Document... | D.. | Document... | P.. | Bu... | Da... | CAD Gross | CashDiscount | CDPer. |
|---|---|---|---|---|---|---|---|---|
| 1900000000 | KR | 04/22/2019 | 31 | | 11- | 1,500.00- | | |
| 1900000001 | KR | 04/22/2019 | 31 | | 11- | 1,189.00- | 23.78- | 2.000 |
| 1900000002 | KR | 04/22/2019 | 31 | | 11- | 1,189.00- | 23.78- | 2.000 |
| 1900000003 | KR | 04/22/2019 | 31 | | 11- | 1,189.00- | 23.78- | 2.000 |
| 1900000004 | KR | 04/24/2019 | 31 | | 13- | 3,450.00- | 69.00- | 2.000 |

< >

🔧 📋 📊 📈 ≡ ⇄ 📱 📱 Am... | Gross<... | Currency | ✎ Items | ✎ Items | ✎ Disc. | ✎ Disc.

Processing Status

| Number of Items | 5 | Amount Entered | 1,450.00- |
|---|---|---|---|
| Display from Item | 1 | Assigned | 1,500.00- |
| Reason Code | | Difference Postings | |
| Display in clearing currency | | Not Assigned | 50.00 |

Fig 7

Simulate the posting:

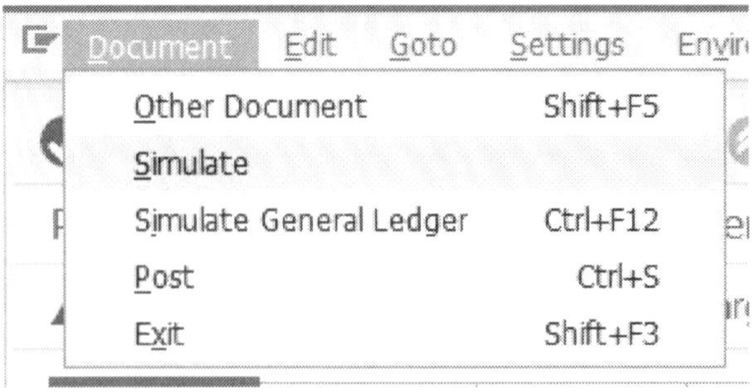

| ☞ | Document | Edit | Goto | Settings | Envir |
|---|---|---|---|---|---|
| | Other Document | | | Shift+F5 | |
| | Simulate | | | | |
| | Simulate General Ledger | | | Ctrl+F12 | |
| | Post | | | Ctrl+S | |
| | Exit | | | Shift+F3 | |

Fig 8

## Post Outgoing Payments Display Overview

⊟  ⠿ Display Currency    ⓘ Taxes    ⟲ Reset

| Document Date | 04/25/2019 | Type | KZ | Company Code | SFE1 |
|---|---|---|---|---|---|
| Posting Date | 04/25/2019 | Period | 4 | Currency | CAD |
| Document Number | INTERNAL | Fiscal Year | 2019 | Translation dte | 04/25/2019 |
| Reference | | | | Cross-CC Number | |
| Doc.Header Text | | | | Trading part.BA | |

Items in document currency

| | PK | BusA | Acct | | CAD | Amount | Tax amnt |
|---|---|---|---|---|---|---|---|
| 001 | 50 | | 0000107000 | Bank A/c | | 1,450.00- | |
| 002 | 50 | | 0000900200 | Over Payment Acc | | 50.00- | |
| 003 | 25 | | 0000100000 | WOOD SUPPLIER | | 1,500.00 | |

Fig 9

We see the difference is being posted to the over payment account as a credit (posting key 50) to the over payment account it determined from the configuration. This is counter intuitive – it hits the over payment account because it is a 'profit' to the customer i.e. SFE1 (same as an overpayment would be to us from our customer).

Post the document and the vendor's payable report clears this document completely:

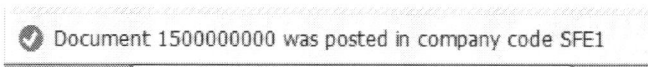

✓ Document 1500000000 was posted in company code SFE1

Fig 10

## Vendor Line Item Display

👓  ✏ ⚏ ▦  ⯐ ⯑ ⬚  ▼ ≜ ≛  ▦ ⊞ ⯐  Σ ½ ⊡ ⊡  ⓘ ⓘ Se

| Vendor | 100000 |
|---|---|
| Company Code | SFE1 |
| Name | WOOD SUPPLIER |
| City | toronto |

| St | Assignment | Document | Doc. Type | Doc..Date | DD | Amount in Local Crcy | LCurr | Clrng doc. |
|---|---|---|---|---|---|---|---|---|
| ● | | 1900000001 | KR | 04/22/2019 | | 1,189.00- | CAD | |
| | | 1900000002 | KR | 04/22/2019 | | 1,189.00- | CAD | |
| | | 1900000003 | KR | 04/22/2019 | | 1,189.00- | CAD | |
| | | 1900000004 | KR | 04/24/2019 | | 3,450.00- | CAD | |
| | | | | | | 7,017.00- | CAD | |
| | Account 100000 | | | | | 7,017.00- | CAD | |
| | | | | | | 7,017.00- | CAD | |

Fig 11

# III.     Posting with cash discount and underpaying the vendor

In F-53 enter the amount we will pay the vendor:

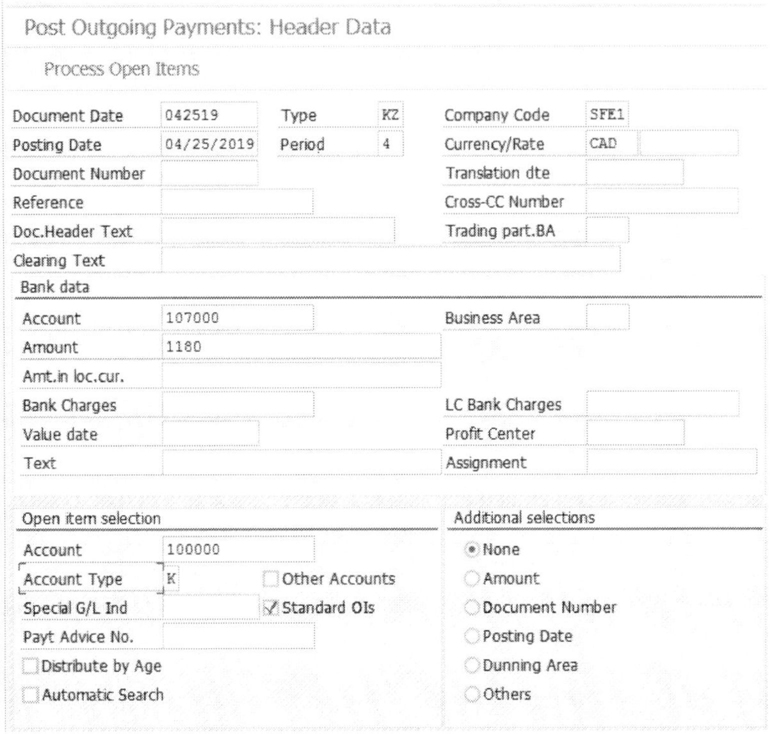

## Post Outgoing Payments: Header Data

### Process Open Items

| | | | | | |
|---|---|---|---|---|---|
| Document Date | 042519 | Type | KZ | Company Code | SFE1 |
| Posting Date | 04/25/2019 | Period | 4 | Currency/Rate | CAD |
| Document Number | | | | Translation dte | |
| Reference | | | | Cross-CC Number | |
| Doc.Header Text | | | | Trading part.BA | |
| Clearing Text | | | | | |

### Bank data

| | | | |
|---|---|---|---|
| Account | 107000 | Business Area | |
| Amount | 1180 | | |
| Amt.in loc.cur. | | | |
| Bank Charges | | LC Bank Charges | |
| Value date | | Profit Center | |
| Text | | Assignment | |

| Open item selection | | | Additional selections |
|---|---|---|---|
| Account | 100000 | | ⦿ None |
| Account Type | K | ☐ Other Accounts | ○ Amount |
| Special G/L Ind | | ☑ Standard OIs | ○ Document Number |
| Payt Advice No. | | | ○ Posting Date |
| ☐ Distribute by Age | | | ○ Dunning Area |
| ☐ Automatic Search | | | ○ Others |

Fig 12

# Process Open Items:

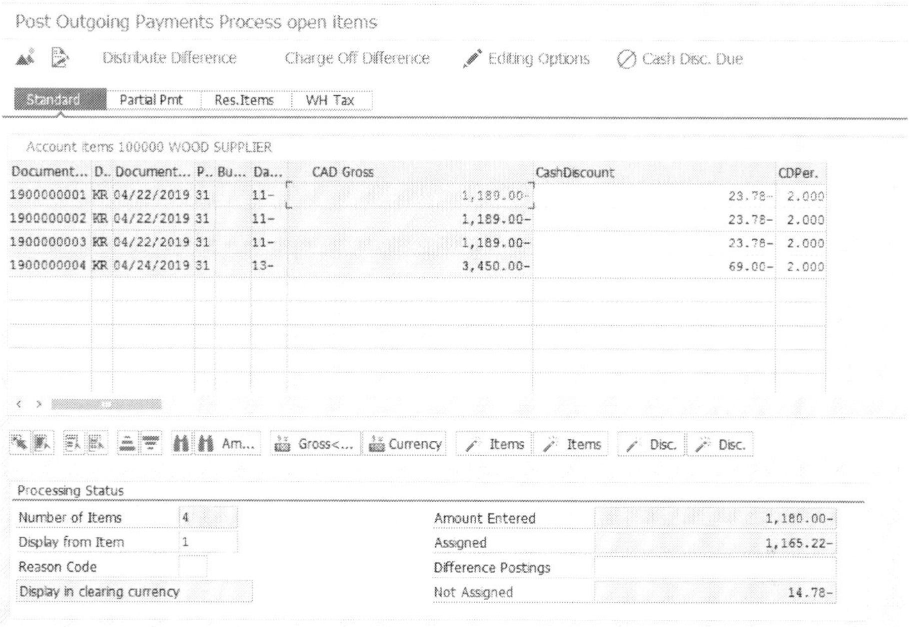

Fig 13

Let us assume the first invoice below is being paid off with this amount of $1,150. The invoice is $1,189 and since we are paying within the terms, we are also entitled to a cash discount of 2 % = $23.78.

| | |
|---|---|
| Amount Entered | 1,180.00- |
| Assigned | 1,165.22- |
| Difference Postings | |
| Not Assigned | 14.78- |

Fig 14

The Not Assigned amount of $14.78 will then be required to post to the under payment account. Let us simulate this event:

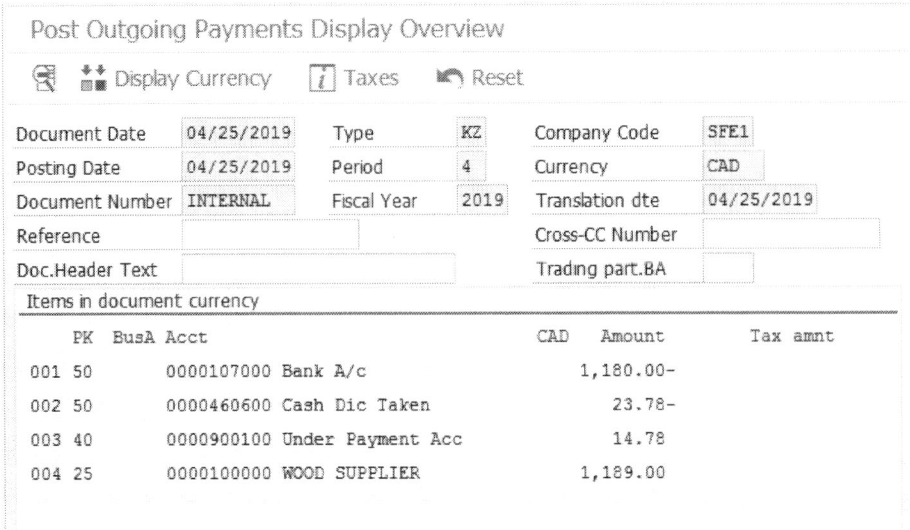

## Post Outgoing Payments Display Overview

| Display Currency | | Taxes | | Reset | | | |
|---|---|---|---|---|---|---|---|
| Document Date | 04/25/2019 | Type | KZ | Company Code | SFE1 | | |
| Posting Date | 04/25/2019 | Period | 4 | Currency | CAD | | |
| Document Number | INTERNAL | Fiscal Year | 2019 | Translation dte | 04/25/2019 | | |
| Reference | | | | Cross-CC Number | | | |
| Doc.Header Text | | | | Trading part.BA | | | |

Items in document currency

| PK | BusA | Acct | | CAD | Amount | Tax amnt |
|---|---|---|---|---|---|---|
| 001 50 | | 0000107000 | Bank A/c | | 1,180.00- | |
| 002 50 | | 0000460600 | Cash Dic Taken | | 23.78- | |
| 003 40 | | 0000900100 | Under Payment Acc | | 14.78 | |
| 004 25 | | 0000100000 | WOOD SUPPLIER | | 1,189.00 | |

Fig 15

Post:

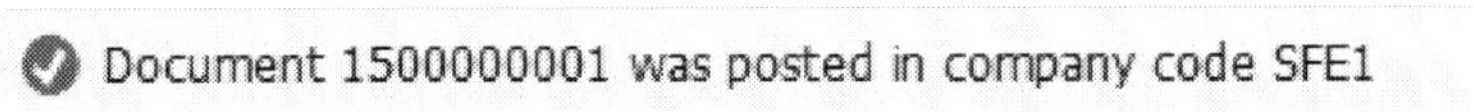

Document 1500000001 was posted in company code SFE1

Fig 16

The AP statement removes the line altogether:

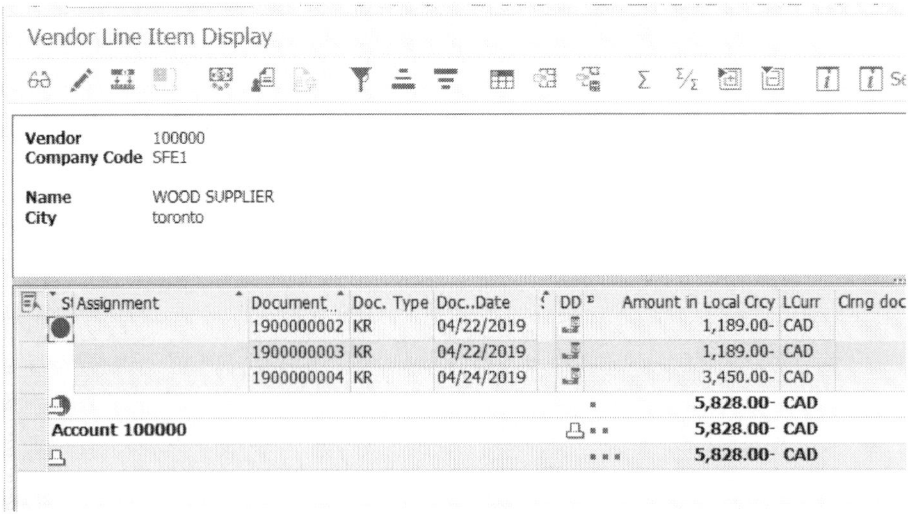

## Vendor Line Item Display

| Vendor | 100000 |
|---|---|
| Company Code | SFE1 |
| Name | WOOD SUPPLIER |
| City | toronto |

| St | Assignment | Document | Doc. Type | Doc..Date | DD | Amount in Local Crcy | LCurr | Clrng doc |
|---|---|---|---|---|---|---|---|---|
| | | 1900000002 | KR | 04/22/2019 | | 1,189.00- | CAD | |
| | | 1900000003 | KR | 04/22/2019 | | 1,189.00- | CAD | |
| | | 1900000004 | KR | 04/24/2019 | | 3,450.00- | CAD | |
| | | | | | | 5,828.00- | CAD | |
| | Account 100000 | | | | | 5,828.00- | CAD | |
| | | | | | | 5,828.00- | CAD | |

Fig 17

226

# HANDLING DOWN PAYMENTS TO

# VENDORS (C/U)

Down payments (aka advance payments) are often used to pay vendors for turnkey projects or asset purchases. These are treated differently in SAP compared to normal vendor payments for trade payables. Down payments made to vendors remain on the book as current assets till adjusted/cleared against the actual invoice.

|       |                                                          |
| ----- | -------------------------------------------------------- |
| I.    | Define Reconciliation Account for Vendor Down Payment    |
| II.   | Making the Down Payment to Vendor                        |
| III.  | Displaying the Balances for confirmation of postings     |
| IV.   | Receiving the Invoice against Down Payment made          |
| V.    | Displaying the balances                                  |
| VI.   | Clearing the Down Payment made                           |
| VII.  | Displaying the Balances for confirmation of postings     |
| VIII. | Clear the Vendor's Account                               |

I is a one- time configuration, the rest are all transactions. II, IV, VI and VIII are the actual postings in the process. III, V and VII are included only to confirm the process is going well.

All are discussed in sequence.

# I. Define Reconciliation Account for Vendor Down Payment (C)

T Code SPRO

They require their own reconciliation account, under the normal payables one for reporting separately on the Balance sheet.

Like the customer or vendor reconciliation accounts, this down payment reconciliation, account is also a configuration; to do that, follow the path:

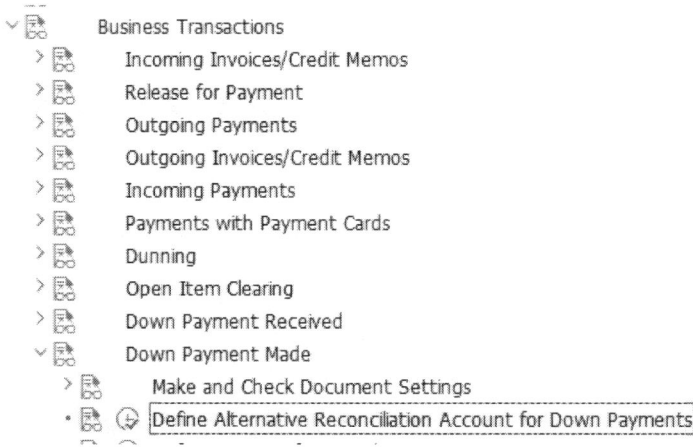

Fig 1

## Maintain Accounting Configuration : Special G/L - List

| Acct Type | Sp.G/LInd. | Name | Description |
|---|---|---|---|
| K | A | DP, CA | Down Payments, Current Assets |
| K | B | DP, FA | Down Payments, Financ'l Assets |
| K | F | Pmt req | Down Payment Requests |
| K | I | DP, IA | Down Payments, Intang. Assets |
| K | M | DP, TA | Down Payments, Tangible Assets |
| K | O | DP, A | Down Payments, Amortization |
| K | V | DP, S | Down Payments, Stocks |
| K | X | DP, WI | Down Payment, Without Invoice |

Fig 2

Double click on the line corresponding to the current assets (the only one we will define here) and enter your CoA in the window that pops up:

Fig 3

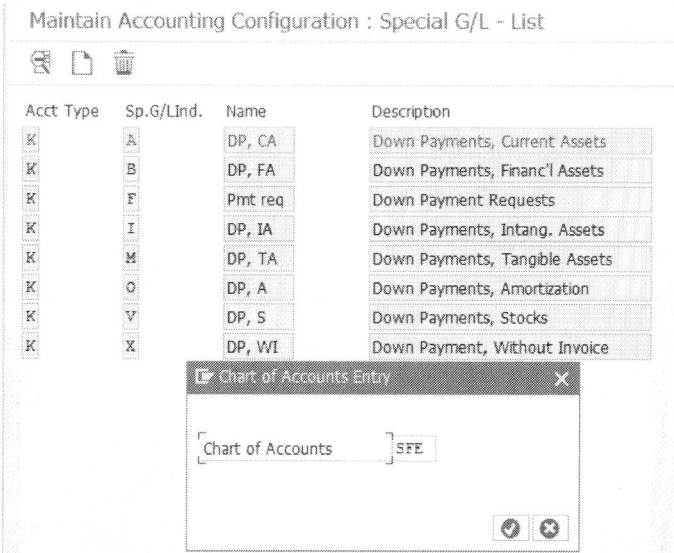

Fig 4

Let's say we use 213000 as this sp G/L account to capture these down payments:

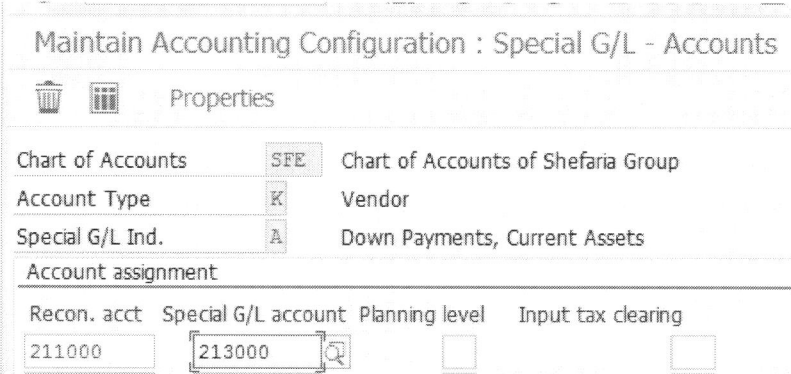

Fig 5

Save the data in the transport.

Next, to ensure it is properly configured, click on Properties:

Properties to verify the correct posting keys are there:

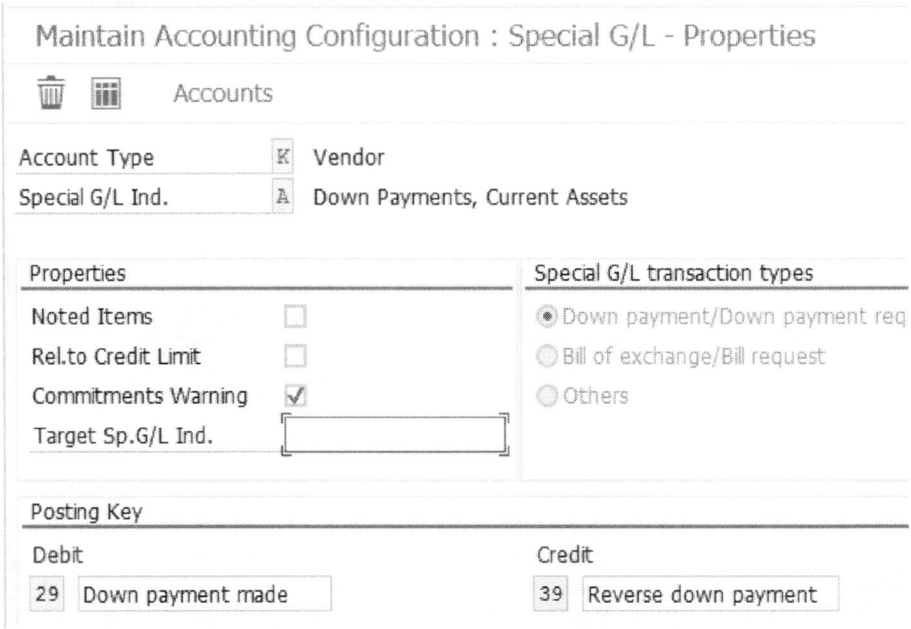

Maintain Accounting Configuration : Special G/L - Properties

🗑 🏛  Accounts

Account Type        K  Vendor
Special G/L Ind.     A  Down Payments, Current Assets

| Properties | | Special G/L transaction types |
|---|---|---|
| Noted Items | ☐ | ◉ Down payment/Down payment req |
| Rel.to Credit Limit | ☐ | ○ Bill of exchange/Bill request |
| Commitments Warning | ✓ | ○ Others |
| Target Sp.G/L Ind. | | |

Posting Key

Debit                            Credit
29  Down payment made           39  Reverse down payment

Fig 5

The correct posting keys 29 and 39 are allocated by SAP automatically.

Next step is to define these reconciliation G/L accounts 211000 and 213000 in your co code as you did the other G/L accounts, bearing in mind these are Balance sheet accounts. Both will be reconciliation accounts, we will use 213000 as the account for *Trade Payables - Special purchases* and 211000 for *Trade Payables – Domestic*.

## II. Making the down Payment to the Vendor (U)

T Code F-48

Now that we have configured the down payment account, we are ready to make a down payment to a vendor – that down payment will be held as a current assets till settled.

The T Code to make down payments is F-48 or follow the menu path:

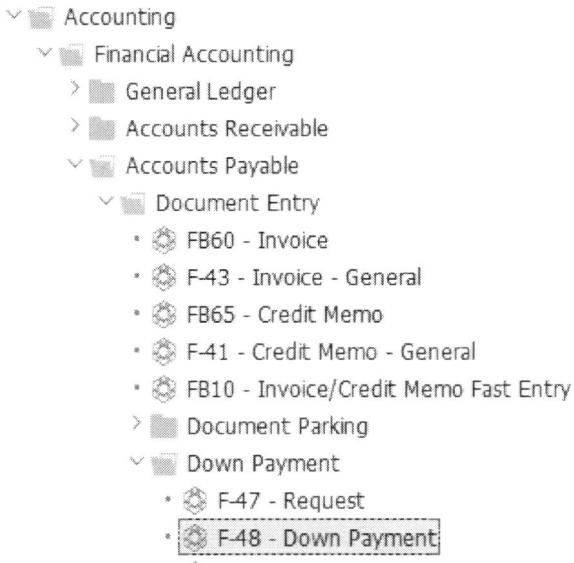

```
˅ 🖥 Accounting
    ˅ 🖥 Financial Accounting
        > 📁 General Ledger
        > 📁 Accounts Receivable
        ˅ 🖥 Accounts Payable
            ˅ 🖥 Document Entry
                • ⚙ FB60 - Invoice
                • ⚙ F-43 - Invoice - General
                • ⚙ FB65 - Credit Memo
                • ⚙ F-41 - Credit Memo - General
                • ⚙ FB10 - Invoice/Credit Memo Fast Entry
                > 📁 Document Parking
                ˅ 🖥 Down Payment
                    • ⚙ F-47 - Request
                    • ⚙ F-48 - Down Payment
```

Fig 6

The screen opens like this:

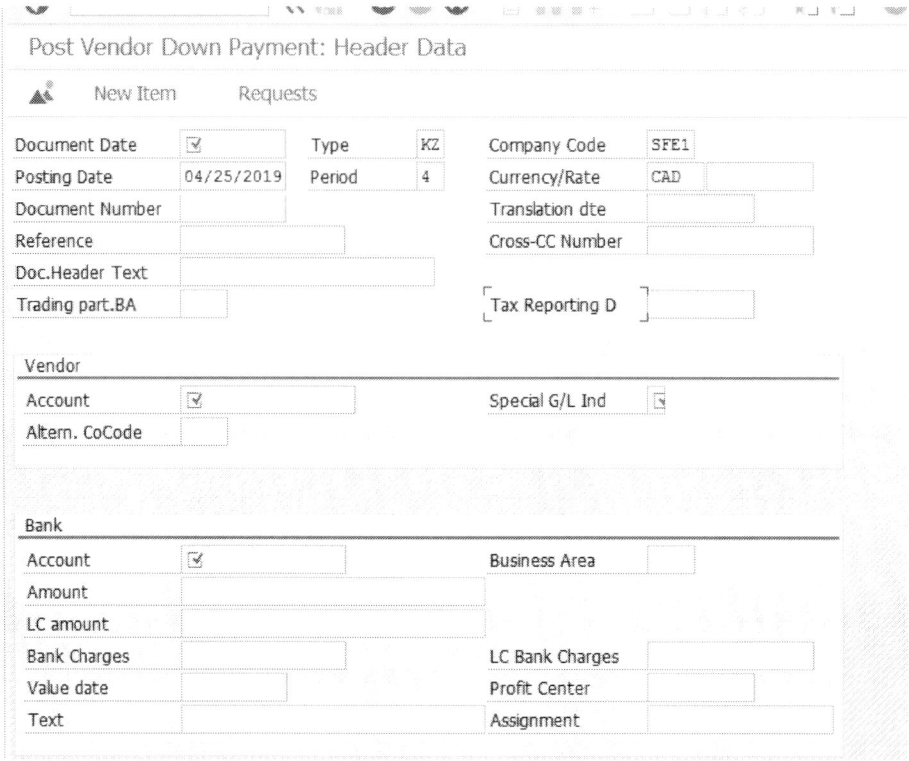

Fig 7

Enter the following information:

- Date
- Vendor account
- Bank GL account # which will hold this down payment and the value date if mandatory. This date belongs to Treasury to monitor cash requirements and availability
- CC
- Amount and currency
- The Spl acct indicator will be 'A' which is SAP standard for Down Payment:

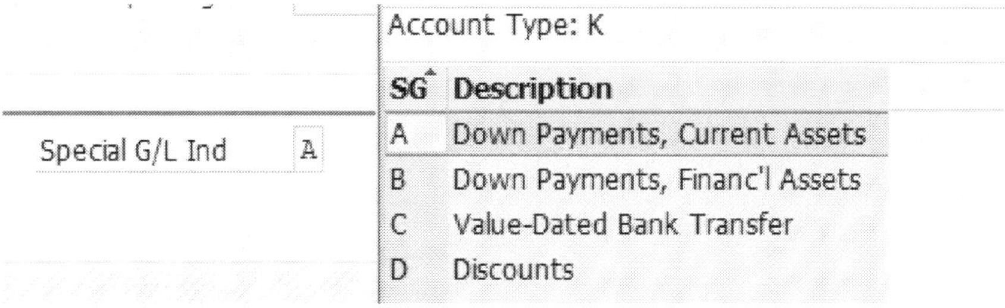

Account Type: K

| SG | Description |
|---|---|
| A | Down Payments, Current Assets |
| B | Down Payments, Financ'l Assets |
| C | Value-Dated Bank Transfer |
| D | Discounts |

Special G/L Ind: A

Fig 8

Enter the data as below to post this down payment. Notes can also be entered to describe the nature/reason for this payment.

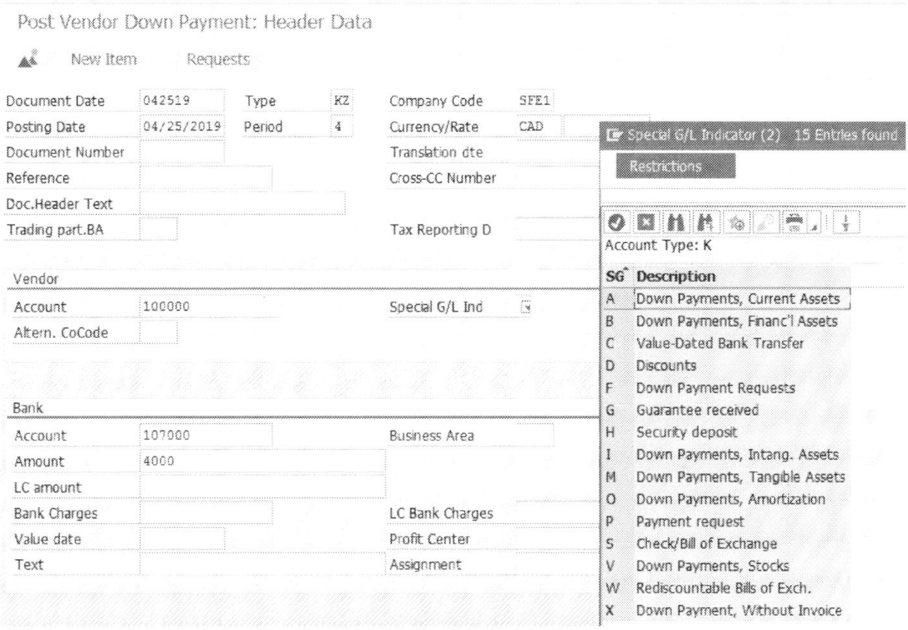

Fig 9

Hit Enter and the system takes us to the next screen:

Enter the amount or a * which is all this screen requires:

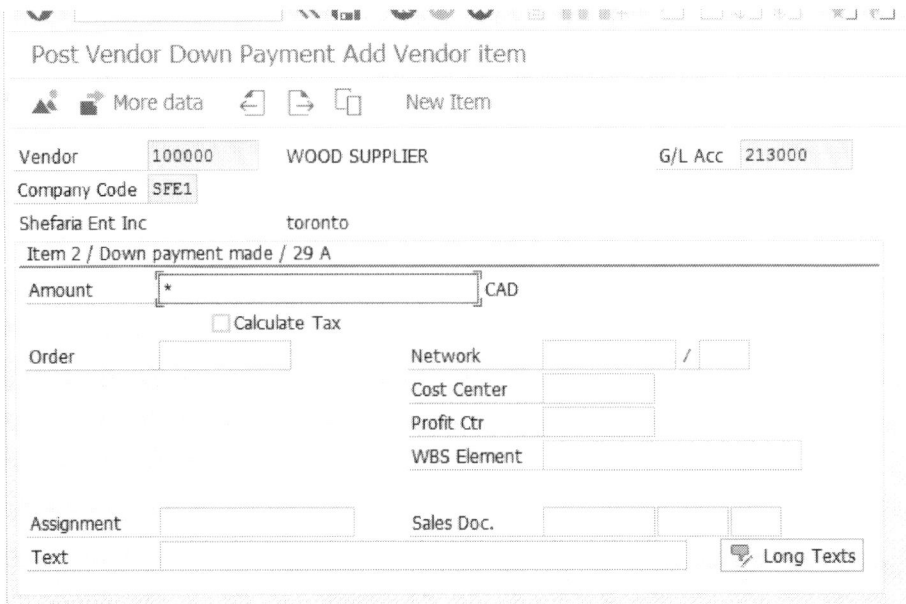

Fig 10

Note how SAP found the G/L account 213000 by itself to post to for reconciliation. It found it from the configuration we did earlier.

Now we have the option again to simulate this document for any errors before posting it:

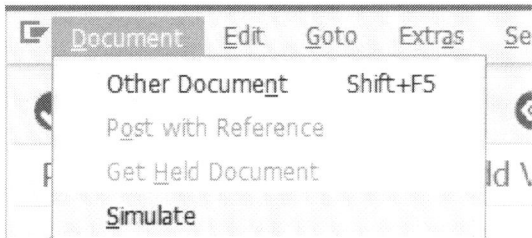

Fig 11

If everything looks fine:

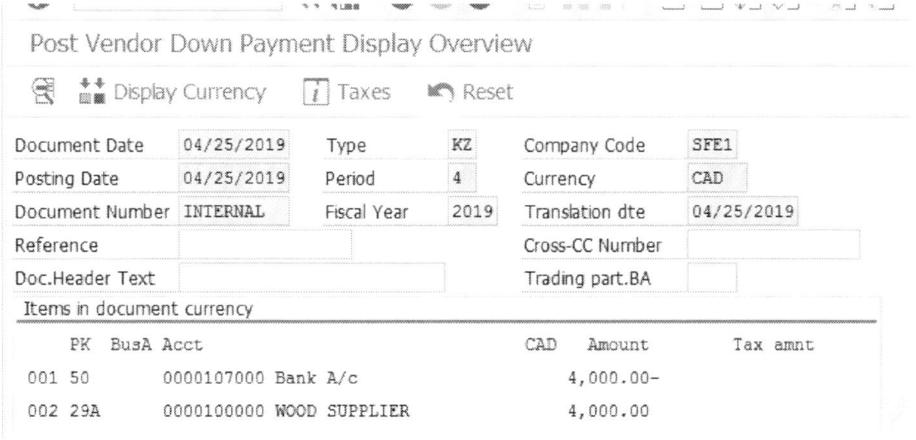

**Post Vendor Down Payment Display Overview**

🔲 ⠠⠠ Display Currency   ⓘ Taxes   ↶ Reset

| | | | | | |
|---|---|---|---|---|---|
| Document Date | 04/25/2019 | Type | KZ | Company Code | SFE1 |
| Posting Date | 04/25/2019 | Period | 4 | Currency | CAD |
| Document Number | INTERNAL | Fiscal Year | 2019 | Translation dte | 04/25/2019 |
| Reference | | | | Cross-CC Number | |
| Doc.Header Text | | | | Trading part.BA | |

Items in document currency

| PK | BusA | Acct | | CAD | Amount | Tax amnt |
|---|---|---|---|---|---|---|
| 001 | 50 | 0000107000 | Bank A/c | | 4,000.00- | |
| 002 | 29A | 0000100000 | WOOD SUPPLIER | | 4,000.00 | |

Fig 12

Save the document and we get the number at the bottom:

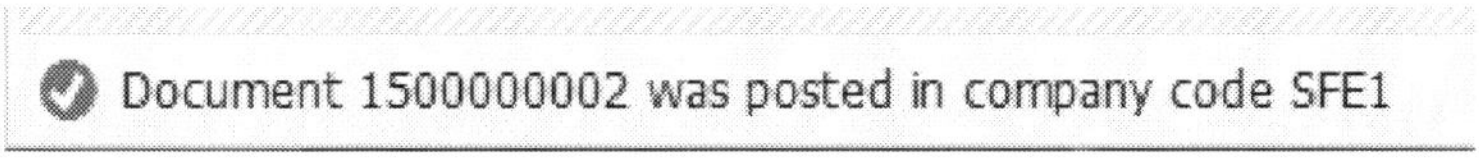

✅ Document 1500000002 was posted in company code SFE1

Fig 13

## III. DISPLAYING THE BALANCES FOR CONFIRMATION OF POSTINGS (U)

T Code FK10N

We can now display the balances in the vendor account via the transaction FK10N or the path:

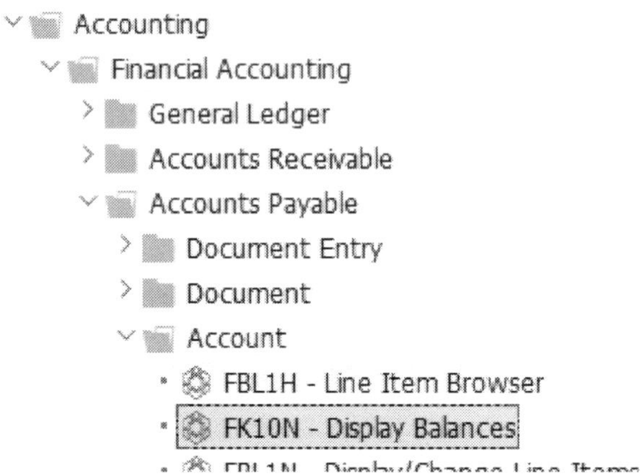

Fig 14

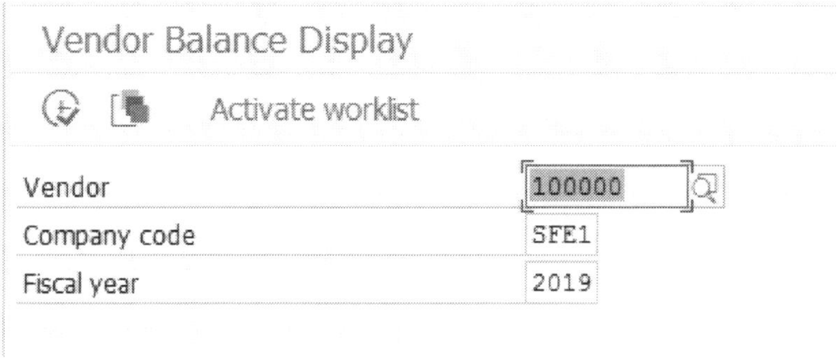

Fig 15

Execute and the results give all the balances against this vendor: The default screen will show the normal transaction balances:

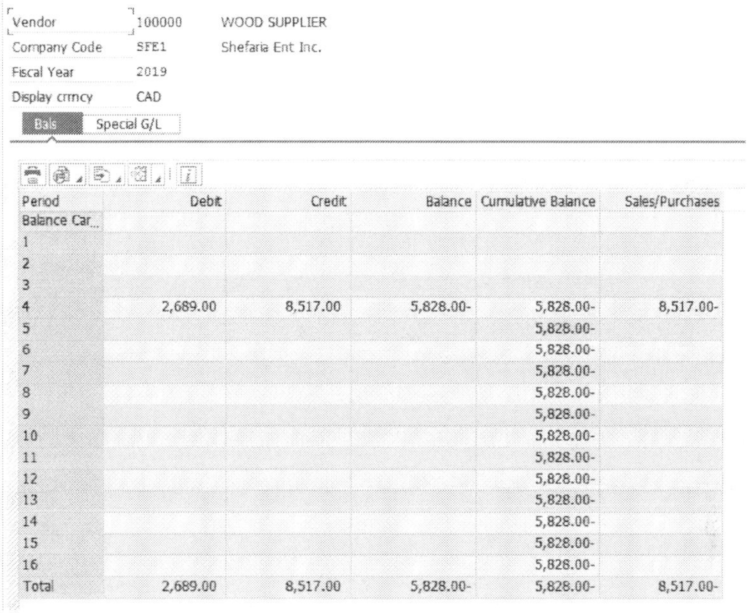

| Period | Debit | Credit | Balance | Cumulative Balance | Sales/Purchases |
|--------|-------|--------|---------|--------------------|-----------------|
| Balance Car... | | | | | |
| 1 | | | | | |
| 2 | | | | | |
| 3 | | | | | |
| 4 | 2,689.00 | 8,517.00 | 5,828.00- | 5,828.00- | 8,517.00- |
| 5 | | | | 5,828.00- | |
| 6 | | | | 5,828.00- | |
| 7 | | | | 5,828.00- | |
| 8 | | | | 5,828.00- | |
| 9 | | | | 5,828.00- | |
| 10 | | | | 5,828.00- | |
| 11 | | | | 5,828.00- | |
| 12 | | | | 5,828.00- | |
| 13 | | | | 5,828.00- | |
| 14 | | | | 5,828.00- | |
| 15 | | | | 5,828.00- | |
| 16 | | | | 5,828.00- | |
| Total | 2,689.00 | 8,517.00 | 5,828.00- | 5,828.00- | 8,517.00- |

Vendor: 100000 WOOD SUPPLIER
Company Code: SFE1 Shefaria Ent Inc.
Fiscal Year: 2019
Display crrncy: CAD

Fig 16

Clicking on the Special G/L tab - [Bals] [Special G/L] will give us these down payments:

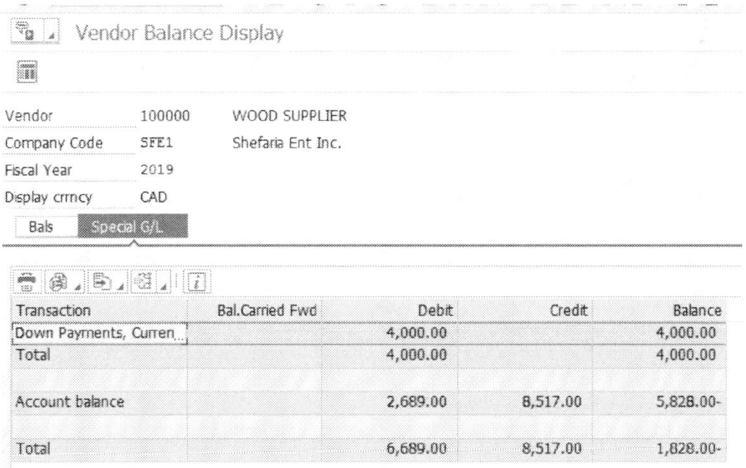

**Vendor Balance Display**

Vendor: 100000 WOOD SUPPLIER
Company Code: SFE1 Shefaria Ent Inc.
Fiscal Year: 2019
Display crrncy: CAD

| Transaction | Bal.Carried Fwd | Debit | Credit | Balance |
|-------------|-----------------|-------|--------|---------|
| Down Payments, Curren... | | 4,000.00 | | 4,000.00 |
| Total | | 4,000.00 | | 4,000.00 |
| | | | | |
| Account balance | | 2,689.00 | 8,517.00 | 5,828.00- |
| | | | | |
| Total | | 6,689.00 | 8,517.00 | 1,828.00- |

Fig 17

As usual, double click on the Total line and you see the detailed breakdown of that balance:

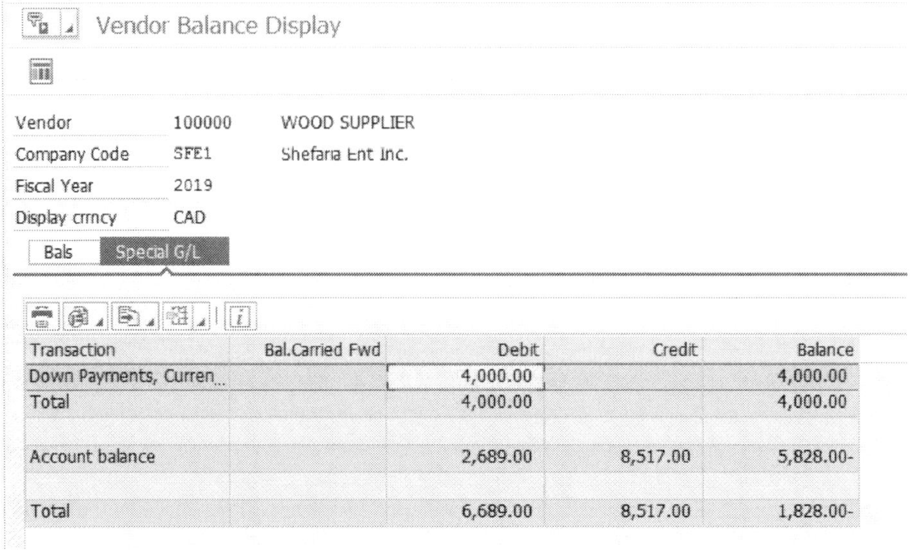

**Vendor Balance Display**

| Vendor | 100000 | WOOD SUPPLIER |
| Company Code | SFE1 | Shefaria Ent Inc. |
| Fiscal Year | 2019 | |
| Display crrncy | CAD | |

Bals | Special G/L

| Transaction | Bal.Carried Fwd | Debit | Credit | Balance |
|---|---|---|---|---|
| Down Payments, Curren... | | 4,000.00 | | 4,000.00 |
| Total | | 4,000.00 | | 4,000.00 |
| Account balance | | 2,689.00 | 8,517.00 | 5,828.00- |
| Total | | 6,689.00 | 8,517.00 | 1,828.00- |

Fig 18

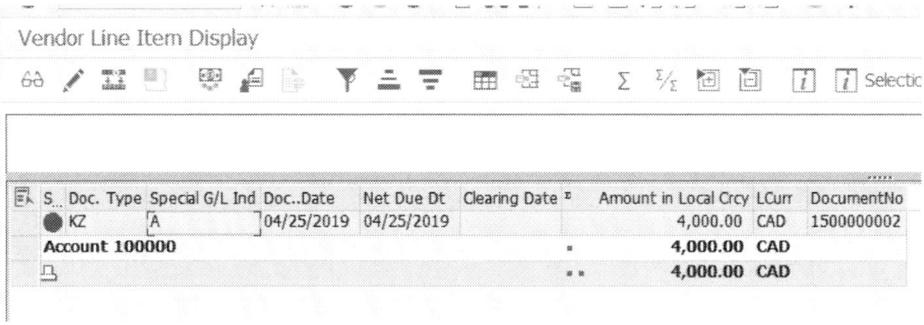

**Vendor Line Item Display**

| S | Doc. Type | Special G/L Ind | Doc..Date | Net Due Dt | Clearing Date | Σ | Amount in Local Crcy | LCurr | DocumentNo |
|---|---|---|---|---|---|---|---|---|---|
| ● KZ | A | | 04/25/2019 | 04/25/2019 | | | 4,000.00 | CAD | 1500000002 |
| Account 100000 | | | | | | ▪ | 4,000.00 | CAD | |
| ⅃ | | | | | | ▪ ▪ | 4,000.00 | CAD | |

Fig 19

Note the document # we just entered at the top as document type KZ. The letter A is symbolic of the Spl G/L indicator

## IV. Receiving/booking the Invoice against the Down Payment made (U)

T Code FB60

Now, the vendor provides the invoice against the down payment we already made and we need to adjust that against the debit balance in the vendor account.

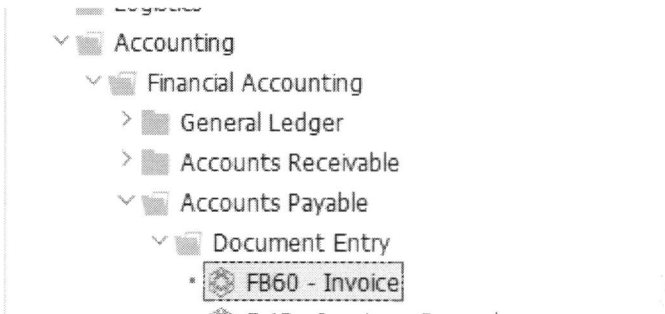

Fig 20

We debit the purchase account

Fig 21

On hitting Enter, we get an information message:

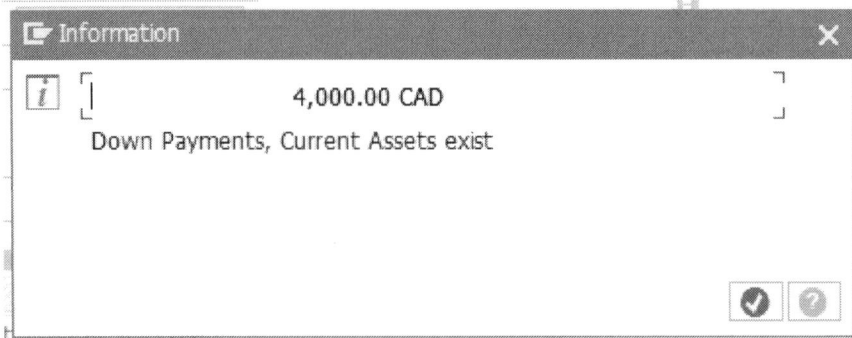

Fig 22

*** *This amount shown in the message can be different if multiple down payments have been posted to the vendor account, which have not been cleared yet.*

Hit Enter again:

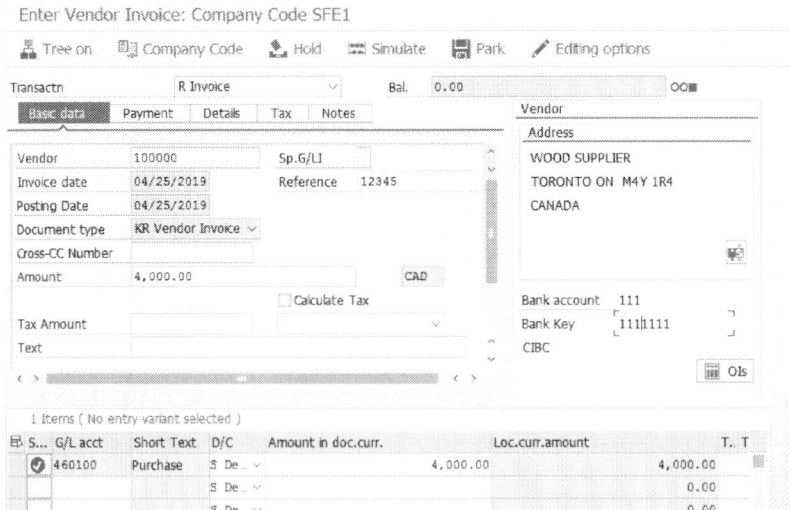

Fig 23

and save it:

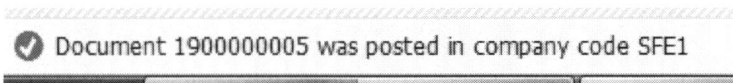

Document 1900000005 was posted in company code SFE1

# V. DISPLAYING THE BALANCES (U)

T Code FK10N

If you check FK10N again, we notice the payables having gone up with this invoice (compare Fig 16 with Fig 24 below to verify).

| Vendor | 100000 | WOOD SUPPLIER |
|---|---|---|
| Company Code | SFE1 | Shefaria Ent Inc. |
| Fiscal Year | 2019 | |
| Display crrncy | CAD | |

Bals    Special G/L

| Period | Debit | Credit | Balance | Cumulative Balance | Sales/Purchases |
|---|---|---|---|---|---|
| Balance Car... | | | | | |
| 1 | | | | | |
| 2 | | | | | |
| 3 | | | | | |
| 4 | 2,689.00 | 12,517.00 | 9,828.00- | 9,828.00- | 12,517.00- |
| 5 | | | | 9,828.00- | |
| 6 | | | | 9,828.00- | |
| 7 | | | | 9,828.00- | |
| 8 | | | | 9,828.00- | |
| 9 | | | | 9,828.00- | |
| 10 | | | | 9,828.00- | |
| 11 | | | | 9,828.00- | |
| 12 | | | | 9,828.00- | |
| 13 | | | | 9,828.00- | |
| 14 | | | | 9,828.00- | |
| 15 | | | | 9,828.00- | |
| 16 | | | | 9,828.00- | |
| Total | 2,689.00 | 12,517.00 | 9,828.00- | 9,828.00- | 12,517.00- |

Fig 24

# VI. CLEARING THE DOWN PAYMENT MADE TO VENDOR (U)

T Code F-54

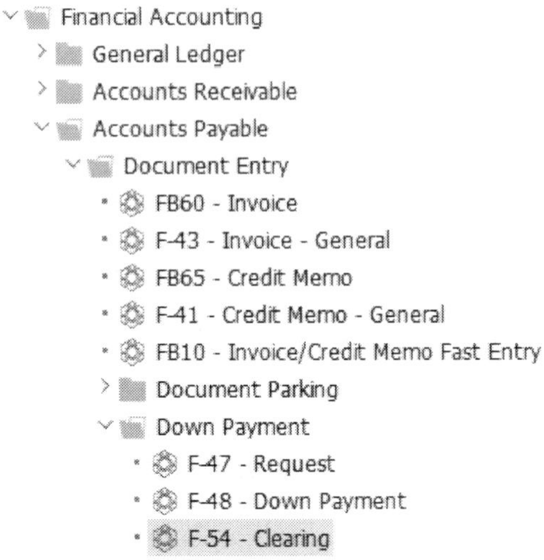

Fig 25

Enter the relevant data:

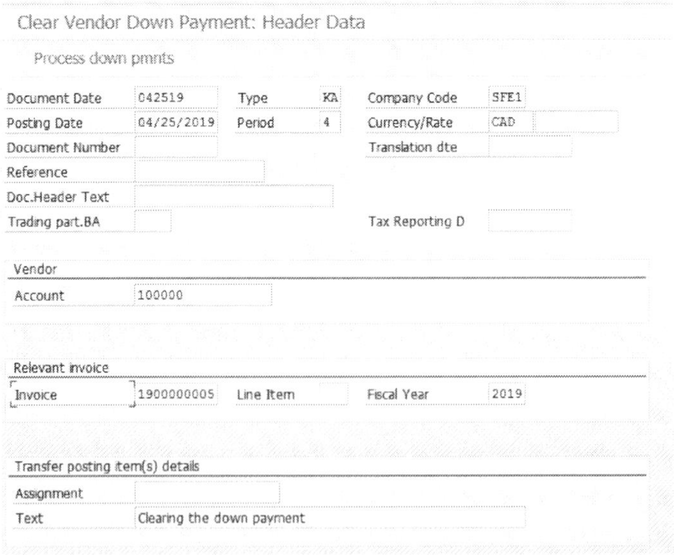

Fig 26

Note the # we use – the posting # we got earlier to say that we will be clearing against this internal document #.

Click on the button Process down pmnts to display the down payments outstanding that can be adjusted – note SAP got the posting from the document # because that is linked to the original document #

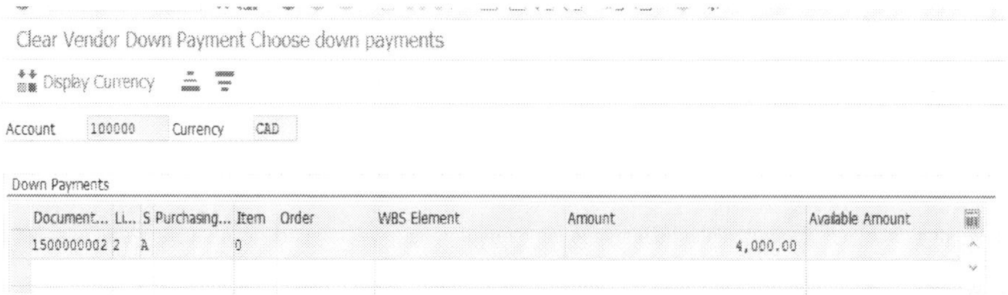

Clear Vendor Down Payment Choose down payments

Display Currency

| Account | 100000 | Currency | CAD |

Down Payments

| Document... | Li... | S | Purchasing... | Item | Order | WBS Element | Amount | Available Amount | |
|---|---|---|---|---|---|---|---|---|---|
| 1500000002 | 2 | A | | 0 | | | | 4,000.00 | |

Fig 27

Enter the amount to clear in the Transfer posting column (scroll to the right to view it if you need to), press Enter and verify the bottom total changes to that same amount in

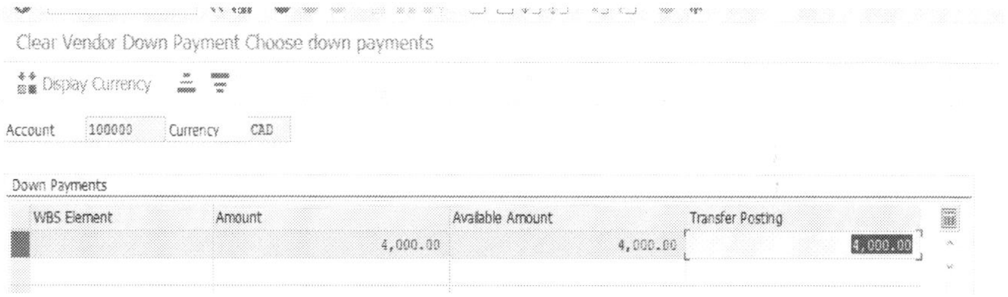

Clear Vendor Down Payment Choose down payments

Display Currency

| Account | 100000 | Currency | CAD |

Down Payments

| WBS Element | Amount | Available Amount | Transfer Posting | |
|---|---|---|---|---|
| | 4,000.00 | 4,000.00 | 4,000.00 | |

Fig 28

243

Again, we can simulate the document:

```
Clear Vendor Down Payment Display Overview
  [icon] [icon] Display Currency  [i] Taxes  [icon] Reset

Document Date      04/25/2019   Type        KA      Company Code      SFE1
Posting Date       04/25/2019   Period      4       Currency          CAD
Document Number    INTERNAL     Fiscal Year 2019    Translation dte   04/25/2019
Reference                                           Cross-CC Number
Doc.Header Text                                     Trading part.BA
  Items in document currency
     PK  BusA Acct                                  CAD    Amount         Tax amnt
  001 39A      0000100000 WOOD SUPPLIER                   4,000.00-
  002 26       0000100000 WOOD SUPPLIER                   4,000.00
```

Fig 29

If everything looks right, post it by saving it:

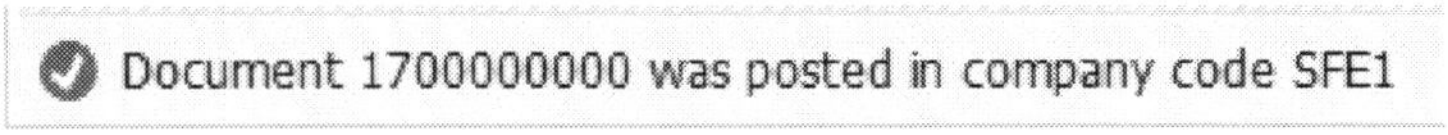

Document 1700000000 was posted in company code SFE1

Fig 30

T Code FK10N

Click on the tab Special G/L:

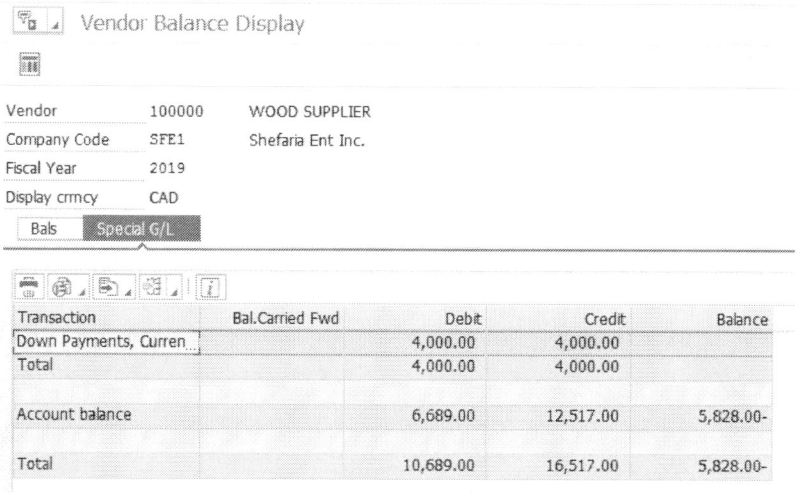

Vendor Balance Display

| | | |
|---|---|---|
| Vendor | 100000 | WOOD SUPPLIER |
| Company Code | SFE1 | Shefaria Ent Inc. |
| Fiscal Year | 2019 | |
| Display crrncy | CAD | |

Bals | Special G/L

| Transaction | Bal.Carried Fwd | Debit | Credit | Balance |
|---|---|---|---|---|
| Down Payments, Curren... | | 4,000.00 | 4,000.00 | |
| Total | | 4,000.00 | 4,000.00 | |
| | | | | |
| Account balance | | 6,689.00 | 12,517.00 | 5,828.00- |
| | | | | |
| Total | | 10,689.00 | 16,517.00 | 5,828.00- |

Fig 31

We notice that the amount of $4,000 has now moved from the column Balance to Credit in the vendor. Compare with Fig 18.

Double click on the Balance line:

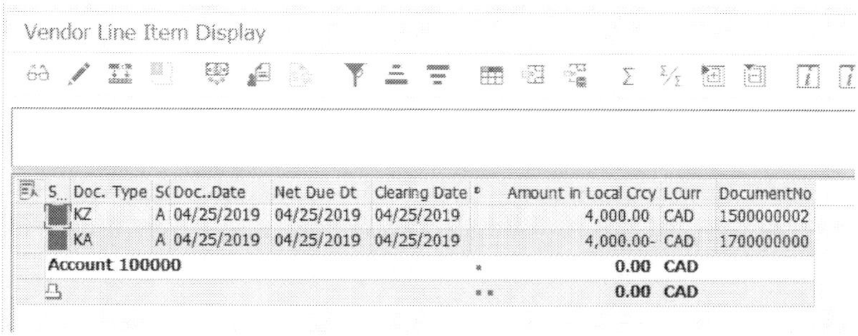

Vendor Line Item Display

| S.. | Doc. Type | S( | Doc..Date | Net Due Dt | Clearing Date | | Amount in Local Crcy | LCurr | DocumentNo |
|---|---|---|---|---|---|---|---|---|---|
| | KZ | A | 04/25/2019 | 04/25/2019 | 04/25/2019 | | 4,000.00 | CAD | 1500000002 |
| | KA | A | 04/25/2019 | 04/25/2019 | 04/25/2019 | | 4,000.00- | CAD | 1700000000 |
| **Account 100000** | | | | | | * | **0.00** | **CAD** | |
| | | | | | | ** | **0.00** | **CAD** | |

Fig 32

The 2 highlighted cancelling entries of 10,000 each are revealed above. Note the reference of the clearing document 1700000000 in the document No 1500000002.

# VIII. CLEARING THE VENDOR'S ACCOUNT (U)

T Code F-44

This is the last step in the process of down payments – to clear the vendor account. F-44 or follow the path:

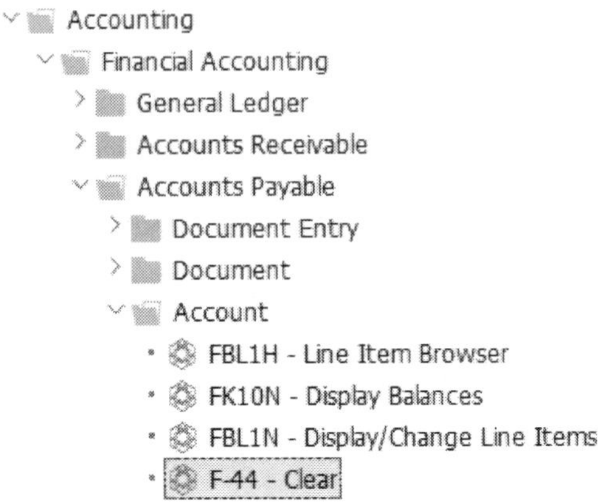

- ∨ 🗀 Accounting
  - ∨ 🗀 Financial Accounting
    - > 🗀 General Ledger
    - > 🗀 Accounts Receivable
    - ∨ 🗀 Accounts Payable
      - > 🗀 Document Entry
      - > 🗀 Document
      - ∨ 🗀 Account
        - • ⬡ FBL1H - Line Item Browser
        - • ⬡ FK10N - Display Balances
        - • ⬡ FBL1N - Display/Change Line Items
        - • ⬡ F-44 - Clear

Fig 33

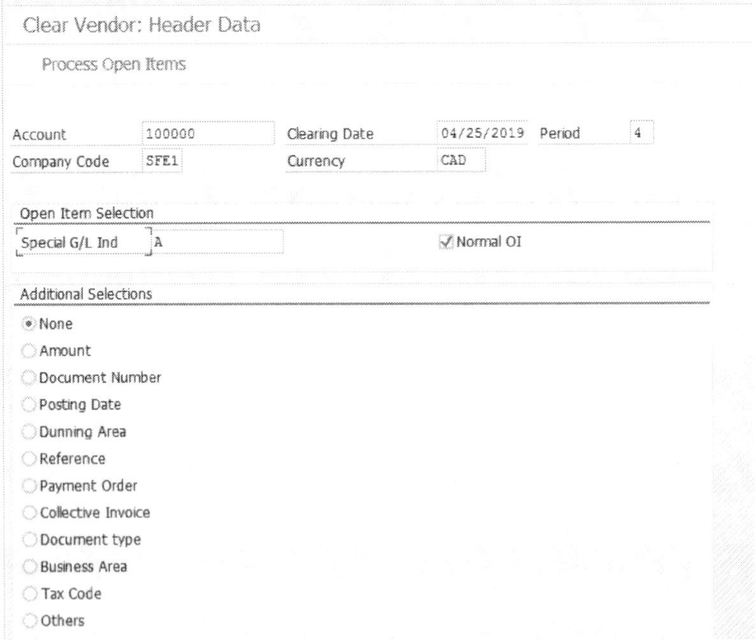

Clear Vendor: Header Data

Process Open Items

| Account | 100000 | Clearing Date | 04/25/2019 | Period | 4 |
|---------|--------|---------------|------------|--------|---|
| Company Code | SFE1 | Currency | CAD | | |

Open Item Selection

Special G/L Ind    A                                    ✓ Normal OI

Additional Selections

- ⦿ None
- ○ Amount
- ○ Document Number
- ○ Posting Date
- ○ Dunning Area
- ○ Reference
- ○ Payment Order
- ○ Collective Invoice
- ○ Document type
- ○ Business Area
- ○ Tax Code
- ○ Others

Fig 34

Enter the vendor account # as above and click on the tab
Process Open Items

To display all the invoices pending in the vendor account for clearing.

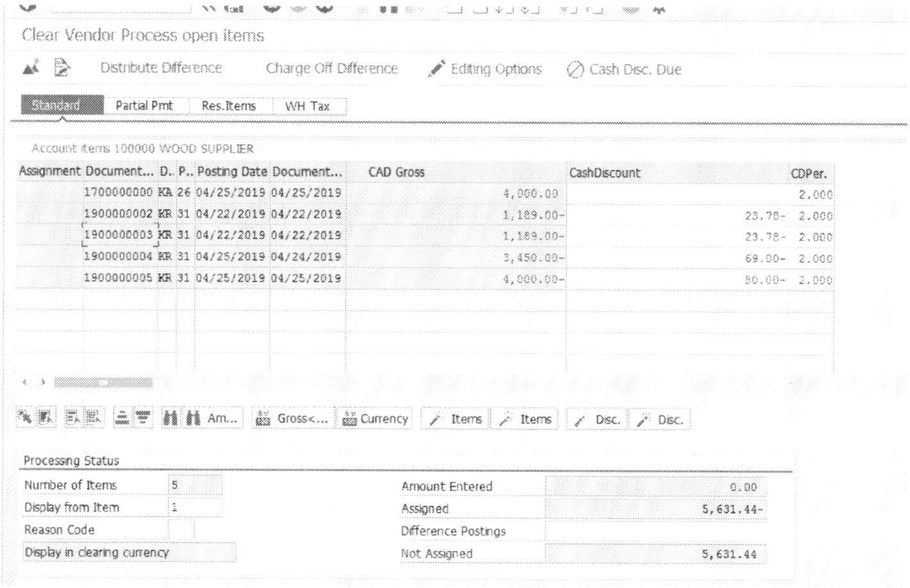

Fig 35

Since there are many entries here, we first need to choose our correct ones that we want to clear. We know they are 1900000005 from the vendor's invoice reference document (FB60) and 1700000000 from clearing (F-54). Therefore, we need to select them first. Some items may be on the next screen so have to be found by scrolling in the right bar.

Select the ones you need to square off -eliminate the cash discount if any, as it is not relevant to this situation.

Clear Vendor Process open items

A̿ ▷    Distribute Difference    Charge Off Difference    ✏ Editing Options    ⊘ Cash Disc. Due

| Standard | Partial Pmt | Res.Items | WH Tax |

Account items 100000 WOOD SUPPLIER

| Assignment | Document... | D.. | P.. | Posting Date | Document... | CAD Gross | CashDiscount | CDPer. |
|---|---|---|---|---|---|---|---|---|
| | 1700000000 | KA | 26 | 04/25/2019 | 04/25/2019 | 4,000.00 | | 2.000 |
| | 1900000002 | KR | 31 | 04/22/2019 | 04/22/2019 | 1,189.00- | 23.78- | 2.000 |
| | 1900000003 | KR | 31 | 04/22/2019 | 04/22/2019 | 1,189.00- | 23.78- | 2.000 |
| | 1900000004 | KR | 31 | 04/25/2019 | 04/24/2019 | 3,450.00- | 69.00- | 2.000 |
| | 1900000005 | KR | 31 | 04/25/2019 | 04/25/2019 | 4,000.00- | | |

< >  ▭

⯐⯐ ⯐⯐ ⯐⯐ ⯐⯐ ⯐⯐ Am...  Gross<...  Currency  ✏ Items  ✏ Items  ✏ Disc.  ✏ Disc.

Processing Status

| | | | |
|---|---|---|---|
| Number of Items | S | Amount Entered | 0.00 |
| Display from Item | 1 | Assigned | 0.00 |
| Reason Code | | Difference Postings | |
| Display in clearing currency | | Not Assigned | 0.00 |

Fig 36

Ensure that the not assigned amount is 0 as above.

At this point, we are ready to clear these 2 by saving the posting. This is a special posting, which does not post any line item #s but merely takes them out of the pending reports. This clearing once done, cannot be reversed either and the down payment process needs to begin again if required to. Again, SAP gives us the option to simulate the document:

| 🖙 | Document | Edit | Goto | Settings | Environment |
|---|---|---|---|---|---|
| | Other Document | | | Shift+F5 | |
| | Simulate | | | | |
| | Simulate General Ledger | | | Ctrl+F12 | |
| | Post | | | Ctrl+S | |
| | Exit | | | Shift+F3 | |
| | Standard | Partial Pmt | Res.Items | WH Tax | |

Fig 37

248

As stated, this simulation screen will have no line items like all the others we saw:

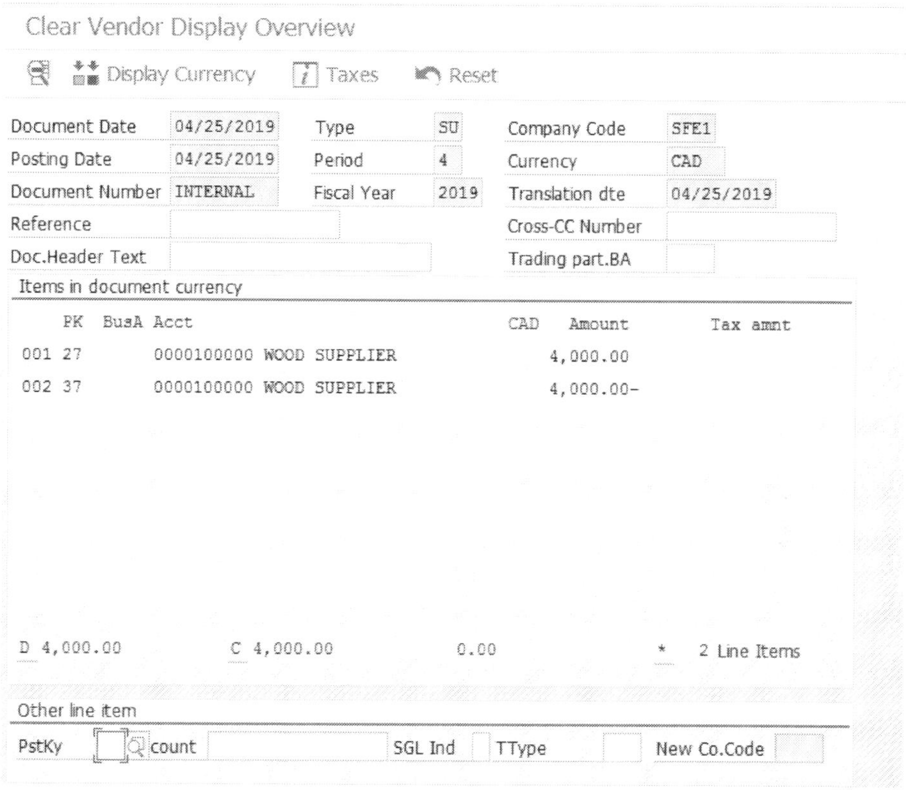

Clear Vendor Display Overview

🗄 ⁑ Display Currency  ⃞ Taxes  ↩ Reset

| Document Date | 04/25/2019 | Type | SU | Company Code | SFE1 |
| Posting Date | 04/25/2019 | Period | 4 | Currency | CAD |
| Document Number | INTERNAL | Fiscal Year | 2019 | Translation dte | 04/25/2019 |
| Reference | | | | Cross-CC Number | |
| Doc.Header Text | | | | Trading part.BA | |

Items in document currency

| | PK | BusA | Acct | | CAD | Amount | | Tax amnt |
| 001 | 27 | | 0000100000 | WOOD SUPPLIER | | 4,000.00 | | |
| 002 | 37 | | 0000100000 | WOOD SUPPLIER | | 4,000.00- | | |

D 4,000.00        C 4,000.00        0.00        *  2 Line Items

Other line item

| PstKy | | count | | SGL Ind | TType | | New Co.Code | |

Fig 38

This screen is blank because it creates no line items as the 2 lines are being netted off completely with each other. If there were to be differences of any kind, line items would be created for them. Since SAP showed no errors, we can now post the document by saving it. We get the posting number at the bottom:

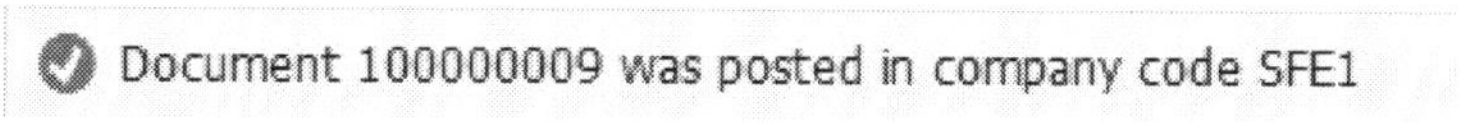

✅ Document 100000009 was posted in company code SFE1

Fig 39

Note from the # that this is a normal accounting document.

To verify the posting indeed took place and that the down payment was adjusted against the vendor invoice, we can look up FBL1N/H:

**Vendor Line Item Browser**

General Restrictions

| | | | |
|---|---|---|---|
| Company Code | SFE1 | to | |
| Vendor | 100000 | to | |

Line Item Selection

Status

○ Open Items

Details for selection of Open Items

| Open Items at Key Date | 04/25/2019 |
|---|---|

◉ Cleared Items

Details for selection of Cleared Items

| Clearing Date | 04/25/2019 | to | |
|---|---|---|---|
| Open Items at Key Date | | | |

Fig 40

In addition, execute. We see both our documents here:

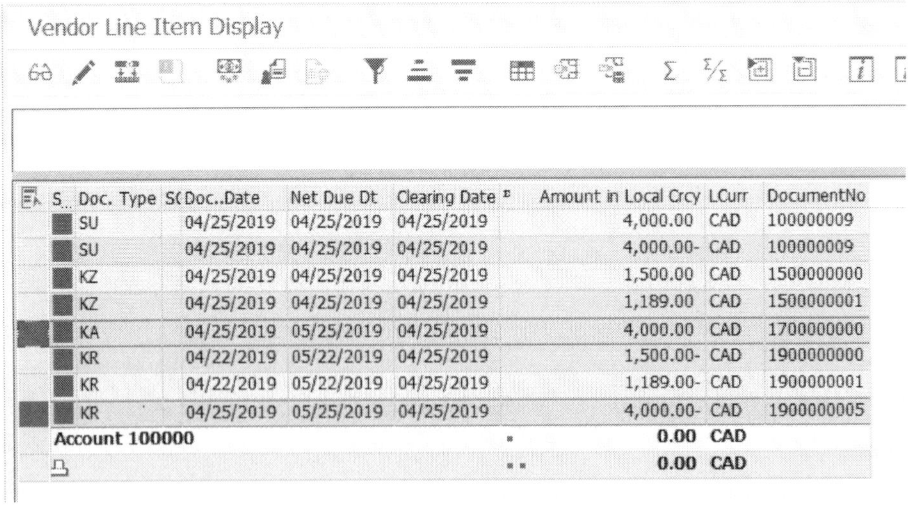

**Vendor Line Item Display**

| S | Doc. Type | S( Doc..Date | Net Due Dt | Clearing Date | Amount in Local Crcy | LCurr | DocumentNo |
|---|---|---|---|---|---|---|---|
| | SU | 04/25/2019 | 04/25/2019 | 04/25/2019 | 4,000.00 | CAD | 100000009 |
| | SU | 04/25/2019 | 04/25/2019 | 04/25/2019 | 4,000.00- | CAD | 100000009 |
| | KZ | 04/25/2019 | 04/25/2019 | 04/25/2019 | 1,500.00 | CAD | 1500000000 |
| | KZ | 04/25/2019 | 04/25/2019 | 04/25/2019 | 1,189.00 | CAD | 1500000001 |
| | KA | 04/25/2019 | 05/25/2019 | 04/25/2019 | 4,000.00 | CAD | 1700000000 |
| | KR | 04/22/2019 | 05/22/2019 | 04/25/2019 | 1,500.00- | CAD | 1900000000 |
| | KR | 04/22/2019 | 05/22/2019 | 04/25/2019 | 1,189.00- | CAD | 1900000001 |
| | KR | 04/25/2019 | 05/25/2019 | 04/25/2019 | 4,000.00- | CAD | 1900000005 |
| Account 100000 | | | | | 0.00 | CAD | |
| | | | | | 0.00 | CAD | |

Fig 41

# HANDLING DOWN PAYMENTS FROM

# CUSTOMERS (C/U)

The same way as we pay vendors down payments, customers may also pay us down payments for products like machinery, automobiles etc., primarily the capital expense type purchases.

    I.    Define Reconciliation Account for Customer Down Payment
    II.    Receiving the Down Payment from the customer
    III.    Displaying the Balances for confirmation of postings
    IV.    Sending the Invoice against Down Payment received
    V.    Displaying the balances
    VI.    Clearing the Down Payment received
    VII.    Displaying the Balances for confirmation of postings
    VIII.    Clear the Customer's Account

I is a one- time configuration, the rest are all transactions. II, IV, VI and VIII are the actual postings in the process. III, V and VII are included only to confirm the process is going well.

All are discussed in sequence.

# I. DEFINE RECONCILIATION ACCOUNT FOR CUSTOMER DOWN PAYMENT (C)

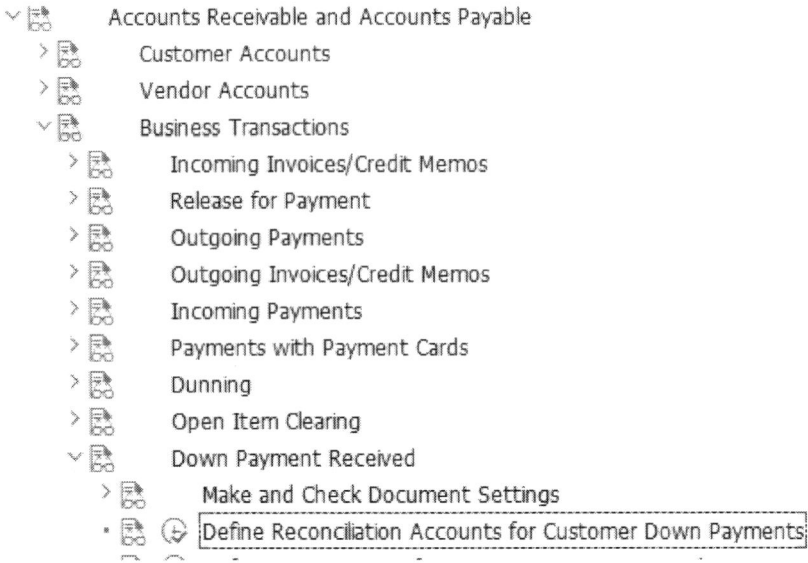

∨ 🗋      Accounts Receivable and Accounts Payable
  › 🗋      Customer Accounts
  › 🗋      Vendor Accounts
  ∨ 🗋      Business Transactions
    › 🗋      Incoming Invoices/Credit Memos
    › 🗋      Release for Payment
    › 🗋      Outgoing Payments
    › 🗋      Outgoing Invoices/Credit Memos
    › 🗋      Incoming Payments
    › 🗋      Payments with Payment Cards
    › 🗋      Dunning
    › 🗋      Open Item Clearing
    ∨ 🗋      Down Payment Received
      › 🗋      Make and Check Document Settings
      • 🗋 ⊙      Define Reconciliation Accounts for Customer Down Payments

Fig 1

Again the Sp G/L indicator is A:

Maintain Accounting Configuration : Special G/L - List

| Acct Type | Sp.G/LInd. | Name | Description |
|---|---|---|---|
| D | A | Dwn p... | Down Payment |
| D | C | SecDep. | RE Rent deposit |
| D | F | Pmt req | Down Payment Request |
| D | G | Guaran. | Guarantees Given |
| D | J | AdPayRe | RE Advance Payment Request |
| D | K | AdPy OC | RE AP Operating Costs |
| D | T | Dwn P... | Down Payment |
| D | U | AdP.SBR | RE AP sales-based rent |

Fig 2

Double click on it:

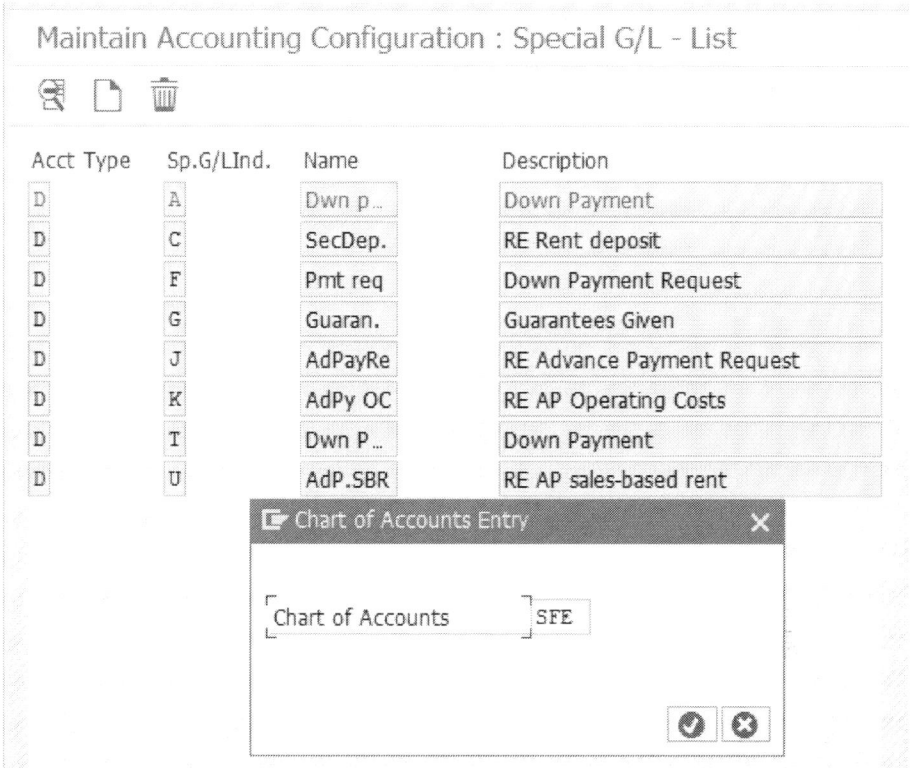

Fig 3

Hit Enter with the following data:

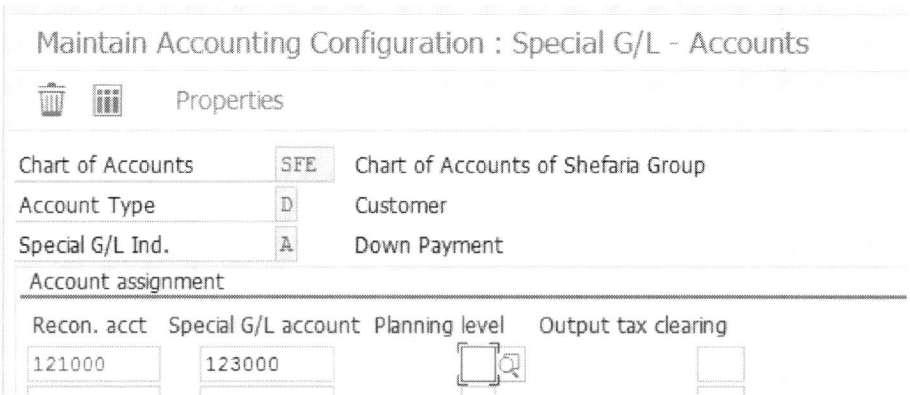

Fig 4

At this point, it is important to ensure the posting keys defined in these accounts are correct. Save the configuration and click on

Properties

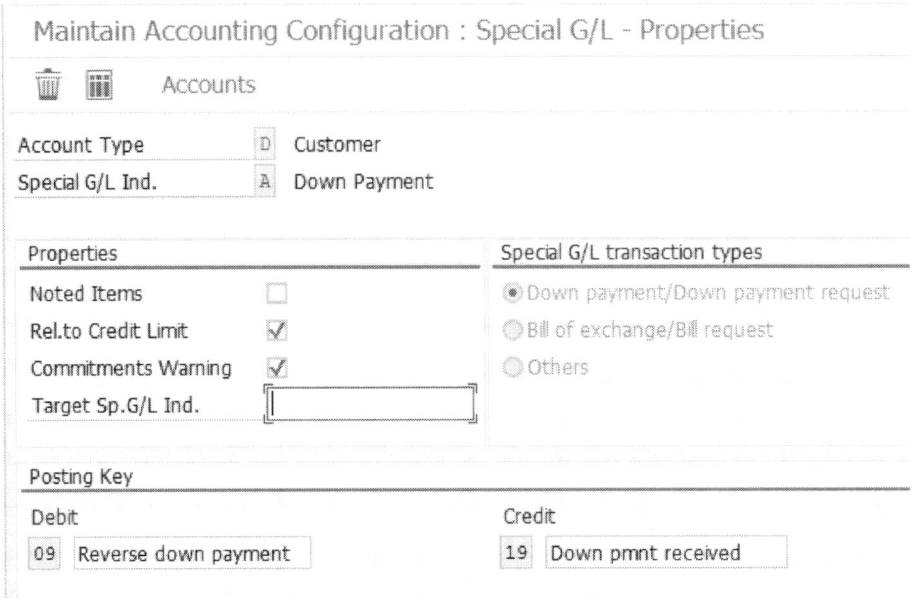

Maintain Accounting Configuration : Special G/L - Properties

🗑 🏛    Accounts

| Account Type | D | Customer |
| Special G/L Ind. | A | Down Payment |

Properties

| Noted Items | ☐ |
| Rel.to Credit Limit | ✓ |
| Commitments Warning | ✓ |
| Target Sp.G/L Ind. | |

Special G/L transaction types

◉ Down payment/Down payment request
◯ Bill of exchange/Bill request
◯ Others

Posting Key

| Debit | | | Credit | | |
| 09 | Reverse down payment | | 19 | Down pmnt received | |

Fig 5

We notice that the posting keys are from the range defined for customers. Ensure the 2 G/L accounts 121000 and 123000 exist in the company code in FS00.

## II.   RECEIVING/BOOKING THE DOWN PAYMENT FROM THE CUSTOMER (U)

T Code  F-29

Or follow the menu path:

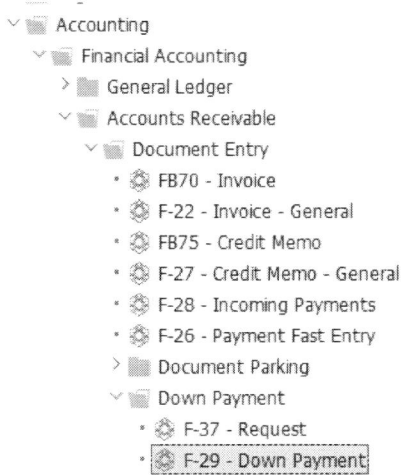

Fig 6

Enter the necessary data as below, notes can also be entered to describe the reason of this payment:

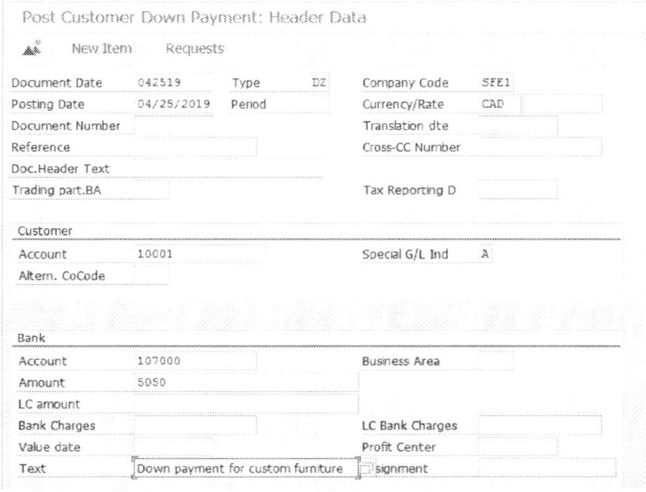

Fig 7

Hit Enter and on the next screen enter the amount again for the contra entry. Note how SAP fetches the G/L account 123000 on it's own based on the configuration we did in the previous step:

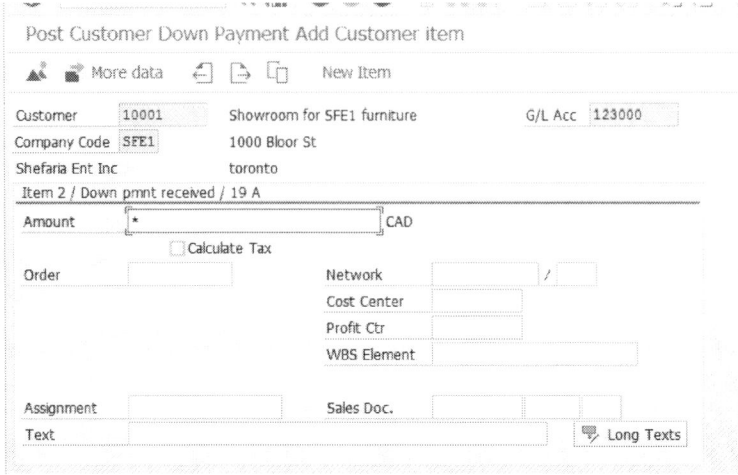

Post Customer Down Payment Add Customer item

More data · New Item

| | | | |
|---|---|---|---|
| Customer | 10001 | Showroom for SFE1 furniture | G/L Acc 123000 |
| Company Code | SFE1 | 1000 Bloor St | |
| Shefaria Ent Inc | | toronto | |

Item 2 / Down pmnt received / 19 A

| Amount | * | CAD |
|---|---|---|
| | □ Calculate Tax | |

| Order | | Network | / |
|---|---|---|---|
| | | Cost Center | |
| | | Profit Ctr | |
| | | WBS Element | |

| Assignment | | Sales Doc. | |
|---|---|---|---|
| Text | | | ⬛ Long Texts |

Fig 8

As always, we can simulate the document before posting:

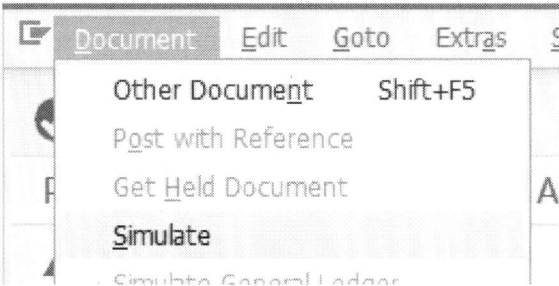

Document    Edit    Goto    Extras    S

Other Document        Shift+F5

Post with Reference

Get Held Document        A

Simulate

Simulate General Ledger

Fig 9

256

**Fig 10**

If the document looks good, post it by saving it to get the document #:

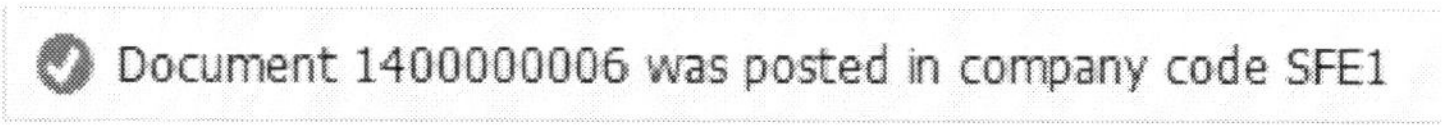

Document 1400000006 was posted in company code SFE1

**Fig 11**

## III. Displaying the Balances for Confirmation of Postings (U)

T Code FD10N or:

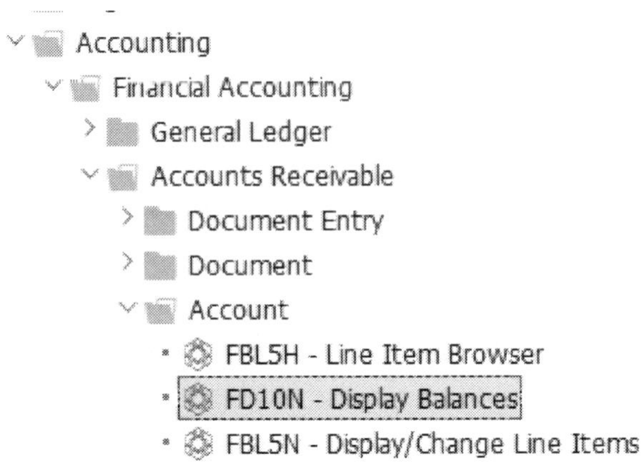

Fig 12

Put the customer number and CC and the year and execute:

Fig 13

The down payment balances are under the special GL tab:

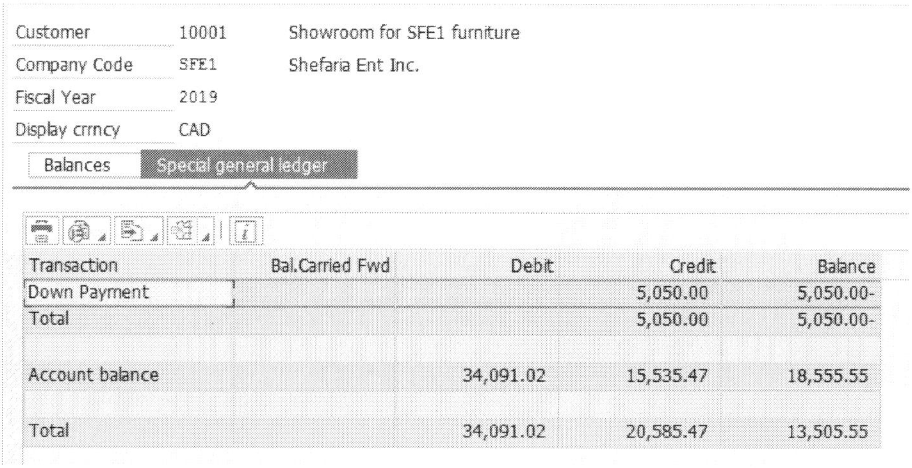

| Customer | 10001 | Showroom for SFE1 furniture |
| Company Code | SFE1 | Shefaria Ent Inc. |
| Fiscal Year | 2019 | |
| Display crrncy | CAD | |

Balances | Special general ledger

| Transaction | Bal.Carried Fwd | Debit | Credit | Balance |
| --- | --- | --- | --- | --- |
| Down Payment | | | 5,050.00 | 5,050.00- |
| Total | | | 5,050.00 | 5,050.00- |
| | | | | |
| Account balance | | 34,091.02 | 15,535.47 | 18,555.55 |
| | | | | |
| Total | | 34,091.02 | 20,585.47 | 13,505.55 |

Fig 14

Double click the Total line to see the latest entry:

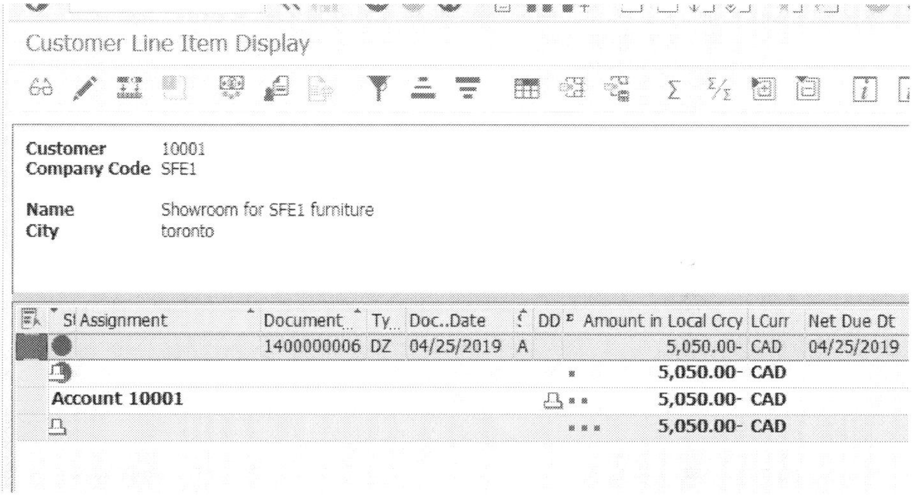

Customer Line Item Display

| Customer | 10001 |
| Company Code | SFE1 |

| Name | Showroom for SFE1 furniture |
| City | toronto |

| St Assignment | Document | Ty | Doc..Date | DD | Amount in Local Crcy | LCurr | Net Due Dt |
| --- | --- | --- | --- | --- | --- | --- | --- |
| | 1400000006 | DZ | 04/25/2019 | A | 5,050.00- | CAD | 04/25/2019 |
| | | | | * | 5,050.00- | CAD | |
| Account 10001 | | | | ** | 5,050.00- | CAD | |
| | | | | *** | 5,050.00- | CAD | |

Fig 15

# IV. Sending the Invoice against the Down Payment received (U)

T Code FB70 or:

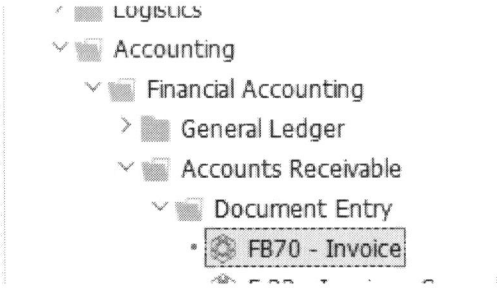

Fig 16

Enter the important data as below to credit the appropriate G/L account for sales against this down payment received:

| | | | | | |
|---|---|---|---|---|---|
| **Enter Customer Invoice: Company Code SFE1** | | | | | |

Transactn  R Invoice

Bal.  0.00

| Basic data | Payment | Details | Tax | Notes |
|---|---|---|---|---|

| | | | |
|---|---|---|---|
| Customer | 10001 | Sp.G/LI | |
| Invoice date | 042519 | Reference | |
| Posting Date | 04/25/2019 | | |
| Document type | DR Customer invoi.. | | |
| Cross-CC Number | | | |
| Amount | 5050 | | CAD |

☐ Calculate Tax

Tax Amount

Text

Company Code   SFE1 Shefaria Ent Inc Toronto

IR coefficient

0 Items ( No entry variant selected )

| S... | G/L acct | Short Text | D/C | Amount in doc.curr. | Loc.curr.amount | T.. T |
|---|---|---|---|---|---|---|
| | 450300 | | H Cr.. | * | 0.00 | |

Fig 17

Hit Enter to ensure zero balance at top right in Green:
An info message will pop up:

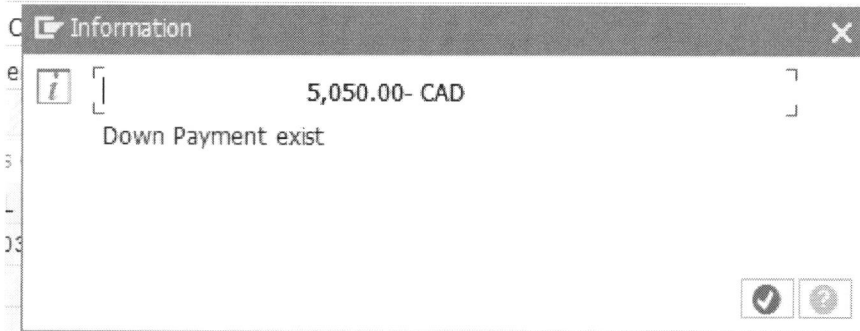

Fig 18

*Note: This amount could (and does) vary depending on how many other down payments exist in the system which have not been settled yet.*

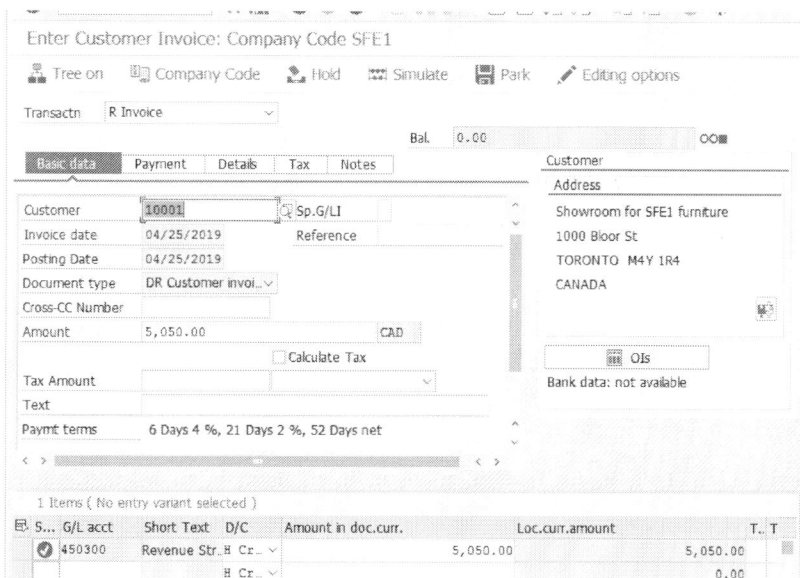

Fig 19

Again, we can simulate this document if we wish to verify the entries or want to make corrections before posting:

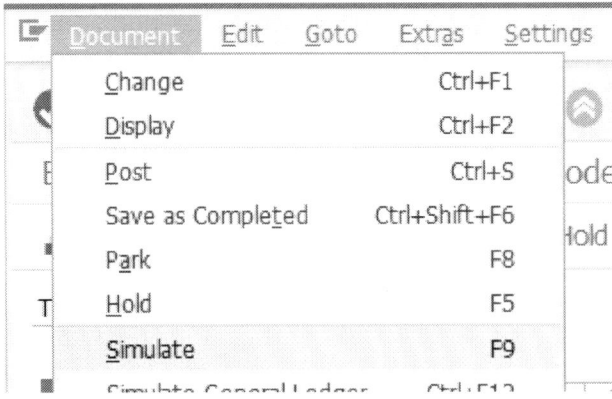

Fig 20

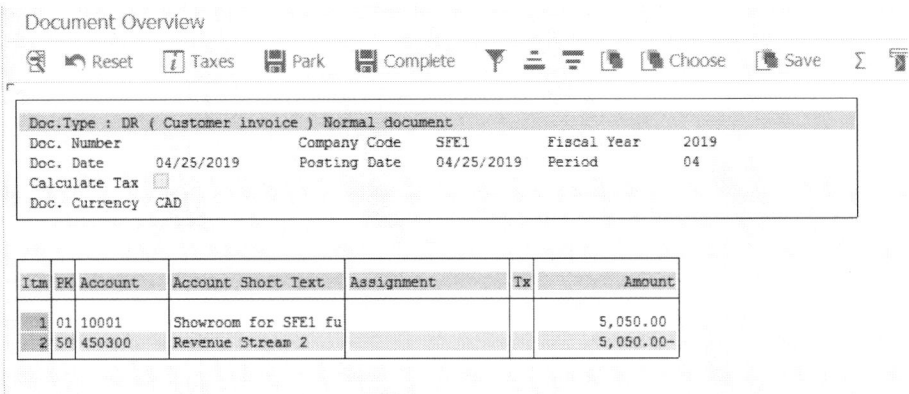

Fig 21

We can now save this document:

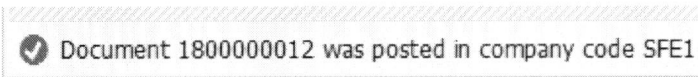

Document 1800000012 was posted in company code SFE1

Fig 22

# V. DISPLAYING THE BALANCES (U)

T Code FD10N:

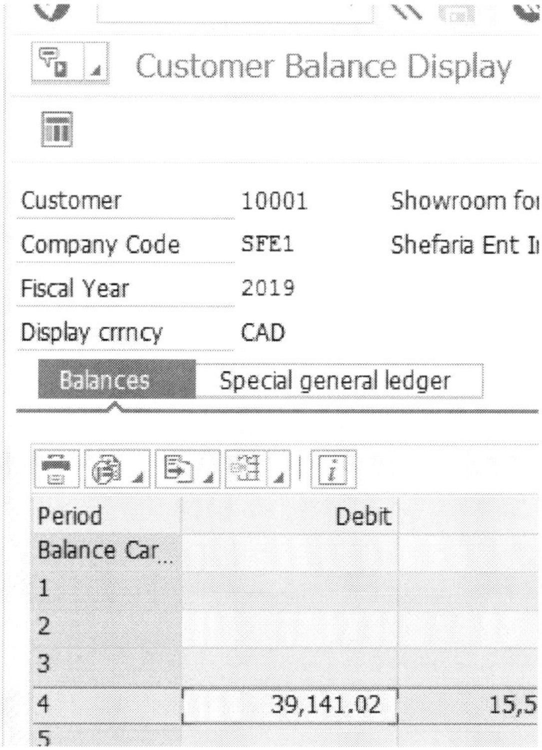

Fig 23

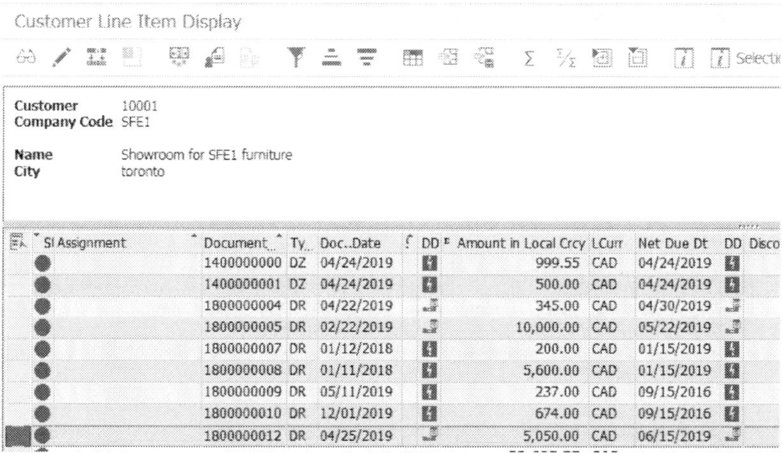

Fig 24

# VI. CLEARING DOWN PAYMENT MADE BY THE CUSTOMER (U)

T Code F-39 or:

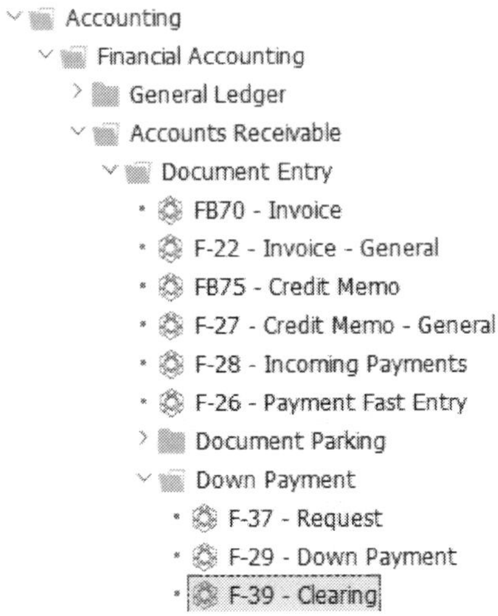

Fig 25

Enter the data as below including the invoice #, which is being cleared:

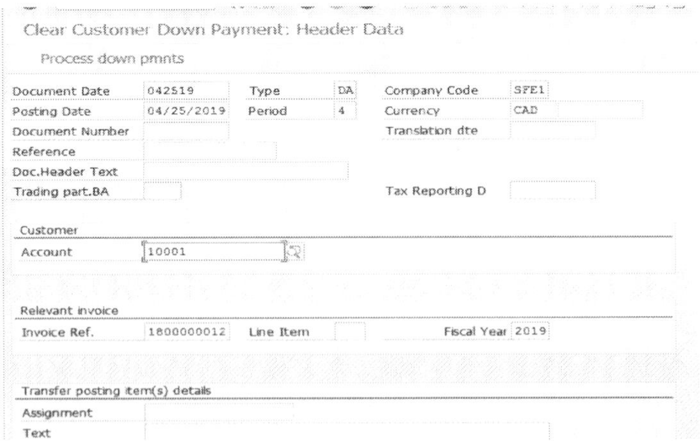

Fig 26

Click on

Now choose the relevant line by doc # (if multiple lines show op) and enter the amount being cleared in the last column:

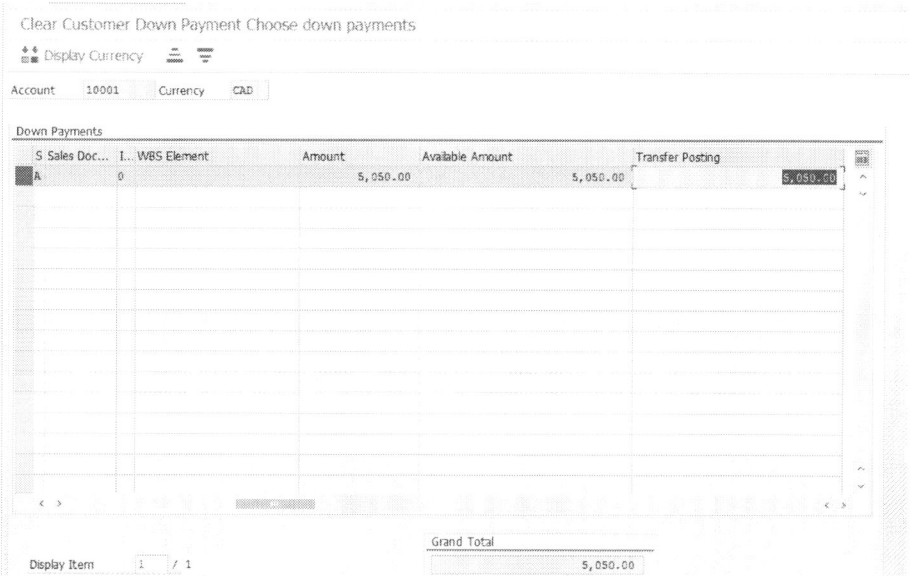

Clear Customer Down Payment Choose down payments

Display Currency

| Account | 10001 | Currency | CAD |

Down Payments

| S | Sales Doc... | I.. | WBS Element | Amount | Available Amount | Transfer Posting | |
|---|---|---|---|---|---|---|---|
| A | 0 | | | 5,050.00 | 5,050.00 | 5,050.00 | |

| Grand Total | |
|---|---|
| | 5,050.00 |

Display Item   1   / 1

Fig 27

Ensure that the total at the bottom is same as the amount being cleared:

Again, we can simulate it:

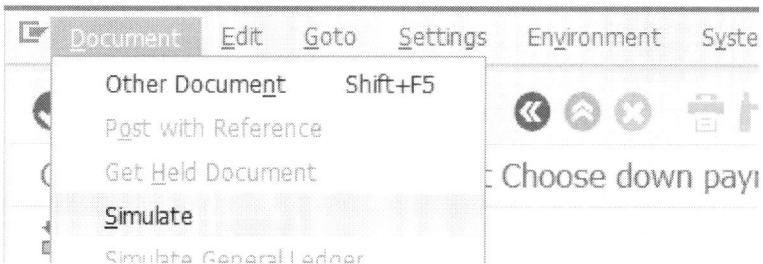

| Document | Edit | Goto | Settings | Environment | Syste |
|---|---|---|---|---|---|
| Other Document | Shift+F5 | | | | |
| Post with Reference | | | | | |
| Get Held Document | | | Choose down payı | | |
| Simulate | | | | | |
| Simulate General Ledger | | | | | |

Fig 28

265

If it looks good, then save it:

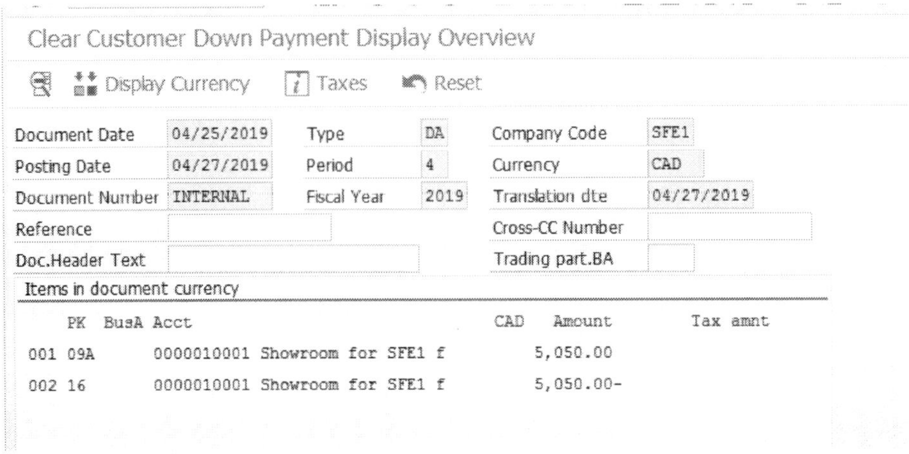

**Clear Customer Down Payment Display Overview**

Display Currency   Taxes   Reset

| Document Date | 04/25/2019 | Type | DA | Company Code | SFE1 |
|---|---|---|---|---|---|
| Posting Date | 04/27/2019 | Period | 4 | Currency | CAD |
| Document Number | INTERNAL | Fiscal Year | 2019 | Translation dte | 04/27/2019 |
| Reference | | | | Cross-CC Number | |
| Doc.Header Text | | | | Trading part.BA | |

Items in document currency

| | PK | BusA | Acct | | CAD | Amount | Tax amnt |
|---|---|---|---|---|---|---|---|
| 001 | 09A | | 0000010001 | Showroom for SFE1 f | | 5,050.00 | |
| 002 | 16 | | 0000010001 | Showroom for SFE1 f | | 5,050.00- | |

**Fig 29**

✅ Document 1600000002 was posted in company code SFE1

# VII. CHECKING THE CUSTOMER BALANCE (U)

T Code: FD10N

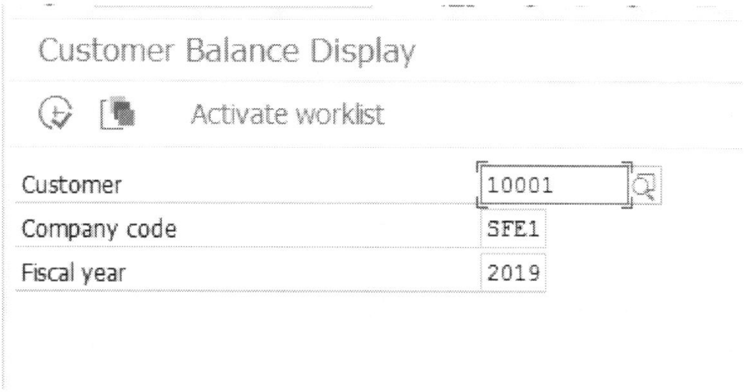

Fig 30

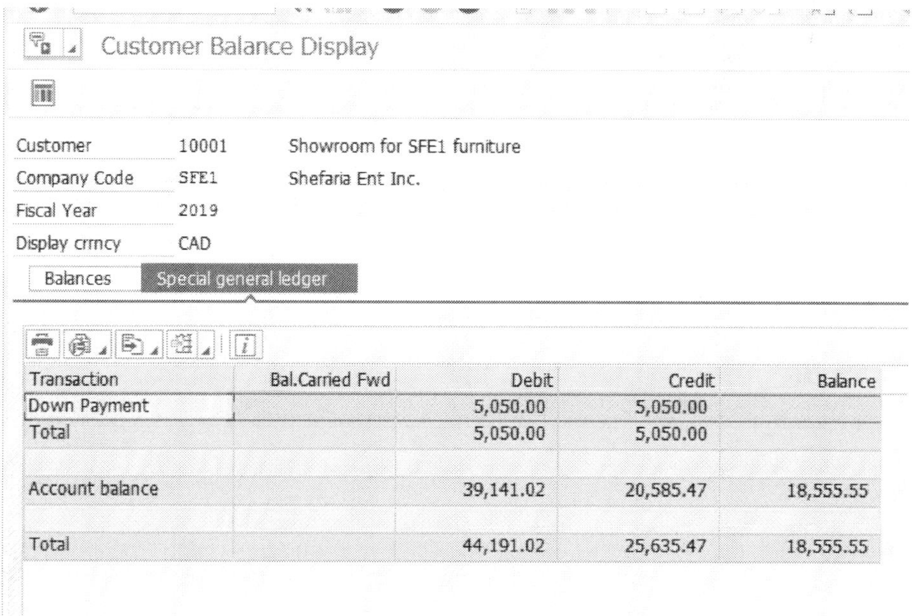

Fig 31

Double click on Total again to confirm the document is cleared.

The 2 highlighted cancelling entries of 5,050 each are revealed above. Note the reference of the clearing document 1600000002 in the document No 1800000012 (Fig 32)

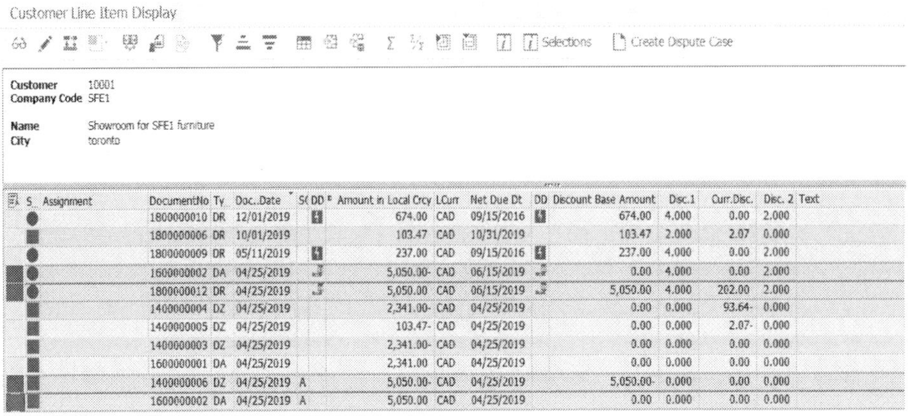

Customer Line Item Display

Customer 10001
Company Code SFE1

Name Showroom for SFE1 furniture
City toronto

| S | Assignment | DocumentNo | Ty | Doc..Date | S(DD | Amount in Local Crcy | LCurr | Net Due Dt | DD | Discount Base Amount | Disc.1 | Curr.Disc. | Disc. 2 | Text |
|---|---|---|---|---|---|---|---|---|---|---|---|---|---|---|
| ● | | 1800000010 | DR | 12/01/2019 | | 674.00 | CAD | 09/15/2016 | | 674.00 | 4.000 | 0.00 | 2.000 | |
| ■ | | 1800000006 | DR | 10/01/2019 | | 103.47 | CAD | 10/31/2019 | | 103.47 | 2.000 | 2.07 | 0.000 | |
| ● | | 1800000009 | DR | 05/11/2019 | | 237.00 | CAD | 09/15/2016 | | 237.00 | 4.000 | 0.00 | 2.000 | |
| ● | | 1600000002 | DA | 04/25/2019 | | 5,050.00- | CAD | 06/15/2019 | | 0.00 | 4.000 | 0.00 | 2.000 | |
| ● | | 1800000012 | DR | 04/25/2019 | | 5,050.00 | CAD | 06/15/2019 | | 5,050.00 | 4.000 | 202.00 | 2.000 | |
| ■ | | 1400000004 | DZ | 04/25/2019 | | 2,341.00- | CAD | 04/25/2019 | | 0.00 | 0.000 | 93.64- | 0.000 | |
| ■ | | 1400000005 | DZ | 04/25/2019 | | 103.47- | CAD | 04/25/2019 | | 0.00 | 0.000 | 2.07- | 0.000 | |
| ■ | | 1400000003 | DZ | 04/25/2019 | | 2,341.00- | CAD | 04/25/2019 | | 0.00 | 0.000 | 0.00 | 0.000 | |
| ■ | | 1600000001 | DA | 04/25/2019 | | 2,341.00 | CAD | 04/25/2019 | | 0.00 | 0.000 | 0.00 | 0.000 | |
| ■ | | 1400000006 | DZ | 04/25/2019 | A | 5,050.00- | CAD | 04/25/2019 | | 5,050.00- | 0.000 | 0.00 | 0.000 | |
| ■ | | 1600000002 | DA | 04/25/2019 | A | 5,050.00 | CAD | 04/25/2019 | | 0.00 | 0.000 | 0.00 | 0.000 | |

Fig 32

# VIII.    Clearing the customer account (U)

T Code: F-32 or:

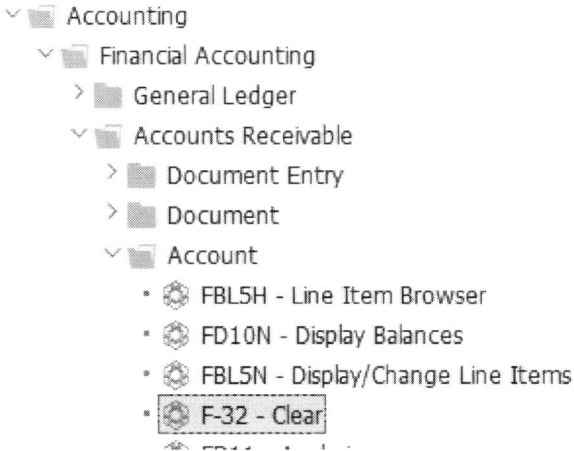

Fig 33

Enter the data as below:

Fig 34

Click on

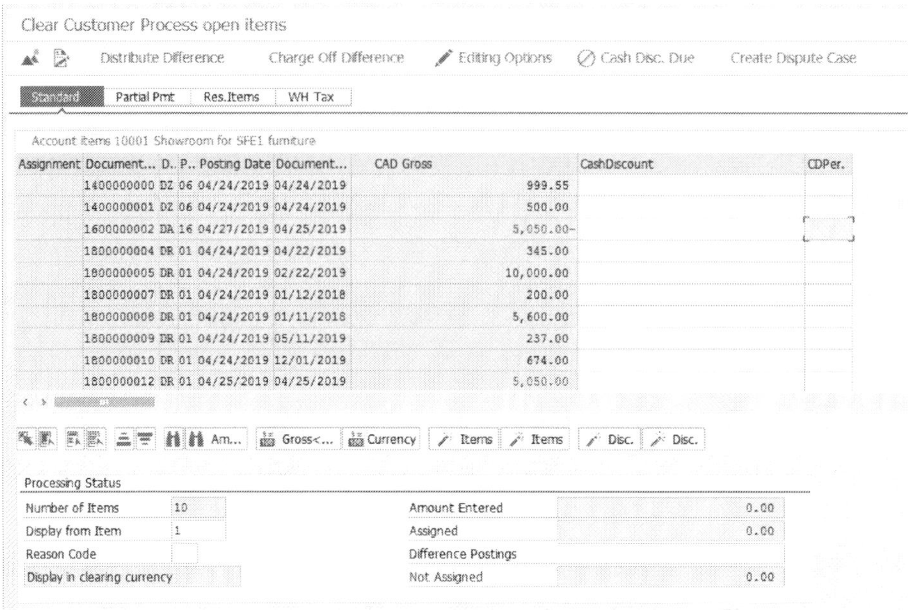

Fig 34

Again, follow the process of selecting/deselecting the required line and ensure the not assigned amount is 0 as above.

Simulate:

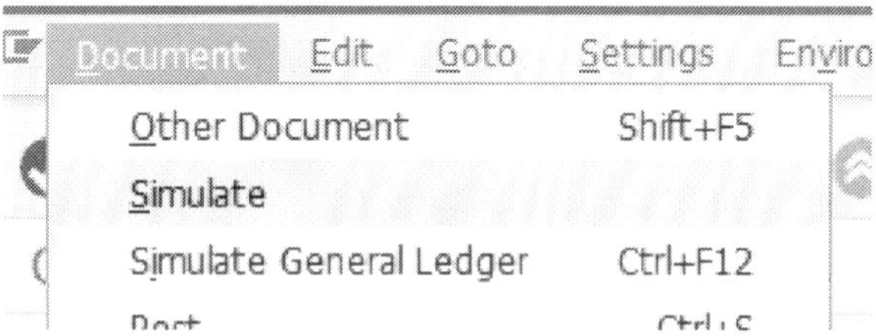

Fig 35

Fig 36

**HANA CHANGE:** In ECC, the system did not show any line items at this stage but only cleared them in the background when F-32 was saved. In HANA, the customer is being debited and credited at the same time using posting keys 07 and 17. The net result is still the i.e. the line items get cleared off the books.

If everything is good, Save it:

Fig 37

Check FD10N again:

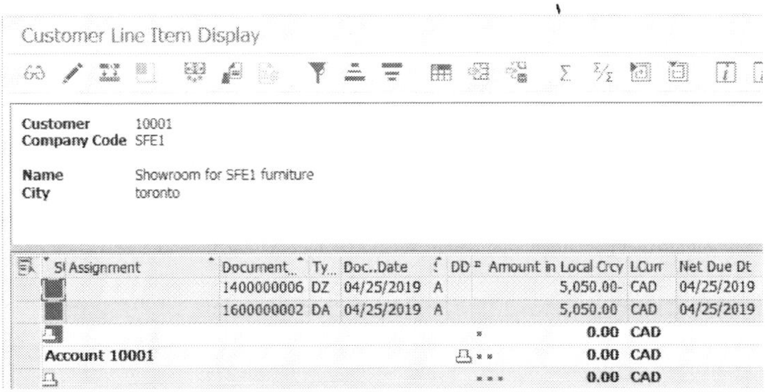

Fig 38

# GOODS RECEIPT (U)

T Code: MIGO

One of the most important transactions and the cusp between Materials Management (MM) and FI, the T Code MIGO is used very frequently in goods based organizations, which buy components or raw materials from vendors. The vendor masters drive how the goods will be received by the company – whether a GR (goods receipt) document must exist before a vendor's invoices can be received in the system or not. Normally this transaction is done by purchasing who verify the goods are in order before receiving them in the system and thereby *indirectly* approving the vendor invoice.

A goods receipt can occur via many ways as an initial transfer of stock, receipt of goods from a vendor, returns from customers etc. For our purpose, to understand the relationship between Materials and Finance, we will cause the GR to create from a Purchase Order (PO) that we will create on a vendor. While the actual detailed creation of the PO, being part of MM, is out of scope of the FI course, we will review some data in the vendor master, which is applicable to this transaction including Purchasing data. In XK01 in ECCor in Transaction BP in HANA, create vendor, let us use the existing vendor to create purchasing views for it. In the previously created BP 9970000030, in the change mode:

Fig 1

Select the role FLVN01 as below:

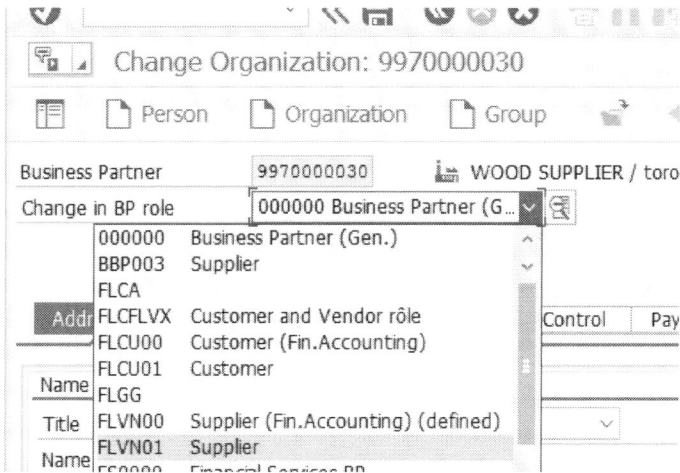

Fig 2

Click on Purchasing Data tab

Fig 3

273

Enter Purchasing Org SFE1:

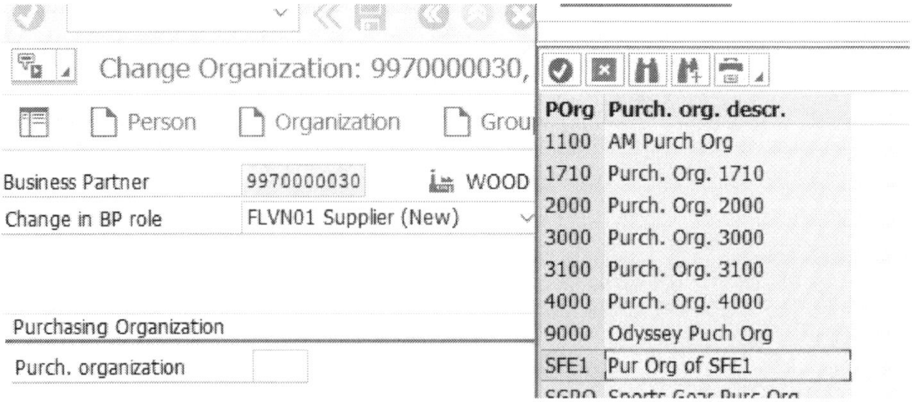

Fig 4

And populate as much data as you can in the tabs below paying special attention to the Purchasing Data tab (this carries most of the data we had in ECC in Purchasing tabs).

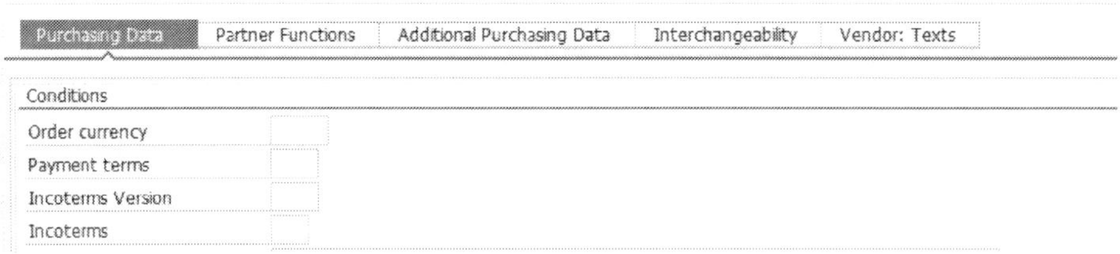

Fig 5

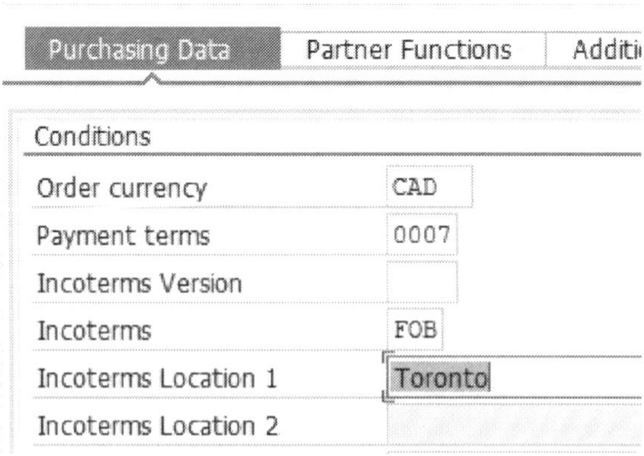

Fig 6

The order currency – used rarely, normally the customer or purchaser decides the ordering currency though this option is available in case the vendor is located overseas and insists on any certain currency that is different from the currency of the buying company. It can be over written in the PO.

The payment terms field in purchasing will take precedence over the payment terms in the accounting screen at time of PO creation.

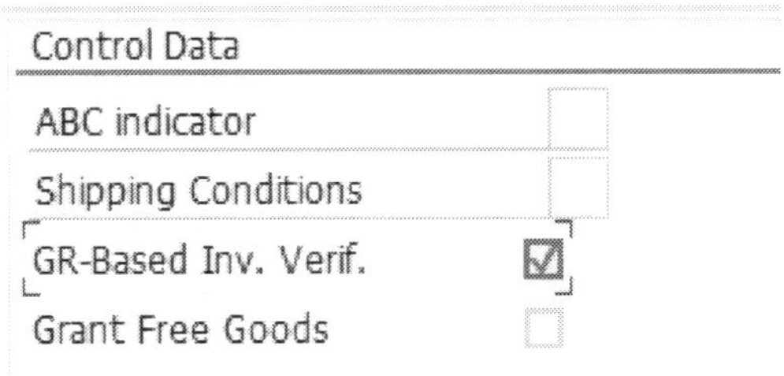

| Control Data | |
| --- | --- |
| ABC indicator | ☐ |
| Shipping Conditions | ☐ |
| GR-Based Inv. Verif. | ☑ |
| Grant Free Goods | ☐ |

Fig 7

GR-Based Inv. Verify. Means until the MIGO transaction has been done (effectively approving the payment for the goods and/or services having been received), the accounting department can't book this invoice (it can be held as an accrual, but not converted into a payable till MIGO is done).

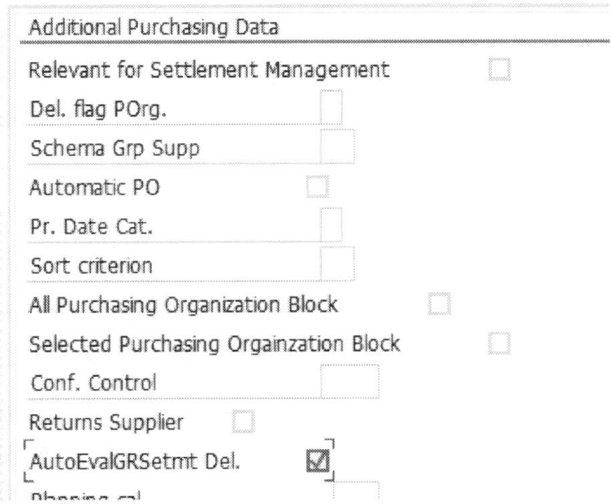

| Additional Purchasing Data | |
| --- | --- |
| Relevant for Settlement Management | ☐ |
| Del. flag POrg. | |
| Schema Grp Supp | |
| Automatic PO | ☐ |
| Pr. Date Cat. | |
| Sort criterion | |
| All Purchasing Organization Block | ☐ |
| Selected Purchasing Orgainzation Block | ☐ |
| Conf. Control | |
| Returns Supplier | ☐ |
| AutoEvalGRSetmt Del. | ☑ |
| Dhaning cal | |

Fig 8

The other buttons are also relevant to accounting depending on what the organization does with the vendor's invoices and how it pays or accrues them. The 2 main ones often used are the ERS (evaluated receipt settlement) in which accruals can be automatically converted to payables and Automatic PO whereby POs can be generated automatically from Purchase requisitions.

For our purpose, we have created a simple PO on an external vendor for material in transaction ME21N the details of which are out of scope of this manual though some of it has been covered in a later section on Framework POs.

There are other data fields that are new but since they fall under the purview of Purchasing, we will skip them here. The vendor is now ready to be used to create POs on and below is one we created for product

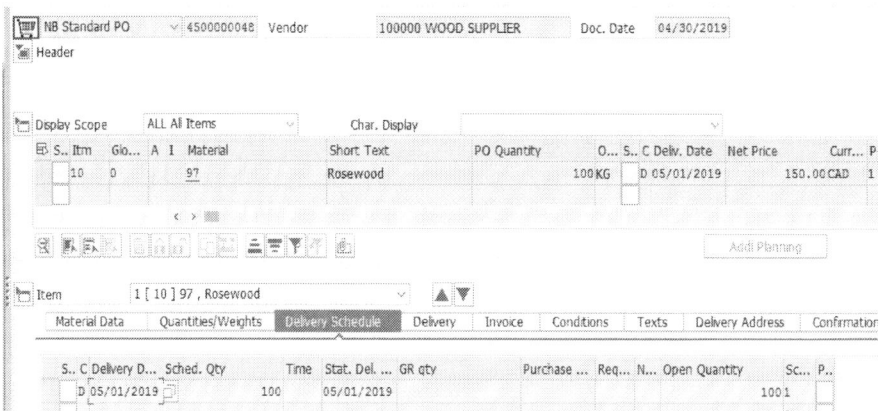

Fig 3

The PO can be displayed in ME23N

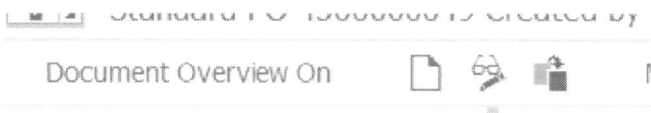

Fig 4

by entering the PO # in the open field by clicking on

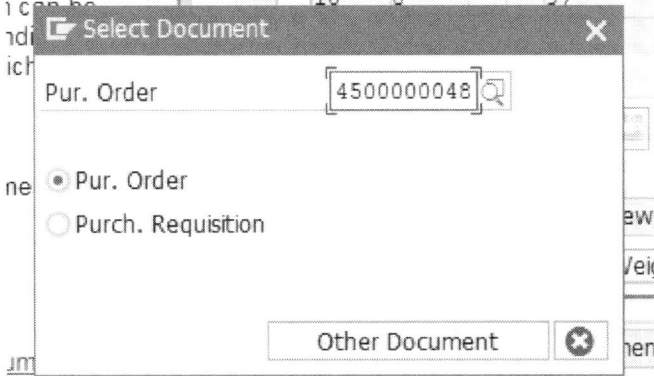

Fig 5

Click on 'Other Document' to view the PO.

From FI perspective, the primary tab of importance at the line item level is Invoice:

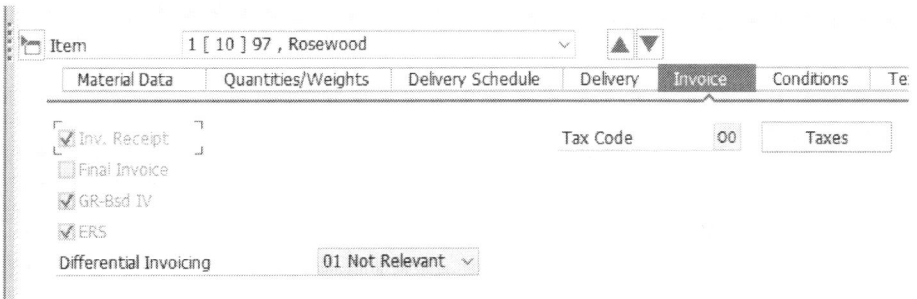

Fig 6

This data, Inv Receipt and GR-Bsd IV as we saw, has defaulted from the vendor master.

Since the PO requires a GR/IR, let us do the GR first via the transaction **MIGO:**

Fig 7

Enter the PO # at the top.

- A crucial field on this screen is the Movement type at the top right. In Materials Management, the entire process of inventory control and movements is driven by Movement type. The SAP standard Movement type for GR from vendors is 101 (for reversals, 102). It is important to note that this 101 default on the MIGO screen is based on the Movement type the user last used. It may be necessary to correct it to the required one. We do have the ability to define our own default values for this screen:

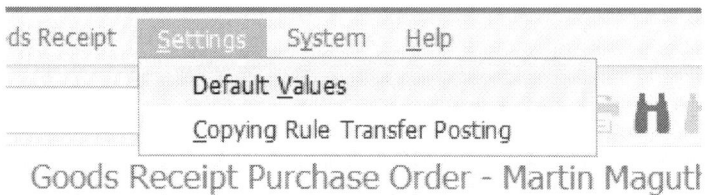

Goods Receipt Purchase Order - Martin Magutl

Fig 8

On clicking Enter, the PO number disappears from the top field and all it's associated data flows into the line item levels at the bottom of the screen:

Fig 9

On the Quantity tab above, you have the option to 'part receive' the goods in case all were not shipped by the vendor. Let us assume we received only 10 out of the 100 kg ordered. Change the quantity from 100 to 10 and click on 'Item OK:

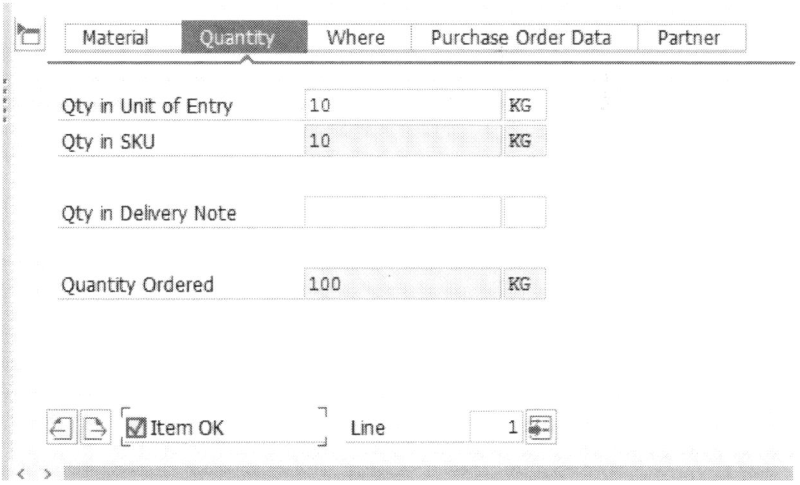

Fig 10

Save to post the document:

Fig 11

This material document would also have posted an accounting document, which can be viewed by going to the material document in MB03 in ECC.

**HANA CHANGE**: Old, tested and used transactions like MB03, MB01, MB1B, MB1C et al are all obsolete in HANA and the system will re-direct you to MIGO. Using MIGO, you can view and/or enter a material document using R02 or you can post the initial stocks using mvt type 561 directly in MIGO.

To view a material document, now use MB51 using any selection criteria you want:

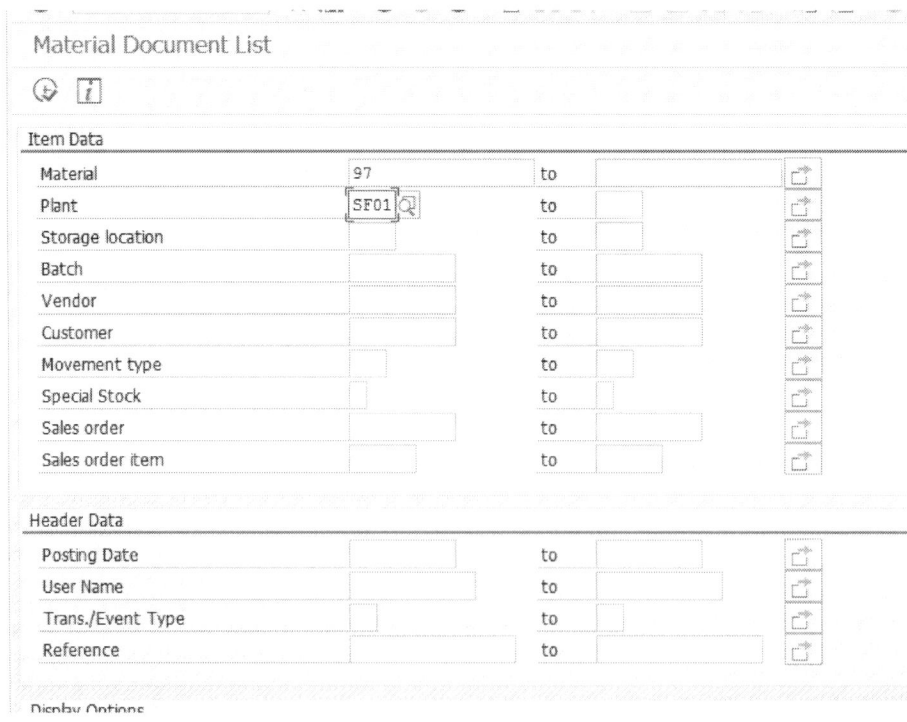

| Material Document List | | |
|---|---|---|
| **Item Data** | | |
| Material | 97 | to |
| Plant | SF01 | to |
| Storage location | | to |
| Batch | | to |
| Vendor | | to |
| Customer | | to |
| Movement type | | to |
| Special Stock | | to |
| Sales order | | to |
| Sales order item | | to |
| **Header Data** | | |
| Posting Date | | to |
| User Name | | to |
| Trans./Event Type | | to |
| Reference | | to |
| Display Options | | |

Fig 12

Alternatively, going back to the PO in ME23N in which a PO History tab would now have appeared at the line item level. This tab is not available unless a subsequent document is posted against the line item.

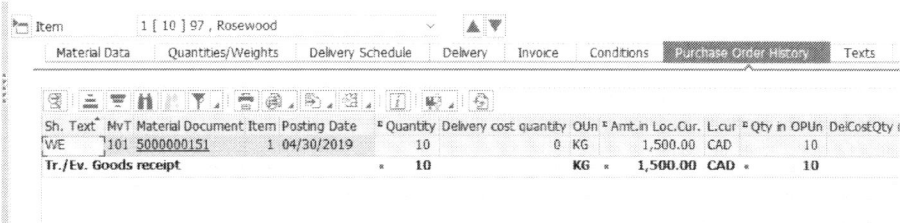

| | | Item | 1 [ 10 ] 97 , Rosewood | | | |
|---|---|---|---|---|---|---|

| Material Data | Quantities/Weights | Delivery Schedule | Delivery | Invoice | Conditions | Purchase Order History | Texts |

| Sh. Text | MvT | Material Document | Item | Posting Date | Quantity | Delivery cost quantity | OUn | Amt.in Loc.Cur. | L.cur | Qty in OPUn | DelCostQty |
|---|---|---|---|---|---|---|---|---|---|---|---|
| WE | 101 | 5000000151 | 1 | 04/30/2019 | 10 | 0 | KG | 1,500.00 | CAD | 10 | |
| Tr./Ev. Goods receipt | | | | | 10 | | KG | 1,500.00 | CAD | 10 | |

Fig 13

Click on the hyperlink (on the Material Doc number) and it takes us into the material document:

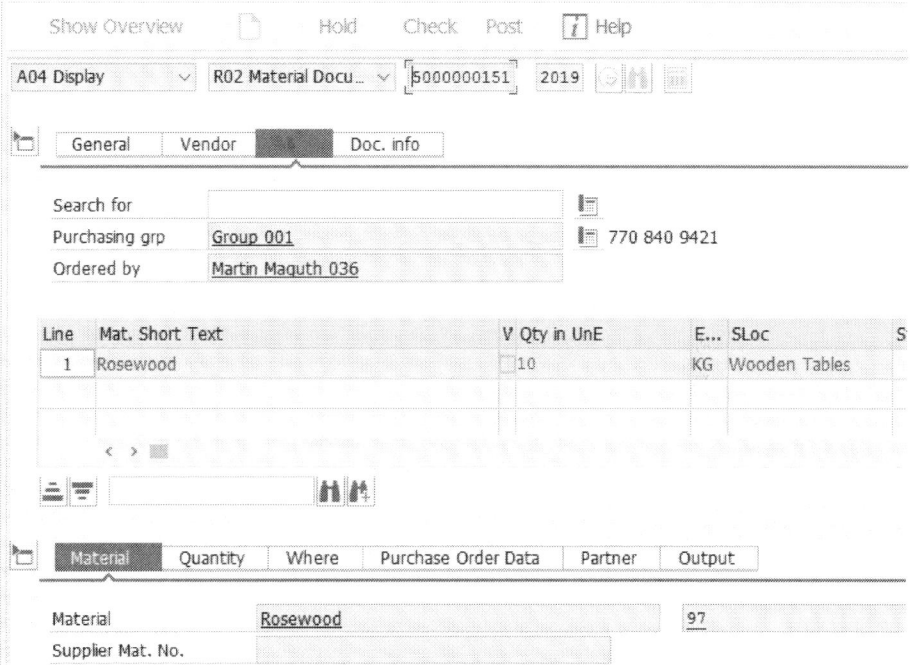

| Show Overview | | Hold | Check | Post | Help |
|---|---|---|---|---|---|

A04 Display ∨ R02 Material Docu... ∨ 5000000151 2019

| General | Vendor | | Doc. info |

Search for
Purchasing grp      Group 001                      770 840 9421
Ordered by          Martin Maguth 036

| Line | Mat. Short Text | V | Qty in UnE | E... | SLoc | S |
|---|---|---|---|---|---|---|
| 1 | Rosewood | | 10 | KG | Wooden Tables | |

| Material | Quantity | Where | Purchase Order Data | Partner | Output |

Material            Rosewood                        97
Supplier Mat. No.

Fig 14

Click on the Doc info tab:

Fig 15

And then on the ⊞ FI Documents

Revealing the accounting document behind it:

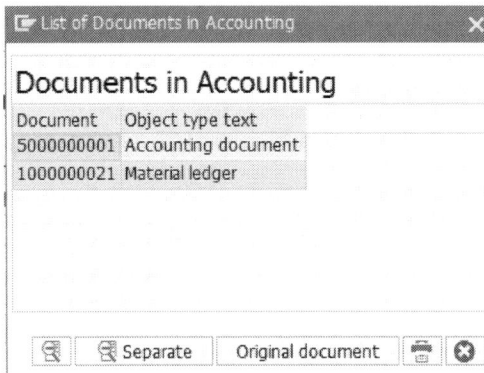

Fig 16

These G/L accounts are configured in transaction OBYC and though strictly a part of MM configuration, this transaction decides most of integration points between MM and FI.

The difference of price variance to G/L 530000 is a result of the price we paid for these items to the vendor and the standard or variable cost we have in the material master of this item in our system.

The details of this calculation are explained next.

Price on the PO is $150.00 per kg which translates to $1,500 as the amount of the goods received that we will pay the vendor:

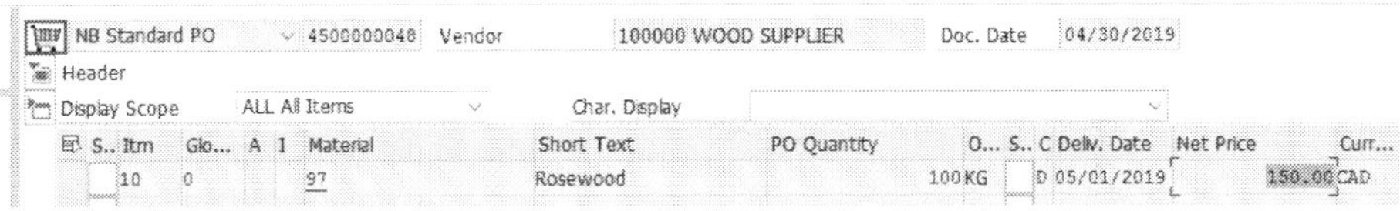

Fig 17

Price in Material Master on Accounting 1 view is 100 per kg which translates to a value of 1,000 for 100 kg of goods received:

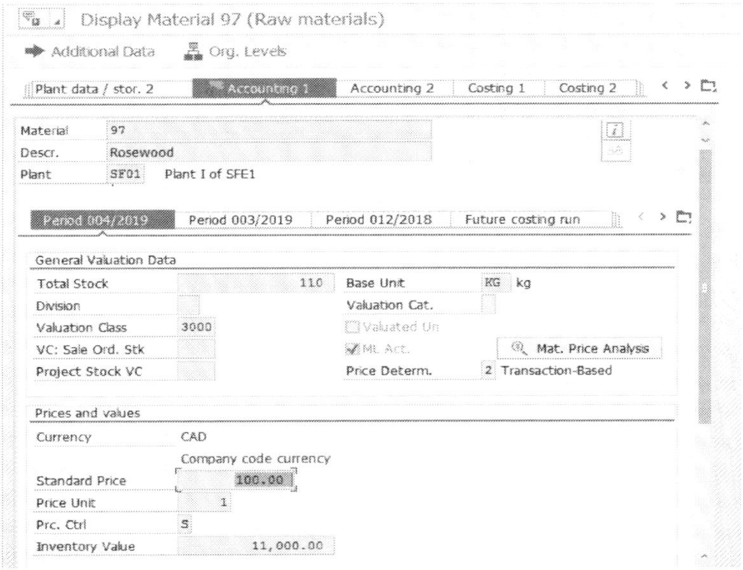

Fig 18

The difference, thus, is the price variance of 500 for buying from this vendor i.e. in this case, a loss to SFE1 since the goods bought for 1,500 are actually valued at 1,000 in the system.

# INVOICE VERIFICATION  (U)

T Code: MIRO

**HANA CHANGE:** In ECC, one could post a vendor invoice any time even if the material posting periods were not open or in the past. With material ledger becoming mandatory in HANA, it is now necessary to align all posting periods i.e. for MM folks, MMPV must be done to enable posting in a new financial period when it opens up.

Unlike MIGO which is primarily performed by the purchasing dept., MIRO is done by Finance/Accounting, as this is the equivalent of booking of vendor invoices for AP based on how the vendor master data is set up.

To explain this process, we will continue working with the same PO. Since MIGO had already occurred, Purchasing has freed up this transaction for FI to take over to book the vendor invoice when it is available against a PO we did MIGO against twice:

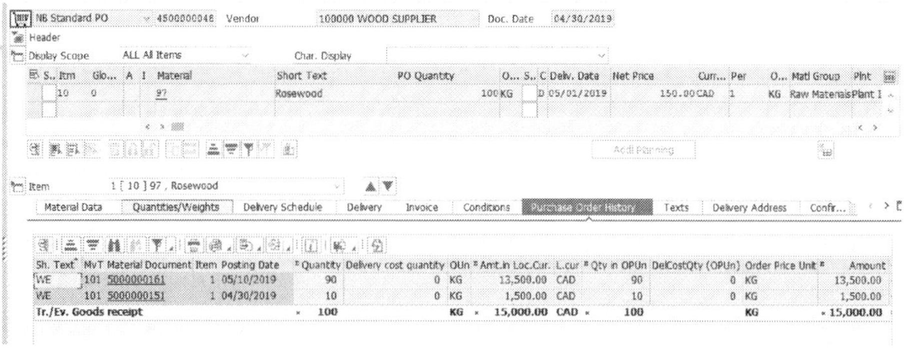

Fig 1

For the purpose of this we will assume the vendor submits the invoice = 1,500 = equal to only one of the line items received so far.

Go to screen for T Code MIRO and enter the Company code in the pop up screen, then the Invoice date, amount of the vendor invoice and the PO number as below and Hit Enter:

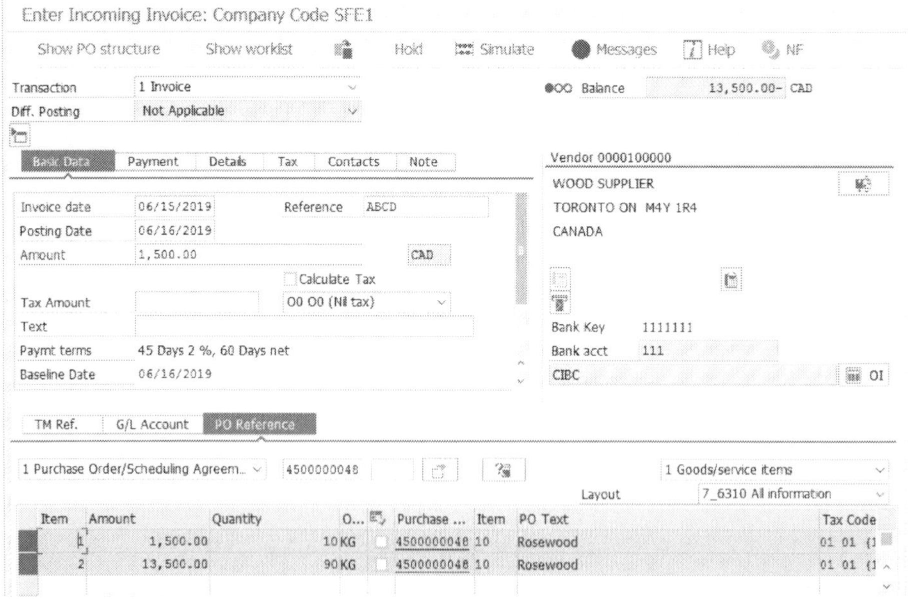

Fig 2

As we see above, when we enter the PO #, the system fetches all the lines against which MIGO has been done and highlights them.

286

However, since the invoice received is only of one of the lines – the first one, we can 'dehighlight' the 2nd line to let it align with the amount of the incoming invoice, on hitting Enter, the amount changes from 15,000 to 1,500 and the document is now balanced (green light at top right).

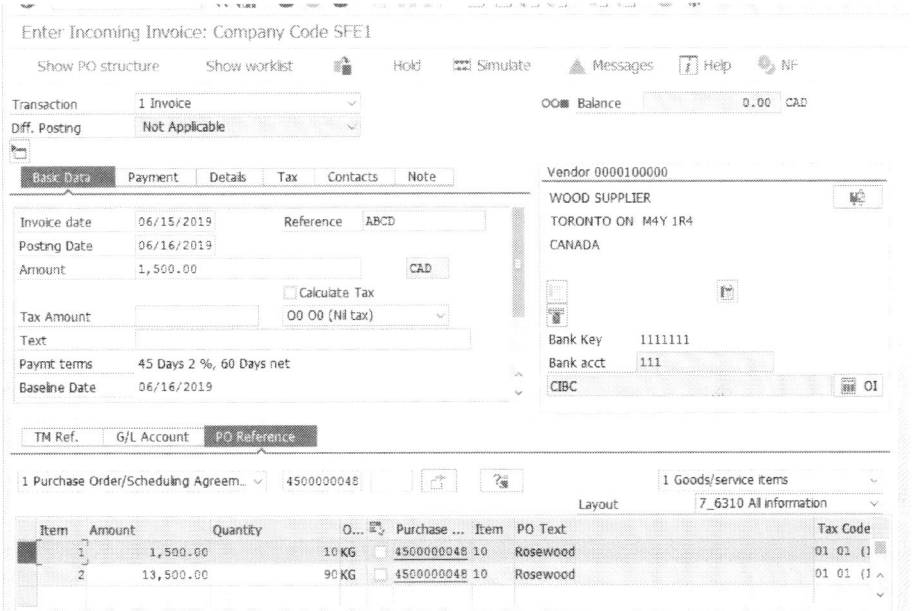

Fig 3

Since the Dr and Cr match we can post it by clicking Save.

Fig 4

We can view this document by:

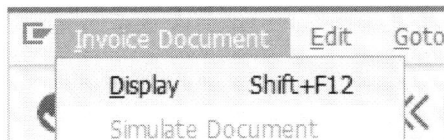

Fig 5

Or in transaction MIR4:

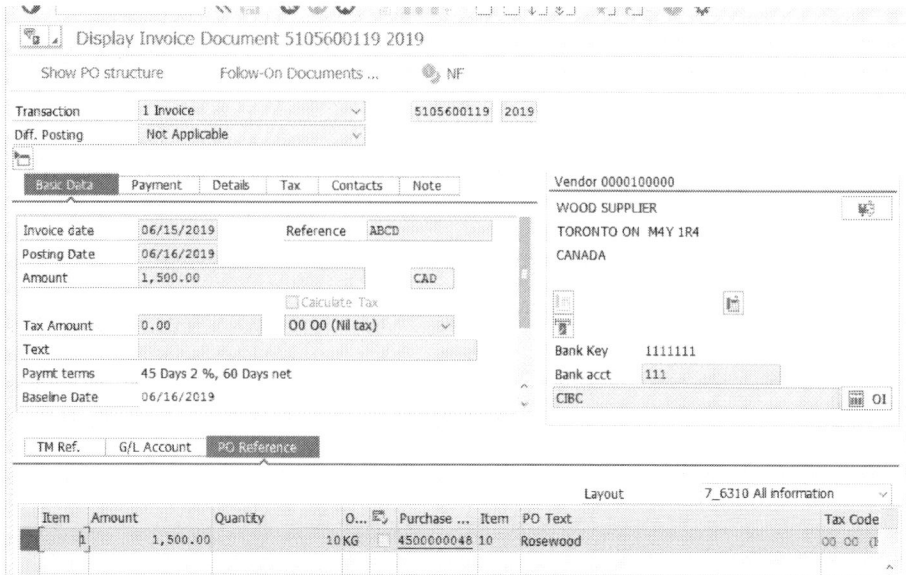

Fig 6

Click on the tab    Follow-On Documents ...

To see the details of the actual accounting document:

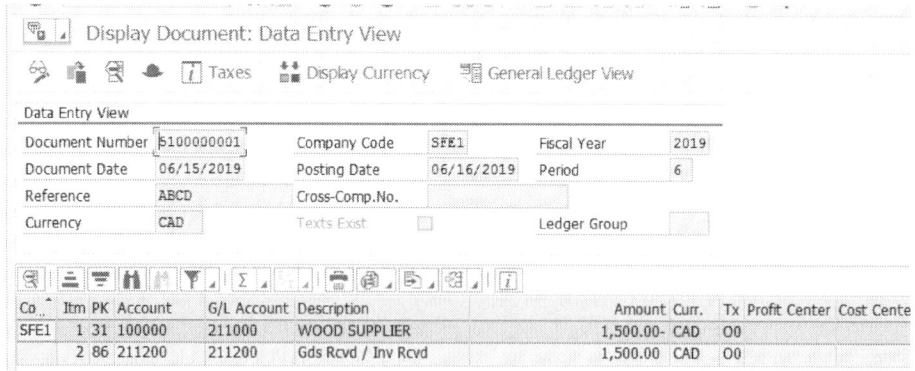

Fig 7

Note that it credited the vendor and cleared the amount in 211200 with a debit, which had earlier been credited when we did the MIGO (goods receipt).

This amount should now show up in the accounts payable to this vendor, which we can look up via FBL1N:

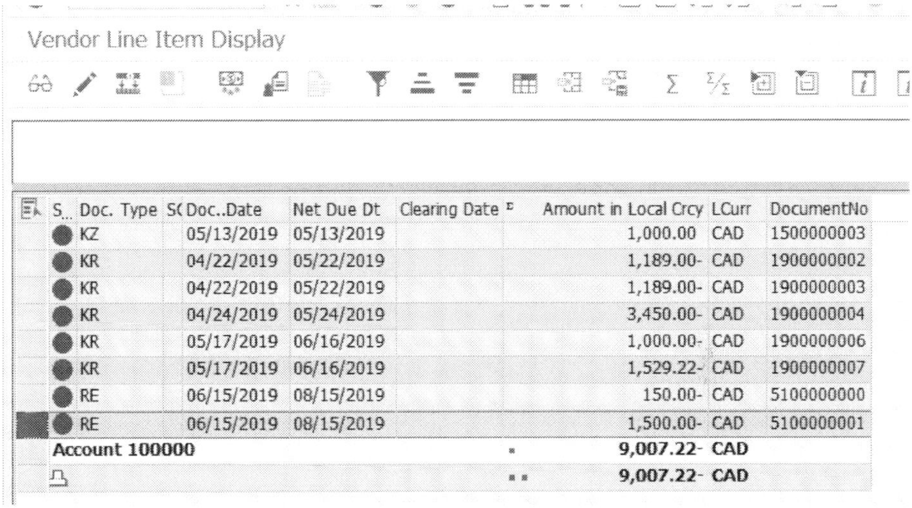

Vendor Line Item Display

| S... | Doc. Type | S( Doc..Date | Net Due Dt | Clearing Date | Amount in Local Crcy | LCurr | DocumentNo |
|---|---|---|---|---|---|---|---|
| KZ | | 05/13/2019 | 05/13/2019 | | 1,000.00 | CAD | 1500000003 |
| KR | | 04/22/2019 | 05/22/2019 | | 1,189.00- | CAD | 1900000002 |
| KR | | 04/22/2019 | 05/22/2019 | | 1,189.00- | CAD | 1900000003 |
| KR | | 04/24/2019 | 05/24/2019 | | 3,450.00- | CAD | 1900000004 |
| KR | | 05/17/2019 | 06/16/2019 | | 1,000.00- | CAD | 1900000006 |
| KR | | 05/17/2019 | 06/16/2019 | | 1,529.22- | CAD | 1900000007 |
| RE | | 06/15/2019 | 08/15/2019 | | 150.00- | CAD | 5100000000 |
| RE | | 06/15/2019 | 08/15/2019 | | 1,500.00- | CAD | 5100000001 |
| Account 100000 | | | | * | 9,007.22- | CAD | |
| | | | | ** | 9,007.22- | CAD | |

Fig 8

289

# EVALUATED INVOICE RECEIPT (U)

T Code MRRL

Often there are vendors whose invoices are converted into payables directly from accruals or after goods have been received, i.e. the company does not wait for the vendor to submit the invoices for the goods or services. SAP has a concept of Evaluated Receipt settlement (ERS) to enable IR (Invoice receipt). The pre-requisite for this is the check on the field **Aut. GR Set Ret** in the Business master for the supplier in purchasing data:

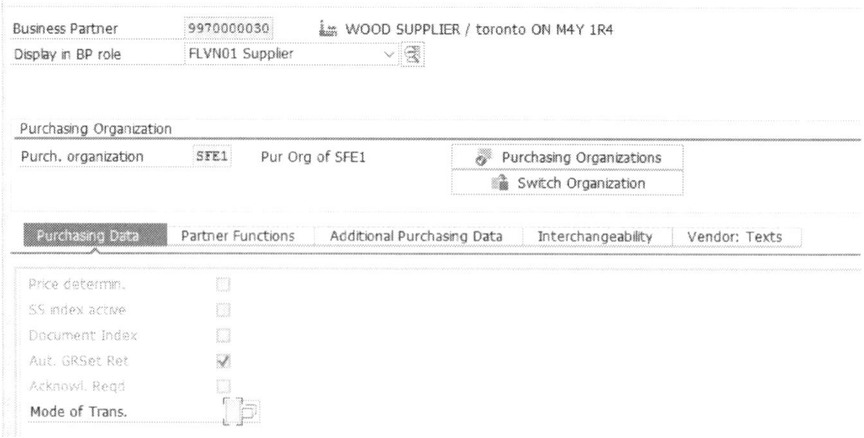

Fig 1

Alternatively, this check can be put in the PO on the line item invoice tab at time of creation or modification. In MM there are purchase info records that are material specific settings, and they over ride what is in the vendor master – in the PIR, we must also ensure that the indicator – No ERS – is NOT set else, that will over ride this setting.

The Goods receipt must exist before this GR can be converted into a payable. Let us do a GR (MIGO) against the same, previous existing PO we used in MIRO. In MIRO, we did an IR for part quantity only. We will do MRRL on the rest of the received quantity. As we notice below, the highlighted line has not yet had an IR against it though the goods have been received.

Fig 2

If we look under the Invoice tab of that line item, we notice the PO is good for MRRL based on the intro section of this topic i..e the pre-requisite has been met:

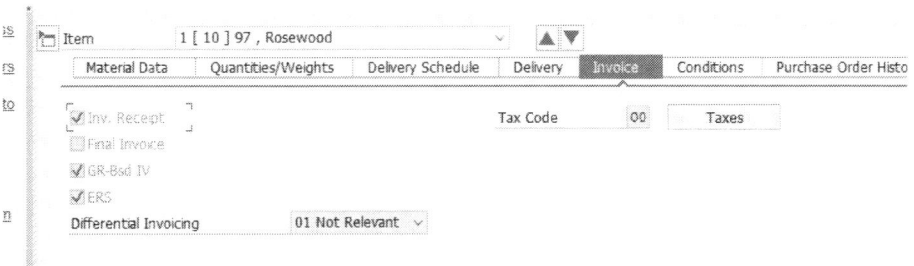

Fig 3

Since the vendor is set up for ERS, we should be able to create the IR without the vendor actually having submitted the invoice. The transaction to run ERS is MRRL. Enter the selection data as necessary and run the transaction. It also gives the ability to first run it in test mode to verify the contents of the documents that will get processed:

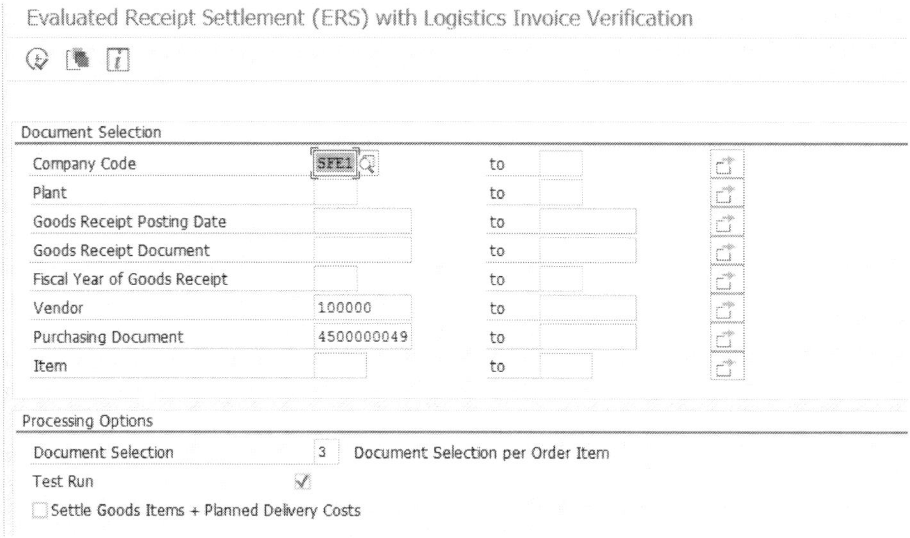

Evaluated Receipt Settlement (ERS) with Logistics Invoice Verification

**Document Selection**

| | | | |
|---|---|---|---|
| Company Code | SFE1 | to | |
| Plant | | to | |
| Goods Receipt Posting Date | | to | |
| Goods Receipt Document | | to | |
| Fiscal Year of Goods Receipt | | to | |
| Vendor | 100000 | to | |
| Purchasing Document | 4500000049 | to | |
| Item | | to | |

**Processing Options**

| | | |
|---|---|---|
| Document Selection | 3 | Document Selection per Order Item |
| Test Run | ✓ | |
| ☐ Settle Goods Items + Planned Delivery Costs | | |

Fig 4

Execute to view in this test mode and we find the line of our PO is ready to create IR:

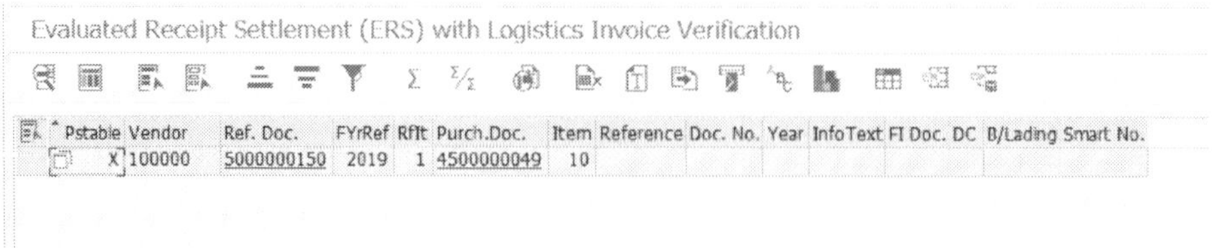

Evaluated Receipt Settlement (ERS) with Logistics Invoice Verification

| Pstable | Vendor | Ref. Doc. | FYrRef | RfIt | Purch.Doc. | Item | Reference Doc. No. | Year | InfoText | FI Doc. | DC | B/Lading | Smart No. |
|---|---|---|---|---|---|---|---|---|---|---|---|---|---|
| X | 100000 | 5000000150 | 2019 | 1 | 4500000049 | 10 | | | | | | | |

Fig 5

The X indicator in the Postable field means this line item will be posted when not run in test mode.  The field Info text blank is an indicator that all is well with this line. Any error would have been reflected in this field.

Now we can go back, remove the test flag, and post it by executing again.

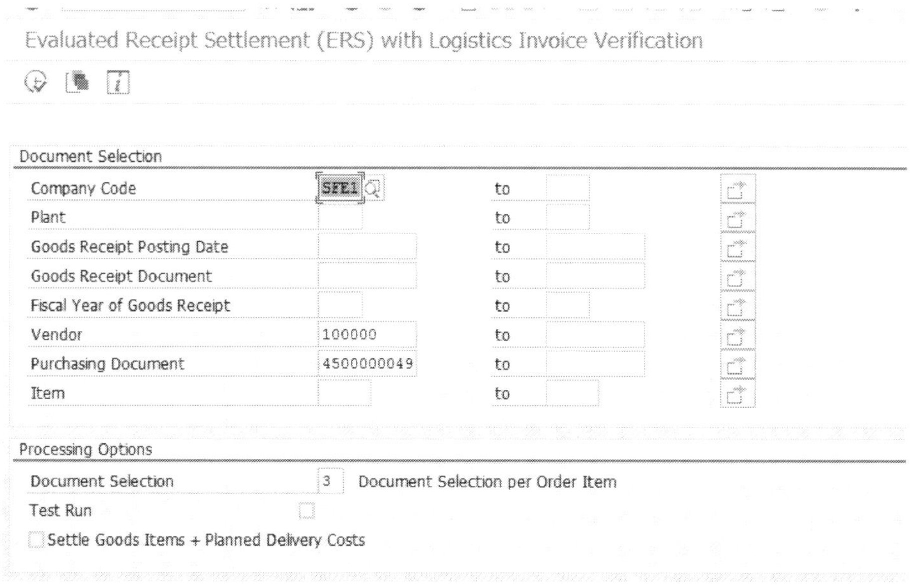

Evaluated Receipt Settlement (ERS) with Logistics Invoice Verification

**Document Selection**

| | | | |
|---|---|---|---|
| Company Code | SFE1 | to | |
| Plant | | to | |
| Goods Receipt Posting Date | | to | |
| Goods Receipt Document | | to | |
| Fiscal Year of Goods Receipt | | to | |
| Vendor | 100000 | to | |
| Purchasing Document | 4500000049 | to | |
| Item | | to | |

**Processing Options**

| | | |
|---|---|---|
| Document Selection | 3 | Document Selection per Order Item |
| Test Run | ☐ | |
| ☐ Settle Goods Items + Planned Delivery Costs | | |

Fig 6

This time, in the real run, it gives the actual Invoice doc # and the FI document #:

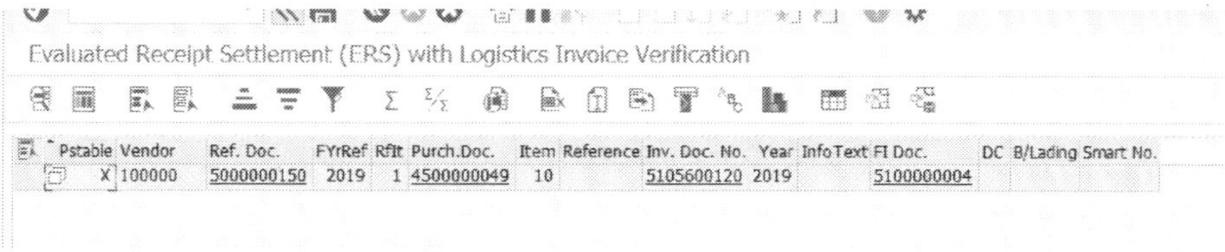

Evaluated Receipt Settlement (ERS) with Logistics Invoice Verification

| Pstable | Vendor | Ref. Doc. | FYrRef | RfIt | Purch.Doc. | Item | Reference | Inv. Doc. No. | Year | InfoText | FI Doc. | DC | B/Lading | Smart No. |
|---|---|---|---|---|---|---|---|---|---|---|---|---|---|---|
| X | 100000 | 5000000150 | 2019 | 1 | 4500000049 | 10 | | 5105600120 | 2019 | | 5100000004 | | | |

Fig 7

293

The PO history for that line item will now reflect this number:

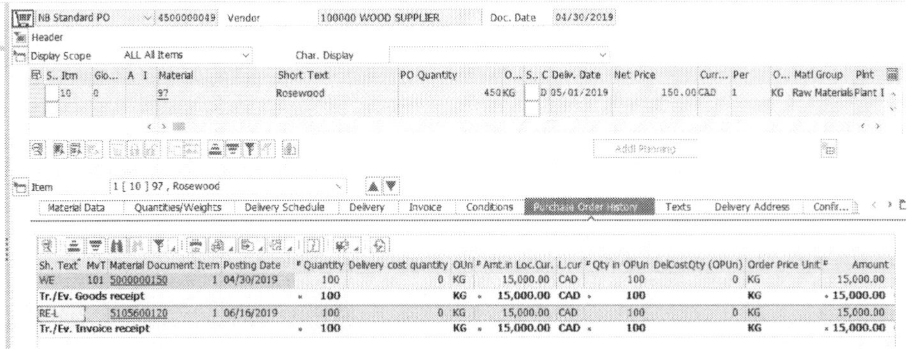

Fig 8

As will the AP of the vendor in FBL1N – the highlighted line below, FI document 5100000004:

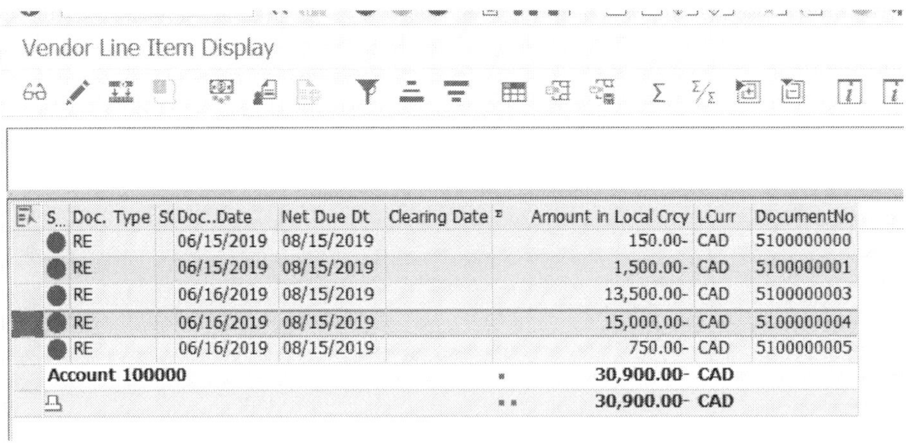

Fig 9

Reversing an ERS is done by creating a credit memo via MIRO. The GR can also be reversed after that if necessary.

E.g. if we now want to reverse this ERS, in MIRO, we choose:

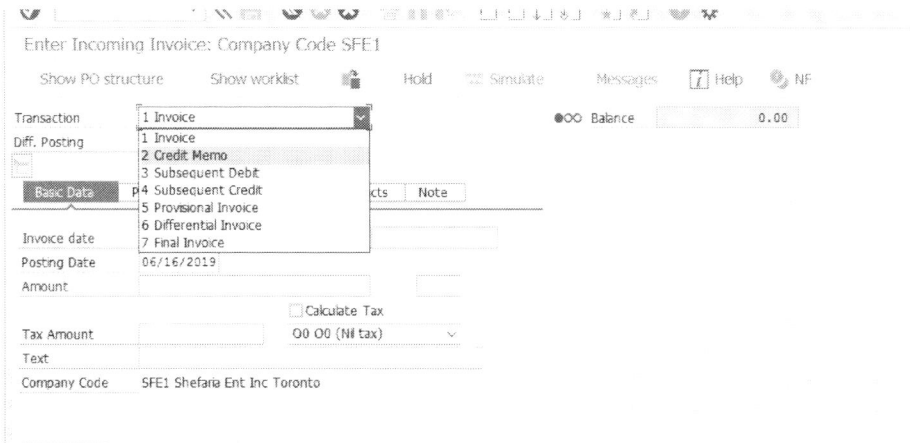

Fig 10

Enter the amount in the Amount column that is being reversed, Hit Enter and the 2 lines against which we have the IR will come up:

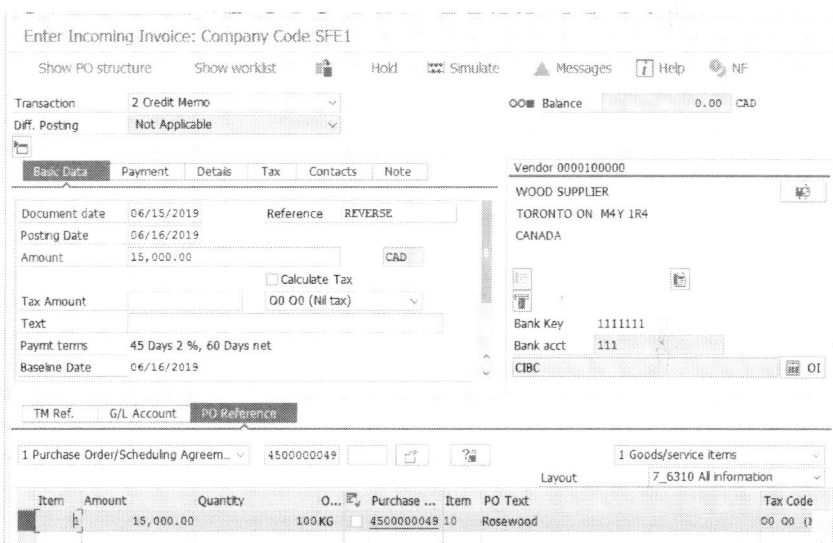

Fig 11

If we just save this, it will reverse both:

Document no. 5105600123 created

Fig 12

If we go back to the PO, we find that the IR has been reversed for both the instances:

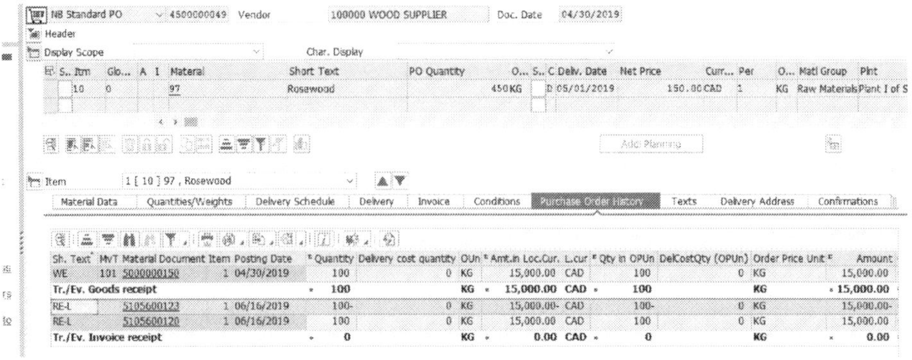

Fig 13

As has the AP in FBL1N:

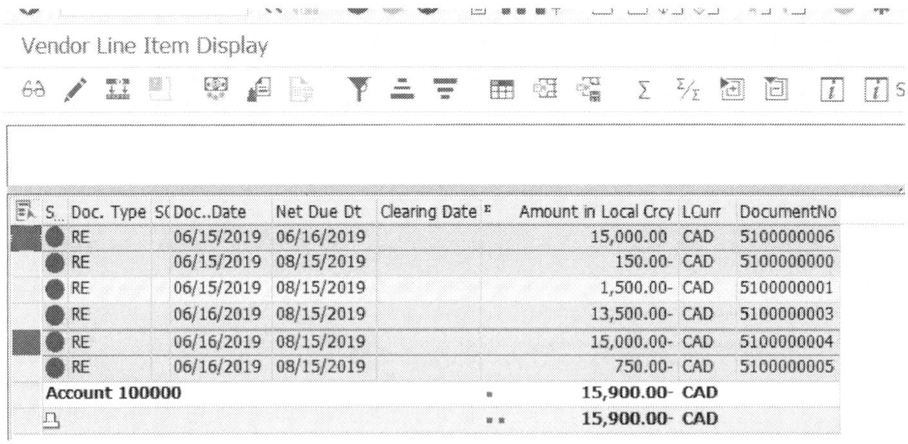

Fig 14

Once an IR done via ERS has been reversed, SAP no longer allows ERS to be done on it again. It has to be now posted manually only via MIRO and can't be done via MRRL.

ERS is very useful to post AP of vendors who provide shipping services; in most cases, the number of invoices is large even though amounts may be small. ERS comes in very handy to prevent manual work and can be run as background jobs to post the AP from the accruals of shipment costs and other service costs.

# PURCHASE ORDER CREATION (U)

T Code ME21N

Purchase Orders for raw materials will usually be created by the Purchasing department and are a part of the MM Module. Certain kind of POs like Framework POs, also referred to as 'Open', 'Blanket', or 'Standing' POs may fall under the purview of Finance. These would typically be POs like for electricity, insurance etc and invoices thus coming in from such vendors, can be paid against these POs bypassing MIGO as there is nothing to *receive*. The POs help track the monies spent on such purchases and make the audit trail clear.

The code to create POs is ME21N. The key is to select the correct PO type, and the main 3 ones are:

1. NB – standard PO used for external vendors and intercompany Purchases
2. UB – stock transport orders used to move material from the same company's one plant to another plant

3. FO – Framework order which is what we will discuss here

Fig 1

There is nothing special required from the vendor perspective for this purpose so we will use the same vendor for this purpose. This vendor need not be set as a GR/IR based payment, as there is no tracking need for the electricity received by the MM department.

On the main ME21N screen, choose FO as the PO type and enter the vendor # as below along with the period this PO will be valid for, normally made yearly but there are no restrictions and it can be practically any period.

Fig 2

Since the service really is not inventoried nor does it require any costing etc, one can freely enter it as the material – here we use – Electricity. The important field is the Account Assignment group – here we say it is K i.e. a cost center must be allocated to this purchase so something can take the hit for the amount associated with it. Further, the plant (SF01) and Material group are mandatory fields. The PO must have a value – e.g. here, 100,000; the quantity is meaningless – has been entered as 1 EA.

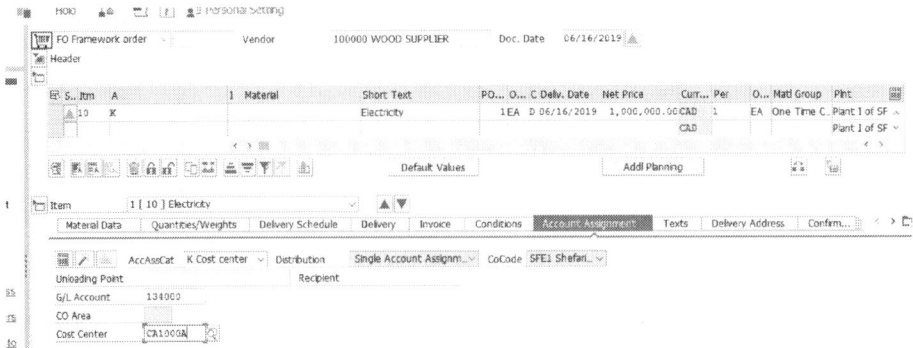

Fig 3

In the line item data, the appropriate cost center is entered:

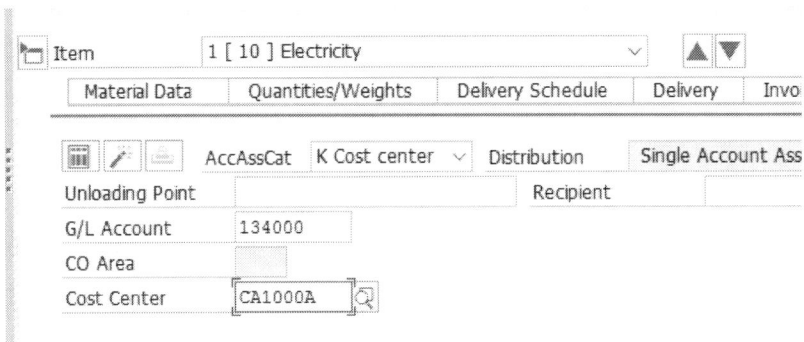

Fig 4

And the required tax under the Invoice tab:

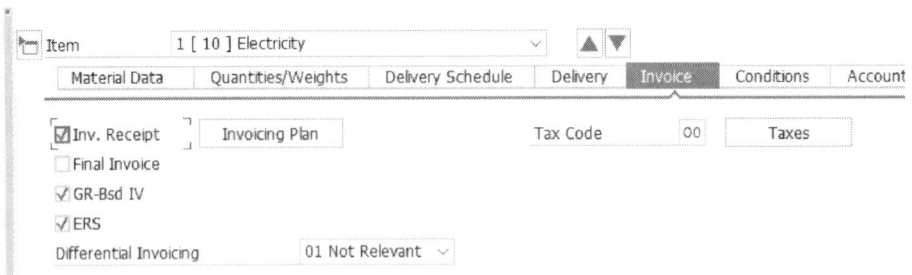

Fig 5

Save the PO to get the number. Normally, your company may desire to have different numbering series for the different kinds of POs just for differentiation purposes.

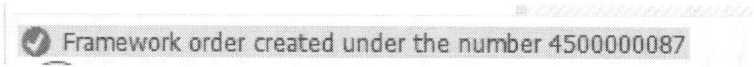

✓ Framework order created under the number 4500000087

Fig 6

The payment of this PO can be made the same way in MIRO as any other goods based PO.

# AUTOMATIC PAYMENT RUNS (C/U)

Automatic payment programs (t code F110) can be set up in SAP to issue checks to vendors and rebates to customers w/o manual intervention to a large extent. It cuts down the time for processing as well as by automating the process; the companies are able to stay on schedules for making payments.

## I.    BANK SETUP IN SAP (C)

T Code SPRO

The first step to enable auto payments is to define from where they will be paid from i.e. the bank accounts. To set up a bank in a CC, follow the path in configuration in Fig 1

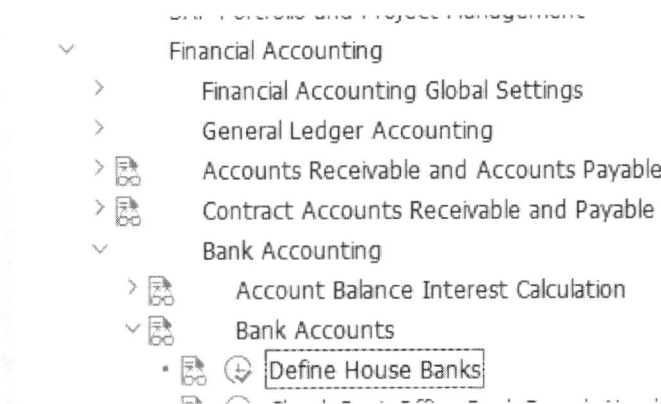

Fig 1

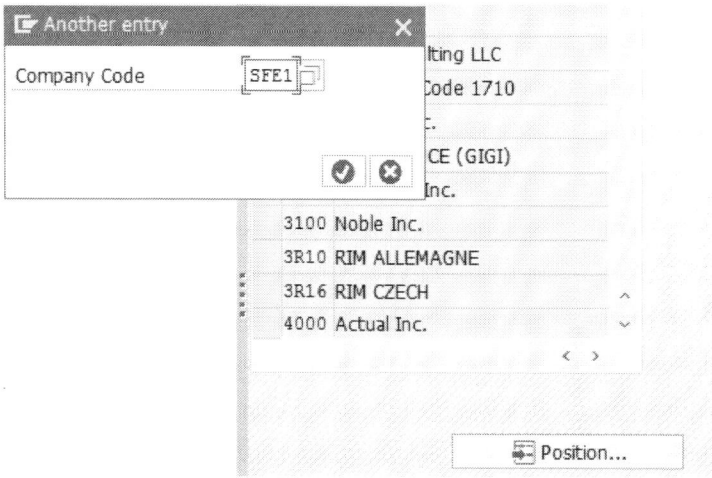

Fig 2

Click Enter and in the new window enter the details of the bank after clicking on New Entries:

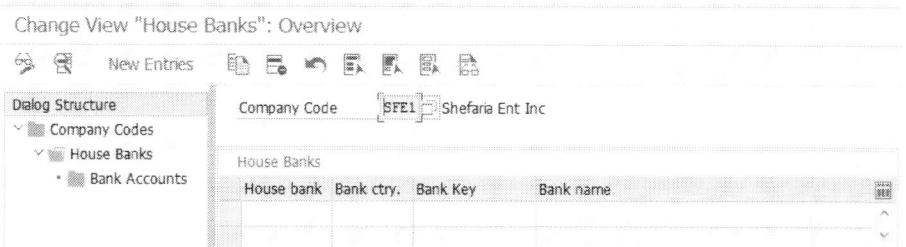

Fig 3

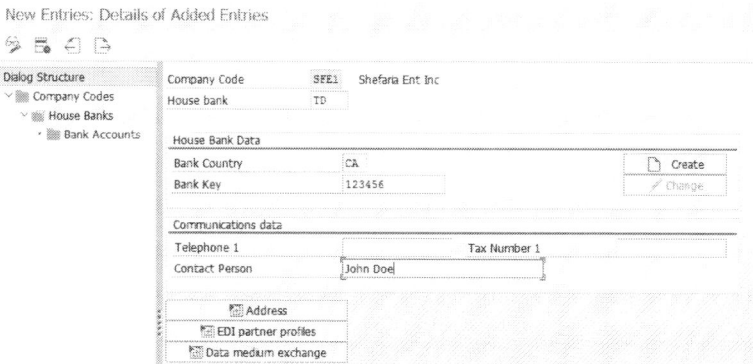

Fig 4

303

The House Bank is the abbreviation for your bank as TD above.

The bank key is the routing # of your bank

Enter telephone and contact person and other details in the address if you wish to and save.

Now double click on Bank Accounts to enter more details in the browser.

**HANA CHANGE:** Since HANA works through Fiori, when you double click on Bank Accounts, the browser opens up to enter the details of the bank through the Net weaver Business client (NWBC).

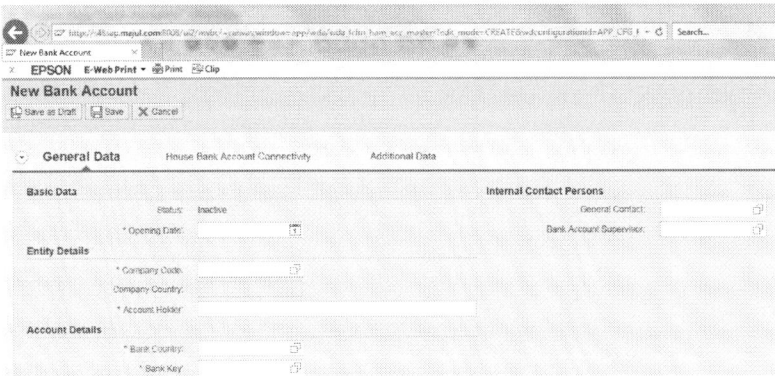

Fig 5

Enter more details relevant to this account and save:

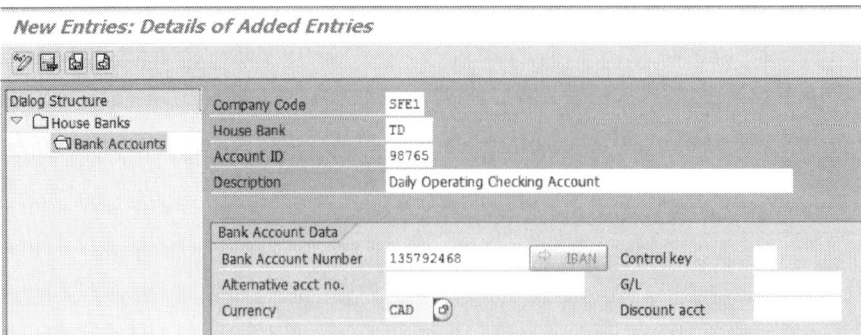

Fig 6

Save the data:

Fig 7

The next configuration step is to set up the Company Codes that will be able to make payments via automatic payment runs. The steps for that are in the path:

Fig 8

Click on New Entries and set up the CC in this table:

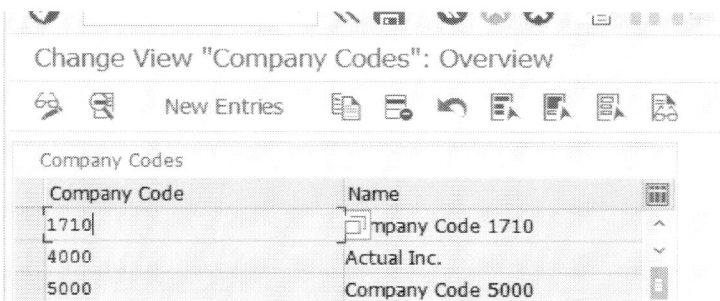

Fig 9

Set up the sending and paying with your CC.

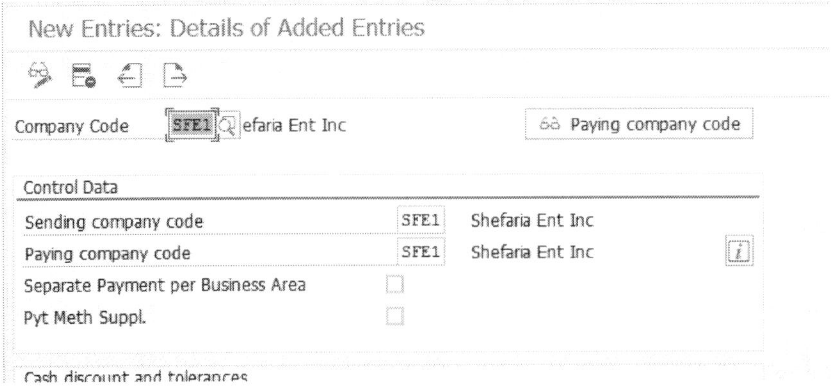

Fig 10

Save.

Now we are required to do some configurations about the details of the paying CC:

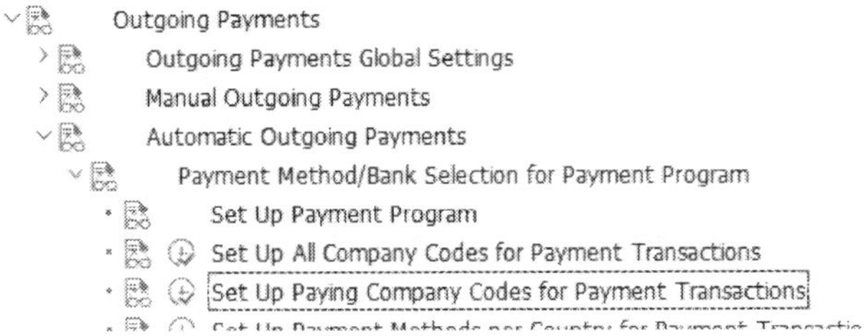

Fig 11

Click on New Entries:

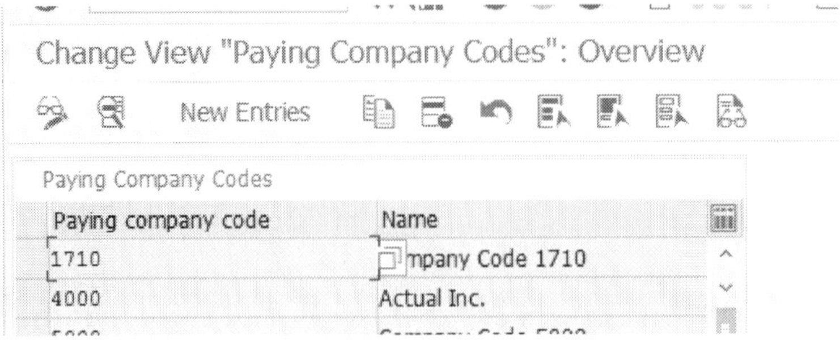

Fig 12

Fig 13

Save.

Next, we set up the methods by which our CC can make payments in the step:

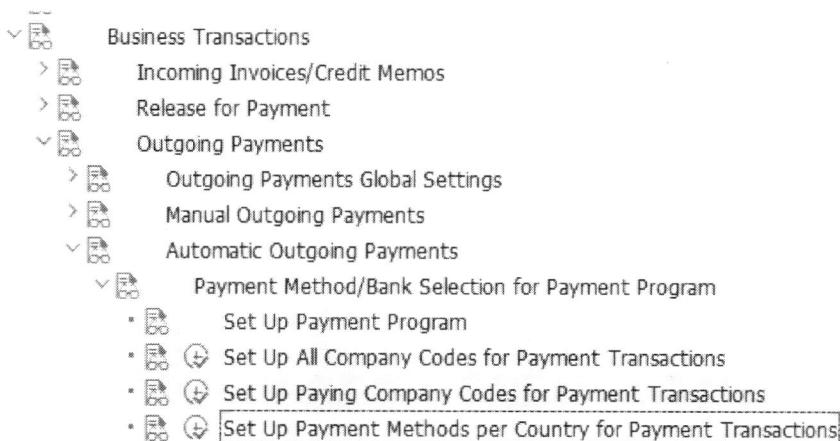

Fig 14

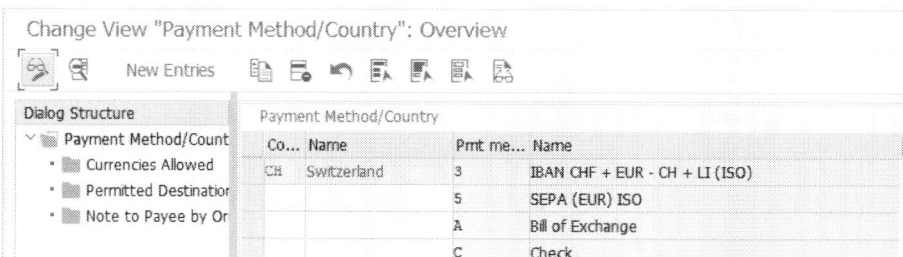

Fig 15

Click on New Entries again in the above screen and add the country and payment method as below:

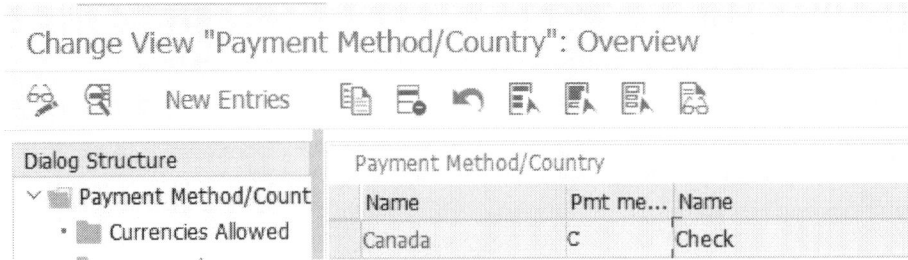

Fig 16

We define that we can make a minimum payment and max payment by Check as above in this CC. Save the configuration.

If you want to allow this CC to make transfers also, then make the relevant entry like for Check:

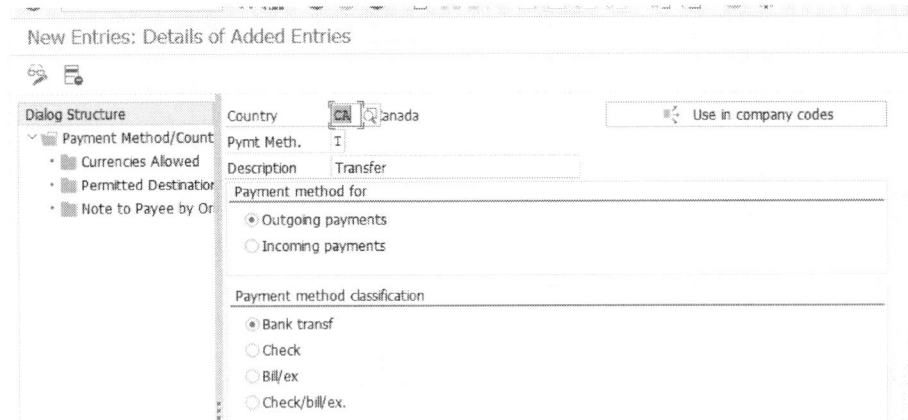

Fig 17

Next step would be to enable the program to understand which bank account to use when processing automatic payments. This is done in the path:

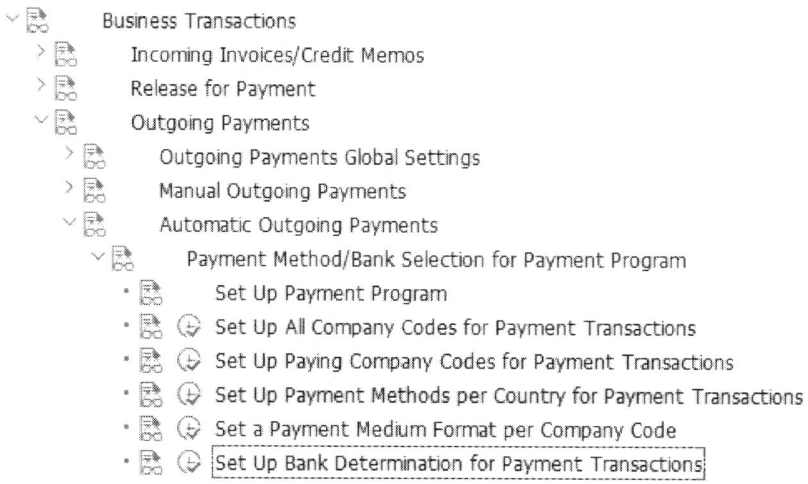

- ⌄ Business Transactions
  - › Incoming Invoices/Credit Memos
  - › Release for Payment
  - ⌄ Outgoing Payments
    - › Outgoing Payments Global Settings
    - › Manual Outgoing Payments
    - ⌄ Automatic Outgoing Payments
      - ⌄ Payment Method/Bank Selection for Payment Program
        - · Set Up Payment Program
        - · ⊕ Set Up All Company Codes for Payment Transactions
        - · ⊕ Set Up Paying Company Codes for Payment Transactions
        - · ⊕ Set Up Payment Methods per Country for Payment Transactions
        - · ⊕ Set a Payment Medium Format per Company Code
        - · ⊕ Set Up Bank Determination for Payment Transactions

Fig 18

Find your CC:

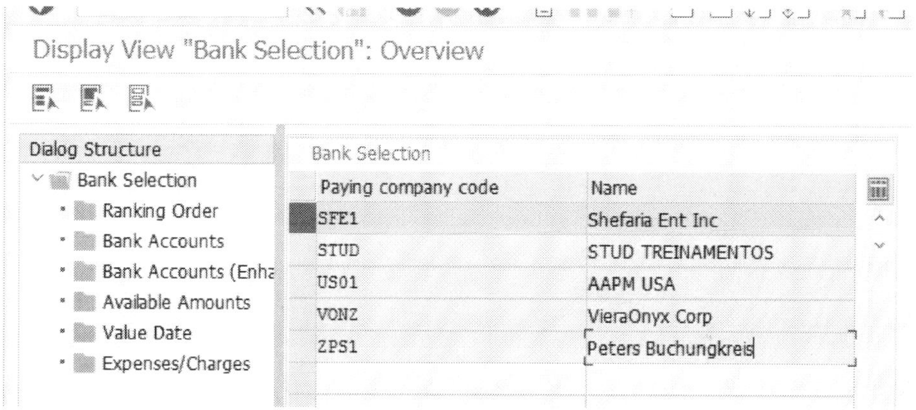

Display View "Bank Selection": Overview

| Dialog Structure | Bank Selection | |
| --- | --- | --- |
| ⌄ Bank Selection | Paying company code | Name |
| · Ranking Order | SFE1 | Shefaria Ent Inc |
| · Bank Accounts | STUD | STUD TREINAMENTOS |
| · Bank Accounts (Enha | US01 | AAPM USA |
| · Available Amounts | VONZ | VieraOnyx Corp |
| · Value Date | ZPS1 | Peters Buchungkreis |
| · Expenses/Charges | | |

Fig 18

309

Double click on the step – Ranking Order as above after highlighting your CC.

The display mode changes to Change mode.

Click on New Entries:

Enter the relevant data for your methods of payment as below:

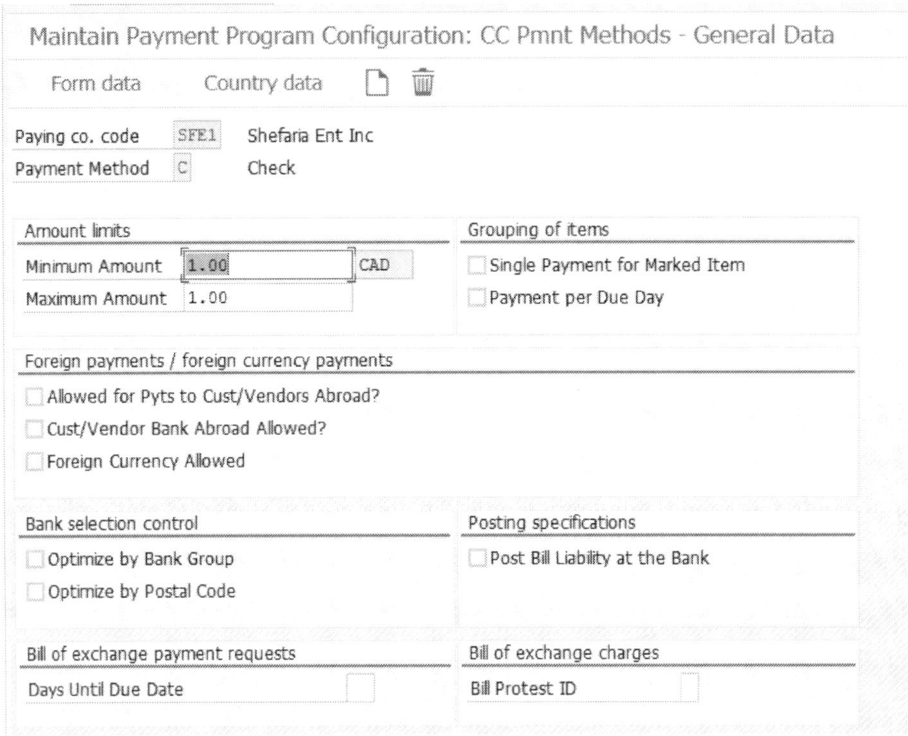

Maintain Payment Program Configuration: CC Pmnt Methods - General Data

| Form data | Country data |
|---|---|

Paying co. code    SFE1    Shefaria Ent Inc
Payment Method    C    Check

**Amount limits**

Minimum Amount    1.00    CAD
Maximum Amount    1.00

**Grouping of items**

☐ Single Payment for Marked Item
☐ Payment per Due Day

**Foreign payments / foreign currency payments**

☐ Allowed for Pyts to Cust/Vendors Abroad?
☐ Cust/Vendor Bank Abroad Allowed?
☐ Foreign Currency Allowed

**Bank selection control**

☐ Optimize by Bank Group
☐ Optimize by Postal Code

**Posting specifications**

☐ Post Bill Liability at the Bank

**Bill of exchange payment requests**

Days Until Due Date

**Bill of exchange charges**

Bill Protest ID

Fig 19

In the above configuration, we are telling SAP program to use this bank as the first priority for cutting checks or sending the payments by transfer.

Save the configuration.

Step back and select the CC again:

310

New Entries: Overview of Added Entries

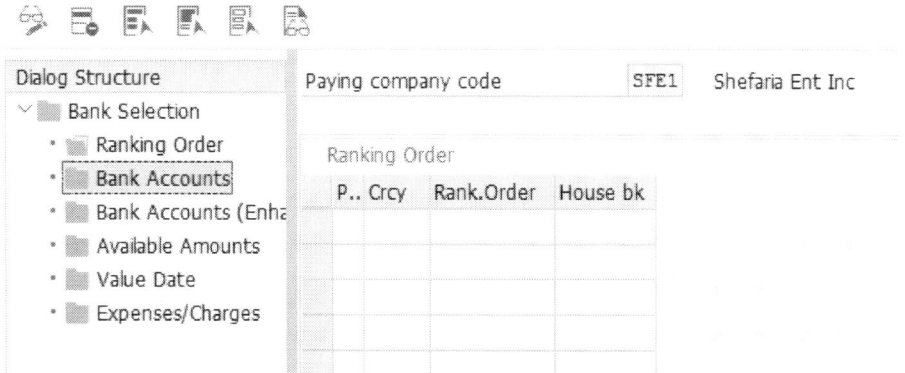

Dialog Structure

Paying company code  SFE1  Shefaria Ent Inc

∨ Bank Selection
 · Ranking Order
 · Bank Accounts
 · Bank Accounts (Enha
 · Available Amounts
 · Value Date
 · Expenses/Charges

Ranking Order

| P.. | Crcy | Rank.Order | House bk |
|-----|------|------------|----------|
|     |      |            |          |

Fig 20

Double click on Bank Accounts:

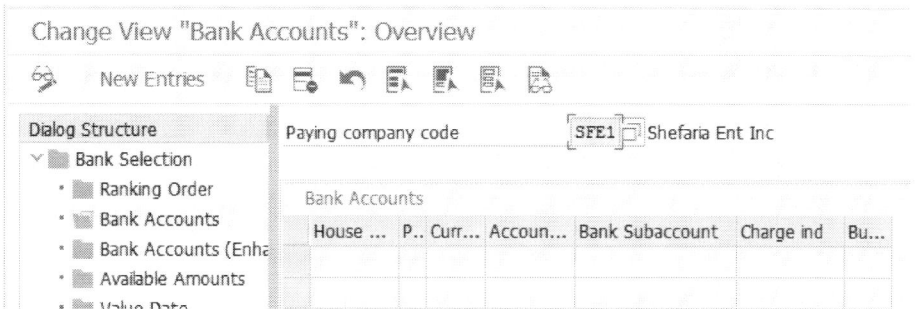

Change View "Bank Accounts": Overview

New Entries

Dialog Structure

Paying company code  SFE1  Shefaria Ent Inc

∨ Bank Selection
 · Ranking Order
 · Bank Accounts
 · Bank Accounts (Enha
 · Available Amounts
 · Value Date

Bank Accounts

| House ... | P.. | Curr... | Accoun... | Bank Subaccount | Charge ind | Bu... |
|-----------|-----|---------|-----------|-----------------|------------|-------|
|           |     |         |           |                 |            |       |

Fig 21

Click on New Entries and make the entries relating to the actual bank that will make the payments; basically, we are selecting what we have already configured:

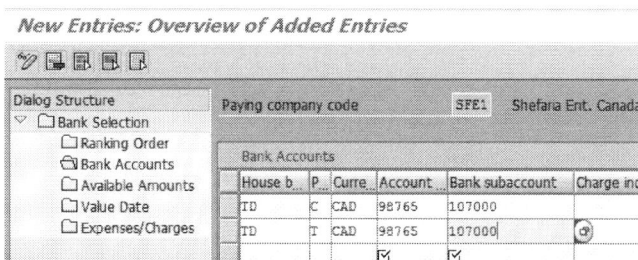

New Entries: Overview of Added Entries

Dialog Structure

Paying company code  SFE1  Shefaria Ent. Canada

∨ Bank Selection
 Ranking Order
 Bank Accounts
 Available Amounts
 Value Date
 Expenses/Charges

Bank Accounts

| House b.. | P.. | Curre.. | Account | Bank subaccount | Charge ind |
|-----------|-----|---------|---------|-----------------|------------|
| TD        | C   | CAD     | 98765   | 107000          |            |
| TD        | T   | CAD     | 98765   | 107000          | ☑          |
|           |     |         | ☑       | ☑               |            |

Fig 22

311

The only exception is the Bank sub-account, which is really the G/L account in the CC that needs to be debited or credited when payments are made to and from it.

Save the data and proceed similarly to the next step of Available Amounts.

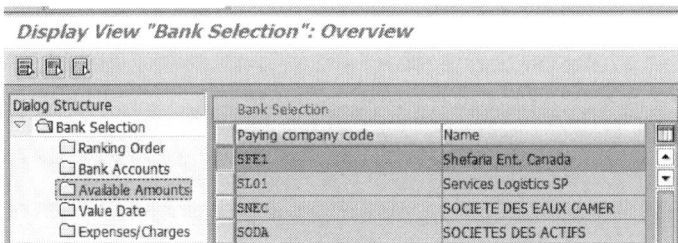

Fig 23

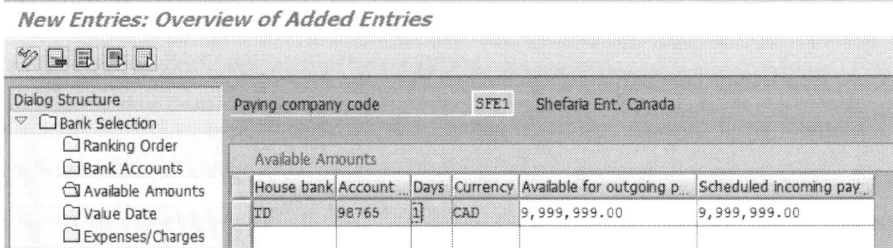

Fig 24

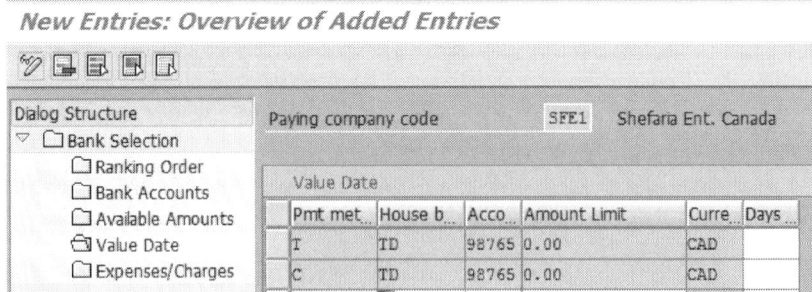

Fig 25

Save.

All the above configuration steps can also be achieved in one area menu related to setting up the CC for auto payments. The t code for that area menu is FBZP:

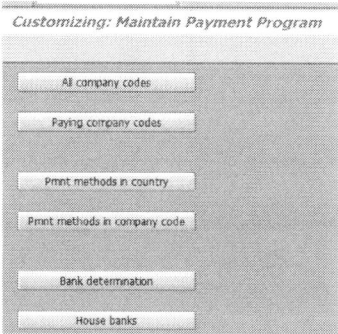

Customizing: Maintain Payment Program

All company codes

Paying company codes

Pmnt methods in country

Pmnt methods in company code

Bank determination

House banks

## II.   CREATING CHECK LOTS (U)

T Code FCHI

Finally, define the check #s in the transaction code FCHI for the house bank and bank account that you will use for making the payments:

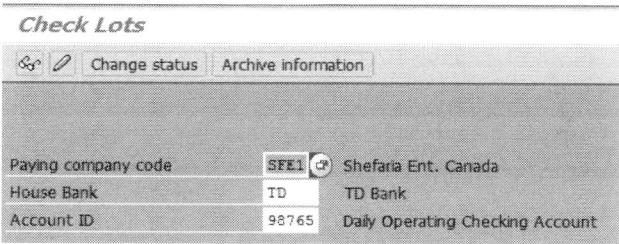

*Check Lots*

&° ⌀  Change status   Archive information

| | | |
|---|---|---|
| Paying company code | SFE1 ⌷ | Shefaria Ent. Canada |
| House Bank | TD | TD Bank |
| Account ID | 98765 | Daily Operating Checking Account |

Fig 26

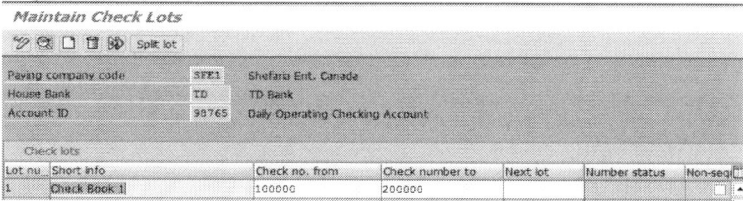

*Maintain Check Lots*

⌂ ⌀ ◻ ⅏ ⅏  Split lot

| | | |
|---|---|---|
| Paying company code | SFE1 | Shefaria Ent. Canada |
| House Bank | TD | TD Bank |
| Account ID | 98765 | Daily Operating Checking Account |

Check lots

| Lot no | Short info | Check no. from | Check number to | Next lot | Number status | Non-seq |
|---|---|---|---|---|---|---|
| 1 | Check Book 1 | 100000 | 200000 | | | ☐ |

Fig 27

313

# III. PAYMENT RUN (U)

T Code F110

To execute the actual payment run for your CC, use transaction F110 or follow the path in the SAP menu:

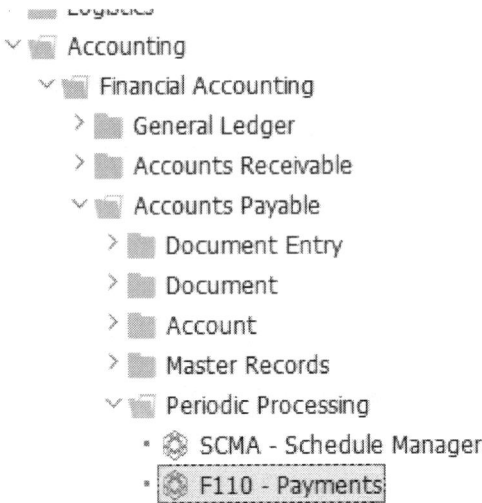

Fig 28

The Identification (Fig 29) is a free text field used to identify the particular run. It can be the name of the person or region or group creating it or anything else the company may prefer as nomenclature.

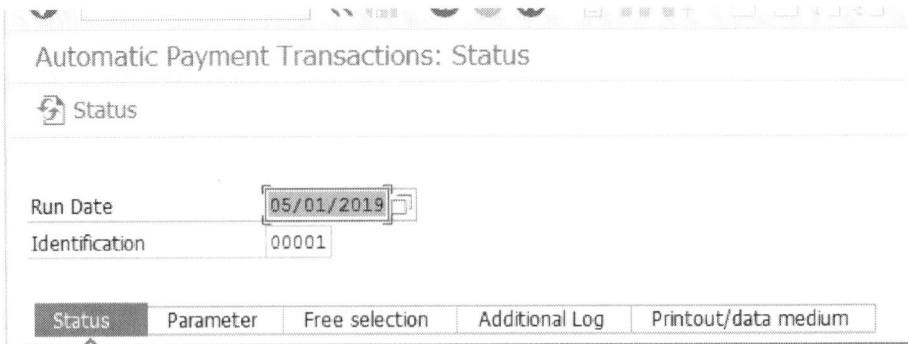

Fig 29

Enter the parameters in each tab as below or your own data:

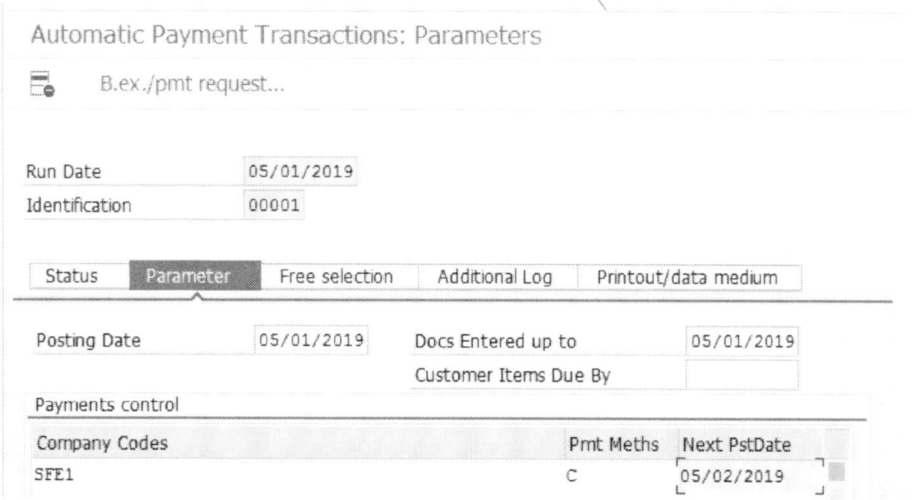

Fig 30

In the Payment Methods field, do a drop down and you can select as many as you want from the available methods by moving the payment method from the possible (right side) to the selected (left side):

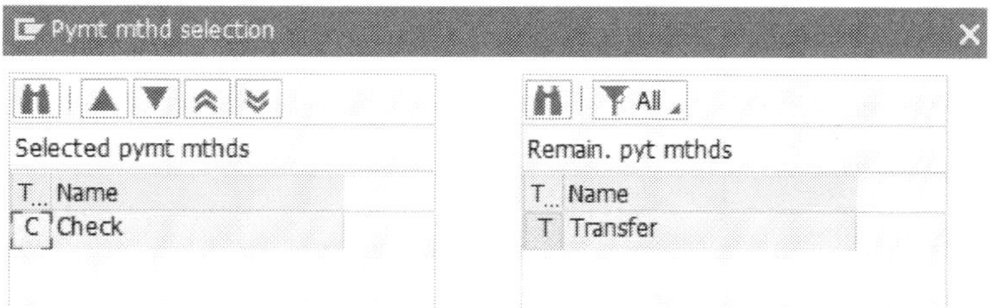

Fig 31

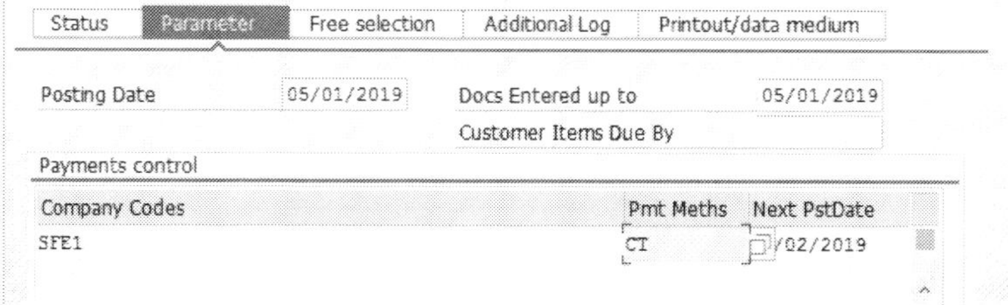

Fig 32

Click on the green arrow for OK:

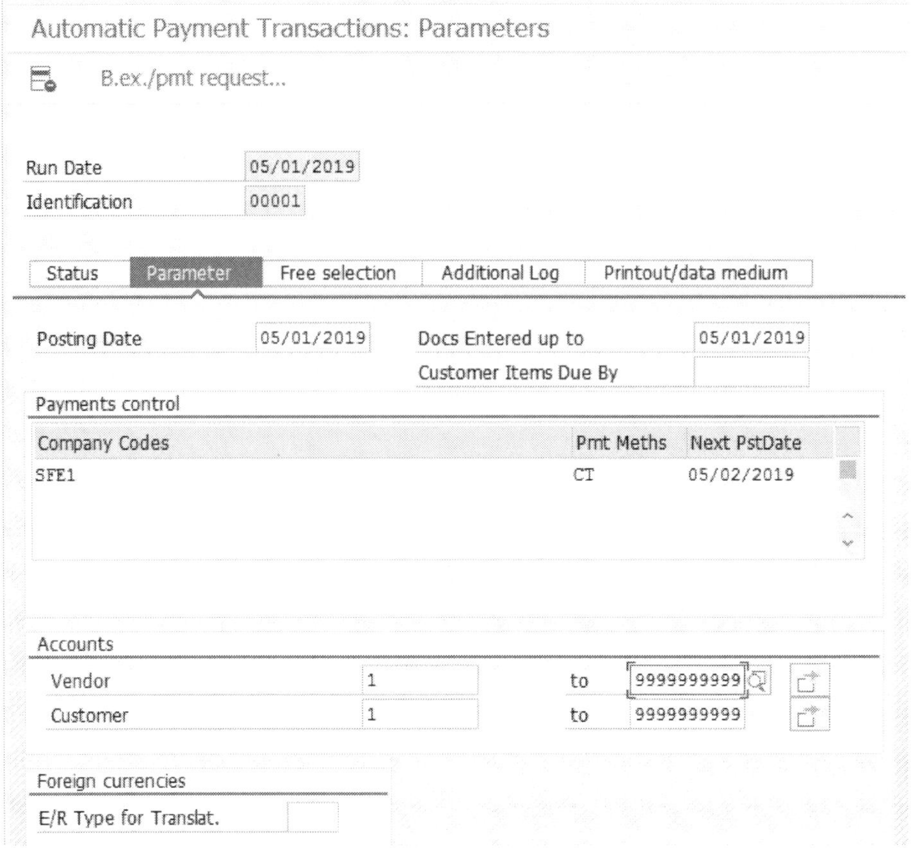

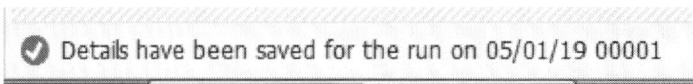

**Automatic Payment Transactions: Parameters**

B.ex./pmt request...

| | |
|---|---|
| Run Date | 05/01/2019 |
| Identification | 00001 |

| Status | Parameter | Free selection | Additional Log | Printout/data medium |
|---|---|---|---|---|

| | | | |
|---|---|---|---|
| Posting Date | 05/01/2019 | Docs Entered up to | 05/01/2019 |
| | | Customer Items Due By | |

**Payments control**

| Company Codes | Pmt Meths | Next PstDate |
|---|---|---|
| SFE1 | CT | 05/02/2019 |

**Accounts**

| | | | |
|---|---|---|---|
| Vendor | 1 | to | 9999999999 |
| Customer | 1 | to | 9999999999 |

**Foreign currencies**

| | |
|---|---|
| E/R Type for Translat. | |

Fig 33

The above tells us that this payment run will make payments for all the due invoices of vendors and/or rebate checks of customers and will make the payments by Check or Transfer as the case may be (usually this value is set in the transaction from the master data from the vendor or customer). You can also restrict the vendors and/or customers to specific ones or ranges here.

Save the payment run.

✓ Details have been saved for the run on 05/01/19 00001

Fig 34

Click on the tab Proposal:

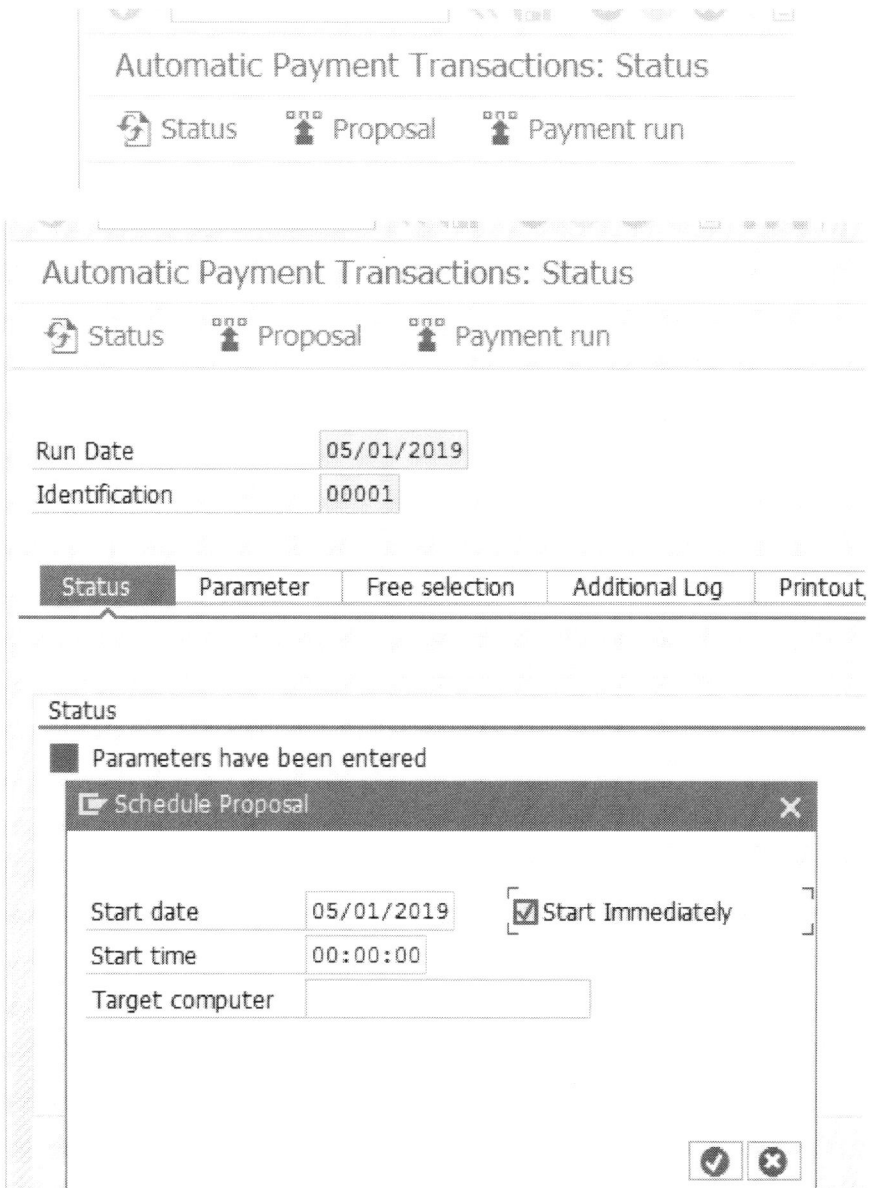

Fig 35

We can either give a future date when this run will take place in the background or we can request it to begin immediately by checking the Start immediately button as above:

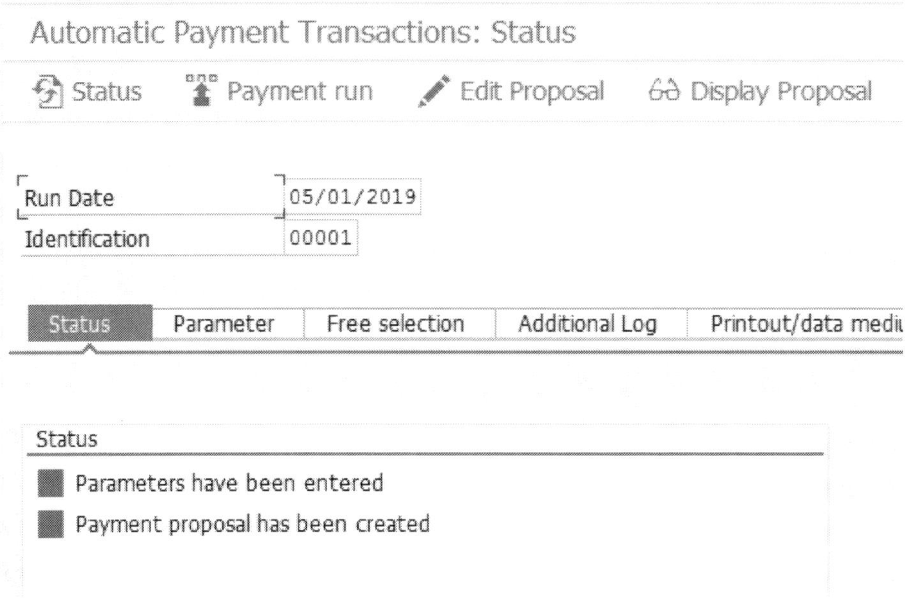

Automatic Payment Transactions: Status

🔁 Status    👤 Payment run    ✏️ Edit Proposal    👓 Display Proposal

| Run Date | 05/01/2019 |
|---|---|
| Identification | 00001 |

| Status | Parameter | Free selection | Additional Log | Printout/data medi |
|---|---|---|---|---|

Status

■ Parameters have been entered
■ Payment proposal has been created

Fig 36

Click on Status refresh after every action to see what status it is at.

🔁 Status

Fig 37

The above tells us that the payment run has completed and all vendors and customers have had their check cut or instructions sent to the bank to send their amounts by transfer.

To verify what was actually done, click on the Proposal button:

📜 Proposal

Fig 39

| Date | Time | Message text | Message class | Messa |
|---|---|---|---|---|
| 23.11.2016 | 00:25:04 | Job started | 00 | 5 |
| 23.11.2016 | 00:25:04 | Step 001 started (program SAPF110S, variant &000000001767, user ID IDES0164) | 00 | 5 |
| 23.11.2016 | 00:25:04 | Log for proposal run for payment on 22.11.2016, identification 00001 | FZ | 4 |
| 23.11.2016 | 00:25:04 | > | FZ | 6 |
| 23.11.2016 | 00:25:04 | > Additional log for vendor 100638 company code 3FE1 | FZ | 6 |
| 23.11.2016 | 00:25:04 | > | FZ | 6 |
| 23.11.2016 | 00:25:04 | > ———————— Due date determination additional log | FZ | 7 |
| 23.11.2016 | 00:25:04 | > Document 1500000026 line item 002 via CAD        2.62 | FZ | 7 |
| 23.11.2016 | 00:25:04 | > Terms of payment: 05.11.2016     0  0.000 %     0  0.000 %     0 | FZ | 7 |
| 23.11.2016 | 00:25:04 | > Item is clearable from 05.11.2016 with payments | FZ | 7 |
| 23.11.2016 | 00:25:04 | > Posting date for this run is 22.11.2016, for next run 23.11.2016 | FZ | 7 |
| 23.11.2016 | 00:25:04 | > Item should be paid now | FZ | 7 |
| 23.11.2016 | 00:25:04 | > Item is due with 0.000 % cash discount | FZ | 7 |
| 23.11.2016 | 00:25:04 | > | FZ | 6 |
| 23.11.2016 | 00:25:04 | > ———————— Due date determination additional log | FZ | 7 |
| 23.11.2016 | 00:25:04 | > Document 1500000026 line item 002 via CAD        250.00 | FZ | 7 |
| 23.11.2016 | 00:25:04 | > Terms of payment: 05.11.2016     0  0.000 %     0  0.000 %     0 | FZ | 7 |
| 23.11.2016 | 00:25:04 | > Item is clearable from 05.11.2016 with payments | FZ | 7 |
| 23.11.2016 | 00:25:04 | > Posting date for this run is 22.11.2016, for next run 23.11.2016 | FZ | 7 |
| 23.11.2016 | 00:25:04 | > Item should be paid now | FZ | 7 |
| 23.11.2016 | 00:25:04 | > Item is due with 0.000 % cash discount | FZ | 7 |

Fig 40

319

# AUTOMATIC CLEARING OF OPEN

# ACCOUNT ITEMS (C/U)

T Code SPRO, F.13

Overview : In SAP the Concept of Automatic clearing simply means an automated process of clearing open items in book of accounts using certain criteria. When doing daily transactions there are many line items in GL/ Vendor / Customer section which remain open due to many reasons.

Following items can be considered as open items :

- GR/IR clearing acounts within a G/L
- Items with witholding tax posting
- Down payments can only be cleared if down payment clearing for the same amount has been posted

The remaining open items are grouped together according to fxed system criteria :

- By company code
- Account type

- Account number
- Reconcilliation Account Number
- Assignment Number
- Currency Key
- Spl. GL Indicators

Clearing takes place when, for the group of line items selected according to the above criteria, the balance in document currency (for customers and vendors) or in update currency (for G/L accounts) is zero. The date for clearing is the clearing date according to your selection specifications. In an update run, if the clearing transaction is successful, the clearing document number is generated by SAP.

During the program run, all accounts in which clearing can be performed are blocked automatically. They get unblocked again after the clearing transaction is over. Accounts that are blocked by other transactions intended for the automatic payment run are not considered in automatic clearing.

**Pre-requisites :** Addressing above criteria we see that F.13 – Automatic Clearing process works on some pre-defined conditions for example if we have raised one invoice for $100 and received payment for $100; in this case, we will have two open line items in the customer account.

Based on three identical information in both open line items.. customer code, amount and invoice number, F.13 turns these open items into cleared items.

We need to define those conditions or basis on which Automatic Clearing will work :

# I. Configuring Automatic Clearing (C)

T Code OB74

In this activity, we enter the criteria for grouping the open items of an account for automatic clearing. The program clears open items of a group if the balance in local and foreign currency is zero.

We enter the following standard criteria:

- The account type
- The account number or number range

We can also enter five additional criteria. We choose the five other criteria from the fields in the main accounting tables BSEG and BKPF. If possible we should choose those fields which are also included in table BSIS (G/L accounts), BSID (customers), or BSIK (vendor). More on the new HANA tables in the concluding sections of this manual including the changes in the very powerful SE16H.

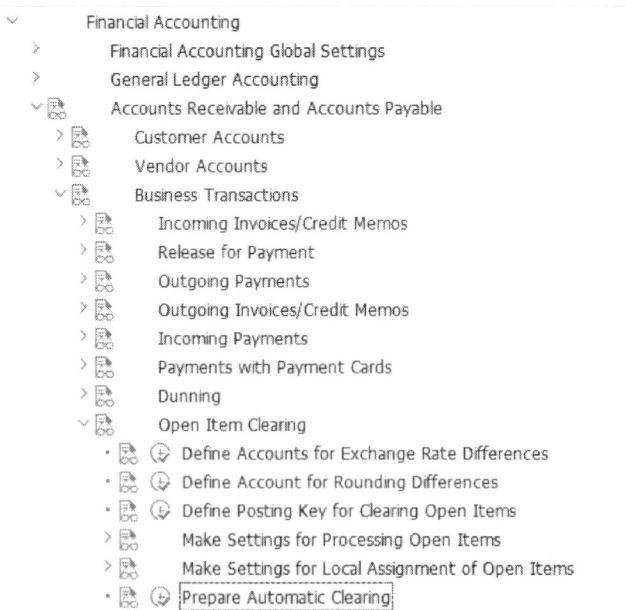

Fig 1

In the following screen we put 4 conditions on which Autoclearing process will work on each account type (Customer , Vendor and GL Account) :

- Assignment Number [ZUONR]
- Reference Number   [XBLNR]
- Trading Partner       [VBUND]
- Purchase Doc No.    [EBELN]

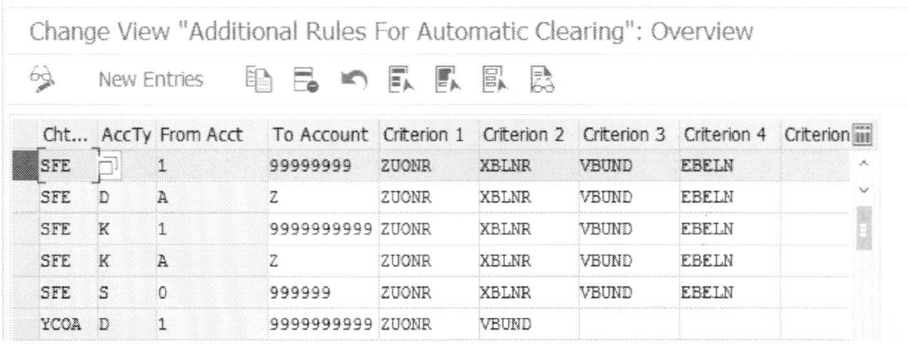

Change View "Additional Rules For Automatic Clearing": Overview

New Entries

| Cht... | AccTy | From Acct | To Account | Criterion 1 | Criterion 2 | Criterion 3 | Criterion 4 | Criterion |
|--------|-------|-----------|------------|-------------|-------------|-------------|-------------|-----------|
| SFE    |       | 1         | 99999999   | ZUONR       | XBLNR       | VBUND       | EBELN       |           |
| SFE    | D     | A         | Z          | ZUONR       | XBLNR       | VBUND       | EBELN       |           |
| SFE    | K     | 1         | 9999999999 | ZUONR       | XBLNR       | VBUND       | EBELN       |           |
| SFE    | K     | A         | Z          | ZUONR       | XBLNR       | VBUND       | EBELN       |           |
| SFE    | S     | 0         | 999999     | ZUONR       | XBLNR       | VBUND       | EBELN       |           |
| YCOA   | D     | 1         | 9999999999 | ZUONR       | VBUND       |             |             |           |

Fig 2

# II. How Automatic Clearing Works

Automatic clearing process only works on Accounts which are mananged as Open Item Management (recall this to be one of the settings in a G/L Account).

During the setup and the execution of Automatic Clearing in the output control we select only those documents that can be cleared; then we obtain a detailed list.

The detail list is a list of the line items and gives information about the open or cleared (or clearable) line items selected. Group of items that comply with the system criteria and the user criteria are summarized. If the clearing conditions have been fulfilled, , in an update run, the clearing document number are displayed if the clearing transaction was successful. If an error occurred during clearing, the message No clearing appears.

Now let's take a scenario : Clearing the Vendor with Customer

**Scenario Overview:** In practice, a specific customer can also be a vendor for the same company code. In this case, open items from the A/P side can be offset with the open items from the A/R side for this specific account. The offset is made using the clearing transaction.

**HANA CHANGE:** In HANA, the vendor and customer master have come together as Business Partners and are set up in the transaction BP as discussed in earlier sections. Change and display are accessed by going to BP and clicking on the icon to recall an existing BP as shown below. Instead of partner functions, we now have Roles that the customer or vendor can assume in the system.

Those who have worked on SAP's CRM system will be well familiar with BP. This, data conversion of customers and vendors from ECC to HANA assumes a lot of significance.

In transaction BP, Click on Person, organization or Group as appropriate. Normally, customers or vendors will be set up as Organizations and contact persons as Persons and Groups as Group.

For our purpose we will use the supplier # 100000 already set up earlier – in it's general data, enter the customer 10001:

Fig 5

Also, in the company code data, check it for netting off with the customer:

Fig 6

In the same way we will now set up Vendor within Customer Master record for the same customer/vendor cobination:

Under BP again : Input the customer account number and the company code. In the tab "Customer: General Data", enter the corresponding vendor number.

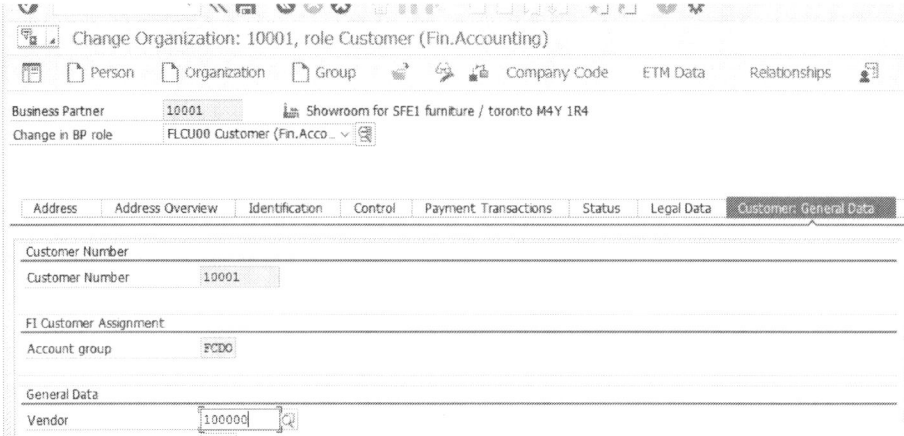

Fig 7

Under the option Company Code Data tab - "Payment transactions", select the "Clrg with vendor." checkbox.

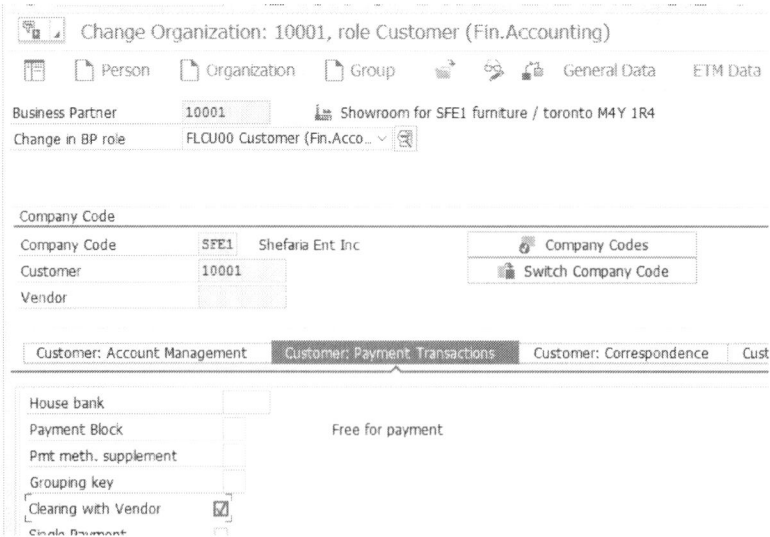

Fig 8

# III. AP, AR, GL Automatic Clearing

T Code F.13

We need to specify Company Code, Fiscal Year, tick Select vendors, customer, GL checkbox, enter vendor & customer account numbers be cleared, and Clearing date. Next, select Test run checkbox in order to have a preview of the proposed items to be cleared.

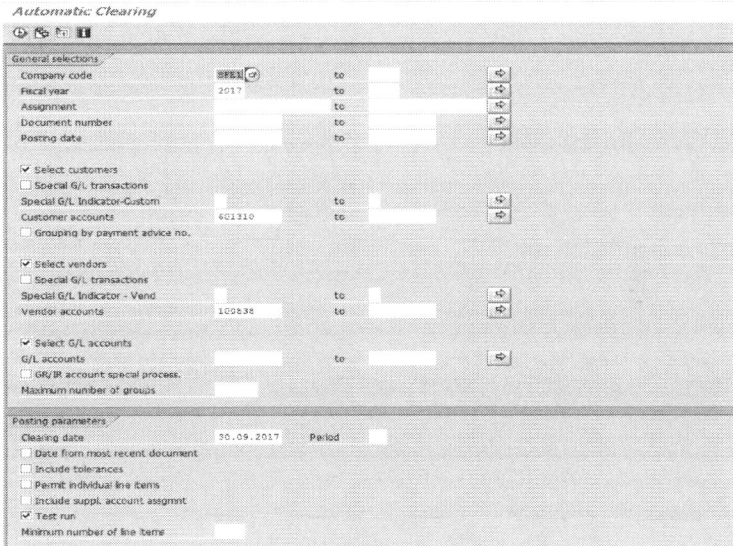

Fig 9

Automatic Clearing Process executed in Test Run to have a preview on list of items to be cleared based on condition grouping.

```
benny                      Automatic Clearing                      Time 10:38:50     Date  30.09.2017
CHENNAI    Test run  " Detail list of open and cleared items      SAPF124 /IDES017  Page           1
*

Company Code          SFE1
Account Type          K
Account number        100838
General Ledger Accou  211000
```

| DocumentNo | Itm | Clearing | Clrng doc. | SG | Crcy | Amount | Doc. Date | BusA | Tr.Prt | Pstng Date |
|---|---|---|---|---|---|---|---|---|---|---|
| 5100000150 | 1 | 30.09.2017 | | | CAD | 5,175.00- | 20170714 | | | 20170715 |
| 5100000151 | 1 | 30.09.2017 | | | CAD | 5,175.00 | 20170714 | | | 20170715 |
| 5100000153 | 1 | 30.09.2017 | | | CAD | 8,625.00 | 20170714 | | | 20170715 |
| 5100000154 | 1 | 30.09.2017 | | | CAD | 8,625.00- | 20170714 | | | 20170715 |
| * | | 30.09.2017 | | | CAD | 0.00 | 20170714 | | | 20170715 |

Fig 10

```
benny                      Automatic Clearing                 Time 11:39:12     Date  30.09.2017
CHENNAI Test run  " Detail list of open and cleared      SAPF124 /IDES017  Page           1
*

Company Code          SFE1
Account Type          S
Account number        200000
General Ledger Accou  200000
```

| DocumentNo | Itm | Clearing | Clrng doc. | SG | Crcy | Amount | Doc. Date | BusA | Tr.Prt |
|---|---|---|---|---|---|---|---|---|---|
| 100000138 | 1 | 30.09.2017 | | | CAD | 5.00- | 20160913 | 0001 | |
| 100000144 | 1 | 30.09.2017 | | | CAD | 5.00 | 20160913 | 0001 | |
| * | | 30.09.2017 | | | CAD | 0.00 | 20160913 | 0001 | |

Fig 11

After checking that there are no mistakes, we will untick it for the final run.

```
benny                      Automatic Clearing                 Time 06:29:58     Date  30.09.2017
CHENNAI                    Test run  " Error Log              SAPF124 /IDES017  Page           5

CoCd AccTy Account number   G/L        Crcy
Program    Scre MT Msg. MsgNo Message Text

                    No errors were logged during clearing in test run
```

Fig 12

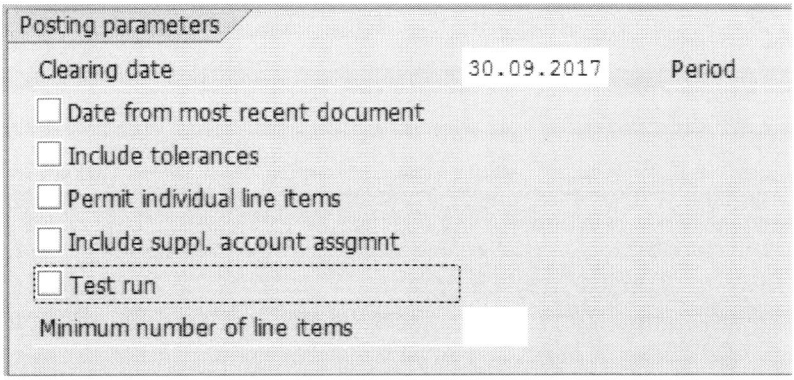

Fig 13

To run the transaction in final run click Execute button for automatic clearing and posting

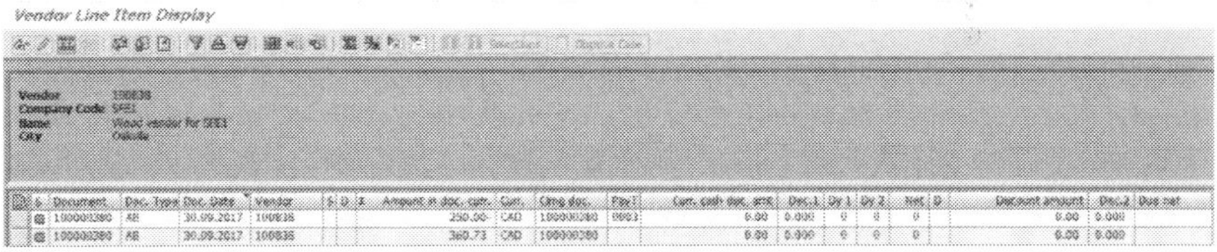

Fig 14

# IV. AUTOCLEAR IN THE FOREGROUND/ BACKGROUND (C)

T Code OBA3

Set Tolerance limit for Amount clearence:

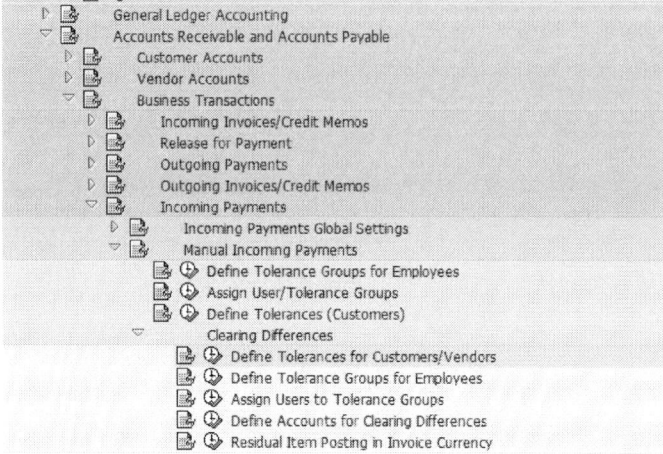

Fig 15

Change View "Customer/Vendor Tolerances": Overview

New Entries

| Company Code | Tolerance group | Name |
|---|---|---|
| SFC1 | SFC1 | Tolerance group of SFC1 |
| SFC2 | | Tolerance group of SFC1 |
| SFC2 | SFC1 | Tolerance group of SFC1 |
| SFE1 | | Tolerance Grp for SFE1 |
| SFE1 | SFE1 | Tolerance Grp for SFE1 |
| SFE2 | | Tolerance Grp for SFE1 |
| SFE2 | SFE1 | Tolerance Grp for SFE1 |

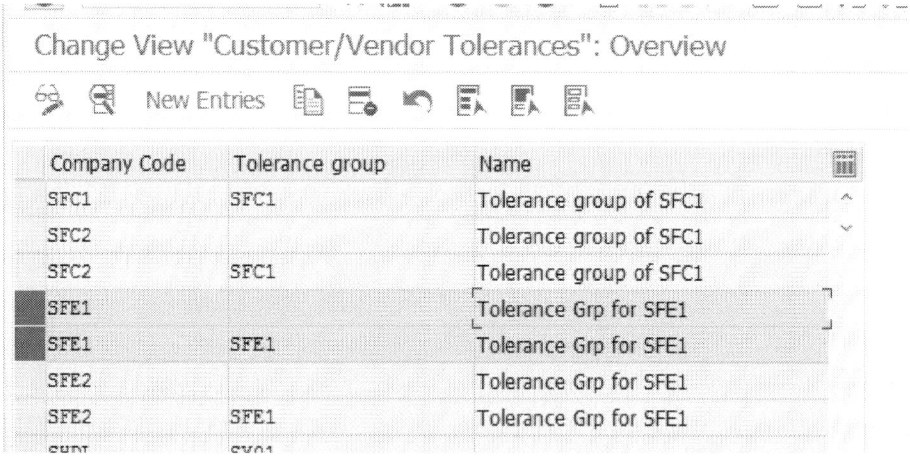

Fig 16

Select New Entries to define new tolerance group for Customers / Vendors

Here we will maintain tolerance limit upto 100 CAD$ as amount difference for autoclearing Customer / Vendor open items.

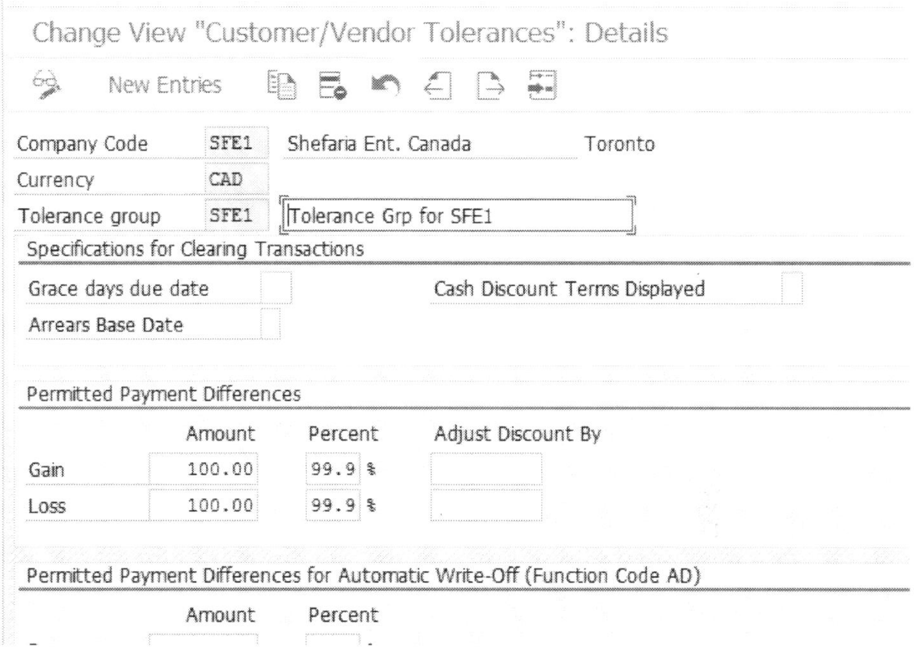

Change View "Customer/Vendor Tolerances": Details

New Entries

| Company Code | SFE1 | Shefaria Ent. Canada | Toronto |
| Currency | CAD | | |
| Tolerance group | SFE1 | Tolerance Grp for SFE1 | |

Specifications for Clearing Transactions

| Grace days due date | | Cash Discount Terms Displayed | |
| Arrears Base Date | | | |

Permitted Payment Differences

| | Amount | Percent | Adjust Discount By |
|------|--------|---------|--------------------|
| Gain | 100.00 | 99.9 % | |
| Loss | 100.00 | 99.9 % | |

Permitted Payment Differences for Automatic Write-Off (Function Code AD)

| | Amount | Percent |
|---|--------|---------|

Fig 17

331

# Assign Tolerance limit for User / Employees (C)

## T Code SPRO

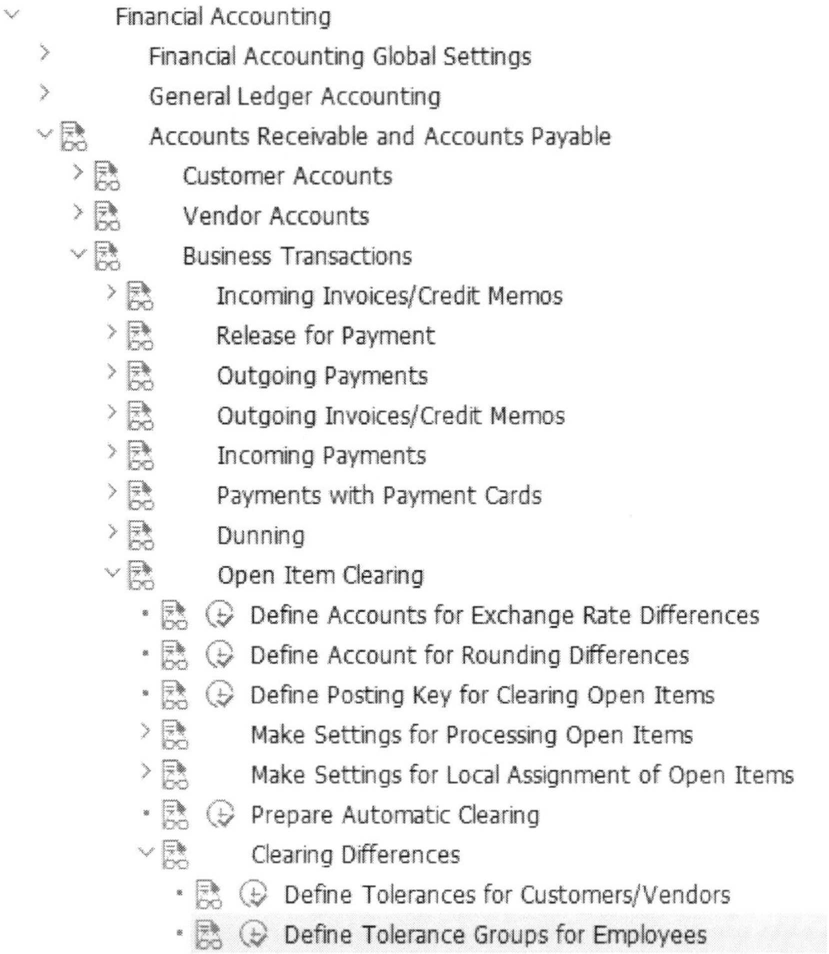

Financial Accounting

    Financial Accounting Global Settings

    General Ledger Accounting

    Accounts Receivable and Accounts Payable

        Customer Accounts

        Vendor Accounts

        Business Transactions

            Incoming Invoices/Credit Memos

            Release for Payment

            Outgoing Payments

            Outgoing Invoices/Credit Memos

            Incoming Payments

            Payments with Payment Cards

            Dunning

            Open Item Clearing

                Define Accounts for Exchange Rate Differences

                Define Account for Rounding Differences

                Define Posting Key for Clearing Open Items

                Make Settings for Processing Open Items

                Make Settings for Local Assignment of Open Items

                Prepare Automatic Clearing

                Clearing Differences

                    Define Tolerances for Customers/Vendors

                    Define Tolerance Groups for Employees

Fig 18

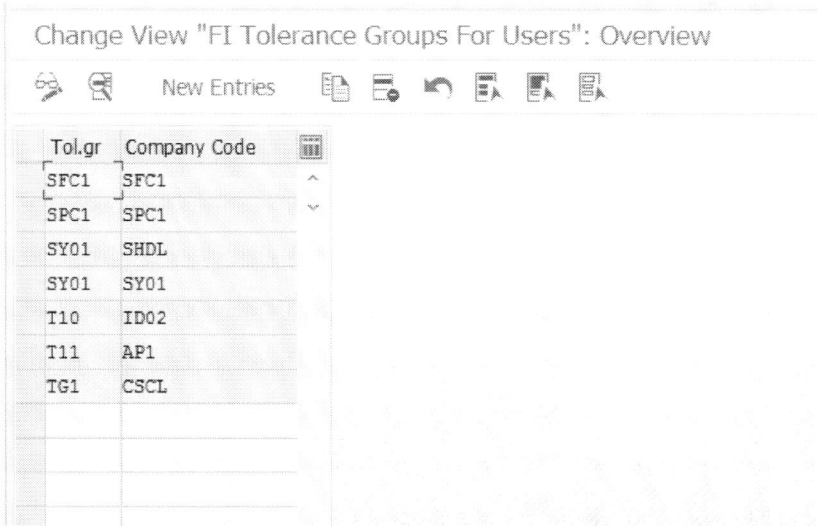

Fig 19

Choose New Entries to define the tolerance group for allowing diferences upto 100 CAD

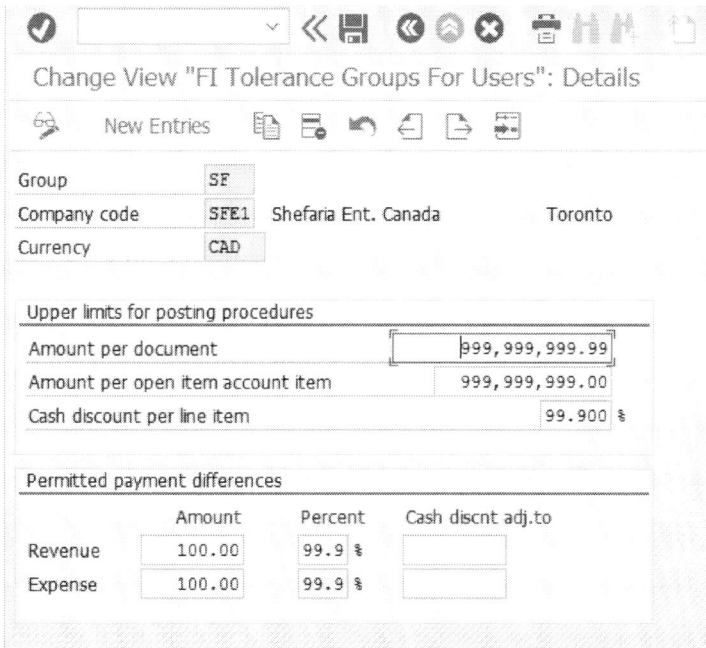

Fig 20

# V. DEFINE TOLERANCE GROUP FOR G/L ACCOUNTS (C)

T Code SPRO

For G/L account clearing, tolerance groups define the limits within which differences are accepted and automatically posted to predefined accounts. The groups defined here can be assigned in the general ledger account master record.

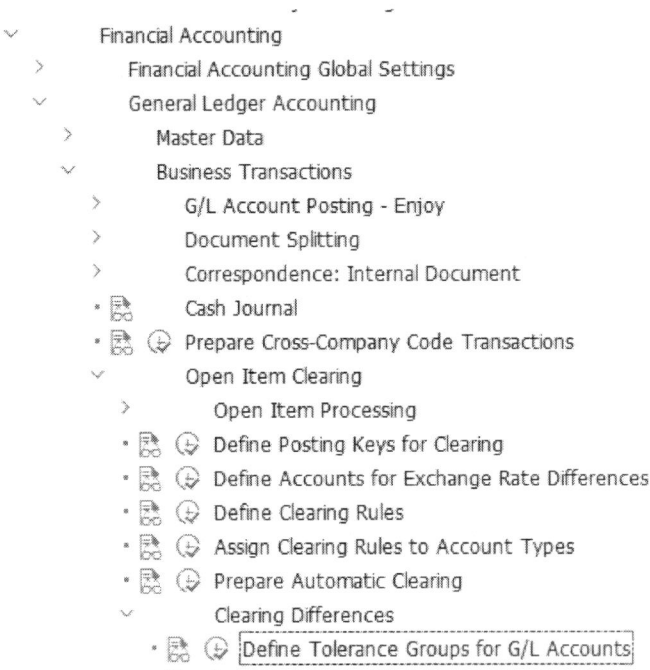

```
⌄    Financial Accounting
  >      Financial Accounting Global Settings
  ⌄      General Ledger Accounting
    >        Master Data
    ⌄        Business Transactions
      >          G/L Account Posting - Enjoy
      >          Document Splitting
      >          Correspondence: Internal Document
    •            Cash Journal
    •            Prepare Cross-Company Code Transactions
      ⌄          Open Item Clearing
        >            Open Item Processing
      •            Define Posting Keys for Clearing
      •            Define Accounts for Exchange Rate Differences
      •            Define Clearing Rules
      •            Assign Clearing Rules to Account Types
      •            Prepare Automatic Clearing
        ⌄            Clearing Differences
        •              Define Tolerance Groups for G/L Accounts
```

Fig 21

| | | Default Tolerance Grp G/L Acct |
|------|------|------|
| SFE1 | | |
| SFE1 | SFE1 | SFE1 Tol Grp |

Setup 2 tolerance groups as shown above using New Entries. One must have the tolerance group field blank and the other have somehting populated in it.

Fig 22

334

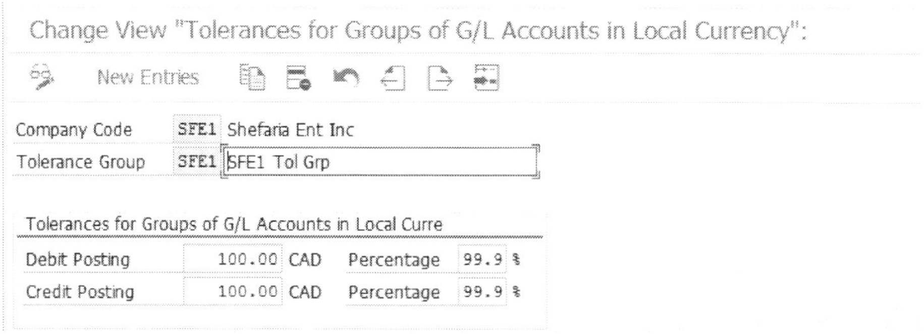

Change View "Tolerances for Groups of G/L Accounts in Local Currency":

New Entries

| Company Code | SFE1 | Shefaria Ent Inc |
| Tolerance Group | SFE1 | SFE1 Tol Grp |

Tolerances for Groups of G/L Accounts in Local Curre

| Debit Posting | 100.00 | CAD | Percentage | 99.9 | % |
| Credit Posting | 100.00 | CAD | Percentage | 99.9 | % |

Fig 23

Click 💾 to save the entries.

# VI. DEFINE ACCOUNTS FOR AUTOPOSTING CLEARING DIFFERENCES (C)

T Code  OBXL

When you are clearing customer/vendor accounts, these tolerance groups specify limits within which differences are accepted and automatically posted to predefined accounts. In this activity you define the accounts to which these differences should be automatically posted.

```
∨    Financial Accounting
  >      Financial Accounting Global Settings
  ∨      General Ledger Accounting
    >        Master Data
    ∨        Business Transactions
      >          G/L Account Posting - Enjoy
      >          Document Splitting
      >          Correspondence: Internal Document
      ·          Cash Journal
      ·          Prepare Cross-Company Code Transactions
      ∨          Open Item Clearing
        >            Open Item Processing
        ·            Define Posting Keys for Clearing
        ·            Define Accounts for Exchange Rate Differences
        ·            Define Clearing Rules
        ·            Assign Clearing Rules to Account Types
        ·            Prepare Automatic Clearing
        ∨            Clearing Differences
          ·              Define Tolerance Groups for G/L Accounts
          ·              Define Tolerance Groups for Employees
          ·              Assign Users to Tolerance Groups
          ·              Create Accounts for Clearing Differences
```

Fig 24

Enter the CoA in the pop up:

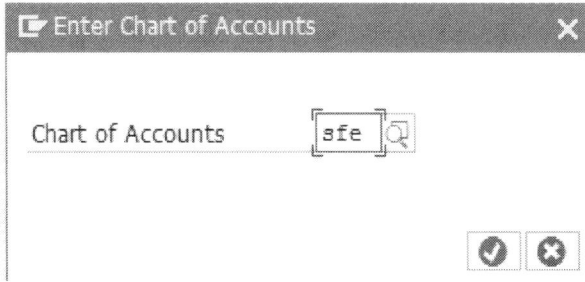

**Enter Chart of Accounts** ✕

Chart of Accounts      sfe

Fig 25

Save the rules as below and define the G/L accounts and save:

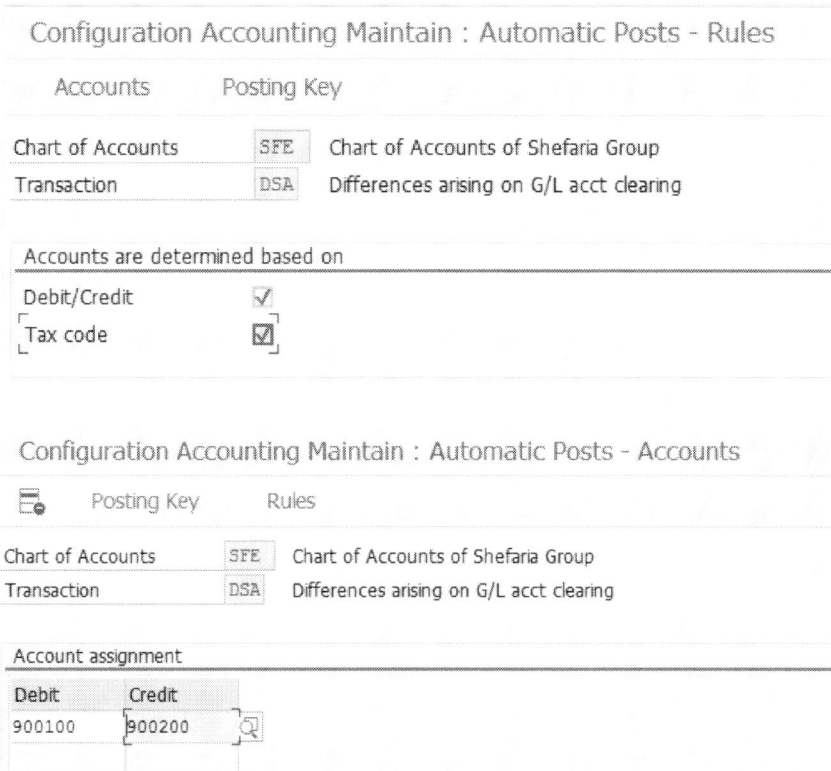

Configuration Accounting Maintain : Automatic Posts - Rules

Accounts      Posting Key

| Chart of Accounts | SFE | Chart of Accounts of Shefaria Group |
| Transaction | DSA | Differences arising on G/L acct clearing |

Accounts are determined based on

| Debit/Credit | ✓ |
| Tax code | ☑ |

Configuration Accounting Maintain : Automatic Posts - Accounts

Posting Key      Rules

| Chart of Accounts | SFE | Chart of Accounts of Shefaria Group |
| Transaction | DSA | Differences arising on G/L acct clearing |

Account assignment

| Debit | Credit |
| --- | --- |
| 900100 | 900200 |

Fig 26

337

# VIII. ACCOUNT DETERMINATION FOR EXCHANGE RATE DIFFERENCE (C)

T Code OB09

Now let us define the accounts for Exchange rate differences. Choose your Chart of Accounts :

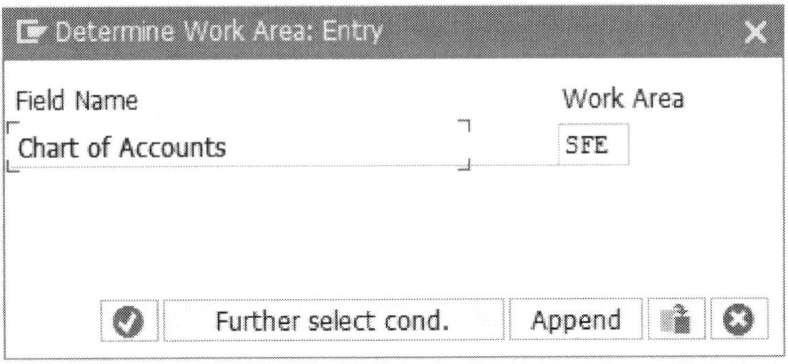

Fig 27

Since we are proceeding with Autoclearing for customer open items we might consider the Customer reconcilliation (GL) account where we will define the account for the realized Exchange rate difference.

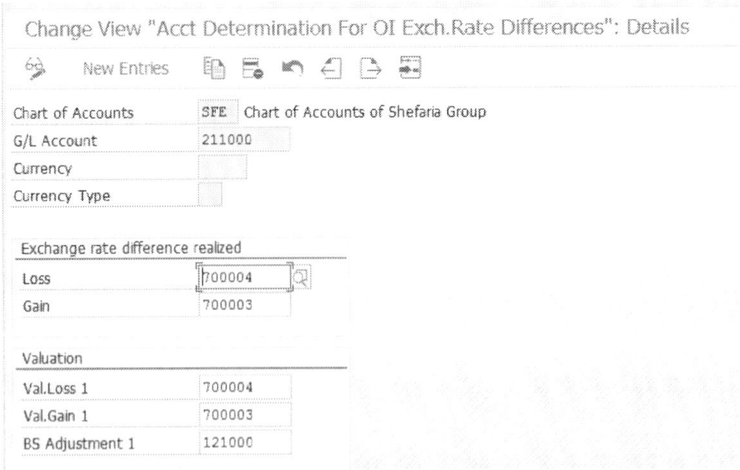

Fig 28

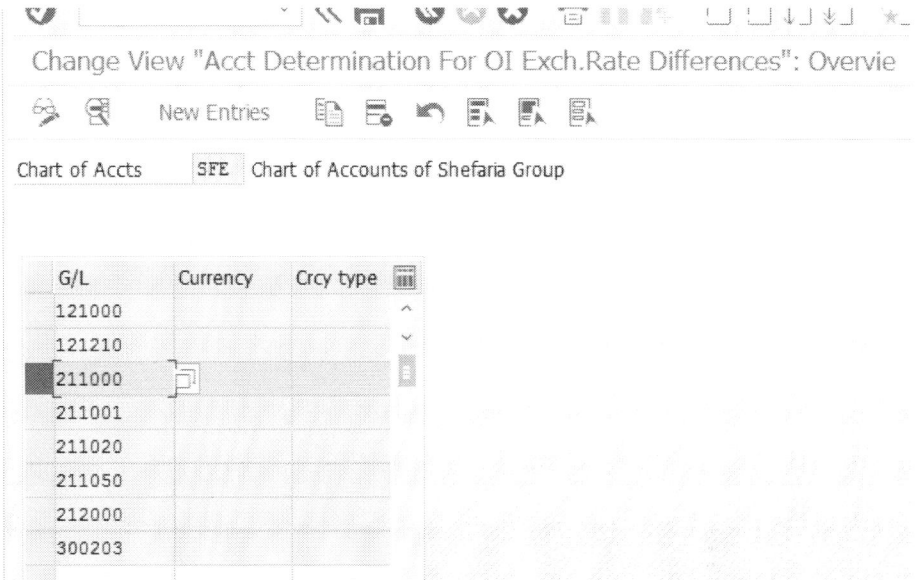

New Entries

Chart of Accts    SFE    Chart of Accounts of Shefaria Group

| G/L | Currency | Crcy type | |
|-----|----------|-----------|---|
| 121000 | | | ^ |
| 121210 | | | v |
| 211000 | | | |
| 211001 | | | |
| 211020 | | | |
| 211050 | | | |
| 212000 | | | |
| 300203 | | | |

Fig 29

Click 🖫 to save the entries.

In this activity we define the accounts for valuating open items here. However, we can only make the necessary settings for these accounts when defining the settings for the closing procedures. This step is important incase the clearing is happening in local currency while the company code has Group Currency different from the local currency, which means the system may identify the Exchange rate Differences. As in this case Company code: SFE1 has group currency [30] active in EUR.

Since F.13 is treated as one of the closing procedures, currency valuation comes into effect during autoclearing for local with additional local currency which is set up as group currency.

# T Code : OB22 in ECC or FINSC_LEDGER in HANA.

## To view the Additional currency set up by Company Code

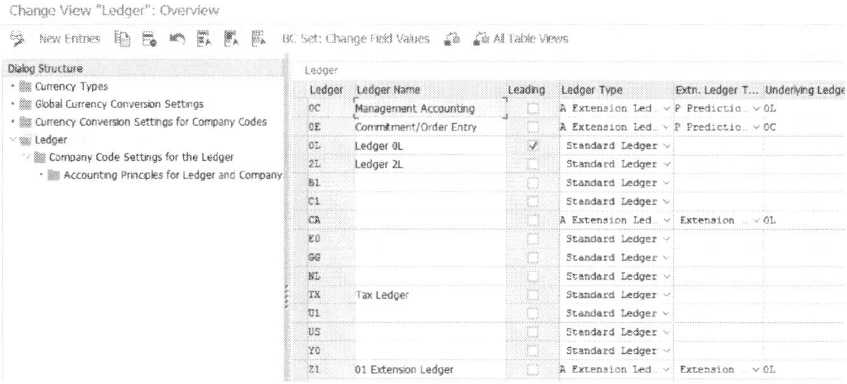

Fig 30

Add the details for the ledger you will use (in our case the standard ledger 0L) for your company code:

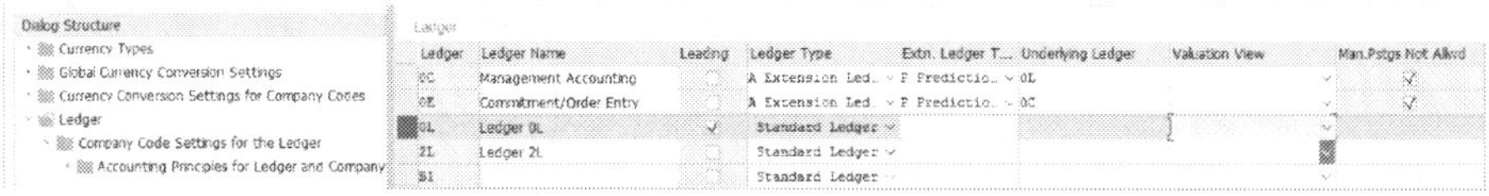

Fig 31

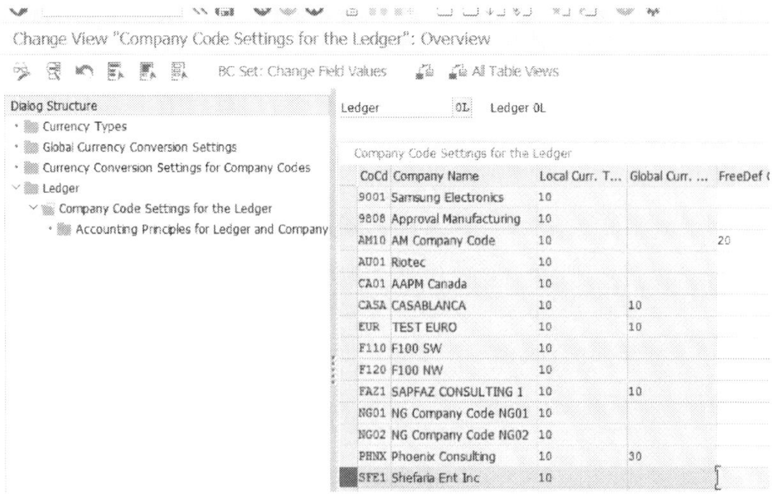

Fig 31

If your group currency is diufferent from this CC currency, use 30 in place of 10 under Global Currency so the ledger can make appropriate conversions.

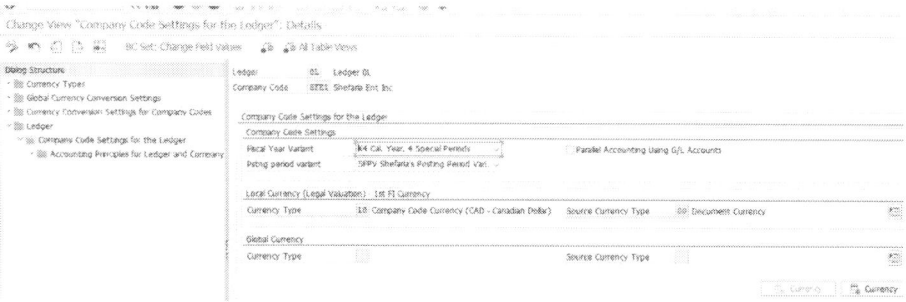

Fig 32

In this section, under this CC data, we will also define the accounting priciples (in our case, GAAP):

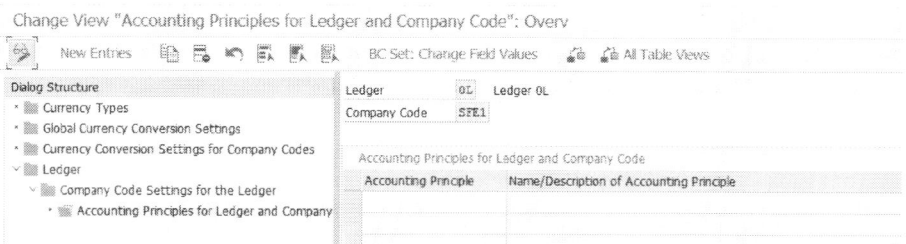

Fig 33

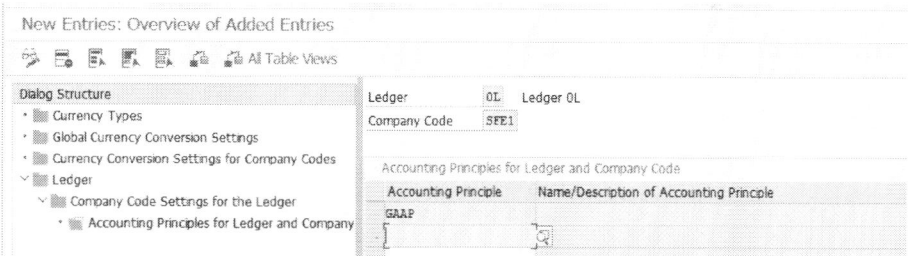

Fig 34

Save. That is all for the configurations in this section and process.

# IX. Execute Autoclearing (U)

T Code F.13

We choose the existing customer which has balances (Fig 35 below of FBL5N) and will autoclear that using the tolerance rules set up earlier.

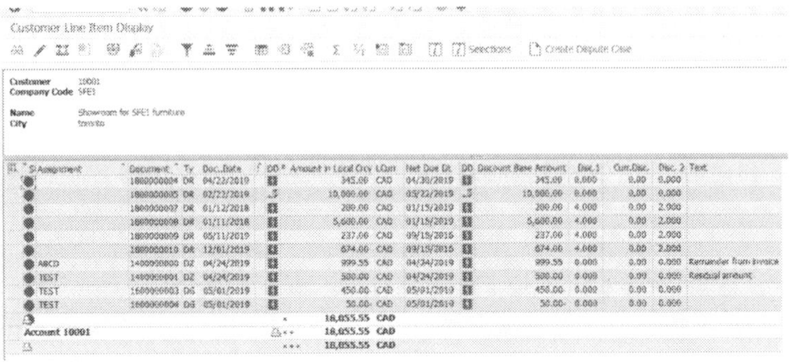


Fig 35

Based on the settings we have done, so long at the data in the fiels ZUONR (Assignment) matches and the line items total out to 0, they will get cleared against each other. As we nmotice above the 3 last lines satisfy this criteria i..e their total is 0 (500-450-50) and they all have the word TEST in the ZUONR (assignment field).

On the F.13 screen, we can clear a customer's line items with the data:

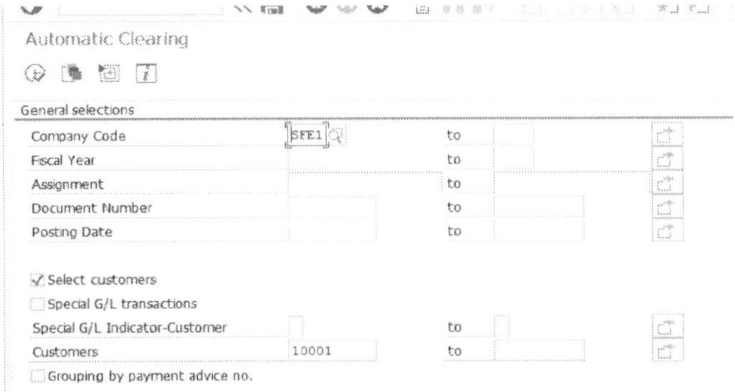


Fig 36

We can also choose the option at the bottom:

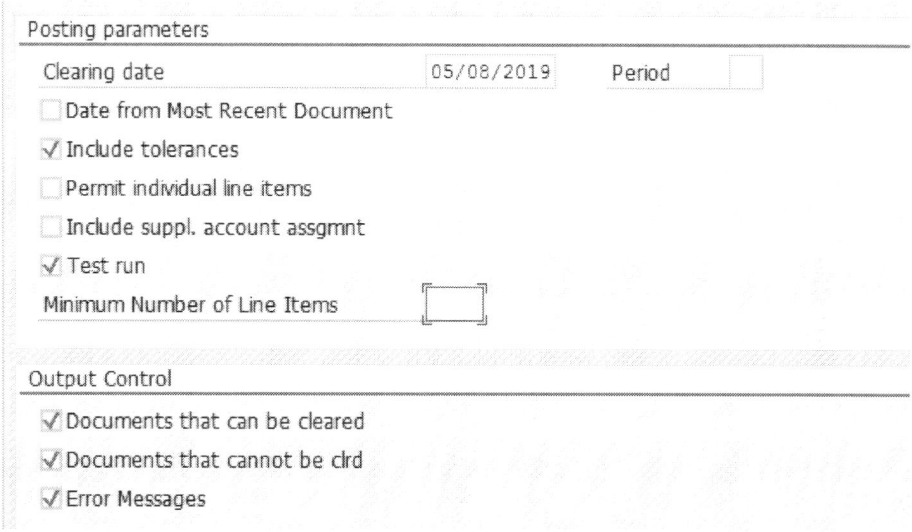

**Posting parameters**

| | | |
|---|---|---|
| Clearing date | 05/08/2019 | Period |
| ☐ Date from Most Recent Document | | |
| ☑ Include tolerances | | |
| ☐ Permit individual line items | | |
| ☐ Include suppl. account assgmnt | | |
| ☑ Test run | | |
| Minimum Number of Line Items | | |

**Output Control**

☑ Documents that can be cleared
☑ Documents that cannot be clrd
☑ Error Messages

Fig 37

This means that SAP will look for the debit/credit totals of the line items based on the common data in the ZUONR fields and will clear them so long at the different between the debit and credit is within the toleranc elimits (in our case, within $ 100).

We can ask for SAP to show all the documents – those that can be cleared, those that can't be cleared and if there are any errors of any kind, we can ask for the error log also as in the screen shot above. Execute:

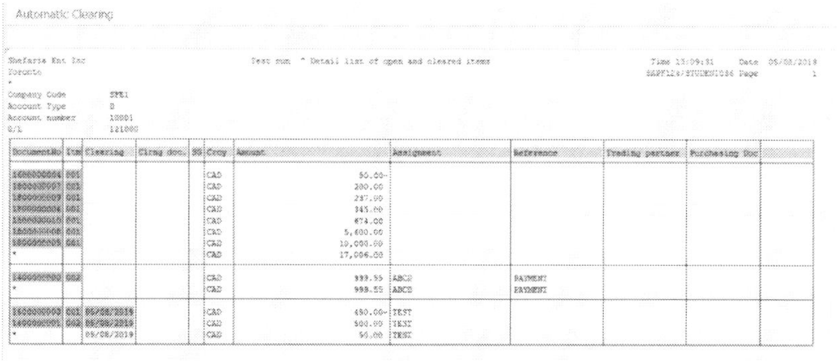

Fig 38

Fig 38 tells us, it will clear one document of 450 with another of negative 500 because the difference is less than 100 i.e. within the tolerance limit.

| | | | | | | |
|---|---|---|---|---|---|---|
| 1600000003 | 001 | 05/08/2019 | | CAD | 450.00- | TEST |
| 1400000001 | 002 | 05/08/2019 | | CAD | 500.00 | TEST |
| * | | 05/08/2019 | | CAD | 50.00 | TEST |

Fig 39

The rest of the documents also show up as that can't be cleared for any reason.

| DocumentNo | Itm | Clearing | Clrng doc. | SG | Crcy | Amount | Assignme |
|---|---|---|---|---|---|---|---|
| 1600000004 | 001 | | | | CAD | 50.00- | |
| 1800000007 | 001 | | | | CAD | 200.00 | |
| 1800000009 | 001 | | | | CAD | 237.00 | |
| 1800000004 | 001 | | | | CAD | 345.00 | |
| 1800000010 | 001 | | | | CAD | 674.00 | |
| 1800000008 | 001 | | | | CAD | 5,600.00 | |
| 1800000005 | 001 | | | | CAD | 10,000.00 | |
| * | | | | | CAD | 17,006.00 | |

Fig 40

The error log at the bottom tells us if there are documents that can be cleared but somehting is holding that up:

| Log text | * | CoCde | AcTyp | Acct no. | Recon.acct | Doc. no. | Itm |
|---|---|---|---|---|---|---|---|
| No G/L account documents selected | | | | | | | |
| No vendor documents selected | | | | | | | |
| Only accounts with debit and credit postings are included | | | | | | | |
| No clearing | | SFE1 | D | 10001 | 121000 | 1400000000 | 002 |
| No clearing (difference too large) | | SFE1 | D | 10001 | 121000 | 1800000005 | 001 |
| Program started by: | " STUDENT036 | | | | | | |
| Start date | " 05/08/2019  Start time  " 13:09:31 | | | | | | |
| Stop date | " 05/08/2019  Stop time  " 13:09:31 | | | | | | |

Fig 41

We can also run in test mode first to check for any possible errors. If no errors are found then we can run in foreground / background to process autoclearing as hown below:

344

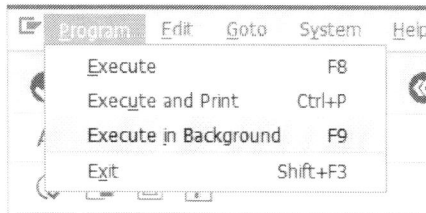

Fig 42

After removing the check and executing the transaction again, the FI Document will be posted as shown at the bottom in Fig 43:

Fig 43

Post processing F.13 - Auto clear : Go to FBL5N again to check the clearence of the customer and as expected, we now see a negative 50 instead of the 2 lines of negative 500 and 450:

Fig 44

# GOODS ISSUE AND IT'S EFFECT ON
# ACCOUNTING (U)

T Code VL02N

In the same way as GR has an effect on accounting, goods issue, which is done when finished goods are shipped out to customers also has an effect too. This effect occurs through the Sales & Distribution module when orders are received and processed by companies. When deliveries are made, they relieve inventory and debit the COGS. Again, since creation of sales orders and deliveries is outside the scope of FI (being part of the SD module), we will limit our understanding to the cusp where SD and FI meet. Some of this will be covered when we do Billing later in this manual.

To understand the implications of master data, we will look at the customer master briefly for the data on the SD side that is important to Finance, apart from what we already constructed when we created the customers. The entire sales activity in SD takes place in a 'sales area', which strictly belongs to the SD module. Every sales area is attached to a CC via the sales organization. When AR is created, it is handed off to Accounting under the CC as a current asset. For the most part, in the sales area data set up in transaction BP in HANA or

XD01 in ECC, only the billing tab is relevant to accounting. We will create our customer now in the sales area of our company:

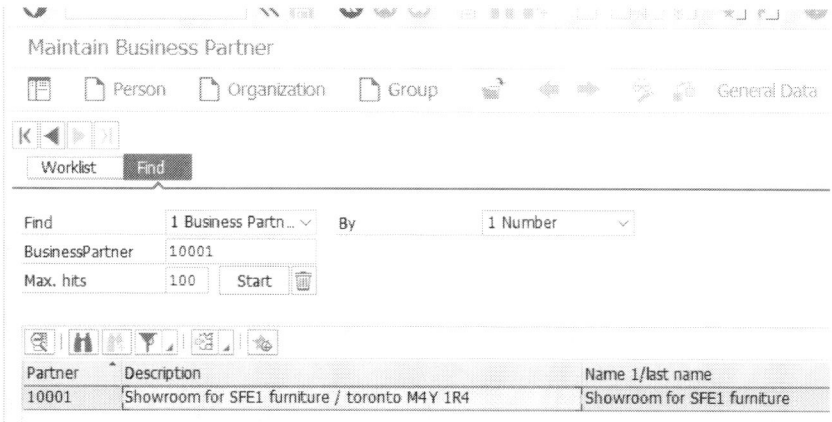

Fig 1

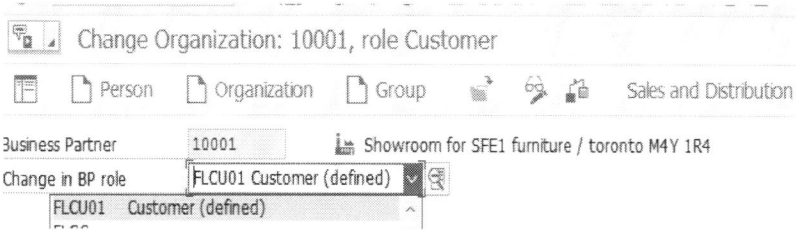

Fig 2

Choose standard BP role FLCU01 or your company defined one as applicable and set up the 'sales area data' for the customer. Our sales area is SFE1-01-F1.

To keep our process simple, we restrict ourselves only to the terms of payment, Incoterms and Acct assignment group under the Billing tab: see Fig 3

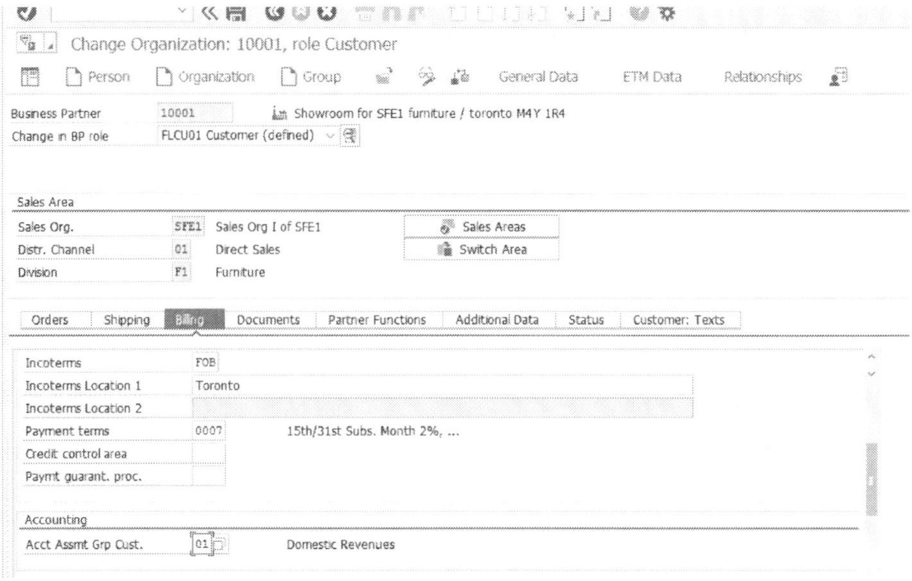

Fig 3

Other fields: the invoicing dates drive the base line date, which in turn drives the time from which the credit terms kick in. One could have an arrangement with the customer to send invoices only once a month, at EOM in which case, a calendar representing that would need to be entered in this field. Often, customers who receive a very high number of invoices may insist on having only an invoice list i.e. a list of invoices; in those scenarios, an appropriate calendar would need to be put in the Invoicing List Dates field.

For the purpose of this manual, a sales order (of order type OR) and a delivery have already been created and the process brought to the point of posting the goods from the delivery. The detailed creation of sales orders and deliveries, being a part of SD, is outside the scope of this manual. The delivery is goods issued (i.e. it's stocks relieved) in a transaction VL02N by pushing the button Post Goods Issue:

348

## Change Outbound Delivery

Post Goods Issue

Outbound Delivery    80000026

**Fig 4**

A message at the bottom says

✅ Delivery 80000026 has been saved

**Fig 5**

Click on the document flow button 🔲 (Fig 3)

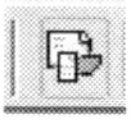

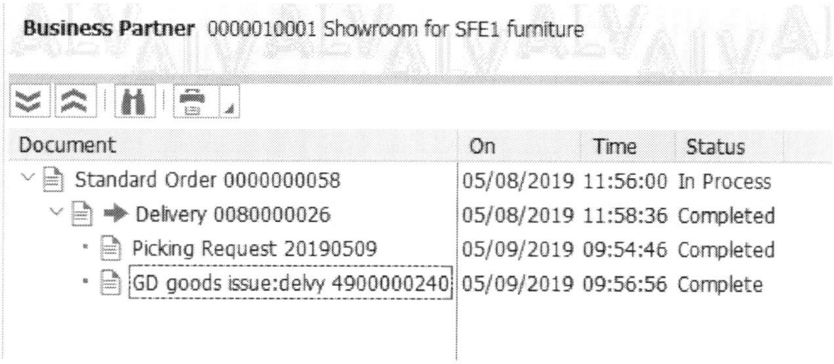

**Business Partner** 0000010001 Showroom for SFE1 furniture

| Document | On | Time | Status |
|---|---|---|---|
| ˅ 📄 Standard Order 0000000058 | 05/08/2019 | 11:56:00 | In Process |
| ˅ 📄 ➡ Delivery 0080000026 | 05/08/2019 | 11:58:36 | Completed |
| · 📄 Picking Request 20190509 | 05/09/2019 | 09:54:46 | Completed |
| · 📄 GD goods issue:delvy 4900000240 | 05/09/2019 | 09:56:56 | Complete |

**Fig 5**

Click on the GD goods issue delivery line and then on

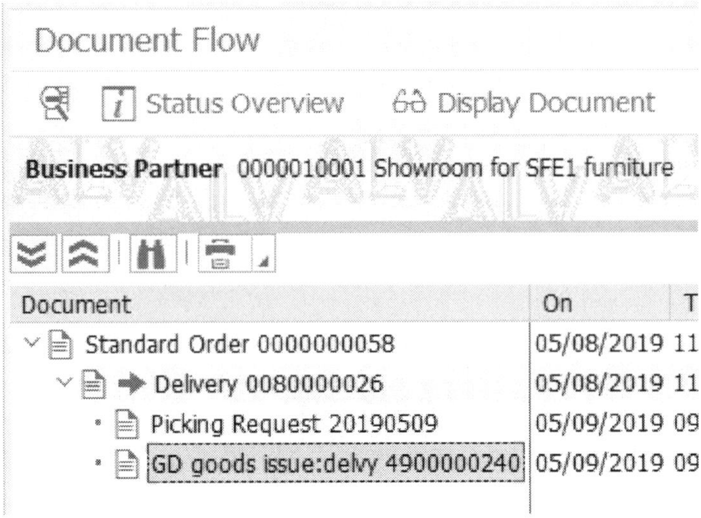

Document Flow

Status Overview    Display Document

**Business Partner** 0000010001 Showroom for SFE1 furniture

| Document | On | T |
|---|---|---|
| Standard Order 0000000058 | 05/08/2019 11 | |
| Delivery 0080000026 | 05/08/2019 11 | |
| Picking Request 20190509 | 05/09/2019 09 | |
| GD goods issue:delvy 4900000240 | 05/09/2019 09 | |

Fig 6

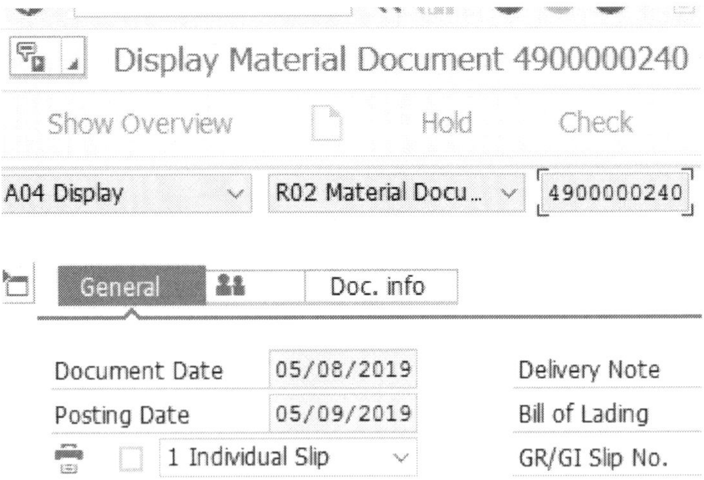

Display Material Document 4900000240

Show Overview          Hold          Check

A04 Display          R02 Material Docu...          4900000240

| General | | Doc. info |
|---|---|---|

| | | | |
|---|---|---|---|
| Document Date | 05/08/2019 | Delivery Note | |
| Posting Date | 05/09/2019 | Bill of Lading | |
| | 1 Individual Slip | GR/GI Slip No. | |

Fig 7

Click on the Doc. info button above

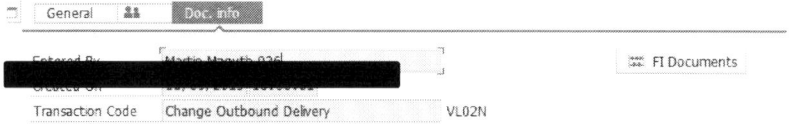

Fig 8

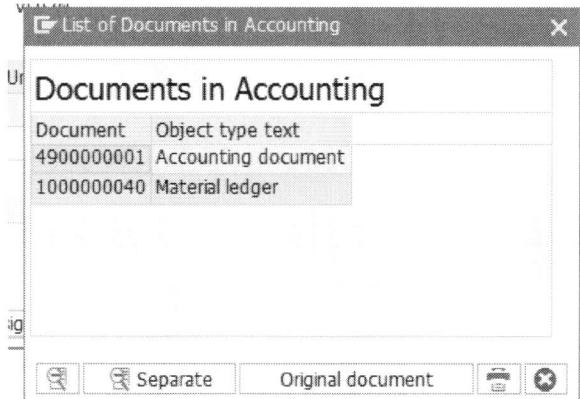

Fig 9

Notice how SAP created the material ledger document also – since ML is mandatory in HANA.

Double click on the Accounting Document.

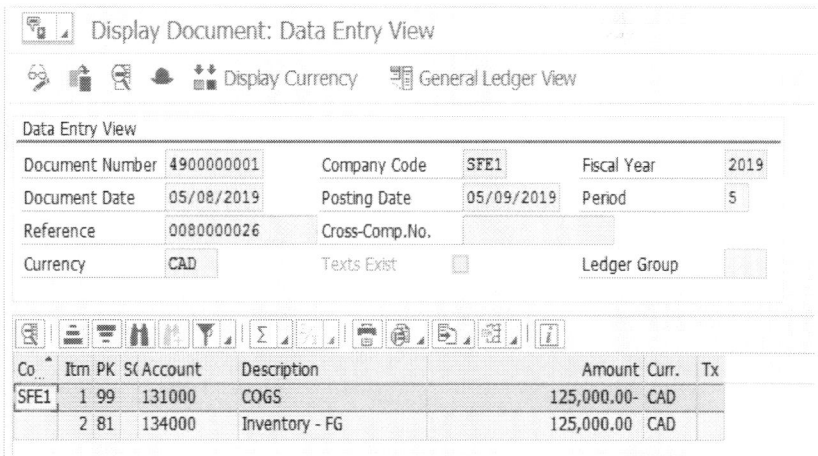

Fig 10

We notice how SAP credited the inventory and debited the COGS. This COGS will form a part of our P & L statement while calculating the periodic profits.

The goods issue in SAP language means the goods now belong to the customer under the custody of the shipper/transporter. Once the inventory is relieved, it is time to invoice the customer. Normally, invoicing is a function that has traditionally been performed by the finance or accounting dept. though in SAP, it falls under the SD module.

# BILLING (U)

Billing in SAP is a function performed in Sales and Distribution. However, in many companies, billing is in reality, done by the Finance or Accounting department. Thus, we will cover billing to some extent in this manual.

In SAP, Billing is a very large sub-module and the term is used as a very generic term to encompass all invoicing, credit/debit memos, pro-forma invoices, inter-company invoicing etc. There are many kinds of billing documents that are set up in SAP to represent different requirements. Further, depending on the process, billing may be done with reference to a delivery where actual physical goods are invoiced or directly from a sales order in cases of services or debit/credit memos.

We will go through in some detail with 2 kinds of billing:

1. Invoicing with reference to deliveries i.e. when tangible, physical goods are sold
2. Invoicing wrt services when services are provided

We will also see how pro-forma invoices are created and debit or credit memos processed in SAP. As also, how data is passed from the SD module to the FI module once billing has taken place.

There are many transactions to do billing. Billing for a single or a few transactions can be done by VF01. Large-scale billing i.e. for many customer and/or documents is done in VF04. VF06 is utilized for creating background jobs for high volume billing. Depending on need, invoicing jobs are set up to run in the background or the users themselves do invoicing.

In the Order to Cash transaction cycle in the SD/FI modules, a transaction typically begins with a sales order or a credit/debit memo request. This sales order may be converted directly into an invoice if it is a services business of via a delivery into invoice if it is shipment of tangible products.

# I. CUSTOMER MASTER DATA WITH RESPECT TO BILLING (U)

T Code BP in HANA or XD01 in ECC

Here, we will understand the order and the customer master's invoicing tab under sales area data in more detail.

A customer master has the following fields under the Sales Area data which are significant for accounting:

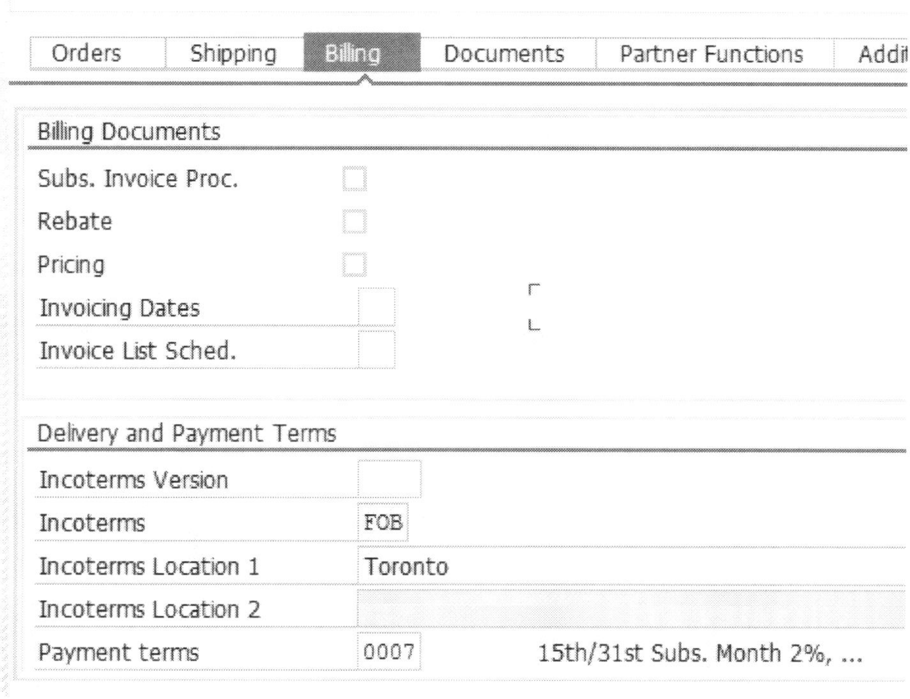

| Orders | Shipping | Billing | Documents | Partner Functions | Addit |
|--------|----------|---------|-----------|-------------------|-------|

**Billing Documents**

Subs. Invoice Proc.

Rebate

Pricing

Invoicing Dates

Invoice List Sched.

**Delivery and Payment Terms**

Incoterms Version

Incoterms    FOB

Incoterms Location 1    Toronto

Incoterms Location 2

Payment terms    0007    15th/31st Subs. Month 2%, ...

Fig 1

***Invoicing dates*** - sometimes customers may insist on getting one invoice for the entire period if there are many transactions. This field can be populated with a calendar that will define the billing date of the invoices. This date will then default into every sales order and invoicing will take place with that same billing date for all the sales orders. The billing date is a precursor to the Baseline date from where the credit terms of the customer begin.

Normally it is kept the same as the billing date though it can be altered. Every invoice in standard SAP leads to an accounting document which is what is reflected in a customer's AR. Usually companies prefer to keep it the same as the invoice number though it can be kept different as per need.

*InvoiceListDates* – invoices, for convenience, when in a high number can be combined into an invoice list. An invoice list is merely a 'list' of the invoices. It is not an accounting document. While pricing can be done in an invoice list and it becomes useful in cases of rebate processing, most organizations will prefer not to do it as it is double maintenance. A calendar similar to the one described earlier is maintained in this field to combine the invoices on that date.

*Incoterms* - Incoterms are internationally agreed shipping terms and have a strong bearing on the freight of the product. Depending on the Inco terms, the freight costs may or may not be a part of the invoice. Thus, these terms get to play a role in the invoking module.

*Terms of Payment* – When defined, these are the credit terms of the customer. The invoice will be due based on these terms, which will be used to calculate the baseline date. Baseline date is the date from which the actual credit clock begins. Usually it will be same as Billing date but need not be.

*Credit control area* – when set, this CCA is the umbrella under which the customer's credit limits are set up. The exposure of open AR, orders not yet executed or in the pipeline, all may together be a part of these credit limits, which will be depleted as more, and more invoicing takes place. Credit notes will, in the reverse way, release more credit limits of the customers.

*Account Assignment group* – is often used to define the G/L accounts to which the revenue relating to product sales, freight, surcharges/discounts etc will be directed to.

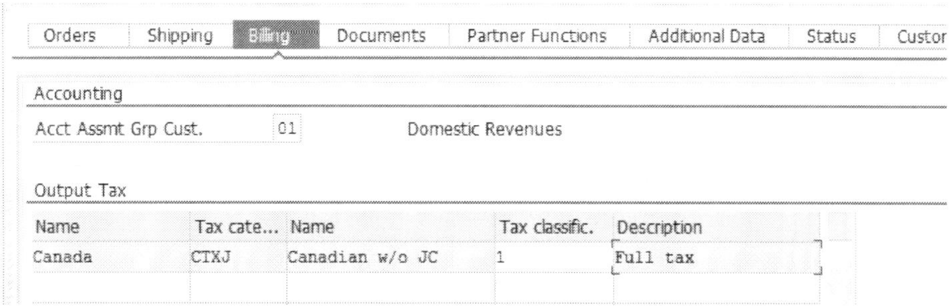

Fig 2

The implication of the tax setup will be discussed in the section of Taxes separately later.

Among the check buttons, one is important:

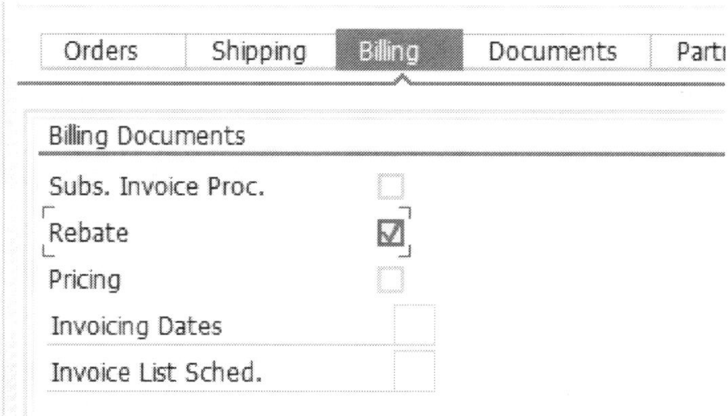

Fig 3

If this is not checked, the customer will not be entitled to rebates.

**ECC Relevancy only:** Partner Functions. Standard SAP has 4 different partner functions or roles that a customer can play in the transaction. The 4 are defined below. They can be, and often are, different in one customer set up. For Finance, the only one relevant is the Payer – the function which will clear the AR.

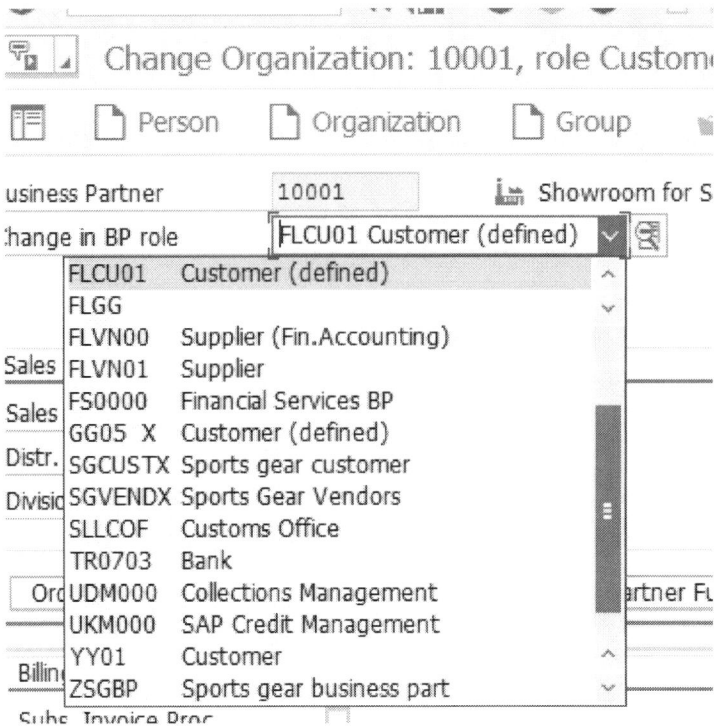

Fig 4

In ECC the primary different partners are:

- Sold to party; the party that usually is the main customer that drives the purchases
- Ship to party; the location of the customer where goods are shipped to or services performed at
- Bill to; where the invoice is sent
- Payer; the one who pays and in whose name the AR is created

They are all linked to each other as necessary in the customer master via the transaction XD01 or VD01.

In HANA, in the BP transaction, instead of partner functions we set up the customers with different 'roles' i.e. if a customer needs to become a payer that role needs to exist for that Business partner number for it to be able to perform that function in SAP.

## II.   DIFFERENT TYPES OF BILLINGS AND BILLING TYPES (U)

The Billing type defines the purpose and behavior of how the transaction will get billed. Standard SAP has many billing types and they can be made to follow different numbering sequences. Many companies may also prefer to have this numbering sequence set up by CCs only for the purpose of identification and separation. The more common billing types in SAP are:

F2   Invoice (F2)
F5   Pro Forma for Order
F8   Pro Forma Inv f Dlv
G2   Credit Memo
IG   Internal Credit Memo
IV   Intercompany billing
L2   Debit Memo
LG   Credit memo list
LR   Invoice list
LRS  Cancel invoice list
S1   Invoice Cancellation

We will look at F2, G2 and F5, the 3 satisfying different purposes.

F2 invoice can be created from a goods issued delivery only or from a sales order only. In the former case, the Actual goods issue date in the delivery serves to become the billing date in the invoice. In the latter case, the billing date flows from the sales order itself.

# III. INVOICING FROM A DELIVERY (U)

T Code VF01

The billing date that the invoice of this delivery will assume is under the Goods movement tab in the delivery in transaction VL03N – the Actual gds mvt date (Fig 5) goes on to become the billing date.

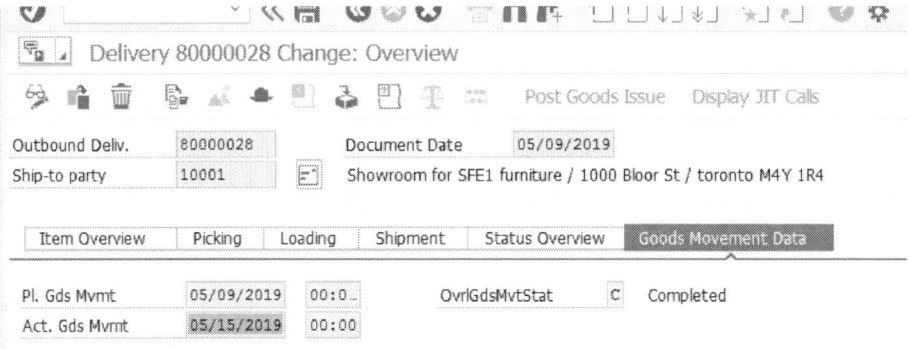

Fig 5

Using the transaction VF01 we will create the invoice from this delivery. In the VF01 screen, enter this delivery number:

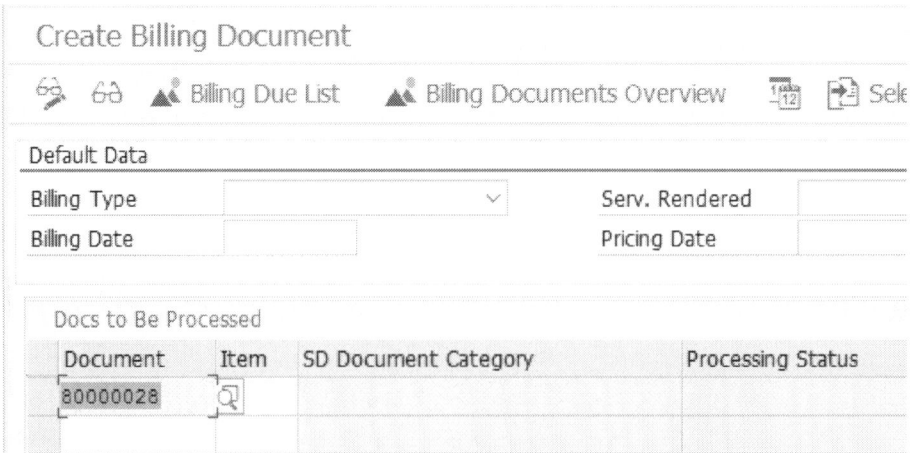

Fig 6

There is normally no need to enter the Billing type unless a billing type different from the system proposed one is required and in that case, certain configurations must be set up already for the billing to happen.

The open fields are the default criteria that can be changed and/or applied to all the deliveries being invoiced in this transaction.

A drop down of the Billing type will give the choices available:

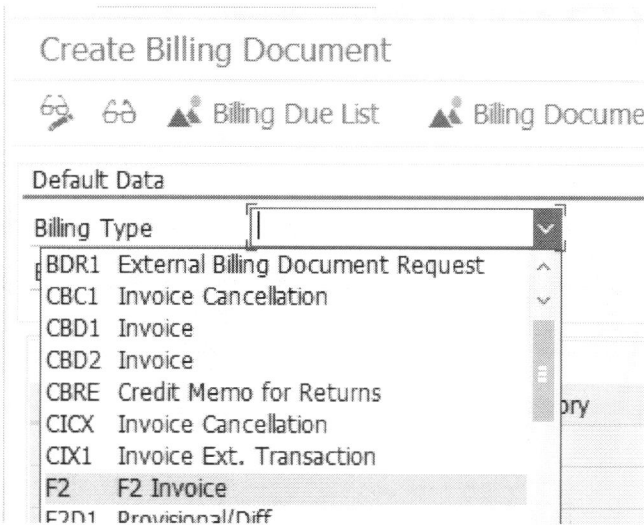

Create Billing Document

Billing Due List    Billing Docume

Default Data

Billing Type

| BDR1 | External Billing Document Request |
| CBC1 | Invoice Cancellation |
| CBD1 | Invoice |
| CBD2 | Invoice |
| CBRE | Credit Memo for Returns |
| CICX | Invoice Cancellation |
| CIX1 | Invoice Ext. Transaction |
| F2 | F2 Invoice |
| F2D1 | Provisional/Diff |

Fig 7

We can enter any dates in the other 3 fields though the billing data must be in the open period for the document to post to accounting. There is no need to define any of this data as it comes from the sales order and/or from the delivery into this invoice.

Multiple deliveries can be entered in the screen at the same time and depending on the configuration set up, some of them may combine to create one invoice e.g. if the customers, billing dates, pricing etc are the same.

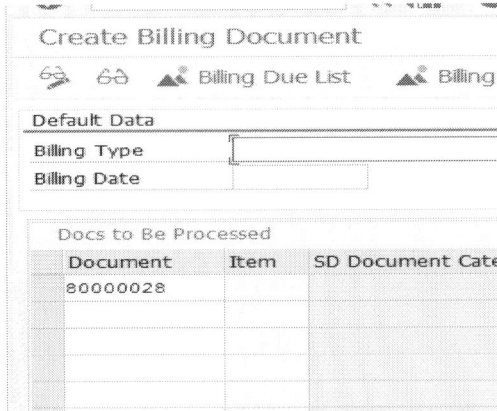

Fig 8

If there are multiple lines on the delivery and we need to create separate invoices for each line or a combination of lines, or we simply want to invoice only a limited number now and the rest

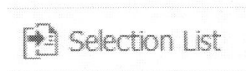

later, the button _____ can be used to 'select' the line items we want to invoice now.

In our example, we will invoice the entire delivery. With the delivery # entered in the screen, Hit Enter:

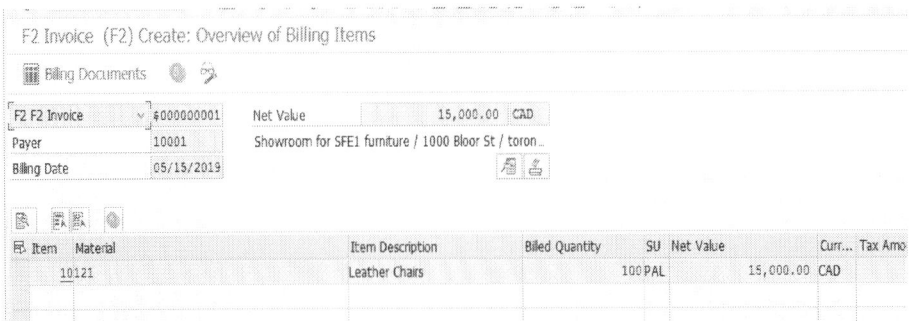

Fig 9

The invoice will get most of the data from the delivery and/or order and may re-determine some depending on how configurations are set up.

Save and the invoice # will show at the bottom:

✅ Document 90000012 saved (

# IV. INVOICING FROM AN ORDER (U)

T Code VF01

In businesses, which do not sell any tangible goods but provide services, orders are created and invoiced directly when the services are completed or based on any other billing plan/schedule. The order is created in the transaction VA01 – use order type OR. We create a sales order for service materials:

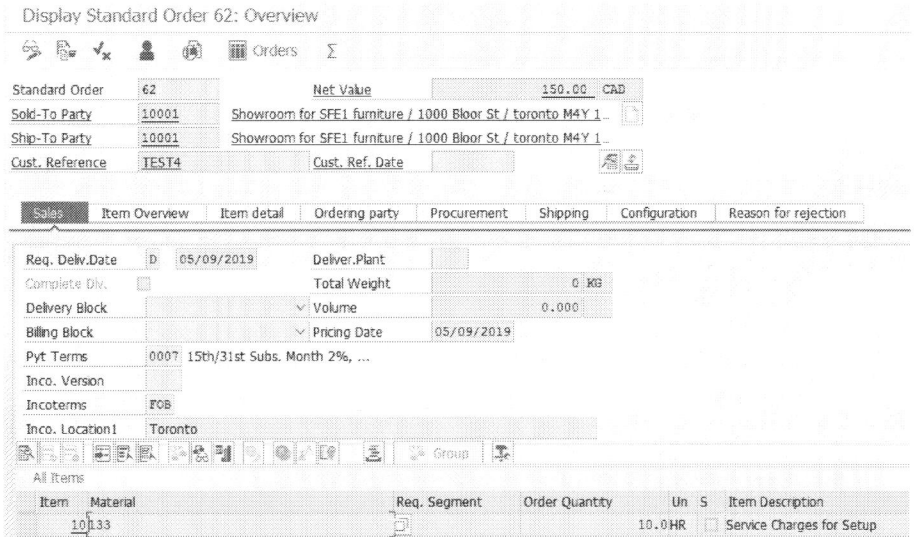

Fig 10

Now this order can be invoiced directly in VF01 bypassing a delivery (because there are no tangible goods to deliver for a service) as we did the delivery earlier:

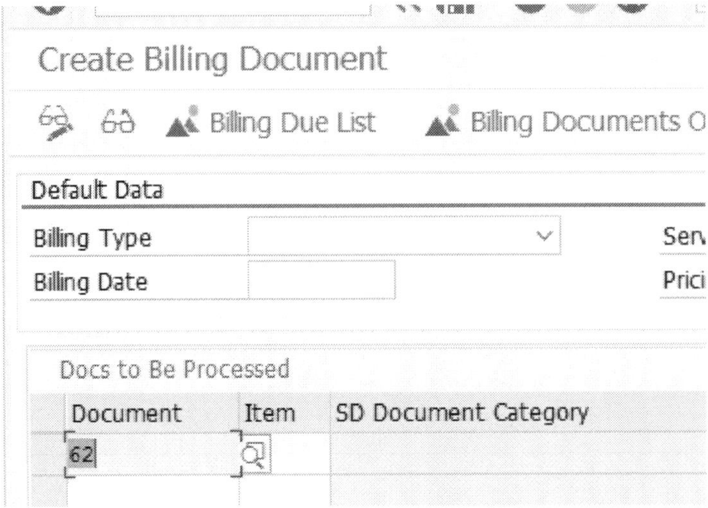

## Create Billing Document

Billing Due List    Billing Documents O

Default Data

| Billing Type | | | Serv |
| Billing Date | | | Prici |

Docs to Be Processed

| Document | Item | SD Document Category |
|----------|------|----------------------|
| 62 | | |

Fig 11

Save:

Document 90000013 has been saved.

Fig 12

# V. Creating Credit memos

T Code VF01

Credit memos may have (at least) 2 origins:

1. Return of goods from the customer
2. Non goods related e.g. price difference

The process will be exactly the same as for invoicing. If the former, it will originate as a returns order from SD leading up to a delivery and this time, instead of Posting goods issue, we will post *Goods receipt*, thus increasing the stocks. SAP will auto determine which billing type to use and create the credit memo wrt to delivery which has been goods receipted.

If the latter, the debit memo request will be created for the difference in price and the credit memo will create directly wrt the credit memo request itself as for issues like price difference, deliveries have no role to play since no material is being returned.

The process of creation is exactly the same as creating the invoices; just differnet billing types are used e.g. standard G2:

Fig 13

# VI.   Important fields on a Billing Document

Most of the header data in the billing document defaults from the customer master and most of the line item data, from the material master.

VF02 is the transaction to make any changes in the existing billing document. VF03 is the transaction to display the billing document.

**Payer:**

Fig 14

As far as Accounting is concerned, the Payer is the only significant customer. A customer master has 4 primary partner functions as we discussed earlier:

- Sold to party
- Ship to party
- Bill to
- Payer

In ECC the above were set up as 'partner functions', in HANA they are called 'roles' – thus, a customer takes the 'role' of a payer, bill to etc.

**Billing Date:**

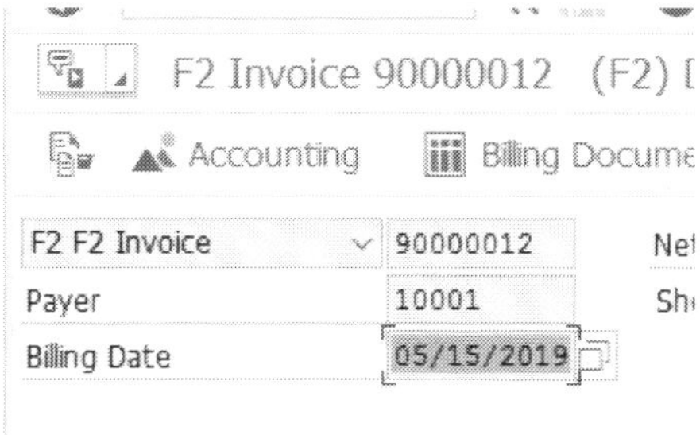

Fig 15

This is also the date when the baseline date usually (can be different is the company desires to give more grace period to customers for payment) begins i.e. when the credit terms of the customer begin.

Under the section Header>Header Detail:

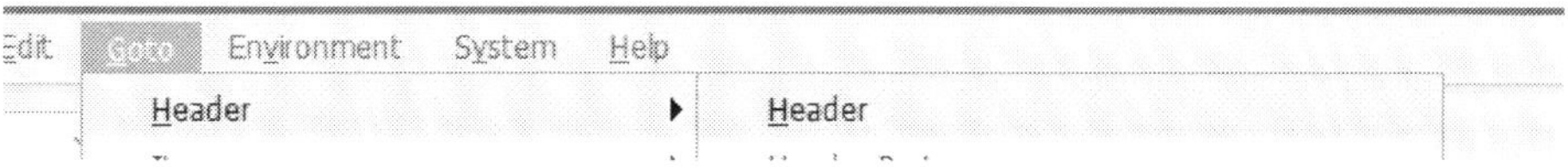

Fig 16

Co Code:

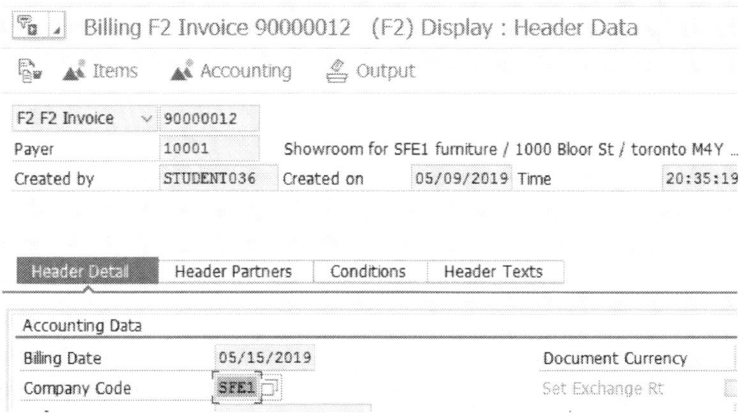

Fig 17

This is the CC responsible for the sales organization that did the transaction. This CC holds the AR and the receivables will form a part of it's current assets. On the Conditions tab, once can see the value of the document along with the taxes:

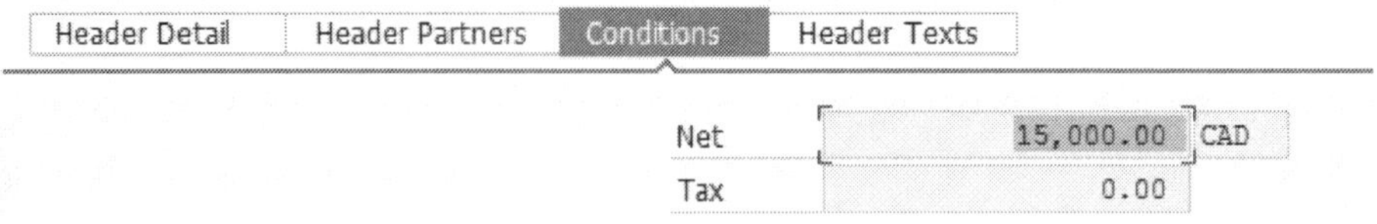

| | | | |
|---|---|---|---|
| | Net | 15,000.00 | CAD |
| | Tax | 0.00 | |

Fig 18

At the line item level, the important fields are:

Fig 19

Service Rendered Date:

| Price Data | | | |
|---|---|---|---|
| Pricing Date | 05/15/2019 | AcctSettleStart | |
| Pr. Ref. Matl | | Serv. Rendered | 05/15/2019 |
| Manual Price | No manual price change | Exchange Rate | 1.00000 |
| Pricing | X Pricing standard | | |

Fig 20

This is the date on which taxes are calculated i.e. the taxes existing on that date in SAP (or external systems) are the valid taxes for this transaction. It is independent of the billing date or date when the order created.

Calculation of taxes is discussed in the next section.

# VII. PRO-FORMA INVOICES (U)

T Code VF01

Occasionally the customer may require a pro-forma invoice for purpose of getting prior approvals for imports, or for customs or bank funding in cases of capital goods etc. 2 standard pro-forma invoices exist in SAP – the F5 created from a sales order and F8 with reference to a delivery. The delivery does not have to be goods issued for this purpose. Pro-forma invoices do not create accounting entries i.e. they never hit AR. Neither can they be cancelled.

## From order, type F5:

Create the sales order (order type called OR) in VA01, all that is needed to enter are the customer, material and quantity and SAP can determine everything else if the configurations and data re set up correctly.

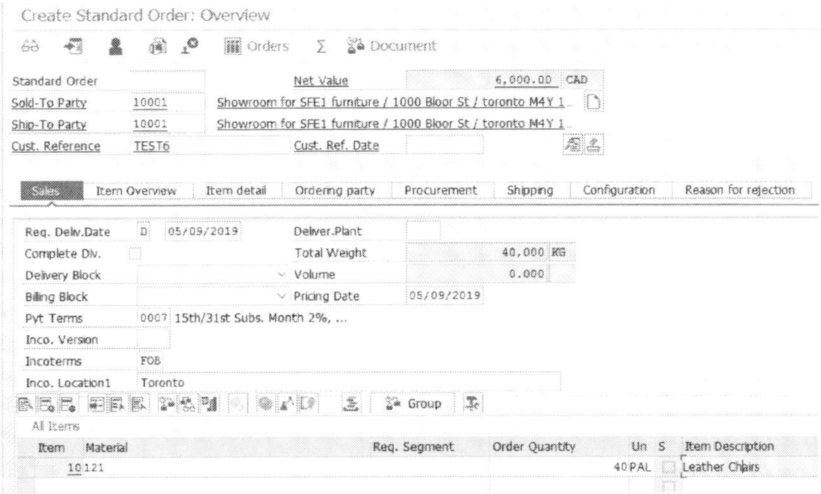

| Create Standard Order: Overview |
| --- |

| Standard Order | | Net Value | 6,000.00 | CAD |
| Sold-To Party | 10001 | Showroom for SFE1 furniture / 1000 Bloor St / toronto M4Y 1 | | |
| Ship-To Party | 10001 | Showroom for SFE1 furniture / 1000 Bloor St / toronto M4Y 1 | | |
| Cust. Reference | TEST6 | Cust. Ref. Date | | |

| Sales | Item Overview | Item detail | Ordering party | Procurement | Shipping | Configuration | Reason for rejection |

| Req. Deliv.Date | D | 05/09/2019 | Deliver.Plant | |
| Complete Dlv. | | | Total Weight | 40,000 KG |
| Delivery Block | | ∨ | Volume | 0.000 |
| Billing Block | | ∨ | Pricing Date | 05/09/2019 |
| Pyt Terms | 0007 | 15th/31st Subs. Month 2%, ... | | |
| Inco. Version | | | | |
| Incoterms | FOB | | | |
| Inco. Location1 | Toronto | | | |

All Items

| Item | Material | Req. Segment | Order Quantity | Un | S | Item Description |
| --- | --- | --- | --- | --- | --- | --- |
| 10 | 121 | | 40 | PAL | | Leather Chairs |

Fig 21

Save

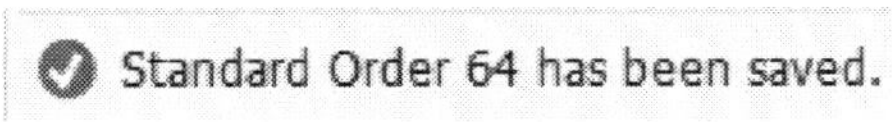

Standard Order 64 has been saved.

Fig 22

In VF01, enter the order # in the Document field and choose F5:

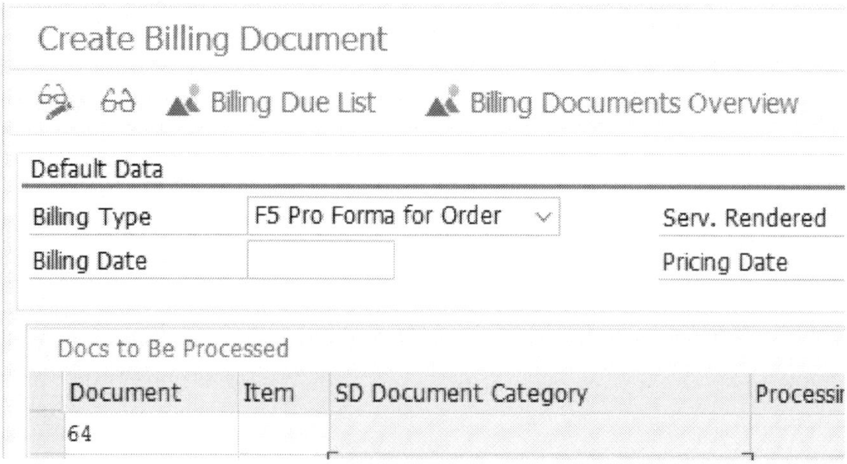

**Create Billing Document**

Billing Due List    Billing Documents Overview

Default Data

| Billing Type | F5 Pro Forma for Order ∨ | Serv. Rendered |
| Billing Date | | Pricing Date |

Docs to Be Processed

| Document | Item | SD Document Category | Processir |
| 64 | | | |

Fig 23

Pro Forma for Order (F5) Create: Overview of Billing Items

Billing Documents

| F5 Pro Forma for Order ∨ | 6000000001 | Net Value | 6,000.00 CAD |
| Payer | 10001 | Showroom for SFE1 furniture / 1000 Bloor St / toron... |
| Billing Date | 05/09/2019 | |

| Item | Material | Item Description | Billed Quantity | SU | Net Value | Curr... | T: |
| 10121 | | Leather Chairs | | 40 PAL | 6,000.00 | CAD | |

Fig 24

Save

Document 90000014 has been saved.

Fig 25

## From delivery, F8:

Sometimes information relating to shipping needs to be given on the pro-forma invoice like palletizing, gross weights, net weights, transporter etc and some of it may be available only in the delivery. In those cases, a delivery is created from the sales order and the pro-forma created wrt to that delivery instead of from the order.

Unlike the real invoice, for a pro-forma invoice the delivery need not be goods issued for the pro-forma to be created from it.
Create the order (type OR) in VA01 and then the delivery in VL01N using that sales order.

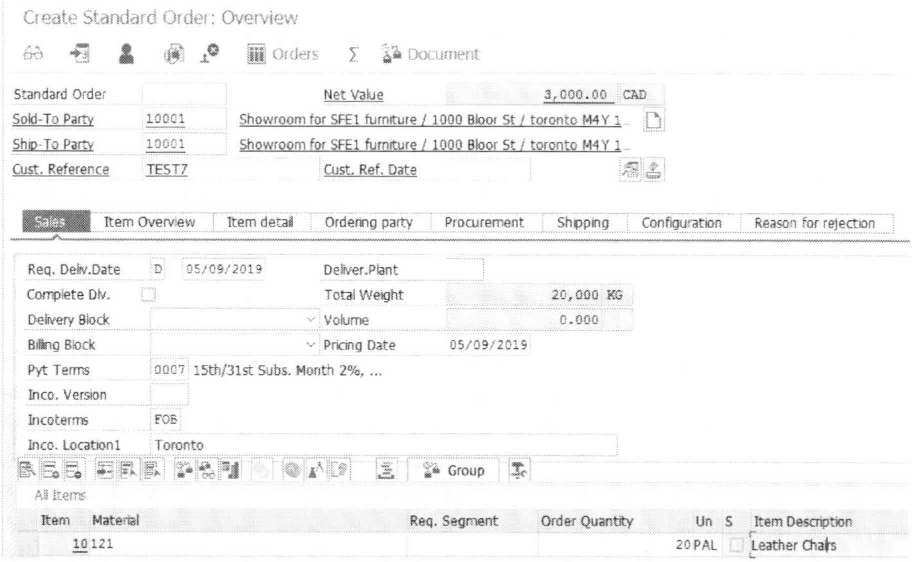

Fig 26

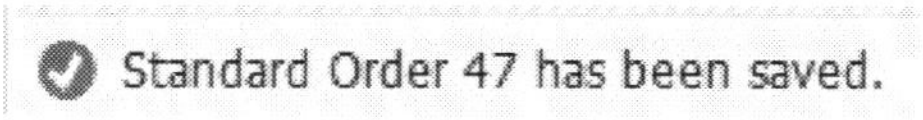

Fig 27

In VL01N create a delivery from this sales order:

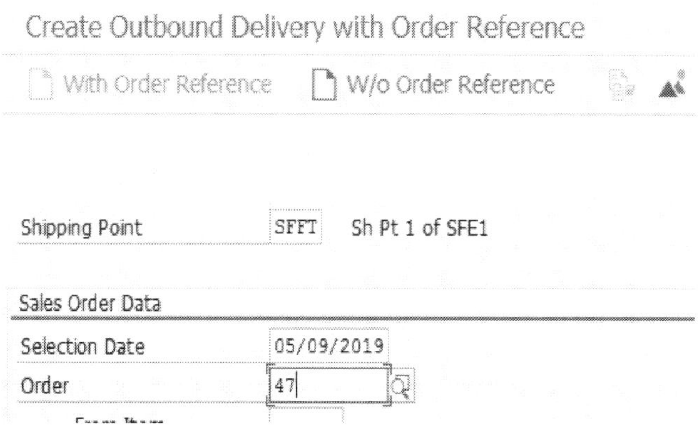

Fig 28

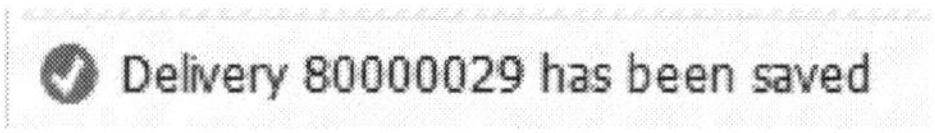

Fig 29

Use this delivery # in VF01, choosing F8 as the Billing type:

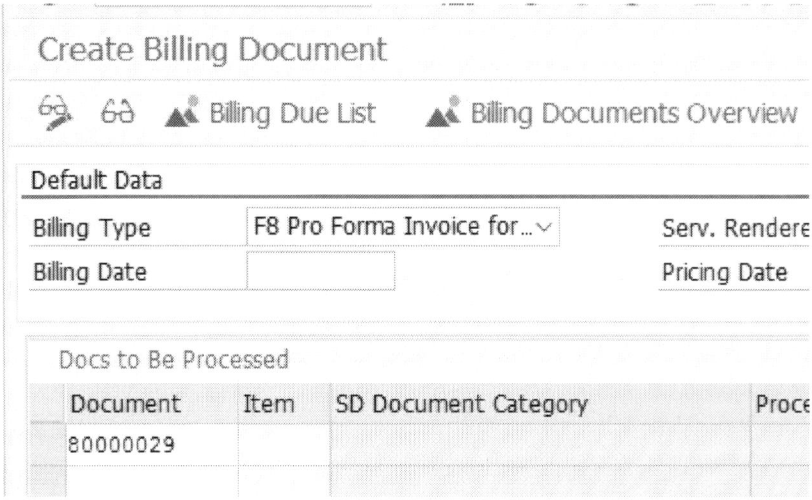

## Create Billing Document

    ◢ Billing Due List    ◢ Billing Documents Overview

### Default Data

| Billing Type | F8 Pro Forma Invoice for... ∨ | | Serv. Rendere |
|---|---|---|---|
| Billing Date | | | Pricing Date |

### Docs to Be Processed

| Document | Item | SD Document Category | Proce |
|---|---|---|---|
| 80000029 | | | |

Fig 30

Hit Enter:

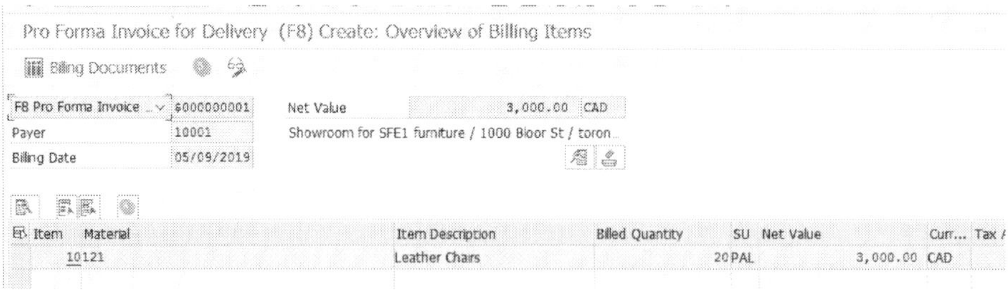

Pro Forma Invoice for Delivery (F8) Create: Overview of Billing Items

▦ Billing Documents ◎ ⊛

| F8 Pro Forma Invoice ... ∨ | 6000000001 | Net Value | 3,000.00 | CAD |
| Payer | 10001 | Showroom for SFE1 furniture / 1000 Bloor St / toron.. |
| Billing Date | 05/09/2019 | |

| Item | Material | Item Description | Billed Quantity | SU | Net Value | Curr... | Tax / |
|---|---|---|---|---|---|---|---|
| 10121 | | Leather Chairs | | 20 PAL | 3,000.00 | CAD | |

Fig 31

Save:

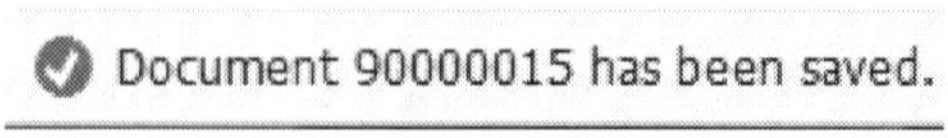

Fig 32

# VIII. Viewing An Invoice (U)

T Code VF03

Although the content of the actual invoice will vary depending on the company's requirements, the process to view them is the same. SAP offers the ability to 'preview' the invoices before the user can decide whether to print or not. Printing can be done in mass scale or individually depending on the volumes.

To look up an individual invoice on the screen go to VF03 (display):

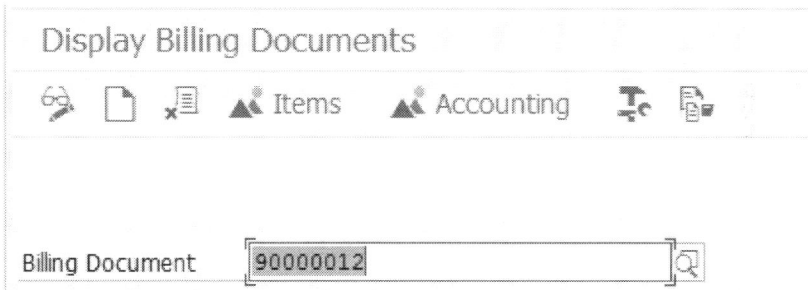

Fig 33

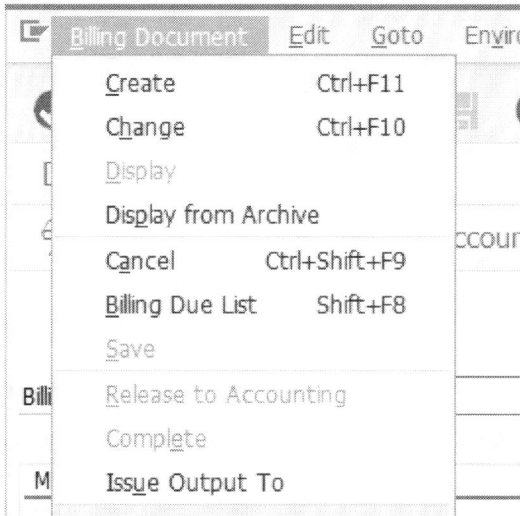

Fig 34

373

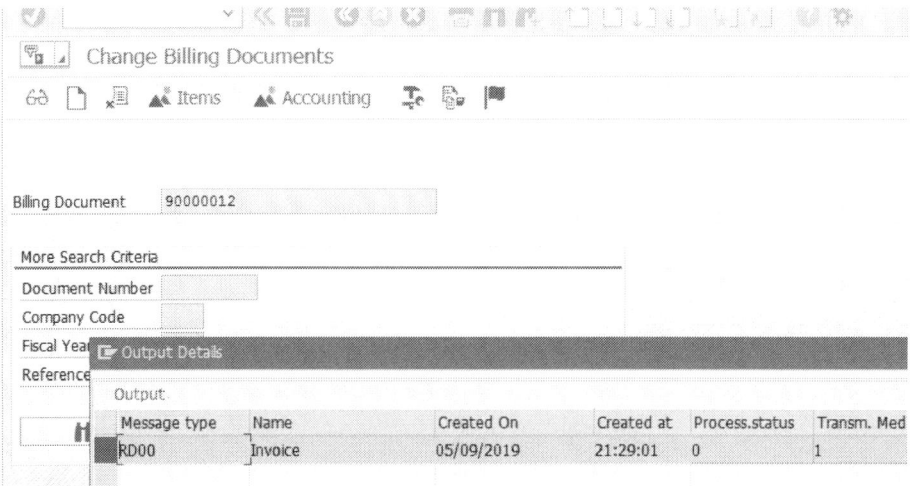

Fig 35

Every company will have it's own Message type (also called Outputs) and often there will be multiple (usually different formats and reasons thereof).

With the appropriate Output highlighted, click on the button

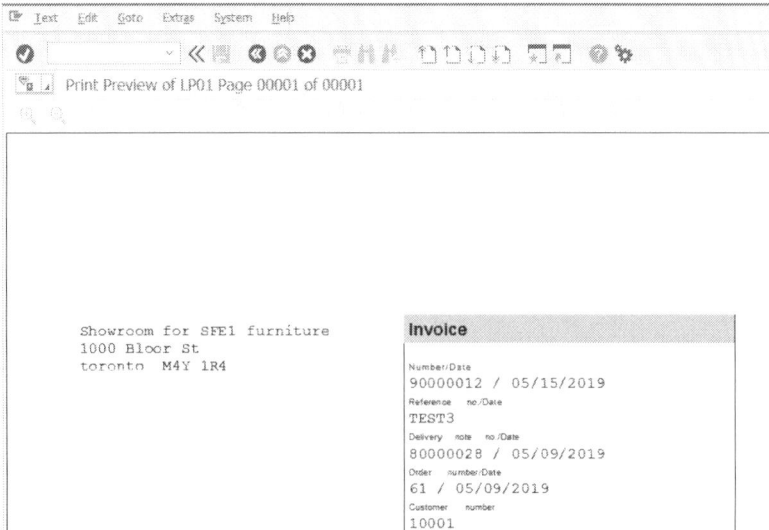

Fig 36

Use scrolling keys to see all the pages if there are multiple.

# IX. Cancelling a Billing Document (U)

T Code VF11

This is done in transaction VF11 which looks like VF01 except for a different header and that here you have to enter the billing document that needs to be cancelled instead of the order # or delivery #:

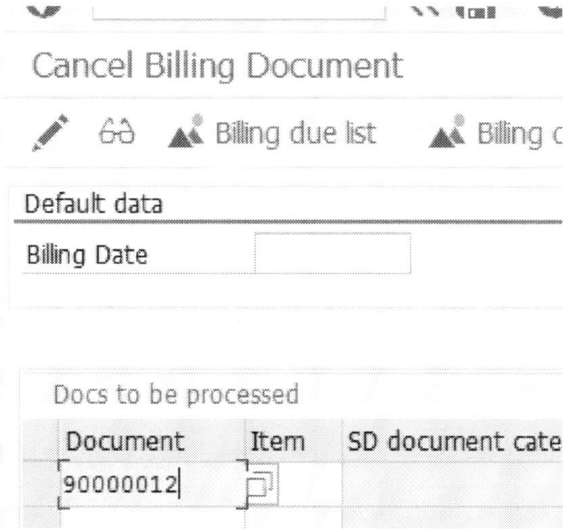

## Cancel Billing Document

&#x270F; &#x6664; Billing due list Billing c

### Default data

Billing Date

### Docs to be processed

| Document | Item | SD document cate |
|----------|------|------------------|
| 90000012 | | |

Fig 37

Hit Enter and Save.

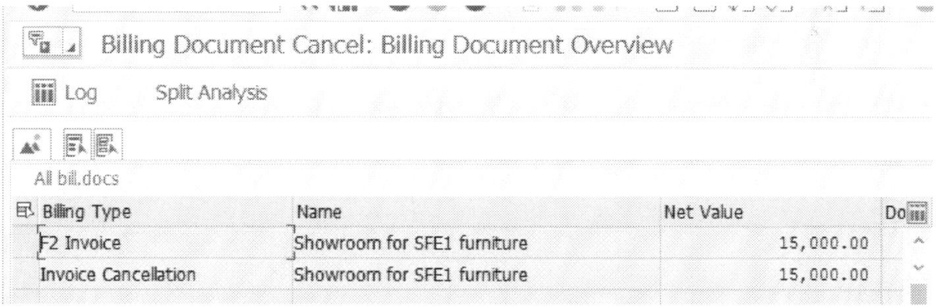

## Billing Document Cancel: Billing Document Overview

Log    Split Analysis

All bill.docs

| Billing Type | Name | Net Value | Do |
|--------------|------|-----------|-----|
| F2 Invoice | Showroom for SFE1 furniture | 15,000.00 | ^ |
| Invoice Cancellation | Showroom for SFE1 furniture | 15,000.00 | v |

Fig 38

&#x2714; Document 90000016 has been saved.

Fig 39

Once an existing billing document is cancelled, it releases the order or the delivery to get billed again. For the most part, in SAP, it is not possible to cancel a preceding document without first cancelling the subsequent document. Thus, it is very important that the data is good from the origin itself, as SAP can be very unforgiving if the data is wrong.

# X. RELEASING BILLING DOCUMENTS TO ACCOUNTING (U)

T Code VFX3

With Billing over, Sales & Distribution hands off the data to accounting. At this cusp is a transaction VFX3 that has to be regularly monitored. Most billing documents will lead up to an accounting document (pro-forma invoices being a notable exception). However, due to various reasons these billing documents get stuck and have to be manually fixed by the users so they can make their way to AR. Some reasons for this are:

1. Old document, billing date is in a closed period.
2. Customer was not extended in the CC i.e. does not have CC data
3. Pricing was not correct
4. G/L account determination for revenue/freight etc. does not exist or is incorrect
5. For exports, certain mandatory foreign trade related data is missing
6. Tax calculations are not correct

And some more that may occur due to company specific custom transactions and data. This data will need to be fixed before these documents can be posted and in some cases, documents will need to be cancelled to re-create them with the correct data.

# XI. ACCOUNTING DOCUMENT

Most invoices will lead to an accounting document if all the data was good in the invoice. The exceptions are special invoices like pro-forma invoices.

In VF03 we can view the invoice we created and it's accounting document:

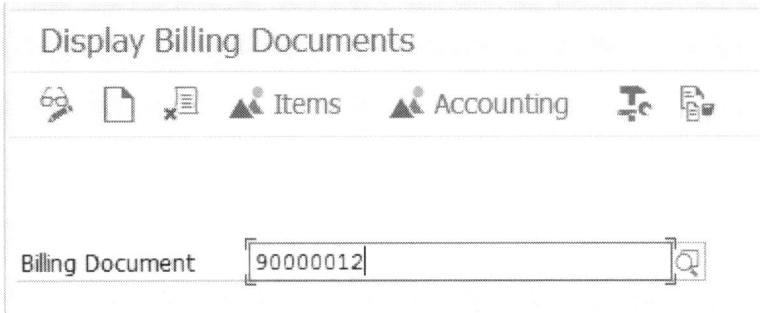

Fig 40

Click on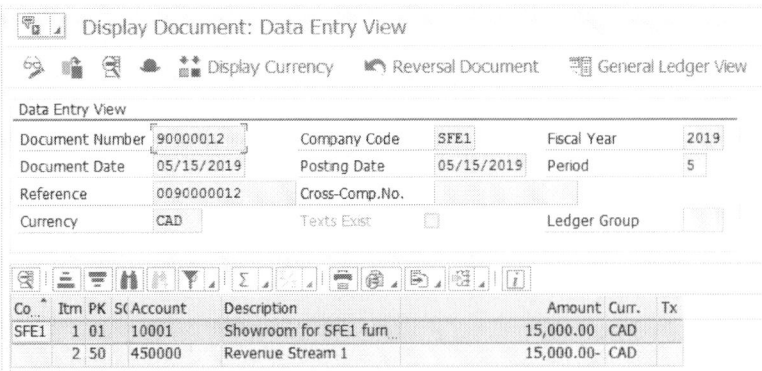

Fig 41

An accounting document is what one sees in the customer's receivables – normally most companies prefer to keep it same as the billing document # to avoid confusion though in SAP it is possible to have both of them as different.

# XII. Relationship Browser

T Code VF03, FB03

A very powerful tool to view the entire chain of transactions is a Relationship browser can be accessed from the accounting document

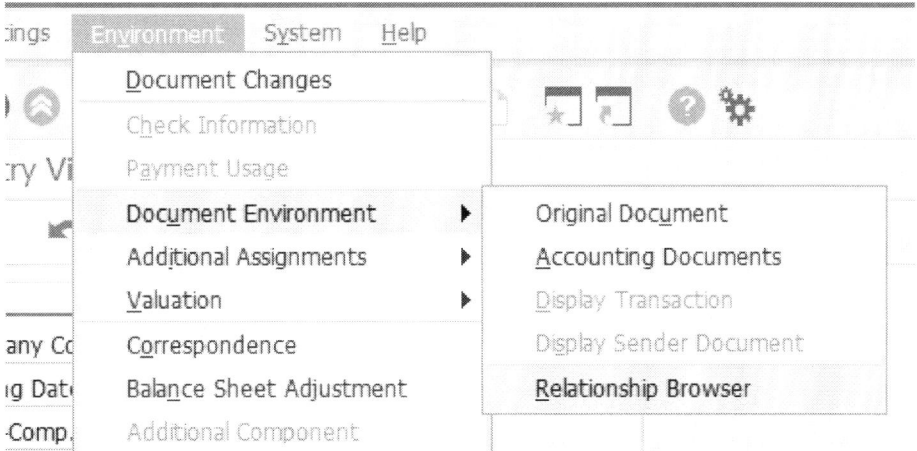

Fig 42

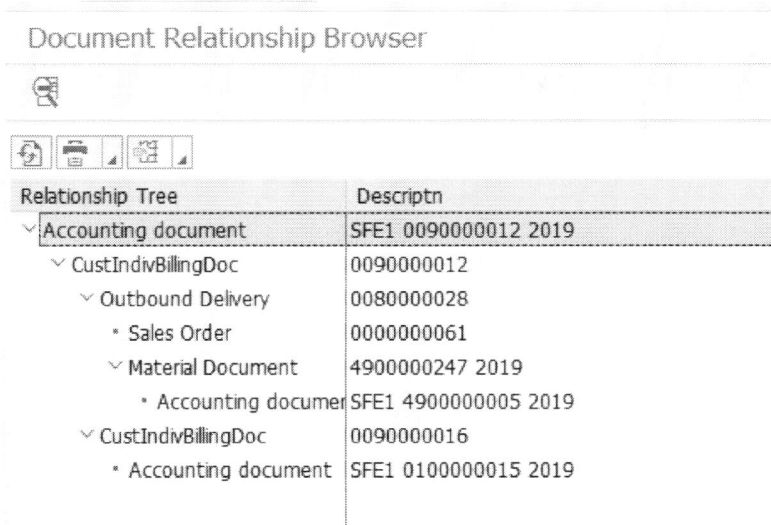

Fig 43

# TAXES IN SAP (U)

## I.      PROCESS (C/U)

T Code SPRO, FTXP

Taxes in SAP are a setup of 3 modules - FI, SD and MM, the main structure and configurations are set up in FI and it is worthwhile to look at the user/functional aspect of this set up. The tax procedure in SAP is set up for each country; it is independent of the CC i.e. all CCs in any certain country can have only one tax procedure.

While not going into the details of the configurations because they are not CC specific, it is important to understand what these tax procedures are and how they are actually implemented in SAP.

Taxes in North America and Europe are calculated in different ways. We will concentrate on the Canadian taxes here which, though calculated the same way as the US ones, are far less complex than US taxation because in Canada it is a 2 tiered structure of Federal and Provincial taxes only while in the US, it is 4 tiered depending on industry, though generally most will fall under 3 tiers. The 4 tiers are state, city, county and district. Very few industries will get the district tax applied. Europe is straight forward with a single VAT being applied.

For this complex taxation and rates, corporations in the US also depend on external services, the 2 most popular being Vertex and Thomson Reuters (also called Sabrix). Often these external systems also keep track of the taxes applied and prepare reports for audits and compliance as well as for filing with the appropriate authorities.

There are 2 primary kinds of taxes in SAP:

- Input tax, used for purchases
- Output tax, used for sales

Depending on the complexity of the company's taxation i.e. based on the customer base and product offering, it may decide to:

- Follow a simple tax procedure whereby all calculations in SAP are done in a standard fashion, not dependent on the exact location of the customer. In Canada or US, this would typically apply to companies, which do business only in the same one province.

- May use the location of the customer if the business is done across provinces or states as the federal tax also will now come into play. This procedure uses Jurisdiction codes, which are provided by the govt. or can be created in SAP and are based on exact locations of the customers since taxes are always applied based on the place of consumption. However, the calculation of them still, would take place within SAP

-

- If the requirement is complex in terms of product and service offerings, which may be subject to different rates of taxation, the company may decide to connect to an external system like Vertex as noted above. The taxes here too, are calculated based on the jurisdiction code however; the calculation does not take place within SAP. Instead, the pertinent data is sent out to the external system via a transmission and the taxation numbers are returned back by that system and applied in SAP. This is usually real time.

Within SAP, the process is driven by tax procedures, tax codes and tax classifications. The mechanism is as follows:

**WHO**: Ship to customer for output tax or purchasing plant for input tax. Taxes are generally applied based on the place of service provided/consumption/use.

**IF**: If tax will be applied. Tax classifications are master data and the customers are given the appropriate tax class in their customer master. Alike, for vendors in the vendor master. The tax classifications are usually simple – 0 means customer is non-taxable and 1 means taxable. Occasionally we may have something additional also, like partial taxation. A similar indicator exists in the material master, which decides if the product or service is taxable, or not. Only when both, customer and material are set as taxable, is the tax applied.

**HOW**: The tax procedure decides this. How will the tax be applied i.e. directly as intra provincial, via jurisdiction codes internally in SAP or from an external system. As we know, we can configure only one tax procedure per country so before SAP is implemented this choice is generally made.

**HOW MUCH**: This is decided by the tax codes or external systems. In a typical taxation setup, the Finance or accounting department sets up these tax codes in a transaction FTXP that replicates the tax procedure being used and sets up the correct tax rates. SD replicates the same for sales and MM for purchases in their respective tax pricing conditions.

To set up taxes in a tax code. Go to transaction FTXP, in the pop up window, say CA (for Canada):

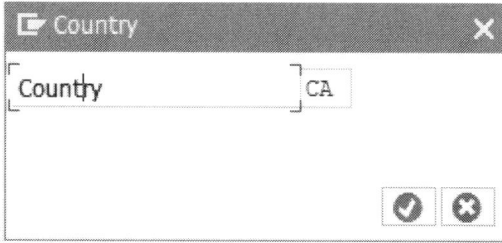

Fig 1

In the window that comes up:

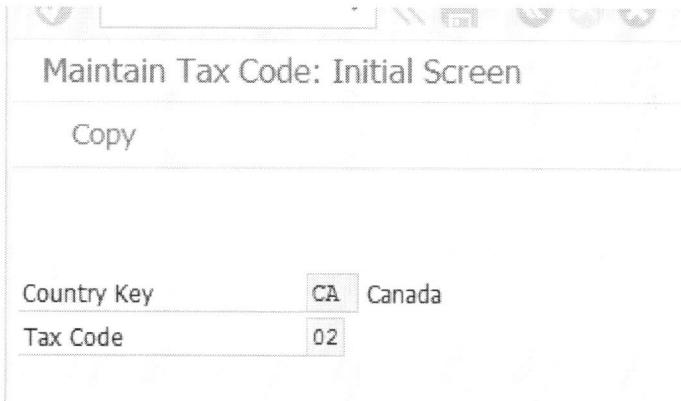

**Maintain Tax Code: Initial Screen**

Copy

| Country Key | CA | Canada |
| Tax Code | 02 | |

Fig 2

Let us enter a 2 digit tax code as above (this can be numeric or alpha numeric) as the one we will set up taxation in. Hit Enter anc click on Properties tab:

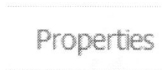

Properties

Fig 3

In the Properties window, enter the tax percentage you want this tax code to apply in the description so that one can know at a glance what this code will do. Also enter if you will use it as an Input tax (V) or Output tax (A).

EU Code as it suggests is required for EU countries only and is provided by the European trade commission

MOSS Tax/RepCtry is also largely associated with EU though many other countries also follow it. It is required for 'reverse taxation' i.e. ifg country A invoices country B for a certain amount of tax, it is country B which will remit it, not country A. This is calles reverse taxation.

| Country Key | CA | Canada |
|---|---|---|
| Tax Code | 02 | |

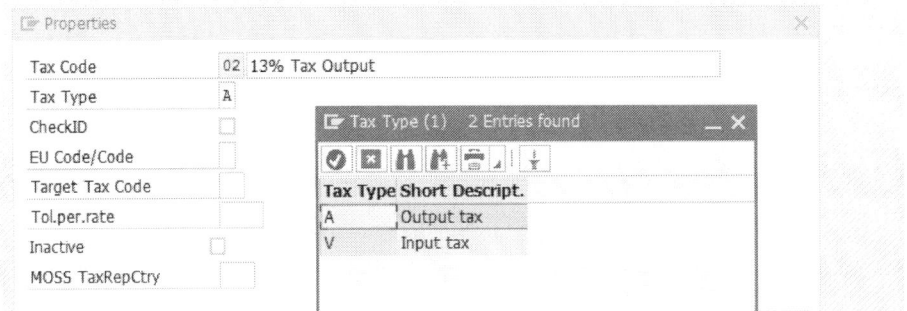

| Properties | × |
|---|---|
| Tax Code | 02 13% Tax Output |
| Tax Type | A |
| CheckID | |
| EU Code/Code | |
| Target Tax Code | |
| Tol.per.rate | |
| Inactive | |
| MOSS TaxRepCtry | |

Tax Type (1)   2 Entries found

| Tax Type | Short Descript. |
|---|---|
| A | Output tax |
| V | Input tax |

Fig 4

On the main screen, enter the percentage of the tax that this tax code will apply at the correct level, here, 13% for Sales.

There can be more conditions hidden and you may need to scroll down to find them:

## Maintain Tax Code: Tax Rates

Properties     Tax accounts     Deactivate line

| | | |
|---|---|---|
| Country Key | CA | Canada |
| Tax Code | 02 | 13% Tax Output |
| Procedure | TAXCA | |
| Tax Type | A | Output tax |

### Percentage rates

| Tax Type | Acct Key | Tax Percent. Rate | Level | From Lvl | Cond. Type |
|---|---|---|---|---|---|
| Base Amount | | | 100 | 0 | BASB |
| * | | | 120 | 0 | |
| * | | | 200 | 100 | |
| A/P Sales Tax 1 Inv. | NVV | | 210 | 120 | JP1I |
| A/P Sales Tax 2 Inv. | NVV | | 220 | 120 | JP2I |
| A/P Sales Tax 3 Inv. | NVV | | 230 | 120 | JP3I |
| A/P Sales Tax 4 Inv. | NVV | | 240 | 120 | JP4I |
| * | | | 300 | 0 | |
| A/P Sales Tax 1 Exp. | VS1 | | 310 | 120 | JP1E |
| A/P Sales Tax 2 Exp. | VS2 | | 320 | 120 | JP2E |
| A/P Sales Tax 3 Exp. | VS3 | | 330 | 120 | JP3E |
| A/P Sales Tax 4 Exp. | VS4 | | 340 | 120 | JP4E |
| * | | | 400 | 0 | |
| A/P Sales Tax 1 Use | MW1 | | 410 | 210 | JP1U |
| A/P Sales Tax 2 Use | MW2 | | 420 | 220 | JP2U |
| A/P Sales Tax 3 Use | MW3 | | 430 | 230 | JP3U |

| Tax Type | Acct Key | Tax Percent. Rate | Level | From Lvl | Cond. Type |
|---|---|---|---|---|---|
| A/P Sales Tax 1 Use | MW1 | | 410 | 210 | JP1U |
| A/P Sales Tax 2 Use | MW2 | | 420 | 220 | JP2U |
| A/P Sales Tax 3 Use | MW3 | | 430 | 230 | JP3U |
| A/P Sales Tax 4 Use | MW4 | | 440 | 240 | JP4U |
| * | | | 500 | 0 | |
| A/R Sales Tax 1 | MW1 | 13.000 | 510 | 120 | JR1 |
| A/R Sales Tax 2 | MW2 | | 520 | 120 | JR2 |
| A/R Sales Tax 3 | MW3 | | 530 | 120 | JR3 |
| A/R Sales Tax 4 | MW4 | | 540 | 120 | JR4 |

Fig 5

385

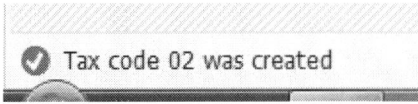

Fig 6

The above is the tax procedure TAXCA being used in our system in Canada. Thus, all CCs in Canada are using this. The main columns denote:

- Tax type – input, output. Though we have set up the input code, the procedure is common to both, input and output.

- Account key. This key is a determining factor of how the tax values are going to post to GLs

- Tax percent rate. You would be most concerned about this field. This is where the actual numbers relating to tax percentages will be entered.

Click on

It asks for the CoA:

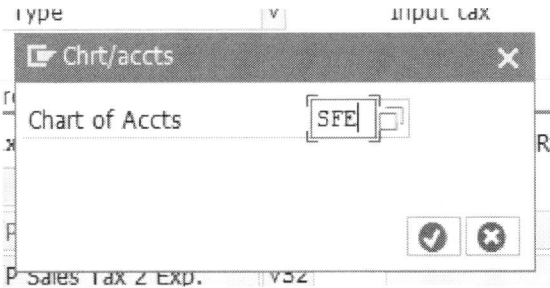

Fig 7

In this field, we have the ability to define the tax G/L accounts where we want the GST/PST/HST etc postings to be made – this GL account configuration defaults from one done in SPRO or transaction code OB40.

We will, however, see how tax can be applied to a sales document only via SD because the tax postings still flow to some G/L. There are 3 steps, all 3 of them are master data.

## II.   MASTER DATA (U)

T Code XD01/XD02, MM01/MM02, VK11/VK12 in ECC and BP, MM01/02, VK11/12 in HANA

Let us ensure our customer is taxable first i.e. it has tax class as 1 for GST. In transaction BP, for the customer's sales area, in the Billing tab, we find the tax classifications set up for the customer.

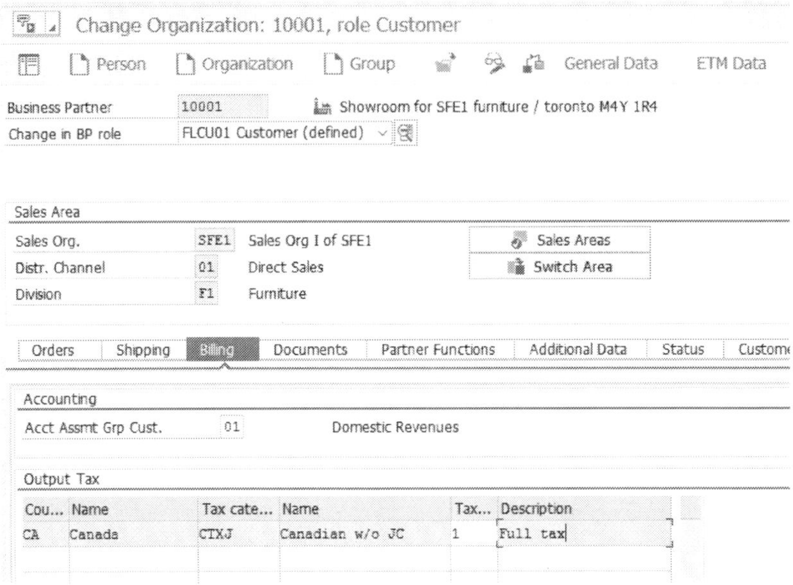

Fig 8

Our material also to taxable as we know taxes get applied only when both are set to taxable in MM02 in Sales: Sales Org 1 data tab as below:

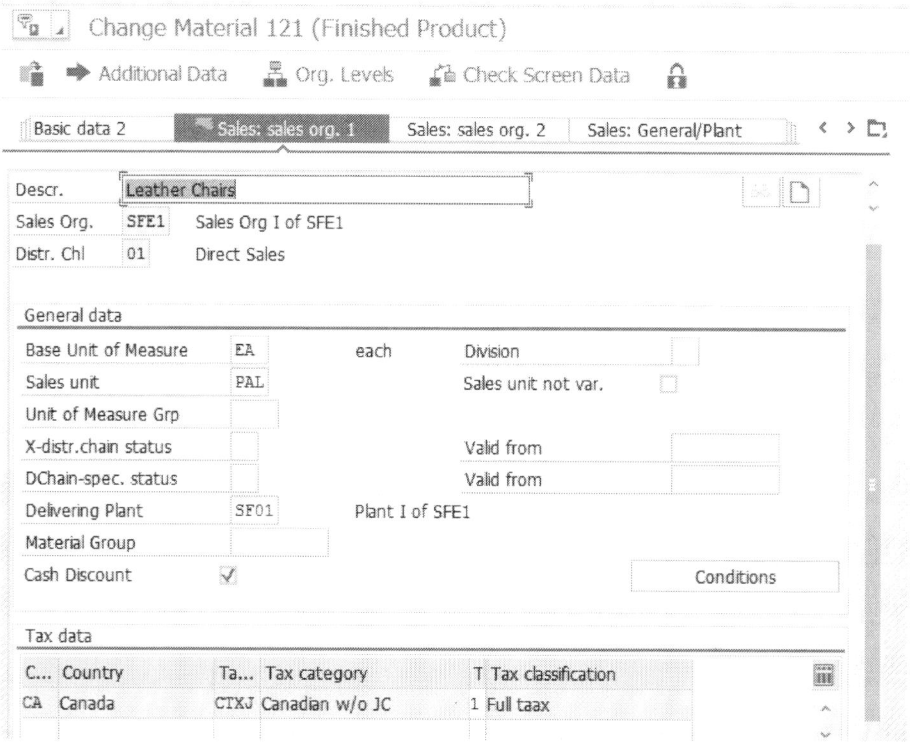

## Change Material 121 (Finished Product)

Additional Data | Org. Levels | Check Screen Data

| Basic data 2 | Sales: sales org. 1 | Sales: sales org. 2 | Sales: General/Plant |

Descr. Leather Chairs

Sales Org. SFE1 Sales Org I of SFE1
Distr. Chl 01 Direct Sales

**General data**

| Base Unit of Measure | EA | each | Division | |
| Sales unit | PAL | | Sales unit not var. | ☐ |
| Unit of Measure Grp | | | | |
| X-distr.chain status | | | Valid from | |
| DChain-spec. status | | | Valid from | |
| Delivering Plant | SF01 | Plant I of SFE1 | | |
| Material Group | | | | |
| Cash Discount | ✓ | | | Conditions |

**Tax data**

| C... Country | Ta... Tax category | T Tax classification | |
| CA Canada | CTXJ Canadian w/o JC | 1 Full taax | |

Fig 9

Next, we set a tax pricing condition for the appropriate condition only on the SD side. This is done in transaction VK11:

Create Condition Records

Condition Information | Key Combination

Condition type    CTXJ    Canadian w/o JC

Fig 10

Hit Enter and choose the 3rd sequence as we are doing domestic sales here:

389

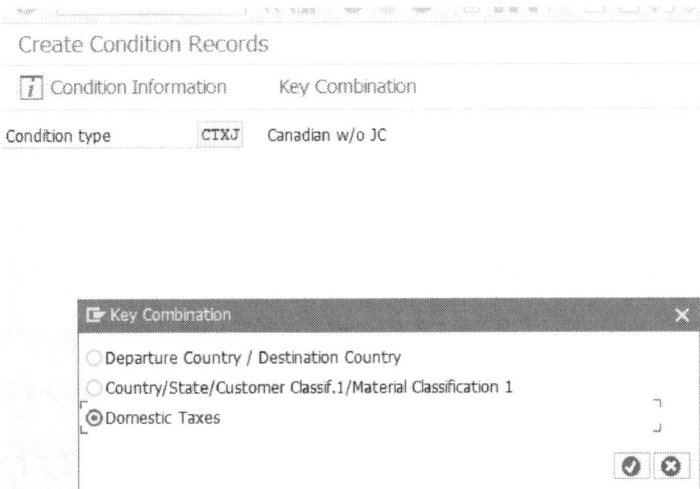

Fig 11

Enter data as below – this merely means that when the customer and material, both are taxable, then apply a tax from tax code

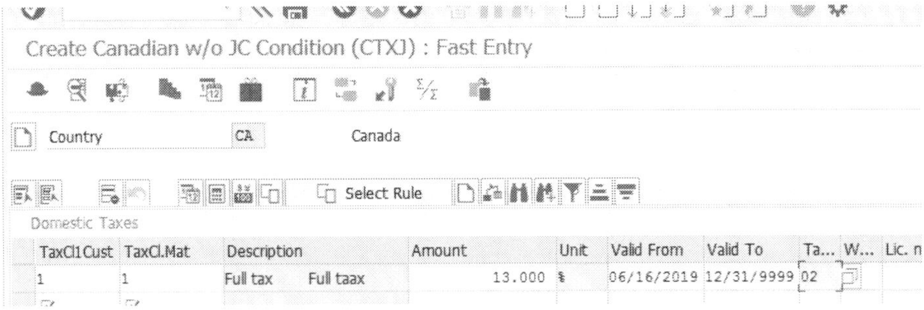

Fig 12

Save. As said in the above section, when the material and customer, both are taxable i.e. the tax class is 1 for both, then apply a domestic tax of 13% based on the tax code 02.

T Code VA01

Let us create a sales order and see the effect:

We see on the pricing screen that the system has now applied the tax we set up:

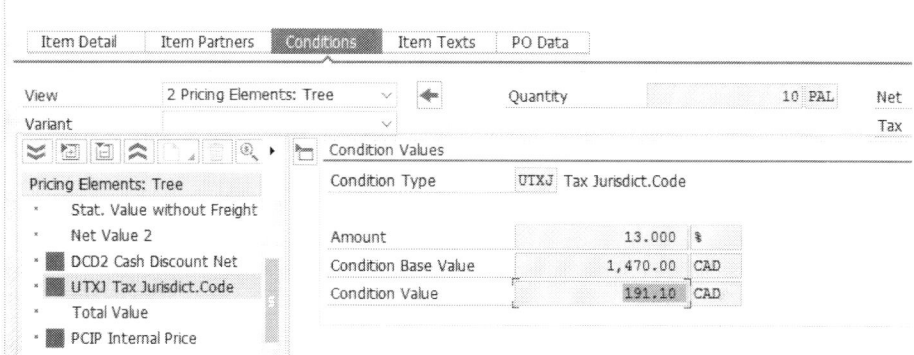

Fig 13

# CUSTOMER STATEMENTS IN SAP (U)

T Code FBL5N, F.27

Most companies send customers' open AR statements at end of the month, quarter or year as the policy may be. Though for the most part, the feel and look of these statements will be specific to the company, with their logos, formatting, information etc, the basic process of running the transaction in SAP to generate statements will likely be the same. In some cases, the companies may also have their own transaction code to run statements en masse for all customers in a Co Code all together. However, standard SAP also does offer the ability to print an individual account statement or multiple statements. Since we will actually not be printing any, we can see the transaction that enables us to see an individual account statement as a pdf document within SAP.

Go to customer AR statement, FBL5N and enter the customer #/s and the date, as on which you want to see the statements:

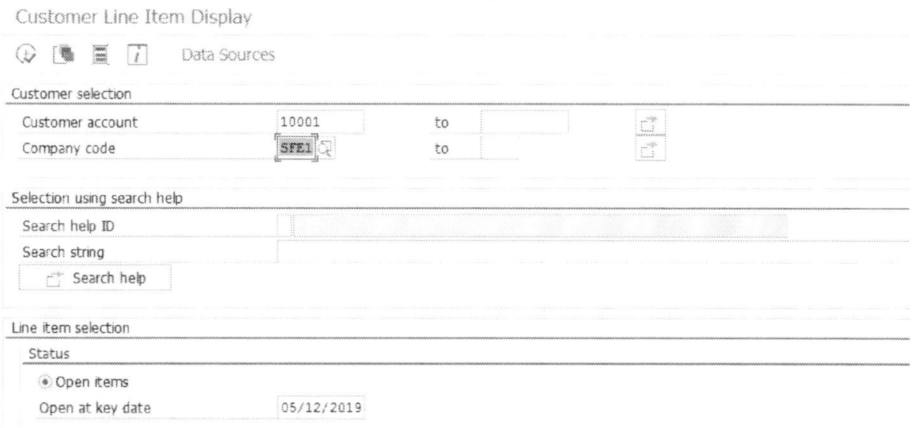

**Customer Line Item Display**

Data Sources

Customer selection

| Customer account | 10001 | to | | |
| Company code | SFE1 | to | | |

Selection using search help

Search help ID

Search string

Search help

Line item selection

Status

◉ Open items

Open at key date    05/12/2019

Fig 1

Execute to get to the detailed line items.

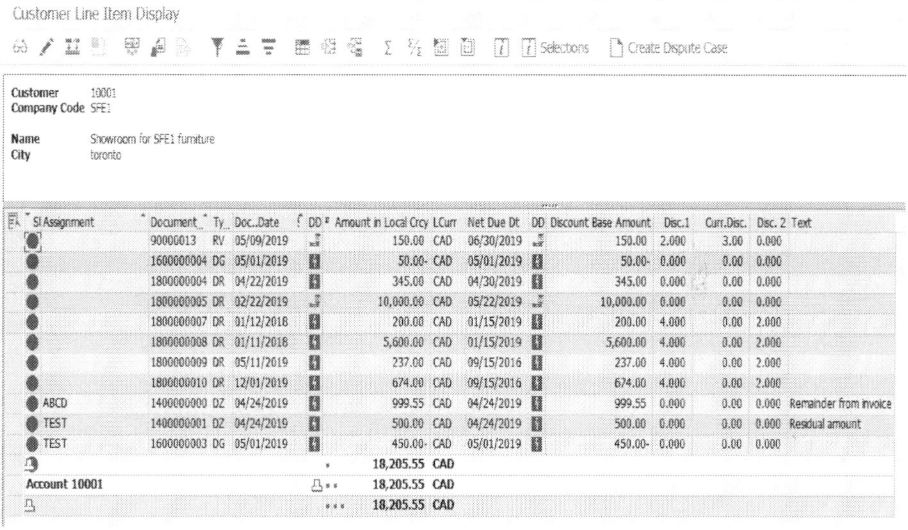

**Customer Line Item Display**

Selections    Create Dispute Case

| Customer | 10001 |
| Company Code | SFE1 |

| Name | Showroom for SFE1 furniture |
| City | toronto |

| St | Assignment | Document | Ty | Doc..Date | DD | Amount in Local Crcy | LCurr | Net Due Dt | DD | Discount Base Amount | Disc.1 | Curr.Disc. | Disc. 2 | Text |
|----|-----------|----------|----|-----------|----|---------------------|-------|-----------|----|--------------------|--------|-----------|--------|------|
| | | 90000013 | RV | 05/09/2019 | | 150.00 | CAD | 06/30/2019 | | 150.00 | 2.000 | 3.00 | 0.000 | |
| | | 1600000004 | DG | 05/01/2019 | | 50.00- | CAD | 05/01/2019 | | 50.00- | 0.000 | 0.00 | 0.000 | |
| | | 1800000004 | DR | 04/22/2019 | | 345.00 | CAD | 04/30/2019 | | 345.00 | 0.000 | 0.00 | 0.000 | |
| | | 1800000005 | DR | 02/22/2019 | | 10,000.00 | CAD | 05/22/2019 | | 10,000.00 | 0.000 | 0.00 | 0.000 | |
| | | 1800000007 | DR | 01/12/2018 | | 200.00 | CAD | 01/15/2019 | | 200.00 | 4.000 | 0.00 | 2.000 | |
| | | 1800000008 | DR | 01/11/2018 | | 5,600.00 | CAD | 01/15/2019 | | 5,600.00 | 4.000 | 0.00 | 2.000 | |
| | | 1800000009 | DR | 05/11/2019 | | 237.00 | CAD | 09/15/2016 | | 237.00 | 4.000 | 0.00 | 2.000 | |
| | | 1800000010 | DR | 12/01/2019 | | 674.00 | CAD | 09/15/2016 | | 674.00 | 4.000 | 0.00 | 2.000 | |
| | ABCD | 1400000000 | DZ | 04/24/2019 | | 999.55 | CAD | 04/24/2019 | | 999.55 | 0.000 | 0.00 | 0.000 | Remainder from invoice |
| | TEST | 1400000001 | DZ | 04/24/2019 | | 500.00 | CAD | 04/24/2019 | | 500.00 | 0.000 | 0.00 | 0.000 | Residual amount |
| | TEST | 1600000003 | DG | 05/01/2019 | | 450.00- | CAD | 05/01/2019 | | 450.00- | 0.000 | 0.00 | 0.000 | |
| | | | | | | 18,205.55 | CAD | | | | | | | |
| Account 10001 | | | | | | 18,205.55 | CAD | | | | | | | |
| | | | | | | 18,205.55 | CAD | | | | | | | |

Fig 2

393

Click on any line item and follow the path below to request a statement:

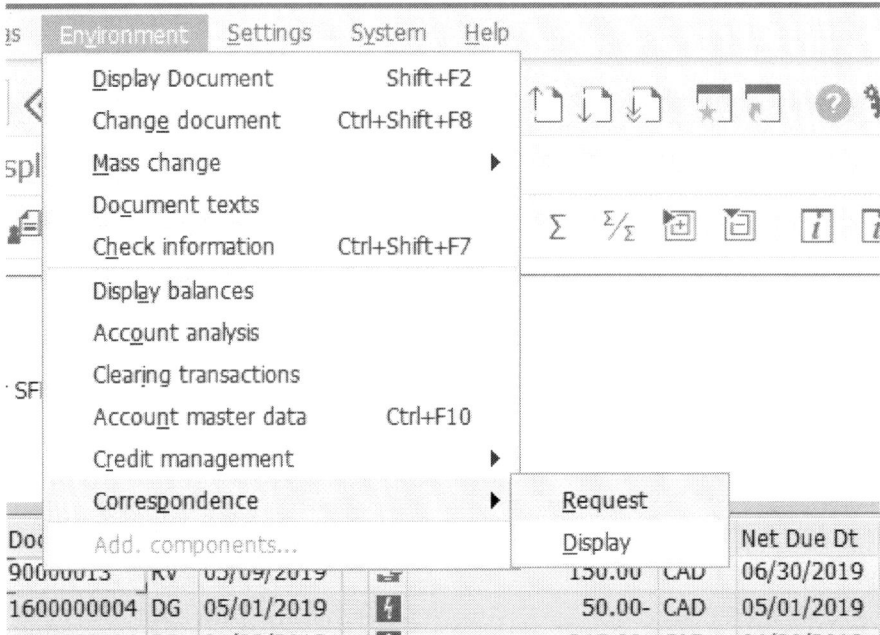

Fig 3

Double click on the SAP06 option. This is the standard SAP one, likely the actual organization may have it's own.

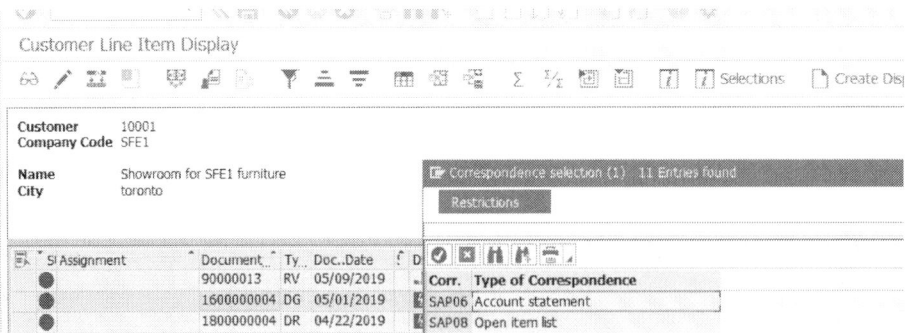

Fig 4

In the window that comes, enter the posting dates of the range of documents you need the statement for:

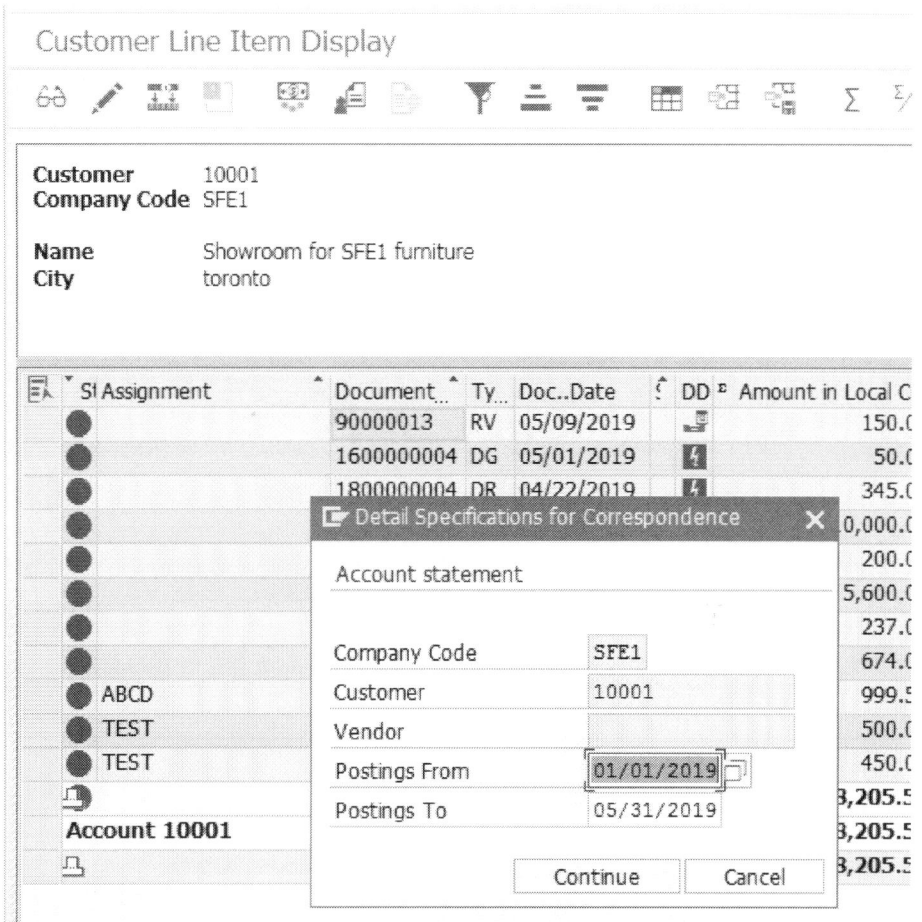

## Customer Line Item Display

Customer        10001
**Company Code** SFE1

**Name**        Showroom for SFE1 furniture
**City**        toronto

| SI Assignment | Document | Ty | Doc..Date | DD | Amount in Local C |
|---|---|---|---|---|---|
| | 90000013 | RV | 05/09/2019 | | 150.( |
| | 1600000004 | DG | 05/01/2019 | | 50.( |
| | 1800000004 | DR | 04/22/2019 | | 345.( |
| | | | | | 0,000.( |
| | | | | | 200.( |
| | | | | | 5,600.( |
| | | | | | 237.( |
| | | | | | 674.( |
| ABCD | | | | | 999.! |
| TEST | | | | | 500.( |
| TEST | | | | | 450.( |
| | | | | | 3,205.! |
| **Account 10001** | | | | | 3,205.! |
| | | | | | 3,205.! |

**Detail Specifications for Correspondence**

Account statement

| | |
|---|---|
| Company Code | SFE1 |
| Customer | 10001 |
| Vendor | |
| Postings From | 01/01/2019 |
| Postings To | 05/31/2019 |

Continue    Cancel

Fig 5

And click on the Continue Button.

A message at the bottom says:

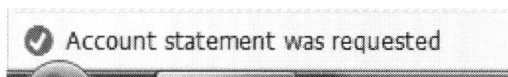

✓ Account statement was requested

Fig 6

Go back to the same path, this time, asking to Display the statement:

395

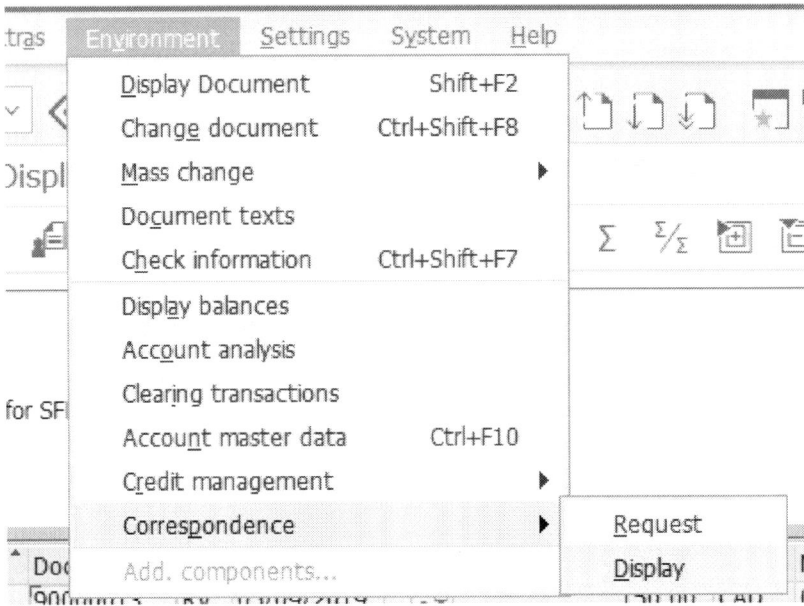

Fig 7

Enter the correct Printer when the window pops up and Click on continue:

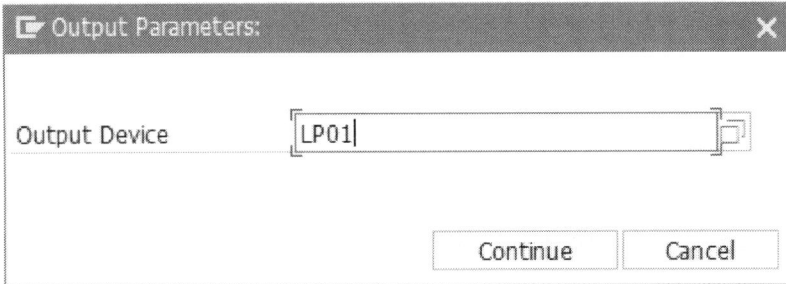

Fig 8

The statement comes up as a Preview:

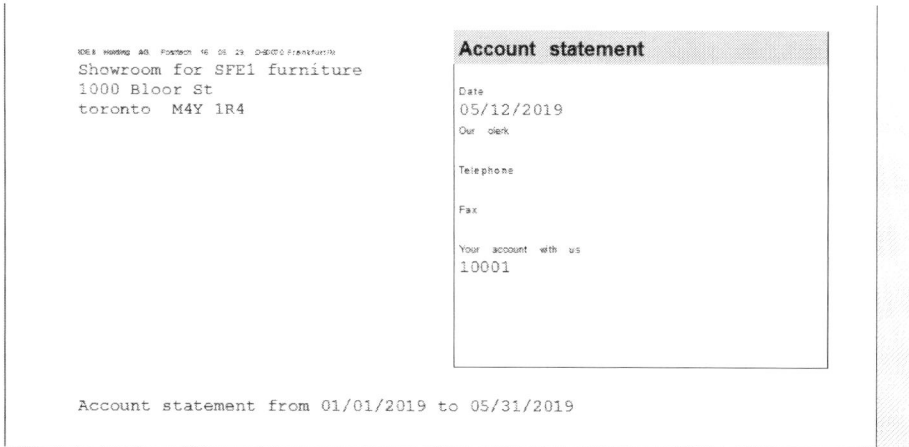

IOE.8 Holding AG. Poartech 46 08 29 D-60070 Frankfurt/M

Showroom for SFE1 furniture
1000 Bloor St
toronto   M4Y 1R4

**Account statement**

Date
05/12/2019

Our  clerk

Telephone

Fax

Your  account  with  us
10001

Account statement from 01/01/2019 to 05/31/2019

Fig 9

You can scroll up and down the pages using the keys

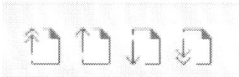

In the real world, when printers are connected in SAP, we can print the statement out using the actual printer. Scroll down to see the actual statement numbers:

| Doc. Number | Doc. Date | Trans- action | Curr- ency | Amount | Clearing |
|---|---|---|---|---|---|
| Balance carried forward 01/01/2019: | | | | 0.00 | |
| 1800000008 | 01/11/2018 | DR | CAD | 5,600.00 | |
| 1800000007 | 01/12/2018 | DR | CAD | 200.00 | |
| 1800000005 | 02/22/2019 | DR | CAD | 10,000.00 | |
| 1800000000 | 04/22/2019 | DR | CAD | 2,000.00 | 1400000000 |
| 1800000003 | 04/22/2019 | DR | CAD | 2,341.00 | 1400000004 |
| 1800000004 | 04/22/2019 | DR | CAD | 345.00 | |
| 1400000001 | 04/24/2019 | DZ | CAD | 500.00 | |
| 1400000001 | 04/24/2019 | DZ | CAD | 7,500.00- | 1400000001 |

Fig 10

We could also choose all postings, not just open AR if in FBL5N, we choose the Posting Dates option instead of the Open as on option:

397

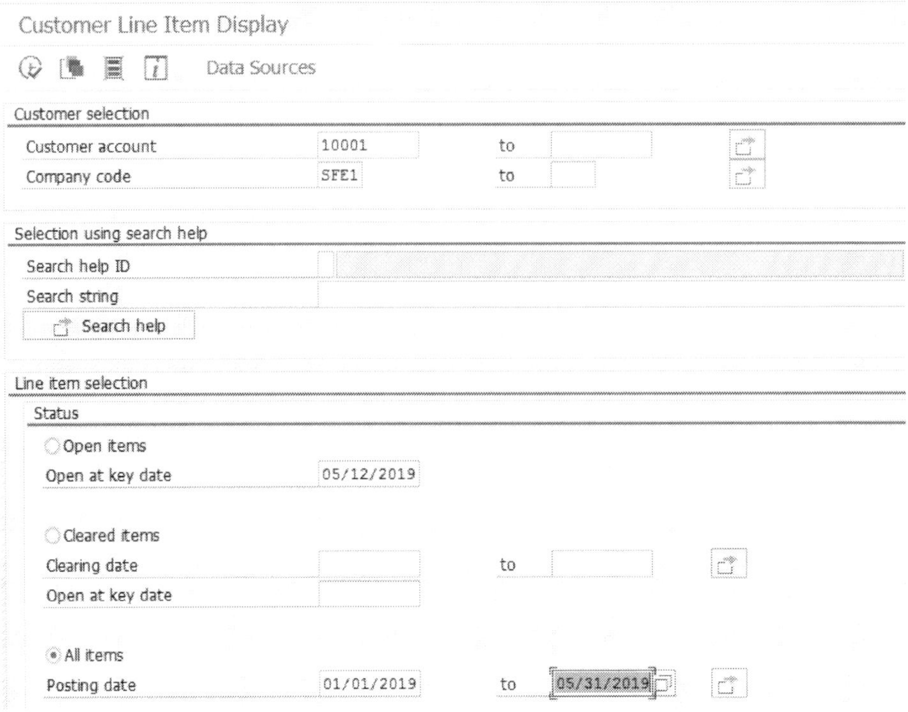

Fig 11

Executing it, we can see the same transactions as we see in the statement plus more though not in chronological order, the green lines being the cleared items:

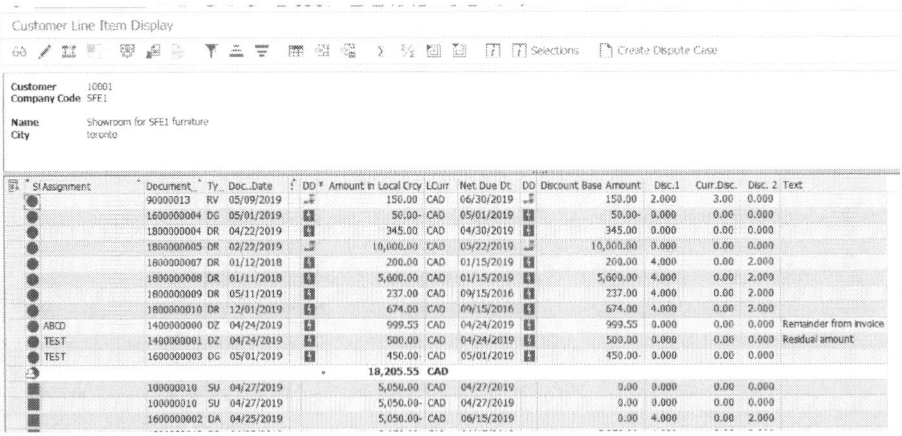

Fig 12

They can be made to show up chronologically by sorting them by Doc. date as below. Place the cursor on that heading and click on the first button in the pair  to sort them by dates:

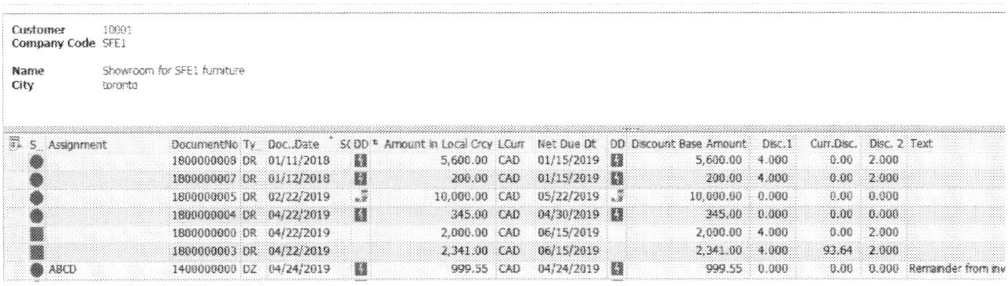

| S. | Assignment | DocumentNo | Ty | Doc..Date | S< | DD | E | Amount in Local Crcy | LCurr | Net Due Dt | Dt | DD | Discount Base Amount | Disc.1 | Curr.Disc. | Disc. 2 | Text |
|---|---|---|---|---|---|---|---|---|---|---|---|---|---|---|---|---|---|
| ● | | 1800000008 | DR | 01/11/2018 | | | | 5,600.00 | CAD | 01/15/2019 | | | 5,600.00 | 4.000 | 0.00 | 2.000 | |
| ● | | 1800000007 | DR | 01/12/2018 | | | | 200.00 | CAD | 01/15/2019 | | | 200.00 | 4.000 | 0.00 | 2.000 | |
| ● | | 1800000005 | DR | 02/22/2019 | | | | 10,000.00 | CAD | 05/22/2019 | | | 10,000.00 | 0.000 | 0.00 | 0.000 | |
| ● | | 1800000004 | DR | 04/22/2019 | | | | 345.00 | CAD | 04/30/2019 | | | 345.00 | 0.000 | 0.00 | 0.000 | |
| ■ | | 1800000000 | DR | 04/22/2019 | | | | 2,000.00 | CAD | 06/15/2019 | | | 2,000.00 | 4.000 | 0.00 | 2.000 | |
| ■ | | 1800000003 | DR | 04/22/2019 | | | | 2,341.00 | CAD | 06/15/2019 | | | 2,341.00 | 4.000 | 93.64 | 2.000 | |
| ● | ABCD | 1400000000 | DZ | 04/24/2019 | | | | 999.55 | CAD | 04/24/2019 | | | 999.55 | 0.000 | 0.00 | 0.000 | Remainder from inv |

Customer 10001
Company Code SFE1

Name Showroom for SFE1 furniture
City toronto

Fig 13

Other than this, we can also use transaction F.27 to directly print or preview statements:

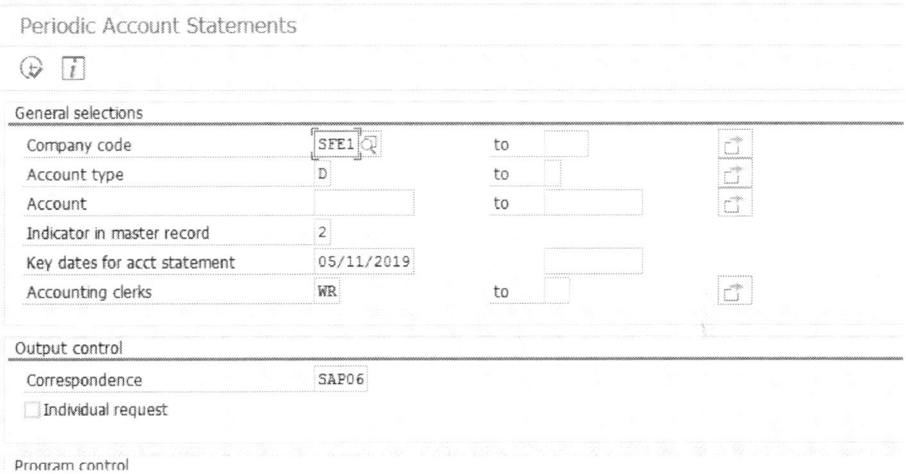

Periodic Account Statements

General selections

| | | | |
|---|---|---|---|
| Company code | SFE1 | to | |
| Account type | D | to | |
| Account | | to | |
| Indicator in master record | 2 | | |
| Key dates for acct statement | 05/11/2019 | | |
| Accounting clerks | WR | to | |

Output control

Correspondence SAP06

☐ Individual request

Program control

Fig 14

The data in the above screen will get validated with the data in the customer master's correspondence tab and gets pulled into the program to create the statements for e.g. this customer has WR as accounting clerk and 2 in the bank statement field:

399

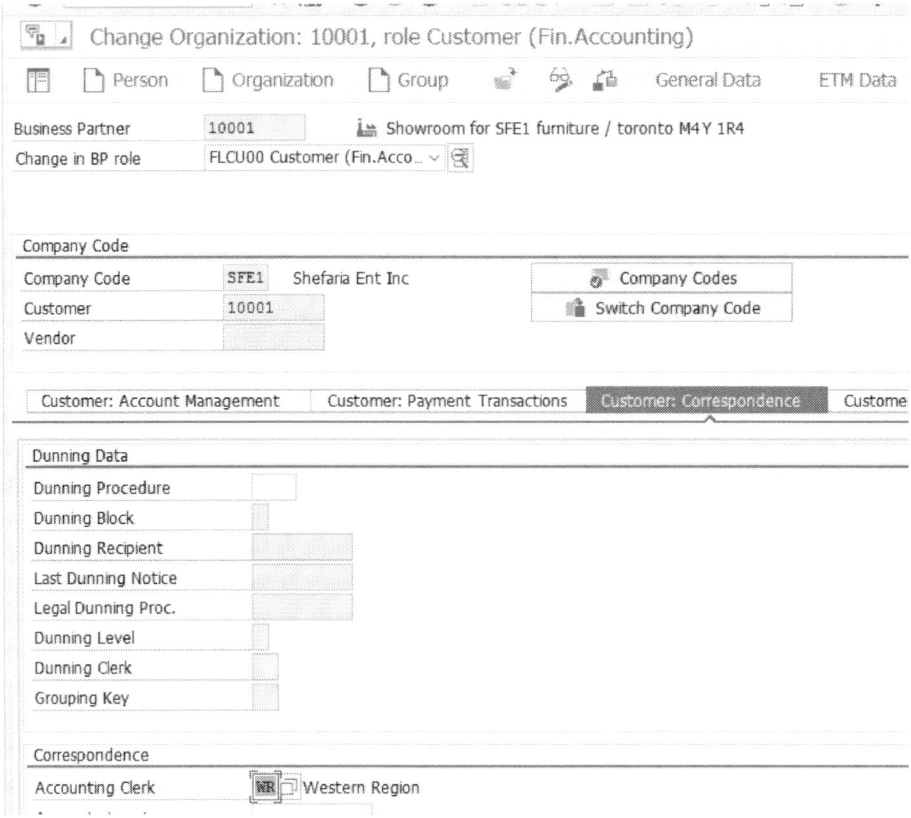

Fig 15

Thus, this customer will get pulled up in the statement (since the variant has asked for all accounting clerks). We could have restricted the data by specific accounting clerk/s.

Executing on this screen, we get the message:

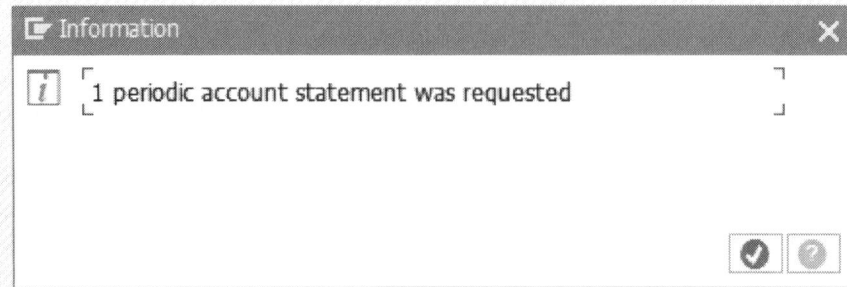

Fig 17

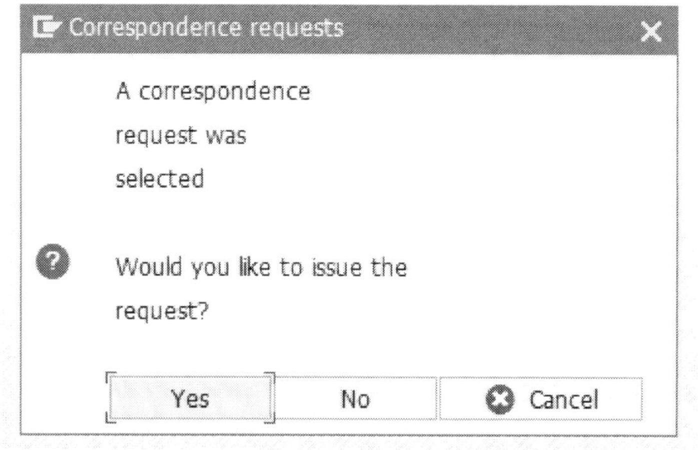

Fig 18

Hit Enter:

Enter the output device in the new screen:

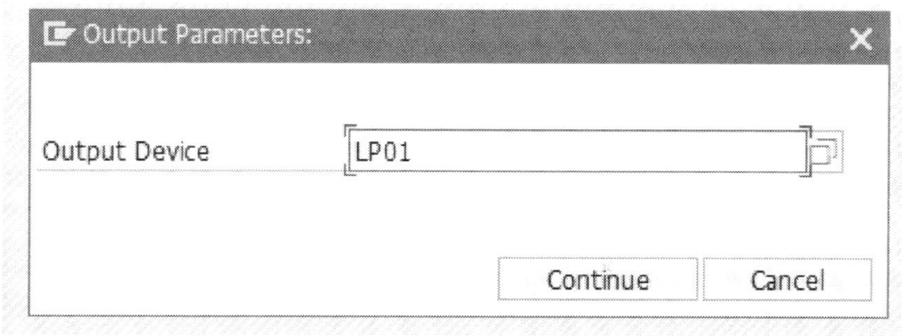

Fig 19

When you see the screen below, you know statements have been generated:

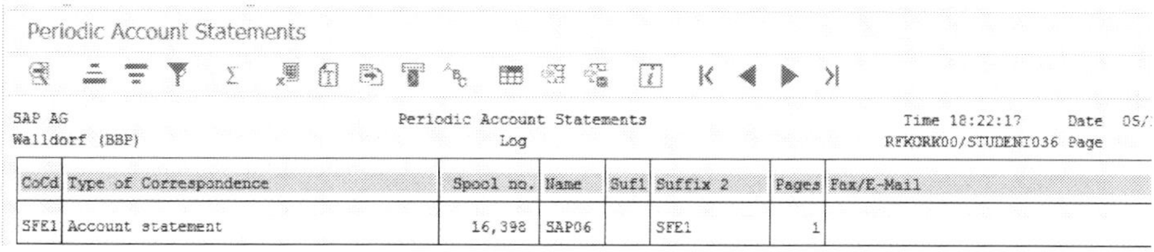

Fig 20

They can be seen in transaction SP02:

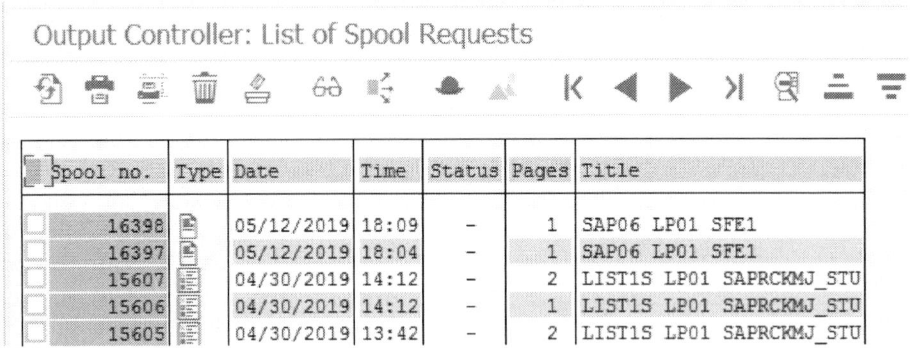

Output Controller: List of Spool Requests

| Spool no. | Type | Date | Time | Status | Pages | Title |
|---|---|---|---|---|---|---|
| 16398 | | 05/12/2019 | 18:09 | – | 1 | SAP06 LP01 SFE1 |
| 16397 | | 05/12/2019 | 18:04 | – | 1 | SAP06 LP01 SFE1 |
| 15607 | | 04/30/2019 | 14:12 | – | 2 | LIST1S LP01 SAPRCKMJ_STU |
| 15606 | | 04/30/2019 | 14:12 | – | 1 | LIST1S LP01 SAPRCKMJ_STU |
| 15605 | | 04/30/2019 | 13:42 | – | 2 | LIST1S LP01 SAPRCKMJ_STU |

Fig 21

Click on  relating to your spool #:

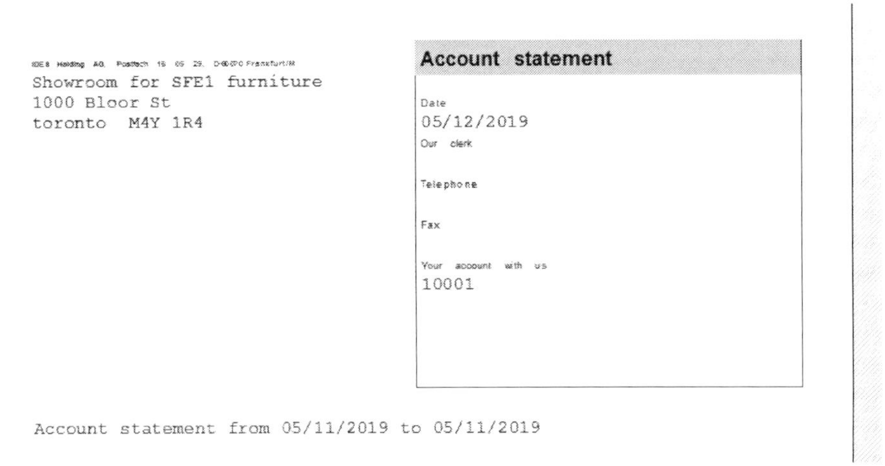

IDES Holding AG. Postfach 15 05 29. D-60-0PO Frankfurt/M
Showroom for SFE1 furniture
1000 Bloor St
toronto  M4Y 1R4

**Account statement**

Date
05/12/2019
Our clerk

Telephone

Fax

Your account with us
10001

Account statement from 05/11/2019 to 05/11/2019

Fig 22

402

# DUNNING (C/U)

T Code SPRO, F150

Invoices and statements sometimes do not get payments from difficult customers. This is where dunning steps in. Simply stated, dunning is a reminder to the customer that payments from them are overdue and they should remit the same to the vendor. The dunning process can also keep track of a customer's payment habits, which can be used in reporting, and decision making on the credit policies a company should adopt to keep receivables in control. There may be customers who buy a lot, pay slow but do pay and do not default. In those cases, the company may want to retain the business, increase the prices marginally to cover for the lost interest and give more than normal credit so their receivables do not affect overdue AR.

Further, this process can also be taken a step forward and this information sent to collection agencies. This is a useful feature for high volume mass product selling companies like cell phone providers, utility companies etc.

While the language on a dunning letter will be company specific like in statements, the process of generating dunning letters in SAP is the same. It involves some configuration set up and master data in the customer's CC data view.

The standard dunning system in SAP covers 4 different customer transactions:

1. Open A/R invoices, including invoices that are partially credited or partially paid
2. Invoices that include installments
3. A/R credit memos
4. Incoming payments that are not based on invoices

# I. DUNNING SETUP (C)

## I. SETUP DUNNING AREA:

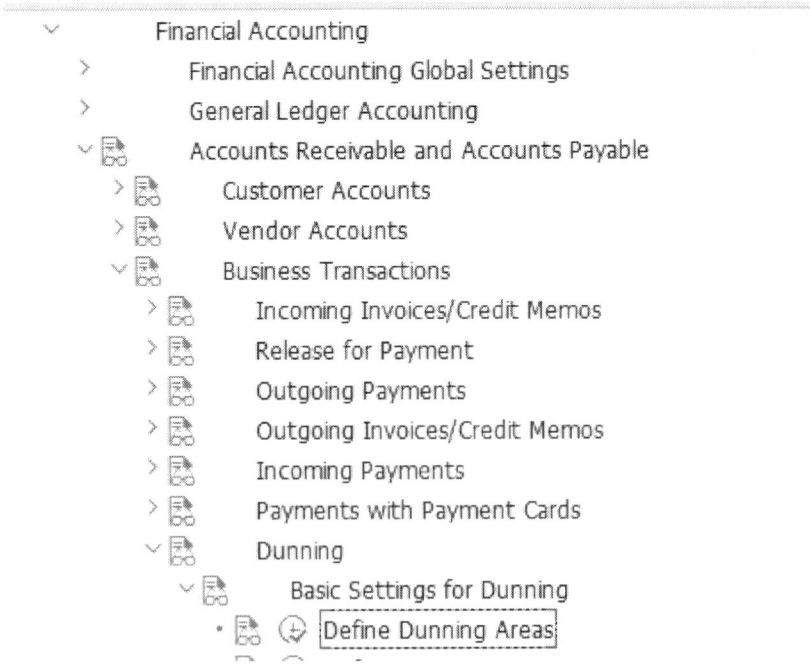

Financial Accounting
> Financial Accounting Global Settings
> General Ledger Accounting
∨ Accounts Receivable and Accounts Payable
> Customer Accounts
> Vendor Accounts
∨ Business Transactions
> Incoming Invoices/Credit Memos
> Release for Payment
> Outgoing Payments
> Outgoing Invoices/Credit Memos
> Incoming Payments
> Payments with Payment Cards
∨ Dunning
∨ Basic Settings for Dunning
• Define Dunning Areas

Fig 1

Dunning areas can be a sales area, a certain profit center, a business area, or can also set up a dunning area for domestic customers or foreign customers etc., the idea really being as to who is responsible for this dunning set up in SAP.

We will set up a generic dunning area for the co code:

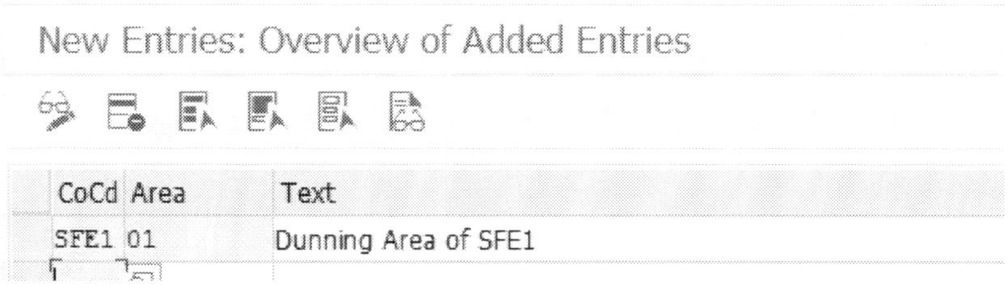

| CoCd | Area | Text |
|------|------|------|
| SFE1 | 01 | Dunning Area of SFE1 |

Fig 2

## II.   DUNNING KEY:

A dunning key defines the levels of dunning that can take place.

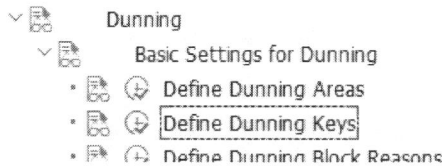

Fig 3

There are pre-defined dunning keys given by SAP, which are normally used.

Check All and Save:

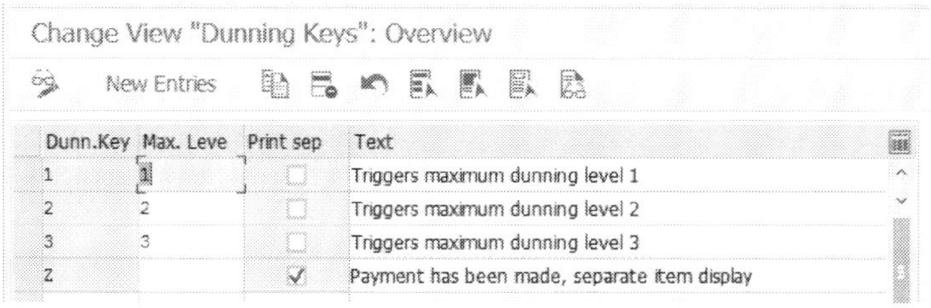

Fig4

With this, we triggered all the dunning levels possible in standard SAP i.e. multiple reminders if necessary can go to the customers so set up to receive them.

### III. DUNNING BLOCKING REASONS:

Certain customers regardless of their payment schedules are too important and are not sent dunning letters to avoid bad unpleasantness. We can define dunning reasons in configuration and then in the customer master, in Correspondence tab, those customers can be assigned some reason or the other for not dunning them. Those customers will then be bypassed during the dunning run and will not be sent letters. They are put on a 'dunning block'.

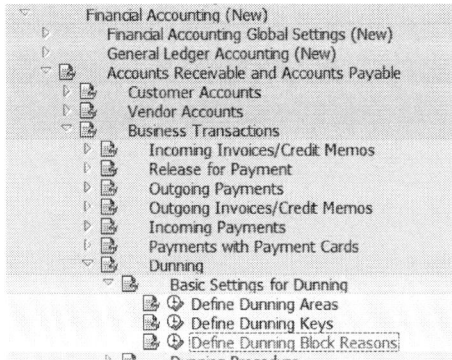

Fig 5

Fig 6

Any of the above reasons (or users can define their own also) can then be assigned in the customer master in the field

Dunning Block can be entered in it's respective field if there is a dunning procedure defined.

**HANA CHANGE**: In ECC we could define the blocking reasons, dunning clerks and other data freely. In HANA however, all these fields are disabled and get enabled only if we enter a dunning procedure in the field. Dunning procedure is explained in the next section.

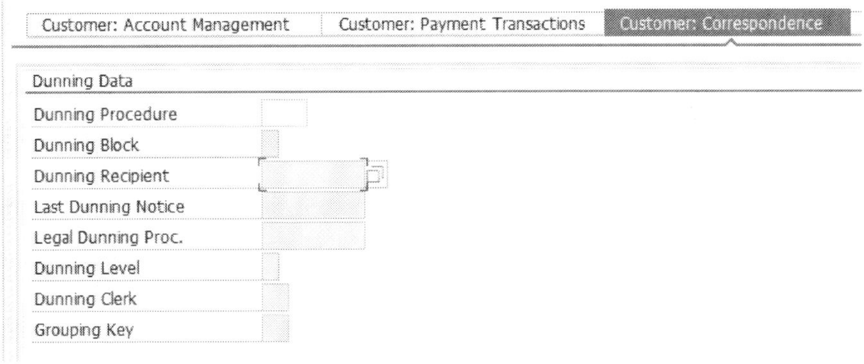

Fig 7 a

With dunning procedure:

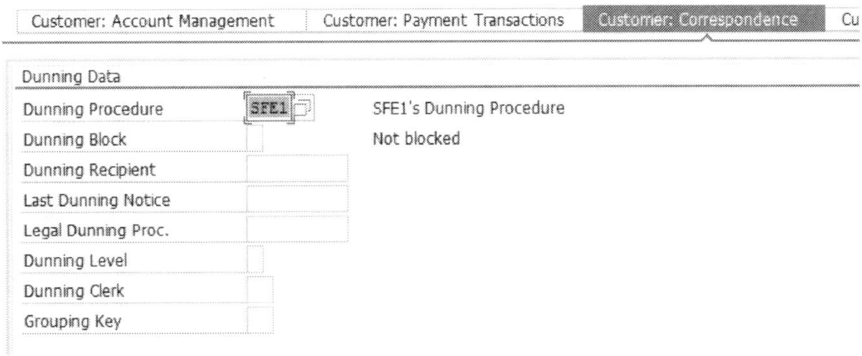

Fig 7 b

## IV.  DUNNING PROCEDURE:

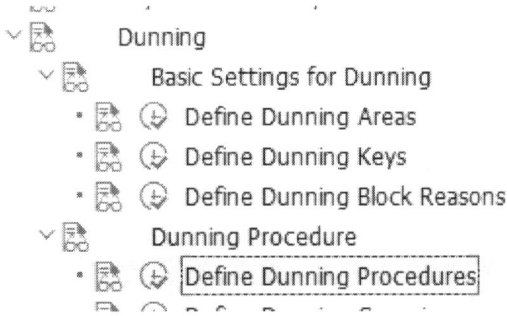

Fig 8

Dunning Procedure defines the process whereby which the customers will be dunned using the dunning keys.

To understand the different drivers in a dunning procedure, let us make our own for our co code:

Fig 9

Click on New Procedure to give it a name and Code:

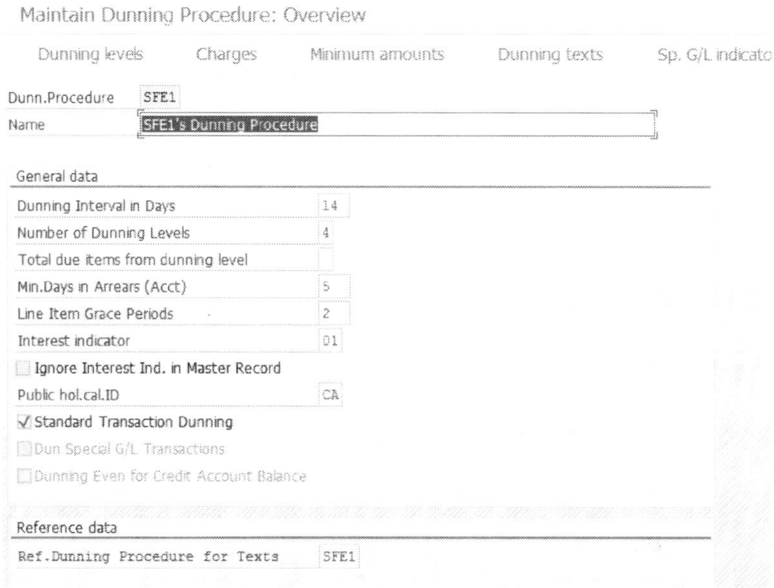

Maintain Dunning Procedure: Overview

Dunning levels    Charges    Minimum amounts    Dunning texts    Sp. G/L indicato

Dunn.Procedure    SFE1
Name              SFE1's Dunning Procedure

General data
Dunning Interval in Days              14
Number of Dunning Levels              4
Total due items from dunning level
Min.Days in Arrears (Acct)            5
Line Item Grace Periods               2
Interest indicator                    01
☐ Ignore Interest Ind. in Master Record
Public hol.cal.ID                     CA
☑ Standard Transaction Dunning
☐ Dun Special G/L Transactions
☐ Dunning Even for Credit Account Balance

Reference data
Ref.Dunning Procedure for Texts       SFE1

Fig 10

(a) The field Dunning Interval in Days defines the # of days in between when the customer receives the next dunning letter. When the dunning job runs, the system checks if this many # of days have passed when the last dunning took place

(b) Dunning levels – the max number of levels of dunning that can be done. 4 is currently the max number in SAP. Normally, if 4 reminders don't lead to the desired results, there is a good chance to write off the amount or pass to a collection agency. However, a company may decide to set up more levels if it feels it will help.

(c) Days in arrears, which at least one item in this account, must have for a dunning notice to be created. These minimum days in arrears have no influence on calculating the days overdue

(d) Line item grace period – if you want to give a grace period of any kind due to delays in post etc. This would then add to the days set in (c) when SAP looks for customers who need to be sent letters in the specific dunning run.

(e) Interest indicator - optional field, we would enter an interest calculation indicator here if we want dunning interest to be calculated for this customer

(f) Check the field Standard Transaction dunning

## V. DEFINE DUNNING CHARGES

Define the Dunning charges to Dunning Procedures Click on the Charges tab

Enter the currency CAD and Hit Enter and enter your respective data as below:

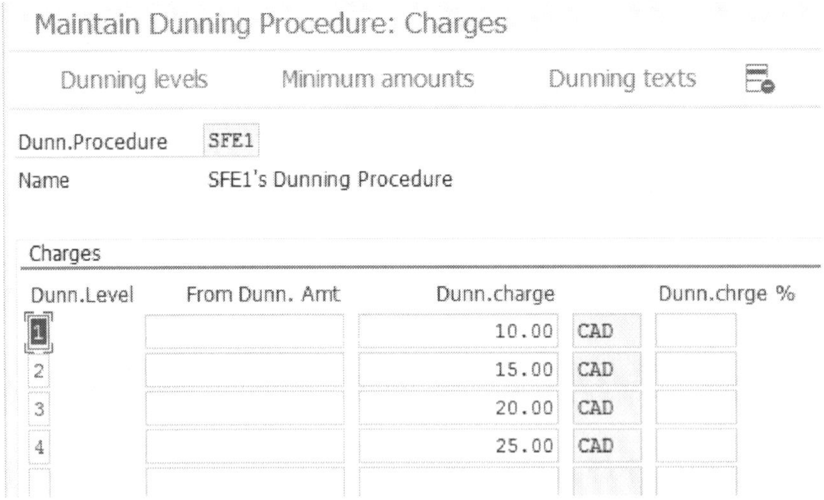

Maintain Dunning Procedure: Charges

| Dunning levels | Minimum amounts | Dunning texts |
| --- | --- | --- |

Dunn.Procedure   SFE1
Name                    SFE1's Dunning Procedure

Charges

| Dunn.Level | From Dunn. Amt | Dunn.charge | | Dunn.chrge % |
| --- | --- | --- | --- | --- |
| 1 | | 10.00 | CAD | |
| 2 | | 15.00 | CAD | |
| 3 | | 20.00 | CAD | |
| 4 | | 25.00 | CAD | |
| | | | | |

Fig 11

410

Dunning charges can be defined in 2 different ways:

(i)    As an absolute amount as in the above case

(ii)   As a % amount. This % amount is calculated by multiplying this % with the total of all overdue items in the dunning notice. The result is the dunning charge in dunning currency.


## VI.    MINIMUM AMOUNTS

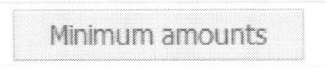

Minimum amounts

The objective of defining Min Amounts is to cover administrative charges associated with dunning the customers.

Maintain Dunning Procedure: Minimum amounts

| Dunning levels | Charges | Dunning texts |
|---|---|---|

Dunn.Procedure    SFE1

Name                      SFE1's Dunning Procedure

Minimum amounts

| Dun | Minimum amnt | Min.Percent. | NoRed. | Min.Amt for Interest | |
|---|---|---|---|---|---|
| 1 | 3.00 | | ☐ | | CAD |
| 2 | 5.00 | | ☐ | | CAD |
| 3 | 7.00 | | ☐ | | CAD |
| 4 | 10.00 | | ☐ | | CAD |
| | | | ☐ | | |

Fig 12

411

Next, we assign what text/letters we will be sent to the customers when we dun them.

Click on *Dunning texts*

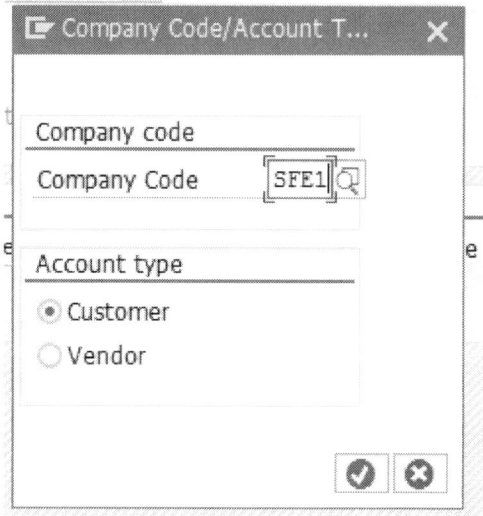

**Company Code/Account T...**   ✕

Company code

Company Code    [SFE1] 🔍

Account type

⦿ Customer
◯ Vendor

✓  ✕

Fig 13

Choose Customer and Click OK

Click on *New company code* to set our CC in the list

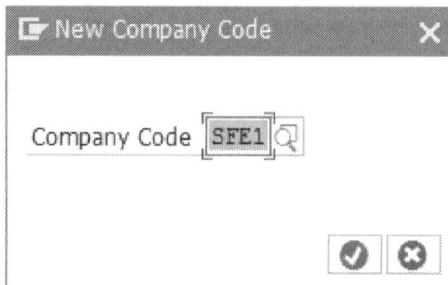

**New Company Code**   ✕

Company Code  [SFE1] 🔍

✓  ✕

Fig 14

Select the 2 options – Dunning by dunning area and Separate Notice per dunning level:

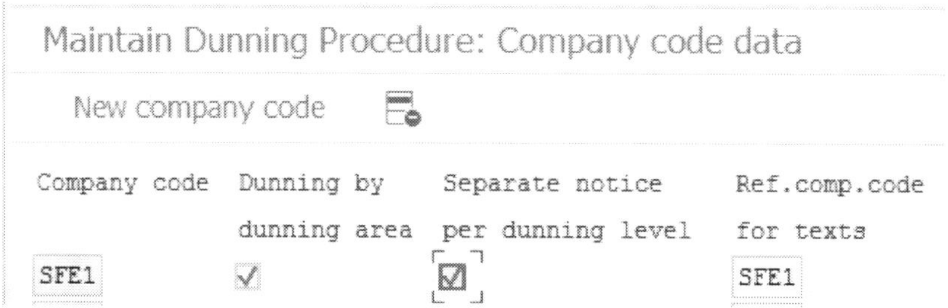

Fig 15

Save the data:

## VIII.  DUNNING LEVELS

The next step is to maintain the actual dunning levels in the dunning procedure. Click on Dunning levels :

Let's assume we want to calculate interest only at the 3rd and 4th level of dunning and give grace of interest on the 1st and 2nd duns:

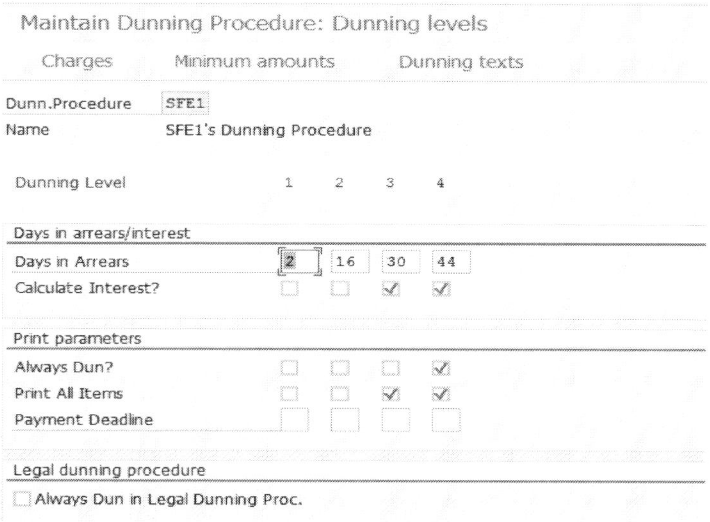

Fig 16

Note the difference of 14 days – this 14 is coming from the time period we defined earlier as the gap between the different duns.

Go back and save the data. The dunning procedure is now ready to be used.

# II. DUNNING THE CUSTOMER (U)

T Code BP in HANA or FD02 in ECC, F150

First, we set up the appropriate master data. Go to transaction BP, change customer's CC data and add the dunning procedure in the Correspondence tab:

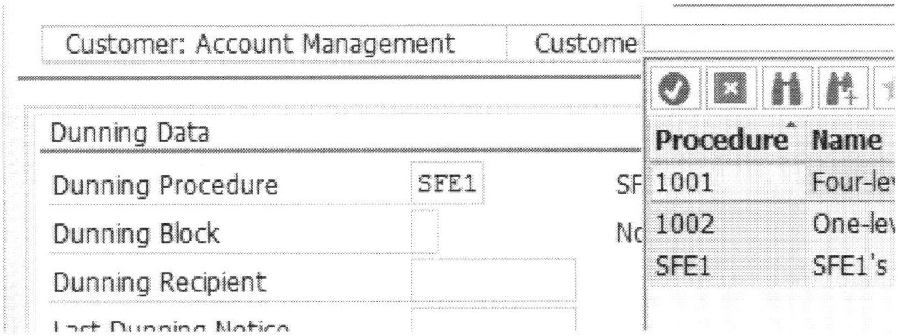

Fig 17

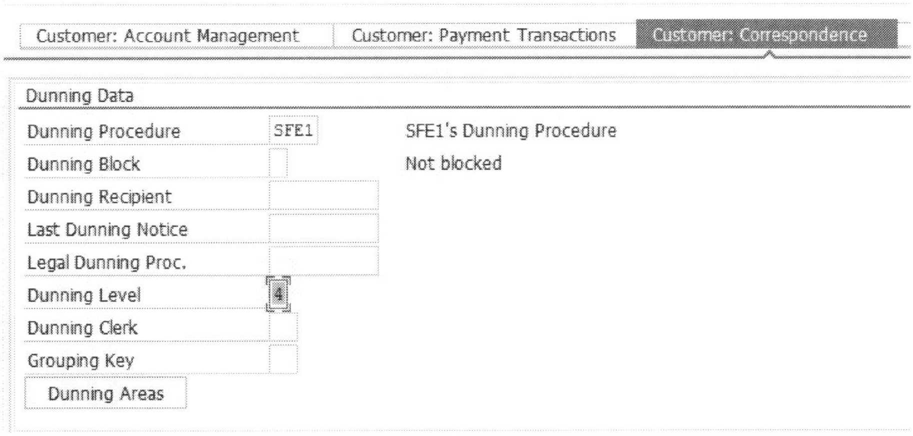

Fig 18

Save.

Once the customer is set up, we are ready to test the dunning process. The t code is F150 for setting up dunning runs for customers collectively or dun individually, or follow the path:

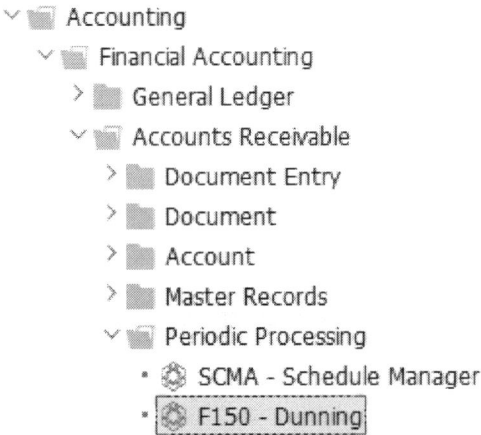

Fig 19

Give the dunning run an ID and the date on which you want it to occur:

Fig 20

Enter the other necessary data in the tabs, esp the Parameter tab:

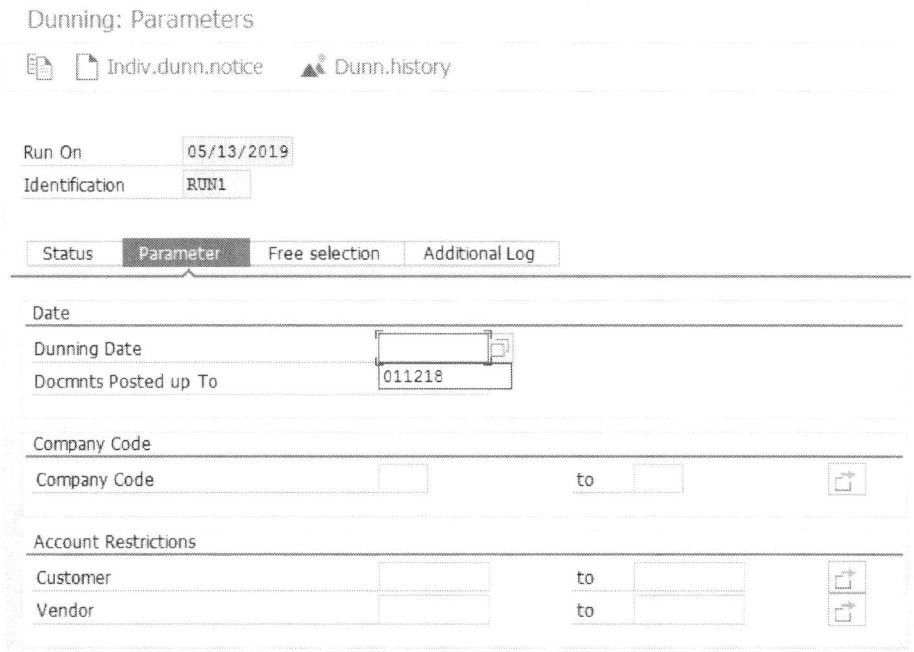

Dunning: Parameters

📇 🗋 Indiv.dunn.notice    🔺 Dunn.history

Run On          05/13/2019
Identification  RUN1

| Status | Parameter | Free selection | Additional Log |

Date

| Dunning Date |  |
| Docmnts Posted up To | 011218 |

Company Code

| Company Code |  | to |  |  |

Account Restrictions

| Customer |  | to |  |  |
| Vendor |  | to |  |  |

Fig 21

The dunning date is the date of issue and also the date from which the arrears are calculated. Documents posted upto date will include all the documents posted till that date.

Account restrictions enable you to exclude or include accounts that should not be dunned or should be dunned. This is different from the exclusions that come in due to data not set in the customer or vendor masters. SAP checks for both – those excluded in the customer master will be excluded as well as those listed here for exclusion will also be excluded. If you want only a few customers to be dunned, then set them up here and SAP will pick up only those for dunning provided they have been set up appropriately in the customer master to be dunned. If a customer is excluded in the customer master then inclusion here will not create dunning letters for them.

417

Dunning: Parameters

📄 Indiv.dunn.notice    ▲ Dunn.history

| Run On | 05/13/2019 |
| Identification | RUN1 |

| Status | Parameter | Free selection | Additional Log |

**Date**

| Dunning Date | 01/01/2019 📅 |
| Docmnts Posted up To | 01/05/2019 |

**Company Code**

| Company Code | SFE1 | to | | ⏩ |

Fig 22

Save the run.

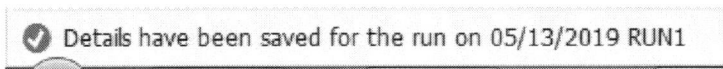
✓ Details have been saved for the run on 05/13/2019 RUN1

Fig 23

Now, a background job will kick in on the above date in this case and create dunning notices for all the appropriately set up customers.

# III. INDIVIDUAL DUNNING NOTICES (U)

T Code F150

We can also see individual notices for any particular customer/s instead of all customers in one run.

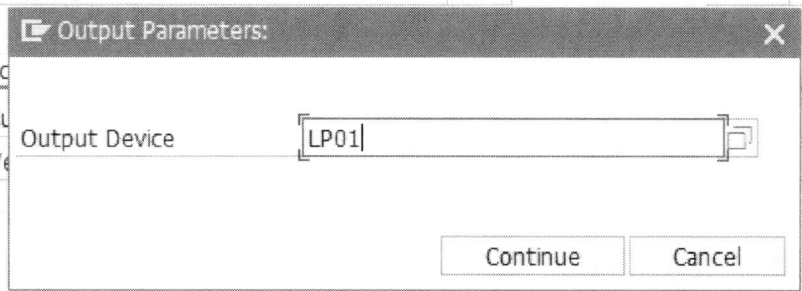

Enter the PDF printer in the window that comes up:

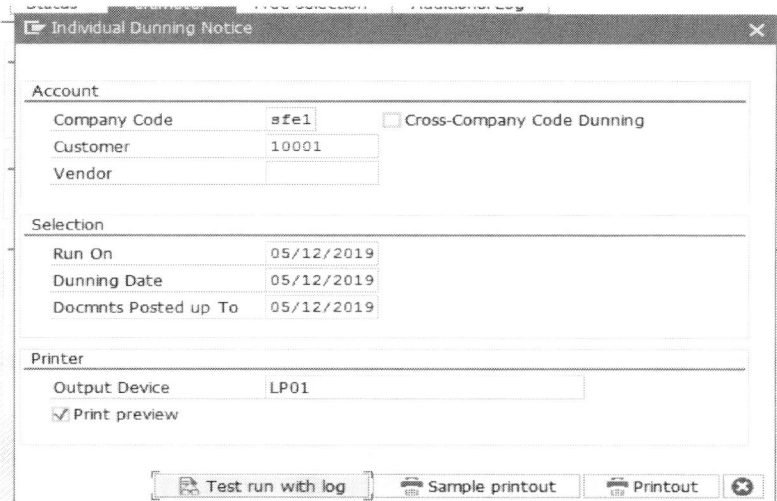

Fig 24

Enter data as:

Fig 25

Click on [🖶 Sample printout]

A very crude letter comes up:

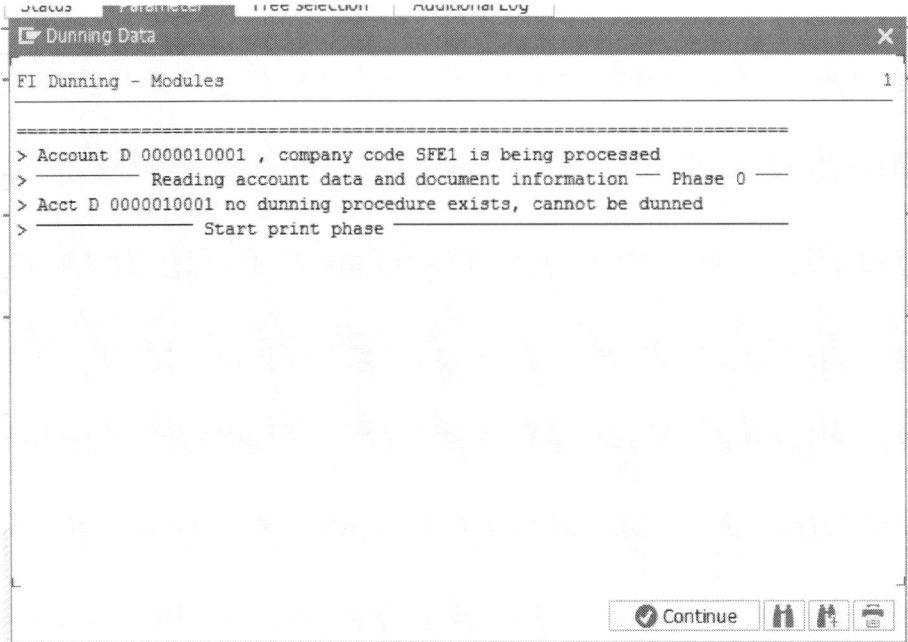

Fig 26

This letter is not a finished product. Normally, companies will develop, align and appropriately place the text in the forms and layouts, which will be created in SAP for this purpose. Here, it is only for demonstration purpose.

# CASH MANAGEMENT – CASH JOURNAL

Cash Management is used to monitor cash flows and to ensure that you have sufficient liquidity to cover your payment obligations.

The cash journal is a sub ledger of Bank Accounting. It is used to manage a company's cash transactions. The system automatically calculates and displays the opening and closing balances, and the receipts and payments totals. User can run several cash journals for each company code. The user can also carry out postings to G/L accounts, as well as vendor and customer accounts.

# I.   CREATE GENERAL LEDGER ACCOUNT (U):

T Code FS01  or the path below takes you to it:

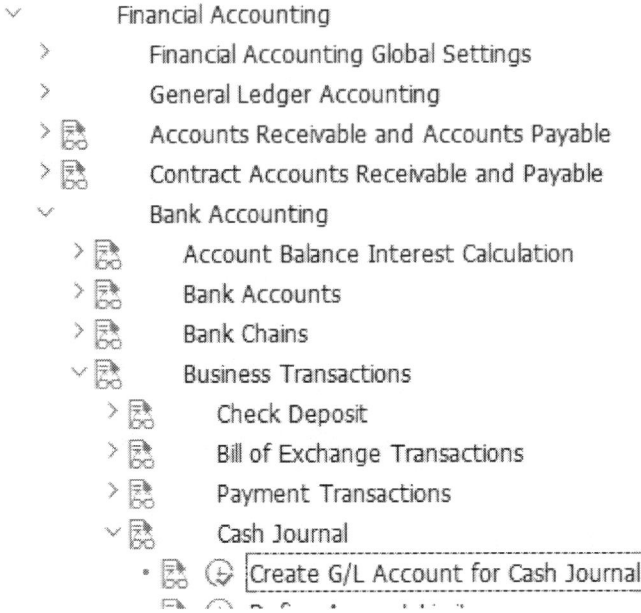

Fig 1

Petty Cash G/L A/C 107100 was created in FS01: we have 3 G/Ls relating to cash:

Fig 2

These GL Accounts will later be used for cash journal postings.

# II. Defining Correspondence Types (C)

T Code SPRO

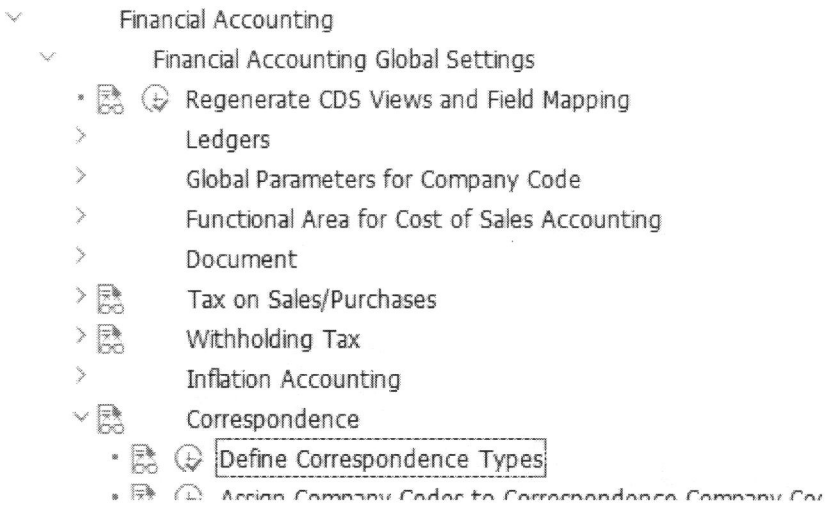

Fig 3

A correspondence type is set up for Company Code : SFE1

Enter    New Entries

Fig 4

Fill up the required fields as shown above and press ⊟ to save the settings. The system will confirm creation of new correspondance type by this message display:

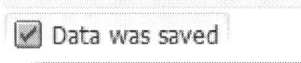

☑ Data was saved

Fig 5

## III. ASSIGNING PROGRAMS FOR CORRESPONDENCE TYPES (C)

T Code SPRO

In this activity, we define the print program and the selection variant corresponding to each correspondence type. The selection variant is used when printing the requested correspondence.

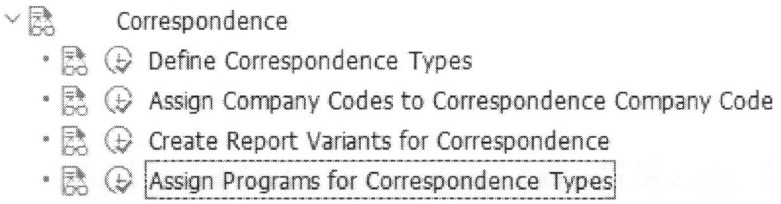

Correspondence
- Define Correspondence Types
- Assign Company Codes to Correspondence Company Code
- Create Report Variants for Correspondence
- Assign Programs for Correspondence Types

Fig 6

In the Change View "Allocate program for automatic correspondence": overview screen, make the new entries :

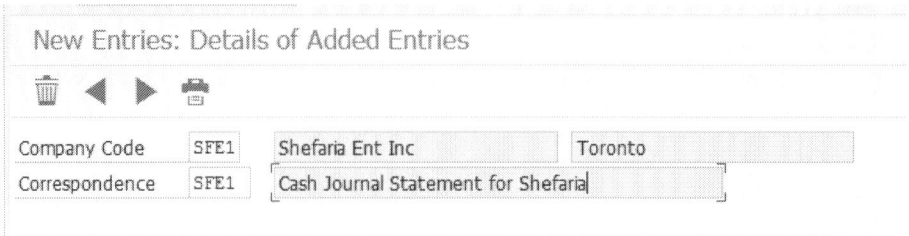

New Entries: Details of Added Entries

🗑 ◀ ▶ 🖨

| Company Code | SFE1 | Shefaria Ent Inc | Toronto |
| Correspondence | SFE1 | Cash Journal Statement for Shefaria | |

Fig 7

424

Enter the following details :

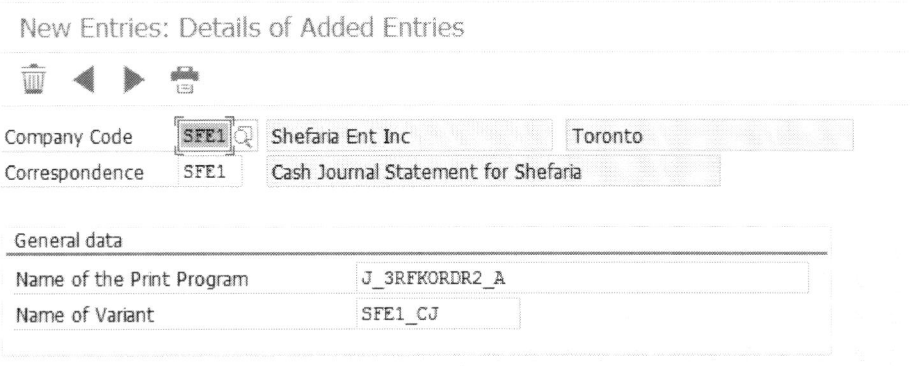
New Entries: Details of Added Entries
Company Code
SFE1
Shefaria Ent Inc
Toronto
Correspondence
SFE1
Cash Journal Statement for Shefaria
General data
Name of the Print Program
J_3RFKORDR2_A
Name of Variant
SFE1_CJ

Fig 8

Save the entries.

# IV. Setting up Limits

HANA CHANGE: In HANA, an minor step/configuration change has been intorduced. Now you can have limits -re-set/defined for the cash journal balances. For our journal, we will set a limit of CAD 10,000. It is one limit, per company code or per transaction. This limit is set per company code, not per the cash journal itself:

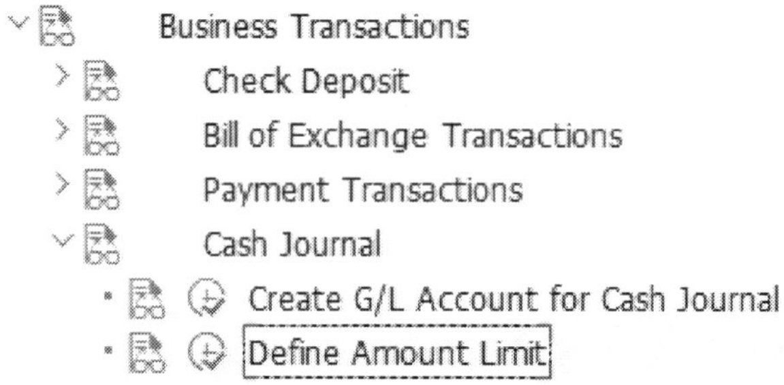

Business Transactions
  > Check Deposit
  > Bill of Exchange Transactions
  > Payment Transactions
  ✓ Cash Journal
      • ⊕ Create G/L Account for Cash Journal
      • ⊕ Define Amount Limit

Fig 9

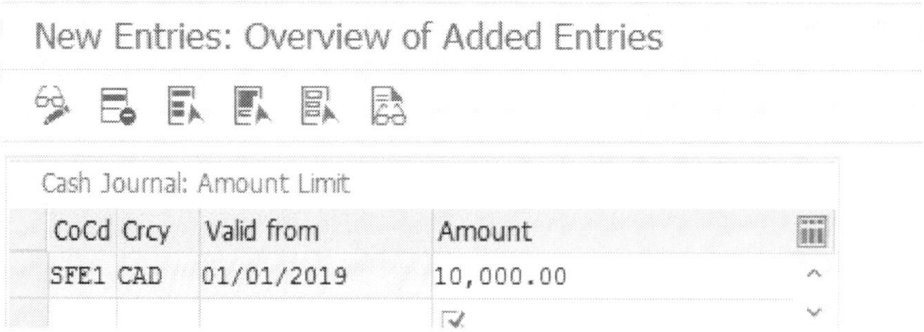

## New Entries: Overview of Added Entries

Cash Journal: Amount Limit

| CoCd | Crcy | Valid from | Amount |  |
|------|------|------------|--------|--|
| SFE1 | CAD | 01/01/2019 | 10,000.00 | |

Fig 10

# V.    DEFINING NUMBER RANGE INTERVALS FOR CASH JOURNAL DOCUMENTS (C)

T Code FBCJC1

A number range is set up for company code SFE1. Access the activity using the T Code or the following navigation path in SPRO:

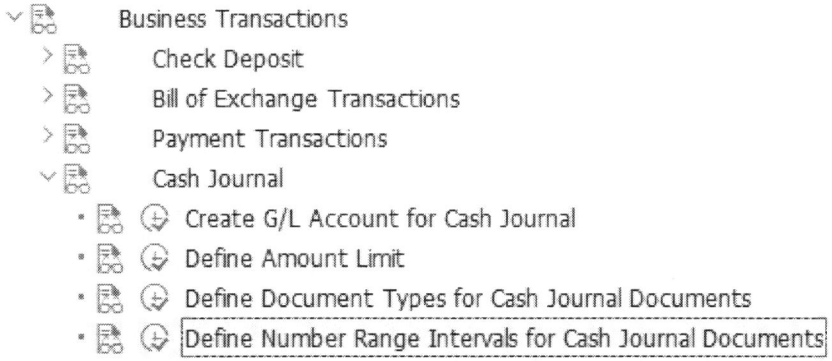

Fig 11

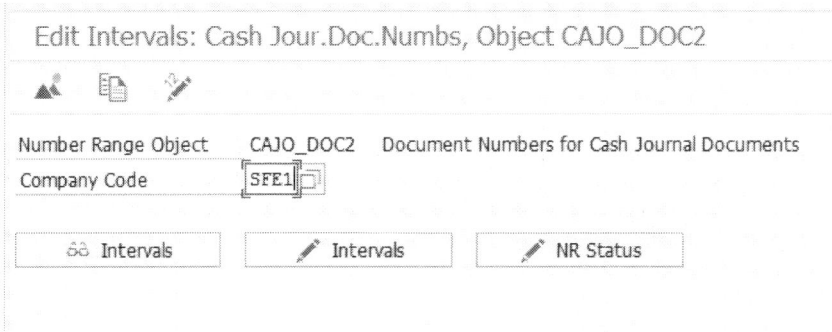

Fig 12

Click [✏ Intervals] and make the following entries :

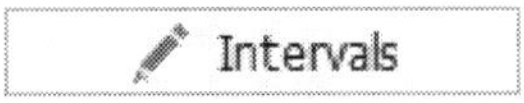

| N.. | From No. | To Number | NR Status | Ext |
|-----|----------|-----------|-----------|-----|
| 01 | 0001000000 | 0001999999 | 0 | ☐ |

Fig 13

Save your entries.

# VI. DEFINE DOCUMENT TYPE FOR CASH JOURNAL DOCUMENTS (C)

T Code OBA7

Or follow the path below in SPRO:

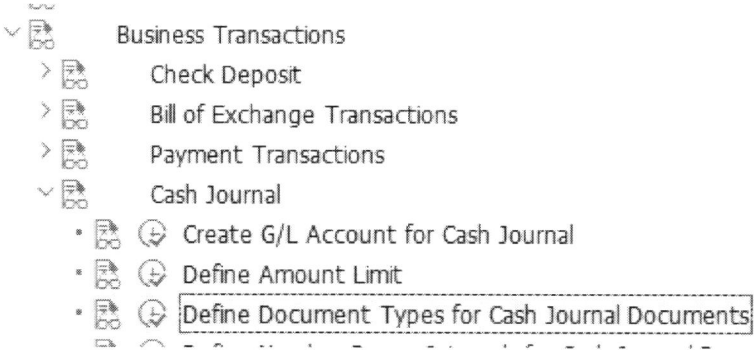

> Business Transactions
> > Check Deposit
> > Bill of Exchange Transactions
> > Payment Transactions
> > Cash Journal
> > · Create G/L Account for Cash Journal
> > · Define Amount Limit
> > · Define Document Types for Cash Journal Documents

Fig 14

We will use the standard document type SK for our purpose:

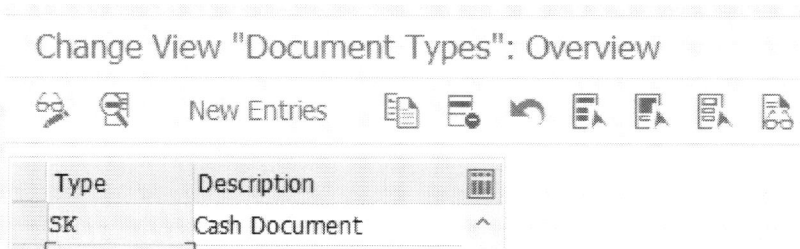

Change View "Document Types": Overview

New Entries

| Type | Description | |
|------|-------------|---|
| SK | Cash Document | ^ |

Fig 15

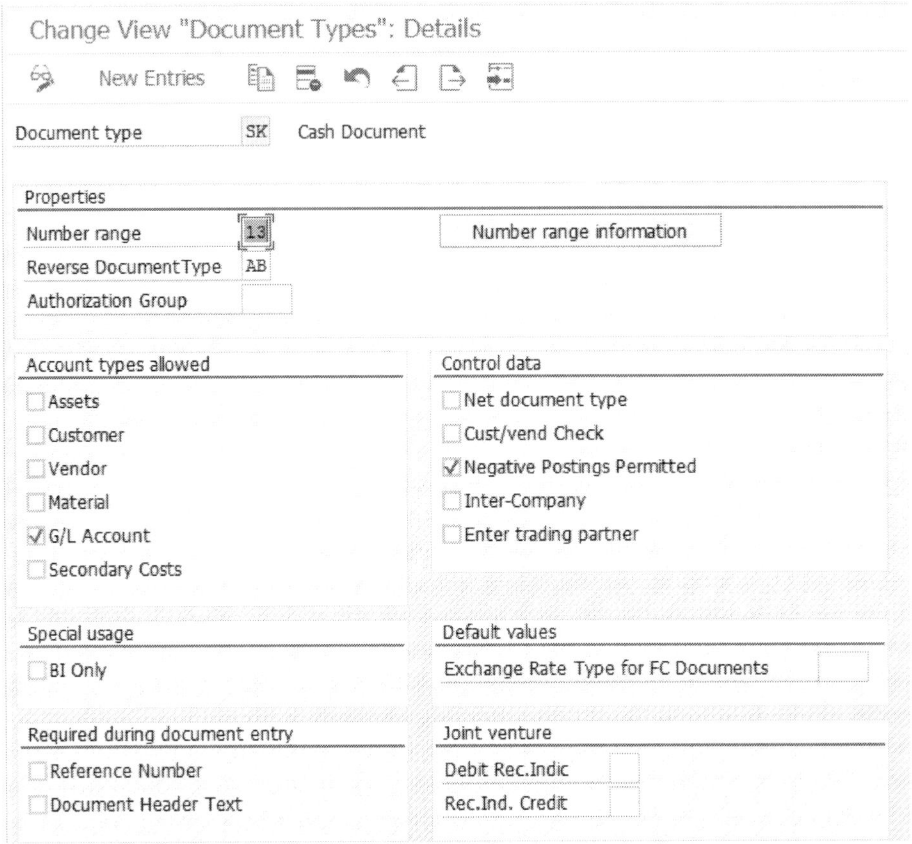

## Change View "Document Types": Details

🔧 New Entries 📋 🗐 🔄 ⬁ ⬀ ⬂

Document type     SK    Cash Document

### Properties

Number range       13            [ Number range information ]
Reverse DocumentType   AB
Authorization Group

### Account types allowed

☐ Assets
☐ Customer
☐ Vendor
☐ Material
☑ G/L Account
☐ Secondary Costs

### Control data

☐ Net document type
☐ Cust/vend Check
☑ Negative Postings Permitted
☐ Inter-Company
☐ Enter trading partner

### Special usage

☐ BI Only

### Default values

Exchange Rate Type for FC Documents

### Required during document entry

☐ Reference Number
☐ Document Header Text

### Joint venture

Debit Rec.Indic
Rec.Ind. Credit

Fig 16

430

# VII. Setting up Cash Journal (C)

T Code FBCJC0

Finally, we need to set up Cash Journal itself. In this set up we will assign GL Account, Document type to the Cash Journal for GL Postings.

In SPRO follow the path below:

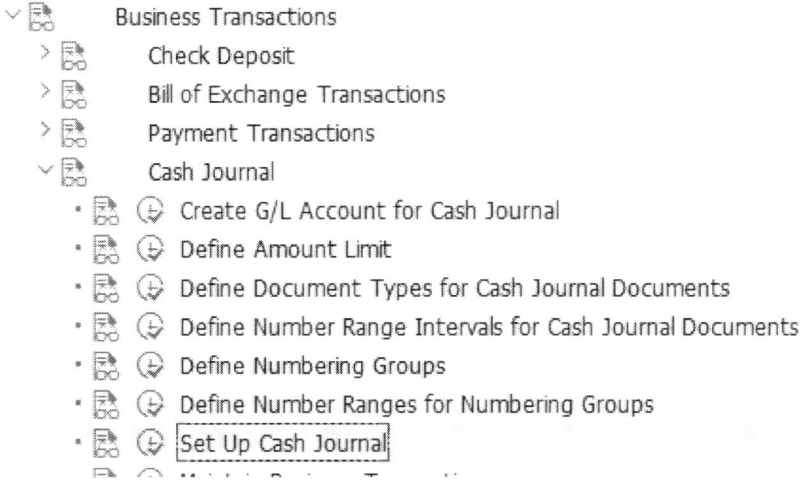

Fig 17

Make the following entries:

Maintain View for Cash Journals

| CoCd | CJ ... | G/L Account | Crcy | Cash Jnl... | D.. | D.. | D.. | D.. | D.. | D.. | Cash ... | Cash ... | Num... | Check ... | Cash journal name | AGrp | Subst. | Si |
|---|---|---|---|---|---|---|---|---|---|---|---|---|---|---|---|---|---|---|
| SFE1 | CJ01 | 100007 | CAD | ☐ | AB | AB | KZ | KZ | DZ | DZ | | | | No | CASH STATEMENT OF SFE1 | | ☐ | |
| | | | | ☐ | | | | | | | | | | No | | | ☐ | |

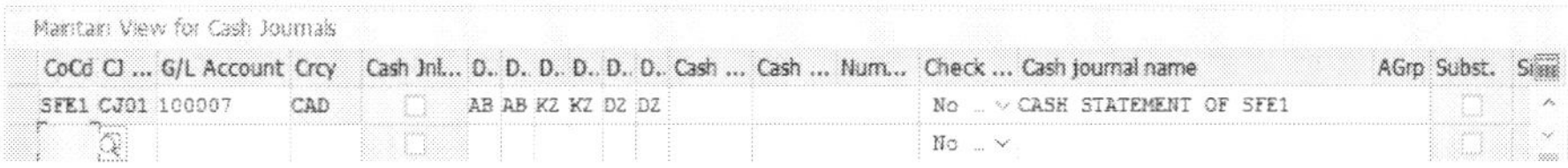

Fig 18

Save the Entries.

# VII. CREATING, CHANGING AND DELETING BUSINESS TRANSACTIONS (C)

T Code FBCJC2

In this activity, we create, change and delete business transactions for the cash journal. In SPRO:

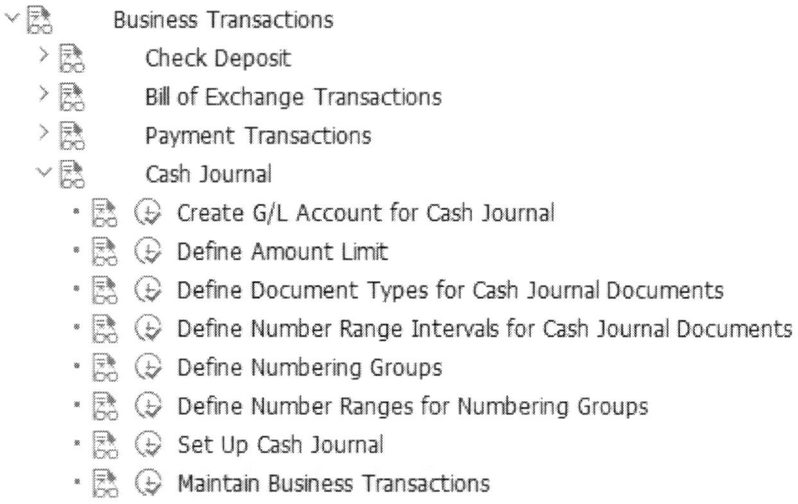

- Business Transactions
  - Check Deposit
  - Bill of Exchange Transactions
  - Payment Transactions
  - Cash Journal
    - Create G/L Account for Cash Journal
    - Define Amount Limit
    - Define Document Types for Cash Journal Documents
    - Define Number Range Intervals for Cash Journal Documents
    - Define Numbering Groups
    - Define Number Ranges for Numbering Groups
    - Set Up Cash Journal
    - Maintain Business Transactions

Fig 19

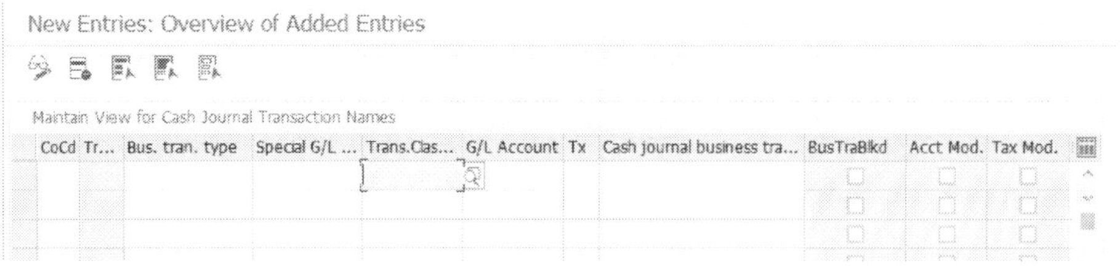

New Entries: Overview of Added Entries

Maintain View for Cash Journal Transaction Names

| CoCd Tr... | Bus. tran. type | Special G/L ... | Trans.Clas... | G/L Account | Tx | Cash journal business tra... | BusTraBlkd | Acct Mod. | Tax Mod. | |
|---|---|---|---|---|---|---|---|---|---|---|
| | | | | | | | | | | |

Fig 20

**HANA CHANGE:** SAP has introduced the ability to separate out the special G/L transaction from the normal ones in the transactions relating to the cash journal. The fields Special G/L and Trans Classification are both new.

Make the following entries, for the purpose of this journal, we will not consider any special G/L:

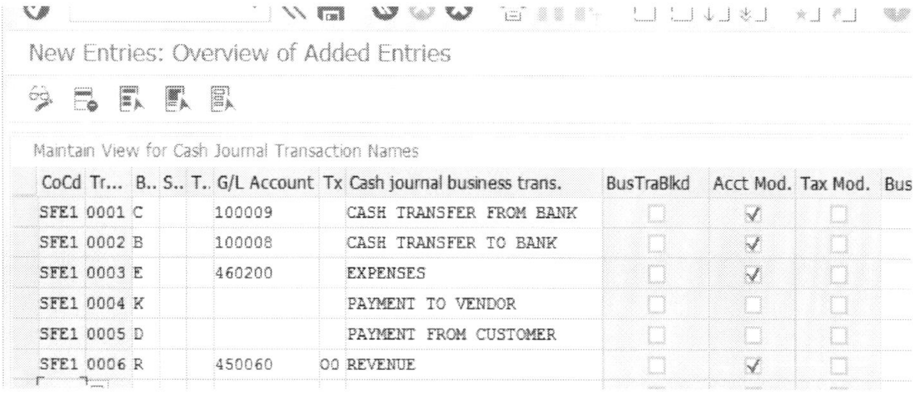

New Entries: Overview of Added Entries

Maintain View for Cash Journal Transaction Names

| CoCd | Tr... | B.. | S.. | T.. | G/L Account | Tx | Cash journal business trans. | BusTraBlkd | Acct Mod. | Tax Mod. | Bus |
|------|-------|-----|-----|-----|-------------|----|-----|------------|-----------|----------|-----|
| SFE1 | 0001 | C | | | 100009 | | CASH TRANSFER FROM BANK | ☐ | ☑ | ☐ | |
| SFE1 | 0002 | B | | | 100008 | | CASH TRANSFER TO BANK | ☐ | ☑ | ☐ | |
| SFE1 | 0003 | E | | | 460200 | | EXPENSES | ☐ | ☑ | ☐ | |
| SFE1 | 0004 | K | | | | | PAYMENT TO VENDOR | ☐ | ☐ | ☐ | |
| SFE1 | 0005 | D | | | | | PAYMENT FROM CUSTOMER | ☐ | ☐ | ☐ | |
| SFE1 | 0006 | R | | | 450060 | OO | REVENUE | ☐ | ☑ | ☐ | |

Fig 21

# VIII. SETTING UP PRINT PARAMETERS FOR CASH JOURNAL (C)

T Code FBCJC3

To print the cash journal and the cash journal receipts, we have to set up the corresponding print program parameters per company code. SAP standard is used. In SPRO:

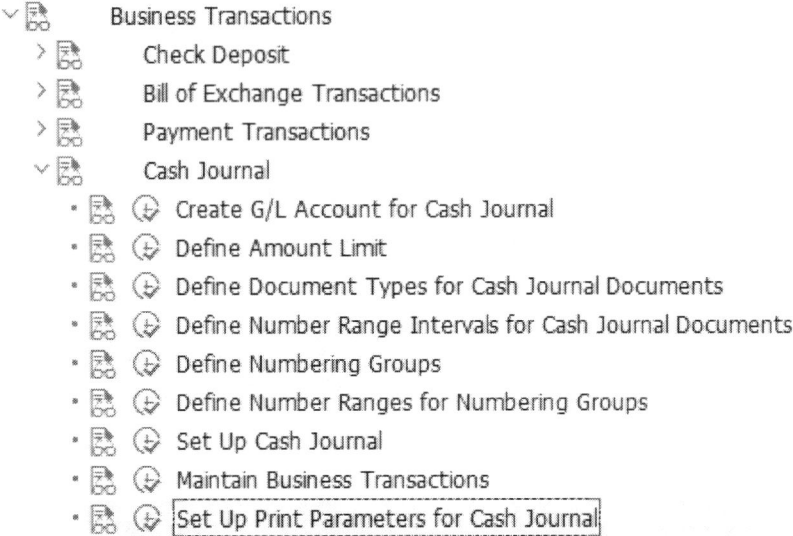

Business Transactions
> Check Deposit
> Bill of Exchange Transactions
> Payment Transactions
> Cash Journal
  · Create G/L Account for Cash Journal
  · Define Amount Limit
  · Define Document Types for Cash Journal Documents
  · Define Number Range Intervals for Cash Journal Documents
  · Define Numbering Groups
  · Define Number Ranges for Numbering Groups
  · Set Up Cash Journal
  · Maintain Business Transactions
  · Set Up Print Parameters for Cash Journal

Fig 22

Choose New Entries option and make the following entries :

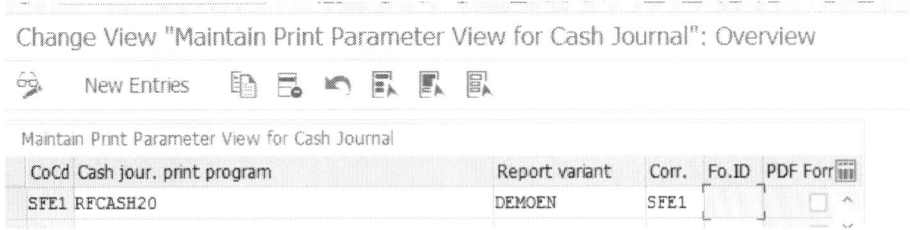

Change View "Maintain Print Parameter View for Cash Journal": Overview

New Entries

Maintain Print Parameter View for Cash Journal

| CoCd | Cash jour. print program | Report variant | Corr. | Fo.ID | PDF Forr |
|------|--------------------------|----------------|-------|-------|----------|
| SFE1 | RFCASH20 | DEMOEN | SFE1 | | |

Fig 23

Save the entries.

434

# IX.     DEFINING SENDER DETAILS FOR CORRESPONDENCE FORM(C)

T Code SPRO

In this activity, you define which texts are to be used in the letter window and the signature line for each company code. This applies to the following:

- Letter header
- Letter footer
- Sender address

Access the activity using one of the following navigation option in SPRO:

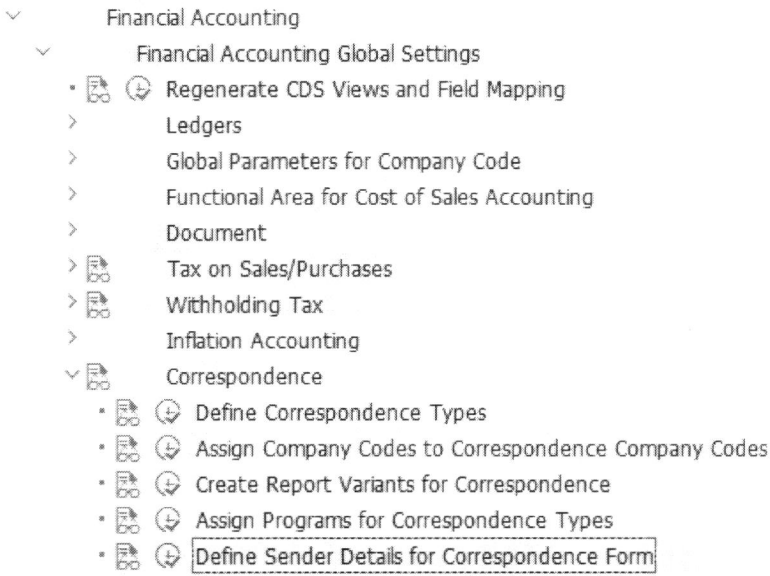

```
⌄      Financial Accounting
  ⌄        Financial Accounting Global Settings
    ·  ▣ ⊕  Regenerate CDS Views and Field Mapping
    >         Ledgers
    >         Global Parameters for Company Code
    >         Functional Area for Cost of Sales Accounting
    >         Document
    > ▣       Tax on Sales/Purchases
    > ▣       Withholding Tax
    >         Inflation Accounting
    ⌄ ▣       Correspondence
      · ▣ ⊕  Define Correspondence Types
      · ▣ ⊕  Assign Company Codes to Correspondence Company Codes
      · ▣ ⊕  Create Report Variants for Correspondence
      · ▣ ⊕  Assign Programs for Correspondence Types
      · ▣ ⊕  Define Sender Details for Correspondence Form
```

Fig 24

Make the following entries and save:

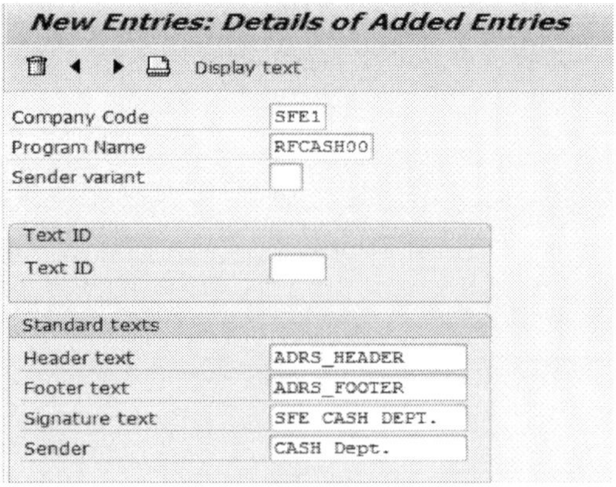


Fig 25

# IV. Cash Journal – User Manual (U)

T Code FBCJ

A Cash Journal can be created to represent a physical "Petty Cash Box" and then, by entering and posting each Cash Payment or Cash Receipt, SAP will automatically update the Cash Balance thereby allowing an easy reconciliation of each Petty Cash box.

Each Cash Journal is linked to a GL Account via Configuration. This GL Account should be set to "Auto Postings only" so that postings can only be made using the Cash Journal and in this way the balance on the GL Account always agrees with the Cash Journal balance. Postings are made according to pre-defined Business Transactions.

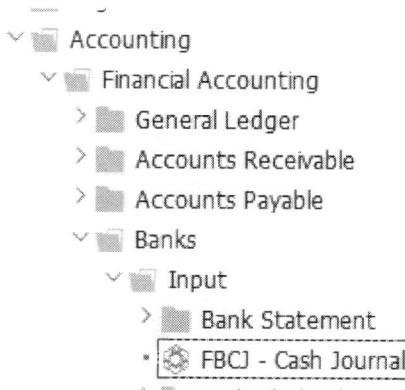

Fig 26

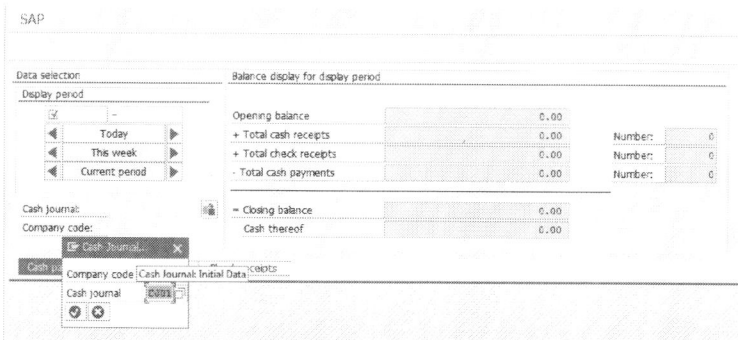

Fig 27

Click ![icon] to update Company Code : SFE1
        Cash Journal     : CJ01

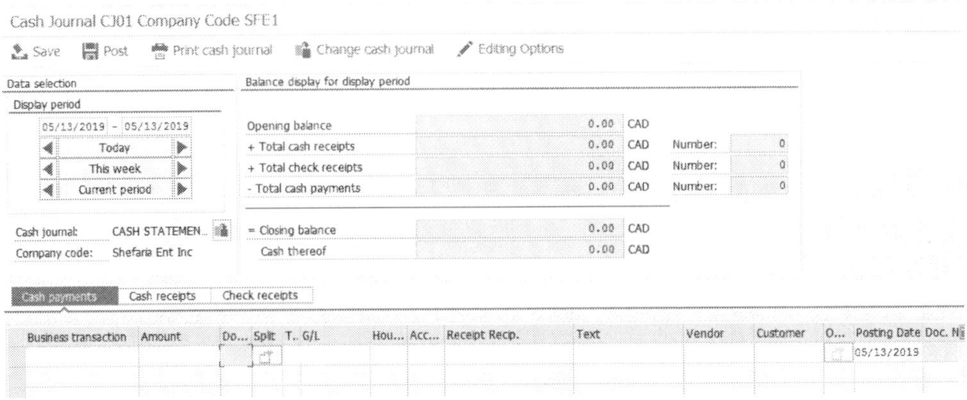

Cash Journal CJ01 Company Code SFE1

Save    Post    Print cash journal    Change cash journal    Editing Options

| Data selection | Balance display for display period | | | | |
|---|---|---|---|---|---|
| Display period | | | | | |
| 05/13/2019 - 05/13/2019 | Opening balance | 0.00 | CAD | | |
| ◄ Today ► | + Total cash receipts | 0.00 | CAD | Number: | 0 |
| ◄ This week ► | + Total check receipts | 0.00 | CAD | Number: | 0 |
| ◄ Current period ► | - Total cash payments | 0.00 | CAD | Number: | 0 |
| Cash journal: CASH STATEMEN_ | = Closing balance | 0.00 | CAD | | |
| Company code: Shefara Ent Inc | Cash thereof | 0.00 | CAD | | |

Cash payments    Cash receipts    Check receipts

| Business transaction | Amount | Do... | Split | T... | G/L | Hou... | Acc... | Receipt Recip. | Text | Vendor | Customer | O... | Posting Date | Doc. N |
|---|---|---|---|---|---|---|---|---|---|---|---|---|---|---|
| | | | | | | | | | | | | | 05/13/2019 | |

Fig 28

Enter the Period for which you are going to run the cash journal

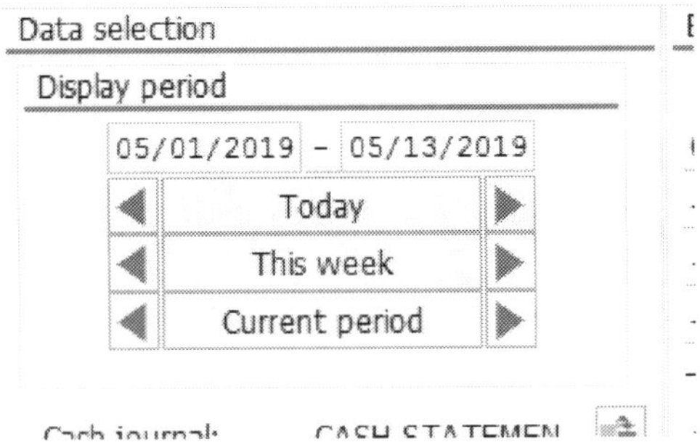

Data selection

Display period

| 05/01/2019 | – | 05/13/2019 |
|---|---|---|
| ◄ Today ► | | |
| ◄ This week ► | | |
| ◄ Current period ► | | |

Cash journal:     CASH STATEMEN

Fig 29

Based on the Period Opening and Closing Balance will be updated.

If we wan to book a customer payment received in Petty cash. Then enter we the following :

Under ![Cash receipts] Select Business Transaction via F4 function:

438

Busines Transaction name

Amount :

Text :     Description of Payment

Customer #:

Posting Date :

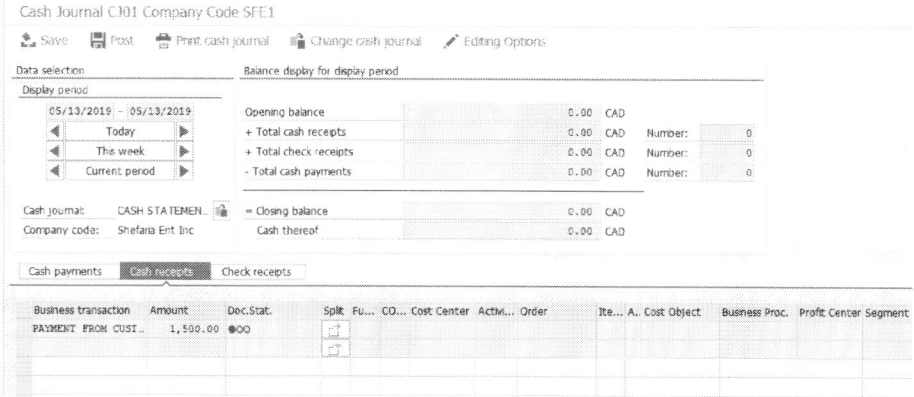

Fig 30

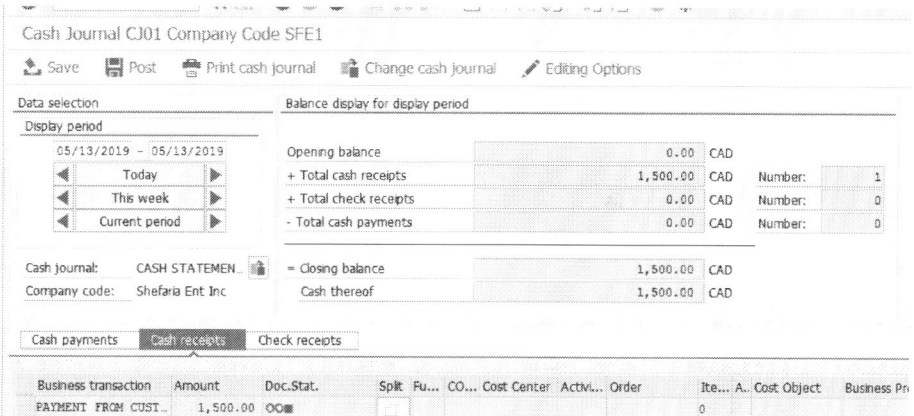

Fig 31

Since we had defined the GL 100007 forpetty cash transactions, when we look up it's balance in FBL3N we find it has gfone up by this amount:

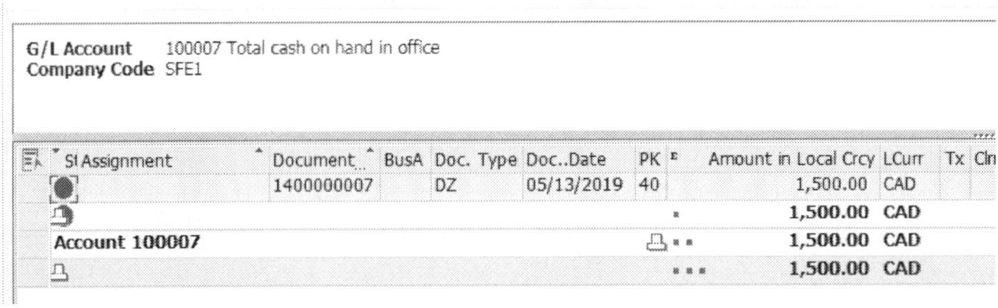
G/L Account 100007 Total cash on hand in office
Company Code SFE1
St Assignment
Document
BusA
Doc. Type
Doc..Date
PK
Amount in Local Crcy
LCurr
Tx
Clr
1400000007
DZ
05/13/2019
40
1,500.00
CAD
1,500.00 CAD
Account 100007
1,500.00 CAD
1,500.00 CAD

Fig 32

Similary for making payment to a vendor choose the following under 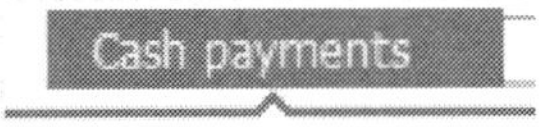
Cash payments
:

Business Transaction : Payment to Vendor and the journal shows thee current balance of 1,500 we got from the customer:

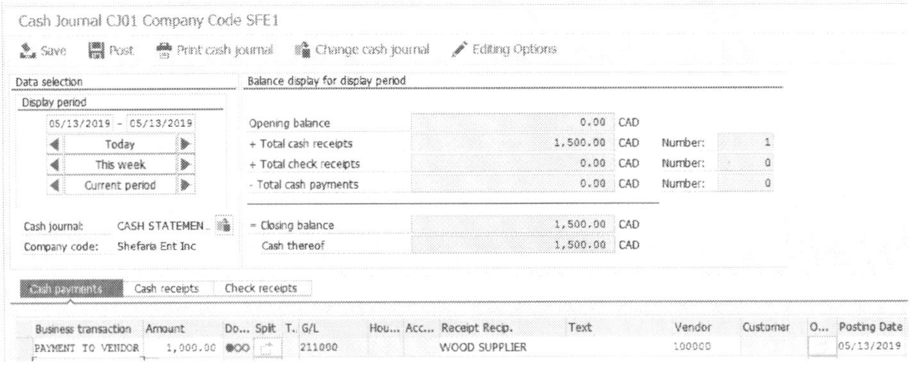
Cash Journal CJ01 Company Code SFE1
Save
Post
Print cash journal
Change cash journal
Editing Options
Data selection
Display period
05/13/2019 - 05/13/2019
Today
This week
Current period
Cash journal: CASH STATEMEN...
Company code: Shefaria Ent Inc
Balance display for display period
Opening balance 0.00 CAD
+ Total cash receipts 1,500.00 CAD Number: 1
+ Total check receipts 0.00 CAD Number: 0
- Total cash payments 0.00 CAD Number: 0
= Closing balance 1,500.00 CAD
Cash thereof 1,500.00 CAD
Cash payments
Cash receipts
Check receipts
Business transaction
Amount
Do...
Split
T.
G/L
Hou...
Acc...
Receipt Recip.
Text
Vendor
Customer
O...
Posting Date
PAYMENT TO VENDOR
1,000.00
211000
WOOD SUPPLIER
100000
05/13/2019

Fig 33

After doing Necessary Cash Journal entries as above, select the entry and Choose Post.

Entry will turn into Green showing it is posted succesfully (Fig 28)

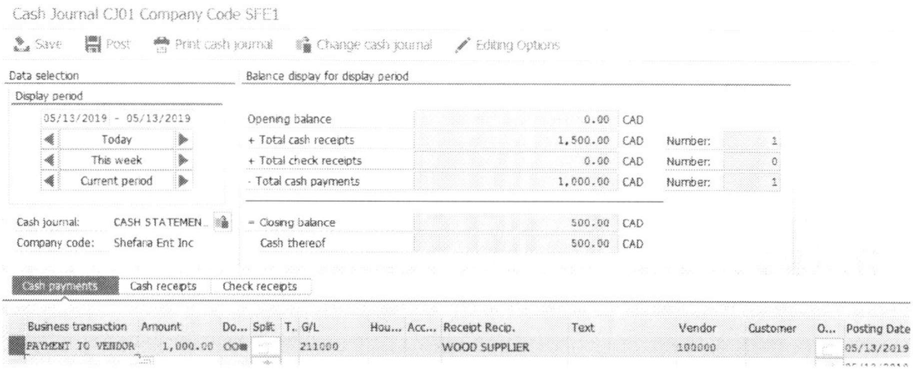

Fig 34

The G/L account total gets updated accordingly:

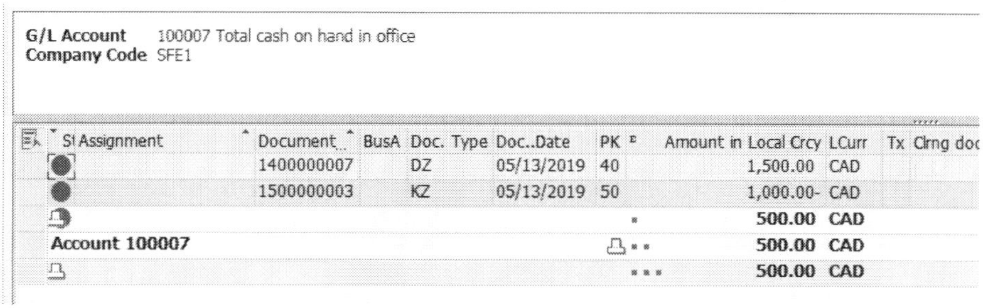

Fig 35

# CUSTOMER NOTED ITEM (U)

## I.    MEMORANDUM (NOTED) ITEM ENTRIES

T Code F-49

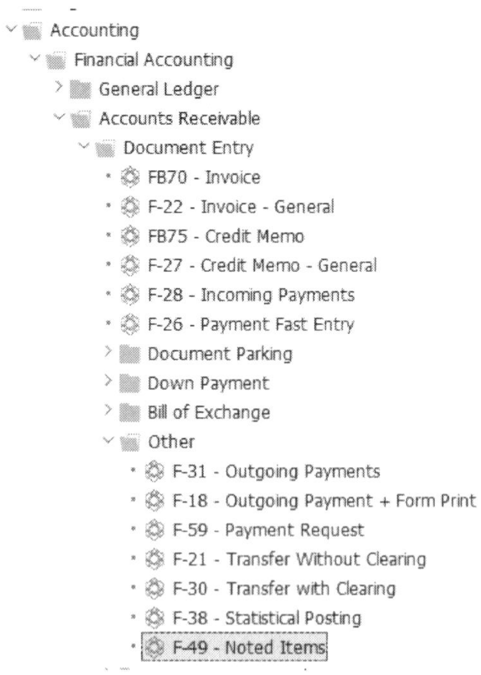

Accounting
- Financial Accounting
  - General Ledger
  - Accounts Receivable
    - Document Entry
      - FB70 - Invoice
      - F-22 - Invoice - General
      - FB75 - Credit Memo
      - F-27 - Credit Memo - General
      - F-28 - Incoming Payments
      - F-26 - Payment Fast Entry
    - Document Parking
    - Down Payment
    - Bill of Exchange
    - Other
      - F-31 - Outgoing Payments
      - F-18 - Outgoing Payment + Form Print
      - F-59 - Payment Request
      - F-21 - Transfer Without Clearing
      - F-30 - Transfer with Clearing
      - F-38 - Statistical Posting
      - F-49 - Noted Items

Fig 1

These can be used for recording Bank Guarantee or any other entries which do not need to be posted to the customer Account and the general ledger A/c. It creates a one line entry only. These entries will have no effect on the Financial Books. We use them only for the purpose of recording and after the purpose is over we can reverse the same.

Create the transaction with the posting key as 09 or 19 using either of the following Special GL Indicators:

L : Letter of Credit
G: Bank Gurantee

Customer Account Number and Amount is to be filled.
Fill in the Bank Guarantee Due Dates so that on the Maturity Date we can reverse it later on.

Scenario : Customer provides bank gurantee. Now to get the payment encashed in real it may take some time. We can record the transaction in a form of entry without impacting the book of accounts. This entry is just for information purposes only.

In the following screen fill up the required details :

Account : Customer Account No.
Reference : We can put Sales Order no or Bank Gurantee ref No
Amount : Bank Gurantee Amount
Text : Free Field for Description

## Customer Noted Item: Header Data

| | | | | | |
|---|---|---|---|---|---|
| Document Date | 05/13/2019 | Type | DA | Company Code | SFE1 |
| Posting Date | 05/15/2019 | Period | 5 | Currency/Rate | CAD |
| Document Number | | | | Translation dte | 05/15/2019 |
| Reference | | | | | |
| Doc.Header Text | | | | | |
| Trading part.BA | | | | | |

**Line Item**

| | | | | |
|---|---|---|---|---|
| Posting Key | 09 | | | |
| Special G/L Ind | G | | | |
| Account | 10001 | | Business Area | |
| Amount | 4,000.00 | | | |
| Amt.in loc.cur. | 4,000.00 | | | |
| Due | 07/13/2019 | | Dunning Key | |
| Dunning Block | | | Dunning Area | |
| Assignment | | | Specl G/L Assgt | |
| Text | Bank Guarantee from customer | | | |

Fig 2

Save:

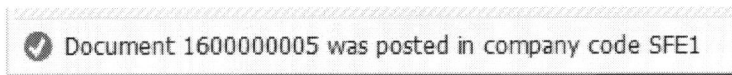

Document 1600000005 was posted in company code SFE1

Fig 3

System saved the entry as NOTED Item :

We can also view the entry in FBL5N with choosing the option 'Noted Items':

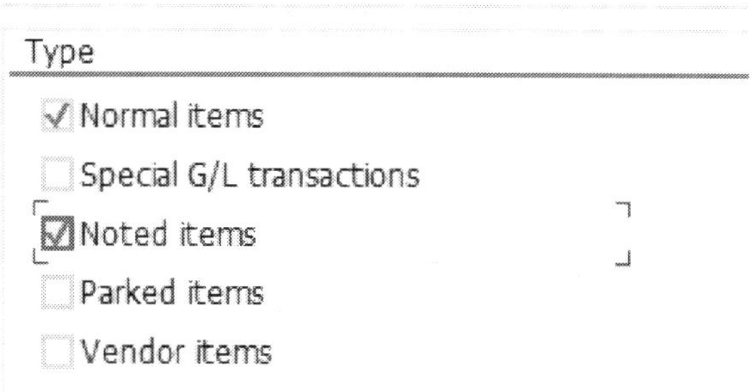

Fig 4

The Special indicator G tells us this is a Bank guarantee:

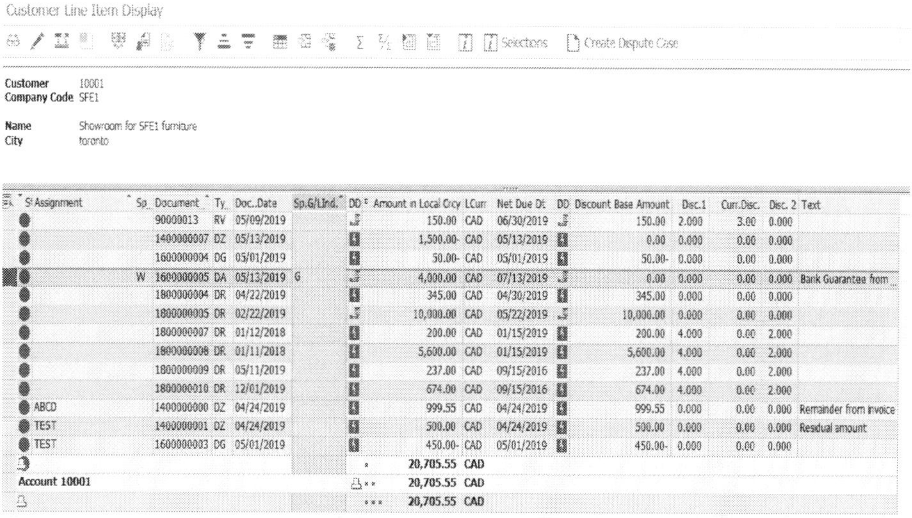

Fig 5

## II. REVERSAL OF NOTED ITEM ENTRIES (U)

T Code FB08

We generally use this option in order to cancel the initial entry/postings or those, which are found to be incorrect. That can be due to many reasons in practical scenarios. SAP provides a list of Reason codes to be selected during reversal; we can choose as applicable:

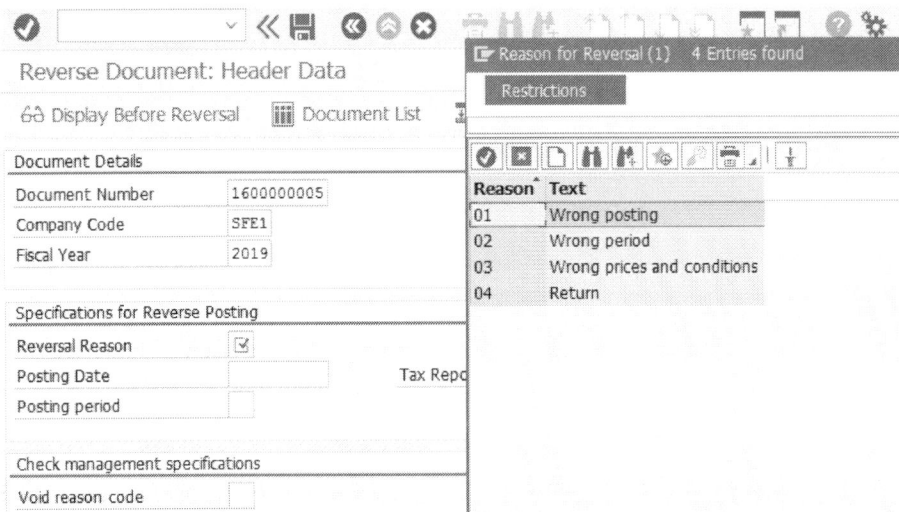

Fig 6

As we reverse the normal documents, we can, in the same way, reverse the Noted Entries also in FB08

Provide the Noted Item Document Number, Company Codes, Fiscal Year and Reversal Reason.

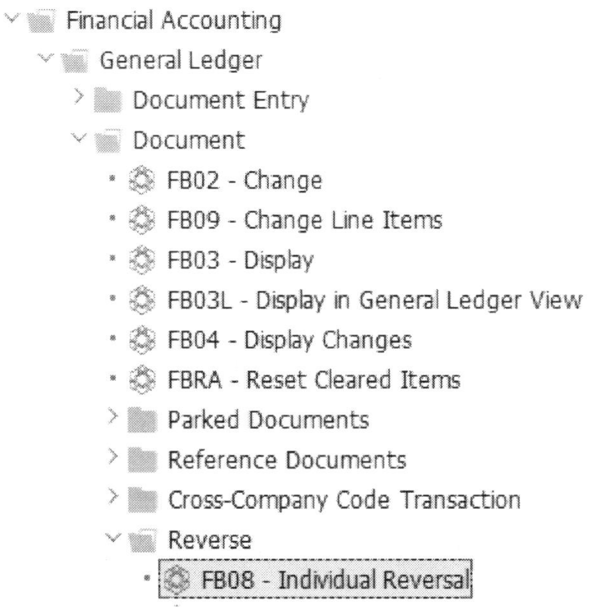

Fig 7

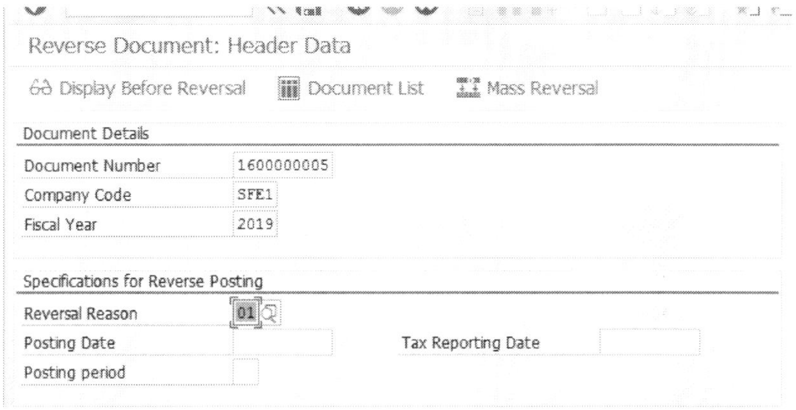

Fig 8

Select 💾 option to save/post the reversal entries. System confirms the posting displaying the following message :

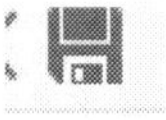

Document 100000016 was posted in company code SFE1

Fig 9

This will clear the old Noted Item entries and the Customer Account will be left with no open items relating tho that entry.

The entry will disappear from FBL5N:

| Customer | 10001 |
|---|---|
| Company Code | SFE1 |
| Name | Showroom for SFE1 furniture |
| City | toronto |

| SI Assignment | Transact. Type | Document | Ty | Doc..Date | DD | Amount in Local Crcy | LCur | Net Due Dt | DD | Discount Base Amount | Disc. 1 | Cur..Disc. | Disc. 2 | Text |
|---|---|---|---|---|---|---|---|---|---|---|---|---|---|---|
| | | 90000013 | RV | 05/09/2019 | | 150.00 | CAD | 06/30/2019 | | 150.00 | 2.000 | 3.00 | 0.000 | |
| | | 1400000007 | DZ | 05/13/2019 | | 1,500.00- | CAD | 05/13/2019 | | 0.00 | 0.000 | 0.00 | 0.000 | |
| | | 1600000004 | DG | 05/01/2019 | | 50.00- | CAD | 05/01/2019 | | 50.00- | 0.000 | 0.00 | 0.000 | |
| | | 1800000004 | DR | 04/22/2019 | | 345.00 | CAD | 04/30/2019 | | 345.00 | 0.000 | 0.00 | 0.000 | |
| | | 1800000005 | DR | 02/22/2019 | | 10,000.00 | CAD | 05/22/2019 | | 10,000.00 | 0.000 | 0.00 | 0.000 | |
| | | 1800000007 | DR | 01/12/2018 | | 200.00 | CAD | 01/15/2019 | | 200.00 | 4.000 | 0.00 | 2.000 | |
| | | 1800000008 | DR | 01/11/2018 | | 5,600.00 | CAD | 01/15/2019 | | 5,600.00 | 4.000 | 0.00 | 2.000 | |
| | | 1800000009 | DR | 05/11/2019 | | 237.00 | CAD | 09/15/2016 | | 237.00 | 4.000 | 0.00 | 2.000 | |
| | | 1800000010 | DR | 12/01/2019 | | 674.00 | CAD | 09/15/2016 | | 674.00 | 4.000 | 0.00 | 2.000 | |
| ABCD | | 1400000000 | DZ | 04/24/2019 | | 999.55 | CAD | 04/24/2019 | | 999.55 | 0.000 | 0.00 | 0.000 | Remainder from invoice |
| TEST | | 1400000001 | DZ | 04/24/2019 | | 500.00 | CAD | 04/24/2019 | | 500.00 | 0.000 | 0.00 | 0.000 | Residual amount |
| TEST | | 1600000003 | DG | 05/01/2019 | | 450.00- | CAD | 05/01/2019 | | 450.00- | 0.000 | 0.00 | 0.000 | |
| | | | | | * | 16,705.55 | CAD | | | | | | | |
| Account 10001 | | | | | ** | 16,705.55 | CAD | | | | | | | |
| | | | | | *** | 16,705.55 | CAD | | | | | | | |

Fig 10

# FOREIGN CURRENCY VALUATION (C/U)

Some companies maintain accounting reports like financial statements in a currency different from the local currency because they are subsidiaries of companies in other countries that have a different currency. Foreign currency valuation is done for preparing the financial statements at a key date. Documents posted in foreign currencies have to be converted to company code currency for preparing the company's financial statements as the company's financial statement can include only those transactions which are posted in company code's operational currency. Hence all the posings which are open items and items which are posted in GL accounts with foreign currency have to be valuated in company code currency. Valuation is performed at the exchange rate on the valuation date. In that way gain or loss is calculated and posted to exchange rate gain/loss accounts. Another scenario where this may be used is when the original invoice to the customer or from a vendor is in one currency but got paid in the other.

Scenario:

- Company Code (Local ) currency : CAD$ (Canadian Dollar)
- Foreign Currency : USD$ (US Dollar)

Pre-requisites:

- Create G/L Accounts for Foreign Currency Valuation Gain & Loss Posting Account
- Maintain Exchange Rate
- Define Valuation Methods
- Foreign Currency Valuation – Automatic Postings for curreign valuation

The report Foreign Currency Valuation provides us with the following functions:

Valuation of foreign currency balance sheet accounts
Valuation of open items in foreign currencies
Saving the exchange rate differences determined from the valuation document Performing the adjustment postings required

**HANA CHANGE:** The ECC transaction code FAGL_FC_VAL in ECC has been replaced with the T code FAGL_FCV in S/4. FAGL_FCV provides with a lot ot addional functionality in that:

1. SAP can determine the document and posting dates automatically if you want it to:

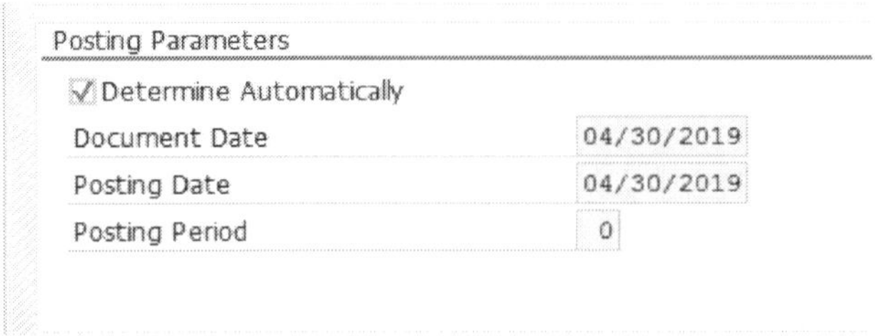

Posting Parameters
☑ Determine Automatically
| | |
|---|---|
| Document Date | 04/30/2019 |
| Posting Date | 04/30/2019 |
| Posting Period | 0 |

Fig 1

2. Now you can choose between different kinds of documents/postings and can also do a similation run apart from the test run itself (which is available in ECC also).

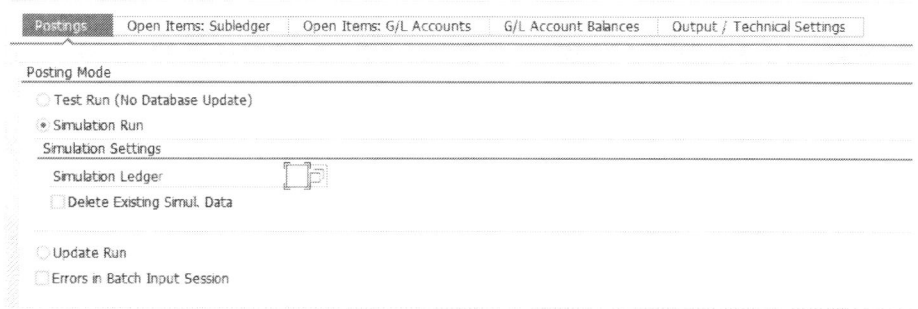

Fig 2

3. Under the Putput/Technical settings, now we have a lot more options relating to how you want the files to be summarized:

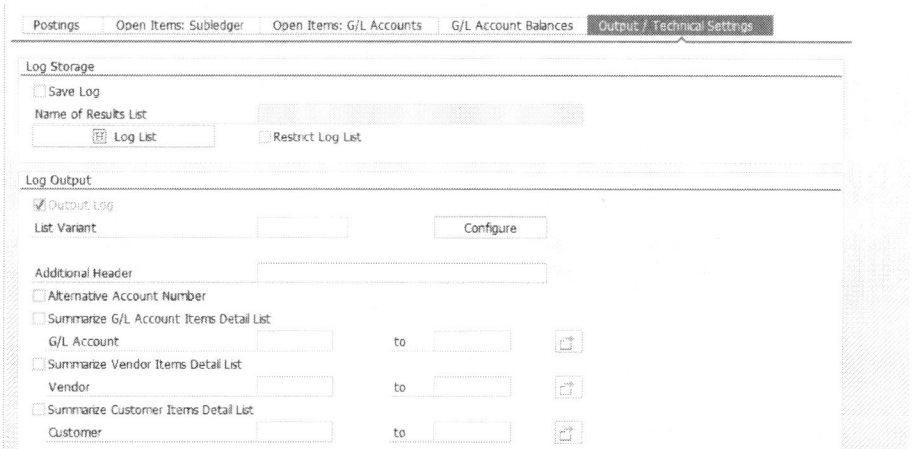

Fig 3

# I. CREATE G/L ACCOUNTS FOR FOREIGN CURRENCY VALUATION GAIN & LOSS POSTING ACCOUNT (U)

Transaction Code : FS00

We need to create this account to assign for Automatic posting during the realization of Gain or Loss derived from Foreign Currency revaluation.

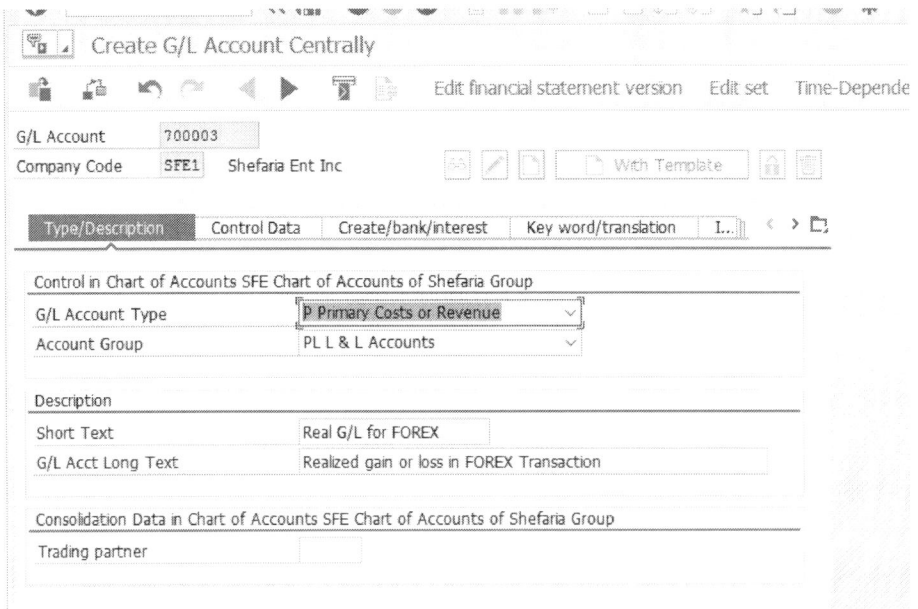

Fig 4

## II.  MAINTAIN EXCHANGE RATE (C/U)

Transaction Code : OB08

Exchange rates are required to:

- Translate foreign currency amounts when posting or clearing
- Determine the gain and loss from exchange rate differences
- Evaluate open items in foreign currency and the foreign currency balance sheet accounts

When we post and clear documents, the system uses the exchange rates defined for rate type **M** to translate the currencies. There must be an entry in the system for this rate type. The exchange rates apply for all company codes i.e. 2 different company codes can't get 2 different exchange rates applicable for the same set of 2 currencies. All the existing exchange rates appear in a table in the Change View Currency Exchange Rates : Overview screen. To change an existing value, we simply overwrite it. Often, companies will take this table out of configuration and make it master data because the rates change frequently and it is not feasible to originate the ex rate from the development system all the time.

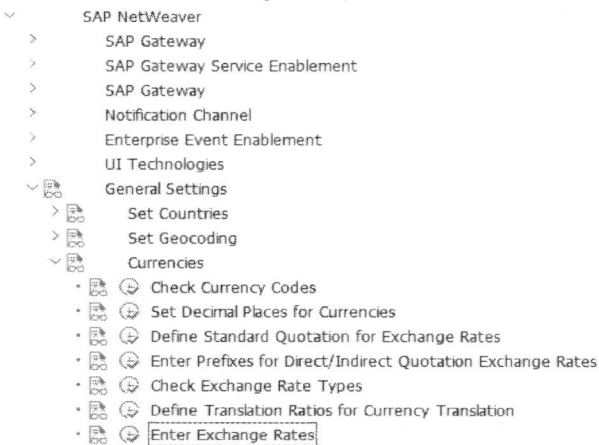

```
        SAP NetWeaver
    >       SAP Gateway
    >       SAP Gateway Service Enablement
    >       SAP Gateway
    >       Notification Channel
    >       Enterprise Event Enablement
    >       UI Technologies
    v       General Settings
      >       Set Countries
      >       Set Geocoding
      v       Currencies
          ·     Check Currency Codes
          ·     Set Decimal Places for Currencies
          ·     Define Standard Quotation for Exchange Rates
          ·     Enter Prefixes for Direct/Indirect Quotation Exchange Rates
          ·     Check Exchange Rate Types
          ·     Define Translation Ratios for Currency Translation
          ·     Enter Exchange Rates
```

Fig 5

453

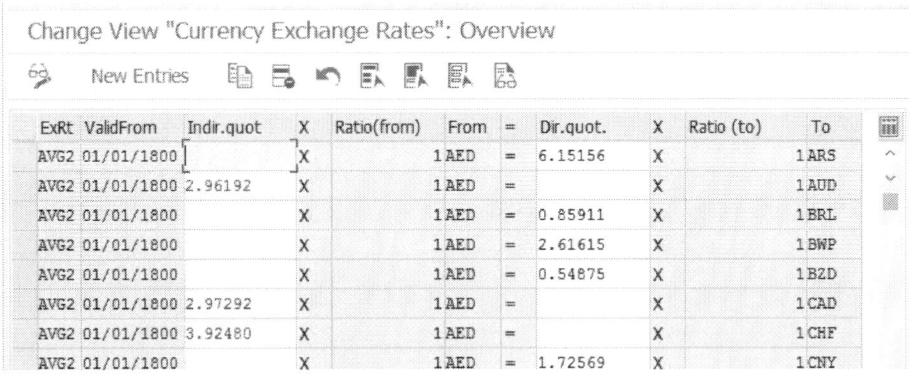

New Entries

| ExRt | ValidFrom | Indir.quot | X | Ratio(from) | From | = | Dir.quot. | X | Ratio (to) | To | |
|------|-----------|------------|---|-------------|------|---|-----------|---|------------|-----|---|
| AVG2 | 01/01/1800 | | X | | 1 AED | = | 6.15156 | X | | 1 ARS | |
| AVG2 | 01/01/1800 | 2.96192 | X | | 1 AED | = | | X | | 1 AUD | |
| AVG2 | 01/01/1800 | | X | | 1 AED | = | 0.85911 | X | | 1 BRL | |
| AVG2 | 01/01/1800 | | X | | 1 AED | = | 2.61615 | X | | 1 BWP | |
| AVG2 | 01/01/1800 | | X | | 1 AED | = | 0.54875 | X | | 1 BZD | |
| AVG2 | 01/01/1800 | 2.97292 | X | | 1 AED | = | | X | | 1 CAD | |
| AVG2 | 01/01/1800 | 3.92480 | X | | 1 AED | = | | X | | 1 CHF | |
| AVG2 | 01/01/1800 | | X | | 1 AED | = | 1.72569 | X | | 1 CNY | |

Fig 6

Click New Entries or update the existing ratio:

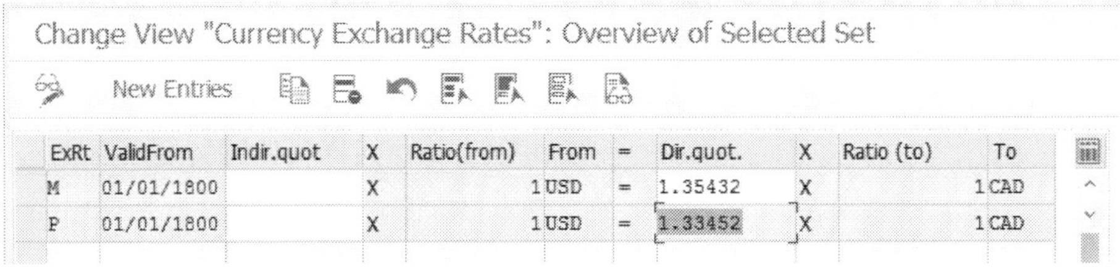

New Entries

| ExRt | ValidFrom | Indir.quot | X | Ratio(from) | From | = | Dir.quot. | X | Ratio (to) | To | |
|------|-----------|------------|---|-------------|------|---|-----------|---|------------|-----|---|
| M | 01/01/1800 | | X | | 1 USD | = | 1.35432 | X | | 1 CAD | |
| P | 01/01/1800 | | X | | 1 USD | = | 1.33452 | X | | 1 CAD | |

Fig 7

Save the entries.

454

# III. Define Valuation Methods (C)

T Code OB59

Foreign Currency valuation can be defined as a procedure for determining at a key date the value of current assets and liabilities posted in a currency different from the CC currency.

Standard SAP already provided various valuation methods. Also we can create our own.

'M' is the average rate of any foreign currency. SAP uses exchange rate type 'M' to value all foreign currency items.

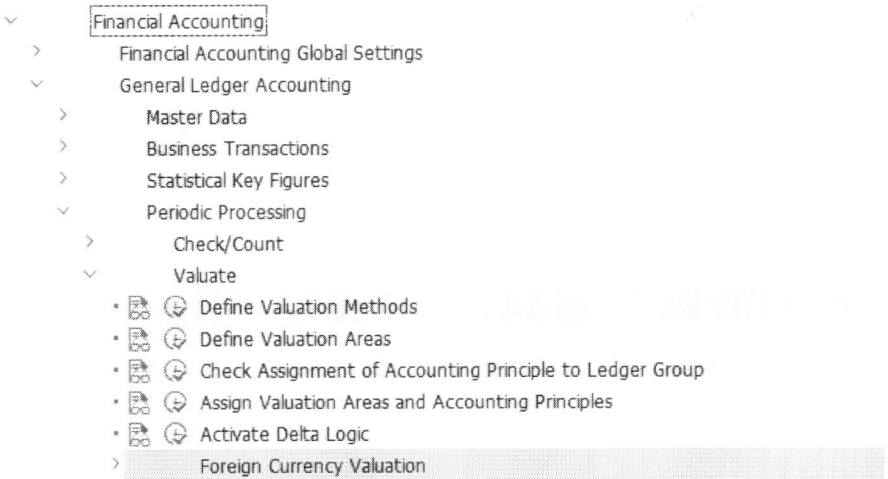

Fig 8

**HANA CHANGE:** The configuration menu for currency valuation which was a part of Business Transactions> Closing has now moved into Periodic closing in HANA. SAP has given a lot of emphasis to the closing activities in S/4 which is likely the cause of this.

Click on New Entries and update the valuation methods with a new Valutation method of your own or choose an existing one. We have set up a new one for vendors and customers:

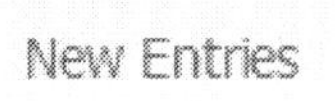

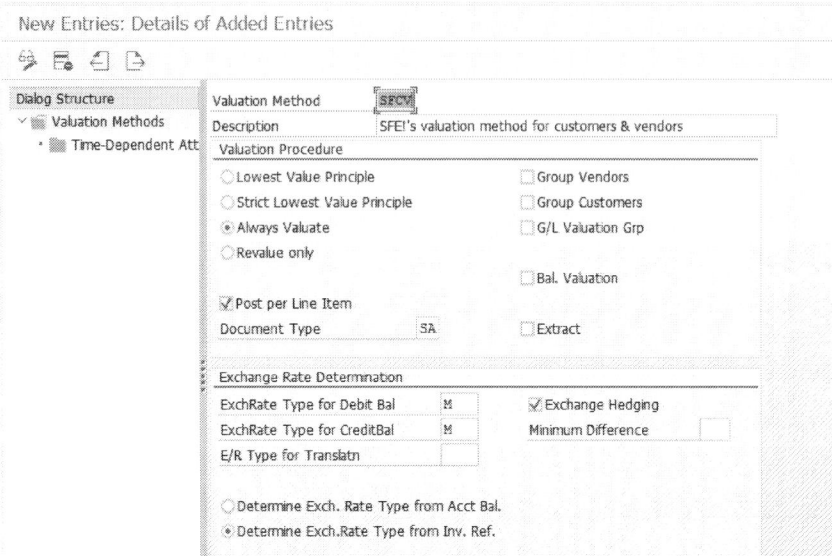

Fig 9

Various Exchange rate type is available with M being the most frequently used.

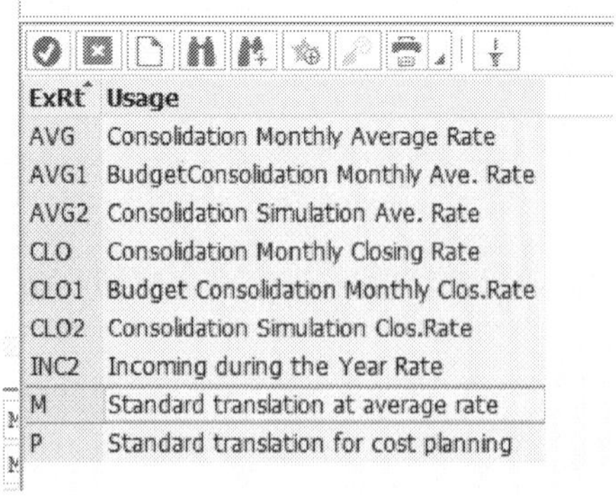

Fig 10

Click ![save icon] to  Save all entries relating to Valuation Method

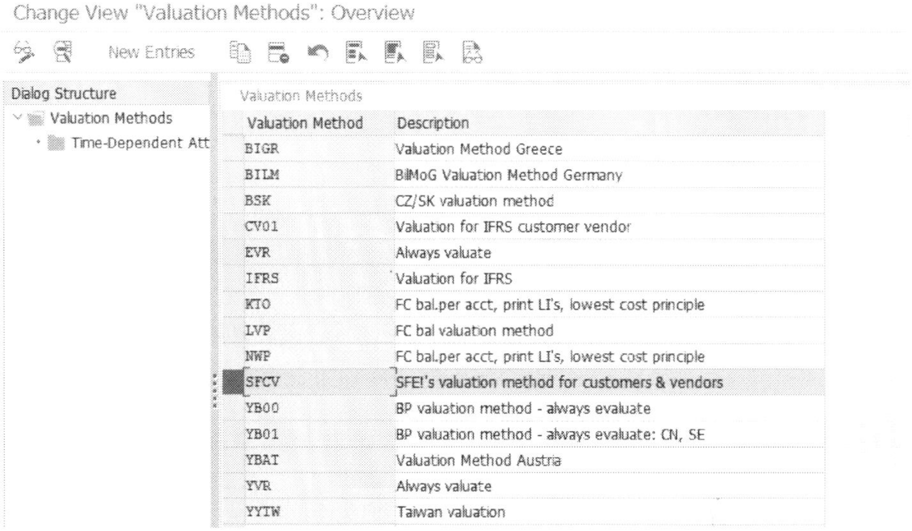

Fig 11

**HANA CHANGE:** Click on the Valuation method and then double click on the Tme dependent attributes in the left window.

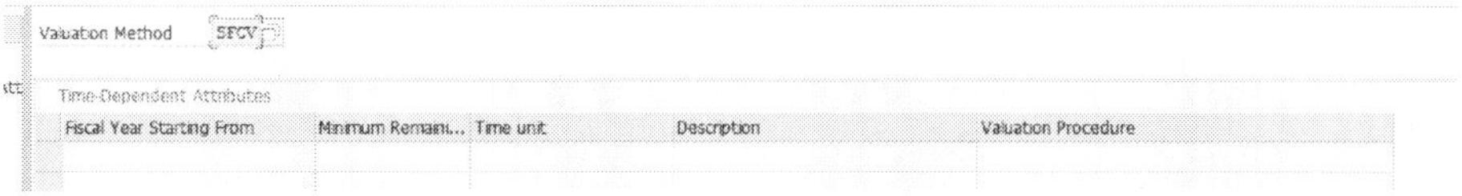

Fig 12

SAP has now provided the ability to have thje option of letting the valuation method begin from a certain data which may fall within the company code's fiscal year and net necessarily coincide with it. This enables us to use different methods for valuating the items, depending on their remaining term e.g. you can begin the valuation from the next full year if the current year is already in the middle. In th eprevious setup, it would have begun immediately.

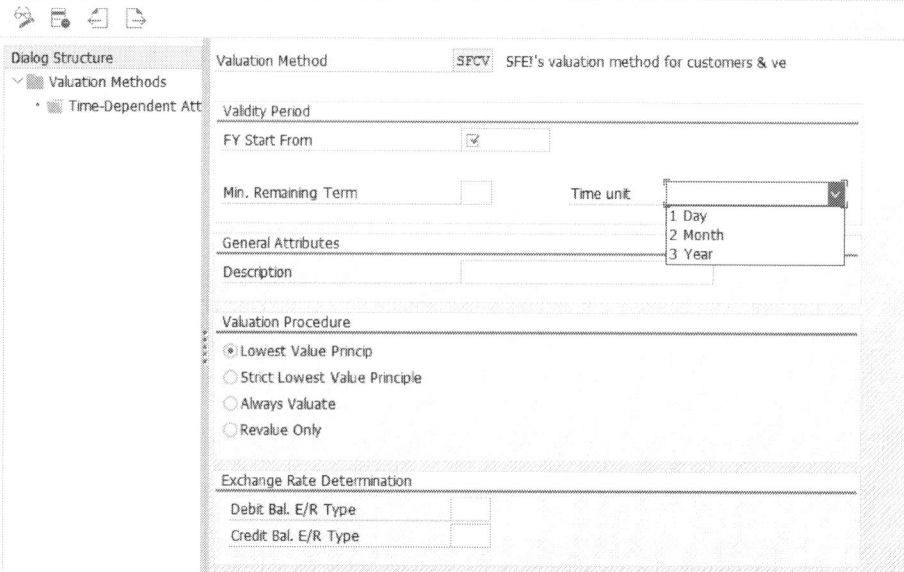

| Dialog Structure | Valuation Method | SFCV | SFE!'s valuation method for customers & ve |
| --- | --- | --- | --- |

∨ ▦ Valuation Methods

• ▦ Time-Dependent Att

Validity Period

FY Start From ☑

| Min. Remaining Term | | Time unit | |
| --- | --- | --- | --- |

1 Day
2 Month
3 Year

General Attributes

Description

Valuation Procedure

◉ Lowest Value Princip
○ Strict Lowest Value Principle
○ Always Valuate
○ Revalue Only

Exchange Rate Determination

Debit Bal. E/R Type

Credit Bal. E/R Type

Fig 13

If one were to use this functionality, next we would configure the accounting principle with the ledger group and make the valuation area get linked to the accounting principle. This functionality is also useful as apart from the standard 0L we can now use different ledger groups that may require different accounting principles with different valuation areas which is common across multi national companies typically following different acounting principles in different countries.

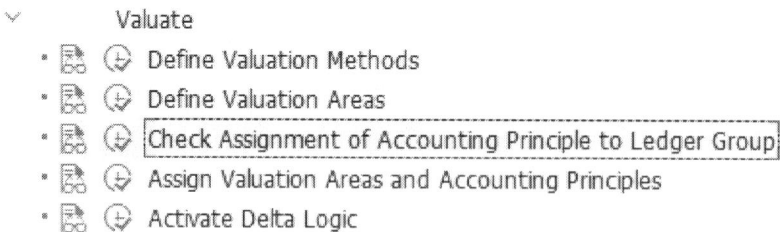

∨ Valuate
• Define Valuation Methods
• Define Valuation Areas
• Check Assignment of Accounting Principle to Ledger Group
• Assign Valuation Areas and Accounting Principles
• Activate Delta Logic

Fig 14

458

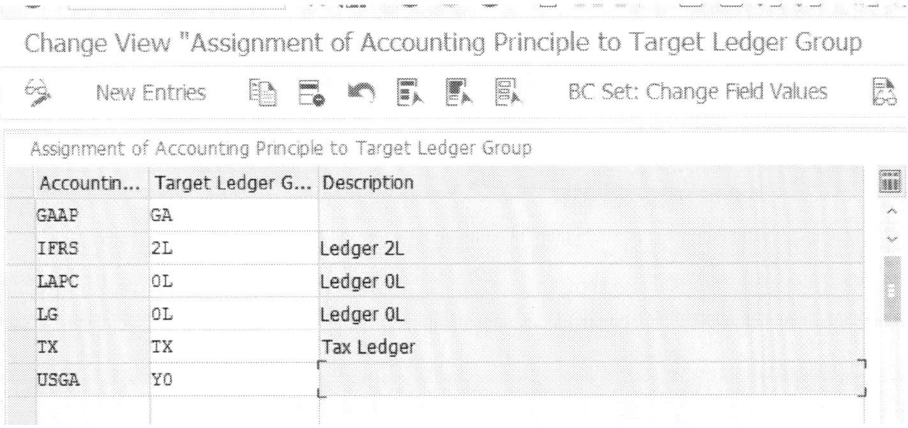

Fig 15

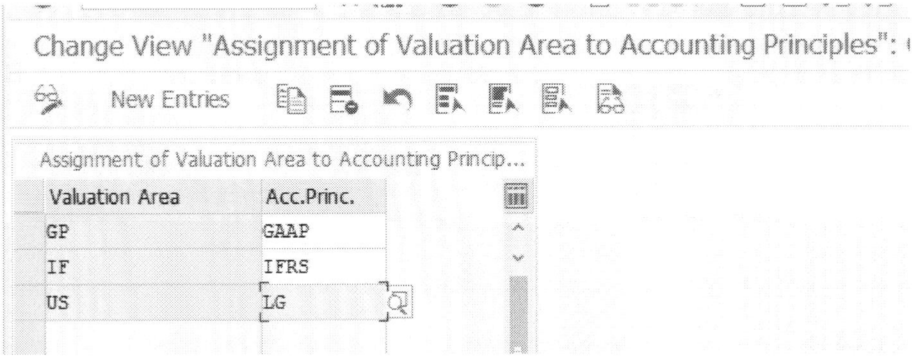

Fig 16

For our purpose we will not be using this to keep the concept of valuation simple.

# IV. Automatic Posting : Assign GL accounts for Foreign Currency valuation (C)

Follow the path below or T Code OBA1

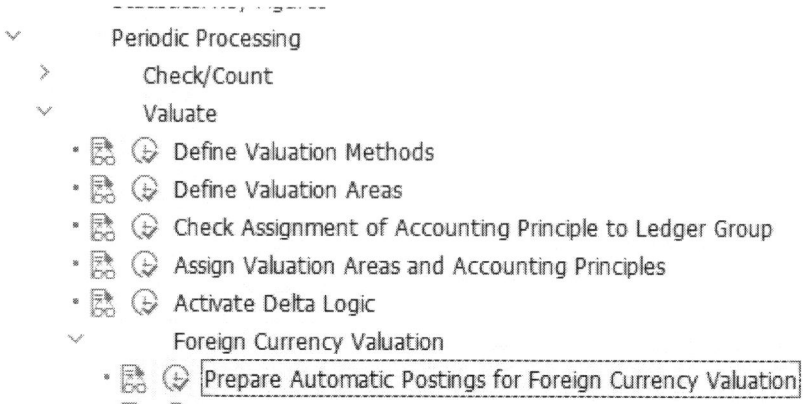

Fig 17

Here the gain and loss account assigned to accounting key KDB and KDF for automatic posting.

| Description | Transaction | Account Determ. | |
|---|---|---|---|
| Document Split for Currency Exchange | CEX | ✓ | |
| Exch. Rate Diff. using Exch. Rate Key | KDB | ✓ | |
| Exchange Rate Dif.: Open Items/GL Acct | KDF | ✓ | |
| Payment difference for altern.currency | KDW | ✓ | |
| Payment diff.for altern.curr.(offset) | KDZ | ✓ | |
| Internal currencies rounding differences | RDF | ✓ | |

Group **FWA** Exchange rate differences

Procedures

Fig 18

Enter the Chart of Accounts and update the following under Transaction Key KDB by double clicking on it.

Expense Account: We need to enter the GL Account Code for Unrealized Foreign Exchange loss. The loss on revaluation is unrealized and will be automatically reversed in the next month.

ER Gains : We need to enter the revenue GL Account for unrealized foreign exchange gain. The loss on revaluation is unrealized and wil be automaticaly reversed in the next month. This is also applicable for Exchange Rate difference in open items e.g. Accounts Receivable and Accounts Payable or we can have a separate account.

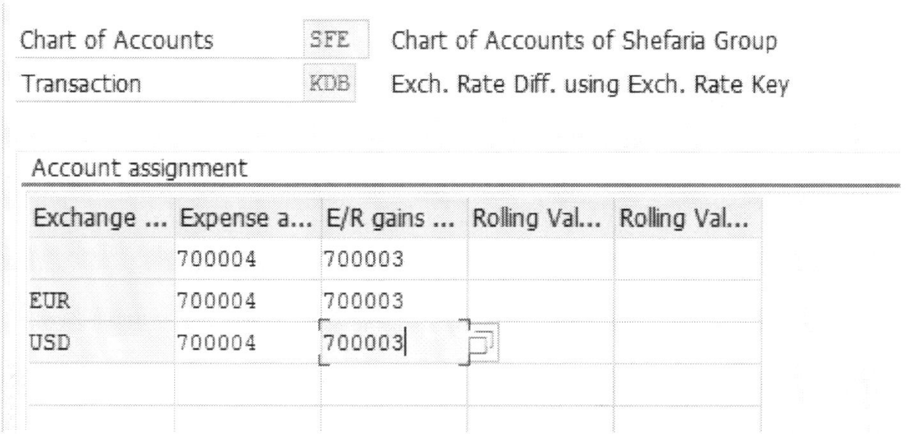

| Chart of Accounts | SFE | Chart of Accounts of Shefaria Group |
| Transaction | KDB | Exch. Rate Diff. using Exch. Rate Key |

Account assignment

| Exchange ... | Expense a... | E/R gains ... | Rolling Val... | Rolling Val... |
|---|---|---|---|---|
|  | 700004 | 700003 |  |  |
| EUR | 700004 | 700003 |  |  |
| USD | 700004 | 700003 |  |  |

Fig 19

Save all entries

Update Transaction Key KDF
Here we update GL Account Code for Accounts receivable and payable (reconcilliation account)

461

Enter 'SFE' as Chart of Accounts in the pop up and Click

New Entries

to update the following:

G/L Account : Balance Sheet Account ( AP , AR, Bank G/L)
Loss          : G/L Account for Forex Loss
Gain          :  G/L Account for Forex gain

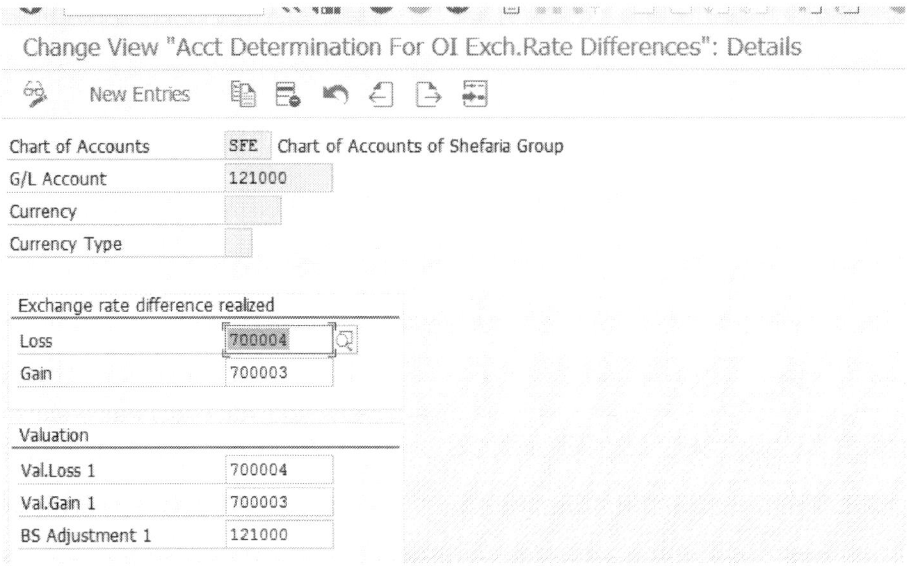

Change View "Acct Determination For OI Exch.Rate Differences": Details

New Entries

| Chart of Accounts | SFE | Chart of Accounts of Shefaria Group |
| G/L Account | 121000 | |
| Currency | | |
| Currency Type | | |

Exchange rate difference realized

| Loss | 700004 |
| Gain | 700003 |

Valuation

| Val.Loss 1 | 700004 |
| Val.Gain 1 | 700003 |
| BS Adjustment 1 | 121000 |

Fig 20

# V. REALISED GAIN LOSS (U)

T Code FB60

Now we can do a transaction to see how this will work:

- Booking Vendor Invoice in Foreign Currency . e.g. in EUR

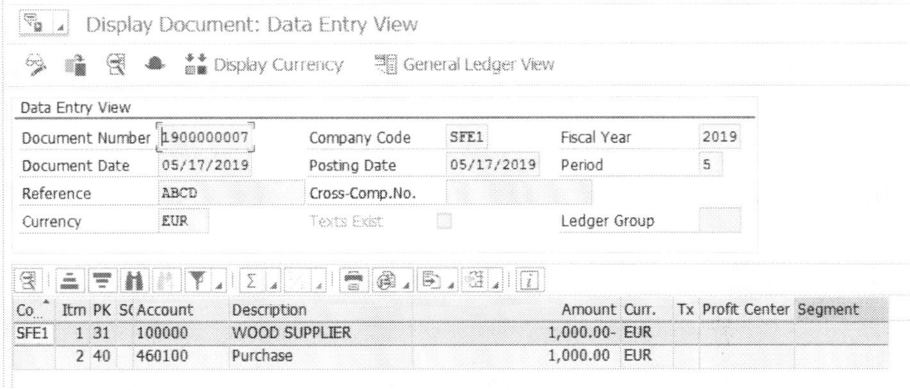

Display Document: Data Entry View
Display Currency
General Ledger View
Data Entry View
Document Number 1900000007
Company Code SFE1
Fiscal Year 2019
Document Date 05/17/2019
Posting Date 05/17/2019
Period 5
Reference ABCD
Cross-Comp.No.
Currency EUR
Texts Exist
Ledger Group
Co... Itm PK S( Account Description Amount Curr. Tx Profit Center Segment
SFE1 1 31 100000 WOOD SUPPLIER 1,000.00- EUR
2 40 460100 Purchase 1,000.00 EUR


Fig 21

When we booked the invoice, SAP looked at the exchange rate and internally booked it in CC currency based on the conversion as below:

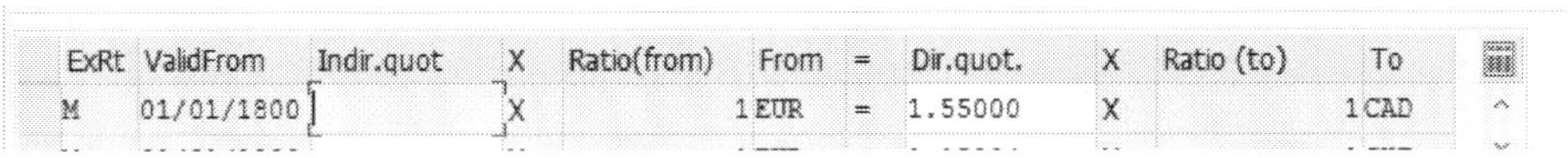

ExRt ValidFrom Indir.quot X Ratio(from) From = Dir.quot. X Ratio (to) To
M 01/01/1800 X 1 EUR = 1.55000 X 1 CAD


Fig 22

# VI. MAKING PAYMENT IN FOREIGN CURRENCY (U)

T Code F-53

At the time of making the payment for the vendor's invoice in the invoice currency, now the system will reverse calculate the exchange rate from one to the other:

Change View "Currency Exchange Rates": Overview

New Entries

| ExRt | ValidFrom | Indir.quot | X | Ratio(from) | From | = | Dir.quot. | X | Ratio (to) | To | |
|------|-----------|------------|---|-------------|------|---|-----------|---|------------|------|---|
| M | 01/01/1800 | 1.52922 | X | | 1 CAD | = | | X | | 1 EUR | |

Fig 23

Below is the similation of this payment:in the document currency:

Post Outgoing Payments Display Overview

Display Currency    Taxes    Reset

| | | | | | | |
|---|---|---|---|---|---|---|
| Document Date | 05/17/2019 | Type | KZ | Company Code | SFE1 | |
| Posting Date | 05/17/2019 | Period | 5 | Currency | EUR | 1.55000 |
| Document Number | INTERNAL | Fiscal Year | 2019 | Translation dte | 05/17/2019 | |
| Reference | 1900000007 | | | Cross-CC Number | | |
| Doc.Header Text | | | | Trading part.BA | | |

Items in document currency

| PK | BusA | Acct | | EUR | Amount | Tax amnt |
|----|------|------|---|-----|--------|----------|
| 001 | 50 | 0000107000 Bank A/c | | | 1,000.00- | |
| 002 | 25 | 0000100000 WOOD SUPPLIER | | | 1,000.00 | |
| 003 | 40 | 0000700004 Real Loss on FOREX | | | 0.00 | |

Fig 24

As we notice above, since the doucment currency and the payment currency is the same, there is no FOREX implication. However, the very presence of the line relating to G/L account relating to FOREX tells us there is something more here. Click on the Display Currency button and we find that there is indeed a loss:

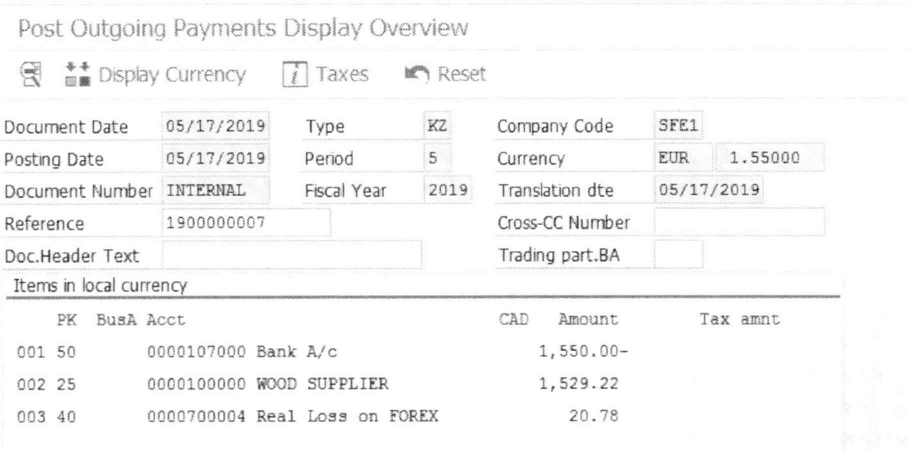

Post Outgoing Payments Display Overview

Display Currency Taxes Reset

| | | | | | |
|---|---|---|---|---|---|
| Document Date | 05/17/2019 | Type | KZ | Company Code | SFE1 |
| Posting Date | 05/17/2019 | Period | 5 | Currency | EUR 1.55000 |
| Document Number | INTERNAL | Fiscal Year | 2019 | Translation dte | 05/17/2019 |
| Reference | 1900000007 | | | Cross-CC Number | |
| Doc.Header Text | | | | Trading part.BA | |

Items in local currency

| | PK | BusA | Acct | CAD Amount | Tax amnt |
|---|---|---|---|---|---|
| 001 | 50 | | 0000107000 Bank A/c | 1,550.00- | |
| 002 | 25 | | 0000100000 WOOD SUPPLIER | 1,529.22 | |
| 003 | 40 | | 0000700004 Real Loss on FOREX | 20.78 | |

Fig 25

This loss (could have been a gain) is based on the buying and selling rates defined earlier in the transaction OC41. Reader is advised to calculate and confirm for themselves.

# VII. Unrealized Gain or Loss (U)

T Code : FAGL_FC_VAL in ECC or FAGL_FCV in HANA.

Or Navigate below:

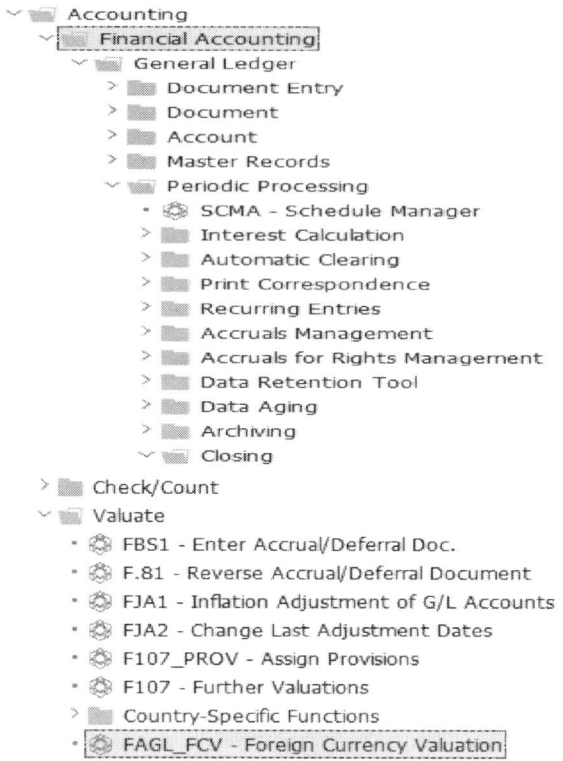

Fig 26

Usage:

All open items in foreign currency are valuated as part of the foreign currency valuation:

- The individual open items of an account in foreign currency form the basis of the valuation i.e. every open item of an account in foreign currency is valuated individually.

- The total difference from all the open items in an account is posted to a financial statement adjustment account.
- The exchange rate profit or loss from the valuation is posted to a separate expense or revenue account for exchange rate differences as an offset posting.

**Features** :

- Unrealized exchange rate differences - When we valuate open items in foreign currency, the exchange rate difference determined is posted as an unrealized exchange rate difference.

- Realized exchange rate differences - For an incoming payment, when we are clear open items, the current exchange rate is determined. Since the exchange differences that were not realized are reversed, the full exchange rate difference is now posted as realized.

- Reversing exchange rate difference postings - On the specified reversal date or in the reversal period, the posted exchange rate differences are automatically reversed by a reverse posting after the valuation run.

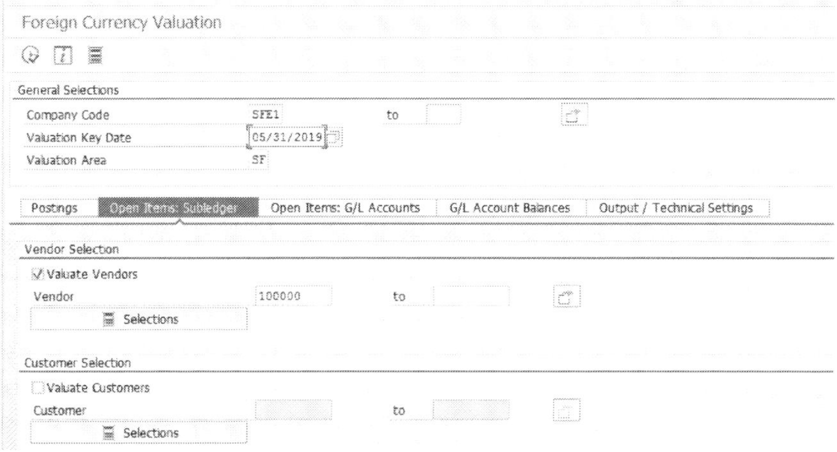

Fig 27

On execution of the report, we find out posting entry as one of the FOREX transactions:

Key Date 05/31/19
Valuation in Company Code Currency (10)
Valuation Area SF / Method SFCV
Test Run / Ledger Group GA

| Lg | AccTy | G/L | Account | DocumentNo | Itm | Amount in FC | Crcy | Amount in LC | LCurr | Revaluat. | BG | Exch. Rat | Typ | Old Difference | New Difference | Amount Posted | Rem. | I |
|---|---|---|---|---|---|---|---|---|---|---|---|---|---|---|---|---|---|---|
| | K | 211000 | 100000 | 1900000007 | 1 | 1,000.00- | EUR | 1,529.22- | CAD | 1.550000 | | 1.529220 | KR | 0.00 | 20.78- | 20.78- | | |
| * | | 211000 | | | | 1,000.00- | EUR | 1,529.22- | CAD | | | | | 0.00 | 20.78- | 20.78- | | |
| ** | | | | | | 1,000.00- | EUR | 1,529.22- | CAD | | | | | 0.00 | 20.78- | 20.78- | | |

Fig 28

# BILL OF EXCHANGE (C/U)

Bills of exchange are a form of short-term finance. If the customer pays by bill of exchange, it does not make payment immediately, but only once the maturity period specified on the bill has elapsed (three months, for example). Bills of exchange can be passed on to third parties for refinancing (bill of exchange usage). A bill of exchange can be discounted at a bank in advance of its due date (discounting). The bank buys the bill of exchange from us. Since it does not receive the amount until the date recorded on the bill, it charges us interest (discount) to cover the period between receiving the bill of exchange and its eventual payment. Some form of handling charge is also usually levied.

- Posting procedure of Bill of Exchange Receivable

There are 3 basic events for which bill of exchange can actually take place.

1. Payment by Bill of Exchange :
   Firstly, the payment by bill of exchange is posted and used to clear the receivable against the customer. There is a now

a bill of exchange receivable, which is recorded on the customer account and the special G/L account.

2. Bill of Exchange Usage
   If the bill of exchange is used for refinancing and is passed on to a bank, then the bill of exchange usage must be posted. The bill of exchange liability (liability to recourse) that you now have is  recorded on special accounts in the system until it has expired.

3. Cancel the Bill of Exchange Liability
   Once the due date of the bill of exchange has elapsed, including any country-specific period for the bill of exchange protest, you can cancel the bill of exchange receivable for your customer and the bill of exchange liability.

# I.  BILL OF EXCHANGE CONFIGURATION (C)

T Code OBYN

Define Alternative Reconciliation account for Account type 'D' and assign the reconciliation and alternative reconciliation GL's –

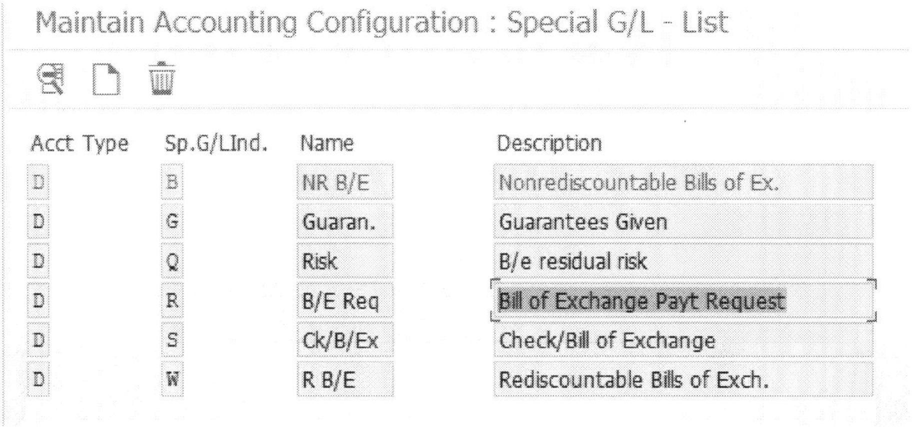

Maintain Accounting Configuration : Special G/L - List

| Acct Type | Sp.G/LInd. | Name | Description |
|-----------|-----------|--------|-------------|
| D | B | NR B/E | Nonrediscountable Bills of Ex. |
| D | G | Guaran. | Guarantees Given |
| D | Q | Risk | B/e residual risk |
| D | R | B/E Req | Bill of Exchange Payt Request |
| D | S | Ck/B/Ex | Check/Bill of Exchange |
| D | W | R B/E | Rediscountable Bills of Exch. |

Fig 1

Enter Chart of Accounts :

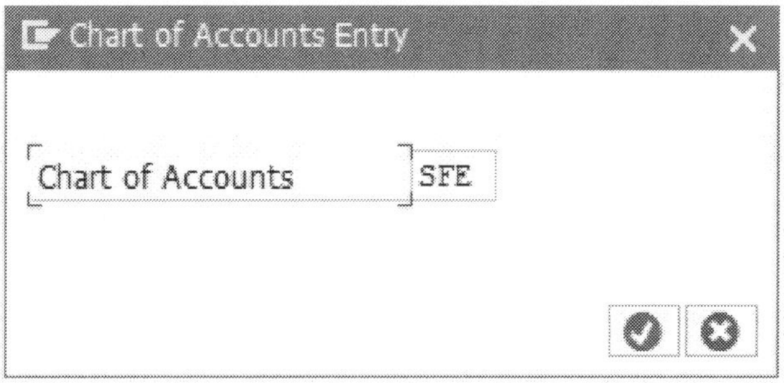

Chart of Accounts Entry

Chart of Accounts    SFE

Fig 2

471

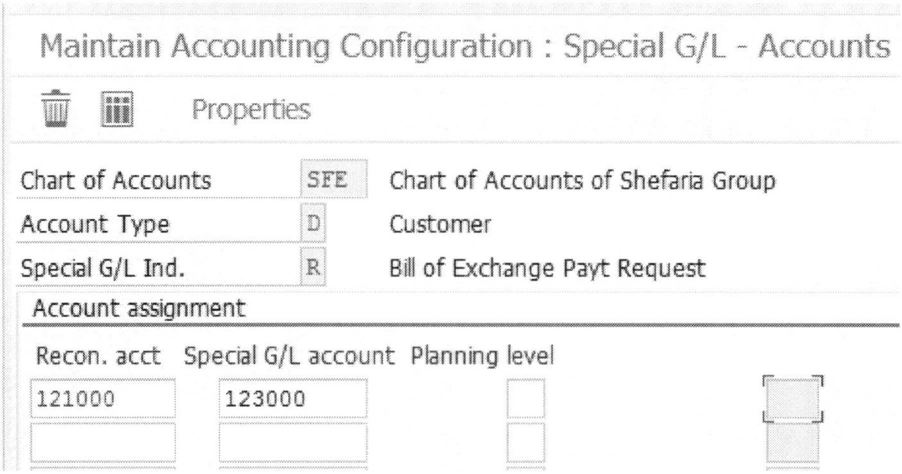
Maintain Accounting Configuration : Special G/L - Accounts
Properties
Chart of Accounts
SFE
Chart of Accounts of Shefaria Group
Account Type
D
Customer
Special G/L Ind.
R
Bill of Exchange Payt Request
Account assignment
Recon. acct
Special G/L account
Planning level
121000
123000

Fig 3

Save the entries

# II. Setup of G/L Account for Bill of Exchange (C/U)

T Code OBYK

Under Balance Sheet group of Accounts create the accounts as needed:

G/l Account : 100068 – Deutsche Bank Bill of exchange discount liability
100069 - Deutsche Bank - Collection of bills of exchange

Next, we link the Bank account and bank discounting account and reconciliation account together:

Change View "Bill Of Exchange Usage Bank SubAccounts": Overview

New Entries

| ChAc | Bank acct | Usage | SGL In | Customer recon. acct | Bank subaccount for liab. |
|---|---|---|---|---|---|
| INT | 113100 | D Discounting | W | | 113107 |
| INT | 113100 | F Forfeiting | B | | 113107 |
| INT | 113100 | F Forfeiting | W | | 113107 |
| INT | 113100 | I Collection | B | | 196600 |
| INT | 113100 | I Collection | W | | 196600 |
| INT | 113200 | D Discounting | B | | 113207 |
| INT | 113200 | D Discounting | W | | 113207 |
| INT | 113200 | F Forfeiting | B | | 113207 |
| INT | 113200 | F Forfeiting | W | | 113207 |
| INT | 113200 | I Collection | B | | 196600 |
| INT | 113200 | I Collection | W | | 196600 |
| INT | 113300 | D Discounting | B | | 113307 |
| INT | 113300 | D Discounting | W | | 113307 |

Fig 4

Click New Entries to update the following:

New Entries: Overview of Added Entries

| ChAc | Bank Acct | Usage | Sp.G/L | Customer Recon. Acct | Bank Subaccount for Liab |
|---|---|---|---|---|---|
| SFE | 100066 | D Discounting | B | | 100068 |
| SFE | 100066 | D Discounting | W | | 100068 |
| SFE | 100066 | F Forfeiting | B | | 100068 |
| SFE | 100066 | F Forfeiting | W | | 100068 |
| SFE | 100066 | I Collection | B | | 100069 |
| SFE | 100066 | I Collection | W | | 100069 |
| SFE | 100067 | D Discounting | B | | 100068 |
| SFE | 100067 | D Discounting | W | | 100068 |
| SFE | 100067 | F Forfeiting | B | | 100068 |
| SFE | 100067 | F Forfeiting | W | | 100068 |
| SFE | 100067 | I Collection | B | | 100069 |
| SFE | 100067 | I Collection | W | | 100069 |
| SFE | 200105 | D Discounting | W | 200110 | 100302 |

Fig 5

# III. ACCEPTANCE OF BILL OF EXCHANGE

## T Code F-36

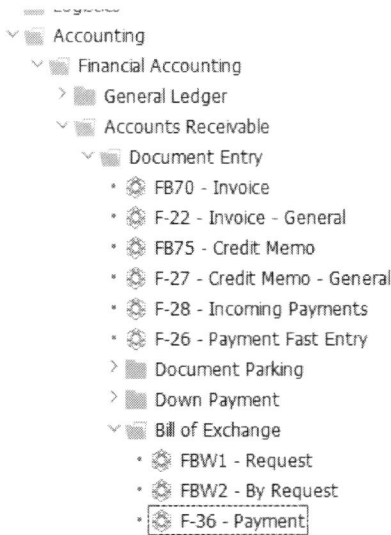

Fig 6

---

Bill of Exchange Payment: Header Data

| Choose open items | Account Model |
| --- | --- |

| | | | | | | |
| --- | --- | --- | --- | --- | --- | --- |
| Document Date | 052119 | Type | D2 | Company Code | SFE1 | |
| Posting Date | 05/19/2019 | Period | 5 | Currency/Rate | CAD | |
| Document Number | | | | Translation dte | | |
| Reference | Invoice # 123 | | | Cross-CC Number | | |
| Doc.Header Text | BOE Payment | | | | | |
| Clearing Text | | | | | | |

Transaction to be processed

○ Outgoing payment
◉ Incoming payment
○ Credit memo
○ Transfer posting with clearing

First line item

| PstKy | 09 | Account | 10001 | SGL Ind | W | TType | |
| --- | --- | --- | --- | --- | --- | --- | --- |

Fig 7

## Bill of Exchange Payment Correct Customer item

| | | | | | |
|---|---|---|---|---|---|
| Customer | 10001 | Showroom for SFE1 furniture | | G/L | 123000 |
| Company Code | SFE1 | 1000 Bloor St | | | |
| Shefaria Ent Inc | | toronto | | | |

**Item 1 / Bill of exchange / 09 W**

| | | |
|---|---|---|
| Amount | 5,600.00 | CAD |
| Assignment | | |
| Text | | 🖉 Long Texts |

**Bill of Exchange Details**

| | | | | | |
|---|---|---|---|---|---|
| Due On | 05/21/2019 ☐ Demand Bl | | Bill/Ex. Status | Planned Usage | ∨ |
| Issue Date | ☐ Accepted | | Bill Protest ID | | |
| Drawer | Shefaria Ent Inc | | Toronto | | ON |
| Drawee | Showroom for SFE1 furniture | | toronto | | |
| Domicile | | | | | |
| Cent.Bnk Loc | | | | | |
| Bank Country | | | | | |

Fig 8

Click on Process Open Items at the top of the above menu:

## Bill of Exchange Payment Correct Customer item

| | | | | | |
|---|---|---|---|---|---|
| Customer | 10001 | Showroom for SFE1 furniture | | G/L | 123000 |
| Company Code | SFE1 | 1000 Bloor St | | | |
| Shefaria Ent Inc | | toronto | | | |

**Item 1 / Bill of exchange / 09 W**

| | | |
|---|---|---|
| Amount | 5,600.00 | CAD |
| Assignment | | |
| Text | | 🖉 Long Texts |

**Bill of Exchange Details**

| | | | | | |
|---|---|---|---|---|---|
| Due On | 05/21/2019 ☐ Demand Bl | | Bill/Ex. Status | Planned Usage | ∨ |
| Issue Date | ☐ Accepted | | Bill Protest ID | | |
| Drawer | Shefaria Ent Inc | | Toronto | | ON |
| Drawee | Showroom for SFE1 furniture | | toronto | | |
| Domicile | | | | | |
| Cent.Bnk Loc | | | | | |
| Bank Country | | | | | |

Fig 9

Apply the amount to the open invoice you need to, same way as you would provess F-28:

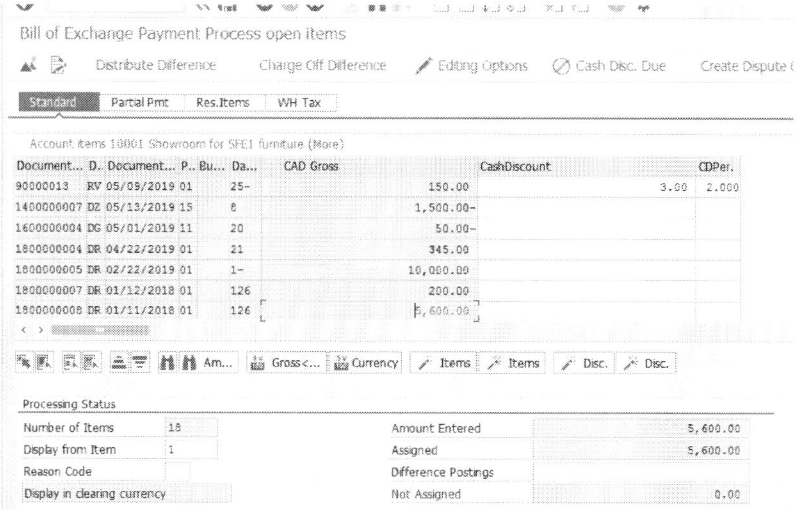

Fig 10

Simulate the Transaction if you want to:

Fig 11

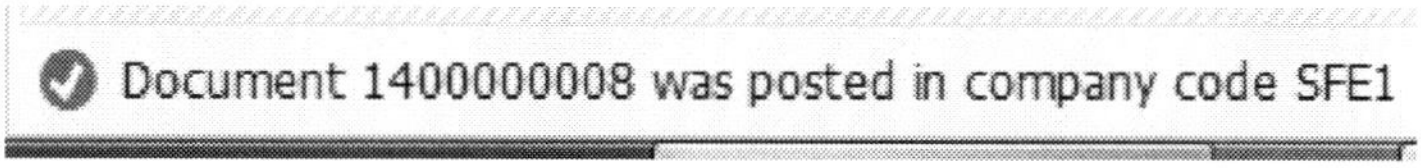

Document 1400000008 was posted in company code SFE1

Fig 12

# IV. BILL DISCOUNTING (U)

T Code F-33

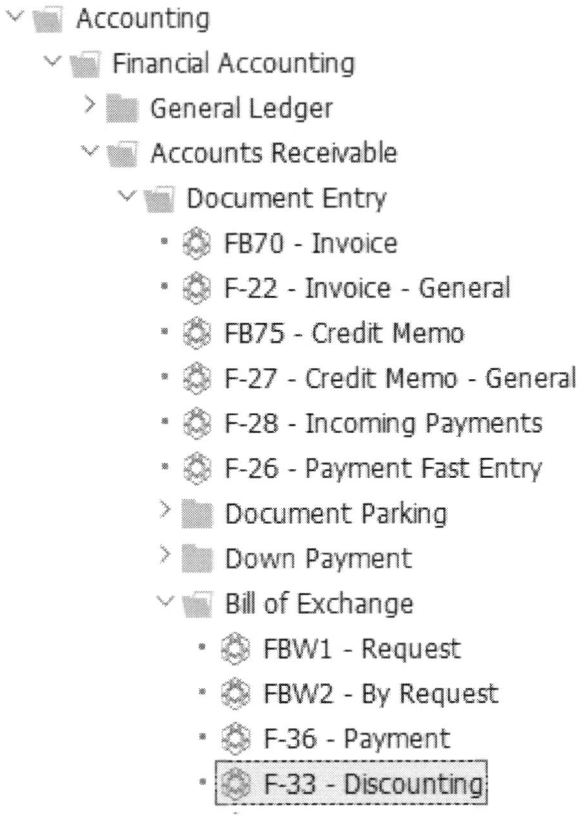

- ∨ 📁 Accounting
  - ∨ 📁 Financial Accounting
    - ⟩ 📁 General Ledger
    - ∨ 📁 Accounts Receivable
      - ∨ 📁 Document Entry
        - • ⚙ FB70 - Invoice
        - • ⚙ F-22 - Invoice - General
        - • ⚙ FB75 - Credit Memo
        - • ⚙ F-27 - Credit Memo - General
        - • ⚙ F-28 - Incoming Payments
        - • ⚙ F-26 - Payment Fast Entry
      - ⟩ 📁 Document Parking
      - ⟩ 📁 Down Payment
      - ∨ 📁 Bill of Exchange
        - • ⚙ FBW1 - Request
        - • ⚙ FBW2 - By Request
        - • ⚙ F-36 - Payment
        - • ⚙ F-33 - Discounting

Fig 13

478

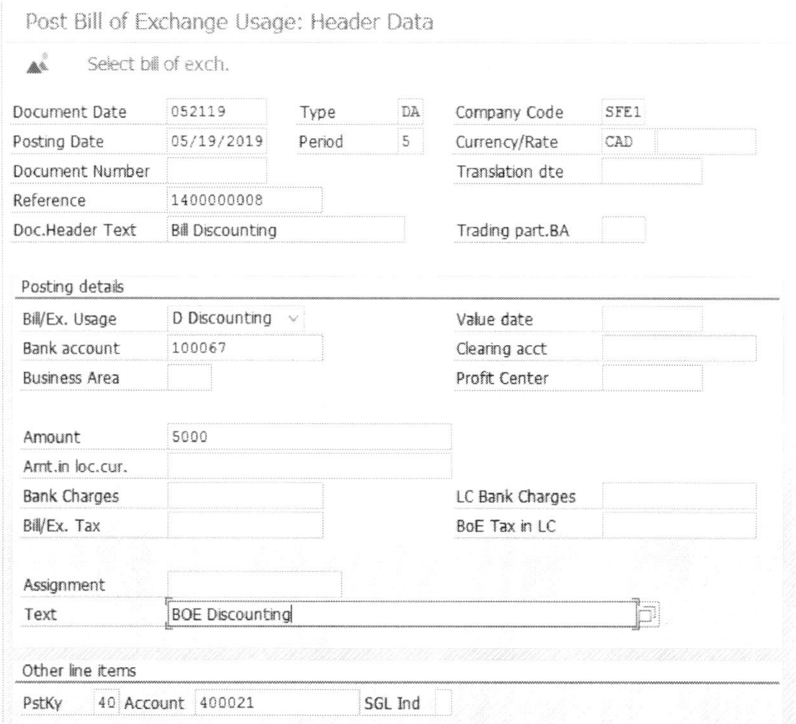

## Post Bill of Exchange Usage: Header Data

Select bill of exch.

| | | | | | | |
|---|---|---|---|---|---|---|
| Document Date | 052119 | Type | DA | Company Code | SFE1 | |
| Posting Date | 05/19/2019 | Period | 5 | Currency/Rate | CAD | |
| Document Number | | | | Translation dte | | |
| Reference | 1400000008 | | | | | |
| Doc.Header Text | Bill Discounting | | | Trading part.BA | | |

### Posting details

| | | | | |
|---|---|---|---|---|
| Bill/Ex. Usage | D Discounting ∨ | | Value date | |
| Bank account | 100067 | | Clearing acct | |
| Business Area | | | Profit Center | |
| | | | | |
| Amount | 5000 | | | |
| Amt.in loc.cur. | | | | |
| Bank Charges | | | LC Bank Charges | |
| Bill/Ex. Tax | | | BoE Tax in LC | |
| | | | | |
| Assignment | | | | |
| Text | BOE Discounting | | | |

### Other line items

PstKy  40  Account  400021  SGL Ind

Fig 14

Posting Key 40 : Use the Bank charges G/L Account as that account will take the hit for this amount.

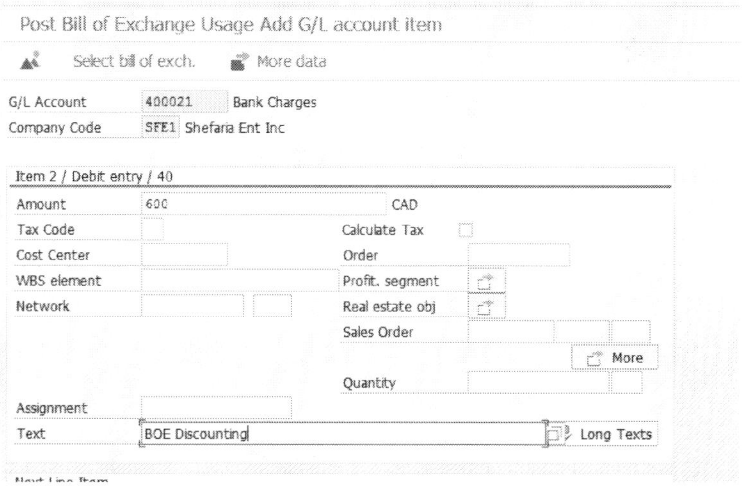

## Post Bill of Exchange Usage Add G/L account item

Select bill of exch.    More data

| | | | |
|---|---|---|---|
| G/L Account | 400021 | Bank Charges | |
| Company Code | SFE1 | Shefaria Ent Inc | |

### Item 2 / Debit entry / 40

| | | | |
|---|---|---|---|
| Amount | 600 | CAD | |
| Tax Code | | Calculate Tax | |
| Cost Center | | Order | |
| WBS element | | Profit. segment | |
| Network | | Real estate obj | |
| | | Sales Order | |
| | | | More |
| | | Quantity | |
| Assignment | | | |
| Text | BOE Discounting | | Long Texts |

Next Line Item

Fig 15

Choose and Enter Bill of Exchange Document No.

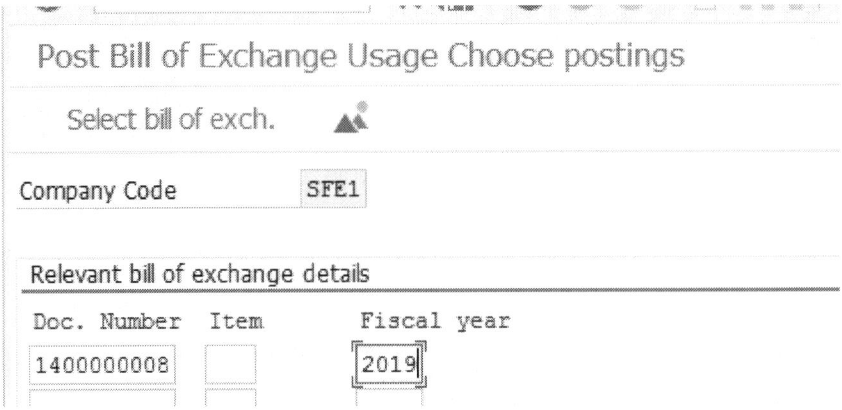

Fig 16

Choose

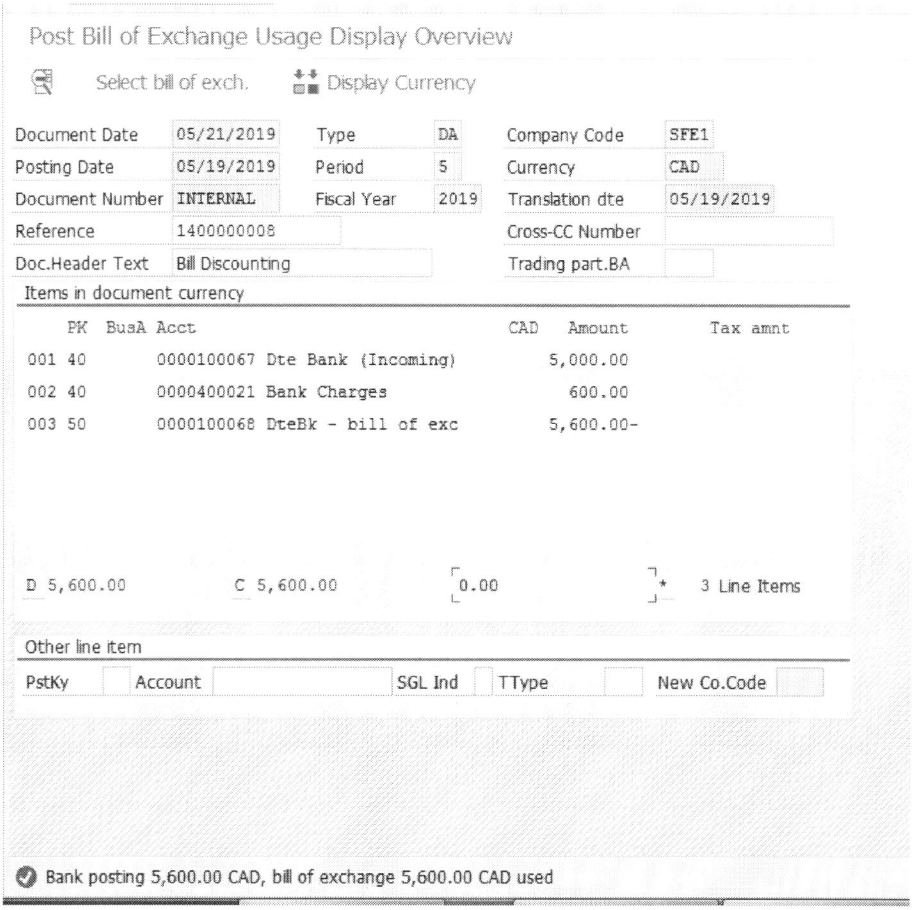
Post Bill of Exchange Usage Display Overview
Select bill of exch.
Display Currency
Document Date 05/21/2019
Type DA
Company Code SFE1
Posting Date 05/19/2019
Period 5
Currency CAD
Document Number INTERNAL
Fiscal Year 2019
Translation dte 05/19/2019
Reference 1400000008
Cross-CC Number
Doc.Header Text Bill Discounting
Trading part.BA
Items in document currency
PK BusA Acct CAD Amount Tax amnt
001 40 0000100067 Dte Bank (Incoming) 5,000.00
002 40 0000400021 Bank Charges 600.00
003 50 0000100068 DteBk - bill of exc 5,600.00-
D 5,600.00
C 5,600.00
0.00
* 3 Line Items
Other line item
PstKy
Account
SGL Ind
TType
New Co.Code
Bank posting 5,600.00 CAD, bill of exchange 5,600.00 CAD used

Fig 17

Post the document with successful Bill of Exchange Discounting

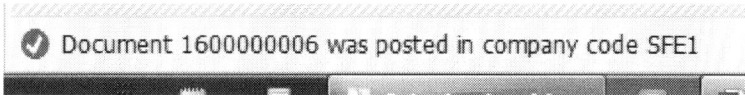

Document 1600000006 was posted in company code SFE1

Fig 18

The interest postion hits the expense account as above.

# BANK RECONCILIATION STATEMENT

# PROCESSING

Bank reconciliation is the process of matching and comparing figures from accounting records in the system with those presented on a bank statement. Less any items which have no relation to the bank statement, the balance of the accounting ledger should reconcile with the balance of the bank statement.

Bank reconciliation allows companies or individuals to compare their account records to the bank's records of their account balance in order to uncover any possible discrepancies.

Standard SAP provides 2 bank reconciliation process :

- ➢ Electronic Bank Reconcilliation
- ➢ Manual Bank Reconcilliation

Electronic Bank statement Process Flow Chart :

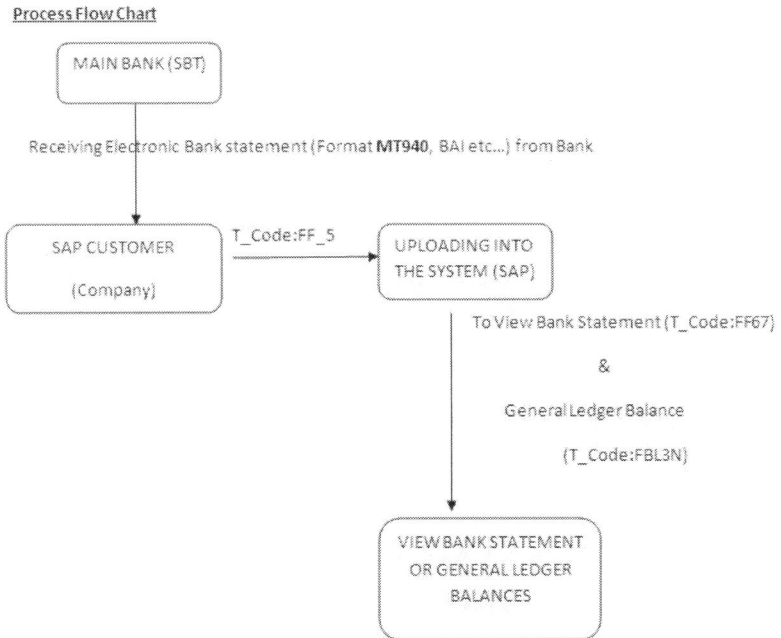

Process Flow Chart

```
        ┌─────────────────────┐
        │  MAIN BANK (SBT)     │
        └─────────────────────┘
                  │
  Receiving Electronic Bank statement (Format MT940, BAI etc...) from Bank
                  │
                  ▼
 ┌──────────────────┐  T_Code:FF_5   ┌──────────────────┐
 │  SAP CUSTOMER    │ ─────────────> │  UPLOADING INTO  │
 │                  │                │  THE SYSTEM (SAP)│
 │  (Company)       │                └──────────────────┘
 └──────────────────┘                         │
                         To View Bank Statement (T_Code:FF67)
                                       &
                              General Ledger Balance
                                  (T_Code:FBL3N)
                                       │
                                       ▼
                         ┌──────────────────────┐
                         │  VIEW BANK STATEMENT  │
                         │  OR GENERAL LEDGER    │
                         │  BALANCES             │
                         └──────────────────────┘
```

Fig 1

Electronic bank statement overview:

- It is an electronic document sent by the bank, which gives details of the transactions done in the account holder's account with the bank.
- The electronic document can be remitted by the bank in the following formats SWIFT, Multi cash, BAI etc.- these are standard formats with specific sets of data
- This statement is used in SAP to do an automatic reconciliation
- The statement is uploaded in SAP and it clears the various Bank clearing accounts

Next step is to configure the Electronic Bank Statement (EBS).

# I.    CREATE HOUSE BANK (C)

Transaction Code FI12

In the SAP system, you use bank ID and account ID to specify bank details. These specifications are used, for example, for automatic payment transactions to determine bank details for payment.

Define your house banks and the corresponding accounts in the system under a bank ID or an account ID. For our understanding of the BNS, we will use the sale bank account we established earlier.

Update Bank Account:

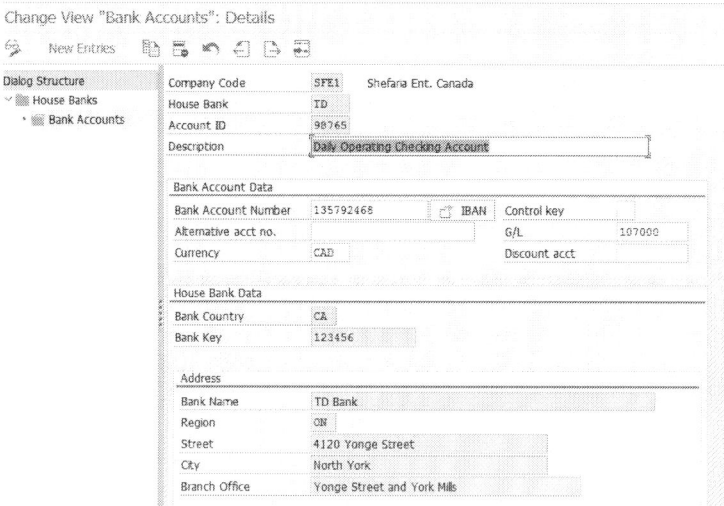

Fig 2

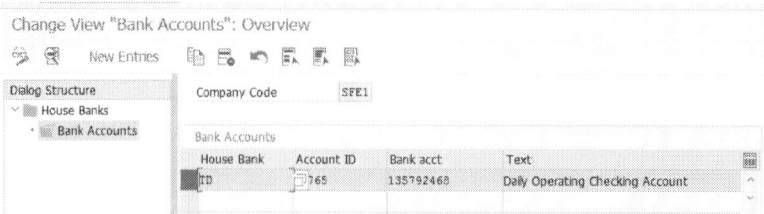

Fig 3

## Electronic Bank Statement (EBS)

In the following activities all the settings necessary for the EBS have been configured in Global Settings for Electronic Bank Statement

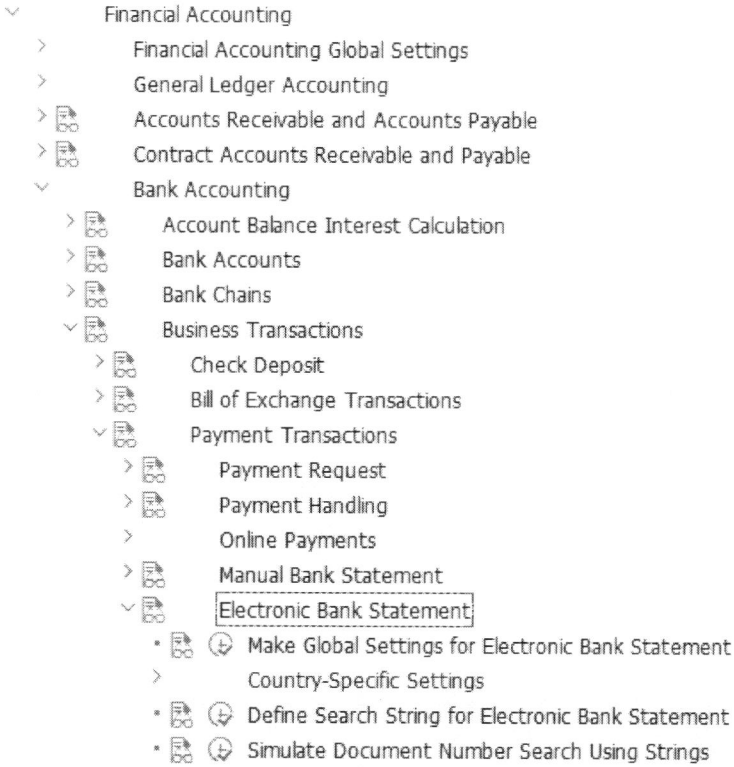

Fig 4

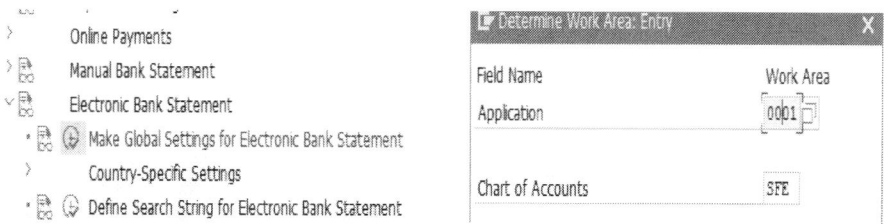

Fig 5

In this activity we make the global settings for the account statement. There are four main steps to be carried out:

- Create account symbol
- Assign accounts to account symbols
- Create keys for posting rules
- Create a transaction type

## II.   CREATE ACCOUNT SYMBOLS (C)

T Code SPRO

In this activity account symbols has been created to define posting specifications. Before the posting rule is used, account symbols are replaced with the relevant accounts to which posting is to be made. Define an ID for each account symbol & enter a description in the text field. Following Account symbols were created :

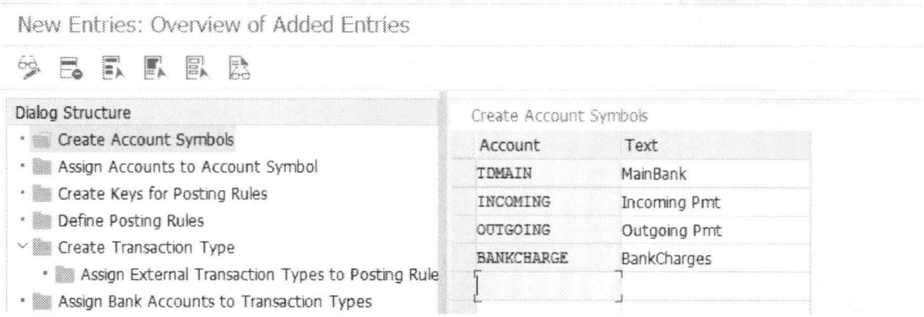

Fig 6

# III. Assign Accounts to Account Symbols (C)

T Code SPRO

In this activity account, determination procedure has been defined for each individual account symbol. Define postings to be triggered by possible transactions in the account statement (such as bank transfer, debit memo). In the posting specifications debit -> credit that has been defined here, we will use the account symbols from step 1, not the G/L account numbers. This prevents similar posting rules being defined several times, as the only difference between them being the accounts to which postings are made.

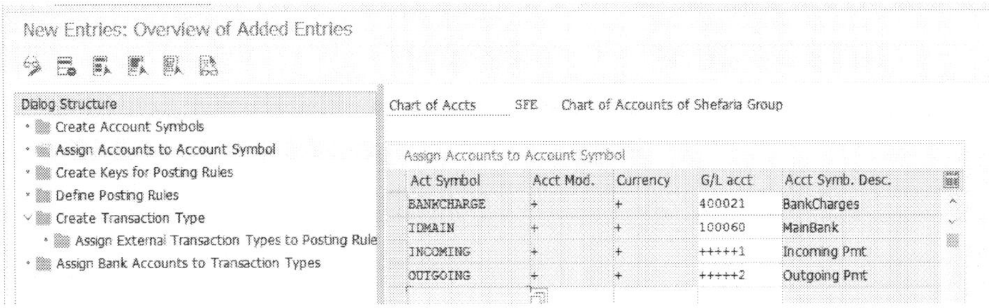

Fig 7

The masking is done using ++++++ for the main bank account. For the sub accounts, all the other digits are masked except the last one. For bank charges, the actual G/L account is entered.

488

# IV. CREATE KEYS FOR POSTING RULES (C)

T Code SPRO

In this activity, separate keys are defined for posting rules to be used for banking transactions.

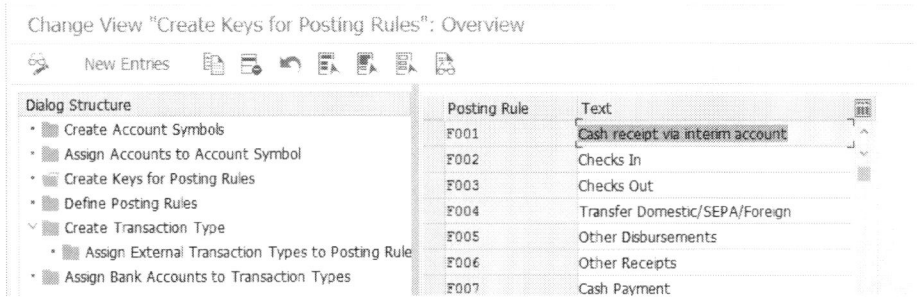

Change View "Create Keys for Posting Rules": Overview

New Entries

| Dialog Structure | Posting Rule | Text |
|---|---|---|
| • Create Account Symbols | F001 | Cash receipt via interim account |
| • Assign Accounts to Account Symbol | F002 | Checks In |
| • Create Keys for Posting Rules | F003 | Checks Out |
| • Define Posting Rules | F004 | Transfer Domestic/SEPA/Foreign |
| ∨ Create Transaction Type | F005 | Other Disbursements |
| • Assign External Transaction Types to Posting Rule | F006 | Other Receipts |
| • Assign Bank Accounts to Transaction Types | F007 | Cash Payment |

Fig 8

Create New Entries:

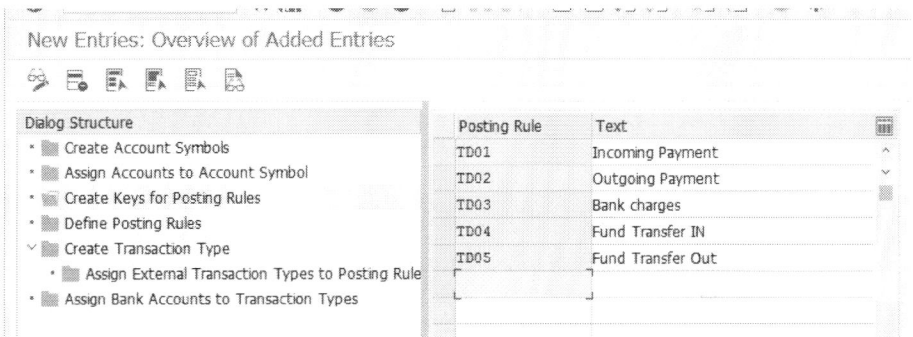

New Entries: Overview of Added Entries

| Dialog Structure | Posting Rule | Text |
|---|---|---|
| • Create Account Symbols | TD01 | Incoming Payment |
| • Assign Accounts to Account Symbol | TD02 | Outgoing Payment |
| • Create Keys for Posting Rules | TD03 | Bank charges |
| • Define Posting Rules | TD04 | Fund Transfer IN |
| ∨ Create Transaction Type | TD05 | Fund Transfer Out |
| • Assign External Transaction Types to Posting Rule | | |
| • Assign Bank Accounts to Transaction Types | | |

Fig 9

# V.   DEFINE POSTING RULES (C)

T Code SPRO

For each posting specifications posting rules has been created which will specify how business transaction is to be posted.

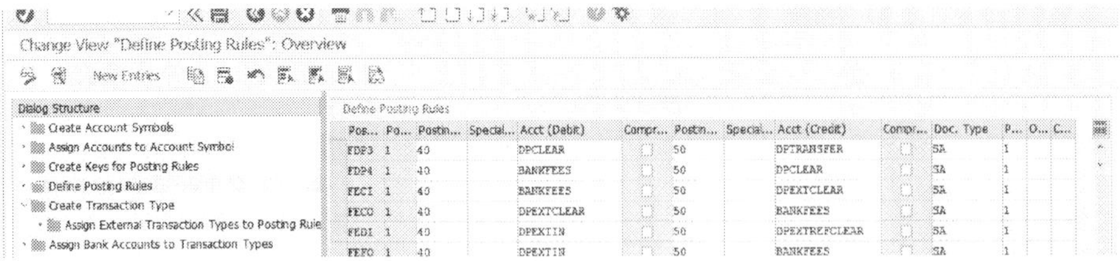

Fig 10

Click New Entries to create new posting rules

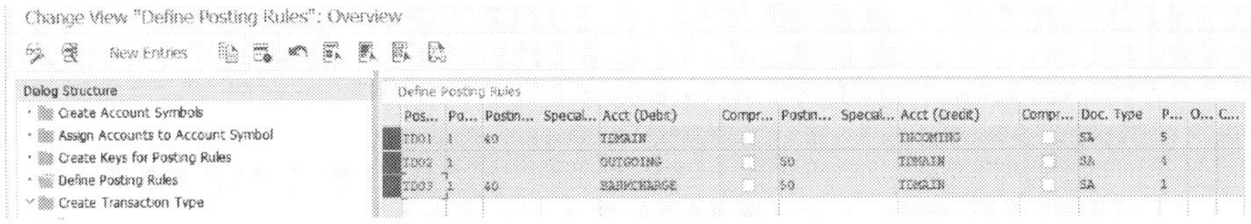

Fig 11

# VI. Create Transaction Types (C)

T Code SPRO

In this activity transaction type: MT940 has been created in order to facilitate Electronic Banking Statement processing.

Fig 12

# VII. ASSIGN EXTERNAL TRANSACTION CODES TO POSTING RULES (C)

T Code SPRO

In this activity (external) business, transaction codes provided by HSBC are assigned to an (internal) posting rule. This means that the same posting specifications can be used for different business transaction codes.

- For each transaction type, a posting rule has been assigned to each external transaction key

- In the "+/- sign" field, enter "+" or "-" to indicate whether payments are incoming or outgoing

- An interpretation algorithm has been defined for open items relating to outgoing payment in order to clear automatically because of the posting.

Choose Transaction type if prompted:

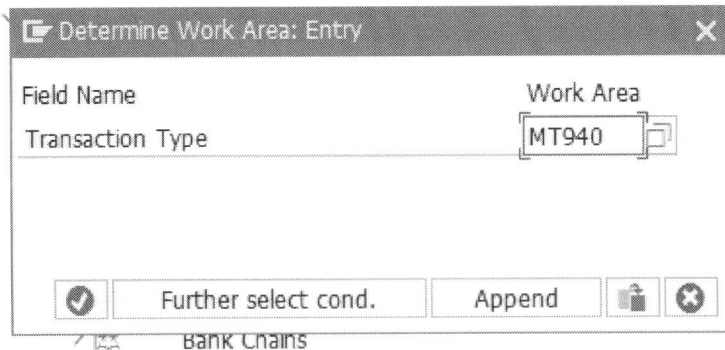

Fig 13

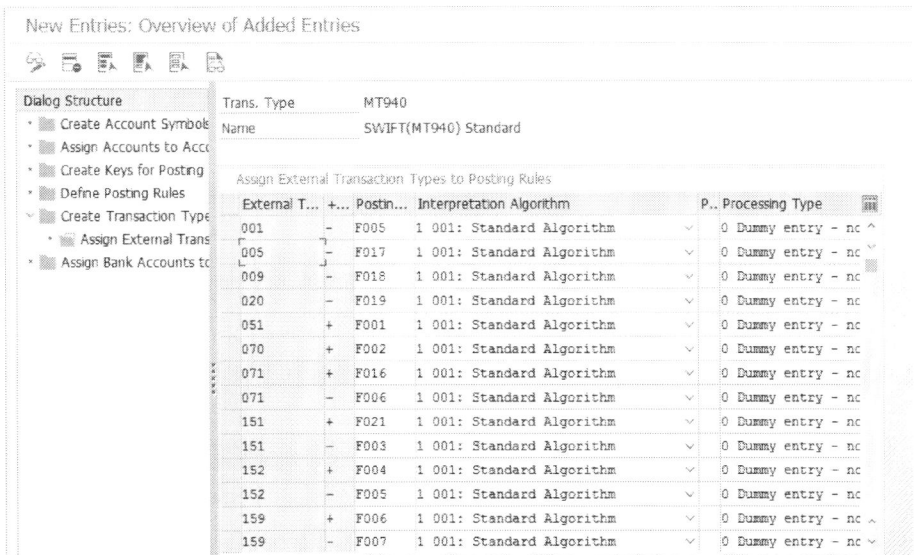

| Dialog Structure | | |
|---|---|---|
| • Create Account Symbol | Trans. Type | MT940 |
| • Assign Accounts to Acc | Name | SWIFT(MT940) Standard |
| • Create Keys for Posting | | |
| • Define Posting Rules | | |
| • Create Transaction Type | | |
| • Assign External Trans | | |
| • Assign Bank Accounts tc | | |

Assign External Transaction Types to Posting Rules

| External T... | +... | Postin... | Interpretation Algorithm | P... | Processing Type |
|---|---|---|---|---|---|
| 001 | – | F005 | 1 001: Standard Algorithm | | 0 Dummy entry – nc |
| 005 | – | F017 | 1 001: Standard Algorithm | | 0 Dummy entry – nc |
| 009 | – | F018 | 1 001: Standard Algorithm | | 0 Dummy entry – nc |
| 020 | – | F019 | 1 001: Standard Algorithm | | 0 Dummy entry – nc |
| 051 | + | F001 | 1 001: Standard Algorithm | | 0 Dummy entry – nc |
| 070 | + | F002 | 1 001: Standard Algorithm | | 0 Dummy entry – nc |
| 071 | + | F016 | 1 001: Standard Algorithm | | 0 Dummy entry – nc |
| 071 | – | F006 | 1 001: Standard Algorithm | | 0 Dummy entry – nc |
| 151 | + | F021 | 1 001: Standard Algorithm | | 0 Dummy entry – nc |
| 151 | – | F003 | 1 001: Standard Algorithm | | 0 Dummy entry – nc |
| 152 | + | F004 | 1 001: Standard Algorithm | | 0 Dummy entry – nc |
| 152 | – | F005 | 1 001: Standard Algorithm | | 0 Dummy entry – nc |
| 159 | + | F006 | 1 001: Standard Algorithm | | 0 Dummy entry – nc |
| 159 | – | F007 | 1 001: Standard Algorithm | | 0 Dummy entry – nc |

Fig 14

Save the entries.

Details of description (MT940 Format)

: 20: Statement Date

: 25: Account Identification Bank ID/account number

: 28C: Statement and/or sequence number

: 60F: Opening Balance

: 61: Statement line field

: 86: Information to account holder

: 62F Closing Balance

# MT940 File Name

The downloaded SWIFT MT940 file will have the similar file name with the following details:

Statement - End of Day (MT940)2019-05-22-

06[1].25.45.876474.940

|   |   |   |   |   |
|---|---|---|---|---|
| A | B | C | D | E |

A = Name of the report

B = Report Download Date

C = Report Download Time, Minutes and Second

D = Random Numbers

E = File Extension

## SWIFT MT940 Layout Specification

The downloaded report will contain the following fields.

| Tag | Field Name Description | Additional Details |
|---|---|---|
| :20: | Transaction reference number 16x | YYMMDD, the statement date of the final closing balance |
| :25: | Account Identification 34x | Internal account number, without '-' |
| :28C: | Statement Number/ Sequence Number | SWIFT Format option C 5n/3n |
| :60 (F/M): | Opening Balance (F) Intermediate (M) 25x | 1a6n3a15n 1a – 'D/C' debit or credit marker |

| Tag | Field Name Description | Additional Details |
|---|---|---|
| | | 6n – Statement Date of the opening balance, YYMMDD<br>3a – Account Currency Code<br>15n – Amount |
| :61: | Statement line 48x<br>(52x – R3.2 onwards) | 6n4n1a15n4a16a16a34a<br>Subfield 1: Transaction Value Date (YYMMDD) (6n)<br>Subfield 2: Transaction Posting Date (MMDD) (4n)<br>Subfield 3: Debit/Credit Marker (1a)<br>Subfield 4: Not applicable<br>Subfield 5: Amount (15n)<br>Subfield 6: Transaction Type (4a)<br>Subfield 7: Reference for Account Owner (16a)<br>Subfield 8: // [Account Servicing Institutions Reference (16a)]<br>Subfield 9: Supplementary Details (34a) |
| :86: | Information to Account Holder 6*65x (unstructured)<br><br>For LVP (Outward) | This field is populated with UNSTRUCTURED information of Transaction Description downloaded from the Bank.<br><br>1. full customer batch reference (Line 1 If available) |

| Tag | Field Name Description | Additional Details |
|-----|------------------------|--------------------|
| | For HVP (Outward) | 2. (ED) - identifer to indicate the end of the customer batch reference<br>3. AUTOPAY OUT - Constant (Line 1)<br>4. Payment setcode (Line 1)<br>5. Payment setcode description (Line 1 if customer reference is NONREF else line 2) |
| | For LVP (Return) | 1. FREE TEXT Beneficiary Name<br>2. Narrative<br>3. Narrative<br>4. Foreign exchange information<br>5. Charges information<br><br>1. Standard Narrative<br>2. Reject Reason<br>3. Payment setcode<br>4. Second Party Identifier |
| :62 (F/M): | Closing Balance (F) Intermediate (M) 25x | 1a6n3a15n<br>1a – 'D/C' debit or credit marker<br>6n – Statement Date of the closing balance, YYMMDD<br>3a – Account Currency Code<br>15n – Amount |

## Transaction code FF_5

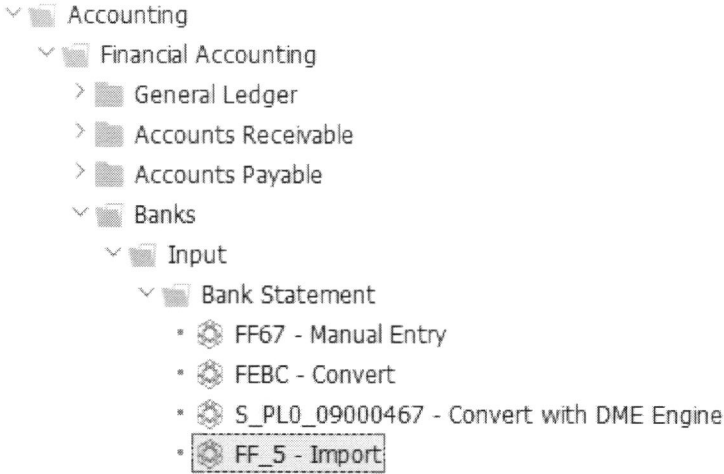

```
∨ 🗀 Accounting
  ∨ 🗀 Financial Accounting
    > 📁 General Ledger
    > 📁 Accounts Receivable
    > 📁 Accounts Payable
    ∨ 🗀 Banks
      ∨ 🗀 Input
        ∨ 🗀 Bank Statement
          • ⬡ FF67 - Manual Entry
          • ⬡ FEBC - Convert
          • ⬡ S_PL0_09000467 - Convert with DME Engine
          • ⬡ FF_5 - Import
```

Fig 15

## Import sample MT940 Statement file from Local Drive / Application server and execute

```
:20:170131
:25:1000111111
:28C:00001/001
:60F:C170101CAD100000
:61:1701050104C3200,00NTRF1400000141      //9001XA90M77B
:86:OMC Inc AUTOPAY IN                          C01
CUSTOMER
:61:1701040103D2000,00NTRF1500000070      //LP KLH920990
:86:wood vendor for SFE1
CABLE      CAD4.00
:61:1701240904C100,00NTRFNONREF           //NONREF
:86:MEPS INTEREST  PAYMENT
INVALID ACCOUNT NUMBER 24174527665
C01 SECID001
:62F:C170131CAD101096.00
```

Fig 16

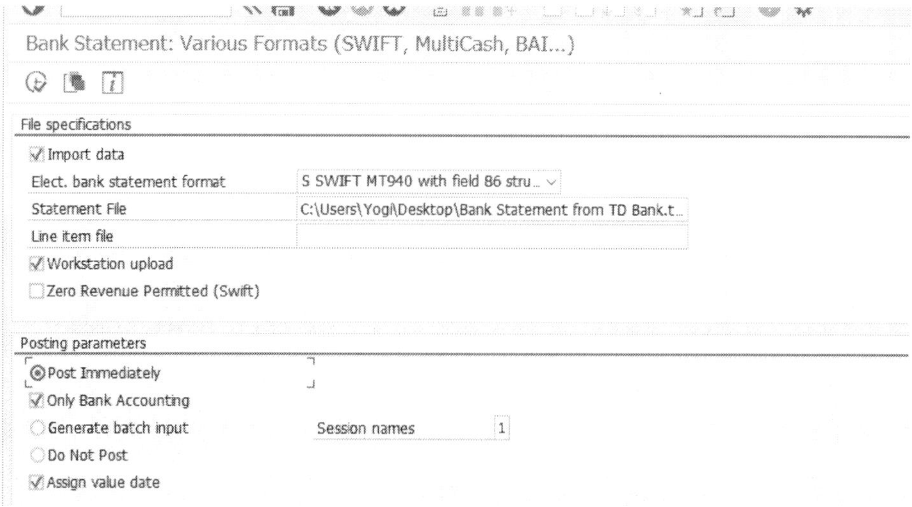

File specifications

☑ Import data

Elect. bank statement format    S SWIFT MT940 with field 86 stru... ∨

Statement File    C:\Users\Yogi\Desktop\Bank Statement from TD Bank.t...

Line item file

☑ Workstation upload

☐ Zero Revenue Permitted (Swift)

Posting parameters

◉ Post Immediately

☑ Only Bank Accounting

○ Generate batch input    Session names    1

○ Do Not Post

☑ Assign value date

Fig 17

Posting Overview: Bank Statement MT940 file has been processed. If some transaction is not posted during MT940 automatic bank reconcilliation it can be later processed via FEBAN – Post Processing

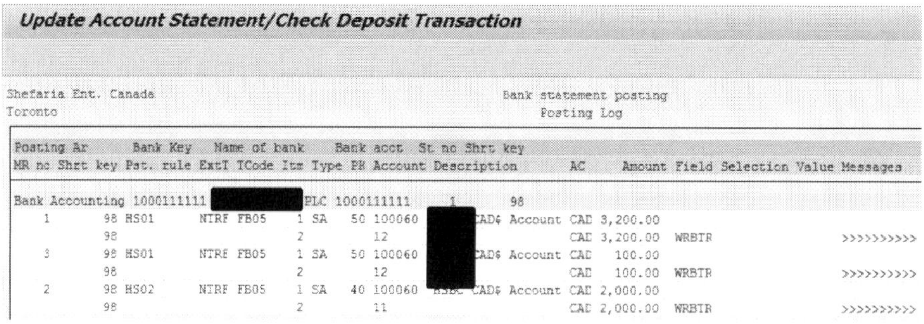

Fig 18

# Update in Bank sub-ledger: confirming Payment Cashed in and Out

### Update Account Statement/Check Deposit Transaction

| Shefaria Ent. Canada | Bank statement posting | Time 12:14:00 | Date 14.03.201 |
| Toronto | Processing Statistics | RFEBKU00/IDES013 Page | |

| Posting Ar | Sessn | Group | FB01 | FB05 | PmtAcc | No Posting | Error | Total | Total Deb. | Total Cred |
|---|---|---|---|---|---|---|---|---|---|---|
| Bank Accounting | | | 0 | 0 | 0 | 0 | 3 | 3 | 3,300.00 | 2,000.00 |
| * Bank Accounting | | | 0 | 0 | 0 | 0 | 3 | 3 | 3,300.00 | 2,000.00 |
| ** Bank Accounting | | | 0 | 0 | 0 | 0 | 3 | 3 | 3,300.00 | 2,000.00 |
| Subledger acctng | | | 0 | 0 | 0 | 3 | 0 | 3 | 3,300.00 | 2,000.00 |
| * Subledger acctng | | | 0 | 0 | 0 | 3 | 0 | 3 | 3,300.00 | 2,000.00 |
| ** Subledger acctng | | | 0 | 0 | 0 | 3 | 0 | 3 | 3,300.00 | 2,000.00 |
| *** | | | 0 | 0 | 0 | 3 | 3 | 6 | 6,600.00 | 4,000.00 |

Fig 19

### Bank Statement: Various Formats (SWIFT, MultiCash, BAI...)

| Shefaria Ent. Canada | | | | | | | Time 12:17:11 | Date 14.03.2017 |
| Toronto | | | | | | | RFEBKA00/IDES013 | Page 1 |

HSBC Canada PLC
Bank no.:     1000111111     Account number: 1000111111     Statement number: 00001     ID:         00000098
House bank:   HSBC           Acct ID:     1-101             Statement date: 31.01.2017  Currency    CAD

Opening Balance    100,000.00
Total Debit          2,000.00
Total Cred.          3,300.00
Clos. Bal.         10,109,600.00

| MR no | Value date | BkPostDate | Payment Notes | Posting Text | Amount | BTC |
|---|---|---|---|---|---|---|
| | | | | Opening Balance | 100,000.00 | |
| 1 | 05.01.2017 | | OMC INC AUTOPAY IN        C01 CUSTOMER | | 3,200.00 | NTRF |
| | | | 9001XA90M77B | | | |
| | | | Reference 1400000141 | | | |
| 2 | 04.01.2017 | | WOOD VENDOR FOR SFE1 CABLE    CAD4.00 | | 2,000.00- | NTRF |
| | | | LP KLH920990 | | | |
| | | | Reference 1500000070 | | | |
| 3 | 24.01.2017 | | MEPS INTEREST  PAYMENT INVALID ACCOUNT NUMBER 241 | | 100.00 | NTRF |
| | | | CID001 | | | |
| | | | NONREF | | | |
| | | | Reference NONREF | | | |
| * | | | | | 101,300.00 | |

Fig 20

# IX. MANUAL BANK RECONCILLIATION (C/U)

## 1. CREATE AND ASSIGN BUSINESS TRANSACTION (C)

T Code SPRO

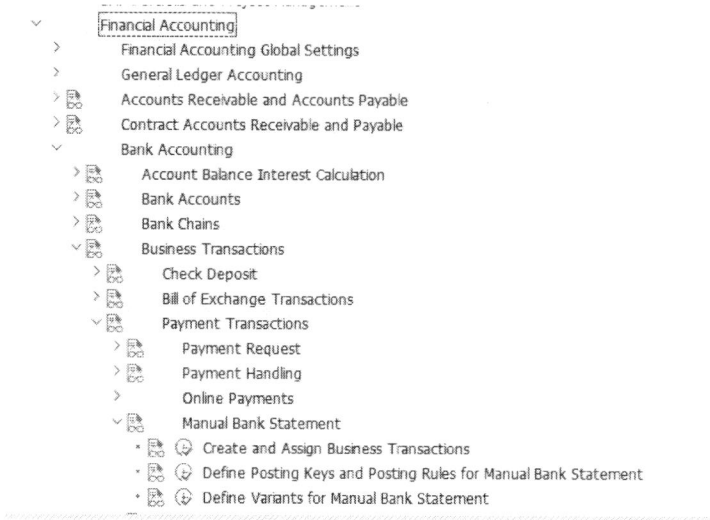

**Fig 21**

Here new Transaction type is defined and assigned with existing Posting rules

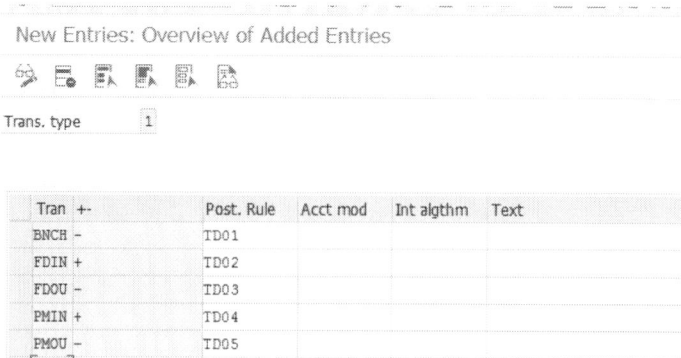

**Fig 22**

## 2. Define Variants for Manual Bank Statement (C)

T Code SPRO

Here we define the required field during bank statement reconciliation processing.

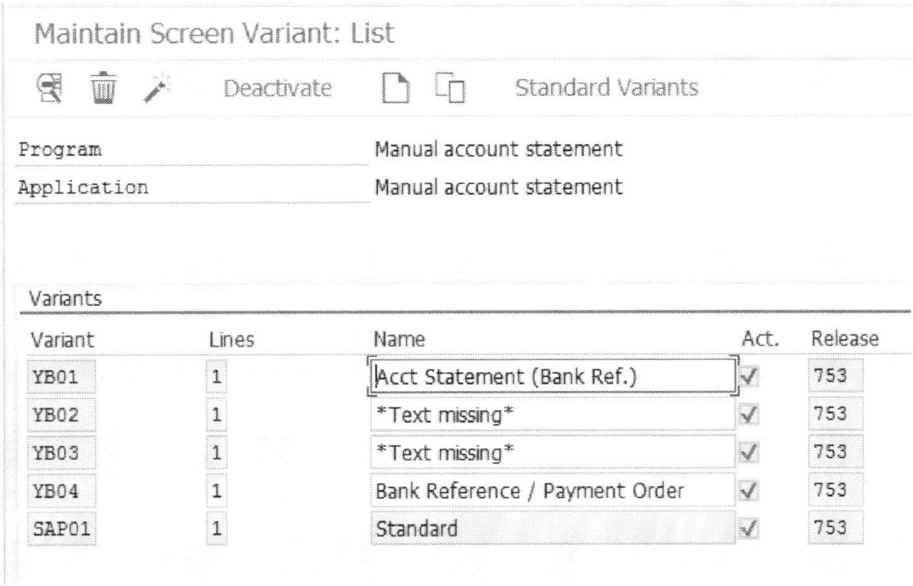

| | Maintain Screen Variant: List | | | | |
|---|---|---|---|---|---|

Deactivate    Standard Variants

| Program | Manual account statement |
|---|---|
| Application | Manual account statement |

Variants

| Variant | Lines | Name | Act. | Release |
|---|---|---|---|---|
| YB01 | 1 | Acct Statement (Bank Ref.) | ✓ | 753 |
| YB02 | 1 | *Text missing* | ✓ | 753 |
| YB03 | 1 | *Text missing* | ✓ | 753 |
| YB04 | 1 | Bank Reference / Payment Order | ✓ | 753 |
| SAP01 | 1 | Standard | ✓ | 753 |

Fig 23

Use [keys] keys to find the fields you want in the new Variant.

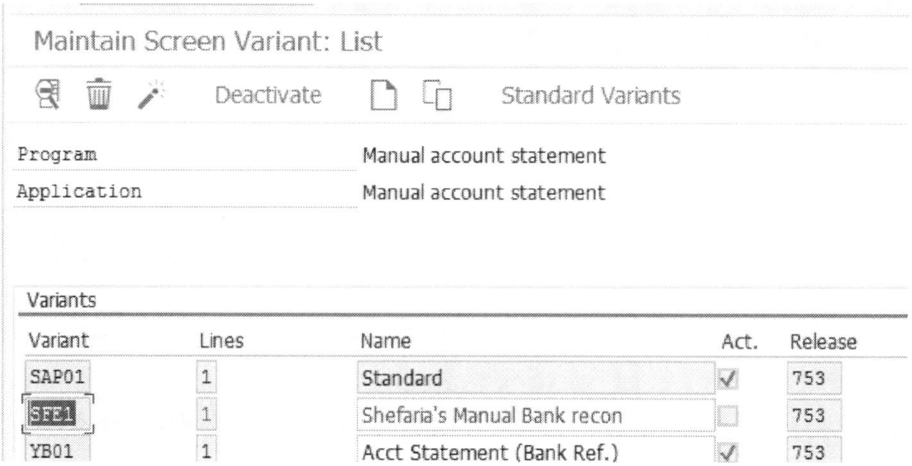

| Program | Manual account statement |
| Application | Manual account statement |

**Variants**

| Variant | Lines | Name | Act. | Release |
|---|---|---|---|---|
| SAP01 | 1 | Standard | ✓ | 753 |
| SFE1 | 1 | Shefaria's Manual Bank recon | ☐ | 753 |
| YB01 | 1 | Acct Statement (Bank Ref.) | ✓ | 753 |

Fig 24

Next, activate the variant using the Activate key:

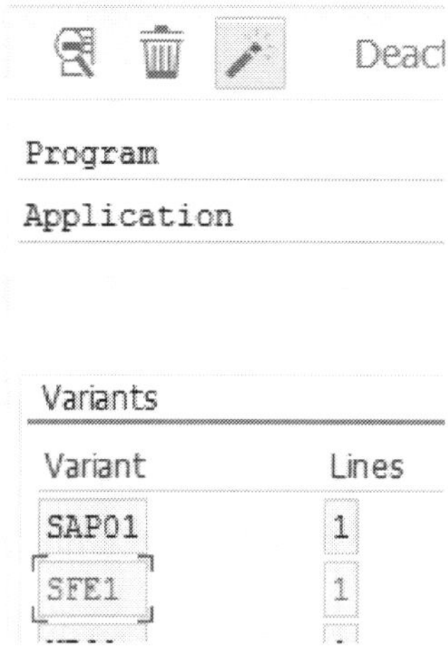

| Program | |
| Application | |

**Variants**

| Variant | Lines |
|---|---|
| SAP01 | 1 |
| SFE1 | 1 |

Fig 25

## 3. PROCESS MANUAL BANK STATEMENT (U)

T Code FF67:

**HANA CHANGE:** The selection screen for manual bank statement processing has a minor change . In ECC, the only options were to process it online or as a background job; in HANA one can set it up as a session also in SM37.

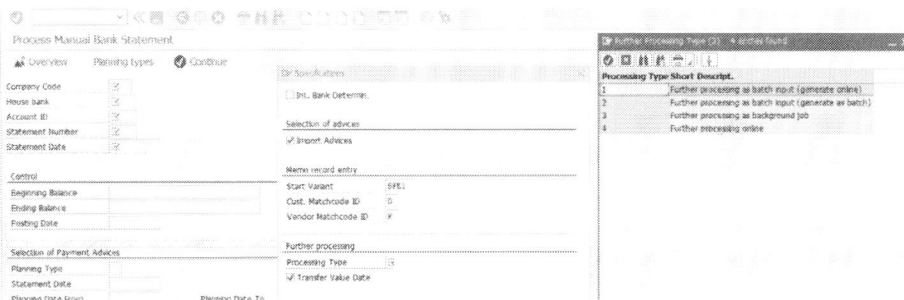

Fig 26

Select relevant Transaction an process the statement reconcilliation

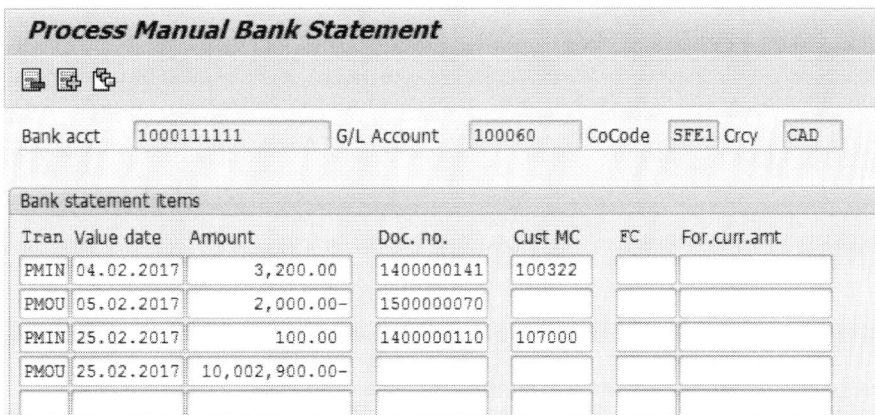

Fig 27

Click Save to save the statement in order to post via further processing.

**Update Account Statement/Check Deposit Transaction**

Shefaria Ent. Canada — Bank statement posting — Time 18:03:28 — Date 14.03.201
Toronto — Processing Statistics — RFEBBU00/IDES013 — Page

| Posting Ar | Sessn | Group | FB01 | FB05 | PmtAcc | No Posting | Error | Total | Total Deb. | Total Cred |
|---|---|---|---|---|---|---|---|---|---|---|
| Bank Accounting | HSBC-1-101 | | 0 | 4 | 0 | 0 | 0 | 4 | 3,300.00 | 10,004,900.00 |
| * Bank Accounting | | | 0 | 4 | 0 | 0 | 0 | 4 | 3,300.00 | 10,004,900.00 |
| ** Bank Accounting | | | 0 | 4 | 0 | 0 | 0 | 4 | 3,300.00 | 10,004,900.00 |
| Subledger acctng | | | 0 | 0 | 0 | 4 | 0 | 4 | 3,300.00 | 10,004,900.00 |
| * Subledger acctng | | | 0 | 0 | 0 | 4 | 0 | 4 | 3,300.00 | 10,004,900.00 |
| ** Subledger acctng | | | 0 | 0 | 0 | 4 | 0 | 4 | 3,300.00 | 10,004,900.00 |
| *** | | | 0 | 4 | 0 | 4 | 0 | 8 | 6,600.00 | 20,009,800.00 |

Fig 28

Click button

Click Overview button. The Manual Bank Statement Overview screen displays

**Manual Bank Statement Overview**

Copy New Statement

Bank Account

| CCode | Name of bank | Bank Key | Acct | | Curr. |
|---|---|---|---|---|---|
| 1000 | Deutsche Bank Gruppe | 50070010 | 10000100 | EUR | EUR |
| 1000 | Deutsche Bank | 62030050 | 7002335300 | EUR | EUR |
| 3000 | Citibank | 134329042 | 30050021 | USD | USD |
| SFE1 | HSBC Canada PLC | 1000111111 | 1000111111 | CAD | CAD |

Fig 32

The overview above confirms the status about Statement Posting.

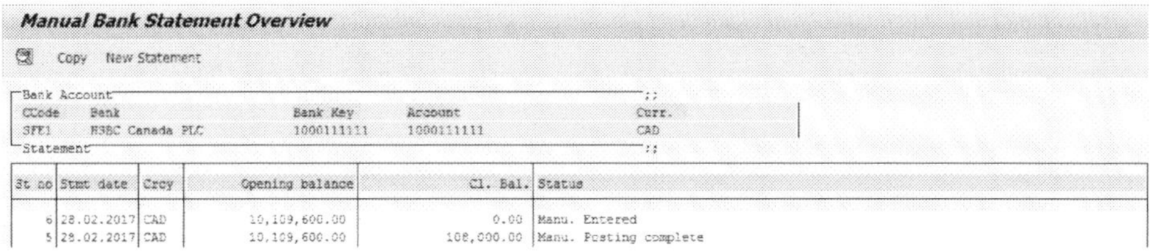

**Manual Bank Statement Overview**

Copy    New Statement

Bank Account
| CCode | Bank | Bank Key | Account | Curr. |
|-------|------|----------|---------|-------|
| 3FE1 | HSBC Canada PLC | 1000111111 | 1000111111 | CAD |

Statement

| St no | Stmt date | Crcy | Opening balance | Cl. Bal. | Status |
|-------|-----------|------|-----------------|----------|--------|
| 6 | 28.02.2017 | CAD | 10,109,600.00 | 0.00 | Manu. Entered |
| 5 | 28.02.2017 | CAD | 10,109,600.00 | 108,000.00 | Manu. Posting complete |

Fig 33

Chose the Statement No. and click [icon] to get the overview of posted items.

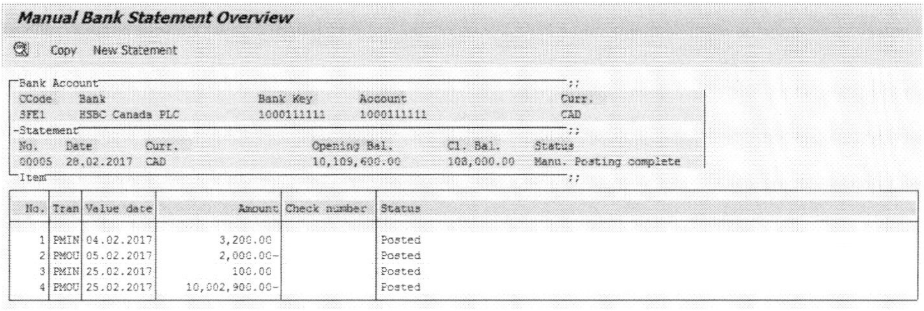

**Manual Bank Statement Overview**

Copy    New Statement

Bank Account
| CCode | Bank | Bank Key | Account | Curr. |
|-------|------|----------|---------|-------|
| 3FE1 | HSBC Canada PLC | 1000111111 | 1000111111 | CAD |

Statement
| No. | Date | Curr. | Opening Bal. | Cl. Bal. | Status |
|-----|------|-------|--------------|----------|--------|
| 00005 | 28.02.2017 | CAD | 10,109,600.00 | 108,000.00 | Manu. Posting complete |

Item

| No. | Tran | Value date | Amount | Check number | Status |
|-----|------|-----------|--------|--------------|--------|
| 1 | PMIN | 04.02.2017 | 3,200.00 | | Posted |
| 2 | PMOU | 05.02.2017 | 2,000.00- | | Posted |
| 3 | PMIN | 25.02.2017 | 100.00 | | Posted |
| 4 | PMOU | 25.02.2017 | 10,002,900.00- | | Posted |

Fig 34

# FINANCIAL STATEMENT VERSIONS (C/U)

This is a very flexible functionality in SAP that enables us to set up the P & L and B/L by configuring the G/L accounts in the statements and then grouping them as needed. We will not go into many details of all here, but will get a good idea of the process involved. In standard SAP, this is a configuration but it is likely that the company will implement this transition because of the high volume of setup and the frequency with which it changes.

This grouping is reflective of how the accounting principles and the laws of the country dictate about this setup – which G/Ls need to be a part of which section or sub-section in the reports.

# I.     SETUP

T Code SPRO

The path to set this up is:

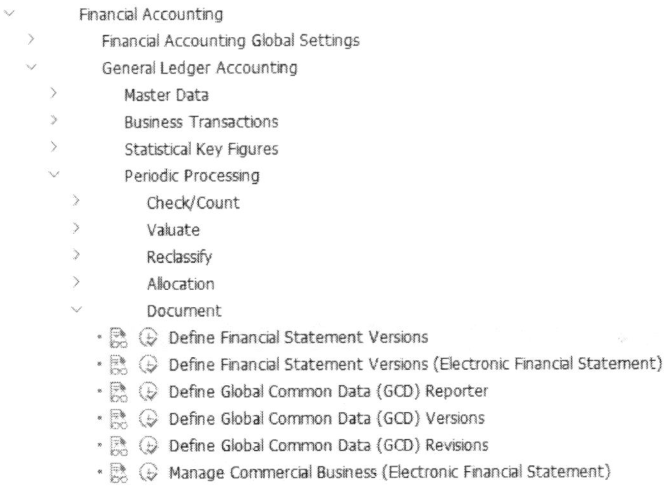

Fig 1

**HANA CHANGE:** Like a lot of other areas in which periodic processing is done, the menu for financial statements has also moved from under document closing in ECC to document periodic processing in HANA, clubbing it under other kinds of closings.

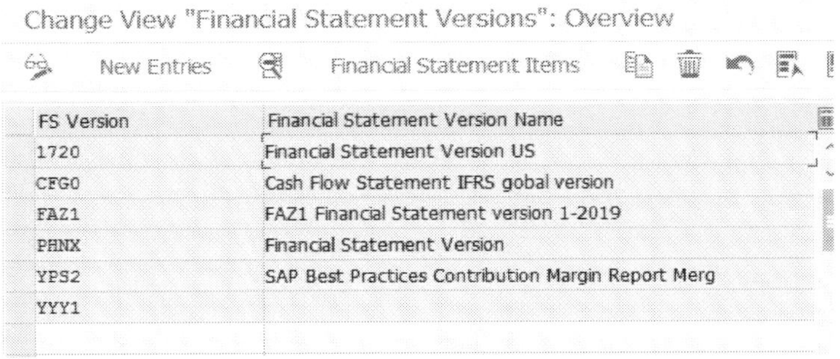

Fig 2

Fig 3

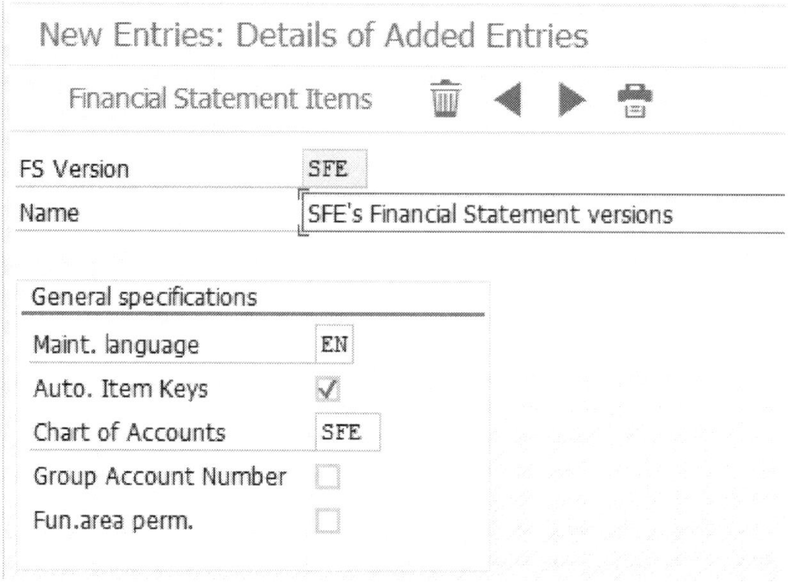

New Entries: Details of Added Entries

Financial Statement Items  🗑  ◀  ▶  🖨

| FS Version | SFE |
| Name | SFE's Financial Statement versions |

General specifications

| Maint. language | EN |
| Auto. Item Keys | ☑ |
| Chart of Accounts | SFE |
| Group Account Number | ☐ |
| Fun.area perm. | ☐ |

Fig 4

Save the configuration.

Change View "Financial Statement Versions": Overview

🔍  New Entries  📋  Financial Statement Items  📑 🗑 ↩

| FS Version | Financial Statement Version Name |
| SFE | SFE's Financial Statement versions |

Fig 5

To configure the BS and P&L as you would like to, select the Fin Statement version and click on Fin. Statement items:

Financial Statement Items

Fig 6

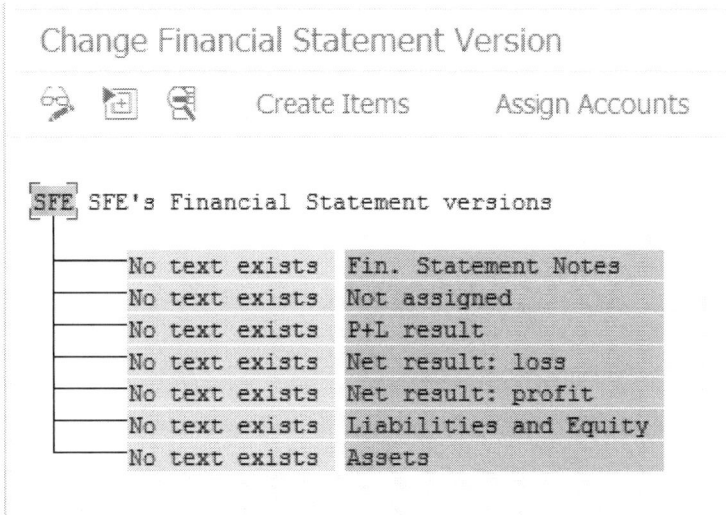

Fig 7

Using the 2 keys:

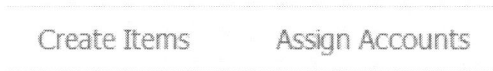

Fig 7

We can create new headings and sub-headings by positioning the cursor at the required place via the key Create Items. E.g. if we want to create a new heading called Fixed Assets under Assets, we will Click on Assets and then on Create Items:

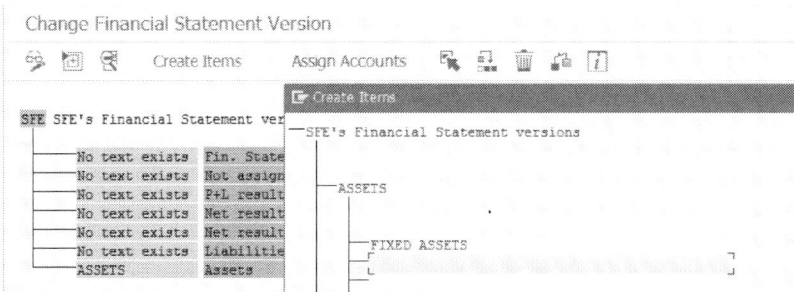

Fig 8

Next, click on Create Items:

Hit Enter and Fixed Assets and Liquid Assets appear as sub-headings of Assets:

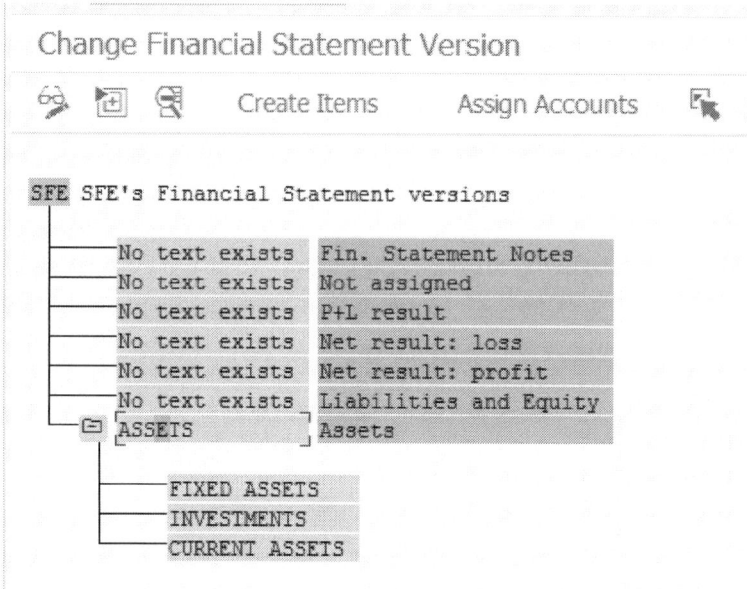

Fig 9

Configuring G/Ls:

Next, we can configure the G/L accounts in each individual sub-heading/bucket. Click on the sub-heading you want to attach the corresponding G/L to, e.g. to Income Statement>Revenue> Revenue from Furniture Division. The click on Assign Accounts:

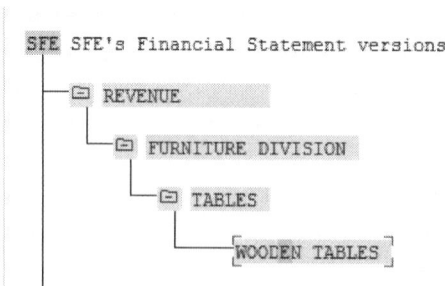

Fig 10

And enter the G/L account e.g. 451011 for this divisions' specific business – granularity here is the choice of the company i.e. at what detail does it want to view and/or report it's P&L and BS components:

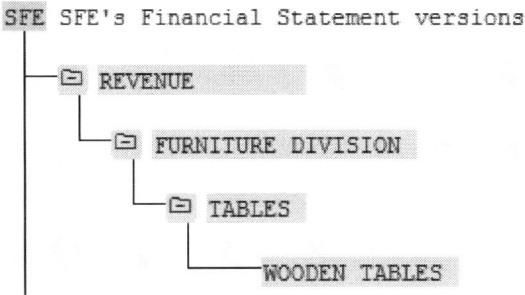

SFE SFE's Financial Statement versions

- REVENUE
  - FURNITURE DIVISION
    - TABLES
      - WOODEN TABLES

Fig 11

Let us define the below accounts as being part of this particular P&L item:

Change Financial Statement Version

Create Items    Assign Accounts

SFE SFE's Financial Statement versions

- REVENUE
  - FURNITURE DIVISION
    - TABLES
      - WOODEN TABLES
        - SFE 0000450000 – 00004500
        - SFE 0000451011 – 00004510

Change Accounts

Item

WOODEN TABLES

| ChAc | From Acct | To Account | D | C |
|------|-----------|-----------|---|---|
| SFE | 450000 | 450000 | ✓ | ✓ |
| SFE | 451011 | 451011 | ✓ | ✓ |
| | | | ☐ | ☐ |
| | | | ☐ | ☐ |

Fig 12

Hit Enter and Save.

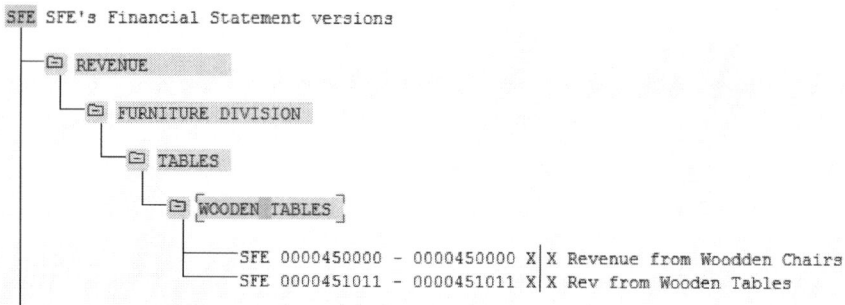

```
SFE  SFE's Financial Statement versions

    ─ ☐ REVENUE

        ─ ☐ FURNITURE DIVISION

            ─ ☐ TABLES

                ─ ☐ WOODEN TABLES

                    ─ SFE 0000450000 - 0000450000 X X Revenue from Woodden Chairs
                    ─ SFE 0000451011 - 0000451011 X X Rev from Wooden Tables
```

Fig 13

Similarly create all the headings/groups and assign the relevant
G/Ls as above. The G/Ls can be repeated over the different areas
so long as they follow the norm of P & L and BS numbering
sequences. Save and/or Activate if you are ready:

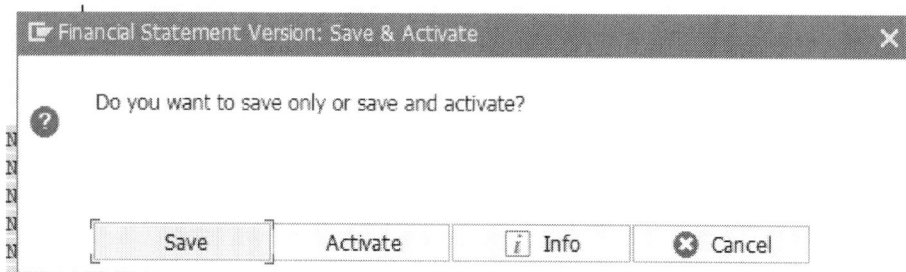

Fig 14

## II. EXECUTING THE FINANCIAL STATEMENT VERSION (U)

T Code S_ALR_87012284

Running the reports created in the financial statement versions is done via the transaction menu under Closing:

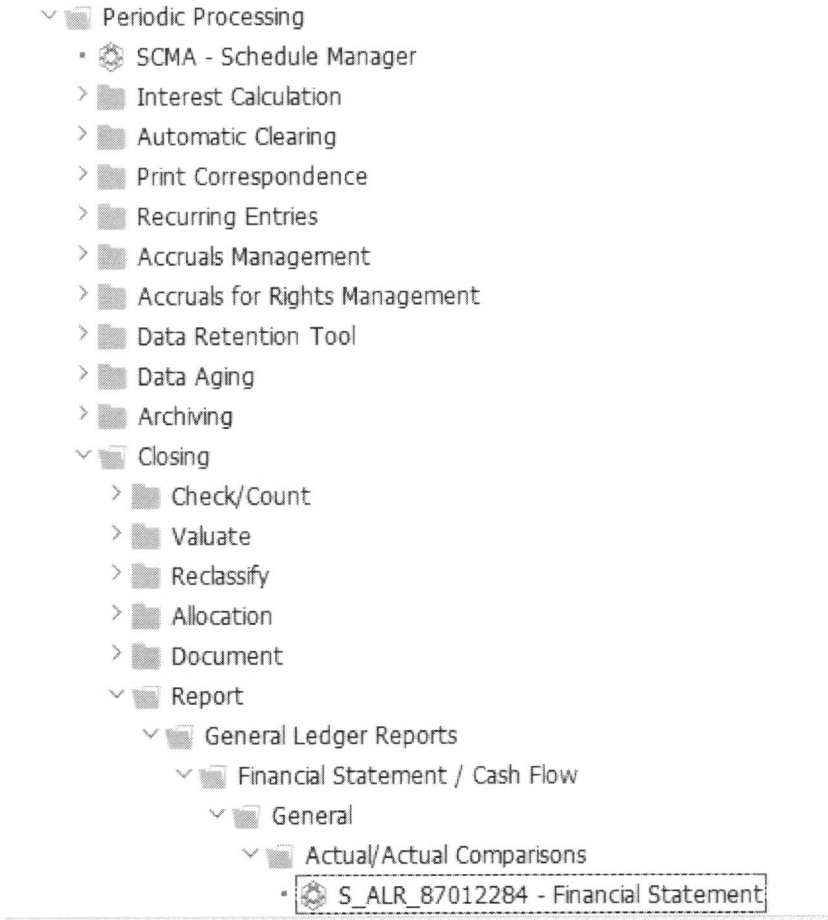

```
∨ 📁 Periodic Processing
    · ⚙ SCMA - Schedule Manager
    > 📁 Interest Calculation
    > 📁 Automatic Clearing
    > 📁 Print Correspondence
    > 📁 Recurring Entries
    > 📁 Accruals Management
    > 📁 Accruals for Rights Management
    > 📁 Data Retention Tool
    > 📁 Data Aging
    > 📁 Archiving
    ∨ 📁 Closing
        > 📁 Check/Count
        > 📁 Valuate
        > 📁 Reclassify
        > 📁 Allocation
        > 📁 Document
        ∨ 📁 Report
            ∨ 📁 General Ledger Reports
                ∨ 📁 Financial Statement / Cash Flow
                    ∨ 📁 General
                        ∨ 📁 Actual/Actual Comparisons
                            · ⚙ S_ALR_87012284 - Financial Statement
```

Fig 14

**HANA CHANGE**: In ECC this report was available under Periodic processing and like many other reports, in HANA, SAP has moved it to under Closing activities.

Enter details as needed:

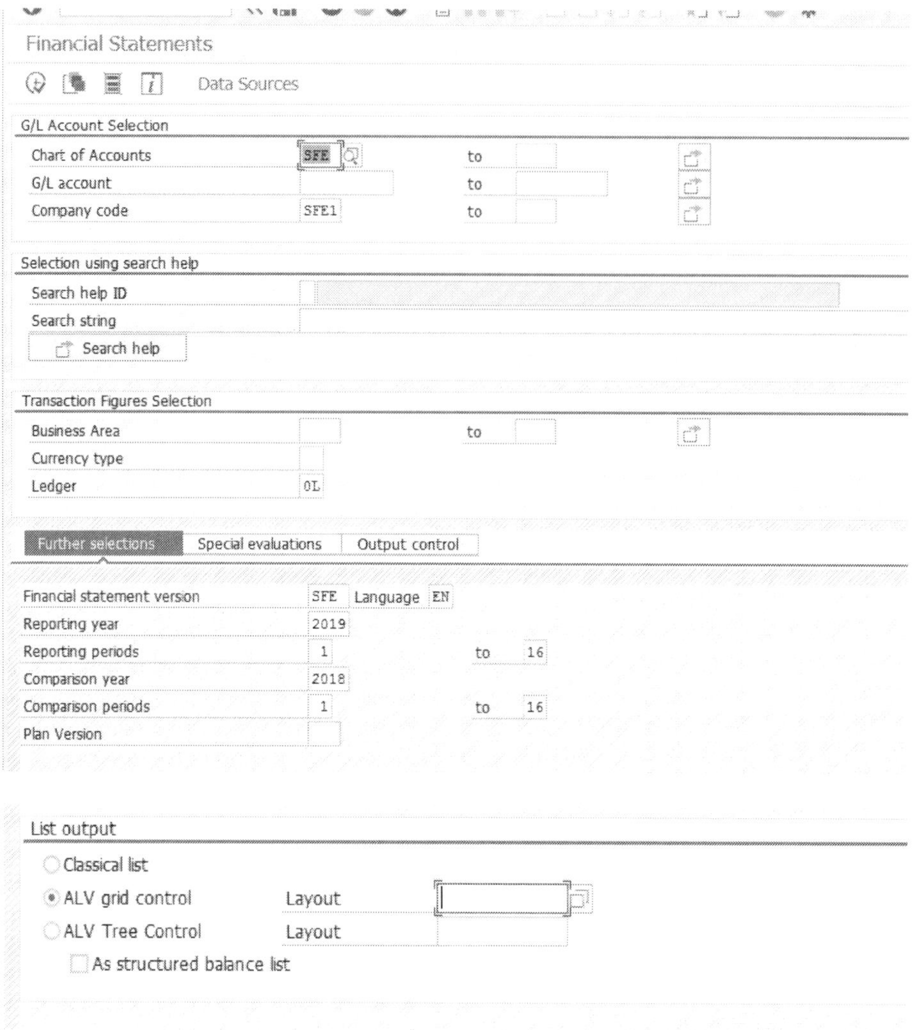

Fig 15

In the new system, the option to how to get the layout is also now available on the main selection screen at the bottom as in Fig 15. Choose whatever you prefer as in this case, ALV Grid.

Depending on how much has been configured, the amounts in the G/Ls will be available to view in their respective headings and sub-headings at the bottom of the report – the data in the upper part is not a part of a formal financial statement version but is only G/L balances.

## SFE's Financial Statement versions

| DL | Ledger |
|---|---|
| 10 | Currency type Company code currency |
| CAD | Amounts in Canadian Dollar |

| FS Item | Text for B/S P&L Item | Tot.Rpt.Pr | Tot.Cmp.Pr | Abs. Difference | Pct.Diff. |
|---|---|---|---|---|---|
| 8 | FURNITURE DIVISION | | | | |
| 14 | 450000 Revenue from Woodden Chairs | 150.00- | 0.00 | 150.00- | |
| 14 | | 150.00- | 0.00 | 150.00- | |
| 13 | | 150.00- | 0.00 | 150.00- | |
| 9 | | 150.00- | 0.00 | 150.00- | |
| 8 | | 150.00- | 0.00 | 150.00- | |
| 2 | 100007 Total cash on hand in office | 500.00 | 0.00 | 500.00 | |
| 2 | 100067 Deutsche Bank (Incoming) | 5,000.00 | 0.00 | 5,000.00 | |
| 2 | 100068 Deutsche Bank - bill of exchange discount liabilit | 5,600.00- | 0.00 | 5,600.00- | |
| 2 | 107000 Bank - TD | 2,109.55- | 0.00 | 2,109.55- | |
| 2 | 121000 Trade Receivables - Domestic | 12,589.55 | 0.00 | 12,589.55 | |
| 2 | 123000 Trade Receivable - Special Purchases | 5,600.00 | 0.00 | 5,600.00 | |
| 2 | 131000 Cost of Goods Sold | 1,171,150.00 | 0.00 | 1,171,150.00 | |
| 2 | 134000 Inventory - Finished Goods | 1,111,350.00- | 0.00 | 1,111,350.00- | |
| 2 | 211000 Trade Payables – Domestic. | 7,357.22- | 0.00 | 7,357.22- | |
| 2 | 211200 Goods Received / Invoice Received | 89,850.00- | 0.00 | 89,850.00- | |
| 2 | 400021 Bank Charges | 600.00 | 0.00 | 600.00 | |
| 2 | 450300 Revenue from Woodden Chairs (Manual adj) | 36,784.47- | 0.00 | 36,784.47- | |
| 2 | 450600 Cash Discount given to customers | 95.71 | 0.00 | 95.71 | |

Fig 16

# COST CENTER ACCOUNTING (U)

Controlling provides us with information for management decision-making. It facilitates coordination, monitoring and optimization of processes and resources in an organization. This involves recording both the consumption of production factors and the services provided by an organization.

In SAP Controlling Cost Center Accounting Concept determines where costs are incurred in the organization. To achieve this aim, costs are assigned to the sub areas of the organization where they have the most influence. By creating and assigning cost elements to cost centers, we not only make cost controlling possible, but also provide data for other application components in Controlling, such as Cost Object Controlling. We can also use a variety of allocation methods for allocating the collected costs of the given cost center/s to other controlling objects.

# I. CREATE COST CENTER

T Code   KS01

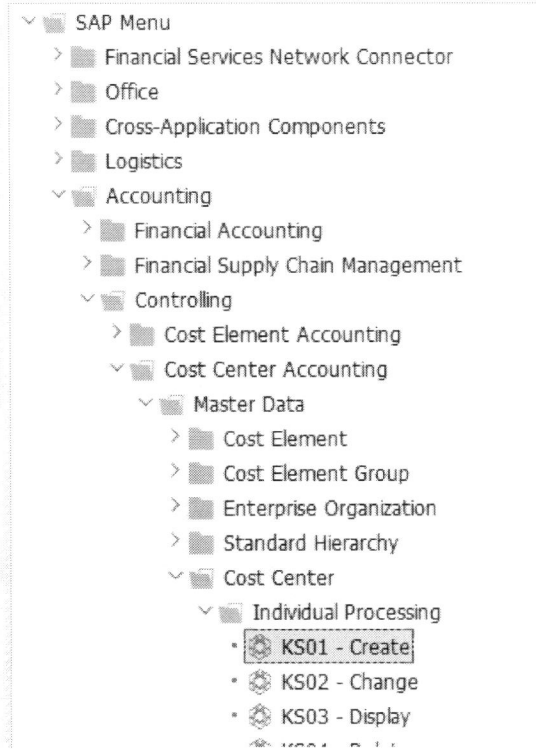

Fig 1

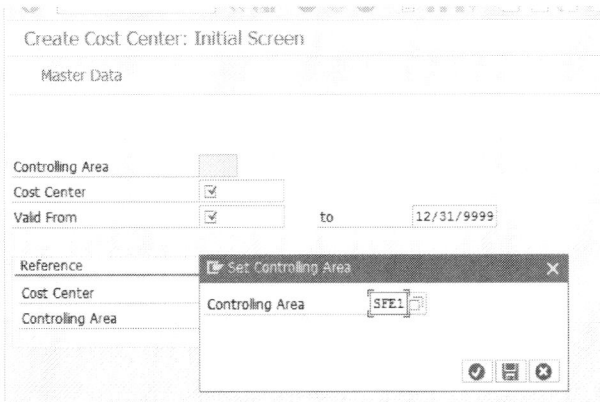

Fig 2

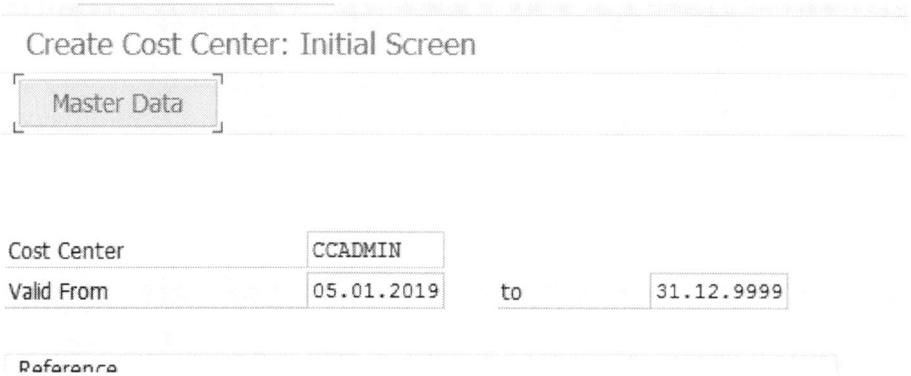

Create Cost Center: Initial Screen

Master Data

| Cost Center | CCADMIN | | |
|---|---|---|---|
| Valid From | 05.01.2019 | to | 31.12.9999 |

Reference

Fig 3

Enter the necessary details as below:

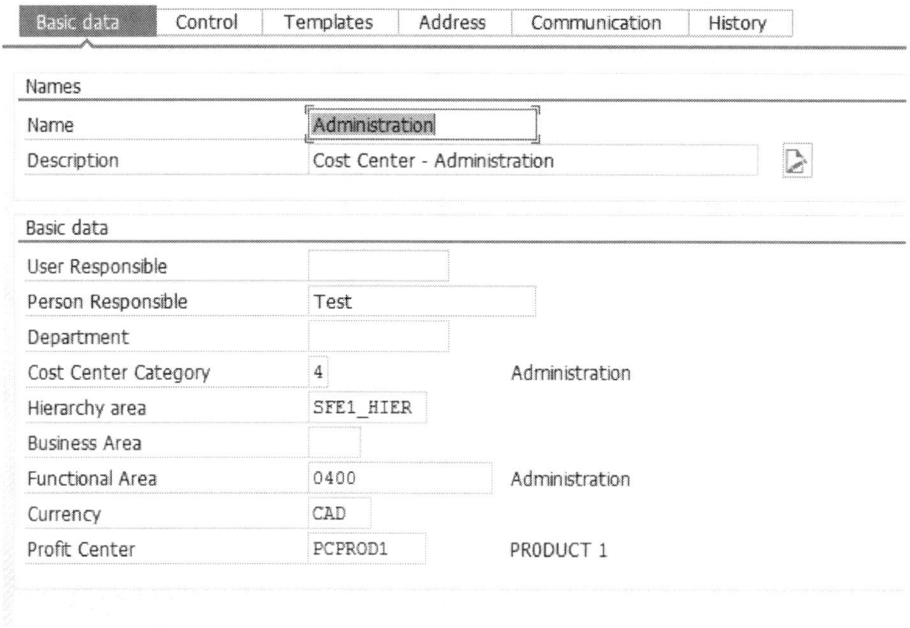

| Basic data | Control | Templates | Address | Communication | History |
|---|---|---|---|---|---|

Names

| Name | Administration |
|---|---|
| Description | Cost Center - Administration |

Basic data

| User Responsible | |
|---|---|
| Person Responsible | Test |
| Department | |
| Cost Center Category | 4 | Administration |
| Hierarchy area | SFE1_HIER |
| Business Area | |
| Functional Area | 0400 | Administration |
| Currency | CAD |
| Profit Center | PCPROD1 | PRODUCT 1 |

Fig 4

A cost center can also be set up specifically for a profit center. Profit centers are discussed in the next section.

Go to the Next TAB : CONTROL make following settings to tell the system what kind of costs it will track:

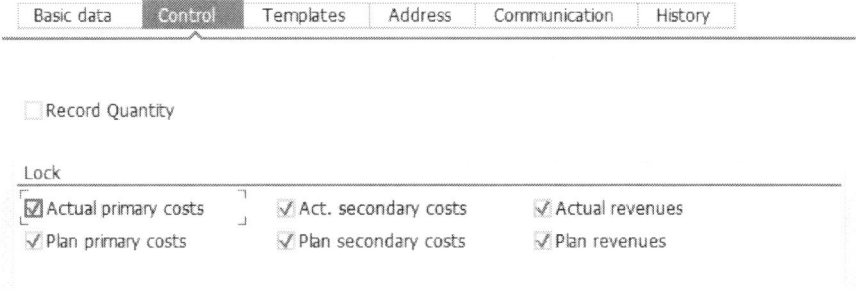

Fig 5

Select Save to finish creation of Cost Center: Administration . System confirms with the message of save.

## II.   USING THE COST CENTER IN TRANSACTIONS

T Code FB60 as an example only. The cost centers can be used can be used anywhere inline items of accounting documents ans are often also used to for document splitting).

In Cost Center Tab we select applicable Cost Center from the list or enter the one we just created - CCADMIN

Fig 7

# III. Reporting on Cost Centers

T Code KSB1

To look up the postings made to the different cost centers, we use the t-code KSB1 or follow the path:

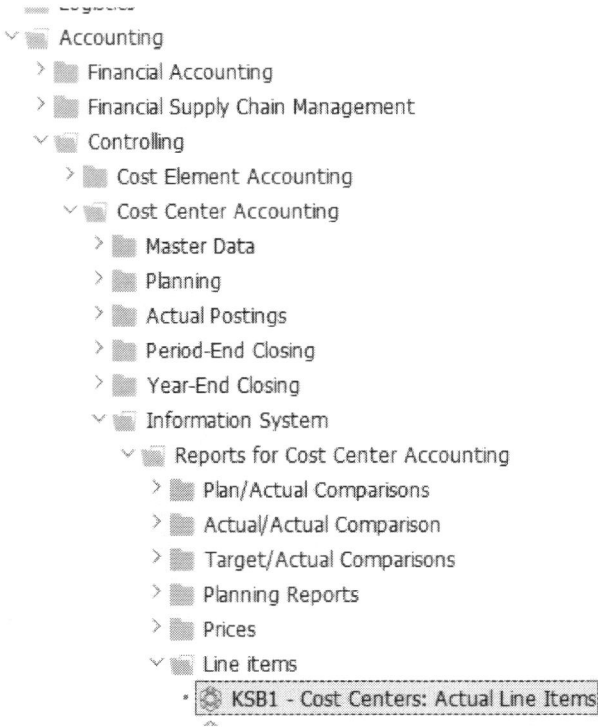

```
    Logistics
  v  Accounting
    >  Financial Accounting
    >  Financial Supply Chain Management
    v  Controlling
      >  Cost Element Accounting
      v  Cost Center Accounting
        >  Master Data
        >  Planning
        >  Actual Postings
        >  Period-End Closing
        >  Year-End Closing
        v  Information System
          v  Reports for Cost Center Accounting
            >  Plan/Actual Comparisons
            >  Actual/Actual Comparison
            >  Target/Actual Comparisons
            >  Planning Reports
            >  Prices
            v  Line items
              ·  KSB1 - Cost Centers: Actual Line Items
```

Fig 8

Enter the Controlling Area and other selection criteria e.g. dates, which cost centers etc:

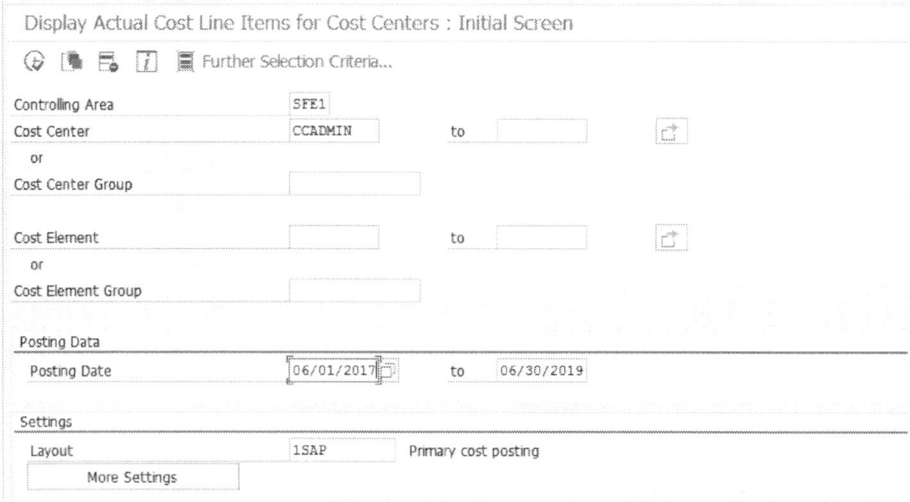

Fig 9

The executable report gives you the postings done to those cost centers:

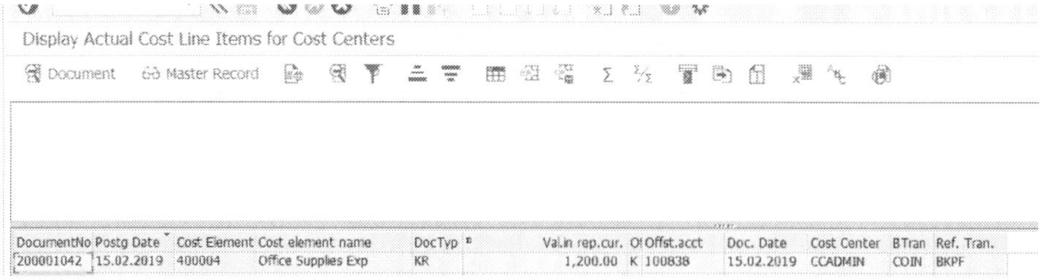

Fig 10

Many other reposts exists for budgeting purposes in which the cost allocations budgeted can be compared with the actuals that took place via the transactions. These reports form a few of the basis of management accounting.

# PROFIT CENTER ACCOUNTING (U)

A profit center is a management-oriented organizational unit used for internal controlling purposes. Dividing the company up into profit centers allows us to analyze areas of responsibility and to delegate responsibility to decentralized units, thus treating them as "companies within the company".

Thus, while a cost center is a subunit of a company that is responsible only for its costs, a profit center is a subunit of a company that is responsible for revenues *and* costs.

Example of cost centers are the production departments and the service departments within a factory and administrative departments such as IT and accounting.

Often a division of a company is a profit center because it has control over its revenues, costs, and the resulting profits.

Cost centers and profit centers are usually associated with planning and control in a decentralized company.

# I.  CREATE PROFIT CENTER

T Code  KE51 or the path:

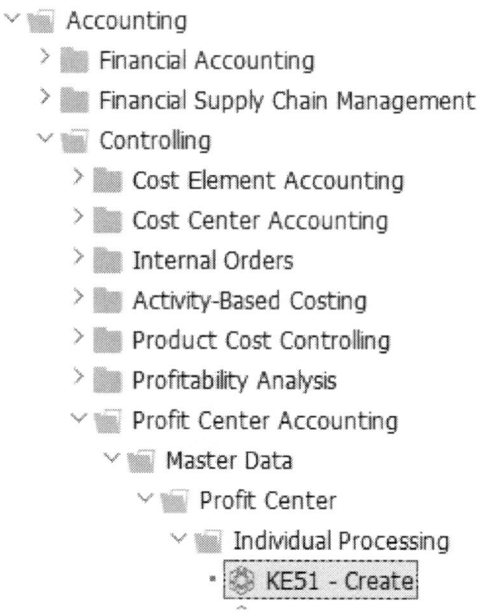

Fig 1

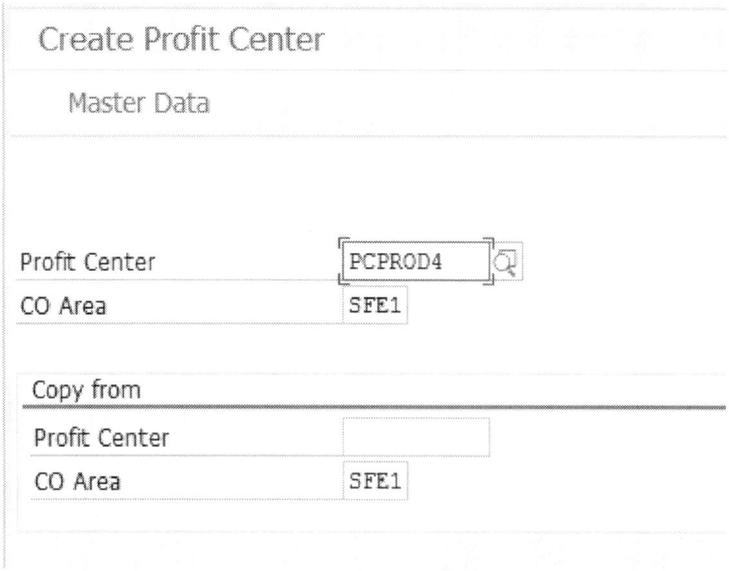

Fig 2

Press Enter and key in the following or similar entries to create Profit Center

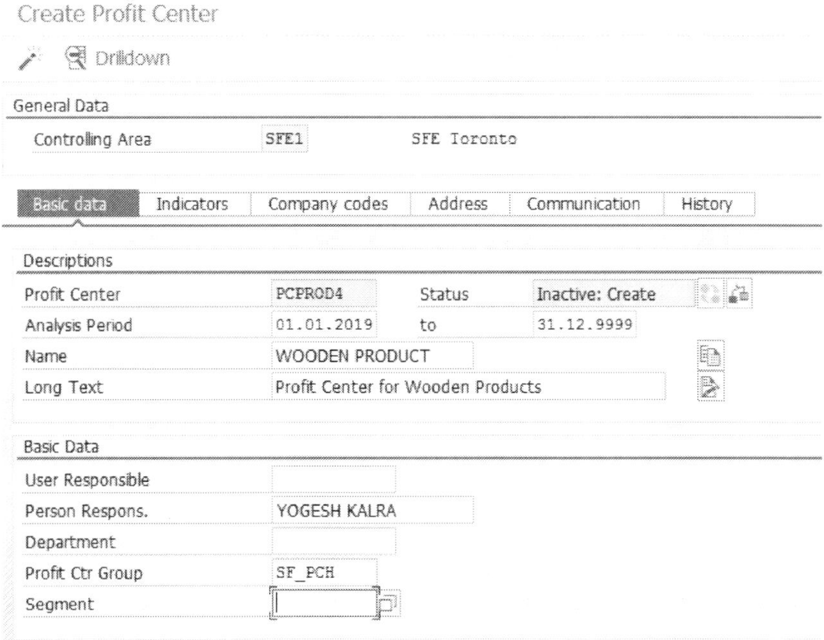

Create Profit Center

Drilldown

General Data

| Controlling Area | SFE1 | SFE Toronto |
|---|---|---|

| Basic data | Indicators | Company codes | Address | Communication | History |

Descriptions

| Profit Center | PCPROD4 | Status | Inactive: Create |
|---|---|---|---|
| Analysis Period | 01.01.2019 | to | 31.12.9999 |
| Name | WOODEN PRODUCT | | |
| Long Text | Profit Center for Wooden Products | | |

Basic Data

| User Responsible | |
|---|---|
| Person Respons. | YOGESH KALRA |
| Department | |
| Profit Ctr Group | SF_PCH |
| Segment | |

Fig 3

Go to CC tab and confirm the following settings for the active organization for which this profit Center is to be created. This is the way Profit centers are made to be used by different CCs.

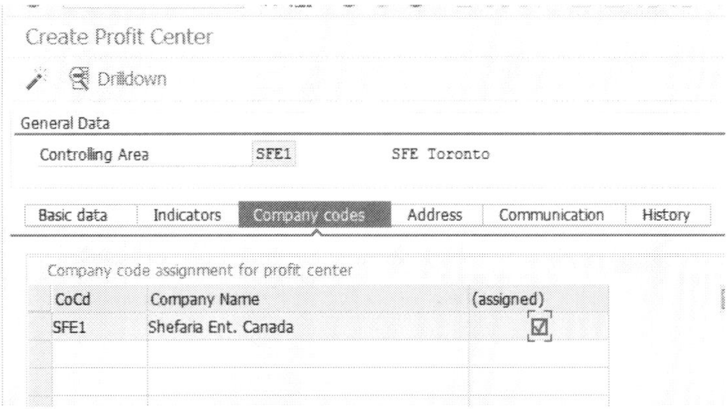

Create Profit Center

Drilldown

General Data

| Controlling Area | SFE1 | SFE Toronto |
|---|---|---|

| Basic data | Indicators | Company codes | Address | Communication | History |

Company code assignment for profit center

| CoCd | Company Name | (assigned) |
|---|---|---|
| SFE1 | Shefaria Ent. Canada | ☑ |
| | | |

Fig 4

After checking all entries click  to activate the Proift center. The activation enables the usage of the profit center. The system will confirm with the following message :

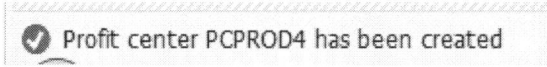
Profit center PCPROD4 has been created

# II. USING THE PROFIT CENTER IN TRANSACTIONS

T Code FB70 (example only, the PrCtr can be used anywhere in any posting where you see the field).

Sales & Revenue is subjected to booking in respective Profit center.

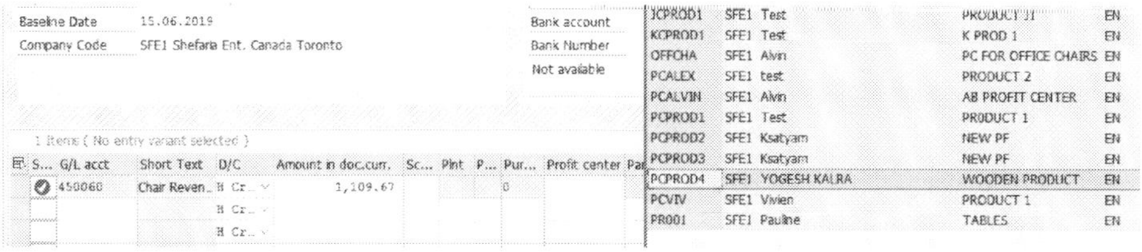

Fig 6

Here we used the Revenue from Sales GL : 450060 and is subjected to profit center booking .

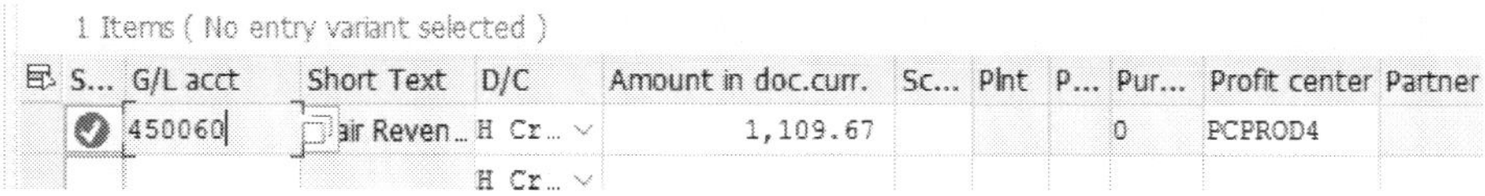

Fig 7

Select ▦ Simulate to process the entry :

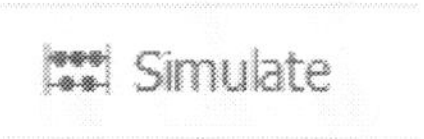

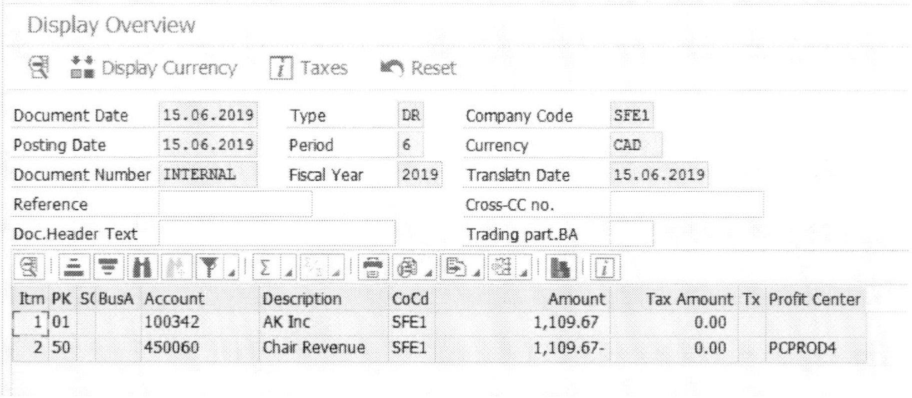

## Fig 8

## Save to post the entry to the Profit Center PCPROD4

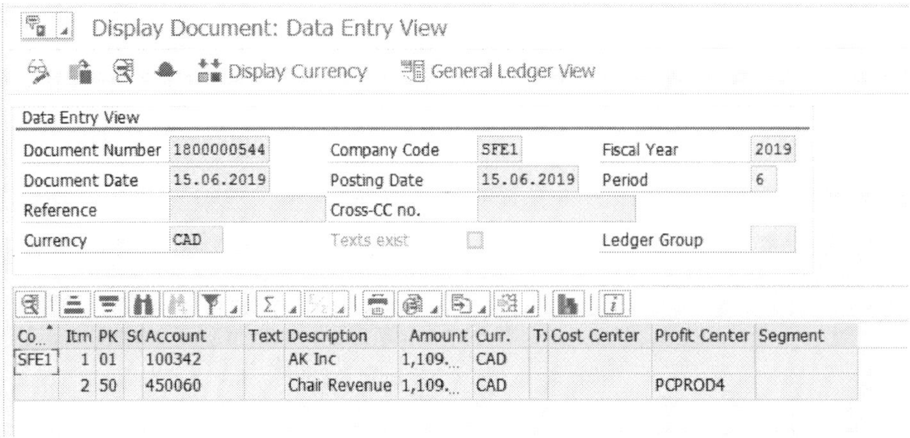

Display Document: Data Entry View

Display Currency   General Ledger View

Data Entry View

| | | | | | |
|---|---|---|---|---|---|
| Document Number | 1800000544 | Company Code | SFE1 | Fiscal Year | 2019 |
| Document Date | 15.06.2019 | Posting Date | 15.06.2019 | Period | 6 |
| Reference | | Cross-CC no. | | | |
| Currency | CAD | Texts exist | ☐ | Ledger Group | |

| Co. | Itm | PK | SC | Account | Text | Description | Amount | Curr. | T | Cost Center | Profit Center | Segment |
|-----|-----|----|----|---------|------|-------------|--------|-------|---|-------------|---------------|---------|
| SFE1 | 1 | 01 | | 100342 | | AK Inc | 1,109... | CAD | | | | |
| | 2 | 50 | | 450060 | | Chair Revenue | 1,109... | CAD | | | PCPROD4 | |

## Fig 9

# III. Reporting on Profit Centers

T Code KE5Z or FAGLL03

Like the cost centers, profit centers can also be reported on for the purpose of analysis and management decision making.

Follow the path:

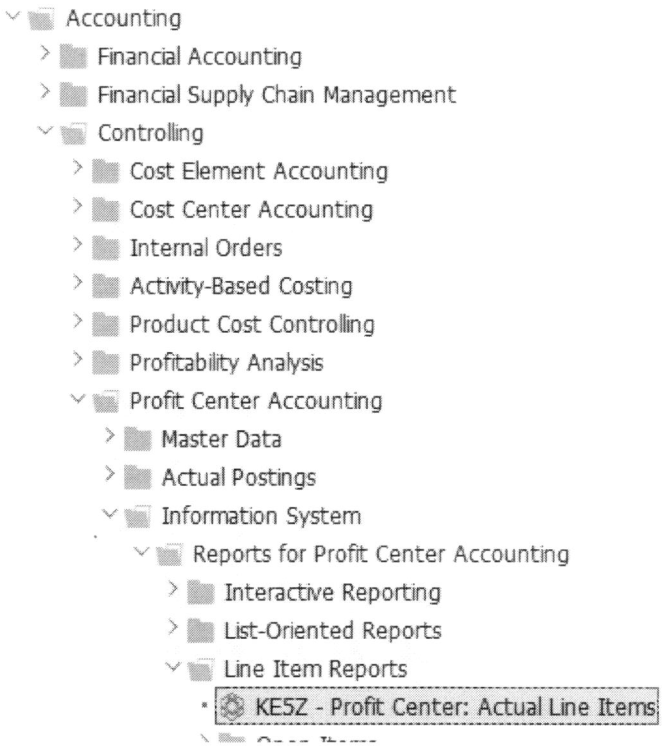

```
∨ 📁 Accounting
    > 📁 Financial Accounting
    > 📁 Financial Supply Chain Management
    ∨ 📁 Controlling
        > 📁 Cost Element Accounting
        > 📁 Cost Center Accounting
        > 📁 Internal Orders
        > 📁 Activity-Based Costing
        > 📁 Product Cost Controlling
        > 📁 Profitability Analysis
        ∨ 📁 Profit Center Accounting
            > 📁 Master Data
            > 📁 Actual Postings
            ∨ 📁 Information System
                ∨ 📁 Reports for Profit Center Accounting
                    > 📁 Interactive Reporting
                    > 📁 List-Oriented Reports
                    ∨ 📁 Line Item Reports
                        · ⚙ KE5Z - Profit Center: Actual Line Items
                          ⌐ ▩ Open Items
```

Fig 10

# Enter the data as needed on the screen:

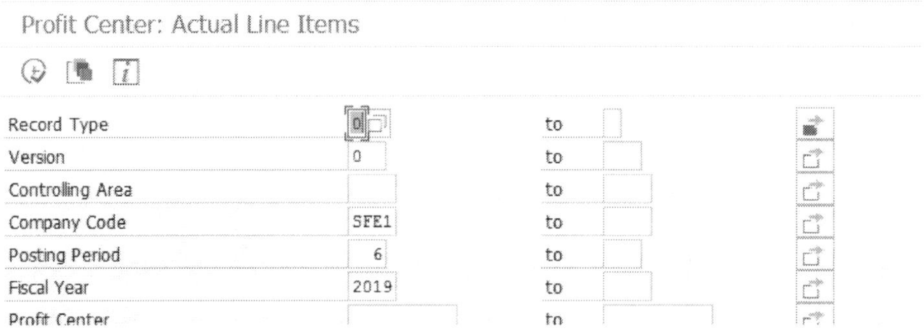

**Profit Center: Actual Line Items**

| | |  | | |
|---|---|---|---|---|
| Record Type | 0 | to | | |
| Version | 0 | to | | |
| Controlling Area | | to | | |
| Company Code | SFE1 | to | | |
| Posting Period | 6 | to | | |
| Fiscal Year | 2019 | to | | |
| Profit Center | | to | | |

Fig 11

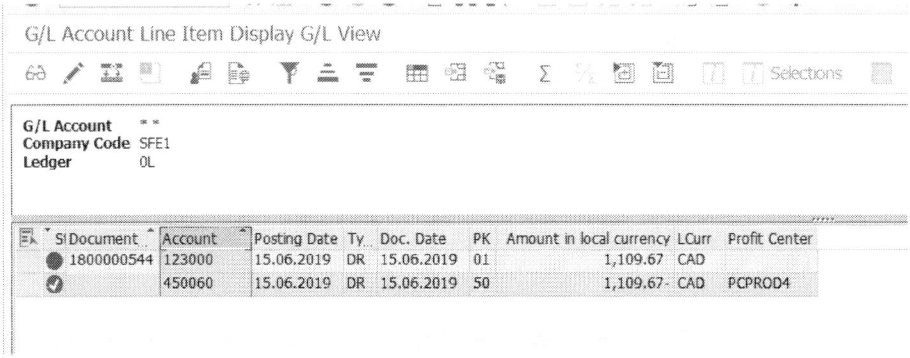

**G/L Account Line Item Display G/L View**

G/L Account    * *
Company Code   SFE1
Ledger      0L

| | S! Document | Account | Posting Date | Ty | Doc. Date | PK | Amount in local currency | LCurr | Profit Center |
|---|---|---|---|---|---|---|---|---|---|
| ● | 1800000544 | 123000 | 15.06.2019 | DR | 15.06.2019 | 01 | 1,109.67 | CAD | |
| ✓ | | 450060 | 15.06.2019 | DR | 15.06.2019 | 50 | 1,109.67- | CAD | PCPROD4 |

Fig 12

# CROSS – APPLICATION AND GENERAL
# COMPONENTS IN SAP (U)

## I.  VARIANTS (U)

Variants are variations of input and output screens. They are not cross application components but 'common' components. Most of the screens in SAP behave similarly for the purpose of creating variants. The purpose of variants is twofold:

- To enable the user to save time by setting up screens with roughly the same data that may be needed every time the transaction is run. In that respect, these input variants can be treated as master data.

- To let different users who may be using the same transaction have their differentiation from each other in terms of inputs and outputs by naming their variants as suitable to them.

  There are 2 primary kinds of variants, best explained with examples.

# 1. SELECTION/INPUT VARIANTS

Let us call the standard SAP transition to look up account balances, FBL3N:

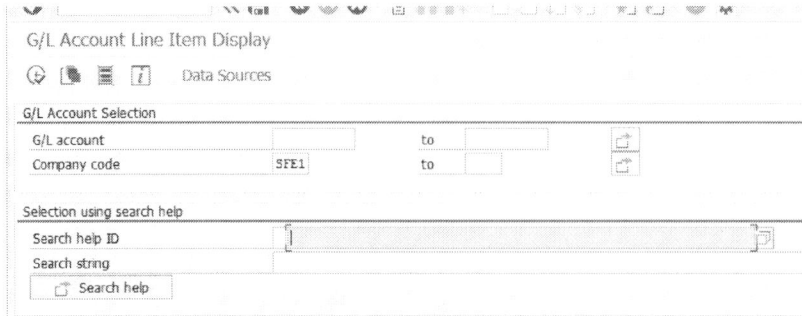

Fig 1

Let us assume that as an accounts person, one responsible for the company code SFE1 and for G/L accounts 100000 to 199999. A simple variant can be set up with these values:

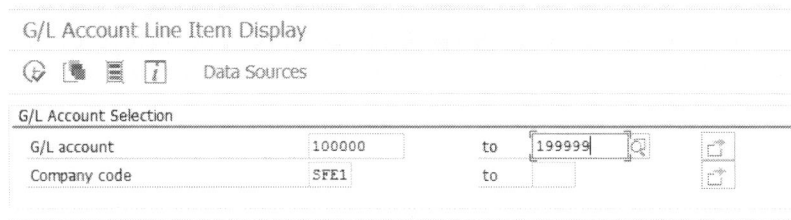

Fig 2

Save the values either by clicking on Save or:

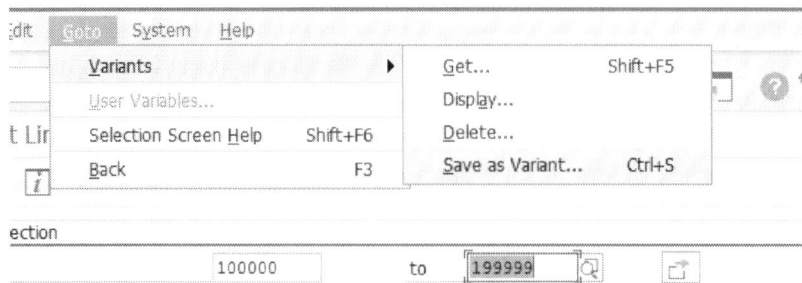

Fig 3

Give it a name that makes sense to you:

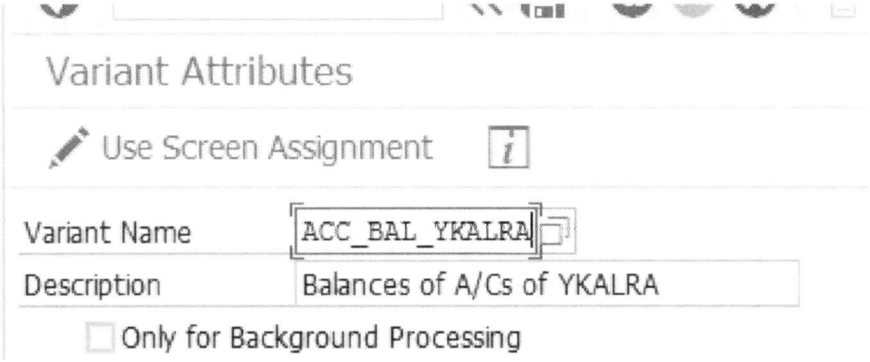

Fig 4

Save it:

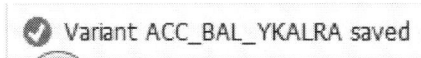

Next time when you call the transaction FBL3N simply click on the

button   and double click on your variant to call up the same information you entered:

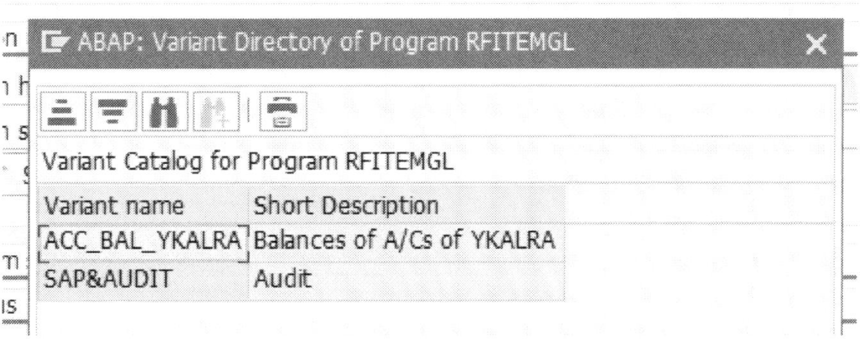

Fig 5

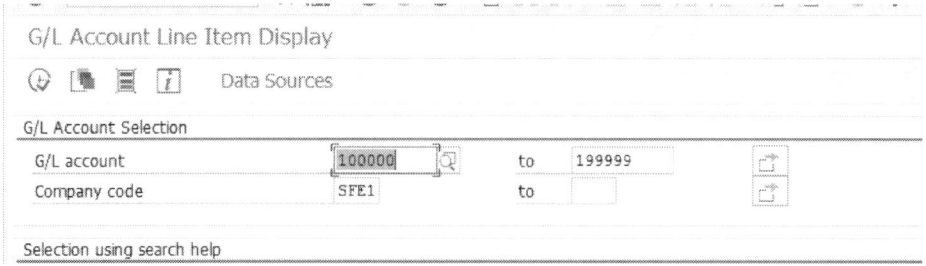

Fig 6

The above was a simple example of a variant. The inputs can be further defined using the feature of multiple values using the

icon

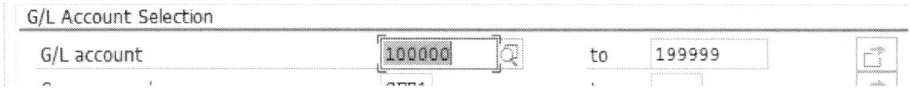

**Fig 7**

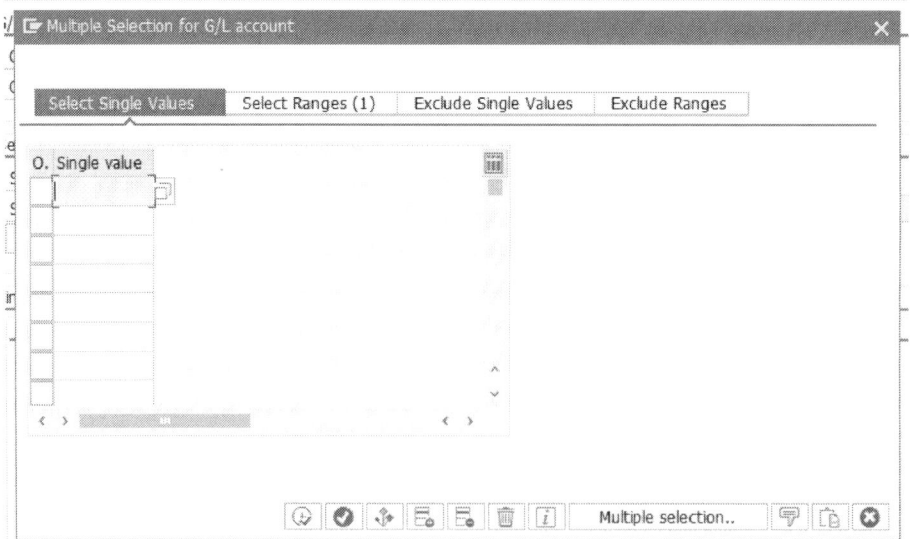

Fig 8

As we notice above, there are 4 tabs:

1. Select single values – here, G/L accounts. You can keep adding the G/Ls you want the balances for, manually or, copy them from a spreadsheet and paste them using the icon ▥. We can also use the button to upload a text file though this is seldom used as the same objective can be achieved by the simpler copy/paste feature.

2. Select Intervals – this is what we have chosen in our current variant:

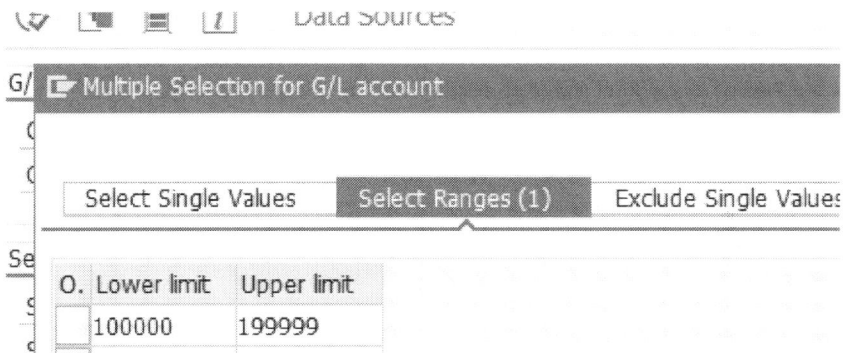

Fig 9

As seen in Fig 9, multiple intervals of different ranges can be chosen.

3 and 4 – Exclude single values and exclude ranges – work exactly the same way as 1 and 2 except these are for excluding the G/L accounts while 1 and 2 were for including them.

## 2. Output/Display Variant

Let us stay with our same variant and execute the report using the button Execute:

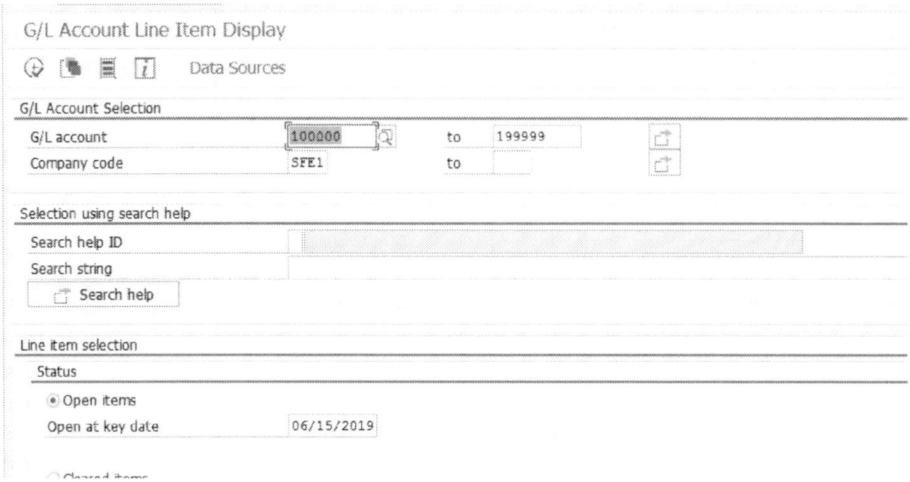

Fig 10

Some kind of a layout emerges based on what the default is:

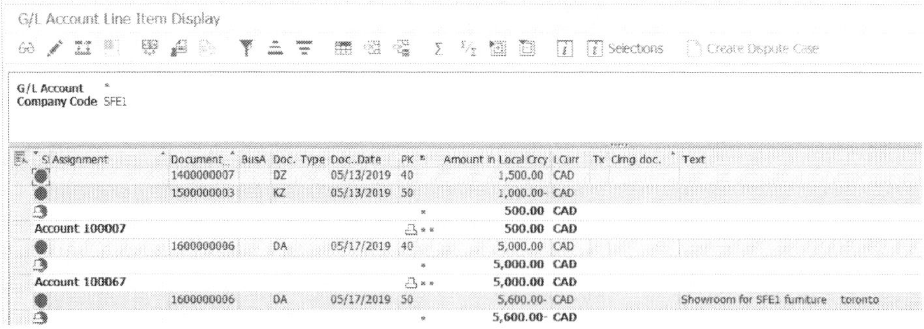

Fig 11

The above is the display of the report based on some parameters. Let us see what they are and how this can be customized to our requirement as it may not be suitable for the data we need.

The first is how to display. As seen above, this is an Excel friendly layout. It can be changed to a more generic layout using:

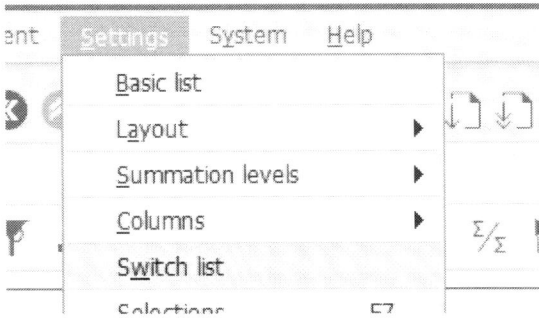

Fig 12

G/L Account Line Item Display

G/L Account 100007 Total cash on hand in office
Company Code SFE1

| | St | Assignment | DocumentNo | BusA | Type | Doc..Date | PK | Amount in Local Crcy | LCurr | Tx | Clrng doc. | Text |
|---|---|---|---|---|---|---|---|---|---|---|---|---|
| | ● | | 1400000007 | | DZ | 05/13/2019 | 40 | 1,500.00 | CAD | | | |
| | ● | | 1500000003 | | KZ | 05/13/2019 | 50 | 1,000.00- | CAD | | | |
| * | ● | | | | | | | 500.00 | CAD | | | |
| ** Account 100007 | | | | | | | | 500.00 | CAD | | | |

G/L Account 100067 Deutsche Bank (Incoming)
Company Code SFE1

| | St | Assignment | DocumentNo | BusA | Type | Doc..Date | PK | Amount in Local Crcy | LCurr | Tx | Clrng doc. | Text |
|---|---|---|---|---|---|---|---|---|---|---|---|---|

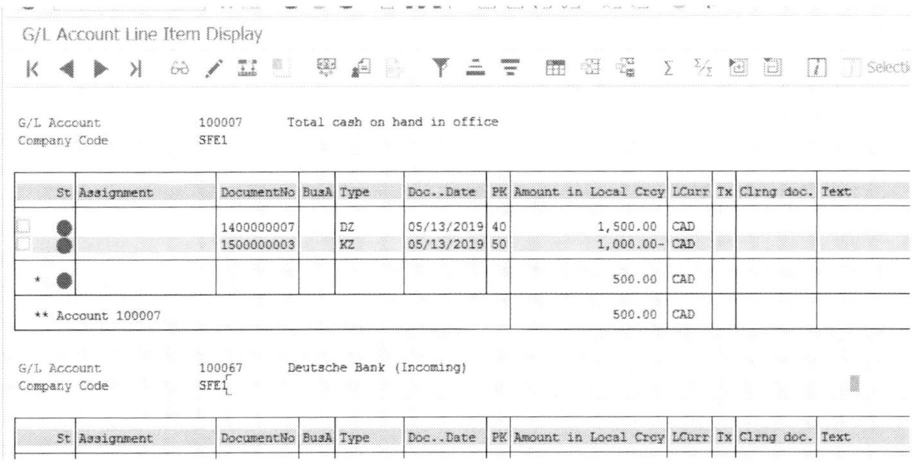

Fig 13

Most people will prefer the Excel type grid so we work with that.

Below are the primary icons (many are Windows based and thus, familiar) that we will work with.

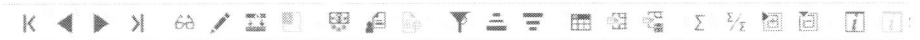

Fig 14

The SAP specific ones,  refer to how the layouts can be created and saved. As we notice, the columns currently available to us in this report are:

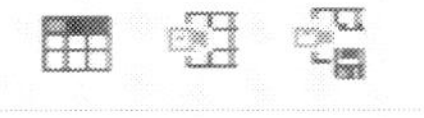

Fig 15

The source of these columns are SAP tables – in this case, accounting tables (next section, ideally, to be visited only once you have finished the rest of this book).

If we wish to add/delete or re-arrange any of these columns, click on ⊞ to change the layout:

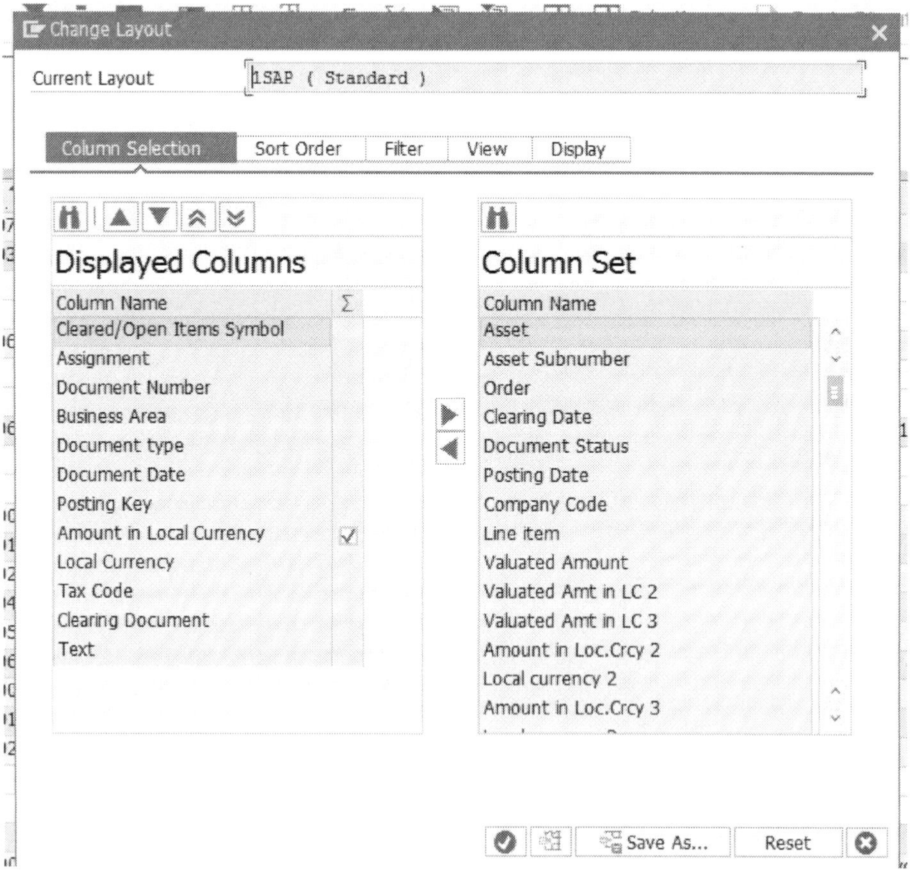

Fig 16

538

As you notice, the section on the left is the list of the columns displayed in the order from top to bottom > left to right in the report. The right section is the list of more fields/columns available though it is not necessary that all of them hold data. If you wish to see something new/additional or want to hide any, just double click on it and it flips from one column to the other as clicked.

The keys 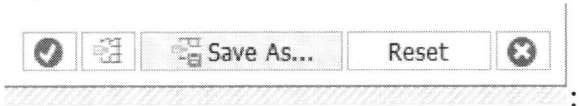 are useful to find, or move up or down the list.

Once we are satisfied with what we require in your report and want to save it with the ides of recalling it every time (same way as the input variant), click on Save As at the bottom:

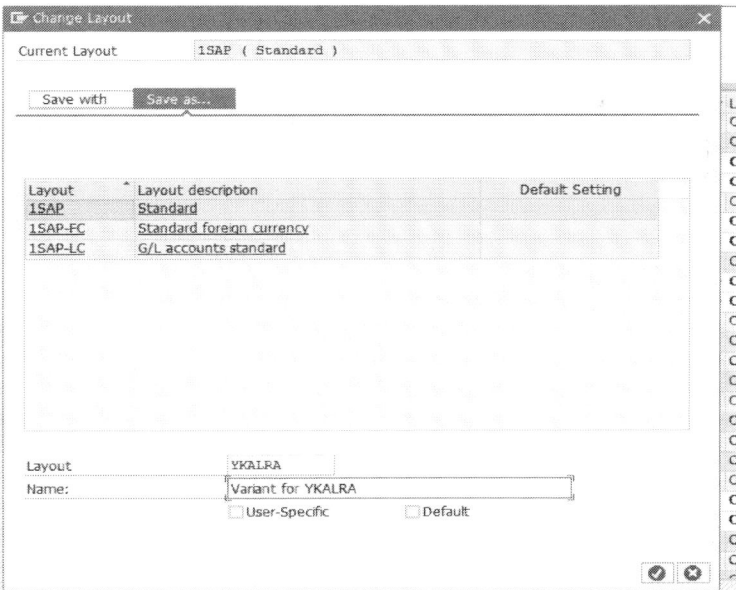

Fig 17

Give it a name:

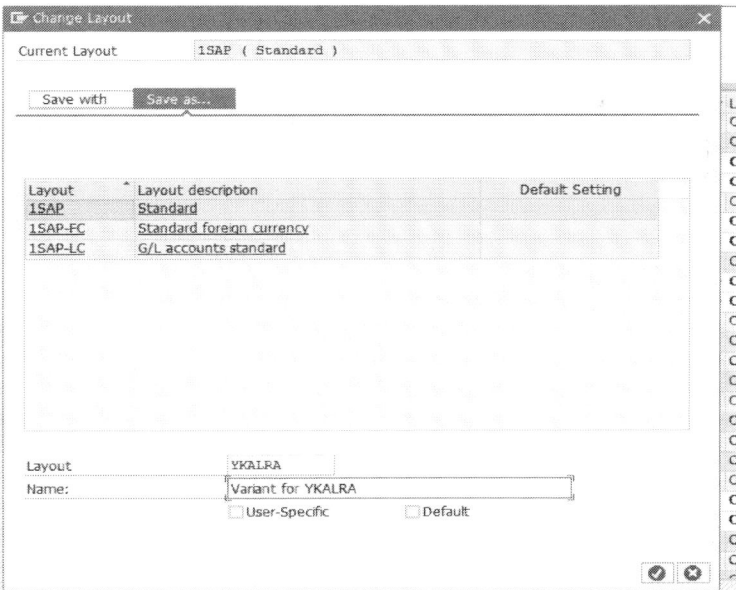

Fig 18

We can only use one of the buttons:

☐ User-Specific          ☐ Default

Fig 19

To save as specific to you OR as a default layout. It is highly recommended not to save as a default layout otherwise everyone will see only that as a default and will have to change it to their requirements which will not be a very kind act towards other users.

So we save this as user specific:

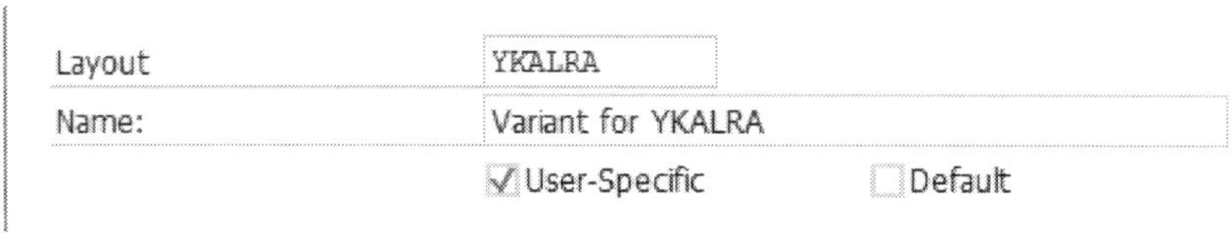

| Layout | YKALRA |
|---|---|
| Name: | Variant for YKALRA |

☑ User-Specific          ☐ Default

Fig 20

Fig 21

Next time we run this report, we can call for our display variant using the icon ⌗ : (See Fig 14)

Click on the hyperlink of your variant as below:

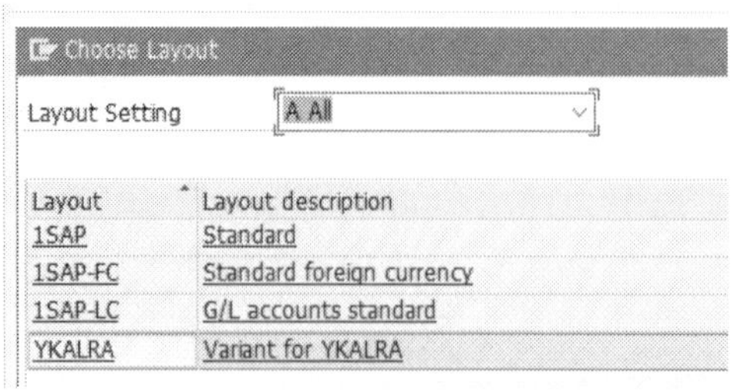

☞ Choose Layout

| Layout Setting | A All ⌄ |
|---|---|

| Layout | Layout description |
|---|---|
| 1SAP | Standard |
| 1SAP-FC | Standard foreign currency |
| 1SAP-LC | G/L accounts standard |
| YKALRA | Variant for YKALRA |

Fig 22

The message displayed at the bottom is:

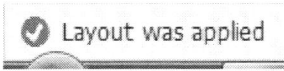

Fig 23

This ensures whatever we had asked for in the layout SFE1 is now on screen displayed for us.

For the most part, this variant functionality in SAP is exactly the same across all screens and all modules thereby making your life infinitely easier.

Not only do variants help us save time, they can also present us with data relating to the documents themselves e.g. by checking any particular line, you can go straight into the document and even change it for whatever is possible to be changed as shown in the previous section. Select the line item and then Click on Environment> Display Document:

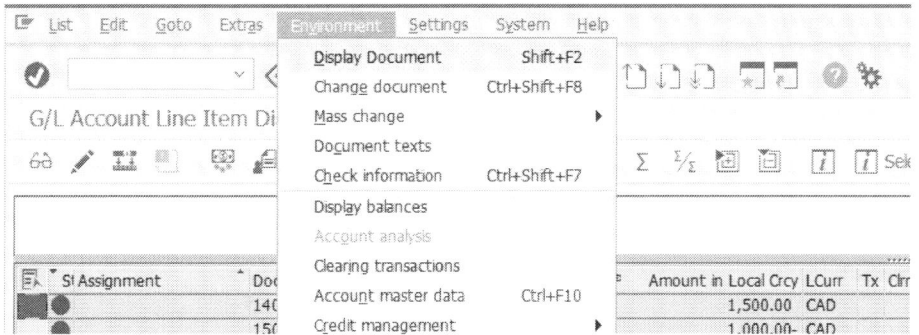

Fig 24

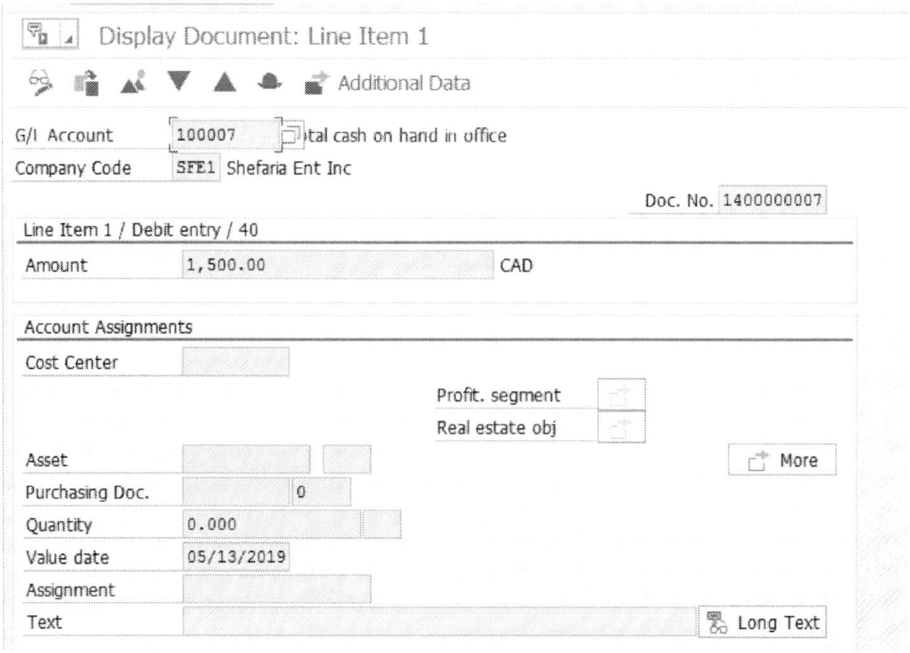

## Display Document: Line Item 1

Additional Data

| | | |
|---|---|---|
| G/l Account | 100007 | tal cash on hand in office |
| Company Code | SFE1 | Shefaria Ent Inc |

Doc. No. 1400000007

### Line Item 1 / Debit entry / 40

| Amount | 1,500.00 | CAD |
|---|---|---|

### Account Assignments

| | |
|---|---|
| Cost Center | |

Profit. segment

Real estate obj

| | |
|---|---|
| Asset | |
| Purchasing Doc. | 0 |
| Quantity | 0.000 |
| Value date | 05/13/2019 |
| Assignment | |
| Text | |

More

Long Text

Fig 25

Printed in Poland
by Amazon Fulfillment
Poland Sp. z o.o., Wrocław